Richmond-Petersburg Campaign

Dear Nadia,
May you see our
History and Travel the
world.

Tim Amoroso
816-585-8231
March 2025

P.S. you have
awesome/
eyes!

The U.S. Army War College
Guides to Civil War Battles

Guide to the
Richmond-Petersburg Campaign

Edited by
Charles R. Bowery, Jr.
and Ethan S. Rafuse

Maps by
Steven Stanley

University Press of Kansas

Published by the University Press of Kansas (Lawrence, Kansas 66045),
which was organized by the Kansas Board of Regents and is operated and
funded by Emporia State University, Fort Hays State University, Kansas State
University, Pittsburg State University, the University of Kansas, and Wichita
State University

Library of Congress Cataloging-in-Publication Data

Guide to the Richmond-Petersburg Campaign/edited by Charles R. Bowery Jr.
and Ethan S. Rafuse; maps by Steven Stanley.
    pages cm.—(U.S. Army War College guides to Civil War battles)
    Includes bibliographical references and index.
    ISBN 978-0-7006-1959-7 (cloth : alk. paper)—ISBN 978-0-7006-1960-3
(pbk. : alk. paper) 1. Petersburg (Va.)—History—Siege, 1864–1865.
2. Richmond (Va.)—History—Siege, 1864–1865. 3. Petersburg National
Battlefield (Va.)—Tours. 4. Richmond National Battlefield Park (Va.)
—Tours. 5. Battlefields—Virginia—Petersburg Region—Guidebooks.
6. Battlefields—Virginia—Richmond Region—Guidebooks. I. Bowery,
Charles R. II. Rafuse, Ethan Sepp, 1968– III. Stanley, Steven.
    E476.93.G85 2014
    975.5'03—dc23

                                                        2013049561

British Library Cataloguing-in-Publication Data is available.

Printed in the United States of America

10 9 8 7 6 5 4 3 2 1

The paper used in this publication is recycled and contains 30 percent post-
consumer waste. It is acid free and meets the minimum requirements of the
American National Standard for Permanence of Paper for Printed Library
Materials Z39.48-1992.

TO OUR FATHERS:

Charles R. Bowery, Sr. (1930–2008)

Robert W. Rafuse, Jr. (1936–2014)

CONTENTS

List of Maps and Illustrations   *xi*
Acknowledgments   *xv*
How to Use This Book   *xix*
Visitor Center   *xxi*
The Battlefield Today   *xxiii*
Introduction   *1*

PART I: PETERSBURG NATIONAL BATTLEFIELD

First Petersburg   9
    Summary of Principal Events, 13–18 June 1864   10
    1. Battery No. 6   10
    2. Battery No. 5   20
    3. Battery No. 8   24
    4. Battery No. 9   28
    5. Harrison's Creek   38
    6. First Maine Heavy Artillery Monument   49
    7. Taylor Farm   57

The Battle of Fort Stedman   71
    Summary of Principal Events, 6 February–25 March 1865   72
    1. Colquitt's Salient   72
    2. Planning the Assault   76
    3. The Assault on Fort Stedman   79
    4. The Capture of Fort Stedman   81
    5. The Federal Counterattack   84
    6. The Failure of the Attack   98

The Battle of the Crater   103
    Summary of Principal Events, 19 June–31 July 1864   103
    1. Taylor Farm   105
    2. The Mine   107
    3. The Crater   116
    4. The Mahone Monument   132
    5. The Crater   138

PART II: EXCURSIONS

Excursion 1: From Cold Harbor to Petersburg   147
  Summary of Principal Events, 27 May–15 June 1864   147
  1. Cold Harbor   148
  2. Long Bridge   152
  3. Glendale   154
  4. Crossing the James   157
  5. Baylor Farm   159

Excursion 2: City Point   167
  1. Appomattox Overlook   169
  2. Grant's Cabin   177
  3. The Wharf   185

Excursion 3: Deep Bottom   197
  Summary of Principal Events, 18 June–7 October 1864   199
  1. Deep Bottom   202
  2. Strawberry Plains   208
  3. The Darby/Enroughty Farm   213
  4. Fussell's Mill   223
  5. The Capture of the Rockbridge Artillery   229
  6. New Market Heights and Fussell's Mill   232
  7. Cavalry Engagement on the Charles City Road   241

Excursion 4: Fort Harrison and Darbytown Road   249
  Summary of Principal Events, 1 September–8 October 1864   249
  1. Deep Bottom   251
  2. New Market Heights   253
  3. Laurel Hill and the Tenth Corps Attack   258
  4. Fort Gilmer   261
  5. Varina Road   265
  6. Fort Harrison   269
  7. Fort Hoke   278
  8. Darbytown Road, 7 October 1864   280

Excursion 5: Westward Movements 287

Summary of Principal Events, 18 June 1864–7 February 1865 288

1. Fort Davis 293
2. Fort Alexander Hays 296
3. Richard Bland College 302
4. Globe Tavern 304
5. Fort Wadsworth 309
6. Oak Grove Church 321
7. Reams Station Battlefield 332
8. Sharon Church 342
9. Fort Archer 347
10. Fort Urmston 354
11. Fort Fisher 358
12. Dabney's Mill 363
13. Burgess's Mill 367
14. Hatcher's Run 375

Excursion 6: The Fall of Petersburg 389

Summary of Principal Events, 6 February–3 April 1865 390

1. Dinwiddie Church of the Nazarene 392
2. Lewis Farm 397
3. White Oak Road 402
4. Dinwiddie Court-House 410
5. Chamberlain's Bed 420
6. The Federal Plan, 1 April 1865 423
7. The Shad Bake and the Confederate Plan 428
8. The Angle 432
9. The Waterloo of the Confederacy 437
10. Munford's Stand 441
11. Sutherland Station 443
12. Fort Gregg 451

Appendix I: Order of Battle—15 June 1864 463
Appendix II: Order of Battle—29 September 1864 469
Appendix III: Order of Battle—1–2 April 1865 475
Bibliography 481
Index 485

MAPS AND ILLUSTRATIONS

Maps

Richmond-Petersburg overview   xxiv

First Petersburg overview   11

First Petersburg, June 15, 1864   21

First Petersburg, June 16, 1864   34

First Petersburg, June 17, 1864   40

First Petersburg, June 18, 1864: Morning attacks   50

First Petersburg, June 18, 1864: Afternoon attacks   59

Fort Stedman and the Crater overview   73

Fort Stedman, March 25, 1865: First and second phases   75

Fort Stedman, March 25, 1865: Last phase   85

The Battle of the Crater, July 30, 1864   108

Cold Harbor to Petersburg overview   150

City Point overview   167

City Point, 1864–1865   168

Confederate and Union Lines near Deep Bottom   203

First Deep Bottom, July 28, 1864   214

Second Deep Bottom, August 14–17, 1864   225

New Market Heights, September 29, 1864: First and second
phases   252

New Market Heights, September 29, 1864: Final phase   256

Fort Harrison–Chaffin's Farm, September 29–30, 1864   260

Fort Harrison–Chaffin's Farm, September 30, 1864   273

Darbytown Road, October 7, 1864   282

Westward movements overview   289

Jerusalem Plank Road, June 22, 1864   297

Weldon Railroad, August 18, 1864   306

Weldon Railroad, August 19, 1864   311

Weldon Railroad, August 21, 1864   315

Wilson-Kautz Raid, June 22–30, 1864   323

Reams Station, August 25, 1864: First assault   333

Reams Station, August 25, 1864: Second and third assaults 338

Peebles Farm: Union advance 343

Peebles Farm, September 30–October 2, 1864 352

First Battle of Squirrel Level Road, October 1, 1864 356

Boydton Plank Road, October 27, 1864 368

Boydton Plank Road, October 28, 1864 376

Hatcher's Run, February 5, 1865 378

Hatcher's Run, February 6, 1865 382

Hatcher's Run, February 7, 1865 386

Fall of Petersburg overview 392

Positions of the armies, March 25, 1865 394

Lewis Farm, March 29, 1865 398

White Oak Road, March 31, 1865: First and second phases 403

White Oak Road, March 31, 1865: Third and fourth phases 407

Dinwiddie Court-House, March 31, 1865 411

Five Forks, April 1, 1865 424

Sutherland Station, April 2, 1865 446

Breakthrough at Petersburg–Fort Gregg, April 2, 1865 453

Illustrations

Wartime Petersburg, Virginia (USAMHI) xviii

Lt. Gen. Ulysses S. Grant (USAMHI) 13

Maj. Gen. William F. "Baldy" Smith (USAMHI) 16

Gen. Pierre G. T. Beauregard (USAMHI) 19

"The Dictator" in front of Petersburg (USAMHI) 25

Confederate positions captured by the Union Eighteenth Corps, June 15, 1864 (USAMHI) 28

Fort Stedman (USAMHI) 80

Maj. Gen. John F. Hartranft and staff (USAMHI) 91

Gen. Robert E. Lee (USAMHI) 99

Details of the Mine (*Battles and Leaders of the Civil War*, Vol. IV, p. 548) 111

Maj. Gen. Ambrose E. Burnside (USAMHI) 117

The Battle of the Crater (USAMHI) 133

Maj. Gen. William Mahone (USAMHI) 137

Interior of the Crater (USAMHI)   142

Post Hospital, City Point (USAMHI)   174

Lt. Gen. Ulysses S. Grant and staff at City Point (USAMHI)   177

City Point (USAMHI)   186

Explosion at City Point (*Harper's Weekly,* August 27, 1864)   195

Richmond, Virginia (USAMHI)   199

Brig. Gen. Francis C. Barlow, Maj. Gen. David B. Birney, Brig.
    Gen. John Gibbon, and Maj. Gen. Winfield Scott Hancock
    (USAMHI)   211

Pontoon bridge at Deep Bottom (USAMHI)   226

Maj. Gen. Benjamin F. Butler (USAMHI)   250

Maj. Gen. Edward O. C. Ord (USAMHI)   254

Fort Burnham, formerly Confederate Fort Harrison
    (USAMHI)   270

Brig. Gen. August V. Kautz and Brig. Gen. Godfrey Weitzel
    (USAMHI)   283

Fort Sedgwick (USAMHI)   294

Fortifications at Fort Davis (USAMHI)   295

Maj. Gen. Gouverneur K. Warren (USAMHI)   313

Front lines of Petersburg (USAMHI)   321

Maj. Gen. Horatio G. Wright, Maj. Gen. Charles Griffin, Maj. Gen.
    George G. Meade, Maj. Gen. John G. Parke, and Maj. Gen.
    Andrew A. Humphreys (USAMHI)   345

150-foot-high signal tower near Petersburg, Virginia
    (USAMHI)   360

Brig. Gen. Joshua L. Chamberlain (USAMHI)   401

Maj. Gen. Philip H. Sheridan, Lt. Col. James W. Forsyth, Maj. Gen.
    Wesley Merritt, Brig. Gen. Thomas C. Devin, Maj. Gen. George A.
    Custer (USAMHI)   412

Maj. Gen. George E. Pickett (USAMHI)   431

Maj. Gen. Horatio G. Wright (USAMHI)   448

Capture of Confederate works at Petersburg (USAMHI)   462

ACKNOWLEDGMENTS

There is perhaps no more gratifying aspect of the task of bring-ing a book to completion than the opportunity to thank the many people whose help and support made it possible. First on the list is our good friend Brig. Gen. (ret.) Jack Mountcastle, who on learning of our interest in doing a volume on the Richmond and Petersburg Cam-paigns for this distinguished series put us in contact with Leonard J. Fullenkamp at the Army War College. Len's response to our proposal was gratifyingly positive—indeed perhaps more so than was merited at the time. More importantly, throughout the process of putting this volume together he has been a source of sage advice and guidance. It is with great pleasure that we not only express appreciation for his efforts on behalf of this project but count him among our friends in the profession. We also thank Ruth Gordon of the Army War College Foundation for the support the foundation and she personally have given our efforts from the time this project was conceived. For their help gathering the images from the collections at the magnificent U.S. Army Heritage and Education Center that appear in the book, we thank Louise Arnold-Friend, Richard Baker, Jack Giblin, and Gary Johnson.

One of the most appealing aspects of putting together a volume in this series, of course, was the knowledge that it would give us an op-portunity to work with Mike Briggs of the University Press of Kansas. Mike brings to any project more professional skill as an editor than anyone could hope for. He has been a good friend for many years, even when compelled to extend us more patience and faith that this would finally get done than we probably merited. We also thank Kelly Chrisman Jacques, Rebecca J. Murray, Jane Raese, and Mike Kehoe of the University Press of Kansas for all they did to help us through the process of turning the decidedly rough manuscript we submitted to them into a finished book. We are especially appreciative to Connie Oehring for going above and beyond in her inestimably important work as copy editor.

Our work received invaluable support from a number of folks who took time from their busy schedules to share their particular exper-tise on the Richmond and Petersburg Campaigns. First among these is Christopher Calkins, who since handing over the reins as chief of interpretation at Petersburg National Battlefield (which are now in the able hands of Chris Bryce, a long-ago comrade of Ethan's at Manassas National Battlefield) has been the driving force behind creating a first-rate battlefield experience at Sailor's Creek. Chris welcomed us into his lair at the battlefield and into his home, shared his expertise on the campaign and park, and provided invaluable feedback on large sections of the guide that enabled us to correct a number of points that needed it. We cannot express our appreciation strongly enough for all Chris did to support this project. The same can be said in regard to Robert E. L. Krick, whose encyclopedic knowledge of the battlefields north of the James River, many of which are not interpreted in any way and are not strictly within his area of responsibility at Richmond National Battlefield Park, was also of inestimable assistance to our efforts. For Charles, who grew up on the battlefields north of the river, this project was a labor of love. Without Bob's help this guide would not be as accurate or as comprehensive as it is in its treatment of those battlefields.

We also appreciate the support we received from Christopher Stowe, who as both a good friend and the historian on the U.S. Army Command and General Staff College's (CGSC's) teaching team at Fort Lee could not avoid being heavily involved in this project. Chris accompanied us on drives and walks around the battlefield, generously shared his own tremendous expertise on the campaign, read and critiqued drafts of the guide, and was a boon companion throughout. We also thank Steve Stanley, who produced the excellent maps that accompany the text and, in his dealings with us, demonstrated fully an "infinite capacity for taking pains."

The roots of this project extend back over a decade to when we worked together on the faculty at the U.S. Military Academy (USMA) at West Point, during which time we benefited from the leadership provided to the department and its military division by Robert Doughty, Lance Betros, and Matthew Moten. While on the faculty at USMA, we had our first opportunities to collaborate during staff rides of the Richmond and Petersburg battlefields. One of the most gratifying aspects of these rides was the opportunity to work with Will Greene of the incomparable Pamplin Historical Park. Will is currently working on a multivolume study of the Petersburg Campaign that will undoubtedly set a new standard for scholarship on the subject. Anyone who knows Will can attest to his generosity in sharing his incredible expertise on all aspects of the Civil War, one of the many qualities that make him one of the truly great people in the field.

Fortuitously, a great deal of the groundwork for this project had already been laid even before it was conceived thanks to Ethan's spending three months teaching at the CGSC campus at Fort Lee, Virginia. During that time he took students and other members of the faculty around the Petersburg battlefields on numerous occasions. We thank them for serving as initial sounding boards, and we also thank the members of the CGSC faculty then and since who have supported work on this project, especially Fort Lee teaching team leaders Neal Bralley and Bob Kennedy and James Willbanks, Richard Barbuto, and Christopher Gabel, who make the Department of Military History such a great place to work. We are also thankful for the efforts of the various commanding officers and mentors who provided Charles with the time and opportunity to work on the guide. The most important of these is Brig. Gen. Timothy J. Edens, who was his mentor and commanding officer during his longest combat deployment and whose guidance has made him a better soldier and leader in ways too numerous to mention. His two bosses at the U.S. Army Aviation Center, Col. (ret.) Jimmy Meacham and Col. Shawn Prickett, have also mentored him along the way.

Our greatest appreciation, of course, is for the support we have received from our families during the years it took this project to come to fruition. Rachel and Corinne Lee Rafuse were always there with support for their husband and father while he worked on this project. Mary Ann Bowery has endured her husband's fascination with the Civil War with patience and good humor and has always been his sounding board and reality check.

Wartime Petersburg, Virginia (USAMHI)

HOW TO USE THIS BOOK

This guide is designed to enable you to have an enjoyable and productive visit to the sites associated with the Richmond-Petersburg Campaign of 1864–1865. The environs of Richmond and Petersburg can be frustrating and confusing places for the visitor seeking to follow the course and gain a full understanding of the campaign and its major operations, which took place over hundreds of square miles of Tidewater and Southside Virginia. Further complicating efforts to gain a full understanding of this massive and complex campaign is the fact that a relatively small percentage of the area where operations took place is under National Park Service ownership and management. Moreover, much of this area consists of noncontiguous parcels of ground surrounded by private property, while industrial and suburban development radiates in all directions from both Richmond and Petersburg, with industrial parks, factories, housing developments, street grids, and highways having changed much of the area forever. With patience, curiosity, and this book, however, the modern visitor will be able to visit most places of true significance and find even in this highly developed area patches of hallowed ground that have changed very little from their wartime appearance.

Although the reader will gain a good understanding of the Richmond-Petersburg Campaign from reading this book and exploring the sites where the campaign's course and outcome were determined, this book is not intended to be a strict narrative history. Readers will benefit from reviewing one of the many published narrative accounts of the Civil War in general and the Richmond-Petersburg Campaign in particular before and after their visit.

In order to give the reader a full understanding of events, the stops are arranged in a way that makes as much geographical and chronological sense as possible, something the modern road network and the often disjointed manner in which the campaign unfolded make impossible to do exactly. The itinerary in this book, along with the detailed directions to and between each stop, is designed to overcome problems posed by the modern road network as much as possible and to facilitate efforts to get around the area in a clear, logical fashion. As with previous volumes in this series, at each stand you will find excerpts from official reports, memoirs, and other primary materials that describe the action, with enough intrusion by the editors as is necessary to clarify or amplify points made in those documents.

The first section of the book is designed to accompany readers as they explore the main section of Petersburg National Battlefield, which includes sites of importance to the First, Third, and Final Petersburg Offensives. Separate excursions enable the reader to explore and gain a better understanding of the significance of the many important sites outside this area and are structured to enable the visitor to study each independently or as part of a comprehensive study of the Richmond-Petersburg Campaign.

The core tour covering the engagements that took place in the Eastern Front segment of Petersburg National Battlefield (First Petersburg, Fort Stedman, the Crater) is structured to enable the reader to do a study of them in a single day, which is about how long the Westward Movements excursion requires as well. The other excursions will take less time. It is always preferable to study military operations in the order in which they unfolded, though in this case geography makes that difficult—indeed prohibitively so unless one has many days to devote to their study. For readers who want to take a chronological approach and have time to do so, we suggest beginning with From Cold Harbor to Petersburg, followed by First Petersburg, City Point, Deep Bottom, the Crater, Westward Movements, Fort Harrison–Darbytown Road, Fort Stedman, and the Fall of Petersburg. If readers wish to just study the operations south of the James and Appomattox rivers in chronological order, they can start with First Petersburg, then visit the Crater and City Point, followed by the Westward Movements and Fall of Petersburg excursions. Focused study on operations north of the James involves (in sequence) the following excursions: From Cold Harbor to Petersburg, Deep Bottom, and Fort Harrison–Darbytown Road.

We have provided full names and military ranks whenever an individual is mentioned for the first time, with all Confederate names italicized.

VISITOR CENTER

The National Park Service Visitor Center at Petersburg is the point of departure for the main section of the book and all of the excursions. It is easily accessible from Interstates 95 and 295 via Virginia Route 36, which at various points is named Oaklawn Boulevard, Washington Street, and Wythe Street. Your visitor fee, payable at the gatehouse at the top of the exit from Route 36 or the front desk in the Visitor Center, is valid for seven consecutive days.

The Visitor Center contains a well-stocked bookstore, a museum displaying artifacts from the siege, and a small theater for audiovisual programs. The National Park Service staff on site here organizes a regular schedule of short tours and events.

THE BATTLEFIELD TODAY

The main battlefield area at Petersburg National Battlefield, also known as the Eastern Front segment, is serviced by a park road that begins at the Visitor Center and continues south and west to modern Crater Road (U.S. 301), which in 1864–1865 was known as the Jerusalem Plank Road, in the vicinity of Blandford Church. Because the park road is mostly one-way, visitors cannot visit all of the sites by car in exact chronological order without retracing some steps on foot. Following the park road, the visitor is able to see three main groups of features. The first begins at the area around the Visitor Center and extends down to the Taylor House site. It primarily supports study of the First Battle of Petersburg of June 15–18, 1864. At Fort Stedman, the focus is on where the Confederates launched an unsuccessful offensive on March 25, 1865. Finally, the section of the park between the Taylor House and exit from the park onto Crater Road focuses on what is undoubtedly the most famous episode of the entire campaign, the Battle of the Crater on July 30, 1864.

Much of the campaign south of the James River in 1864–1865 revolved around efforts by the Federals to gain control of the logistical network south and west of Petersburg that linked the town and its defenders with the Carolinas. Sites associated with these operations make up what is known as the Western Front section of the Petersburg National Battlefield and are covered in the Westward Movements and Fall of Petersburg excursions. The Western Front section of Petersburg National Battlefield consists largely of the remnants of forts constructed by the Federals as they extended their lines westward and the park road linking them and ultimately takes you to the Five Forks unit of Petersburg National Battlefield. The National Park Service also owns the tip of land at the confluence of the Appomattox and James Rivers known as City Point, where Union headquarters was located for much of the campaign, and Fort Gregg, which played a critical role in the final phase of the campaign. The last major segment south of the James that belongs to the National Park Service is the site of the April 1, 1865, engagement at Five Forks. North of the James River, the National Park Service owns only sites associated with the September–October 1864 fight for Fort Harrison, which is operated as part of the Richmond National Battlefield Park, and the Confederate defensive line.

Although the National Park Service's holdings are extensive, much of the ground where significant operations took place around Richmond and Petersburg between June 1864 and April 1865 is outside National Park Service control. Fortunately, in addition to these National Park Service sites, a number of sites of importance to the Richmond-Petersburg Campaign remain accessible to the public, thanks to the efforts of private preservation groups, the work of local park authorities, and simple good fortune, and retain enough of their historical flavor to be of value to the student studying the campaign.

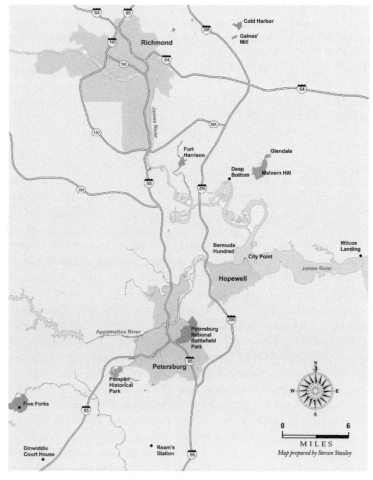

Richmond-Petersburg overview

INTRODUCTION

As the sun rose over the Virginia tidewater on June 15, 1864, a magnificent scene played out along the banks of the historic James River. Engineers from the Union army had constructed a 2,100-foot-long pontoon bridge connecting the north and south banks of the river. As dawn approached, thousands of blue-clad troops, countless batteries of artillery, and scores of wagons began taking advantage of this engineering marvel to move from the north to the south side of the river. By noon on June 15, wrote one witness:

> The approaches to the river on both banks were covered with masses of troops moving briskly to their positions or waiting patiently their turn to cross. . . . The bright sun, shining through a clear sky upon the scene, cast its sheen upon the water, was reflected from the burnished gun-barrels and glittering cannon, and brought out with increased brilliancy the gay colors of the waving banners. The calmly flowing river reflected the blue of the heavens, and mirrored on its surface the beauties of nature that bordered it. . . . It was a matchless pageant that could not fail to inspire all beholders with the grandeur of achievement and the majesty of military power.[1]

At one point that morning, a lean, bearded man of medium height and a determined though decidedly unprepossessing appearance ascended the bluff overlooking the north bank of the river, clasped his hands behind his back, and began to take in the scene. Usually a cigar was tightly clamped between his teeth, but not on this occasion. One of his subordinates later suspected that the absence of the cigar and his "profound silence" were evidence that Lt. Gen. Ulysses S. Grant, supreme commander of all the armies of the United States, "was lost in the contemplation of the spectacle" playing out below him. More than that was undoubtedly on Grant's mind, however. He had brought his army to the banks of the James River not for a "matchless pageant" but to put it in position to strike a blow against what he had

---

[1] Horace Porter, *Campaigning with Grant* (New York: Century, 1897), pp. 199–200.

determined to be the decisive point of the war in Virginia. That point was the town of Petersburg.[2]

At one moment during the brutal Overland Campaign, which had preceded the arrival of Grant and his army at Wilcox's Landing, Grant's counterpart, Gen. *Robert E. Lee*, had remarked to a subordinate: "We must destroy this army of Grant's before he gets to James River. If he gets there, it will become a siege, and then it will be a mere question of time."[3] *Lee's* prescient words, rather than the acute appreciation for the power of contingency in military operations that undoubtedly weighed on Grant's mind in June 1864, have been associated with the campaign for Richmond and Petersburg ever since, lending it an air of inevitability that has contributed to the campaign's relatively minor place in our historical consciousness. Indeed, a survey of the literature produced in more than 150 years since the Civil War began could understandably lead one to conclude the campaign for Richmond and Petersburg was of considerably less significance than other episodes on the road to Union victory, such as Shiloh, Chickamauga, and Gettysburg. Moreover, one of the defining characteristic of the campaign in the minds of most students of the war—the extensive system of trenches north and south of the James River that the armies built and occupied throughout the campaign—has fostered an image of a stagnant and somewhat uneventful campaign of position that contrasts starkly with the dramatic maneuvers and fighting of the earlier Overland Campaign and the dynamic pursuit that would later corner *Lee's* army at Appomattox.

Yet the campaign was much more than simply a siege—indeed, a compelling case can be made for disposing of this term altogether if we are to properly understand what happened south and north of the James River between June 1864 and April 1865. Indeed, in many ways the Petersburg Campaign encapsulated all that the Civil War was militarily and all that it would become in the last years of the conflict. In its conduct it saw elements of the premodern and the modern, and the ultimate course the campaign took was by no means determined at its outcome.

The Confederate armies that occupied the Petersburg and Richmond fortifications in mid-June 1864 were very different from those

---

[2] Ibid., pp. 37, 198–201.

[3] Jubal A. Early, "The Campaigns of Gen. Robert E. Lee. An Address . . . before Washington and Lee University, January 19th, 1872," in Gary W. Gallagher, ed., *Lee the Soldier* (Lincoln: University of Nebraska Press, 1996), p. 65.

that had started the spring campaign in early May. They were only a shadow of the magnificent forces that had foiled one Union offensive after another in Virginia and at one point had even carried the war to the banks of the Susquehanna River in Pennsylvania. Weeks of marching and fighting from the banks of the Rapidan River to the outskirts of Richmond had ground *Lee's* magnificent Army of Northern Virginia down to fewer than 40,000 men. Nonetheless, what remained was a hard core of steadfast veterans. The leadership of the army was tough and capable and had been forged into a relatively smoothly operating team, largely due to its absolute confidence in *Lee's* generalship. These factors made *Lee's* small army like a wounded animal, limited perhaps in its striking power but still dangerous. Consequently, although the line of contact between the two eastern armies had shifted 60 miles to the south since May, in the minds of the participants the issue was still very much in doubt. Although they had not experienced the carnage and intensity of combat undergone by the Army of Northern Virginia, the forces guarding Richmond and Petersburg that had been operating under the command of *Pierre G. T. Beauregard* had also suffered during the course of the spring campaigns.

Things were hardly going swimmingly on the Federal side of the line in June 1864. The Army of the Potomac had also changed and suffered a great deal in the weeks leading up to June 15. As they made their way south from the Rapidan River, the Federals fought both the rebels and among themselves, and the army's high command had a history of being riven with dissension. Before beginning operations in 1864, Grant had decided to place his headquarters in the field with the Army of the Potomac and, during the early stages of the Overland Campaign, had gradually taken operational and tactical control of an army that belonged, on paper at least, to Maj. Gen. George Gordon Meade, the victor of Gettysburg. This ambiguous command relationship did not sit completely well with either man. Although they were in almost complete accord regarding how operations had been conducted since the establishment of their command relationship a few months earlier, tensions had emerged in the relationship between Grant and Meade, and between them and their subordinate commanders, by the time they began maneuvering the Army of the Potomac toward Petersburg.

The butcher's bill for this movement was staggering, almost beyond comprehension even for a Northern populace seemingly inured to years of war. Between crossing the Rapidan River on May 4 and the time it began crossing the James, Meade's army suffered more than 50,000 casualties and experienced naught but frustration in its attempt to bring *Lee* to battle under advantageous conditions. During the failed campaign along the James in May and June, the Union Army of the James commanded by Maj. Gen. Benjamin F. Butler had suffered casualties—albeit in much lower numbers than had the Army of the Potomac—as well as the embarrassment of experiencing defeat at the hands of an inferior force and being penned up in their entrenchments around Bermuda Hundred, in Grant's words, "as if . . . in a bottle strongly corked."[4]

In the course of the Overland and Bermuda Hundred Campaigns, the Union Armies of the James and the Potomac had lost as many men as *Lee* and *Beauregard* had in their entire combined force. The high casualties and failure of Grant's strategy to achieve decisive victories had also taken a heavy toll on Northern morale, which boded ill for the Union cause in a war that Lincoln had accurately defined in 1861 as "essentially a People's contest."[5] As if this were not enough, three-year enlistments in both Meade's and Butler's armies were expiring while personality conflicts, rivalries between Eastern and Western officers as well as between political and West Point–trained officers, and spats over the conduct of the Overland Campaign had fostered tensions, resentments, and suspicions among Union army, corps, and division commanders.

After failing miserably in his attempt to break the Confederate lines at Cold Harbor on June 3, Grant decided once again not to stay in place and lick his wounds or to fall back but to move east and south. Once across the James, Grant would attempt to take Petersburg, the terminus of four railroads and Richmond's lifeline to the Deep South. The attempt failed, but it proved to be but the opening phase of a ten-month campaign that produced significant fighting on both sides of the James River. During that period *Lee* struggled to avoid, and then to break, the noose that the Federals doggedly endeavored to fashion around the neck of his army. When the campaign ended in April 1865, the surrender of *Lee's* army was indeed but a matter of time—a week, to be exact.

The popular impression of the Richmond-Petersburg Campaign of 1864–1865 is of a dull campaign of siegework, punctuated by the

<hr />

[4] Bruce Catton, *Grant Takes Command* (Boston: Little, Brown, 1968), p. 247.

[5] Abraham Lincoln, "Message to Congress," July 4, 1861, in Roy P. Basler, ed., *The Collected Works of Abraham Lincoln*, 9 vols. (New Brunswick, N.J.: Rutgers University Press, 1953–1955). Volume 4, p. 438.

spectacular and curious Union fiasco at the Crater, that offers little of interest beyond a foretaste of the dreary trench warfare of World War I. This was not the case. There was, to be sure, extensive use of fortifications, and the fight at the Crater did occur, but the campaign also saw large segments of the Union and Confederate armies battle for control of the railroads and roads around Richmond and Petersburg. These engagements tested the tactical and operational savvy of leaders on both sides. Moreover, Union and Confederate cavalry ranged far and wide over the Virginia landscape over the course of the campaign. Grant's conduct of the campaign, which relied heavily on support from the navy and entailed a massive logistical effort, also offers an example of joint operations and a compelling illustration of the critical role of logistics in the conduct of major military operations.

The fighting around Richmond and Petersburg also saw the first use of African American soldiers in frontline combat in the Eastern Theater of the Civil War. Throughout the war, debate over the use of the U.S. Colored Troops was inextricably intertwined with larger political dynamics in both the North and the South, though there is no debate about the bravery African American troops demonstrated during the course of their service in the Union Army. Thus, the Richmond-Petersburg Campaign shaped and was shaped by many of the political and social dynamics that produced and fueled the Civil War. The purpose of this book is to help the reader better understand this campaign and the fields where its course and outcome were determined.

PART I
PETERSBURG NATIONAL BATTLEFIELD

FIRST PETERSBURG

This section of the guide takes you over the ground where the outcome of the First Petersburg Offensive of June 15–18, 1864, was decided. This ground also saw combat in the Battle of Fort Stedman of March 1865 and the July 1864 Battle of the Crater (also known as the Third Petersburg Offensive). Because of the one-way road through the park, it is not possible to do the First Petersburg section and then easily backtrack to do the Crater and Fort Stedman engagements in the sequence in which they occurred. Thus, in order to avoid potential confusion, this section will not address the Crater and Fort Stedman but will refer readers to other sections that do when they are on the ground associated with those actions. This arrangement gives readers the option of staying chronologically true in focusing solely on the First Petersburg Offensive or endeavoring to do all three of the engagements in line with the geography and road network.

The First Petersburg Offensive marked the transition from the Overland and Bermuda Hundred Campaigns of May and June 1864 to the Richmond-Petersburg Campaign of June 1864 to April 1865. In the course of the Overland Campaign, which saw brutal fighting in engagements at the Wilderness, Spotsylvania, the North Anna River, and around Cold Harbor, Union forces commanded by Lt. Gen. Ulysses S. Grant and Maj. Gen. George G. Meade lost nearly 60,000 killed, wounded, and missing while Gen. *Robert E. Lee's* Confederate Army of Northern Virginia suffered losses of about 33,000. The campaign began with an attempt by Grant's forces during the first week of May to turn *Lee's* right, which *Lee* successfully prevented by bringing the Federals to battle in the Wilderness. Grant would make four more unsuccessful attempts to maneuver around *Lee's* right that would be thwarted in bloody fighting and carry the two armies to the outskirts of Richmond by the first week of June. While this was going on, another Federal army, Maj. Gen. Benjamin F. Butler's Army of the James, moved up the James River to City Point and Bermuda Hundred and made an attempt to seize Richmond and the railroads linking the Confederate capital with Petersburg. This attempt was thwarted in mid-May by a much smaller force, scraped together by Confederate authorities under the command of Gen. *Pierre G. T. Beauregard,* that forced Butler's command back to a fortified position in the Bermuda Hundred peninsula.

After a futile attempt to break *Lee's* lines with a direct assault at Cold Harbor on June 3, Grant decided to make another grand turning movement. Meade's Army of the Potomac would march south from Cold Harbor, cross the James, and link up with elements from Butler's army to attack Petersburg. If successful, this operation would give the Federals possession of a city whose rail connections to the Carolinas were critical to the ability of the South to continue the fight in Virginia. Its failure would condemn both sides to a nine-month campaign around Richmond and Petersburg. Although ultimately a decisive Union victory that ended with the surrender of *Lee's* army only a week later, the Richmond-Petersburg Campaign cost both sides dearly in both lives and treasure.

SUMMARY OF PRINCIPAL EVENTS, 13–18 JUNE 1864

June 13–July 31—The Richmond (Virginia) Campaign

June 13—Skirmish at White Oak Swamp, Lt. Gen. *Richard S. Ewell*, C.S. Army, assigned to command of the Department of Richmond, vice Maj. Gen. *Robert Ransom Jr.* ordered to Department of Western Virginia; skirmish at Riddell's Shop

14—Skirmish near Harrison's Landing

15—Skirmish at Malvern Hill; skirmish near Smith's Store; Brig. Gen. Alfred H. Terry, U.S. Army, in temporary command of Tenth Army Corps, vice Maj. Gen. Quincy A. Gillmore

15–18—Assaults on the Petersburg lines

16—Action on the Bermuda Hundred front

16–17—Actions at Fort Clifton

17—Skirmish on the Bermuda Hundred front

18—Skirmish at King and Queen Court-House; Maj. Gen. David B. Birney, U.S. Army, in temporary command of Second Army Corps; Brig. Gen. William T. H. Brooks, U.S. Army, assumes command of Tenth Army Corps

19–July 31—Siege of Petersburg and Richmond

STOP 1: BATTERY NO. 6

From the Visitor Center entrance, walk on the paved path to the flagpole, then proceed straight to the parking lot. Cross the parking lot, and walk about 100 yards to a point just past a sign reading, "Site of Confederate Battery 6," which is about 10 yards to the left of the single cannon. Battery No. 5 is about 300 yards to your left. Stop here and face the treeline.

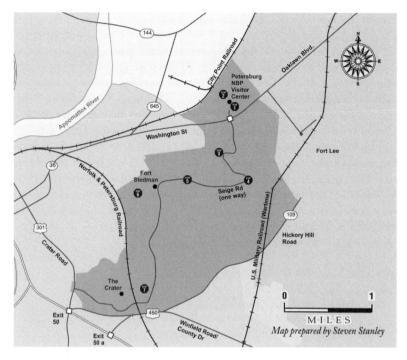

First Petersburg overview

This was the location of the sixth in a 10-mile line of fifty-five forts or batteries that, connected by trenches, began on the Appomattox River east of Petersburg and ended on the Appomattox west of the city in June 1864. The line was initially laid out by Lt. Col. *Walter Stevens* and Col. *J. F. Gilmer* during the second half of 1862, and construction was largely completed under the direction of Capt. *Charles Dimmock* by the summer of 1863. Efforts to conform the "Dimmock Line" to the terrain around Petersburg had the effect of creating a number of salients in the line that were vulnerable to cross fire and attack from three directions. Among the most prominent of these was the one incorporating Batteries 4, 5, 6, and 7, which covered the approach to the town along the City Point Railroad. Federal forces commanded by Maj. Gen. William F. "Baldy" Smith would follow the railroad in their advance on Petersburg on June 15, 1864.

The arrival of Smith's command in front of Petersburg was the product of a grand movement conceived by Union general-in-chief Lt. Gen. Ulysses S. Grant that began on the evening of June 12. That night the Second, Fifth, Sixth, and Ninth Corps of Maj. Gen. George G.

Meade's Army of the Potomac evacuated their trenches in front of Cold Harbor and began pushing south across the Chickahominy River en route to the James River. Meanwhile, the Eighteenth Corps from Maj. Gen. Benjamin F. Butler's Army of the James marched from Cold Harbor east to White House on the Pamunkey River, where it boarded transports that would take it to Bermuda Hundred. During the morning of June 14, the Second Corps began crossing the James at Wilcox's Landing on boats while Federal engineers constructed a magnificent pontoon bridge just downriver connecting the end of the Wyanoke Peninsula with the southern bank of the river nearly 2,000 feet away.

The approximately 14,000 men of Smith's Eighteenth Corps began their advance toward Petersburg from City Point early on the morning of June 15. Maj. Gen. Winfield Scott Hancock's Second Corps, which had completed its crossing of the James at five that morning, was to march to Smith's assistance.

TO THE GATES OF PETERSBURG

Lt. Gen. Ulysses S. Grant, USA, commanding Armies of the United States, to Maj. Gen. Henry W. Halleck, Chief of Staff at Washington, 1:30 p.m., June 14, 1864

Our forces will commence crossing the James to-day. The enemy shows no signs yet of having brought troops to the south side of Richmond. I will have Petersburg secured, if possible, before they get there in much force. Our movement from Cold Harbor to the James River has been made with great celerity and so far without loss of accident. [U.S. War Department, *The War of the Rebellion: A Compilation of the Official Records of the Union and Confederate Armies*, 70 vols. in 128 parts and index (Washington, D.C.: Government Printing Office, 1880–1901), series 1, volume XL, part 1, p. 12. Hereafter cited as *O.R.*; all references are to series 1 unless otherwise noted.]

Report of Lt. Gen. Ulysses S. Grant, USA, commanding Armies of the United States

My idea, from the start, had been to beat *Lee's* army north of Richmond if possible; then, after destroying his lines of communication north of the James River, to transfer the army to the south side and besiege *Lee* in Richmond or follow him south if he should retreat. After the battle of the Wilderness it was evident that the enemy deemed it of the first importance to run no risks with the army he then had. He acted purely on the defensive

Lt. Gen. Ulysses S. Grant (USAMHI)

behind breast-works, or feebly on the offensive immediately in front of them, and where in case of repulse he could easily retire behind them. Without a greater sacrifice of life than I was willing to make, all could not be accomplished that I had designed north of Richmond. I therefore determined to . . . move the army to the south side of the James River, by the enemy's right flank, where I felt I could cut off all his sources of supply except by the [James River and Kanawha] canal. . . .

Attaching great importance to the possession of Petersburg, I sent back to Bermuda Hundred and City Point General Smith's command by water, via the White House, to reach there in advance of the Army of the Potomac. This was for the express purpose of securing Petersburg before the enemy, becoming aware of our intention, could re-enforce the place. The movement from Cold Harbor commenced after dark on the evening of the 12th; one division of cavalry, under General [James H.] Wilson, and the Fifth Corps crossed the Chickahominy at Long Bridge, and moved out to White Oak Swamp, to cover the crossings of the other corps. The advance corps reached James River, at Wilcox's Landing and Charles City Court-House, on the night of the 13th. . . .

The Second Corps commenced crossing the James River on the morning of the 14th by ferry-boats at Wilcox's Landing. The laying of the pontoon bridge was completed about midnight of the 14th, and the crossing of the balance of the army was rapidly pushed forward by both bridge and ferry. After the crossing had commenced, I proceeded by a steamer to Bermuda Hundred to give the necessary orders for the immediate capture of Petersburg. The instructions to General Butler were verbal, and were for him to send General Smith immediately, that night, with all the troops he could give him without sacrificing the position he then held. I told him that I would return at once to the Army of the Potomac, hasten its crossing, and throw it forward to Petersburg by divisions as rapidly as it could be done; that we could re-enforce our armies more rapidly there than the enemy could bring troops against us. General Smith got off as directed, and confronted the enemy's pickets near Petersburg before daylight next morning. [*O.R.*, XLVI, part 1, pp. 21, 23.]

Smith's command advanced toward Petersburg on June 15 in two columns. The division commanded by Brig. Gen. Edward W. Hinks, an all–African American unit, followed the City Point Road, while just north of them Brig. Gen. William T. H. Brooks's and Brig. Gen. John H. Martindale's divisions crossed the Appomattox River at Point of Rocks and then followed the City Point Railroad south and west toward Petersburg. Screening the advance was a force of 2,500 cavalry commanded by Brig. Gen. August V. Kautz. Before moving on Petersburg, Smith was assured by his superiors that he would encounter little if any resistance. Thus, it was with some consternation that he received news from Kautz that, at around six a.m., the cavalry had been brought to a halt only a few miles from City Point by Confederate rifle pits located on the Baylor Farm, which were occupied by four pieces of artillery and Confederate cavalry commanded by Brig. Gen. *James Dearing.*

At Smith's direction, Hinks moved his command forward, deployed it with Col. Samuel Duncan's brigade in the lead, and ordered it to attack *Dearing's* position. Intense and accurate Confederate artillery fire and marshy, wooded terrain combined to frustrate Duncan's first attack, but he eventually managed to get two regiments into a position from which they could crush the Confederate left. *Dearing* responded by ordering his men to pull back toward Petersburg. Although they lost one of their guns, *Dearing* and his men had held off the Federals for nearly two hours, during which he sent a message to his superiors back at Petersburg reporting that a large Union force was heading toward them.

Report of Maj. Gen. William F. Smith, USA, commanding Eighteenth Corps, Army of the James

About 4 a.m. the head of my column left Broadway. Near Baylor's farm our cavalry came upon the enemy's artillery and infantry. General Kautz being unable to dislodge them, General Hinks was ordered to make the attack. The rifle-pits were gallantly carried by General Hinks' command and one piece of artillery captured. My command was then ordered to move forward according to the original orders of the day. [*O.R.*, XL, part 1, p. 705.]

Report of Brig. Gen. Edward W. Hinks, USA, commanding Third Division, Eighteenth Corps, Army of the James

About 5 o'clock, General Kautz's cavalry column having passed, my division was ordered into column and proceeded as far as the railroad, when its march was obstructed by a halt of the cavalry, and sharp firing of musketry and artillery was heard toward the front. I immediately made a personal reconnaissance and found that the enemy had opened fire from a position in Baylor's field, which commanded the road, as it debouched from the wood and swamp, near Perkinson's Saw Mill, and that the head of the cavalry column had been driven in. Having reported the state of affairs to General Smith, I was ordered to deploy in two lines of battle, with skirmishers in front, and force a passage of the swamp. Duncan's brigade was formed on the first line, [Col. John H.]Holman's

Maj. Gen. William F. "Baldy" Smith (USAMHI)

in the second. Considerable delay was occasioned by the difficulty in getting the Fifth Massachusetts Cavalry into line by reason of its awkwardness in maneuver, it being composed of new recruits, and drilled only in [Philip St. George] Cooke's single rank cavalry formation, which entirely unfitted it to act as infantry in line.

The lines, however, being formed, I ordered an advance, having directed [Capt. James R.] Angel's battery into a position from which its guns were brought to bear upon the enemy over our advancing lines. The wood and swamp, through which ran a creek, was extremely difficult of passage, but the advance was finally made by most of the regiment, though furiously assailed with spherical case, canister, and musketry along the whole line. Some confusion, however, arose among the regiments upon the left of the road, and a few of the men fell back to the open space of ground. The enemy was found to be in a hastily constructed work, occupying a very strong position in Baylor's field, with four pieces of artillery and some force of infantry in the field-works, and two pieces of artillery, with supports, upon the crest of the hill on the right. The distance from the edge of the woods to the works was about 400 yards over open, rising ground, which was speedily overcome, when the enemy fled toward Petersburg, leaving in our hands one 12-pounder gun. This line was carried at a little later than 8 a.m. [*O.R.*, XL, part 1, p. 721.]

Report of Col. Joseph B. Kiddoo, Twenty-second U.S. Colored Troops, Second Brigade, Hinks's Division, Eighteenth Corps, Army of the James

On the morning of the 15th I moved with the rest of the brigade from Spring Hill on the City Point road. Approaching the enemy's advanced line of rifle-pits near Baylor's house, I received orders from the colonel commanding the brigade to form line of battle and advance, the Fifth U.S. Colored Troops [USCT] being at the same time on my right and the Fourth U.S. Colored Troops on my left. I also received orders from the colonel commanding to be ready to charge when ordered. After I had gotten under the fire of the enemy's artillery, concluding that on account of the broken nature of the ground orders could not reach me to charge, or that I could not be found, I took the responsibility and ordered my regiment to charge the line of rifle-pits in my front. The effect with which the enemy's artillery was playing upon my line was the strongest inducement for me to give this order. The charge was gallantly made, and that portion of the rifle-pits in front of my line possessed, together with one 12-pounder howitzer, from the fire of which my men suffered severely while coming from the woods. [*O.R.* XL, part 1, p. 724.]

The site of the Baylor Farm is interpreted by a battlefield wayside marker at the Hopewell Visitor Center, which is located about 3 miles east of the entrance to the Park Tour Road off Route 36.

Narrative of Gen. Pierre G. T. Beauregard, CSA, commanding Department of North Carolina and South Carolina [and Defenses of Petersbzurg]

As prompt and energetic action became more and more imperative, and as I could no longer doubt the presence of Smith's corps with Butler's forces, I sent one of my aides, Colonel *Samuel B. Paul,* to General *Lee* with instructions to explain to him the exact situation. General *Lee's* answer to Colonel *Paul* was not encouraging. He said that I must be in error in believing the enemy had thrown a large force on the south side of the James; that the troops referred to by me could be but a few of Smith's corps going back to Butler's lines. Strange to say, at the very time General *Lee* was thus expressing himself to Colonel *Paul,* the whole of Smith's corps was actually assaulting the Petersburg lines. But General *Lee* finally said that he had already issued orders for the return of [Maj. Gen. *Robert*] *Hoke's* division; that he would do all he could to aid me, and even come himself should the necessity arise.

The Confederate forces opposed to Smith's corps on the 15th of June consisted of the 26th, 34th, and 46th Virginia regiments, the 64th Georgia, the 23d South Carolina, [Lt. Col. *Fletcher H.*] *Archer's* militia, [*Cullen A.*] *Battle's* and [*William H.*] *Wood's* battalions, [Capt. *Nathaniel A.*] *Sturdivant's* battery, *Dearing's* small command of cavalry, and some other transient forces, having a real effective for duty of 2,200 only. These troops occupied the Petersburg line on the left from Battery No. 1 to what was called Butterworth's Bridge, toward the right, and had to be so stationed as to allow but one man for every 4½ yards. From that bridge to the Appomattox [west of Petersburg]—a distance of fully 4½ miles—the line was defenseless.

Early in the morning—at about 7 o'clock—General *Dearing,* on the Broadway and City Point roads, reported his regiment engaged with a large force of the enemy. The stand made by our handful of cavalry, near their breastworks, was most creditable to themselves and to their gallant commander, and the enemy's ranks, at that point, were much thinned by the accurate firing of the battery under [Capt. *Edward*] *Graham.* But the weight of numbers soon produced its almost inevitable result, and, in spite of the desperate efforts of our men, the cavalry breastworks were flanked and finally abandoned by us, with the loss of one howitzer. Still, *Dearing's* encounter with the enemy, at that moment and on

Gen. Pierre G. T. Beauregard (USAMHI)

that part of the field, was of incalculable advantage to the defenders of our line, inasmuch as it afforded time for additional preparation and the distribution of new orders by [Brig. Gen. *Henry A.*]
Wise. [Robert Underwood Johnson and Clarence Clough Buell,
eds., *Battles and Leaders of the Civil War,* 4 vols. (New York: The Century Company, 1884–1887). Volume IV, p. 540. Hereafter cited as
Battles and Leaders.]

Report of Brig. Gen. Henry A. Wise, CSA, commanding Wise's Brigade, Department of North Carolina and South Carolina

The following forces were engaged: The Twenty-sixth, Thirty-fourth, Forty-sixth Virginia, Sixty-fourth Georgia, Company F, Twenty-third South Carolina, *Archer's* Militia [Third Battalion Virginia Reserves], *Battle's* [Forty-Fourth Battalion Virginia Infantry] and *Wood's* [Battalion Virginia Reserves] Battalions, *Sturdivant's* [Virginia Light] Battery, *Dearing's* Cavalry [Brigade], and other transient forces, making a total strength of 2,738, but a really effective one of 2,200 men of all arms. . . . At 7 a.m. on June 15, General *Dearing* [informed] General *Wise* that his forces were hotly engaged with the enemy on the Broadway and City Point Roads, not far from their forks. General Wise took command of the right, from Battery 23 to Butterworth's Bridge.

The cavalry made a handsome stand at their breastworks, and *Graham's* [Virginia Horse Artillery] Battery did great execution among the enemy's ranks. But they advanced in such overwhelming force that, although their assaults were several times repulsed, they prevailed in flanking our cavalry breastworks, which were finally abandoned, with the loss of one howitzer. [Janet B. Hewett et al., eds., *Supplement to the Official Records of the Union and Confederate Armies,* 51 vols. (Wilmington, N.C.: Broadfoot Publishing, 1994–1997). *Part I—Reports,* volume VII, pp. 284–285. Hereafter cited as *O.R. Supplement.*]

From Battery No. 6, turn left and walk over to Battery No. 5, following the trace of the old Dimmock Line, which should be indicated by the high grass to your right. Rejoin the paved path as it enters Battery No. 5, and follow it over to a cannon facing toward the woods. Stop here, and face the tree line.

STOP 2: BATTERY NO. 5

THE UNION ASSAULT, 15 JUNE 1864

After successfully overcoming the Confederate position at the Baylor Farm, Smith pushed his command forward as Brig. Gen. *Henry Wise* concentrated his approximately 2,000 men in the eastern defenses of the Dimmock Line. Smith's three divisions reached the Confederate defensive line around noon, but their commander decided to conduct a thorough reconnaissance before launching his attack,

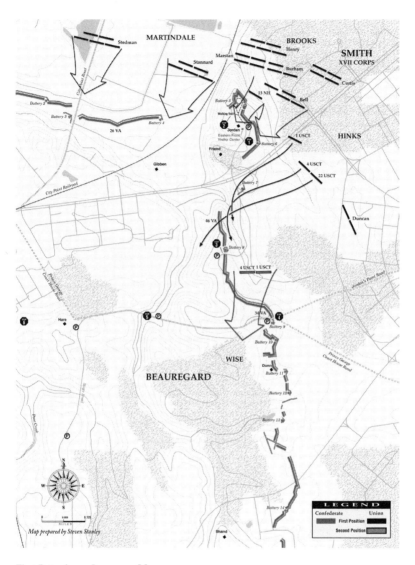

First Petersburg, June 15, 1864

while the Confederate defenders frantically shuffled their forces to meet the threat.

Narrative of General Beauregard, continued

At 10 o'clock a.m. the skirmishing had assumed very alarming proportions. To the urgent demands of General *Wise* for reenforcements, I was enabled at last to answer that part of *Hoke's* division was on the way from Drewry's Bluff and would be in time to save the day, if our men could stand their ordeal, hard as it was, a little while longer. . . .

All along the line, from one end to the other, the order was given "to hold on at all hazards!" It was obeyed with the resolute fortitude of veterans, though many of the troops thus engaged, with such odds against them, had hardly been under fire before. At 12 m., and as late as 2 p.m., our center was vigorously pressed, as though the Norfolk and Petersburg Railroad were the immediate object of the onset. General *Wise* now closed the line from his right to strengthen Colonel *J[ohn] T[homas] Goode* and, with him the 34th Virginia; while, at the same time and with equal perspicacity, he hurried *Wood's* battalion toward the left in support of Colonel *P. R. Page* and his command. [*Battles and Leaders of the Civil War*, IV, p. 540.]

Report of Brigadier General Wise, continued

During that gallant stand of *Dearing's* command, time was gained to make all preparations on the lines, and at about 10 a.m. the skirmishing on the left, began to be serious.

At 12 m. the enemy's cavalry approached our center, dismounted, deployed skirmishers and moved up as infantry. Reinforcements had already been called for from north side of the Appomattox. The repeated reply was to hold on, that reinforcements would be sent. From 12 m. to 2 p.m. the enemy pressed on the center, apparently threatening the [Norfolk and Petersburg] Railroad. The line was, in consequence, closed from the right to support Colonel *Goode* and the Thirty-fourth Virginia. At the same time [Maj. *William*] *Wood's* Battalion was sent to reinforce Colonel [*Powhatan R.*] *Page*, [Twenty-sixth Virginia] on the left. Again additional troops were called for, the reply being that one brigade from [Brig. Gen. *Bushrod R.*] *Johnson's* Division had been ordered on, and that *Hoke's* Division, which had left Drewry's Bluff at 12.15

p.m., would arrive in Petersburg at 5 o'clock p.m. Orders to hold on at all hazards were given all over the lines. [*O.R. Supplement*, VII, pp. 284–285.]

By midafternoon, Smith had decided to concentrate his attack against the salient in the Confederate line near the Jordan House just south of the City Point Railroad in which were located Batteries 4, 5, 6, and 7. He posted Martindale's division on the right, north of the salient; Brooks's in the center, facing the salient directly; and Hinks's division to Brooks's left. After Smith directed his subordinates to make the attack with a heavy skirmish line, rather than the normal line of battle, and a short artillery bombardment, his men went forward at about seven p.m.

Within a few minutes, Brooks's men had torn a huge hole in the Confederate defenses. Taking advantage of a ravine just south of Battery 6, Col. Louis Bell's brigade was able to move into the rear of it and Battery 5, while Brig. Gen. Hiram Burnham's brigade directly assaulted and overran Battery 5. Fortunately for the Confederates, at this point units from *Hoke's* division began arriving on the battlefield and took up a new line east of the Jordan House from which they were able to contain Brooks's success.

Report of Major General Smith, continued

Got into position around the enemy's works at Jordan's house about 1.30 p.m. I found the enemy's artillery so arranged as to have a cross-fire on most of my entire front, and some batteries which I had ordered into position were immediately driven out by enemy's fire. As no engineer officer was ordered to report to me I was obliged to make the reconnaissance in person, and some time was unnecessarily wasted on that account, but not till about 7 p.m. were the final preparations completed for the assault. [*O.R.*, XL, part 1, p. 705.]

Narrative of General Beauregard, continued

The enemy, continuing to mass his columns toward the center of our line, pressed it more and more and concentrated his heaviest assaults upon Batteries Nos. 5, 6, and 7. Thinned out and exhausted as they were, General *Wise's* heroic forces resisted still, with such unflinching stubbornness as to equal the veterans of the Army of Northern Virginia. I was then on the field and only left it when darkness set in. Shortly after 7 p.m. the enemy entered a ravine between Batteries 6 and 7, and succeeded in flanking Battery No. 5. But just then very opportunely appeared, advancing at double-quick, [Brig. Gen. *Johnson*] *Hagood's* gallant South Carolina brigade, followed soon afterward by [Brig. Gen. *Alfred H.*] *Colquitt's*, [*Thomas Lanier*] *Clingman's*, and, in fact, by the whole of *Hoke's* division. They were shown their positions, on a new line selected at that very time by my orders, a short distance in the rear of the captured works, and were kept busy the greatest part of the night throwing up a small epaulement for their additional protection. [*Battles and Leaders*, IV, pp. 540–541.]

Optional excursion: The paved trail you followed to reach this point is part of a 0.6-mile-long loop trail that eventually leads back to the Visitor Center. If you continue to follow it, it will take you to a point where you can see the tracks of the railroad that runs from City Point (modern-day Hopewell) to Petersburg and then to the location of "the Dictator." The Dictator was a 13-inch mortar that was capable of hurling a 225-pound shell over 2 miles; it was later used during the operations around Petersburg to fire on the town. Because of its massive weight, the gun was transported to this point by rail.

Return to your vehicle. Drive out of the parking lot, and proceed down the Park Tour Road past the kiosk and over the bridge. At about 0.2 mile, you will come to a fork in the road. Take the right fork to continue on the one-way Park Tour Road. At 0.4 miles from the parking lot, you will see a pull-off to the right. Stop here, and walk over to the mound of earth that marks the location of Battery No. 8.

STOP 3: BATTERY NO. 8

ATTACK OF THE U.S. COLORED TROOPS, 15 JUNE 1864

While Brooks's men overran Batteries 5 and 6 and a brigade from Martindale's division captured Battery 3, Hinks's division easily drove the Confederates from Battery 7. Two of Hinks's regiments, the First and Twenty-second USCT, then seized Battery 8 and Battery 9. Battery 10 then fell to the Fourth USCT, which led the Confederates to give up Battery 11 as well. There seemed to be nothing that could keep Petersburg out of Union hands before the day was over.

Report of Brigadier General Hinks, continued

At about 2 p.m. by direction of General Smith, the line was extended to the right to connect with General Brooks's line near the point of woods, after which no material change was made in

"The Dictator" in front of Petersburg (USAMHI)

the disposition of troops until preparations were made for the final charge. The enemy kept up an unremitting and very accurate and severe fire of artillery upon my position from the batteries now known as Batteries Nos. 6, 7, 8, 9, and 10. At about 5 o'clock I was informed by General Smith that he intended to charge the works with the skirmish line, and directed me to cause the proper disposition to be made to advance as soon as General Brooks's line commenced to advance.

I immediately directed the skirmish line to be strengthened and sufficiently advanced to gain the most favorable position for the purpose, and to drive in all of the enemy's sharpshooters. At about 7 o'clock an aide from General Smith informed me that the general had directed him to say that General Brooks would be in motion by the time that he (the aide) could reach me, and I, therefore, immediately ordered Colonels Duncan and Holman to commence the assault, which was executed with great gallantry and promptness, resulting in the carrying of all the works from Numbers 7 to Numbers 11 (five in number), and the capture of six guns, with caissons, prisoners, &c. Shortly after the final assault the division was joined on the left by General [David B.] Birney's division, of the Second Corps of the Army of the Potomac, with whom it occupied the works during the night. [*O.R.*, XL, part 1, p. 722.]

Report of Colonel Kiddoo, continued

I took position in the first line and on the left of the Fourth U.S. Colored Troops at about 12 m. In this I lost many men in killed and wounded and one officer killed. One company was thrown out as skirmishers, and at about 4 p.m. I received orders from the colonel commanding to send out three more companies and to form a skirmish line with one pace interval. I complied with said order by sending Major [John B.] Cook, of my regiment, in command of the line. He received orders from the colonel commanding to advance his skirmishers till he felt the enemy's line, and to advance against his works when he saw the lines of General Brooks' command advancing.

Accordingly, at a few minutes before sundown, Major Cook, seeing the line of General Brooks advancing, reports to me that he ordered his line to advance and charge the work in his immediate front, now known as Battery No. 7. He further reports that both officers, and men cheerfully obeyed this order and advanced on the run till they got so far under the guns of the battery as to be sheltered from their fire. At this juncture Major Cook ordered his line to break to the right and left, in order to gain the rear of the work. This was promptly done, and Captain [Jacob B.] Force and Lieutenant [William D.] Milliken, of my regiment, were the first to enter the work in the rear. These officers, as well as Major Cook, report to me that there were two 12-pounder howitzers and one iron piece in the fort when they entered it. The skirmishers of the First were on the left of Major Cook's line, and those of the Fourth were on the right, portions of both of which entered the fort after the men of my regiment had possessed it.

When the skirmish line advanced I received orders from the colonel commanding to take the rest of my command to its support. I moved out on the double-quick, and finding Battery No. 7 in our possession I turned my attention to Battery No. 8. I found Lieutenant-Colonel [Elias] Wright, First U.S. Colored Troops, with a portion of his skirmish line occupying a small lunette between Batteries Nos. 7 and 8, which had been abandoned by the enemy. I proposed that we unite our commands and charge Battery No. 8. He thought it not safe, but proposed to support me if I would do so. I immediately formed a column of companies, left a few of my men on the parapet of the lunette to engage the gunners on Battery No. 8, which were in easy range, and who were playing with some effect upon my men as they were forming for the charge.

The charge was made across a deep and swampy ravine. The enemy immediately ceased firing his artillery and took the parapets of the fort and rifle-pit as infantrymen. My men wavered at first under the hot fire of the enemy, but soon, on seeing their colors on the opposite side of the ravine, pushed rapidly up and passed the rifle-pits and fort. Lieutenant-Colonel Wright came to my support when I had advanced part the way up the opposite side of the ravine and at a time when I was most heavily pressed. The enemy left me one 12-pounder howitzer in the fort, which was immediately turned against Battery No. 9. Lieutenant [William H.] Short, whom I left in care of the wounded and to bury the dead, reports that he buried 11 and brought away 43 wounded. The enemy retreated to Battery No. 9, reformed and advanced apparently to take the work he had just lost. I formed all the men of both regiments and advanced to meet him, and drove him back. At this juncture I would have advanced against Battery No. 9 had it not been that company commanders assured me that the ammunition was about expended. At about 9 o'clock I was relieved by troops of the Second Corps, when I rejoined my brigade. [*O.R.*, XL, part 1, pp. 724–725.]

Report of Brigadier General Wise, continued

From 3 to 5 p.m., the enemy continued to press the center, and, as was expected, concentrated upon Batteries 5, 6, and 7, where the works were "ineffably and contemptibly weak." At 7.10 p.m., they entered a ravine between Nos. 6 and 7 and flanked No. 5. The line then broke from 3 to No. 11 inclusive. The whole line on the right was then ordered to close on the left, up to Battery No. 14; Batteries 1 and 2 being still ours. The Fifty-ninth Virginia arriving at that time, was sent on the City Point Road towards Battery No. 2, to arrest the retreat of the line to the left. Between 8 and 9 p.m., General *Hagood's* Brigade of *Hoke's* Division

Confederate positions captured by the Union Eighteenth Corps, June 15, 1864 (USAMHI)

arrived and, soon after, General *Hoke* himself, who took command. . . . The casualties in *Wise's* Brigade, on June 15, amounted to twelve killed, sixty-two wounded and 129 missing. Only three regiments engaged. Ten guns were lost from Batteries 2, 5, 7, 8, and 9. [*O.R. Supplement*, VII, p. 286.]

Return to your vehicle, and drive on the Park Tour Road for 0.3 mile to the parking area on the left for Battery No. 9.

STOP 4: BATTERY NO. 9

THE FIGHTING ENDS, 15 JUNE 1864

Despite the great successes achieved by Brooks's, Martindale's, and Hinks's assaults, Smith made no effort that night to exploit them. Although a fresh Confederate division, *Hoke's*, arrived on the field and was able to establish a new defensive line, the arrival of Hancock's corps around nine p.m. more than compensated for this. Hancock's movements had been held up by confusion in the Union chain of command that had delayed the commencement of his march. The Second Corps then had to march 14 miles through severe heat that caused many in its ranks to drop out during the march. Hancock himself was suffering severe pain from a groin wound he had suffered at Gettysburg that still had not completely healed and forced him to ride in a wagon. For his part, Smith's judgment and energy that day were impaired by a severe case of dysentery. Thus, when the two ailing generals got together that evening, they decided they were content with what had been achieved on June 15; they chose to rest their tired troops and consolidate their positions.

Report of Major General Smith, continued

In about twenty minutes the works at Jordan's house and on its left were carried by the divisions of Generals Brooks and Hinks, capturing guns, caissons, horses, ammunition, colors, camp and garrison equipage, and intrenching tools and prisoners. Some heavy profile works in rear of the line captured still keeping up a galling artillery fire I ordered the colored troops to carry them by assault. This was gallantly done. About this time I learned that General Martindale, on my right, with [Brig. Gen. George J.] Stannard's brigade, in advance, had carried the enemy's works between Jordan's house and the Appomattox, capturing two pieces of artillery, with teams, caissons, &c., complete. By this time darkness had set in, and having learned some time before that re-enforcements were rapidly coming in from Richmond, and deeming that I held important points of the enemy's line of works, I thought it prudent to make no farther advance, and made my dispositions to hold what I already had. About midnight [Maj. Gen. John] Gibbon's division, of the Second Corps, came up to relieve the part of my too extended lines. [O.R., XL, part 1, p. 705.]

Narrative of General Beauregard, continued

Strange to say, General Smith contented himself with breaking into our lines, and attempted nothing further that night. All the more strange was this inaction on his part, since General Hancock, with his strong and well-equipped Second Army Corps, had also been hurried to Petersburg and was actually there, or in the immediate vicinity of the town, on the evening of the 15th. He had informed General Smith of the arrival of his command and of the readiness of two of his divisions—Birney's and Gibbon's—to give him whatever assistance he might require.

Petersburg at that hour was clearly at the mercy of the Federal commander, who had all but captured it, and only failed of final success because he could not realize the fact of the unparalleled disparity between the two contending forces. Although the result of the fighting of the 15th had demonstrated that 2200 Confederates successfully withheld nearly a whole day the repeated assaults of at least 18,000 Federals, it followed, none the less, that Hancock's corps, being now in our front, with fully 28,000 men,—which raised the enemy's force against Petersburg to a grand total of 46,000,—our chance of resistance, the next morning and in the course of the next day, even after the advent of *Hoke's* division, was by far too uncertain to be counted on, unless strong additional reenforcements could reach us in time. [*Battles and Leaders,* IV, p. 541.]

Report of Maj. Gen. Winfield Scott Hancock, USA, commanding Second Corps, Army of the Potomac

At 6.30 p.m. the head of Birney's division had arrived at the Bryant house, on Bailey's Creek, about one mile in rear of the position of Hinks' division, of the Eighteenth Corps. Leaving Birney and Gibbon instructions to move forward as soon as they could ascertain at what point their assistance was required, I rode forward to the field, where I met General Smith, who described to me the operations of the day, and pointed out as well as he could in the dusk of the evening the position of the enemy's lines he had carried. I now informed him that two divisions of my troops were close at hand and ready for any further movements which in his judgment and knowledge of the field should be made. General Smith requested me to relieve his troops in the front line of works which he had carried, so that the enemy should encounter fresh troops should they attempt their recapture. He was then of the opinion that the enemy had been reenforced during the evening. In accordance with this request, I at once directed Birney and Gibbon to move up and occupy the captured earth-works from the Friend house, on the right, to the Dunn house, on the left of the Prince George road. By the time this movement was completed it was 11 p.m., too late and dark for any immediate advance. At midnight I instructed Generals Birney and Gibbon that if any commanding points were held by the enemy between their positions and the Appomattox they should be attacked and taken at or before daylight. I was extremely anxious that all the ground between my line and the river should be in our possession before the enemy could get his heavy re-enforcements up. [*O.R.*, XL, part 1, p. 305.]

THE BATTLE OF 16 JUNE 1864

By dawn on June 16, *Beauregard* had his troops in a new line that had been selected by General *Hagood* the previous evening. The Hagood Line was located west of Harrison's Creek and connected to the old Dimmock Line near Batteries 2 and 12. *Hoke's* division held the Confederate left, with *Hagood's* brigade positioned between the Appomattox and the Prince George Court-House Road and Brig. Gen. *Alfred H. Colquitt's* brigade to *Hagood's* right. *James G. Martin's* and *Thomas Lanier Clingman's* brigades extended the line southward, and *Wise's* battered command held the far right. By midmorning, *Beauregard's* numbers had increased to about 10,000 due to the arrival of Brig. Gen. *Bushrod Johnson's* division from Bermuda Hundred, which left the Confederate Howlett Line at Bermuda Hundred for all intents and purposes undefended. General *Lee* responded to *Beauregard's* move by ordering Lt. Gen. *Richard H. Anderson* and one of the divisions from his corps to take *Johnson's* place.

Even with the arrival of *Johnson's* command, *Beauregard* was still in a tight spot. Smith's and Hancock's commands, which occupied the positions in the Dimmock Line the former had seized the night before, outnumbered *Beauregard's* command by three to one. However, upon taking charge of the situation during the afternoon, Army of the Potomac commander Maj. Gen. George Meade directed Smith and Hancock not to attack until Maj. Gen. Ambrose Burnside's Ninth Corps reached the field. During the morning Col. Thomas W. Egan's brigade conducted a reconnaissance south of the Prince George Court House Road that seized Battery No. 12 but was severely battered by a brigade from *Johnson's* division that had just reached the field.

During the early afternoon, two of Burnside's divisions arrived on the field exhausted from a march through brutal heat. Meade immediately went to work preparing an assault. At six p.m., Birney's and [Brig. Gen. Francis C.] Barlow's divisions from Hancock's corps attacked the Confederates, with the former targeting the Confederate line near where it intersected with the Prince George Court House Road and Barlow attacking south of the road near the Avery and Shand Houses. Both attacks managed to achieve temporary penetrations of the Confederate line; however, the Federals could not exploit them. Although, by the time the fighting ended they had possession of two more batteries in the Dimmock Line.

Report of Brigadier General Wise, continued

A new line was formed during the night from Battery No. 2 through Friend's Field to the woods, and thence through them across the road leading to Dunn's House, and thence on the road to Webb's House.

Hoke's Division was placed on the left, *Clingman's* brigade forming its right. On *Clingman's* right was *Wise's* Brigade. The right of *Wise's* Brigade terminated on the apex of a high hill, between which and Webb's house there is a deep ravine. An interval of a quarter mile was left across the ravine. General *Wise* called the attention of General *Hoke* and General *Johnson* to that fact. He was told that a regiment would be sent from [Brig. Gen. *Stephen D.*] *Elliott's* Brigade to fill it. But on the night of June 16, as late as 10 p.m., that gap had not been filled. [*O.R. Supplement*, VII, p. 287.]

Report of Brig. Gen. Johnson Hagood, CSA, commanding Hagood's Brigade, Hoke's Division, Department of North Carolina and South Carolina

On the evening of the 15th about dark my brigade arrived at Petersburg by the Richmond and Petersburg Railroad, and I was at General *Beauregard's* headquarters reporting for orders when a courier announced that the enemy had carried the defenses from No. 3 to No. 7, inclusive, and that our troops were retreating. I was ordered to move out immediately upon the City Point road and take a position to cover that approach to the city, and upon which a new defensive line could be taken. It was after dark, and being unacquainted with the country, and unable to learn much from the confused and contradictory accounts of the volunteer guides who accompanied me, I halted my command at the junction of the City Point and Prince George roads and rode forward myself to reconnoiter the country. With the aid of a map opportunely sent me by Colonel [*David B.*] *Harris*, chief of engineers, I finally determined upon the line of the creek which empties into the Appomattox in rear of No. 1, and the west fork of which crosses the line near No. 15, and established my command upon it.

General *Colquitt's* brigade and the other brigades arriving shortly afterward were established in succession upon this line, General *Hoke* having approved the selection, and by daylight the position was partially intrenched. Colonel [*William B.*] *Tabb's* regiment, of *Wise's* brigade, held the lines from No. 1 to No. 2, and was relieved by one of my regiments (Twenty-seventh South Carolina). This made my line in echelon, with the echelon thrown forward on the left. Discovering this at daylight, and that this portion of the line was completely enfiladed by the guns of the enemy established at No. 7, I withdrew this regiment also to the west side of the creek. The new line now held by our forces was the chord of the arc of the abandoned works. I also brought in and sent to the ordnance officer two field pieces, spiked, that had been abandoned by our troops the day before. [*O.R.*, XL, part 1, p. 801.]

Report of Major General Hancock, continued

It was not until about 6 a.m. on the 16th that Generals Birney and Gibbon advanced to reconnoiter the ground in their front, by which time the enemy had moved a considerable body of fresh troops on the field, had occupied the large redoubt and rifle-pits in front of the Avery house, and had greatly strengthened their positions at all important points. During this first advance on the morning of the 16th, [Col. Thomas W.] Egan's brigade, of Birney's division, made a spirited attack upon the enemy, who held a small redoubt on Birney's left, which was carried by Egan in his usual intrepid manner. Barlow's division arrived on the field about daylight, and took position on Birney's left, extending toward the Norfolk and Petersburg Railroad. . . .

During the forenoon of the 16th I was instructed by Lieutenant-General Grant, in the absence of General Meade and himself, to take command of all the troops in front of Petersburg, and to push forward a reconnoitering force in my front for the purpose of discovering the most favorable point at which to make an attack. I was ordered to be prepared to commence the attack at 6 p.m. In the mean time General Burnside had been directed to mass his corps upon my left, in readiness to assist in an assault upon the enemy when it should be determined, or to aid me in the event of my being assailed. [*O.R.*, XL, part 1, pp. 305–306.]

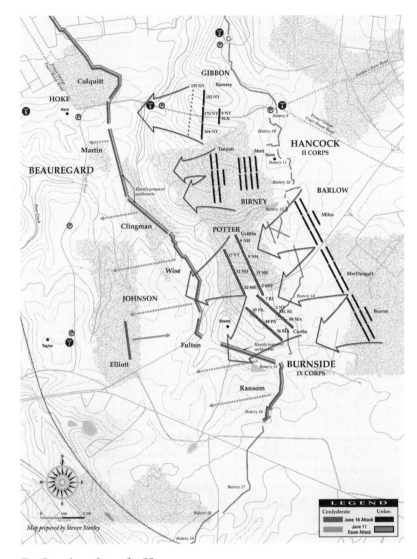

First Petersburg, June 16, 1864

Report of Brig. Gen. Regis de Trobriand, USA, commanding First Brigade, Third Division, Second Corps, Army of the Potomac

On the morning of the 16th instant, at daylight, the enemy opened upon us with their batteries, killing and wounding a considerable number of the brigade. The brigade was at once formed, and an assaulting column, consisting of the Seventeenth Maine and Twentieth Indiana Volunteers, was ordered to charge and take the enemy's works in our front. An advance was made, but the position being one of great strength and held by a large force, it was found impossible to carry it. The line was reformed, and a second attempt, with a larger force, was unsuccessful. The enemy were too strong and their position impregnable to the small force brought against it. The gallantry of the charging party was not equal to taking a position which a whole division afterward failed to carry. The brigade then formed a line at right angles to the line deserted by the enemy. Here Colonel Egan, commanding brigade, was severely wounded, and Colonel [Henry J.] Madill, One hundred and forty-first Pennsylvania Volunteers, assumed command of the brigade. This position the brigade held until 5 p.m. [*O.R.*, XL, part 1, pp. 390–391.]

Report of Maj. Gen. George G. Meade, USA, commanding Army of the Potomac

Early on the morning of the 16th I proceeded to City Point, and from thence to Petersburg, meeting, when about half way to the latter place, the lieutenant-general commanding, by whom I was instructed to take command of the troops then in front of Petersburg, and, if practicable, push the enemy across the Appomattox. At the same time orders, were sent to [Maj. Gen. Horatio G.] Wright to move up his artillery and one division of his infantry to Petersburg, and to take the other two divisions by water to City Point. Proceeding on I reached Petersburg about 2 p.m., and after communicating with corps commanders orders were given for an assault by Hancock and Burnside at 6 p.m., Smith demonstrating, he having reported an assault not expedient on his front. The assault was made, as directed, by Hancock, and resulted in taking and holding part of the enemy's line. The fighting continued till late in the night. [*O.R.*, XL, part 1, pp. 167–168.]

Report of Major General Hancock, continued

The reconnaissance ordered by General Grant was made by General Birney on the left of the Prince George road, and in front of the hill on which the Hare house stood, which was then held by the enemy.

It was decided by Major-General Meade, who had now arrived upon the field, that the attack should be made at that point. Very sharp skirmishing, accompanied by artillery fire, continued along my front until 6 p.m., when, in accordance with instructions from the major-general commanding, I directed Generals Birney, Barlow, and Gibbon to advance and assault the enemy in front and to the left of the Hare house. My troops were supported by two brigades of the Ninth Corps and by two of the Eighteenth Corps. The advance was spirited and forcible, and resulted, after a fierce conflict, in which our troops suffered heavily, in driving the enemy back some distance along our whole line. The severe fighting ceased at dark, although the enemy made several vigorous attempts during the night to retake the ground which he had lost; in this, however was foiled, as our troops had entrenched themselves at dark and repelled all efforts to dislodge them. [*O.R.*, XL, part 1, p. 306.]

Report of Col. John Ramsey, USA, commanding Second Brigade, Second Division, Second Corps, Army of the Potomac

On the morning of the 15th resumed our march. Marching in the direction of Petersburg, Va., arrived at the outer line of works of that city, which had been captured same day [by] General Hinks' division of colored troops. We remained behind those works and the Petersburg road until the following evening, the 16th. On that evening three brigades of the corps were selected to make an assault upon the works in front of the city. My brigade was selected to represent the Second Division, and I [was] directed to report to Major General D. B. Birney, he being temporarily in command of the corps.[6] In accordance with instructions from him my brigade was moved in front of the works, deployed into two lines of the battle, One hundred and fifty-fifth New York

---

[6] Hancock was compelled to temporarily relinquish command of his corps on June 16 and at other points during the operations around Petersburg because of a bad wound he had suffered at Gettysburg that had not yet fully healed.

Volunteers deployed as skirmishers left of skirmish line, and lines of battle resting on the road above mentioned. I moved forward precisely at 6 p.m., the hour indicated, driving in the enemy's pickets until we came in front of their works and under the fire of their line of battle. We emerged from the woods into the field and moved toward the enemy's works, and as far in that direction, and there holding a position in advance of either of the other brigades which participated in the assault. [*O.R.*, XL, part 1, p. 377.]

Narrative of General Beauregard, continued

Without awaiting an answer from the authorities at Richmond to my urgent representations, I ordered General *Bushrod R. Johnson* to evacuate the lines in front of Bermuda Hundred at the dawn of day on the 16th, leaving pickets and skirmishers to cover the movement until daylight, or later if necessary, and to march as rapidly as possible with his entire force to the assistance of Petersburg. The emergency justified this action. I had previously [1:45 p.m.] communicated with General *[Braxton] Bragg* upon this point, and had asked the War Department to elect between the Bermuda Hundred line and Petersburg, as, under the present circumstances, I could no longer hold both. The War Department had given me no answer, clearly intending that I should assume the responsibility of the measure, which I did. Scarcely two hours after *Johnson's* division had abandoned its position at Bermuda Hundred, Butler's forces drove off the Confederate pickets left there, as already stated, and took full possession of the lines.

By the 16th of June three Federal corps—Smith's, Hancock's, and Burnside's,—aggregating about 66,000 men, confronted our lines. Opposed to them I had, after the arrival of *Johnson's* division, about 10 a.m., an effective of not more than 10,000 men of all arms.

Through a sense of duty I addressed the following telegram, June 16th, 7:45 a.m. to General *Lee:* "Prisoner captured this a.m. reports that he belongs to Hancock's corps (Second), and that it crossed day before yesterday and last night from Harrison's Landing. Could we not have more reenforcements here?"

No direct answer was received to the above. But in reply to another dispatch of mine, June 16th, 4 p.m, relative to the tugs and transports of the enemy seen that day by Major [*George H.*] *Terrett,* General *Lee* sent this message: "The transports you mention have probably returned Butler's troops. Has Grant been seen crossing

James River?" This shows that *Lee* was still uncertain as to his adversary's movements, and, notwithstanding the information already furnished him, could not realize that the Federals had crossed the James, and that three of their corps were actually assaulting the Petersburg lines. General Hancock, the ranking Federal officer present, had been instructed by General Meade not to begin operations before the arrival of Burnside's command. Hence the tardiness of the enemy's attack, which was not made till after 5 o'clock p.m., though Burnside had reached Petersburg according to his own report, at 10 o'clock a.m.

The engagement lasted fully three hours, much vigor being displayed by the Federals, while the Confederates confronted them with fortitude, knowing that they were fighting against overwhelming odds, constantly increasing. Birney's division of Hancock's corps finally broke into part of our line and effected a lodgment. The contest, with varying results, was carried on until after nightfall, with advantage to us on the left and some serious loss on the right. It then slackened and gradually came to an end. In the meantime [Maj. Gen. Gouverneur] Warren's corps, the Fifth, had also come up, but too late to take a part in the action of the day. Its presence before our lines swelled the enemy's aggregate to about 90,000, against which stood a barrier of not even 10,000 exhausted, half-starved men, who had gone through two days of constant hard fighting and many sleepless nights in the trenches. [*Battles and Leaders*, IV, pp. 541–542.]

To drive to Harrison's Creek, leave the parking area and drive .06 mile to the parking area on the right.

STOP 5: HARRISON'S CREEK

THE BATTLE OF 17 JUNE 1864

Still enjoying a tremendous advantage in numbers, the Federals resumed their effort against the Hagood Line early on June 17. Around daybreak Brig. Gen. Robert Potter's division from Burnside's command launched an assault from the area around the Shand House that managed to seize another battery in the Dimmock Line and 600 prisoners. Unfortunately, divisions from the Ninth Corps and Second Corps that were supposed to assist the attack failed to arrive in time to exploit Potter's success. An afternoon assault by Brig. Gen. Orlando Wilcox's division of the Ninth Corps in the same area likewise failed to achieve a breakthrough. Meanwhile, north of the Appomattox, the Confederates reclaimed possession of the Howlett Line at Bermuda Hundred.

The last of Burnside's divisions, Brig. Gen. James Ledlie's, made an attack around six p.m. that managed to seize about a quarter mile of the Hagood Line before a strong Confederate counterattack shortly before midnight drove the Federals back to their original lines. Shortly thereafter, finally convinced that night that Grant had moved his entire force south of the James, *Lee* ordered the bulk of his army to Petersburg as Meade developed plans for an assault by his entire command at daybreak.

Report of Major General Meade, continued

At early dawn of the 17th of June a gallant assault was made by the Ninth Corps, capturing a redoubt, 4 guns, several colors, and many prisoners. During the night of the 16th [Brig. Gen. Thomas H.] Neill's division, Sixth Corps, arrived, relieving Brooks' division, of the Eighteenth, who, accompanied by Major-General Smith, returned to Bermuda Hundred, leaving General Martindale in command of Smith's troops. Warren, with the Fifth Corps, also came up during the night of the 16th, and was posted on the left of the Ninth Corps. During all of the 17th the enemy was vigorously pressed, Martindale pushing him back on the right, and the whole line gradually advancing. [*O.R.*, XL, part 1, p. 168.]

Report of Major General Hancock, continued

On the morning of the 17th General Barlow advanced against the enemy in conjunction with General Burnside, and succeeded in pushing forward his line considerably after some sharp fighting. Birney and Gibbon on the right also moved forward, driving the enemy from the hill on which the Hare house stood and occupied it. (Fort Stedman was afterward erected on that hill.) The enemy made frequent efforts to retake the Hare house during the day, but were handsomely repelled on each occasion. In the evening, about 6 p.m., General Barlow again participated in an attack with General Burnside's corps, in which Barlow's division lost heavily in killed, wounded, and prisoners.

The night of the 17th of June I was compelled to turn over my command on account of disability from my wound, which during the entire campaign had given me great annoyance, and at times had prevented me from taking that active part in the movement

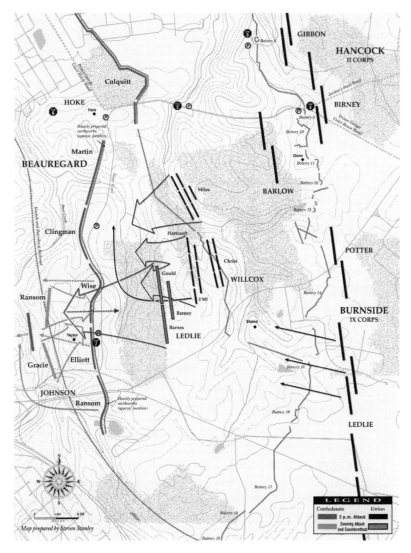

Map prepared by Steven Stanley

First Petersburg, June 17, 1864

of my troops which I desired to do. I relinquished the command
to Major-General Birney, the next senior general officer present
in my corps. [*O.R.*, XL, part 1, pp. 306–307.]

For an optional walk, you can either read the following reports here or cross the
Park Tour Road to enter the trail that runs along Harrison Creek. Follow this trail
for about a half mile (it is marked by yellow slashes on the trees) to a point just
past where a second trail joins it from the left and the trail begins to head down
to the bed of Harrison Creek. Stop here.

Report of Maj. Gen. Ambrose E. Burnside, USA, commanding Ninth Corps, Army of the Potomac

At about 8 p.m. on the 15th we started under orders to re-
enforce Generals Hancock and Smith near Petersburg, crossing
the James River on the pontoon bridge above Fort Powhatan. We
marched up the road nearest the river until we reached the Old
Court-House, when we turned to the left, our advance reaching
a position occupied by our troops about 10 a.m. on the 16th.
About 1 p.m., after a consultation and reconnaissance with General [John G.] Barnard, our troops were placed in position on
the extreme left. Soon after this orders were received to be in
readiness to support an attack which was to be made at 4 p.m.
by a part of General Hancock's corps. During this attack General [Charles] Griffin's brigade, of General Potter's division, was
ordered to report to General Barlow. His place as support was
supplied by [Gen. John] Hartranft's brigade, of [Gen. Orlando]
Willcox's division. During the night heavy skirmishing was kept
up, but nothing of importance occurred in our front. General
Potter was directed to make his dispositions to attack at a very
early hour in the morning, and, if possible, carry the enemy's line
in his immediate front just on the left of the Second Corps. The
First Division, General Ledlie, was to support the attack.

At 3 o'clock on the morning of the 17th the two brigades of
General Potter dashed forward in most gallant style, carrying all
the lines and redoubts of the enemy on the ridge upon which
stood the Shands house, capturing 4 pieces of artillery, 5 colors,
600 prisoners, and 1,500 stand of small-arms. Our people pushed
forward until they found the enemy in a new and very strong position, when General Potter took up a line in advance of that which

he had just carried, pushing his pickets close up to the enemy's new line. There was considerable delay in getting up the troops of the First Division owing to the obstacles which intervened between this division and General Potter's, the whole ground being covered by fallen timber, over which it was very difficult to pass in the dark. Had it been possible to have supported General Potter's gallant charge, the victory would have been probably much more decisive. Soon after daylight General Willcox was directed to attack the enemy's works in front of the Shands house. His two brigades were formed in the ravine which intervened between the Shands house and the enemy's lines.

A misunderstanding in reference to the point of attack caused some delay. Soon after, however, the troops were in position to move in the direction contemplated. General Hartranft's brigade, leading, dashed forward in a most vigorous manner, its left reaching the enemy's main line of rifle-pits, but owing to the severe fire of musketry and artillery from the enemy, especially to our left and the great loss which it inflicted, his brigade was compelled to give way to the right, a portion of them falling back through the line of General Barlow's division. Colonel [Benjamin] Christ's brigade, which had gained a position about midway between the ravine and the enemy's line, bravely held its ground during the day under a most galling fire of the enemy, which resulted in a severe loss. On the afternoon of this day, say at 4 o'clock, General Ledlie's division was directed to assault the enemy's position at about the same point, which it did in a handsome manner. Supported by artillery, which had been placed in position, the line was carried and held till 10 o'clock at night, when his advance was driven in by an overpowering force of the enemy, our men being much fatigued from long marches and constant fighting. A portion of Colonel Christ's brigade, of the Third Division, participated in this attack, and General [Samuel] Crawford, of the Fifth Corps, rendered very efficient aid on the left. We captured in this action 100 prisoners and 1 stand of colors. [*O.R.*, XL, part 1, pp. 522–523.]

Report of Brig. Gen. Robert Potter, USA, commanding Second Division, Ninth Corps, Army of the Potomac

Having received orders to renew the attack before daylight in the morning, I determined to attack near the Shands house.

Griffin's brigade was formed on the right, with the Seventeenth Vermont, Eleventh New Hampshire, and Thirty-second Maine in the first line, with the Sixth and Ninth New Hampshire, Thirty-first Maine, and Second Maryland in support. [Col. John] Curtin formed his brigade with the Forty-fifth and Forty-eighth Pennsylvania and Thirty-sixth Massachusetts in front, supported by the Seventh Rhode Island, Second New York Mounted Rifles, and Fifty-eighth Massachusetts Regiments. Griffin moved directly on the house and orchard to the right, Curtin moved to the left of the house and toward the Redoubt No —. Canteens and cups were packed in haversacks to prevent noise, and orders were given to rely upon the bayonet, and not fire a shot. The brigades moved promptly at 3 a.m., and rushed at once on the enemy's works, carrying their lines, taking 4 pieces of cannon, 5 colors, some 600 prisoners, and about 1,500 stand of small-arms. We pursued the enemy some distance, but having no support, and finding the enemy in a new position, we took up a line in advance of the position we had carried, the left resting on a redoubt in that line, pushing our skirmishers as far to the front as practicable. We continued our skirmishing all day, and in the afternoon I placed a battery in position near my front at the Shands house, and other batteries were placed in position in the rear of the line at various points to cover the attack made by the First and Third Divisions, and I held my division in readiness to assist them. [*O.R.*, XL, part 1, p. 545.]

Report of Brig. Gen. Orlando Willcox, USA, commanding Third Division, Ninth Corps, Army of the Potomac

On the morning of the 17th Hartranft reported back, and I was ordered to attack the enemy in their works on the right of the Avery house and in front of Shands' house. At the latter point there was a good position for a battery, which I requested to place there, but time would not allow. My two brigades were formed partly in the ravine in front of Shands' and partly on the crest beyond. Major-General Burnside indicated the point of attack on the enemy's breast-works in an open field. Fixing this required point caused a little delay, by the necessary movement of troops, in the tangled ravine, farther to the right than that at first indicated by General [John G.] Parke, chief of staff. Major J. St. Clair Morton, chief engineer of the corps, accompanied the commander of my leading brigade (General Hartranft), and verified the point, compass in hand, after Hartranft's line was formed on the edge of the field. The direction indicated was so unfortunate that, as soon as my lines started from the brow of the ravine, they were swept by an enfilading fire of canister from a rebel battery, nearly opposite Shands' house. Our artillery did nothing at the critical moment. My troops advanced at a double-quick, unsupported in any manner whatever. A cloud of blinding dust was raised by the enemy's artillery missiles. Hartranft's left struck the enemy's pits, but melted away in a moment. But eighteen out of ninety-five survived in the ranks of the left companies of the left regiment, and out of 1,890 men, which composed his lines, but 1,050 came out, and a few afterward through the Second Corps works on my right. Among the killed was the gallant Morton. Hartranft's line having thus melted out of sight, Colonel Christ halted, and held his brigade, lying down, about half way from the ravine to the enemy's works. This position the brave troops of Christ's brigade continued to hold until night, when they performed important service. In the evening, with guns in position at the Shands house, the First Division moved over the same ground, but taking a better direction, with Crawford's division, Fifth Corps, on their left. [*O.R.*, XL, part 1, pp. 571–572.]

Report of Brig. Gen. James H. Ledlie, USA, commanding First Division, Ninth Corps, Army of the Potomac

At daylight on the morning of the 17th I was ordered to move forward in support of General Potter, who was then advancing on the enemy's works, comprising Battery 14, with its connecting lines of defense. I immediately ordered forward my division, and occupied Battery 15 and Battery 16, with the earthworks connecting. With the exception of several slight changes, my division remained in the last named position until about 4 p.m., when I was ordered to support an attack to be made by the Third Division, under General Willcox, and accordingly moved my command to the ravine in front, and to the right of the Shands house.

The Third Division not having succeeded in its attack, I was ordered about 5.30 p.m. to form my division for a charge upon the enemy's works, which were from 300 to 500 yards west of the ravine. I ordered the First Brigade, under Colonel J. P. Gould, and the Second Brigade, under Lieutenant Colonel Joseph H. Barnes, to form in line of battle below the crest of the hill west of the ravine, and placed the Twenty-first Massachusetts Volunteers on the right of the line, the left connecting with the main line of battle, but forming a line at an angle of about 45 degrees to the main line, to cover any flank movement that might be made by the enemy on my right, and the left of the Second Brigade was ordered to be thrown back at about the same angle for the accomplishment of the same object on my left. The Third Brigade, under Lieutenant Colonel B. G. Barney, was formed in two lines about 100 paces in rear of the First and Second Brigades. The One hundredth Pennsylvania Volunteers, under Lieutenant-Colonel [Matthew M.] Dawson, were thrown out as skirmishers and covered the front of nearly the whole line. At this juncture the enemy's batteries—one in front of the extreme left of my line, one still farther to the left, and one some distance on the right (all of which swept the position we were about to storm)—opened with shell and canister upon my lines, killing and wounding 32 men before I advanced.

The skirmishers were then temporarily withdrawn; but in a short time afterward they were thrown forward, and I gave the order for the charge, with directions to my command not to fire a shot until reaching the enemy's lines. The line was then moved forward with bayonets fixed, charging at a run over the entire distance with steadiness and bravery. The Third Brigade followed enthusiastically, gaining distance at some points on the first line. The men charged the works fiercely and bravely, mounting the parapet and leaping quite over the ditch into the enemy's lines, where the fight became a hand-to-hand conflict, my men using the bayonet and breech, and succeeded in carrying the works in handsome style. The troops pressed forward and also succeeded in taking another line of the enemy's works, running at a slight angle to the main line, and refusing at a point about midway between that and the woods in rear. The enemy then kept up a desultory fire for several hours from the woods, which was steadily returned by my command. Too much praise cannot be accorded the men making this charge, subject as they were not only to a terrible fire of shell and canister from the batteries previously referred to (which raked the whole of the field from the ravine to the enemy's works), but to heavy and continuous volleys of musketry, without discharging a single piece in defense until the object of the charge was accomplished.

About 9 p.m. the following regiments of the Third Division reported to me for duty: First Michigan Sharpshooters, Captain L. C. Rhines; Second Michigan Volunteers, Colonel William Humphrey; Thirty-eighth Wisconsin Volunteers, Lieutenant Colonel C. K. Pier, and the Sixtieth Ohio Volunteers, under Major M. P. Avery. All these regiments, except the First Michigan Sharpshooters, were placed upon the right of my line, and the last-named regiment was placed on the extreme left, and in these positions they all rendered important service. About 10 p.m. the enemy made a charge upon my lines, which was repulsed, my command capturing 5 officers and 71 enlisted men, together with a stand of colors belonging to the Thirty-fifth North Carolina Infantry. I then called upon the corps commander for support and was informed by him that General Crawford had been ordered forward with his division to support me, and was also informed that General Barlow would move forward and connect with my right, but these movements were not made at 12 midnight. About this time the enemy concentrated in front of my lines and charged fiercely, at the same time massing on my left, which was entirely unprotected, compelling my men to fall back to their advanced line of rifle-pits, which they held until morning, when it was found that the enemy had retreated from our front. [*O.R.*, XL, part 1, pp. 532–533.]

Report of Brig. Gen. Samuel W. Crawford, USA, commanding Third Division, Fifth Corps, Army of the Potomac

I at 6.45 p.m. moved my command to the support of General Ledlie's command, First Division, Ninth Army Corps, the Third Brigade, of my command, Colonel [James] Carle commanding, in the advance, and the First and Second Brigades in supporting distance. It was reported to me that General Ledlie's division occupied and held the enemy's line of breast-works. The Third Brigade on advancing found this report to be erroneous, General Ledlie occupying only the enemy's skirmish line. Colonel Carle advanced in front of General Ledlie's line, and by a gallant effort succeeded in capturing the Thirty-ninth Regiment North Carolina Troops, the commanding officer of which surrendered to Colonel Carle, himself, regiment, and colors. These prisoners were sent to the rear by Colonel Carle, and turned over to one of my aides, and seized by General Ledlie from him. I respectfully insist that the prisoners and colors of the Thirty-ninth Regiment North Carolina Troops were taken by Colonel Carle, and he alone should receive credit for the same. General Ledlie's line having fallen back, and not deeming it prudent for Colonel Carle to remain in his advanced and exposed position, I ordered Colonel [Peter] Lyle, commanding First Brigade, to relieve him with a strong skirmish line, and to place his line of battle on a prolongation of General Ledlie's line. [*O.R.*, XL, part 1, p. 472.]

Report of Brig. Gen. Thomas L. Clingman, CSA, commanding Clingman's Brigade, Hoke's Division

My brigade formed the right wing of Major General *Hoke's* Division and immediately on my right was placed General *Wise's* Brigade. . . . During the day, there had been several feeble demonstrations of the enemy, which had been repulsed at once; but about 6.30 o'clock the enemy advanced in great force, partly in my front and also directly in front of the line of General *Wise's* Brigade. The pickets were driven in and the line began to fire, but in less than five minutes, as I think, I heard exclamations, "our men are giving way on the right;" and on looking in that direction, I saw with the greatest astonishment, the troops running from the line of General *Wise's* Brigade back to the rear. I could see plainly the regiments next to me, and probably a portion of the second one of the brigade. By the time, however, the men had run about 100 yards to the rear, I saw an officer come up, with what I took to be about one company following him, and from the trench, wave his hand, seemingly calling back the fugitives. . . . A number did return toward the trenches, but just as they were about entering them, the enemy appeared advancing from the front, and were, I think, within 100 yards, or rather less. I could see one of their flags and what appeared to be about one regiment coming up towards the works. Those who were getting back to the trenches, immediately fled again to the rear. . . . These occurances took place just before sunset. I moved my brigade somewhat to the right along the trenches and ordered Lieutenant-Colonel [*William Stewart*] *Devane*, of the Sixty first [North Carolina] Regiment of my brigade, to take four companies to the right and rear of my line to check, if possible, the movement of the enemy. They had by this time not only filled the abandoned trenches of General *Wise's* Brigade, but had also advanced a heavy force beyond them towards the city, for a short distance. . . .

I immediately afterwards carried from my left wing half of the Fifty-first [North Carolina] Regiment, under command of

Colonel [*Hector McAllister*] *McKethan*, up to the right. They swept around from the rear, and driving back the enemy, entered the trenches to the right of the line held by Colonel *Devane*, with the assistance of Captain [*Samuel D.*] *Preston*. This occurred a little before dark, and from that time the enemy were kept out of the trenches entirely, as far up as our line of fire extended. . . . The enemy for a period of two hours made repeated advances in heavy force against my entire front, but especially against the right. They did not, however, at any time approach nearer than twenty yards of the right, commanded by Captain [*James W.*] *Lippitt*, but were always driven back by his fire in front, chiefly by the oblique enfilading fire of my entire brigade, which could reach them as soon as they came up the hill into the field and cut them to pieces, so that after two or three volleys, they invariably broke and ran to the rear. These movements, with attacks occasionally along my whole front, were kept up until nearly 10 o'clock when they ceased, the enemy keeping themselves back where they could be sheltered by the hill in front of the right. [*O.R. Supplement*, VII, pp. 305–306.]

Lieutenant General Grant to Major General Halleck, 11 a.m., June 17, 1864

The Ninth Army Corps this morning carried two more redoubts, forming part of the defenses of Petersburg, capturing 450 prisoners and 4 guns. Our successes are being followed up. . . . The Eighteenth Corps (Smith's) was transported from White House to Bermuda Hundred by water, moved out near to Petersburg the night of its arrival, and surprised or rather captured the very strong works northeast of Petersburg before sufficient force could be got in there by the enemy to hold them. He was joined the night following this capture by the Second Corps, which in turn captured more of the enemy's redoubts farther south, and this corps was followed by the Ninth, with the result above stated. All the troops are now up except two divisions covering the wagon trains, and they will be up to-night. The enemy in their endeavor to re-enforce Petersburg abandoned their intrenchments in front of Bermuda Hundred. They no doubt expected troops from north of the James River to take their place before we discovered it. General Butler took advantage of this and moved a force at once upon the railroad and plank road between Richmond and Petersburg, which I hope to retain possession of. [*O.R.*, XL, part 1, pp. 12–13.]

Return to your vehicle, and drive 0.3 mile along the Park Tour Road to the parking area for Fort Stedman on your right. Walk to the paved trail, and turn right. As you walk, note the foundations for the wartime Hare House to the left of the trail. Upon reaching an intersection in the trail, continue straight ahead to the monument to the First Maine Heavy Artillery.

STOP 6: FIRST MAINE HEAVY ARTILLERY MONUMENT

THE BATTLE OF 18 JUNE 1864

Finally, at 4:30 a.m., the Federal high command managed to get their forces in front of Petersburg, advancing in force. When they went forward, however, they found the Hagood Line empty. During the night *Beauregard* had pulled his command back to a new, much stronger line laid out by Col. *David B. Harris* and [Col.] *Hilary P. Jones* the day before that extended from the Appomattox River to the location of Battery No. 25 in the Dimmock Line near the Jerusalem Plank Road. The Federals then pawed their way forward as Gen. *Robert E. Lee*, finally convinced that Grant was making his main effort against Petersburg, rushed nearly his entire command to *Beauregard's* assistance.

Narrative of General Beauregard, continued

The firing lasted, on the 17th, until a little after 11 o'clock p.m. Just before that time I had ordered all the camp-fires to be brightly lighted, with sentinels well thrown forward and as near as possible to the enemy's. Then, at about 12:30 a.m., on the 18th, began the retrograde movement, which, notwithstanding the exhaustion of our troops and their sore disappointment at receiving no further reenforcements, was safely and silently executed, with uncommonly good order and precision, though the greatest caution had to be used in order to retire unnoticed from so close a contact with so strong an adversary.

The digging of trenches was begun by the men as soon as they reached their new position. Axes, as well as spades; bayonets and knives, as well as axes,—in fact, every utensil that could be found,—were used. And when all was over, or nearly so, with much anxiety still, but with comparative relief, nevertheless, I hurried off this telegram to General *Lee* [18th, 12:40 a.m.]: "All quiet at present. I expect renewal of attack in morning. My troops are becoming much exhausted. Without immediate and strong reenforcements, results may be unfavorable. Prisoners report Grant on the field with his whole army."

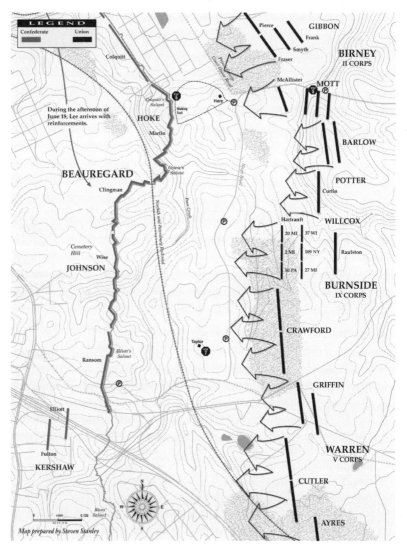

Map prepared by Steven Stanley

First Petersburg, June 18, 1864: Morning attacks

But General *Lee*, although not wholly convinced even at that hour that the Army of the Potomac was already on the south side of the James, long before the dawn of day, on the 18th, and immediately after his conference with Major [*Giles B.*] *Cooke*, sent me this message: "Am not yet satisfied as to General Grant's movements; but upon your representations will move at once to Petersburg." And, in fact, even previous to that hour, on the same night, he had concluded to send [Gen. *Joseph*] *Kershaw's* division to my assistance. The next step taken by General *Lee* was to endeavor to procure sufficient means for the immediate transportation of his troops. The same morning he communicated with General [*Jubal*] *Early* [at Lynchburg], who had not yet returned from his Shenandoah campaign: "Strike as quick as you can, and, if circumstances authorize, carry out the original plan, or move upon Petersburg without delay." Late as had been the credence given by General *Lee* to my representations of Grant's movements, it was, fortunately, not yet too late, by prompt and energetic action, to save Petersburg—and, therefore, Richmond.

General *Kershaw's* division, which proved to be the vanguard of General *Lee's* army, reached Petersburg early Saturday morning, June 18th; it numbered about 5000 men, and, by my orders, was placed on the new line already occupied by our forces with its right on or near the Jerusalem plank-road, extending across the open field and bending back toward the front of the cemetery. [Maj. Gen. *Charles W.*] *Field's* division, of about equal strength, came in some two hours after *Kershaw's*. It had not yet been assigned to its place on the line when *Lee* in person arrived at 11:30 a.m. on that day.

When, early in the morning, the enemy was pushed forward to make the "grand attack ordered for 4 a.m. on the 18th," the retirement of our forces on the previous night from their first positions to the new line of defenses selected by me, as already explained, had so much surprised the assaulting columns as to induce their immediate commanders to additional prudence in their advance and to a complete halt in their operations. . . . We had on our side, after *Kershaw's* arrival, but 15,000 men, no deduction being made for the casualties of the three preceding days. It was only later on, somewhere between 12 m. and 1 p.m., that *Field's* command was put in position on the line, and from that moment to the end of the day our grand total amounted to about 20,000 men.

At noon or thereabout—the predetermined "grand attack" was renewed, although partial disconnected assaults had been made before that hour on several parts of our line, but with no tangible result of any kind. This renewed attack was mainly led by Gibbon's division of Hancock's corps. It proved to be entirely ineffectual. And still another grand attempt was made at 4 p.m., with at least three full Federal corps cooperating: Hancock's on the right, Burnside's in the center, and Warren's on the left. General Meade, in his report, says it was "without success. . . . Later in the day attacks were made by the Fifth and Ninth corps with no better results." The truth is that, despite the overwhelming odds against us, every Federal assault, on the 18th, was met with most signal defeat. . . . I felt sure, therefore, that, for the present at least, Petersburg and Richmond were safe. [*Battles and Leaders*, IV, pp. 543–544.]

Report of Major General Meade, continued

An assault of the whole line was ordered for daylight on the 18th, but on advancing it was found the enemy during the night had retired to a line about a mile nearer the city, the one he now occupies. Orders were immediately given to follow and develop his position, and, so soon as dispositions could be made, to assault. About noon an unsuccessful assault was made by Gibbon's division, Second Corps. Martindale's advance was successful, occupying the enemy's skirmish line and making some prisoners. Major-General Birney, temporarily commanding Second Corps, then organized a formidable column and about 4 p.m. made an attack, but without success. Later in the day attacks were made by the Fifth and Ninth Corps, with no better results. Being satisfied *Lee's* army was before me, and nothing further to be gained by direct attacks, offensive operations ceased and the work of intrenching a line commenced. [*O.R.*, XL, part 1, p. 168.]

THE SECOND CORPS ATTACKS, 18 JUNE 1864

Upon locating the new Confederate line, Meade pressed his subordinates throughout the morning to attack. At about noon, Col. Robert McAllister's brigade of [Brig. Gen. Gershom] Mott's division and Gibbon's division of the Second Corps made separate assaults against the section of the Harris Line near the Hare House that the Confederates repulsed fairly easily. Then, as the Sixth and Eighteenth

Corps to the north and the Ninth and Fifth Corps to the south attacked during the afternoon, the men of the Second Corps resumed their attempts to break the enemy line. Those attempts proved futile. Upon receipt of orders to renew the attack, four brigades refused to comply. Then one unit that did attack, the green First Maine Heavy Artillery, proceeded to demonstrate the folly of doing so. About 4:30 p.m., Maj. Russel B. Shepherd finished forming the regiment in the Prince George Court House Road, then led it forward completely unsupported across a cornfield toward a section of the Confederate line occupied by Brig. Gen. *Alfred Colquitt's* brigade. Ten minutes after the attack commenced, Shepherd's men were falling back, having failed to dent the Confederate line and lost over 600 of the regiment's 900 men. It was the greatest loss of any Union regiment in any engagement during the war and brought the battle on this section of the field to a dismal end for the Federals.

Report of Maj. Gen. John Gibbon, USA, commanding Second Division, Second Corps, Army of the Potomac

On the morning of the 18th the division advanced to the assault at 4 o'clock in two lines, the first composed of the First Brigade, under command of Colonel (now Brigadier General) B[yron] R. Pierce, and the Second Brigade, under command of Colonel John Fraser, One hundred and fortieth Regiment Pennsylvania Volunteers; the second line [Col. Thomas A.] Smyth's brigade, supported by [Col. Paul] Frank's brigade, of the First Division, all on the right of the Prince George Court-House road. The enemy having fallen back the division was pushed ahead, but soon came upon a strong line of works, on which (Smyth's brigade being deployed to the right) two ineffectual assaults were made with heavy loss, Brigadier General Pierce and Colonel Ramsey being wounded. Later in the day another assault was made by Mott's division on the left of the road, Fraser's brigade being sent to assist in it. [*O.R.*, XL, part 1, p. 366.]

Narrative of Col. Robert McAllister, USA, commanding Eleventh New Jersey, Third Brigade, Third Division, Second Corps, Army of the Potomac

➤ We received orders to be ready for a charge at early dawn, I was to have my Brigade in two lines and lead the advance. We went over the enemy's breastworks without much opposition and drove them about ¾ of a mile, when we run up against another line of works much more formidable. Here we met with hard opposition and had to halt and fortify in order to protect ourselves.

This second line of works was built to lead us into a death trap. I halted my Brigade; alone and personally I went to reconnoiter this second line of the enemy's works. I found them very strong—in the form of a half moon with guns planted to enfilade our flanks as we advanced. I went back and informed Col. [Byron R.] Pierce of the situation and told him that to advance into that death trap would be fatal to the Brigade. I asked him to come and reconnoiter with me and see if I was not correct. He did so and came to the same conclusion. He went back to inform our superior officers of the situation.

I knew nothing more till I was ordered to charge. It was about 11 a.m., when we charged, my Brigade leading the van. The Rebels poured down upon us lead and iron by musketry and cannon that cut our men down like hail cuts the grain and grass. We had to advance a long distance up a cleared plain. Our ranks melted away, and we could not advance further. We dropped down and those who were not killed or wounded—or who had not fallen back—began digging little pits. We remained there for two or more hours. We were then ordered back and lost many men in retiring. Each regiment planted its Colors in line of battle.

I sent word back to Genl. Mott: "I can go no further. What shall I do?" He answered: "Remain where you are until further orders." After a time he sent the order to us to fall back. I returned under a severe fire and reported to Genl. Mott with my Brigade.

He directed me where to form, saying: "We are going to make a charge. You may be needed." "Where is my old 3rd Brigade?" I asked. He replied: "They are going in just where you came out." "God help them!" I exclaimed. "Why?" Mott asked. "It is a death trap," I said, "A brigade can't live in there for five minutes." Just as I said this, an aide rode up. "Move your troops forward to the charge," he said to Genl. Mott.

The order was given; and thus was made the disastrous charge of the 1st Maine Heavy Artillery. Two or three other brigades, my old Brigade amongst them, were brought up to help in the charge, but they failed worse than we did. The slaughter was terrible. This Division lost in the battles of yesterday far more than 1,000 men. . . . After the Maine Heavies retired, the ground was strewn with wounded and dying crying "Water! Water!" No help or relief could be sent them. . . . Hundreds of our wounded thus died in our sight. We could hear their cries for help, yet we could not rescue them or give them the relief that might have saved their lives. . . . It was perfectly heartrending. [James I. Robertson, ed., *The Civil War Letters of General Robert McAllister* (New Brunswick, N.J.: Rutgers University Press, 1965), pp. 443–445.]

Report of Capt. Thomas C. Thompson, USA, commanding Seventh New Jersey Infantry, Third Brigade, Third Division, Second Corps, Army of the Potomac

Remained idle during the greater part of the 17th, and at night moved to the right of the road and there remained all night. During the night the enemy abandoned the line of works in front and fell back to another line beyond the old . . . road. At daylight on the 18th, when their retreat was discovered, the regiment joined in the advance, and upon arriving beside the road halted and erected a small rifle-pit. No movement of consequence took place during the day until about 4 p.m., the brigade having massed by the roadside, just to the right of the O. P. Hare house, when an attempt was made to carry the enemy's rifle-pits, but was repulsed. The First Maine Heavy Artillery lead the column, the Sixteenth Massachusetts following, and this regiment behind the latter regiment. The Sixteenth Massachusetts failed to follow the First Maine, whereupon Major [Frederick] Cooper ordered the regiment forward, but not being properly supported did not advance beyond the Hare house. After the failure of this charge the brigade was withdrawn to the rear. [*O.R.*, XL, part 1, p. 418.]

Narrative of Brig. Gen. Johnson Hagood, CSA, commanding Hagood's Brigade, Hoke's Division, Department of North Carolina and South Carolina

General *Beauregard* . . . had determined on taking a more compact and shorter line of defence than the one now occupied, and during these two days' fighting it had been partially prepared for occupation. It was this last line which was held during the siege that ensued. It was some 800 yards nearer the city, and, like the line of the first taken, was the chord to an arc of the original defences, still more of which were now abandoned.

This line was at first a simple trench with the parapet on the farther side of it, and though it was afterwards amplified it retained the general character of a trench, and was always known as "The Trenches," in distinction from the portion of the original works held by us. These last were artillery redoubts, connected by infantry breastworks. These "trenches" opposed Grant's front of attack, the remaining portion of the *enciente* was not assailed until perhaps the closing day of the siege of '65.

At 1:30 a.m., on the 18th, *Hagood's* brigade moved back on the new line to the position assigned it. . . . His left was on the Appomattox, thence running off southward, nearly at right angles to the river, his line crossed the City Point road and extended to the westward end of the eminence known as Hare's Hill, where *Colquitt* prolonged the general line. The New Market race course was in front of the right of the brigade, and the approach to its position was generally level. By daylight, the Confederates were quietly in position and diligently strengthening their incomplete works.

Shortly after daylight, the enemy advanced upon our old works, and finding them abandoned, came on with vociferous cheers. As soon as their skirmishers encountered ours in their new position, their line of battle halted, and heavy skirmishing commenced. This continued until about 2 p.m., the skirmishers alternately driving each other. The brigade lost several killed and wounded and a few prisoners, but inflicted an equal or greater loss upon the enemy and captured between twenty-five and thirty prisoners.

At 2 p.m., the enemy formed for assault upon the portion of the brigade between the river and the City Point road, and a little later moved forward. A regiment was pushed up along the bank of the river under cover of the grove and buildings of the Younger Hare. It came in column and, as soon as its head was uncovered, endeavored to deploy. The rest of their force attempted to come forward in line of battle. A rapid fire was opened on the column, as soon as it showed itself, and upon those in line at about 300 yards. The column never succeeded in deploying and the line broke after advancing about fifty yards under fire. They were rallied and again brought forward, but were repulsed in confusion and with heavy loss. The voices of the Federal officers in command could be plainly heard. The Twenty-first, Twenty-seventh and Eleventh regiments repulsed this attack.

South of the City Point road, the Seventh battalion and Twenty-fifth regiment were not at this time attacked. Later in the afternoon, when the enemy made a general assault upon the Confederate lines to the right, the Twenty-fifth fired a few volleys obliquely into the assaulting lines moving over Hare's Hill upon *Colquitt*. The skirmishing here, however, in the morning was particularly heavy and obstinate. Major [*James H.*] *Rion* commanded the brigade skirmishers and distinguished himself by his usual gallantry and address. He was wounded in the arm, but continued in the field till night. Lieutenant [*R. F.*] *Felder*, of the Twenty-fifth, was also wounded and Lieutenant [*William A.*] *Harvey*, of the Seventh battalion, was killed. [Johnson Hagood, *Memoirs of the War of Secession: From the Original Manuscripts of Johnson Hagood* (Columbia, S.C.: The State Company, 1910), pp. 269–270.]

To visit Fort Stedman: If you wish to examine the fighting that took place on this ground in March 1865, continue on the trail that took you to the monument until you come to a T intersection. Turn right, and walk to the small monument for Colquitt's Salient just beyond the end of the paved trail. Stop at the monument, turn around to face toward the parking area, and turn to the section of the guide on Fort Stedman. Note: Due to the one-way park road, you will not have a chance to backtrack to this area from any of the other sites within the Petersburg National Battlefield's Eastern Front section.

To visit the Taylor Farm: If you do not wish to study the fighting at Fort Stedman in March 1865, continue on the trail that took you to the monument until you come to a T intersection. Turn left at the intersection, and return to the parking area. Proceed 1.0 mile on the Park Tour Road to the parking area for the Taylor Farm on the right. Walk toward the ruins of the Taylor House for about 250 yards, then over to the line of guns. Stop at the guns, and face west (the direction they are pointing) toward the low ground through which the railroad and Poor Creek run.

STOP 7: TAYLOR FARM

This is also the first stop for the Crater section of this guide.

THE NINTH CORPS ATTACKS, 18 JUNE 1864

As the Union Second Corps was coming to grief in its attacks at the Hare House and Prince George Court House Road, to the north Maj. Gen. Horatio Wright's Sixth Corps and Smith's Eighteenth Corps made a feeble attack on the Confederate lines astride and north of the City Point Road. Meanwhile, south of the Second Corps, Burnside's

Ninth Corps and Maj. Gen. Gouverneur Warren's Fifth Corps attempted to break the Confederate lines in their front. Around noon,
Willcox's division from the Ninth Corps advanced over the grounds of
the Taylor Farm into the cut of the Norfolk and Petersburg Railroad.
There they were joined on their left by Brig. Gen. Samuel Crawford's
division of the Fifth Corps and part of Brig. Gen. Charles Griffin's.
While in the cut, Willcox's men began to take fire from Confederates
in the section of the Harris Line that crossed the railroad north of
their position. Prodded by Meade, Burnside ordered Willcox and a
brigade from Potter's division to advance from the railroad cut. They
were able to push across Poor Creek, with one brigade getting within
125 yards of a salient in the Confederate lines occupied by Capt. *Richard G. Pegram's* battery and *Stephen D. Elliott's* South Carolina brigade
but could go no further.

Narrative of Capt. Richard G. Pegram, CSA, commanding Petersburg Battery (Virginia), Department of North Carolina and Southern Virginia

In the afternoon of the 17th of June, 1864, my battery having been withdrawn on the 16th instant from our lines near the
Howlett house, in Chesterfield, and ordered to Petersburg, I was
directed to place it in position at the spot subsequently known as
the "Crater." My orders were to act as a support to our troops in
the event that they should be driven from the lines near the Avery
house which were then occupied by them and which were constantly assailed by the enemy. On the morning of the 18th, before
day-light—it may have been earlier in the night—the Avery house
line was evacuated by our troops and they fell back to the new line,
which had been selected by Col. *D. B. Harris,* and of which the
position I occupied constituted a part, although my guns were a
little in advance of this line, because, when I loaded them, I knew
nothing about the selected line. . . . When I located my guns on
the evening of the 17th, as I have already stated, I knew nothing
about the establishment of our new line. About eleven o'clock
that night Col. *Harris* approached me and informed me that I was
a short distance in advance of our new line and then pointed out
the new line to me. I saw there a battery staked out for my guns
with traverses of such thickness as would require a large force to
complete it in a day, and, as I was informed that I need look for no
assistance from our infantry who, when they fell back, would have

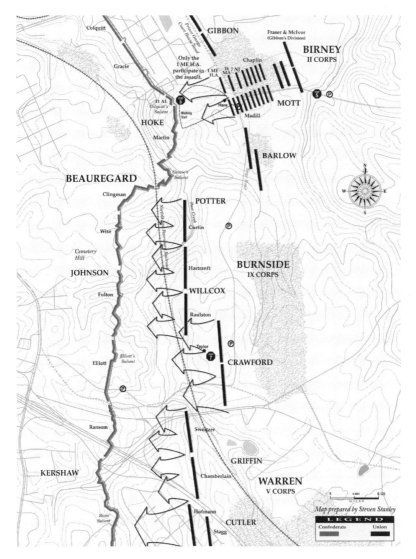

First Petersburg, June 18, 1864: Afternoon attacks

to construct works for their own protection, and, as my own men were worn out with the labor of constructing the pits I had had prepared, and, if they had been perfectly fresh, would have been unable then to make much progress in the construction of the work intended for my guns before the enemy's probable advance, I was compelled to hold on to the position I had already taken, in the pits I then occupied with my guns.

The pits occupied by my guns were not connected by rifle-pits with each other, or with our infantry line on either flank, as we had neither the time nor the labor necessary for their construction, and consequently this was a weak spot in our line. [George S. Bernard, ed., *War Talks of Confederate Veterans* (Petersburg, Va.: Fenn and Owen, 1892), pp. 207–208.]

Report of Major General Burnside, continued

A general attack was ordered by the major-general commanding the Army of the Potomac for 4 a.m. on the 18th, and General Willcox was ordered to take the advance of this corps, supported by General Potter. On pushing out the skirmishers in advance of the attacking column it was discovered that the enemy had withdrawn from the line on the open ground in front of the Shands house, but their skirmishers were found in the woods that intervened between it and the Taylor house.

General Willcox's division, with the First Brigade of the Second Division, steadily advanced through the woods under a heavy fire of musketry and artillery, driving the enemy back to the cut in the railroad beyond the Taylor house. From the open ground in front of this house it was discovered that the enemy had a strongly intrenched line beyond the railroad around the base of Cemetery Hill, which line bore off in the direction of the Hare house, crossing to this side of the railroad at a point nearly opposite our right, the enemy's skirmishers still occupying the railroad cut as well as a deep ravine which crossed the cut at a small angle immediately in our front. After some very severe fighting on the part of these two divisions the enemy was driven from a portion of the cut.

At 3 p.m. a general attack was ordered by the major-general commanding the Army of the Potomac, which resulted on the part of this corps in driving the enemy entirely out of the cut and ravine, and establishing our extreme advance within about 100 yards of the enemy's main line beyond the railroad. No better fighting has been done during the war than was done by the divisions of Generals Potter and Willcox during this attack, the railroad cut and ravine presenting formidable obstacles to the advance. General Parke, my chief of staff, had the more immediate directions of these divisions during that day. The troops of General Hancock, on our right, and General Warren, on our left, fully co-operated with us in this engagement. Our losses in the engagements of the 16th, 17th, and 18th were very severe, among which were many of our best commanding officers of brigade and regiments. The advanced position gained by us was held as an intrenched skirmish line, and our main line between the Second and Fifth Corps passed by the Taylor house. [*O.R.*, XL, part 1, p. 523.]

Report of Brigadier General Willcox, continued

June 18, at 4.30 a.m. I was ordered to move forward again and attack. A party of skirmishers was sent out in advance to feel for the enemy, and reported that the latter had fallen back, and with skirmishers deployed I moved on, Hartranft's brigade in front, across the fields and into the woods, toward the Taylor house. In the woods we encountered the enemy's skirmishers and a brisk shelling from their batteries across the Norfolk railroad. We drove back their skirmishers steadily out of the woods and into the cut of the Norfolk railroad, which formed a deep cover. On coming to the edge of the open field near the Taylor house, we found that the enemy had built a strong line of intrenchments beyond the railway cut and a winding ravine, through which ran a small creek, whose banks, immediately in my front, were steep and covered with wood and thicket. Here, then, were two lines of obstacles interposed between me and the enemy's works. Moreover, the advance to the railroad was over an open field exposed to fire.

The enemy's line was about 800 yards from the Taylor house, running along the foot of Cemetery Hill, turning to our right toward the Hare house, and crossing the railway at a point where a gun in position swept the railroad cutting for some distance. I brought up [Capt. Jacob] Roemer's battery and put part of it in position to command this gun, and part to reply to a battery which fired upon the left and front. General Crawford's division, Fifth Corps, had advanced through the woods in connection with me, and on my left, and Potter's (Second) division, Ninth Corps, now came up to support me. I ordered Hartranft to carry the railroad cut, which he did in good style. Crawford's troops did the same on our left.

After this General Barlow's division, Second Corps, came up on my right, and I proposed to Crawford and Barlow to make a general attack on the works at 12. Crawford acceded, but Barlow replied that he had no orders to attack. I considered a vigorous attack on Barlow's front essential to my success, as I was exposed to a heavy enfilading fire from the works that there curved around my right. The enemy's sharpshooters were picking off my men in the cut every moment, notwithstanding the traverses we threw up.

At 3 p.m. a general attack was ordered by the major-general commanding the army, and Hartranft began to move his command again, with Curtin's brigade, of Potter's division, on his right, and Colonel [William C.] Raulston, Twenty-fourth New York (dismounted) Cavalry (now commanding Christ's brigade), supporting. The railway bank was quite high and so steep that holes had to be dug in the side of it for the men to plant their feet, and as soon as a man showed his head he came under fire. This, of course, led to vexatious labor and delay in order to prepare the line to climb the bank simultaneously. On the extreme left, where the bank was lower, the movement began at once, and here the troops got as far as the ravine, driving out the enemy at the same time with the Fifth Corps troops.

Every preparation being made, under a galling fire, at 5.30 the whole of the division and part of Curtin's brigade made a determined advance. The whole ground from the railroad to the ravine was carried, officers and men falling at every step. The ravine was crossed, the crest beyond gained, and under the fire of a heavy line of battle my heroic troops fought their way up to within 125 yards of the enemy's intrenchments and held their ground. There were not over 1,000 uninjured left in the ranks to intrench themselves when night came on. [*O.R.*, XL, part 1, pp. 572–573.]

Report of Brig. Gen. John F. Hartranft, USA, commanding First Brigade, Third Division, Ninth Corps, Army of the Potomac

Advanced in good order to the Norfolk railroad cut, followed by Raulston's brigade, which also entered the cut. The enemy's sharpshooters commanded this cut from the right. A traverse was at once built across the cut on the right of the line, by tearing up the track and ties. Between 3 and 4 p.m. an order was received to advance upon the enemy's works without regard to the troops on our right or left. The enemy's line was about 300 yards in advance. A little stream of water, forming a ravine, with trees on the opposite side of the bank, intervened. This railroad cut was about fifteen to twenty feet deep, and the sides almost perpendicular. Steps and holes had to be made in the same so as to enable the troops to climb up on the bank, which was commanded by the enemy from his mainline, but the trees intervening offered some cover from his view. Many, however, were killed and wounded here. The troops of the entire division were in condition to make but a feeble attack; the regiments scarcely averaged 100 men. The losses had been very heavy in killed and wounded during the day and the day before, and many stragglers were still back.

Between 5 and 6 p.m. the whole division was out of the cut and in the ravine in advance. I now ordered the troops forward to attack; also ordered Colonel Curtin, First Brigade of Potter's division, to advance part of his brigade to the ravine. The division moved forward to attack, until reaching the summit of the opposite bank of the ravine, about 125 yards from the enemy's line. At this point my line became exposed to the full view of the enemy, whose fire was too severe to attempt farther advance. This position was, however, held and intrenched during the night, and was the nearest point to the enemy's line gained by the army on that day. [*O.R.*, XL, part 1, pp. 577–578.]

Journal of Maj. Gen. Bushrod Rust Johnson, CSA, commanding
Johnson's Division, Department of North Carolina and Southern Virginia

Enemy seen advancing 7.30 a.m. . . . at that hour opened first gun from section of *Pegram's* Battery on right of Baxter's Road. [Capt. *John O.*] *Miller's* section on right and *Pegram's* four Napoleons on left joined in fire. First shot cut a regiment in two. Firing all very good. The enemy's line, about one brigade of Yankee's about crest of hill east side of Taylor's Creek in front of Taylor's House, was driven by flank at double-quick to *Wise's* left in the woods by artillery alone. At first shot, Yankee's line was down. Enemy massed in the woods. Brought up four batteries . . . opened first battery about 8 o'clock. All these batteries commenced 10 o'clock from their new position—battery of two Napoleons and two 10-pounder Parrott guns on right of road. Fired on seven Yankee guns on crest of hill. . . . Artillery practice continued all day. Sharpshooters and skirmishers advanced about 10 o'clock. Our skirmishers were driven from slope in front of Taylor's House about 3 o'clock to railroad (we had men of enemy's battery found on crest of hill). At 9 or 10 o'clock a.m. skirmishers advanced from enemy's lines at 10 a.m. and drove in our advanced skirmishers to the second line of skirmishers on west side of Taylor's Creek.

In afternoon, enemy's skirmishers descended the slope to railroad and advanced across the creek. At about 4 p.m. enemy's skirmishers advanced on . . . Taylor's Creek, and drove in our skirmishers to their work. The enemy made a charge in two lines of about one brigade near *Elliott's* right artillery and infantry repulsed the charge easily, except for [those] which enlodged in ravine. General *Elliott* sent out two companies and drove them off. About 6.30 p.m. found regular lines of enemy's batteries with one color of United States and one state flag. The regiment in front of *Pegram's* four guns at about 200 yards and the fight commenced with artillery and infantry. Soon five enemy's colors were counted, perhaps but the regiments' or one brigade. Commenced entrenching in edge of woods below brow of hill north of Baxter's Road and were soon under cover with skirmishers advanced. On the right of the road . . . about one brigade charged up to battery and *Elliott's* Brigade charged up within fifty yards of our works, exposed . . . canister and flank fire from *Elliott's* Brigade and were driven back, repulsed, in disorder with great loss [of] men to top of hill on east of Taylor's Creek. They then formed a line of skirmishers which advanced about dusk to within fifty yards of *Elliott's* works (he having not thrown out skirmishers) [and] established a line which was not reported to me; [they] removed their wounded and dead. The enemy's loss was very heavy. [*O.R. Supplement,* VII, pp. 277–278.]

Narrative of Captain Pegram, continued

When the enemy's infantry advanced they proceeded to throw small parties at a time into the railroad cut of the Norfolk and Petersburg railroad, between the Baxter Road and the point at which the railroad crosses Taylor's Creek, where they would be protected from our fire, and where they could in this way gradually accumulate a considerable force. The distance from the railroad to the low ground or meadow west of the railroad to the point where they would be protected by the slope of the hill occupied by us, and at some little distance from the brow of which our line had been located, was inconsiderable, and after the enemy had massed a sufficient force in this cut, an operation which the fire from my guns and other artillery on our lines delayed, somewhere about one or two o'clock in the afternoon (I think), they advanced across the meadow west of the railroad cut, and established their line. . . . After nightfall, on the 18th, Gen. *Bushrod Johnson* sent a regiment or battalion of infantry for my immediate support, and these troops with some loss succeeded in constructing the necessary rifle-pits, after which I felt that my position could be successfully held against any effort the enemy might make for its capture by direct assault. From the time of the establishment of their line in front of the line occupied by my guns and the infantry to my right and left, the enemy kept up an almost constant and often furious musketry fire upon our lines until the morning of the Crater explosion. [Bernard, ed., *War Talks of Confederate Veterans*, pp. 207–208.]

THE FIFTH CORPS ATTACKS, 18 JUNE 1864

By the time Warren's Fifth Corps was ready to participate in the June 18 offensive, two divisions from *Lee's* army had reached Petersburg and extended the Confederate position to and beyond the Jerusalem Plank Road. Preparatory to his attack, Warren moved many of his men forward to the cut through which the Norfolk and Petersburg ran, with Crawford's division connecting with Burnside's command near the Taylor Farm, Brig. Gen. Charles Griffin's division on Crawford's left, and Brig. Gen. Lysander Cutler on the far left of the entire army. None of the attacks they delivered during the afternoon reached the Confederate lines, with much of the Fifth Corps exhibiting the sort of reluctance to attack entrenched positions that had been evident in the Second Corps's efforts near the Hare House. The First Petersburg Offensive was over.

Report of Brig. Gen. Lysander Cutler, USA, commanding Fourth Division, Fifth Corps, Army of the Potomac

On the 17th I sent the One hundred and forty-seventh New York to picket the Blackwater, and moved my command forward and went into position on the left of the Ninth Corps, my left extending toward the Blackwater, and intrenched within about 600 yards of the enemy's works. At daylight on the 18th I was ordered to move on the enemy's works. The order was immediately executed. The enemy's first and second lines were found to have been abandoned during the night. A few men who were left asleep only were found. I pushed my skirmishers and line of battle forward across the Norfolk railroad, and found the enemy on the crest beyond and in front of Petersburg. The enemy had set fire to the bridges across the railroad cut as they retired. I immediately rebuilt the bridge in my front to enable the batteries to come up.

Having formed my command on the left of the railroad in two lines, I moved forward, my right resting on the road, and drove in the enemy's pickets on his works in front of the town, General [Romeyn B.] Ayres' (Second) division having in the mean time come in on my left. At 2.50 p.m. an order was received to advance on the enemy's works; at 3 o'clock an order saying the movement was general. I immediately put my command in position to advance and at 3.20 moved forward, my Second Brigade (Colonel [J. William] Hofmann) leading, supported by my First Brigade (Colonel [Edward S.] Bragg). General Ayres, of the Second Division, did not receive the order in time to enable him to move simultaneously with me. My command suffered severely both by direct and flank fire of both infantry and artillery, and though a part of both brigades got within about seventy-five yards of the enemy's works they were unable to carry them. My men held the ground gained until dark, when, in obedience of orders, I withdrew the most advanced portions of my command and intrenched, connecting with Griffin on my right and Ayres on my left. In this affair I lost in killed and wounded about one-third of the men I had with me, and among them many valuable officers. [*O.R.*, XL, part 1, pp. 473–474.]

Report of Col. William S. Tilton, USA, commanding First Brigade, First Division, Fifth Corps, Army of the Potomac

June 18, at 5 a.m. broke camp and marched to the front, stacking arms in rear of Second Corps, when we made coffee. At 8 a.m. the brigade advanced to the front and left to take up a line before the enemy's works on new ground. My regiment (22nd Massachusetts) was detailed to skirmish to the front and drive in the rebel pickets. I deployed in an open field near Colonel Avery's house, with my right resting on the Norfolk turnpike road.

We pushed forward to the Norfolk railroad, which crossed the pike and to a ravine beyond, where the right of my line, being more exposed than the left, was driven back. The left, however, under Major [Mason W.] Burt, held its own, having shelter in rear of a crest. I thereupon strengthened my right with 100 men from the Sixty-second Pennsylvania; went in again, when I succeeded in driving the rebel skirmishers out of the ravine into one beyond.

About 12 m. [Jacob B.] Sweitzer's brigade moved toward and took position in this last ravine, all the regiments but one being on the right of the road. The First Brigade, Colonel [Joshua] Chamberlain, then advanced to the ravine and took position on the left of Colonel Sweitzer's brigade. This was done under a very heavy fire, and the brigade lost more than 200 men, including Colonel Chamberlain, who was wounded. . . . There it was, just before dark, that I was placed in command with orders to charge when troops on my right and left did. . . . I immediately proceeded to reconnoiter the ground, and communicate with the brigade commanders upon my right and left. Colonel Hofmann on the left, commanding a brigade in Cutler's division, assured me of his cooperation at the right moment.

The Eighty-third Pennsylvania, Forty-fourth New York, and Sixteenth Michigan Regiments, of [Brig. Gen. Joseph J.] Bartlett's brigade, were now sent me as a support. I removed the One hundred and eighty-seventh Pennsylvania, which had formed my second line, to the left of my front line, and placed Bartlett's three regiments in my second line, with orders to intrench and clear up the bushes in their front. After waiting anxiously the movement of the brigade on my right, I finally received notice that it had been suspended. [*O.R.*, XL, part 1, pp. 455–457.]

Report of Col. J. William Hofmann, USA, commanding Second Brigade, First Division, Fifth Corps, Army of the Potomac

At 4 a.m. on the morning of the 18th the brigade moved forward to attack the works of the enemy. It was soon ascertained that the enemy had withdrawn during the night, and that he had also abandoned his second line of works about a quarter of a mile in rear of the first line. Upon moving forward the skirmish line the enemy was found posted in rear of a third line of works, his skirmishers thrown forward to near the railroad. The brigade was moved to the west side of the railroad, and formed in line of battle in a wood, the right of the brigade resting on the railroad, and subsequently moved to the front of the woods and in rear of a hill.

At 3 p.m. the brigade was formed in line of battle on the crest of a hill, and moved forward to charge the works of the enemy, then about 700 yards in our front. In order to reach the enemy's works it was necessary to cross a ravine about 200 yards in front of the works. The line moved forward with spirit. The enemy immediately opened with musketry and spherical case, and, as we approached nearer, with canister. When the line had arrived near the ravine the loss had already been very great, for the troops were exposed to a fire not only in front but upon both flanks. As the line was descending the near slope of the ravine it broke; many returned. About 200 reached the opposite slope of the ravine, where they found shelter by lying close to the ground. Lieutenant-Colonel [George] Harney was the only regimental commander that reached this point. My horse was killed a moment before the line broke, and I did not reach the opposite side of the ravine. The officers now rallied the men in rear of the crest, from which the line had moved when the charge commenced. About 450 men were formed in line. An order was received at 4 p.m. to prepare for a second charge at 5.30 p.m. It was subsequently suspended. The troops in the ravine remained until dark, when they were withdrawn. Pickets were now thrown out to the foot of the ravine, a new line of battle formed and advanced to the crest of the hill, and breast-works were thrown up. [*O.R.*, XL, part 1, p. 476.]

Narrative of General Beauregard, *continued*

Scarcely two hours after General *Lee's* arrival I rode with him to what was known as the City Reservoir, on a commanding elevation, toward the right of our line. A good view of the surrounding country could be had from this point, and the whole field was there spread out before us like a map. I explained to General *Lee* and showed him the relative positions of our troops and of those of the enemy. I also pointed out to him the new and shorter line then occupied by us, and gave my reasons for its location there. They were these:

First, that it kept the enemy's batteries at a greater distance from the besieged town. Second. That it would act as a covered way (as the phrase is in the regular fortifications) should we deem it advisable to construct better works on the higher ground in the rear. In the meantime we could construct a series of batteries to protect our front line by flanking and over-shooting fires; and we could throw up infantry parapets for our reserves, whenever we should have additional troops. Third. That the new line gave a close infantry and artillery fire on the reverse slope of Taylor's Creek and ravine, which would prevent the construction of boyaux of approaches and parallels for a regular attack.

General *Lee*, whose capacity as a military engineer was universally acknowledged—and none appreciated it more than I did—was entirely of my opinion. Thus the new defensive line selected by me, which my own troops had been holding for twelve hours before the arrival of General *Lee* at Petersburg, and which his troops occupied as they came in, was maintained unchanged as to location—though much strengthened and improved thereafter—until the end of the war.

After those explanations to General *Lee*, and while still examining the field, I proposed to him that, as soon as [Lt. Gen. *Ambrose P.*] *Hill's* and [Maj. Gen. *Richard H.*] *Anderson's* corps should arrive, our entire disposable force be thrown upon the left and rear of the Federal army before it began to fortify its position. General *Lee*, after some hesitation, pronounced himself against this plan. He thought it was wiser, under the circumstances, to allow some rest to his troops (those present as well as those still coming up) after the long march all would have gone through with; and he stated as a further reason for his objection, that our best policy— one, he said, which had thus far proved successful to him—would be to maintain the defensive as heretofore. I urged that the Federal troops were at least as much exhausted as ours, and that their ignorance of the locality would give us a marked advantage over them; that their spirits were jaded, and ours brightened just then by the fact of the junction of his army with my forces; and that the enemy was not yet intrenched. But I was then only second in command, and my views did not prevail.

The evening of the 18th was quiet. There was no further attempt on the part of General Meade to assault our lines. He was "satisfied," as he said in his report, that there was "nothing more to be gained by direct attacks." The spade took the place of the musket, and the regular siege was begun. It was only raised April 2, 1865. [*Battles and Leaders*, IV, p. 544.]

To return to the Visitor Center, follow the park road to its terminus at Crater Road. Turn right onto Crater Road, and proceed 0.8 mile to Wythe Street. Turn right, and drive 2.2 miles on Route 36 (Wythe Street/Washington Street [Wythe Street intersects and then is named Washington Street]) to the exit to Petersburg National Battlefield on your right, then proceed to the parking area for the Visitor Center.

THE BATTLE OF FORT STEDMAN

This section of the guide provides directions and materials necessary to do a focused study of the March 1865 Battle of Fort Stedman.
Due to the configuration of Petersburg National Battlefield, it is very
difficult to study the campaign in a fashion that allows a visitor to follow it in a strictly chronological sequence. Thus, readers will be given
the option of studying the Battle of Fort Stedman as a stand-alone
engagement or breaking off from their study of the June 1864 First
Petersburg Offensive to examine the Fort Stedman fighting and then
return to the First Petersburg materials. A study of Fort Stedman also
provides a natural starting point for an examination of the actions
leading to the fall of Richmond and Petersburg; directions linking this
section to the Fall of Petersburg excursion may be found at the end of
this section of the guide.

The Battle of Fort Stedman came after a winter of great hardship
for the Army of Northern Virginia and the Confederate cause. The
year 1864 had been a period of steady deterioration for the cause of
Southern independence, with the North achieving decisive victories
in the Shenandoah Valley and elsewhere. As March 1865 opened, Lt.
Gen. Ulysses S. Grant was marshaling his forces and preparing for
a major operation against Confederate communications south and
west of Petersburg, an operation that he anticipated would seal the
outcome of the campaign. Gen. *Robert E. Lee*, meanwhile, had been
warning Richmond that the fragility of his force and the weakness of
its position were leading him to the conclusion that the only prospect
for avoiding total defeat would be to try to escape toward North Carolina to link up with a Confederate force commanded by Gen. *Joseph E.
Johnston. Lee* thought he and *Johnston* together might be able to decisively defeat Union forces in North Carolina commanded by Maj.
Gen. William T. Sherman, then do the same to Grant. It was a desperate stratagem by a desperate man leading a desperate cause, but there
were, as he saw it, precious few other viable options.

To make a move to join *Johnston* possible, *Lee* recognized that he
would have to induce Grant to loosen the tight grip his army had
established around much of Petersburg. Thus was born the idea for
an attack on the Federal lines around Fort Stedman. A strong attack
and breakthrough here, *Lee* hoped, might enable a Confederate force

to pose such a threat to the railroad that supplied much of the Army of the Potomac that Grant would be compelled to contract his lines. This, *Lee* hoped, might create just enough space to make a relatively clean escape from Petersburg possible. Like the larger plan to escape to continue the fight in conjunction with *Johnston's* force, it was a desperate stratagem.

SUMMARY OF PRINCIPAL EVENTS, 6 FEBRUARY– 25 MARCH 1865

February

6—Maj. Gen. Edward O. C. Ord, U.S. Army, assigned to command of the Department of Virginia

9—Gen. *Robert E. Lee* assumes command of the Confederate Armies

26—Maj. Gen. Winfield S. Hancock, U.S. Army, assigned to the command of the Department of West Virginia and temporarily of all the troops of the Middle Military Division not under the immediate command of Maj. Gen. Philip Sheridan

27–March 28—Expedition from Winchester to the front of Petersburg, Va.

March

25—Assault on Fort Stedman

From the Visitor Center, drive out of the parking lot and, after passing through the kiosk and crossing the bridge, take the right fork onto the Park Tour Road. From the fork, proceed 1.6 miles until you reach the parking area on the right. Walk on the trail to the right of Fort Stedman out to the small monument to Colquitt's Salient that is in front of some earthworks just beyond where the paved trail ends. Stop here and turn to face Fort Stedman.

STOP 1: COLQUITT'S SALIENT

Report of Lt. Gen. Ulysses S. Grant, USA, commanding Armies of the United States

From this time [the 27 October 1864 battle at Hatcher's Run, southwest of Petersburg] forward the operations in front of Petersburg and Richmond, until the spring campaign of 1865, were confined to the defense and extension of our lines and to offensive movements for crippling the enemy's lines of communication

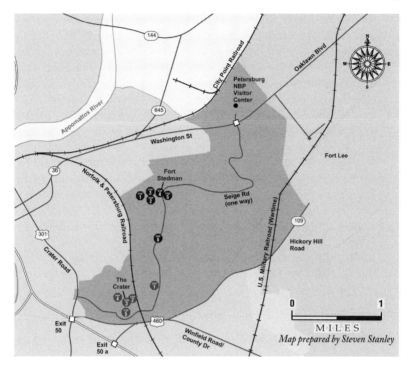

Fort Stedman and the Crater overview

and to prevent his detaching any considerable force to send south. By the 7th of February our lines were extended to Hatcher's Run, and the Weldon railroad had been destroyed to Hicksford. . . .

By the first of February General Sherman's whole army was in motion from Savannah. He captured Columbia, S.C. on the 17th; thence moved on Goldsborough, N.C., via Fayetteville. . . . On the 18th (19th) the combined forces of the enemy, under *Joe Johnston*, attached his advance at Bentonville. . . . On the night of the 21st the enemy retreated to Smithfield . . . from there Sherman continued to Goldsborough. . . .

General Sheridan moved from Winchester on the 27th of February, with two divisions of cavalry, numbering about 5,000 each. . . . After the long march by General Sheridan's cavalry over winter roads, it was necessary to rest and refit at White House. At this time the greatest source of uneasiness to me was the fear that the enemy would leave his strong lines about Petersburg and

Richmond for the purpose of uniting with *Johnston*, before he was driven from them by battle or I was prepared to make an effectual pursuit. On the 24th of March General Sheridan moved from White House, crossed the James River at Jones' Landing, and formed a junction with the Army of the Potomac in front of Petersburg on the 27th. During this move General Ord sent forces to cover the crossings of the Chickahominy. On the 24th of March the following instructions for a general movement of the armies operating against Richmond were issued. [U.S. War Department, *The War of the Rebellion: A Compilation of the Official Records of the Union and Confederate Armies*, 70 vols. in 128 parts and index (Washington, D.C.: Government Printing Office, 1880–1901), series 1, volume XLVI, part 1, pp. 31–32, 48–50. Hereafter cited as *O.R.*; all references are to series 1 unless otherwise noted.]

Reminiscences of Col. Edward Porter Alexander, CSA, Chief of Artillery, First Corps, Army of Northern Virginia

And so the time passed until the end of March with only one hostile incident. This was an incident very characteristic of Gen. *Lee* for it seems to me one of the greatest instances of audacity which the war produced. It was nothing less than an attempt to surprize & seize Fort Stedman, one of Grant's specially prepared forts, near the right of his line around Petersburg. Having taken that fort an effort was to be made to roll up Grant's line to the right, while forces should also be sent to the left to destroy the pontoon bridges over the Appomattox & to burn wharves, storehouses, &c. at City Point.

A great compliment was paid Gen. [*John B.*] *Gordon* in selecting him to command this assault. Indeed I think the very idea of the scheme is, in itself, an immense compliment to our whole army, that Gen. *Lee* believed it equal to such an undertaking. [Gary W. Gallagher, ed., *Fighting for the Confederacy: The Personal Recollections of General Edward Porter Alexander* (Chapel Hill: The University of North Carolina Press, 1989), 506–507.]

Narrative of Maj. Gen. John B. Gordon, CSA, commanding Second Corps, Army of Northern Virginia

If there was a weak point in those defences, I was expected to find it. If such a point could be found, I was expected to submit to General *Lee* some plan by which it would be feasible, or at

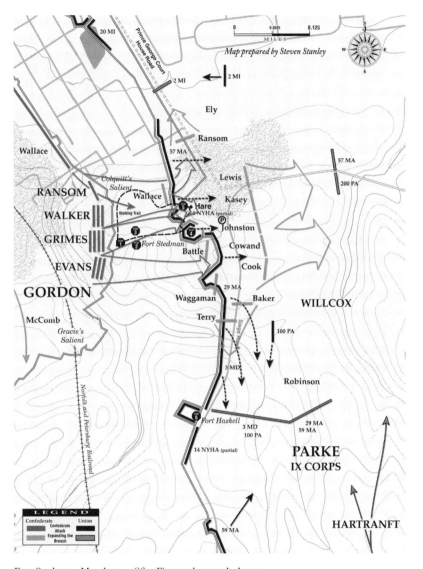

Fort Stedman, March 25, 1865: First and second phases

least possible, for his depleted army to assail it successfully. . . . It required a week of laborious examination and intense thought to enable me to . . . [decide] that Fort Stedman on Grant's lines was the most inviting point for attack and Colquitt's Salient on *Lee's* lines the proper place from which to sally. . . . The purpose of the movement was not simply the capture of Fort Stedman and the breastworks flanking it. The prisoners and guns we might thus capture would not justify the peril of the undertaking. The tremendous possibility was the disintegration of the whole left wing of the Federal army, or at least the dealing of such a staggering blow upon it as would disable it temporarily, enabling us to withdraw from Petersburg in safety and join *Johnston* in North Carolina. The capture of the fort was . . . simply the opening of a road through the wilderness of hostile works nearest to us in order that my corps and the additional forces to be sent me could pass toward the rear of Grant's lines and then turn upon his flanks. [John B. Gordon, *Reminiscences of the Civil War* (New York: Charles Scribner's Sons, 1903), pp. 398–413.]

Walk forward onto the low ground to the right in front of you. You are now in the area between the Union and Confederate lines that was home to a series of picket positions, or listening posts, maintained by both sides. This piece of terrain was to play a major role in the Confederate assault.

STOP 2: PLANNING THE ASSAULT

Narrative of Major General Gordon, continued

[I informed General *Lee*] that "During the week of investigation I have learned the name of every officer of rank in my front. I propose to select three officers from my corps, who are to command each a body of 100 men. These officers are to assume the names of three Union officers who are in and near Fort Stedman. When I have carried Fort Stedman, each of these selected officers is to rush in the darkness to the rear with his 100 men, shouting: 'The Rebels have carried Fort Stedman and our front lines!' They are to maintain no regular order, but each body of 100 is to keep close to its leader. As these three officers strike the line of infantry in rear of the fort and at different points, they will be halted; but each of them will at once represent himself as the Union officer whose name he bears, and is to repeat: 'The

Rebels have captured our works, and I am ordered by General [Napoleon B. McLaughlen] to rush back to the fort in rear and hold it at all hazards.' . . . Each body of 100 men will thus pass the supporting line of Union infantry and go to the rear of the fort to which I will direct the leader. They are to enter, overpower the Union guards, and take possession of the fort. Thus the three forts will be captured." . . . There was a long discussion of the chances and the serious difficulties in this desperate adventure. These were fully recognized by General *Lee.* . . . He directed me to proceed with the selection of my men for the different parts of the programme, but not to notify them until he had made search for the guides and had thought the whole plan over. Twenty-four hours later occurred the final conference before the attack. . . . Lee had thought of all the chances: he had found three men . . . for the three guides; he had selected different troops to send me from other corps, making, with mine, nearly one half of his army, and had decided that we should make one supreme effort to break the cordon tightening around us. These troops were to come from [Lt. Gen. *James*] *Longstreet's* and [Lt. Gen.] *A. P. Hill's* corps. A body of cavalry was to be sent me, which, in case we succeeded in getting into the three rear forts, was to ride across the broken gap at Fort Stedman, and then gallop to the rear, destroy Grant's railroad and telegraph lines, and cut away his pontoons across the river, while the infantry swept down the rear of the Union intrenchments. . . .

All night my troops were moving and concentrating behind Colquitt's Salient. For hours Mrs. Gordon sat in her room in Petersburg, tearing strips of white cloth to tie across the breasts of the leading detachments, that they might recognize each other in the darkness and in the hand-to-hand battle expected at the Federal breastworks and inside the fort. The fifty heavy keen-edged axes were placed in the hands of the fifty brave and stalwart fellows who were to lead the column and hew down Grant's obstructions. The strips of white cloth were tied upon them, and they were ready for the desperate plunge.

The chosen 300, in three companies, under the three officers bearing names of Union officers, were also bedecked with the white cotton Confederate scarfs. To each of these companies was assigned one of the three selected guides. . . . The column of attack was arranged in the following order: the 50 axemen in front, and immediately behind and close to them the selected 300. Next came the different commands of infantry who were to move in compact column close behind the 300, the cavalry being held in reserve until the way for them was cleared. . . . At 4 a.m. I stood on the top of the breastworks, with no one at my side except a single private soldier with rifle in hand, who was to fire the signal shot for the headlong rush. This night charge on the fort was to be across the intervening space covered with ditches, in one of which stood the watchful Federal pickets. There still remained near my works some of the débris of our obstructions, which had not been completely removed and which I feared might retard the rapid exit of my men; and I ordered it cleared away. The noise made by this removal, though slight, attracted the attention of a Union picket who stood on guard only a few rods from me, and he called out: "What are you doing over there, Johnny? What is that noise? Answer quick or I'll shoot."

The pickets of the two armies were so close together at this point that there was an understanding between them, either expressed or implied, that they would not shoot each other down except when necessary. The call of this Union picket filled me with apprehension. I expected him to fire and start the entire picket-line to firing, thus giving the alarm to the fort, the capture of which depended largely upon the secrecy of my movement. The quick mother-wit of the private soldier at my side came to my relief. In an instant he replied: "Never mind, Yank. Lie down and go to sleep. We are just gathering a little corn. You know rations are mighty short over here." There was a narrow strip of corn which the bullets had not shot away still standing between the lines. The Union picket promptly answered: "All right, Johnny; go ahead and get your corn. I'll not shoot at you while you are drawing your rations." . . . My troops stood in close column, ready for the hazardous rush upon Fort Stedman. While the fraternal dialogue in reference to drawing rations from the cornfield was progressing between the Union picket and the resourceful private at my side, the last of the obstructions in my front were removed, and I ordered the private to fire the signal for the assault. [Gordon, *Reminiscences*, pp. 398–413.]

Report of Maj. Gen. John G. Parke, USA, commanding Ninth Corps, Army of the Potomac

The line held by this corps extended from the Appomattox on the right, with pickets stretching some three miles down the river, to Fort Howard on the left, a distance of about seven miles. The line was occupied by the First Division, Bvt. Major General O[rlando] B. Willcox, commanding, extending from the Appomattox to Fort Meikel, and the Second Division, Bvt. Major General R[obert] B. Potter commanding, extended from Fort Meikel to Fort Howard. The Third Division, Brigadier General J[ohn] F. Hartranft commanding, was held in reserve, its right regiment being posted near the Dunn House Battery, and its left regiment between Forts Hays and Howard. The intrenchments held by Willcox's division and the First Brigade of Potter's, were very nearly as placed when the positions were originally gained by our troops, under fire, and in so close proximity to the enemy that the work was necessarily very defective. This was especially the case with Fort Stedman, where our line crossed the Prince George Court-House road. This is a small work without bastions, with Battery Number 10 immediately adjoining, the battery open in the rear, and the ground in rear of the fort nearly as high as its parapet. The opposing lines are here about 150 yards apart, the picket-lines about fifty yards. This portion of the line was held by the Third Brigade, First Division, Bvt. Brigadier General N. B. McLaughlen commanding. [*O.R.*, XLVI, part 1, pp. 316–317.]

Remain in place with a view up the slope toward Fort Stedman.

STOP 3: THE ASSAULT ON FORT STEDMAN

Narrative of Major General Gordon, continued

As the solitary signal shot rang out in the stillness, my alert pickets, who had crept close to the Union sentinels, sprang like sinewy Ajaxes upon them and prevented the discharge of a single alarm shot. Had these faithful Union sentinels been permitted to fire alarm guns, my dense columns, while rushing upon the fort, would have been torn into fragments by the heavy guns. Simultaneously with the seizing and silencing of the Federal sentinels, my stalwart axemen leaped over our breastworks, closely followed by the selected 300 and the packed column of infantry . . . soon was heard the thud of the heavy axes as my brave fellows slashed down the Federal obstructions. The next moment the infantry sprang upon the Union breastworks and into the fort, overpowering the gunners before their destructive charges could be emptied

Fort Stedman (USAMHI)

into the mass of Confederates. They turned this captured artillery upon the flanking lines on each side of the fort, clearing the
Union breastworks of their defenders for some distance in both
directions. Up to this point, the success had exceeded my most
sanguine expectations. We had taken Fort Stedman and a long
line of breastworks on either side. We had captured nine heavy
cannon, eleven mortars, nearly 1000 prisoners . . . with the loss of
less than half a dozen men. [Gordon, *Reminiscences*, pp. 398–413.]

Report of Asst. Surg. Samuel Adams, USA, Medical Inspector

At 4.30 o'clock on the morning of the 25th instant the enemy
made an assault on the lines at Fort Stedman in three columns;
one column swept down to the left toward Battery Numbers 9,
one to the right toward Fort Haskell, while a third moved forward
directly toward Fort Stedman. The enemy had been coming in
for several nights, bringing their guns and equipments with them;
on this occasion they came in squads, as deserters to our pickets,
and by this ruse the picket-line at this point was enveloped and

captured before the alarm could be given to the main line. The pickets were active and on the alert, and had been visited by the officer of the picket, Captain [John F.] Burch, Third Maryland Veteran Volunteers, at 4 a.m. There was no neglect or want of vigilance on the part of the pickets of this division. The attack was made on the Second and Third Brigades of the First Division, Major-General Willcox commanding. The alarm was soon conveyed to the main line, and the troops were ready and in line to meet the assault promptly. The enemy swept over the parapet and overpowered the garrison of Battery 10, killing and capturing the cannoneers at their guns; they then pushed forward to Fort Stedman, capturing its guns and the garrison, composed of one battalion of the Fourteenth New York Heavy Artillery. [*O.R.*, XLVI, part 1, p. 320.]

Walk to Fort Stedman, following the paved trail that took you out to Colquitt's Salient. Just before you reach the parking lot, turn right toward the Fort Stedman monument, then turn right again to enter Fort Stedman. After entering the fort, follow the paved trail around to a point between the second and third cannon. Stop and face in the direction toward which they are pointed.

STOP 4: THE CAPTURE OF FORT STEDMAN

Narrative of Major General Gordon, continued

From the fort I sent word to General *Lee*, who was on a hill in the rear, that we were in the works and that the 300 were on their way to the lines in the rear. Soon I received a message from one of these three officers . . . that he had passed the line of Federal infantry without trouble by representing himself as Colonel —— of the Hundredth Pennsylvania, but that he could not find his fort, as the guide had been lost in the rush upon Stedman. I soon received a similar message from the other two, and so notified General Lee. [Gordon, *Reminiscences*, pp. 398–413.]

Narrative of Maj. Gen. James A. Walker, CSA, commanding Early's Division, Second Corps, Army of Northern Virginia

As the head of the column entered Fort Stedman the resistance wholly ceased, and in the dim light of the coming dawn the fleeing enemy could be seen on every side, hastening to the protection of the second line of forts. Our being in possession of Fort Stedman made the enemy's breastworks on either side and

82] THE BATTLE OF FORT STEDMAN

as far as the neighboring forts untenable and they were rapidly
abandoned. A strong skirmish line of Confederates was at once
thrown forward towards the second line of the enemy's works,
and got within easy musket range, but though they were guarded
by a small force it was too large to be dislodged by skirmishers.
[*Southern Historical Society Papers*, 52 vols. (Millwood, N.Y.: Kraus
reprint, 1876–1959), volume XXXI, pp. 27–29. Hereafter cited
as *SHSP.*]

Report of Bvt. Maj. Gen. Orlando B. Willcox, USA, commanding First Division, Ninth Corps, Army of the Potomac

At 4.15 o'clock on the morning of the 25th ultimo the enemy
attacked the entrenchments held by the Third Brigade of this division. The brigade picket officer . . . reports that he visited the
picket-line at 4 o'clock of that a.m. and saw that the men were on
the alert. After visiting the line he returned to his headquarters in
front of Fort Stedman and Battery No. 11. He states that in a few
minutes after his return a man of the lookout gave notice that the
enemy were approaching. At the same time the men on the post
fired their pieces. One column moved toward the right of Battery No. 10, a second column moved toward a point between Fort
Stedman and Battery No. 11, a third column moved direct toward
Stedman. These columns were preceded by a strong storming
party, which broke through the pickets, clubbing their muskets,
and made opening in the abatis. The trench guards made sufficient resistance to arouse the garrisons of the inclosed works in
the immediate neighborhood, but the column which struck to the
right of Battery No. 10 quickly succeeded in breaking through
and effecting an entrance into that battery, which is entirely open
in the rear. [*O.R.*, XLVI, part 1, pp. 322–324.]

Report of Bvt. Brig. Gen. Napoleon B. McLaughlen, USA, Fifty-seventh Massachusetts Infantry, commanding Third Brigade, First Division, Ninth Corps, Army of the Potomac

On hearing the noise of the attack that morning, I awoke
my staff and dispatched them to various parts of the line to get
the troops under arms, and proceeded myself to Fort Haskell,
garrisoned by a battalion of the Fourteenth New York Heavy Artillery, whom I found on the alert and ready to resist an attack.
I then turned down the line to the right, passing the One hundredth Pennsylvania Volunteers, who were already in their works,
and Battery 12, finding everything right, and reached the mortar

battery Number 11, in which were no guns, and which was occupied by the Twenty-ninth Massachusetts Veteran Volunteers. Here
I found Major [Charles T.] Richardson, of that regiment, who
told me that the battery was in the enemy's hands, and that his
command had just been driven from it. I at once sent orders to
the Fifty-ninth Massachusetts Veteran Volunteers, the only regiment of my brigade not in the line of works, to report to me at
double-quick, and to Battery 12 to turn their mortars on Battery
11, which was done, three shots being fired.

On the arrival of the Fifty-ninth I put them into the work
with fixed bayonets and recaptured it at once. Supposing that I
had restored the only break in the line, I crossed the parapet into
Fort Stedman on the right, and meeting some men coming over
the curtains, whom in the darkness I supposed to be a part of the
picket, I established them inside the work, giving directions with
regard to position and firing, all of which were instantly obeyed.
In a few minutes I saw a man crossing the parapet, whose uniform
in the dawning light I recognized to be the enemy's, and I halted
him, asking his regiment. This called attention to myself, and the
next moment, I was surrounded by the rebels, whom I had supposed to be my men, and sent to the rear, where I found General
Gordon, to whom I delivered my sword, and was sent by him to Petersburg. While standing by General *Gordon* four brigades moved
forward toward our works, their commanders reporting to him.
While there Captain [Henry L.] Swords, of the First Division staff,
was brought up, having been captured in Fort Stedman, where he
had been directed in search of me, and also Lieutenant [Thomas]
Sturgis, of my staff, whom I had sent to the left and ordered to
report to me at Fort Stedman.

From Petersburg I was sent by rail the same day to the Libby
Prison at Richmond, Va., and remained there until the afternoon
of April 2, when I, with the other officers confined there, was
paroled and sent to this place via Fortress Monroe, where we arrived this morning. There were 16 officers of my brigade captured besides myself, and about 480 enlisted men, all of whom
are paroled. I have not the slightest fault to find with any of the
troops of my command. All were vigilant and on the alert, both
officers and men, and all was done that lay within the bounds of
possibility. The enemy, aware of the recent order allowing deserters to bring in their arms, approached my picket-line under that
disguise, in small squads, and thus surprised the pickets, capturing them without any alarm being given. I would say, further, that

I have personal knowledge that there were three divisions massed to break my brigade line, those of [Maj. Gen. *Bushrod R.*] *Johnson* and *Gordon* making the attack, and the third being held in reserve, with cavalry and batteries in support. [*O.R.*, XLVI, part 1, pp. 331–332.]

Report of Maj. George M. Randall, USA, Fourteenth New York Heavy Artillery, Ninth Corps, Army of the Potomac

At 3 a.m. the officers of my command were informed by a sergeant of the picket that the enemy were advancing on our works in my immediate front. I at once ordered my command to the works. On reaching them I found that some few men of the enemy were on the works to the right of Battery No. 10, who made a most desperate attempt to gain possession. My command opened fire, and succeeded in foiling their attempt. The enemy were re-enforced, and made another desperate attempt. A few had gained our works, but these were captured and sent to the rear. I ordered my men to use their bayonets and the butts of their muskets, which they did most gallantly, fighting hand to hand with the enemy. The next attack was made on Fort Stedman, and notwithstanding the darkness of the night and the suddenness of the attack, succeeded in checking them at these points. The third attack, the enemy met with better success, they having flanked us on our right and left, and charging us at daybreak with overwhelming force, made it necessary for my men to retreat, which they did, toward the first battalion of my regiment, now at Fort Haskell. [*O.R.*, XLVI, part 1, p. 341.]

After taking time to look around the interior of Fort Stedman, exit the fort via the walking path and return to the Pennsylvania Monument located near the parking area. You may choose to read the materials for the next stop at this location or, if you wish, continue on to Fort Haskell, located approximately one-quarter mile to the south along the park road. Keep in mind that the park road is one-way, so it would be best to walk if you wish to return to Fort Stedman without driving back via the Visitor Center.

STOP 5: THE FEDERAL COUNTERATTACK

Report of Major General Parke, continued

As soon as it became evident at my headquarters that the enemy were attacking, I dispatched aides-de-camp to communicate

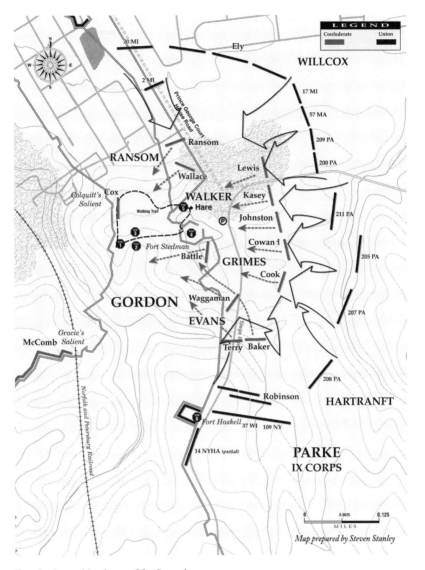

Fort Stedman, March 25, 1865: Last phase

with General Willcox and McLaughlen, ordered General Hartranft to concentrate his right brigade and re-enforce General Willcox, and ordered General [John C.] Tidball, chief of artillery, to place his reserve batteries in position on the hills in rear of the point attacked. On receiving a report from General Willcox and from members of my own staff of the state of affairs, I ordered up General Hartranft's other brigade, informed General Willcox that he would be re-enforced by the Third Division, and directed him to at once reoccupy the works taken. General Hartranft concentrated his division with commendable promptitude, his left regiment having to move a distance of five miles, he in the meantime promptly and gallantly attacking with a regiment of his right brigade, the Two hundredth Pennsylvania, assisted by detachments from McLaughlen's and [Lt. Col. Ralph] Ely's brigades, of Willcox's division, checking the enemy's skirmishers, who were advancing toward Meade's Station, and driving them back to the line of works.

The column of the enemy which turned to the left hand after entering our line, proceeded along the trenches in the direction of Battery Numbers 9, taking the Fifty-seventh Massachusetts in flank and rear, and driving them from the trenches. The left of the Second Michigan, the left regiment of Ely's brigade, of Willcox's division, was also somewhat broken, but the regiment promptly rallied, and fought the enemy over the traverses so stoutly that time was gained to bring up re-enforcements from the right of the brigade, and form a strong line perpendicular to the intrenchments, with right resting near Battery 9. This line of troops, assisted by the artillery from Numbers 9, Numbers 5, and McGilvery, repulsed with loss a heavy assault on Battery 9, and stopped all farther advance of the enemy in that direction. The picket-line was held up to a point to the left of Battery 9 throughout the engagement.

The rebel column which moved from Fort Stedman toward Fort Haskell met no better success. It gained temporary possession of Mortar Batteries 11 and 12, but the garrisons of those works, the Twenty-ninth Massachusetts and One hundredth Pennsylvania, quickly rallied on the left, and formed in conjunction with troops withdrawn from his left by Colonel [Samuel] Harriman, commanding First Brigade, Willcox's division, a line perpendicular to the intrenchments, connecting on their right with Hartranft's troops and with left resting near Fort Haskell, checking all farther progress of the enemy, and slowly driving him back. He made several desperate assaults on Fort Haskell, but was bloodily repulsed.

At 7.30 a.m. the position of affairs was this: We had regained Batteries 11 and 12, and had drawn a cordon of troops around Fort Stedman and Battery 10, forcing the masses of the enemy back into those works where they were exposed to, and suffered greatly from, a concentrated fire from all the artillery in position bearing on those points and the reserve batteries on the hill in rear. This cordon was composed of Hartranft's division, with regiments from McLaughlen's and Ely's brigades on either flank. [*O.R.*, XLVI, part 1, pp. 317–318.]

Report of Bvt. Maj. Gen. Orlando B. Willcox, USA, commanding First Division, Ninth Corps, Army of the Potomac

The right column, with the aid of troops from Stedman, now succeeded in gaining Battery Number 11. Their left column turned down the works to their left toward Battery Number 9, taking the Fifty-seventh Massachusetts in the trenches in flank and rear, capturing a part of them. The remainder retired to the rear, reassembled, and afterward did good work as skirmishers, with General Hartranft's troops. The Second Michigan fought the enemy on this flank from their bomb-proofs and traverses in the most spirited manner, until they were drawn in by order of their brigade commander, Bvt. Colonel Ralph Ely, to Battery Numbers 9, which, though small, is an inclosed work.

In pursuance with my orders Colonel Ely deployed, perpendicular to and to the rear of his entrenchments, a portion of the First Michigan Sharpshooters as skirmishers, promptly taking them from the right of our line for this purpose. I also directed him to press the enemy on his left as much as possible. Finding themselves opposed in this direction the enemy halted for more of their troops to come up, and the ground vacated by the Second Michigan remained unoccupied by either party. The enemy's skirmishers now came down the hill directly to the rear of Stedman, and moved toward my headquarters at the Friend house, the Dunn House Battery, and in the direction of Meade's Station, and this, for a time, rendered my communication with the Third Brigade long and circuitous. Meantime, I had ordered out the Seventeenth Michigan Engineer Regiment, at my headquarters, and sent word to the commanding officers of the Two hundredth and Two hundred and ninth Pennsylvania—encamped between Meade's Station and Dunn House Battery—to move, respectively, one to the Friend house, the other in front of the Dunn House Battery. These regiments promptly appeared.

Brigadier-General Hartranft commanding the Third Division, now came up in person, and I requested him to move his available force direct upon the fort. He promptly and gallantly took command of the two regiments already out, without waiting for the rest of his command. I ordered the Seventeenth Michigan to deploy as skirmishers on his right. This regiment, with only 100 men in its ranks, under command of Major [Joseph A.] Mathews, moved forward at the same time with General Hartranft's line, capturing most of the enemy's skirmishers in their front, about twenty-five in number, and inclining to the right, connected with the skirmishers of Ely's brigade.

While Hartranft was operating in rear of Stedman the enemy's force, which had moved down toward Battery 9 and halted, was re-enforced by [Brig. Gen. *Matthew W.*] *Ransom's* brigade, and opened an attack upon that battery. This attack was handsomely repulsed by my skirmishers and troops of the Second Brigade in Battery Number 9, assisted by the artillery, particularly one piece of Roemer's battery, under Major [Jacob] Roemer himself. The enemy attempted to retreat back to his own entrenchments, when they were charged by detachments of the Second Michigan, who captured some prisoners. Troops of the Twentieth and Second Michigan also threw themselves into the picket-line of the Second Brigade, and poured such a fire on the flanks of the retreating enemy that over 300 threw down their arms and surrendered themselves on the spot. On our left the enemy proceeded through the trenches, driving before them the Twenty-ninth Massachusetts, a small regiment, which made the best resistance it could, over its traverses and works, being attacked in front, flank, and rear. From Battery Numbers 11 they proceeded toward Battery Numbers 12 in the same manner, killing, wounding, and capturing a part of the One hundredth Pennsylvania Veteran Volunteers. In this attack Colonel [Joseph H.] Pentecost, commanding One hundredth Pennsylvania, was mortally wounded. A part of this regiment was deployed as skirmishers in the rear, and a part went into Fort Haskell. Brevet Colonel [Gilbert P.] Robinson took a part of the Third Maryland from a portion of his line on the left of Haskell and deployed it on the left of the skirmish line of the One hundredth Pennsylvania. Soon afterward Colonel Robinson, by my direction, assumed command of the Third Brigade.

I would here state that last winter, when it was thought that the enemy were mining toward Stedman, I gave directions to the brigade commanders that in the event of the line being broken at Stedman or any other point, they should immediately take out troops where they could best be spared from their respective fronts and attack the flanks of the enemy, and by no means to abandon their works. This order was handsomely carried out by the brigade and regimental commanders on this occasion, and led to the most beneficial results.

In pursuance with this order, Colonel Harriman, commanding First Brigade of this division, and posted on the left of the Third Brigade, ordered up the One hundred and ninth New York and Thirty-seventh Wisconsin Volunteers to report to General McLaughlen, but, as General McLaughlen could not be found, these two regiments were formed in line in rear of the skirmishers already mentioned and entrenched themselves to resist the large force moving down the rear of the line toward Haskell. The enemy was now confronted on this flank by the troops in Fort Haskell and the skirmishers of the One hundredth Pennsylvania and Third Maryland. The enemy made three advances on Haskell, all of which were gloriously repulsed. Meantime several ineffectual attempts were made by General Hartranft with a portion of his division to regain Fort Stedman by an advance on the rear of that work, but very soon after the repulse of the enemy at Fort Haskell the Second Brigade, of Hartranft's division, came up and formed on his left, the left of this brigade stretching toward Haskell. On the appearance of this new line the enemy, already repulsed on both flanks and considerably demoralized by the fire of our well-served artillery, were seen breaking away in small detachments from Stedman back to their own lines. This was quickly perceived by our troops on all sides. Major [Norman] Maxwell, One hundredth Pennsylvania, with the skirmishers of his regiment, under Captains [John L.] Johnson and [David P.] Book, and those of the Third Maryland, under Captain [Joseph F.] Carter, immediately started along the trenches toward Stedman, capturing a large number of prisoners in the bomb-proofs from Battery Numbers 12 to Battery Numbers 10. The first Union colors on the recaptured fort were planted there by Sergeant [Charles] Oliver, One hundredth Pennsylvania, who captured a stand of rebel colors, at the same point and at the same time, with his own hands.

Hartranft's line advanced rapidly, enveloping the rear of the works. The Seventeenth Michigan, on the extreme right, dashed forward and gained the trenches lately occupied by the

Fifty-seventh Massachusetts but now held by the enemy, capturing prisoners on that side. The retreat of the enemy was soon cut off by the troops of this division gaining the rear of the main body along the parapet of the works, and a large number of prisoners and some colors were captured by the troops of both divisions. One thousand and five prisoners, besides some of the wounded, fell into the hands of my own command, also seven stand of the enemy's colors, together with one of our own flag-staffs recaptured. [*O.R.*, XLVI, part 1, pp. 322–324.]

Report of Bvt. Maj. Gen. John F. Hartranft, USA, commanding Third Division, Ninth Corps, Army of the Potomac

Immediately upon hearing the alarm on the right of the line, which was about 4.30 a.m., Captain [Prosper] Dalien, of my staff, who was on duty as staff officer of the day, was sent from my headquarters, which were at the Avery house, to Colonel Harriman and Brigadier-General McLaughlen, commanding brigades in the First Division, and ascertain the cause of the alarm; at the same time orders were sent to my brigade commanders, and their commands were under arms ready for any emergency. The position of my division, which consists of two brigades, was as follows: One regiment, the Two hundredth Pennsylvania Volunteers, near the Dunn House Battery; the Two hundred and ninth Pennsylvania Volunteers, at Meade's Station; the Two hundred and eighth Pennsylvania Volunteers, on the right of the Avery house; the Two hundred and fifth and Two hundred and seventh Regiments Pennsylvania Volunteers, on the army line railroad, near Fort Prescott, and the Two hundred and eleventh Pennsylvania Volunteers, near the railroad, about half way between Forts Alex, Hays and Howard. At 5.10 a.m. Captain Dalien returned to headquarters with a dispatch from General McLaughlen's headquarters, and of which the following is a copy:

HEADQUARTERS THIRD BRIGADE, FIRST DIVISION, NINTH ARMY CORPS, March 25, 1865.

GENERAL: The enemy have attacked our lines and carried a portion of its works (from Battery 11 and Stedman to the right). They are now moving towards the Appomattox. General on the lines.

Very respectfully, your obedient servant,

CLARKE,

Acting Assistant Adjutant-General.

Maj. Gen. John F. Hartranft and staff (USAMHI)

A few moments afterward I received dispatch from Major-General Parke, of which the following is a copy:

> HEADQUARTERS NINTH ARMY CORPS, March 25, 1865—5.15 a.m.
>
> GENERAL: The general commanding directs that you move the brigade at Meade's Station to re-enforce General Willcox, in order to recapture a battery reported to be taken by the enemy on his front and near Fort Stedman.
>
> Very respectfully, your obedient servant,
> J. L. VAN BUREN,
> Brevet Colonel and Aide-de-Camp.

I immediately started in person to the right, and at the same time ordered the Two hundred and eighth Regiment Pennsylvania Volunteers to report to General McLaughlen. I then went to communicate with Major-General Willcox, commanding First Division, whose headquarters were at the Friend house. I found the Two hundred and ninth Pennsylvania Volunteers moving toward General Willcox's headquarters and the Two hundredth

Pennsylvania Volunteers had already moved out of camp and had
halted with the right resting near the Dunn House Battery. This
was done by the order of Major-General Willcox, the regiment
having had directions to obey the orders of General Willcox in
case of an attack, to avoid delay, the distance to my headquarters being so great owing to the length of the line covered by
my command. I asked General Willcox to send one of his staff
to direct the Two hundred and ninth Pennsylvania Volunteers,
and he designated Captain [Levi C.] Brackett, aide-de-camp, to
perform this duty, who led the regiment by the flank down the
road to the left of the Friend house. It was now sufficiently light
to see the enemy's skirmishers advancing from the rear and our
right of Fort Stedman toward the ravine and covering the main
road leading from Stedman to the Ninth Corps hospitals. Seeing
this movement of the enemy's skirmishers, and finding a small
party of men from the Fifty-seventh Massachusetts Volunteers in
front of the Two hundredth Pennsylvania Volunteers, under command of a captain, engaging them, and from whom I ascertained
that this detachment had been driven its camp and that all that
was left of the regiment had been rallied at that point, I ordered
his detachment to move forward to its old camp, and I immediately advanced the Two hundredth Pennsylvania Volunteers to
the camp of the Fifty-seventh Massachusetts, in rear of Stedman,
without sustaining any very serious damage.

The enemy's line of skirmishers was broken, but he was in
force in the left end of the Fifty-seventh Massachusetts camp, on
the road running in rear of Stedman and in a line of works running about parallel with our line. I sent Major [George] Shorkley,
of my staff, to bring up the Two hundred and ninth Pennsylvania
Volunteers to form a connection on the right of the Two hundredth Pennsylvania Volunteers, and I immediately attacked with
the Two hundredth Pennsylvania Volunteers, but finding the enemy too strong and my right suffering very much from a heavy
fire from Stedman and the troops in the road, the regiment was
forced to retire to an old line of works about forty yards in rear
of and to the right of the Fifty-seventh Massachusetts camp. The
enemy seeing this regiment retire, I feared that he would take
advantage of it and attack me, and I therefore attacked a second
time and gained quite a good position. I held this position for
about twenty minutes, losing very heavily (the loss in this regiment being about 100 at this point), when the line wavered and

fell back to and was rallied on the old line of works from which it had advanced the second time. Here the Two hundred and ninth Pennsylvania Volunteers formed a connection on the right of the Two hundredth Pennsylvania Volunteers, and with the aid of the fire from Battery 9, which had opened, and the Twentieth Michigan, which garrisoned this battery, and the Second and Seventeenth Michigan, of the First Division, which covered the ground between the right of the Two hundred and ninth Pennsylvania Volunteers and Battery 9, I had a strong line, which I determined could be held and check any farther advance in this direction, and I therefore ordered the troops to act on the defensive.

I saw that I could accomplish nothing more with the force I had engaged, and having fully satisfied myself that this advance was not a feint on the part of the enemy, but a serious and determined attack, I dispatched an orderly to bring up my Second Brigade, and I went to confer with General Willcox in regard to the situation. On my way to General Willcox's headquarters I saw Colonel [Charles G.] Loring, of General Parke's staff, through whom I received an order to place my Second Brigade in position on the hill rear of Stedman, and covering Meade's Station. I requested him to communicate with General Willcox, and I proceeded to join my Second Brigade. Two regiments of the Second Brigade, the Two hundred and fifth and Two hundred and seventh Pennsylvania Volunteers, had already been moved to the right as far as the Avery house, on the double-quick, by Major [John D.] Bertolette, assistant adjutant-general (who received the order to do so through Colonel [James L.] Van Buren, aide-de-camp on General Parke's staff), and were by him conducted through the ravine on the right of the Avery house to a point on the right of General McLaughlen's headquarters and in the rear of Fort Stedman under cover. I then went to General McLaughlen's headquarters and found the Two hundred and eighth Pennsylvania Volunteers in a good position on the right of his headquarters, left resting near Fort Haskell and facing northward. Several small detachments of the Third Brigade, First Division, mostly from the One hundredth Regiment Pennsylvania Volunteers, numbering, perhaps, 200 men, were formed on the left of the Two hundred and eighth Pennsylvania Volunteers and between it and Fort Haskell. I also found that the reserves of the First Brigade, First Division, had formed a line on the right of and at right angles with the main line held by that brigade. The Two hundred and fifth and Two hundred and seventh Pennsylvania Volunteers were a short distance to the right of the Two hundred and eighth Pennsylvania Volunteers, and the distance from the left of the Two hundredth Pennsylvania Volunteers to the right of the Second Brigade was probably about 300 yards, which distance was not covered by any troops.

I saw that any further advance on the part of the enemy was impossible under the concentrated infantry fire from the Two hundredth and Two hundred and ninth Regiment Pennsylvania Volunteers and Batteries 9 and McGilvery on the right, and the Two hundred and fifth, Two hundred and seventh, and Two hundred and eighth Regiments Pennsylvania Volunteers and Fort Haskell on the left, and from the field artillery in position on the hills in rear of Stedman, the fire of which was concentrated on the fort, and covering the open space in rear.

It was now about 7.30 a.m., when I received an order from General Parke, through one of his staff, to retake the line. My plan of attack was as follows: Orders were sent out that an assault would be made by my whole division in fifteen minutes, and that the signal for the assault would be the advance of the Two hundred and eleventh Pennsylvania Volunteers from the hill in the rear toward Stedman. Captain [Joseph A.] Hodgkins was directed to advance with the Second Brigade under Colonel [Joseph A.] Mathews, Major Bertolette with the Two hundredth and Two hundred and ninth Pennsylvania Volunteers on the right, and as soon as the Two hundred and eleventh Pennsylvania Volunteers could be put into position it was advanced toward Stedman, under the direction of Captain [Richard A.] Watts, aide-de-camp, in full view of the enemy. This was done for the purpose of attracting the attention and fire of the enemy, and cover the movement of the balance of the division which was to carry the works. This ruse was a complete success. The enemy, seeing the advance of this regiment, numbering about 600 muskets, in such handsome manner, commenced to waver, when the balance of the division charged with a will, in the most gallant style, and in a moment Stedman, Batteries 11 and 12, and the entire line which had been lost, was recaptured with a large number of prisoners, battle-flags, and small-arms. After the troops had commenced moving to make this assault, I received orders not to make it until a division of the Sixth Army Corps, which was on its way to support me, had arrived, but I saw that the enemy had already commenced to waver, and that success was certain.

I, therefore, allowed the lines to charge; besides this, it was doubtful whether I could have communicated with the regiments on the flanks in time to countermand the movement.

From the reports of my subordinate commanders as well as from my own observation, at least 1,500 of the prisoners, and all the battle-flags captured, were taken by and passed to the rear through the lines of my division, but were afterward collected by other troops, while but about 770 prisoners and one battle-flag were credited to my command. The officers and men were so eager to regain the lost ground, and regimental commanders so desirous to maintain their several organizations, which had been somewhat broken after charging through the bomb-proofs and old works around the forts, that little or no attention was paid to the trophies of this brilliant victory.

The officers and men of my division, composed entirely of new troops, deserve great credit for their promptness in moving forward to the point of attack, to which in a great measure is owing the success of the day, and for their gallant conduct throughout the action. [*O.R.*, XLVI, part 1, pp. 345–348.]

Report of Capt. John C. Boughton, USA, Second Michigan Infantry, Ninth Corps, Army of the Potomac

On the morning of the 25th instant, between 4 and 5 o'clock, the regiment was alarmed by messengers sent in from picket by Lieutenant [John] Hardy, who was in command of the line. When I got out, which was 4.30, most of the regiment was under arms in the trench; went to the left and met Lieutenant Hardy coming in from picket. In reply to inquiries, he said the enemy was crossing the line to our left without opposition, and that they would soon be on us. During this time there was some musketry firing near Fort Stedman, but not much, and it was too dark to see well. Before Lieutenant Hardy had passed two men came running from the left, telling that their regiment was all captured, and that the rebels were coming in our rear. I ordered them to be arrested, and stopped their talking. A few minutes later a crowd of men came running down the trench. Supposing they were of one of our regiments, and running from the enemy, I stepped out and ordered them to halt, saying that it was useless to run away, but was answered, carelessly, "It's of no use now; it's all over; you might as well throw down your guns." At the same time one of them placed his hand on my shoulder, saying, "Come with me."

I instantly perceived they were rebels, and answered, "In a minute." Stepping hastily backward, I ordered the men to fire, which they obeyed immediately with good effect. We then fell back behind the first flanker, all except a few who had surrendered and were marched away immediately.

Very soon after they had advanced down the old road in our rear, and opened a fire on us, which obliged us to abandon the two traverses on our left; the companies who had occupied them passed up the line and took shelter in Battery Number 9. I sent a party from the right down the old road in our rear, which checked the enemy's advance on it, and immediately afterward sent Lieutenant [Isaac] Perrine with a company across the old road and to our left and rear. At the same time the regiment reoccupied the traverses which had been abandoned. It was not quite daylight then, but soon after we could see our own troops coming up from the rear, and the enemy retreating to their own works. I then called for volunteers, and when about twenty or twenty-five had responded, I charged down the line with them to the foot of Spring Hill, and cut off the retreat of and captured something over 300 prisoners (I guess at the number, as I did not count them). Lieutenant Perrine, Captain [William] Lang, Lieutenant Hardy, Lieutenant [William F. H.] Holston, and Lieutenant [Charles H.] Rogers rendered most valuable assistance in this movement. Twenty minutes before 7 o'clock we reoccupied the picket-line. [*O.R.*, XLVI, part 1, pp. 327–328.]

Report of Bvt. Maj. Christian Woerner, USA, Third Battery New Jersey Light Artillery, Ninth Corps, Army of the Potomac

Before daylight of yesterday morning much yelling was heard from the direction of Fort Stedman, also much picket-firing from the direction of Forts McGilvery and Stedman. Soon after two guns were fired from Fort Stedman. I did not understand what was going on. Soon after I saw a strong column of infantry marching in close column from Fort Stedman on Fort Haskell, inside of our line of breast-works and between the breast-works and camps, which I supposed to be our infantry, it being still so dark that they could not be distinctly seen. There seemed to be no men along the breast-work, and the advancing column came without resistance to within 100 yards of this fort, when they broke and, covering themselves behind the tents and huts, opened a strong fire on this fort. At the same time several field and mortar batteries of the enemy commenced shelling this fort, and I immediately opened upon the above-mentioned infantry force with canister, in a short time completely silencing them. Now another infantry force was seen forming in the rear of Fort Stedman and advancing in line of battle and with waving colors on Fort Haskell. I brought one of my guns in position in the right corner of this fort, commanding our line between Forts Haskell and Stedman, and fired on them with canister rapidly, inflicting to them severe loss and forcing them to run back toward Fort Stedman and their own lines and to seek shelter behind the tents and huts. Meanwhile our infantry charged up to our breast-works from the rear, and that part of the enemy covering in and behind the huts and tents threw off their arms and surrendered, while the others were retreating in disorder and confusion from Fort Stedman and its vicinity to their lines. This retreating lasted for about half an hour, and I directed the fire of my guns on them with very good effect. At about 7.30 o'clock Fort Stedman was again in possession of our troops and the Union flags in it. [*O.R.*, XLVI, part 1, p. 188.]

Narrative of Major General Walker, continued

It required more than an hour for the entire division to come up and form into line; and it was sunrise before we were ready to advance. . . . By the time the sun was above the horizon the enemy had poured forth from their camps in rear, and filled the forts and breastworks of the second line with troops, both infantry and artillery. They sent out a heavy skirmish line which engaged ours and a brisk and angry skirmish fire was kept up until our troops were withdrawn.

Their artillery, too, came into play, and the guns of their forts in the second line and on our right and left concentrated their fire on Fort Stedman, and such a storm of shot and shell as fell into and around the old fort has seldom been seen. We had failed to carry the second line by surprise; it was manned by four times our numbers and our task was hopeless. Nothing remained but to withdraw to our breastworks. General *Gordon* seemed loath to give up his cherished plans . . . and for an hour or two longer we held our captured fort and breastworks. At last the command came to fall back to our lines, and the troops commenced the retrograde movement, which was a thousand times more hazardous than the advance . . . and the seventy-five yards that lay between Fort Stedman and our shelter was swept by the direct and cross fire of many pieces of artillery posted in both the first and second lines of the enemy's works. . . .

I remained in Fort Stedman . . . until there was no one in the fort except an occasional Confederate passing through. Suddenly I heard a shout, and looking in the direction of the sound I saw a body of Federal infantry coming over the wall of the fort on the opposite side. A few jumps on a double-quick put the wall of the fort between the enemy and myself, and then with a few other belated stragglers I found myself crossing the stormswept space between us and our works . . . it seemed as if I were an hour making that seventy-five yards. [*SHSP*, XXXI, pp. 27–29.]

At this point, you may either return to Fort Stedman or read the materials for the final stop at Fort Haskell. If you remained at Fort Stedman for Stop 5, continue on the paved walking path to the Hare House site in the tree line to your north.

STOP 6: THE FAILURE OF THE ATTACK

Report of Gen. Robert E. Lee, CSA, General-in-Chief of all Confederate armies

At daylight this morning Genl *Gordon* assaulted & carried enemy's works at Hare's Hill, captured nine pieces of artillery, eight mortars, between five & six hundred prisoners, among them one brig. General and a number of officers of lower grade. Enemy's lines were swept away for distance of four or five hundred yards to right & left, and two efforts made to recover captured works were handsomely repulsed; but it was found that the enclosed works in rear, commanding enemy's mainline, could only be taken at great sacrifice, & troops were withdrawn to original position. . . . I was induced to assume the offensive from the belief that the point assailed could be carried without much loss, and the hope that by the seizure of the redoubts in the rear of the enemy's main line, I could sweep along his entrenchments to the south, so that if I could not cause their abandonment, Genl Grant would at least be obliged so to curtail his lines, that upon the approach of Genl Sherman, I might be able to hold our position with a portion of the troops, and with a select body unite with Genl *Johnston* and give him battle. If successful, I would then be able to return to my position, and if unsuccessful I should be in no worse condition, as I should be compelled to withdraw from James River if I

Gen. Robert E. Lee (USAMHI)

quietly awaited his approach. But although the assault upon the fortified works at Hare's Hill was bravely accomplished, the redoubts commanding the line of entrenchments were found enclosed and strongly manned, so that an attempt to carry them must have been attended with great hazards, and even if accomplished, would have caused a great sacrifice of life in the presence of the large reserves which the enemy was hurrying into position. I therefore determined to withdraw the troops, and it was in retiring that they suffered the greatest loss. [Clifford Dowdey and Louis Manarin, eds., *The Wartime Papers of Robert E. Lee* (1961; New York: Da Capo, 1987), pp. 916–917.]

Report of Lieutenant General Grant, continued

Early on the morning of the 25th the enemy assaulted our lines in front of the Ninth Corps (which held from the Appomattox River toward our left) and carried Fort Stedman and a part of the line to the right and left of it, established themselves, and turned the guns of the fort against fuse; but our troops on either flank held their ground until the reserves were brought up, when the enemy was driven back, with a heavy loss in killed and wounded and 1,900 prisoners. Our loss was 68 killed, 37 wounded, and 506 missing. General [George G.] Meade at once ordered the other corps to advance and feel the enemy in their respective fronts. Pushing forward they captured and held the enemy's strongly entrenched picket-line in front of the Second and Sixth Corps and 834 prisoners. The enemy made desperate attempts to retake this line, but without success. Our loss in front of these was 52 killed, 864 wounded, and 207 missing. The enemy's loss in killed and wounded was far greater. [*O.R.*, XLVI, part 1, p. 51.]

Narrative of Major General Gordon, continued

Daylight was coming. Through the failure of the three guides, we had failed to occupy the three forts in the rear, and they were now filled with Federals. Our wretched railroad trains had broken down, and the troops who were coming to my aid did not reach me. The full light of the morning revealed the gathering forces of Grant and the great preponderance of his numbers. It was impossible for me to make further headway with my isolated corps, and General *Lee* directed me to withdraw. . . . This last supreme effort to break the hold of General Grant upon Petersburg and Richmond was the expiring struggle of the Confederate giant, whose strength was nearly exhausted and whose limbs were heavily shackled by the most onerous conditions. *Lee* knew, as we all did, that the chances against us were as a hundred is to one; but we remembered how George Washington, with his band of ragged rebels, had won American independence through trials and sufferings and difficulties, and although they were far less discouraging and insurmountable than those around us, they were nevertheless many and great. It seemed better, therefore, to take the one chance, though it might be one in a thousand, rather than to stand still while the little army was being depleted, its vitality lessening with each setting sun, and its life gradually ebbing, while the great army in its front was growing and strengthening day by day. To wait was certain destruction: it could not be worse if we tried and failed. [Gordon, *Reminiscences*, pp. 398–413.]

To either resume your study of the First Petersburg operations or begin your study of the Battle of the Crater, return to your vehicle. Drive along the park road to the parking area for the Taylor Farm, which will be on the right, 0.9 mile from the Fort Stedman parking area.

To continue your study with the Fall of Petersburg, drive along the park road to its terminus at Crater Road, U.S. Route 301. Turn left and exit immediately onto northbound Interstate 95. After 0.2 mile, exit onto southbound I-85. Drive 2.3 miles, and take exit 65 for Squirrel Level Road, Route 115. At the top of the ramp, turn left, crossing the interstate; proceed 0.2 mile to the intersection with Squirrel Level Road; and turn right. At 2.3 miles from the last turn, bear left to remain on Squirrel Level Road. At 6.3 miles, remain straight ahead as Squirrel Level Road becomes Duncan Road. At 6.9 miles, turn right at the T intersection, remaining on Duncan Road. At 8.6 miles, turn right onto Old Vaughan Road (Route 605). Drive 0.1 mile to Dinwiddie Church of the Nazarene on the right side of the road and pull into the parking area.

To return to the Visitor Center, continue following the park road until you reach its terminus at Crater Road. Turn right onto Crater Road and proceed 0.8 mile to Wythe Street. En route, note Blandford Church on your right; the church contains a magnificent set of original Tiffany stained-glass windows, and the graveyard is the resting place of Confederate Brig. Gen. *William Mahone* and thousands of Confederate soldiers. It is well worth a visit; there is a small admission fee to enter the church. Turn right on Wythe Street and drive 2.2 miles to the exit to Petersburg National Battlefield on your right. Turn left at the top of the exit ramp, and proceed to the parking area for the Visitor Center.

THE BATTLE OF THE CRATER

This section of the guide provides directions and materials necessary to do a focused study of the Battle of the Crater of July 30, 1864. This battle, the most spectacular and best-known episode of the entire Richmond-Petersburg Campaign, was the culminating event of the Third Richmond-Petersburg Offensive of late July 1864. It was the product of a remarkable scheme that was hatched by members of Maj. Gen. Ambrose Burnside's Ninth Corps. It involved digging a mine underneath the Confederate lines and then filling galleries at its end with gunpowder, which when ignited would blow a massive hole in the enemy lines and allow a frontal assault to succeed. It was an inspired if not especially novel concept. Using underground mines against fortified positions was a long-standing practice in Western military history, and in the Vicksburg Campaign of 1863, Union forces had attempted to use mines in a way that anticipated the events of July 1864.

In addition to the magnificent scene produced by the explosion of the mine and the subsequent battle, what made the Battle of the Crater remarkable was the incredible combination of inspired engineering and wretched generalship that shaped its course and outcome. Digging the mine proved a task of unprecedented difficulty but one whose challenges creative Union engineers managed to overcome. Their efforts, and their incorporation into a well-conceived overall plan that involved operations both north and south of the James, would produce one of the greatest spectacles—and tactical opportunities—of the entire war. This opportunity would be lost, however; thrown away by appalling failures in Union leadership. These allowed the Confederates to recover from the initial shock of the explosion of the mine in time to put together and execute a determined response that would turn the Battle of the Crater from a potentially decisive Union victory into a humiliating failure for Union arms—and one of the most tragic episodes of the entire Civil War.

SUMMARY OF PRINCIPAL EVENTS, 19 JUNE–31 JULY 1864

June
18—Skirmish at King and Queen Court-House; Maj. Gen. David B. Birney, U.S. Army, in temporary command of Second Army

Corps; Brig. Gen. William T. H. Brooks, U.S. Army, assumes command of Tenth Army Corps

19–April 3, 1865—Siege of Petersburg and Richmond

20—Skirmish at White House; skirmish at King and Queen Court-House

21—Action at Howlett's Bluff; skirmishes at White House or Saint Peter's Church and Black Creek, or Tunstall's Station

22—Engagement near the Jerusalem Plank Road

22–July 2—Expedition against the South Side and Danville Railroads, with skirmishes at Reams Station (June 22) and at Staunton River Bridge, or Roanoke Station (June 25), and engagements at Sappony Church, or Stony Creek (June 28–29), and at Reams Station (June 29)

23—Skirmish at Jones's Bridge

24—Engagement at Saint Mary's Church; action at Hare's Hill

27—Maj. Gen. Winfield S. Hancock, U.S. Army, resumes command of Second Army Corps

28—Action at Howlett's Bluff

30–July 1—Actions on Four-Mile Creek at Deep Bottom

July

12—Skirmish at Warwick Swamp; skirmish at Turkey Creek

14—Action at Malvern Hill

16—Action at Four-Mile Creek; action at Malvern Hill

17—Skirmish at Herring Creek.

18—Brig. Gen. Alfred H. Terry, U.S. Army, in temporary command of Tenth Army Corps

19—Brig. Gen. John H. Martindale, U.S. Army, in temporary command of Eighteenth Army Corps; vice Maj. Gen. William F. Smith relieved

22—Maj. Gen. Edward O. C. Ord, U.S. Army, assumes command of Eighteenth Army Corps

23—Maj. Gen. David B. Birney, U.S. Army, assumes command of Tenth Army Corps

27—Skirmish near Lee's Mill

27–29—Demonstrations on the north bank of the James River and engagement at Deep Bottom (or Darbytown, Strawberry Plains, and New Market Road)

28—Action at Four-Mile Creek

30—Explosion of the Mine and assault on the Crater; skirmish at Lee's Mill

STOP 1: TAYLOR FARM

Drive out of the Visitor Center parking lot, and, after crossing the bridge over Route 36 and reaching the fork in the road, take the right fork onto the Park Tour Road. Once you are 2.7 miles from the Visitor Center, you will see the parking area for the Taylor Farm on the right. Get out of your vehicle, and follow the trail for about 250 yards toward the line of guns. Stop at the guns, and face west (the direction they are pointing) toward the low ground through which the railroad and Poor Creek run. On the other side of the ravine, the ground slopes up to the Crater, the location of which is indicated by a wood fence.

THE STRATEGIC AND OPERATIONAL SITUATION

In early July 1864, Federal authorities found themselves dealing with a major crisis. A significant Confederate force commanded by Lt. Gen. *Jubal Early* crossed the Potomac River into Maryland from the Shenandoah Valley and advanced to the outskirts of Washington, D.C. In response, Lt. Gen. Ulysses S. Grant was compelled to order one corps then operating against Petersburg and another that was designated for that front to move north to help defend the capital. These units arrived in time to help turn back *Early's* forces in the July 11–12 engagement at Fort Stevens (which President Abraham Lincoln personally witnessed) but were unable to eliminate *Early's* command as a threat. Concerned that if allowed a break from major operations, the Confederate high command might dispatch units from the Richmond-Petersburg front to reinforce its forces in the Shenandoah Valley or Georgia, Grant determined that action was needed. He ordered Maj. Gen. Winfield Scott Hancock's corps from Maj. Gen. George G. Meade's Army of the Potomac north of the James River at Deep Bottom on July 26. This produced three days of maneuvers and fighting that failed to accomplish anything of significance in front of Richmond. What became known as the First Deep Bottom operation did, however, have the effect of inducing the Confederate high command to shift forces from the defense of Petersburg to the defense of Richmond.

To take advantage of this shift, the Union high command moved to implement a plan that had been hatched in mid-June by an enterprising band of Pennsylvania troops in Maj. Gen. Ambrose Burnside's Ninth Corps, which held the section of the Federal line closest to the Confederates. Within a week after the First Petersburg Offensive came to a desultory close for the Federal high command on June 18, 1864, these Pennsylvanians had suggested that a mine be dug from their lines just west of where the Norfolk and Pennsylvania Railroad passed the Taylor Farm to a point under a section of the Confederate works known as [Brig. Gen. *Stephen D.*] *Elliott's* or [Capt. *Richard G.*] *Pegram's* Salient. It would then be filled with gunpowder, which when ignited would blow a hole in the Confederate works large enough to enable an assault to carry them and then press forward to seize Petersburg. Burnside liked the idea and won grudging approval from his superiors to begin work on the mine.

Narrative of Lt. Gen. Ulysses S. Grant, USA, commanding Armies of the United States

On the 25th of June General Burnside had commenced running a mine from about the centre of his front under the Confederate works confronting him. He was induced to do this by Colonel [Henry] Pleasants, of the Pennsylvania Volunteers, whose regiment was mostly composed of miners, and who was himself a practical miner. Burnside had submitted the scheme to Meade and myself, and we both approved of it, as a means of keeping the men occupied. His position was very favorable for carrying on this work, but not so favorable for the operations to follow its completion. The position of the two lines at that point were only about a hundred yards apart with a comparatively deep ravine intervening. In the bottom of this ravine the work commenced. The position was unfavorable in this particular: that the enemy's line at that point was re-entering, so that its front was commanded by their own lines both to the right and left. Then, too, the ground was sloping upward back of the Confederate line for a considerable distance, and it was presumable that the enemy had, at least, a detached work on this highest point.

The work progressed, and on the 23d of July the mine was finished ready for charging; but I had this work of charging deferred until we were ready for it. It was the object, therefore, to get as many of *Lee's* troops away from the south side of the James River as possible. Accordingly, on the 26th, we commenced a movement with Hancock's corps and [Maj. Gen. Philip] Sheridan's cavalry to the north side by the way of Deep Bottom, where [Maj. Gen. Benjamin] Butler had a pontoon bridge laid. The plan, in the main, was to let the cavalry cut loose and, joining with [Brig. Gen. August] Kautz's cavalry of the Army of the James, get by *Lee's* lines and destroy as much as they could of the Virginia Central Railroad, while, in the mean time, the infantry was to move out so as to protect their rear and cover their retreat back when they should have got through with their work. We were successful in drawing the enemy's troops to the north side of the James as I expected. [Ulysses S. Grant, *Personal Memoirs of U.S. Grant*, edited by Brooks D. Simpson (Lincoln: University of Nebraska Press, 1996 [1885]), p. 523.]

Report of Maj. Gen. Ambrose E. Burnside, USA, commanding Ninth Corps, Army of the Potomac

On the 26th of June a letter was received from General [Robert B.] Potter, stating that he believed a mine could be run under the enemy's works, immediately in our front, by which a breach could be made, if it was thought advisable. The suggestion was first made by some non-commissioned officers and privates of the Forty-eighth Pennsylvania Regiment [Lieutenant-Colonel Pleasants], which was composed chiefly of miners from Schuylkill County, Pa., the colonel himself being a skillful and experienced mining engineer. After consultation with General Potter he was authorized to commence the work, and the fact was reported to the commanding general of the Army of the Potomac, who did not specially approve of the work, but rather consented to its advancement. [U.S. War Department, *The War of the Rebellion: A Compilation of the Official Records of the Union and Confederate Armies*, 70 vols. in 128 parts and index (Washington, D.C.: Government Printing Office, 1880–1901), series 1, volume XL, part 1, pp. 523–524. Hereafter cited as *O.R.*; all references are to series 1 unless otherwise noted.]

Return to your vehicle, and proceed on the park road for 0.5 mile to the parking area on your right. After you leave your vehicle, walk on the paved path until you reach a fork. Take the path on the right marked by the sign reading "To Crater via Tunnel" for about 350 yards to the viewing stand overlooking the entrance to the mine. En route, note the Taylor farm on the other side of the ravine through which Poor Creek and the railroad run.

STOP 2: THE MINE

DIGGING THE MINE

Even before word of Grant's approval arrived, Pleasants and his men began work on the mine. Laboring under the supervision of Sgt.

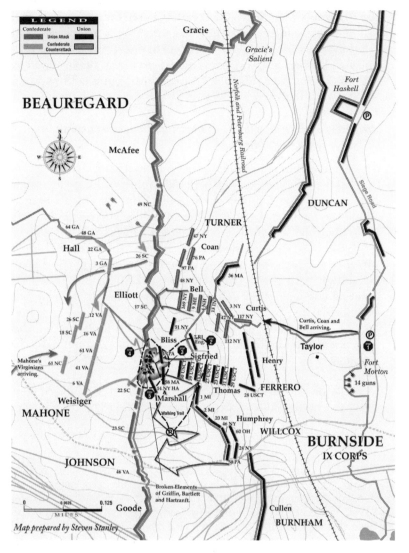

Gracie

Gracie's Salient

Fort Haskell

Norfolk and Petersburg Railroad

BEAUREGARD

McAfee

DUNCAN

Siege Road

49 NC

TURNER

47 NY

Coan

64 GA

48 GA

Hall   22 GA

26 SC

76 PA

3 GA

97 PA

36 MA

48 NY

Elliott

Bell

17 SC

169 NY   9 ME   6 NH   13 TN

3 NY   Curtis

42 NY   117 NY

Curtis, Coan and Bell arriving.

26 SC   12 VA

51 NY

2 RI Eng.

18 SC   16 VA

Bliss

2

112 NY

Taylor

Fort Morton

61 VA

3 SPA

5

Sigfried

Henry

Mahone's Virginians arriving.

61 NC

41 VA

30 USC

39 USCT   23 USCT   31 USCT   29 USCT

14 guns

6 VA

22 SC

58 MA

FERRERO

Weisiger

14 NY HA

5

Thomas   28 USCT

MAHONE

1 Marshall

1 MI

Walking Trail

2 MI

20 MI   Humphrey

46 NY

23 SC

60 OH   WILLCOX

24 NY

BURNSIDE

JOHNSON

46 VA

50 PA

IX CORPS

Broken Elements of Griffin, Bartlett and Hartranft.

Goode

Cullen

BURNHAM

0   0.0625   0.125
MILES

The Battle of the Crater, July 30, 1864

Henry Reese, the men of the Forty-eighth Pennsylvania started work in Poor Creek Ravine about 100 feet behind the Union front line. Working around the clock, they were able to dig over 40 feet of tunnel a day. Initially Reese rewarded each man with "2 good drinks of whiskey" at the end of his shift, but incidents of drunkenness caused him to halt this practice. The mine was, on average, about 4.5 feet high, 4 feet wide at the bottom, and 2 feet wide at the top.

Despite Federal efforts to conceal their work, the Confederates got wind of the project and, under the direction of Capt. *Hugh Douglas*, dug a number of countermines. *Douglas*, however, did not dig them deep enough to locate the Federals. The 510-foot tunnel would be at least 20 feet underground when it reached the Confederate lines in mid-June. On June 17, Pleasants used a theodolite to determine that the mine had in fact reached a point directly below *Elliott's* Salient.

Pleasants's men then went to work on two side galleries. Almost as soon as they began work, however, the sound of Confederate activity above caused the Pennsylvanians working in the tunnel to flee. Pleasants then went into the mine and, after spending a few hours listening to the sounds coming from the Confederate works, determined that the enemy still had not found the mine. Pleasants directed his men to resume work and on the night of June 23 was able to report that the lateral galleries were complete. His men then began filling them with 4 tons of powder (6 had been requested) as Pleasants went about securing the special waterproof safety fuse he had requested. Instead, he learned that he would receive regular blasting fuses. Pleasants decided to make do. On June 28, Pleasants's men had finished loading the mine, and their commander was able to report to Potter and Burnside that the mine was ready.

Report of Lt. Col. Henry Pleasants, USA, Forty-eighth Pennsylvania Infantry, First Brigade, Second Division, Ninth Corps, Army of the Potomac

The mine I excavated in front of the Second Division of the Ninth Corps . . . was commenced at 12 m. the 25th of June, 1864, without tools, lumber, or any of the material requisite for such work. The mining picks were made out of those used by our pioneers; plank I obtained, at first, by tearing down a rebel bridge, and afterward by sending to a saw-mill, five or six miles distant. The material excavated was carried out in hand barrows made out of cracker-boxes. The work progressed rapidly until the 2nd of July, when it reached an extremely wet ground; the timbers gave way and the gallery nearly closed, the roof and floor of the mine nearly meeting. Retimbered it and started again. From this point had to excavate a stratum of marl, whose consistency was like putty, and which caused our progress to be necessarily slow. To avoid this I started an incline plane, and in about 100 feet rose thirteen and a half feet perpendicularly.

On the 17th of July the main gallery was completed, being 510.8 feet in length. The enemy having obtained some knowledge of the mine, and having commenced searching for it, I was ordered to stop mining, which was, however, resumed on the 18th of July by starting the left lateral gallery.

At 6 p.m. July 18 commenced the right lateral gallery; but as the enemy could be heard very plainly working in the fort over us I caused this gallery to be excavated a little beyond and in rear of their work, and gave to it a curved line of direction. The left gallery, being thirty-seven feet long, was stopped at midnight on Friday, July 22; the right gallery, being thirty-eight feet long, was stopped at 6 p.m. July 23. The mine could have been charged and exploded at this time. I employed the men, from that time, in draining, timbering, and placing in position eight magazines, four in each lateral gallery.

Having received the order to charge the mine on the 27th of July, I commenced putting in the powder at 4 p.m., and finished at 10 p.m. . . .

The mine was ventilated at first by having the fresh air go in along the main gallery as far as it was excavated, and to return charged with the gases generated by the breathing and exhalation of the workmen, by the burning of the candles, and by those liberated from the ground, along and in a square tube made of boards, and whose area was sixty inches. This tube led to a perpendicular shaft twenty-two feet high, out of which this vitiated air escaped. At the bottom of this shaft was placed a grating, in which a large fire was kept burning continually, which, by heating the air, rarefied it, and increased its current. Afterward I caused the fresh air to be let in the above-mentioned wooden tube to the end of the work, and the vitiated air to return by the gallery and out of the shaft, placing a partition with a door in the main gallery a little out of the shaft, to prevent its exit by the entrance of the mine. The latter plan was more advantageous, because the gases had to travel a less distance in the mine than before.

As the excavation in the mine progressed, the number of

men required to carry out the material increased, until at last it took nearly every enlisted man in my regiment, which consisted of nearly 400 effective men. The whole amount of material excavated was 18,000 cubic feet.

The great difficulty to surmount was to ascertain the exact distance from the entrance of the mine to the enemy's works, and the course of these works. This was accomplished by making five separate triangulations, which differed but slightly in their result. These triangulations were made in our most advanced line, and within 133 yards of the enemy's line of sharpshooters. [*O.R.*, XL, part 1, pp. 556–558.]

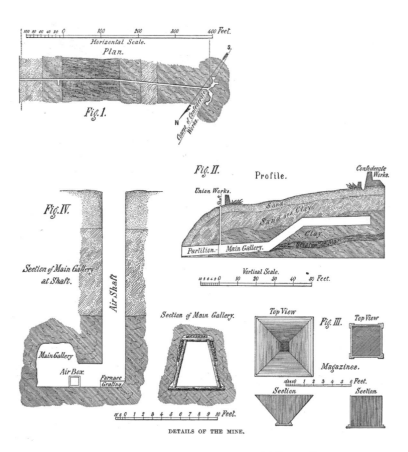

Details of the Mine (*Battles and Leaders of the Civil War,* Vol. IV, p. 548)

PLANNING THE ASSAULT

As Pleasants's men completed their work, his superiors planned for the assault that was to follow. Upon submitting his attack plan to headquarters, Burnside encountered great resistance from Army of the Potomac commander Meade to critical elements of it. When the dispute was brought to Grant, he sided with Meade. A dispirited Burnside then made adjustments to the plan that would prove fatal to the success of the operation.

Narrative of Lieutenant General Grant, continued

The mine was ordered to be charged, and the morning of the 30th of July was the time fixed for its explosion. I gave Meade minute orders on the 24th directing how I wanted the assault conducted, which orders he amplified into general instructions for the guidance of the troops that were to be engaged. Meade's instructions, which I, of course, approved most heartily, were all that I can see now was necessary. The only further precaution which he could have taken, and which he could not foresee, would have been to have different men to execute them. . . . All was ready by the time I had prescribed; and on the 29th Hancock and Sheridan were brought back near the James River with their troops. Under cover of night they started to recross the bridge at Deep Bottom, and to march directly for that part of our lines in front of the mine.

Warren was to hold his line of intrenchments with a sufficient number of men and concentrate the balance on the right next to Burnside's corps, while Ord, now commanding the 18th corps, temporarily under Meade, was to form in the rear of Burnside to support him when he went in. All were to clear off the parapets and the abatis in their front so as to leave the space as open as possible, and be able to charge the moment the mine had been sprung and Burnside had taken possession. Burnside's corps was not to stop in the crater at all but push on to the top of the hill, supported on the right and left by Ord's and Warren's corps. [Grant, *Personal Memoirs*, pp. 524–526.]

Report of Major General Burnside, continued

During the month of July General [Edward] Ferrero's division returned to the corps . . . soon after it was understood that the corps might be ordered to attack, and General Ferrero was informed that in such an event he would be called upon to lead. After considerable conversation upon the subject, the formation suggested by him for the attack by his division was approved, and he was directed to drill his troops in such a manner as to familiarize them with this mode of attack, which he did. . . . On the 26th of July a letter was received requesting a statement of the plan of attack proposed by the corps, the answer to which was. . . .

> My plan would be to explode the mine just before daylight in the morning or about 5 o'clock in the afternoon mass the two brigades of the colored division in rear of my line in column of divisions, double column closed in mass, the head of each brigade resting on the front, and as soon as the explosion has taken place move them forward with instructions for the division to take half distance, and as soon as the leading regiments of the two brigades pass through the gap in the enemy's line, the leading regiment of the right brigade to come into line perpendicular to the enemy's line by the right companies, on the right into line wheel, the left companies on the right into line, and proceed at once down the line of the enemy's works as rapidly as possible, the leading regiment of the left brigade to execute the reverse movement to the left, moving up the enemy's line. The remainders of the two columns to move directly toward the crest in front as rapidly as possible, diverging in such a way as to enable them to deploy into columns of regiments, the right column making as nearly as may be for Cemetery Hill. These columns to be followed by the other divisions of this corps as soon as they can be thrown in. This would involve the necessity of relieving these divisions by other troops before the movement, and of holding columns of other troops in readiness to take our place on the crest in case we gain it and sweep down it. It would be advisable, in my opinion, if we succeed in gaining the crest, to throw the colored division right into the town. There is a necessity for the co-operation, at least in the way of artillery, of the troops on my right and left. Of the extent of this you will necessarily be the judge. I think our chances of success in a plan of this kind are more than even.

On the 28th in conversation with the commanding general he stated that the formation of the troops, as well as the designation of the leading division, did not meet with his approval. After much conversation on the subject the major-general commanding said that he was to visit Lieutenant-General Grant that afternoon, and that a definite answer would be given in the evening.

The next day, the 29th, not far from noon, the major-general commanding called upon me at corps headquarters, saying that it had been decided not to allow General Ferrero's division to take the advance; neither did he approve of the formation which was proposed after the attacking division should have passed over the breach in the enemy's lines. [*O.R.*, XL, part 1, pp. 136, 523–524.]

Narrative of Maj. William H. Powell, USA, Aide-de-Camp, First Division, Ninth Corps, Army of the Potomac

As a diversion Hancock's corps and two divisions of cavalry had crossed to the north side of the James at Deep Bottom and had threatened Richmond. A part of Lee's army was sent from Petersburg to checkmate this move, and when the mine was ready to be sprung Hancock was recalled in haste to Petersburg. . . . With a view of making the attack, the division of colored troops, under General Edward Ferrero, had been drilling for several weeks, General Burnside thinking that they were in better condition to head a charge than either of the white divisions. They had not been in any very active service. . . . General Meade objected to the use of the colored troops on the ground, as he stated, that they were a new division and had never been under fire, while this was an operation requiring the very best troops. General Burnside, however, insisted upon his programme, and the question was referred to General Grant, who confirmed General Meade's views, although he subsequently said in his evidence, before the Committee on the Conduct of the War:

> General Burnside wanted to put his colored division in front, and I believe if he had done so it would have been a success. Still I agreed with General Meade as to his objections to that plan.
>
> General Meade said that if we put the colored troops in front (we had only one division) and it should prove a failure, it would then be said, and very properly, that we were shoving these people ahead to get killed because we did not care anything about them. But that could not be said if we put white troops in front.
>
> The mine was charged with only 8000 pounds of powder, instead of 14,000, as asked for, the amount having been reduced by order of General Meade; and while awaiting the decision of General Grant on the question of the colored troops, precise orders for making and supporting the attack were issued by General Meade.
>
> In the afternoon of the 29th of July, Generals Potter and O[rlando] B.

Willcox met together at General Burnside's headquarters, to talk over the plans of the attack, based upon the idea that the colored troops would lead the charge, and while there the message was received from General Meade that General Grant disapproved of that plan, and that General Burnside must detail one of his white divisions to take the place of the colored division. This was the first break in the original plan. There were then scarcely twelve hours, and half of these at night, in which to make this change and no possible time in which the white troops could be familiarized with the duties expected of them in connection with the assault.

General Burnside was greatly disappointed by this change, but immediately sent for General Ledlie, who had been in command of the First Division only about six weeks. Upon his arrival General Burnside determined that the three commanders of his white divisions should "pull straws," and Ledlie was (as he thought) the unlucky victim. He, however took it good naturedly, and, after receiving special instructions from General Burnside, proceeded with his brigade commanders to ascertain the way to the point of attack. This was not accomplished until after dark on the evening before the explosion.

The order of attack, as proposed by General Burnside, was also changed by direction of General Meade with the approval of General Grant. Instead of moving down to the right and left of the crater of the mine, for the purpose of driving the enemy from their intrenchments, and removing to that extent the danger of flank attacks, General Meade directed that the troops should push at once for the crest of Cemetery Hill. . . . The orders were that Ledlie's division should advance first, pass over the enemy's works, and charge to Cemetery Hill four hundred yards to the right, and approached by a slope comparatively free from obstacles; as soon as the First Division should leave the works the next division (Willcox's) was to advance to the left of Cemetery Hill, so as to protect the left flank of the First Division; and the next division (Potter's) was to move in the same way to the right of Cemetery Hill. The Ninth Corps being out of the way, it was intended that the Fifth and Eighteenth corps should pass through and follow up the movement. [Robert Underwood Johnson and Clarence Clough Buell, eds., *Battles and Leaders of the Civil War*, 4 vols. (New York: The Century Company, 1884–1887). Volume IV, pp. 546–550. Hereafter cited as *Battles and Leaders*.]

To get to the Crater from the viewing platform, continue walking on the paved trail that parallels the tunnel for the mine for about 175 yards. En route, note the location of the Confederate and Federal lines as well as the small depressions on the left marking the location of ventilation shafts.

STOP 3: THE CRATER

What is in front of you is the remains of the Crater, which has been worn down by time and elements to a point where it is much smaller than it was on July 30, 1864. At that time it was approximately 170 feet long, 60 feet wide, and 30 feet deep.

THE MINE EXPLODES

Report of Lieutenant Colonel Pleasants, continued

Having received the order to charge the mine on the 27th of July, I commenced putting in the powder at 4 p.m., and finished at 10 p.m. The tamping was begun at 10 p.m. July 27, and completed at 6 p.m. July 28. Thirty-four feet of main gallery was tamped, and ten feet of the entrance of each of the side galleries; but the space between the magazines was left untamped.

I received orders from corps headquarters, on the 29th of July, to fire the mine at 3.30 a.m. July 30. I lighted the fuse at 3.15 a.m., and having waited till 4.15 a.m. an officer and sergeant of my regiment volunteered to go in and examine into the cause of the delay, and found that the fire had stopped where the fuses were spliced. They relighted it, and at sixteen minutes of 5 the powder exploded.

The charge consisted of 320 kegs of powder, each containing about twenty-five pounds. It was placed in eight magazines connected with each other by troughs half filled with powder. These troughs from the lateral galleries met at the inner end of the main one, and from this point I had three lines of fuses for a distance of ninety-eight feet. Not having fuses as long as required two pieces had to be spliced together to make the required length of each of the lines.

I stood on top of our breast-works and witnessed the effect of the explosion on the enemy. It so completely paralyzed them that the breach was practically 400 or 500 yards in breadth. The rebels in the forts, both on the right and left of the explosion, left their works, and for over an hour not a shot was fired by their artillery. There was no fire from infantry from the front for at least half an

Maj. Gen. Ambrose E. Burnside (USAMHI)

hour; none from the left for twenty minutes, and but few shots from the right. [*O.R.*, XL, part 1, pp. 557–558.]

Narrative of Major Powell, continued

It was a magnificent spectacle, and as the mass of earth went up into the air, carrying with it men, guns, carriages, and timbers, and spread out like an immense cloud as it reached its altitude, so close were the Union lines that the mass appeared as if it would descend immediately upon the troops waiting to make the charge. This caused them to break and scatter to the rear, and about ten minutes were consumed in re-forming for the attack. Not much was lost by this delay, however, as it took nearly that time for the cloud of dust to pass off. The order was then given for the advance. As no part of the Union line of breastworks had been removed (which would have been an arduous as well as hazardous undertaking), the troops clambered over them as best they could. This in itself broke the ranks, and they did not stop to re-form, but pushed ahead toward the crater, about 130 yards distant, the debris from the explosion having covered up the abatis and chevaux-de frise in front of the enemy's works.

Little did these men anticipate what they would see upon arriving there: an enormous hole in the ground about 30 feet deep, 60 feet wide, and 170 feet long, filled with dust, great blocks of clay, guns, broken carriages, projecting timbers, and men buried in various ways—some up to their necks, others to their waists, and some with only their feet and legs protruding from the earth. One of these near me was pulled out, and proved to be a second lieutenant of the battery which had been blown up. The fresh air revived him, and he was soon able to walk and talk. He was very grateful and said that he was asleep when the explosion took place, and only awoke to find himself wriggling up in the air; then a few seconds afterward he felt himself descending, and soon lost consciousness.

The whole scene of the explosion struck every one dumb with astonishment as we arrived at the crest of the debris. [*Battles and Leaders*, IV, pp. 550–551.]

Report of Maj. Gen. Bushrod Johnson, CSA, commanding Johnson's Division, Anderson's Corps, Army of Northern Virginia

On the night of the 28th of July every man in reserve in this division was placed in the trenches. [Brig. Gen. *Alfred*] *Colquitt's* brigade, of [Maj. Gen. *Robert*] *Hoke's* division, was temporarily transferred to my command in exchange for [Brig. Gen. *Archibald*] *Gracie's* brigade and placed on my right. For the purpose of relieving [Maj. Gen. *Charles W.*] *Field's* division from the trenches my line was extended to an attenuation that was deemed barely secure against an ordinary assault. From the left to the right the brigades were stationed in the trenches in the following order, viz: [Brig. Gen. *Matthew*] *Ransom's*, [Brig. Gen. *Stephen*] *Elliott's*, [Brig. Gen. *Henry*] *Wise's*, and *Colquitt's* brigades.

About 4.55 o'clock on the morning of the 30th of July the enemy sprung a large mine under that portion of my line about 200 yards north of the Baxter road, known as *Pegram's* salient. In this salient there were four guns of Captain *Pegram's* battery, and the Eighteenth and Twenty-second South Carolina Regiments, of *Elliott's* brigade, occupied the parapets in the battery and adjacent to it. The Twenty-second South Carolina Regiment extended from a point some seventy yards to the right of the right gun to a point beyond, but near to the left gun of the battery. The Eighteenth was posted on the left of the Twenty-second South Carolina Regiment. The regiments of *Elliott's* brigade were distributed along the parapet from left to right as follows, viz: The Twenty-sixth, Seventeenth, Eighteenth, Twenty-second, and Twenty-third South Carolina Regiments.

To strengthen *Pegram's* salient a second line or trench cavalier had been thrown up in its rear, commanding our front line and the enemy's works at a distance of from 150 to 200 yards. Owing to the extension of our line, already explained, our troops occupied only the front line of our works. The mine, as has been since ascertained, was laid along two wings, extending to the right and left of the main gallery, nearly parallel to the interior crest of our work and beneath the foot of the slope of the banquette, or perhaps farther back, and completely destroyed a portion of the front or main line of our fortification and the right of the trench cavalier. The crater measures 135 feet in length, 97 feet in breadth, and 30 feet deep. The two right guns of *Pegram's* battery were not disturbed by the explosion. The two left guns were thrown out in front of our works, and only eight men out of twenty-eight men and two officers with the battery escaped alive and unhurt. The battery was occupied by five companies of the Twenty-second South Carolina Regiment which were blown up. The Eighteenth South Carolina Regiment, on the left of the battery, had four companies blown up or destroyed by the falling earth. . . . The astonishing effect of the explosion, bursting like a volcano at the feet of the men, and the unweaving of an immense column of more than 100,000 cubic feet of earth to fall around in heavy masses, wounding, crushing, or burying everything within its reach, prevented our men from moving promptly to the mouth of the crater and occupying that part of the trench cavalier which was not destroyed, and over which the debris was scattered. [O.R., XL, part 1, pp. 787–788.]

Narrative of Capt. W. Gordon McCabe, CSA, Pegram's Battalion, Wilcox's Division, Third Corps, Army of Northern Virginia

A slight tremor of the earth for a second, then the rocking as of an earthquake, and with a tremendous burst which rent the sleeping hills beyond, a vast column of earth and smoke shoots upward to a great height, its dark sides flashing out sparks of fire, hangs poised for a moment in mid-air, and then hurtling downward with a roaring sound showers of stones, broken timbers, and blackened limbs, subsides—the gloomy pall of darkening smoke flushing to an angry crimson as it floats away to meet the morning sun.

Pleasants has done his work with terrible completeness, for now the site of the *Elliott* Salient is marked by a horrid chasm, one hundred and thirty-five feet in length, ninety-seven feet in breadth, and thirty feet deep, and its brave garrison, all asleep, save the guards, when thus surprised by sudden death, lie buried beneath the jagged blocks of blackened clay—in all, 256 officers and men of the Eighteenth and Twenty-second South Carolina—two officers and twenty men of *Pegram's* Petersburg battery.

The dread upheaval has rent in twain *Elliott's* brigade, and the men to the right and left of the huge abyss recoil in terror and dismay. Nor shall we censure them, for so terrible was the explosion that even the assaulting column shrank back aghast, and nearly ten minutes elapsed ere it could be reformed. Now a storm of fire bursts in red fury from the Federal front, and in an instant all the valley between the hostile lines lies shrouded in billowing smoke. [*Southern Historical Society Papers*, 52 vols. (Millwood, N.Y.: Kraus reprint, 1876–1959), volume II, pp. 283–284. Hereafter cited as *SHSP.*]

THE UNION ASSAULT

The spectacular success of the mine required a well-executed assault to make the effort and ingenuity that had gone into the project pay off in a decisive Union success. Union artillery immediately opened fire as the 650 men of the Eighteenth and Twenty-second South Carolina of *Elliott's* brigade, 40 percent of whom had been lost—many buried alive from the explosion—and the rest of the Confederate army struggled to respond. After waiting a few minutes for the effects of the explosion to settle, Ledlie's men pushed forward toward the Crater with Col. Elisha G. Marshall's brigade in the lead, followed by Brig. Gen. William F. Bartlett's. Supporting Ledlie's right was Brig. Gen. Simon Griffin's brigade of Potter's division, while Brig. Gen. John Hartranft's brigade of Willcox's division received orders to follow Ledlie.

Problems immediately developed. After leaving their trenches and crossing no-man's-land, Marshall's and Bartlett's commands plunged into the Crater. Almost immediately their ranks became intermingled, and confusion reigned. Making matters worse, Griffin's men veered to the left as they advanced in response to fire from the elements of *Elliott's* brigade and ended up entering the Crater and exacerbating the confusion that prevailed among the Federals. As if this were not bad enough, Hartranft's brigade followed Ledlie's men into the Crater as well. Efforts to resume the advance stalled, frustrated by determined Confederate resistance, a veritable maze of works, and a lack of leadership on the Union side. The man who was supposed to be providing that leadership, Ledlie, was nowhere to be seen and would spend most of the battle drinking in a bomb-proof shelter.

Report of Major General Burnside, continued

The mine sprung at 4.45 a.m. Immediately the leading brigade of the First Division [the Second], under Colonel Marshall, started for the charge. There was a delay of perhaps five minutes in removing the abatis. Clearing that, the brigade advanced rapidly to the fort that had been mined, now a crater of large proportions and an obstacle of great formidableness. Mounting a crest of at least 12 feet above the level of the ground, our men found before them a huge aperture of 150 feet in length by 60 in width, and 25 or 30 in depth, the sides of loose pulverized sand piled up precipitately, from which projected huge blocks of clay. To cross such an obstacle and preserve regimental organization was a sheer impossibility. The lines of the enemy on either side were not single, but involuted and complex, filled with pits, traverses, and bomb-proofs, forming a labyrinth as difficult of passage as the crater itself.

After the training of the previous six weeks it is not to be wondered at that the men should have sought shelter in these defenses. Their regimental organizations were broken, and the officers undertook to reform before advancing. [*O.R.*, XL, part 1, p. 527.]

Report of Brig. Gen. James H. Ledlie, USA, commanding First Division, Ninth Corps, Army of the Potomac

About 1 a.m. on the 30th of July I moved my division from its position on the left of the Tenth Corps to the front occupied by the Second Division of the Ninth Corps. The Second Brigade (composed of the Second Pennsylvania Heavy Artillery, Fourteenth New York Heavy Artillery, Third Maryland Infantry, and the One hundred and seventy-ninth New York Infantry), commanded by Colonel E. G. Marshall, was formed in three lines of battle behind the breast-works of our front line; while the First Brigade [composed of the Twenty-first, Twenty-ninth, Thirty-fifth, Fifty-sixth, Fifty-seventh, and Fifty-ninth Massachusetts Infantry, and One hundredth Pennsylvania], under the command of Brigadier General W. F. Bartlett, was placed in rear, in column formed of three lines of battle, the Thirty-fifth in rear acting as engineer regiment. I then gave instructions to my brigade commanders to the effect that when the order for the charge was given, the column should move through the breach to be made by the mine and then to press forward and occupy the hill beyond, when the Thirty-fifth were to be set at work throwing up intrenchments. At daylight everything was ready, the mine was sprung at 4.45 a.m., and the fortification in my front was utterly demolished. As soon as the debris consequent upon the explosion had fallen to the ground I gave the order for the charge, and my brigades mounted our breast-works and pushed forward gallantly over the slope leading to the enemy's lines, taking possession of the demolished fort and occupying about 100 yards of the enemy's rifle-pits to the left [our right of it], capturing 1 stand of colors and about 50 prisoners. The division was here halted to reform, and hastily constructed traverses to shield the men from a terrible and incessant flank fire, which at the same time afforded our sharpshooters an excellent opportunity for picking off the cannoneers from a battery that enfiladed the position and poured a destructive fire of canister and shrapnel into my line.

At this time the enemy was holding the same line of intrenchments with my own troops, starting from the point where the right of my division rested and extending thence to the left [our right]. It was impossible for my line to advance from this position, as no troops had come up on my right to dislodge the enemy, and had I moved my line forward the enemy would merely by filing to the right in the same trench have occupied my position and poured a deadly fire into my rear. I reported this fact to one of the corps staff officers and soon after received peremptory orders to move my troops forward. I immediately gave the necessary orders, and the brigade commanders had barely got their men into proper position for a charge when the colored troops came running into the crater, and filing through passed into the rifle-pits to the left [our right] of the fort, where my troops now formed for the charge. The colored troops then made a feeble attempt at a charge, but before they accomplished anything the enemy made a fierce attack, and they retreated precipitately into the rifle-pits, breaking my line and crowding the pits to such an extent that it was impossible to reform my line. [*O.R.*, XL, part 1, pp. 535–536.]

Narrative of Bvt. Maj. Charles H. Houghton, USA, Fourteenth New York Heavy Artillery, Third Brigade, First Division, Ninth Corps, Army of the Potomac

Our brigade, commanded by Colonel E. G. Marshall of the 14th New York Artillery, was first in line and formed three lines of battle, the 2d Pennsylvania Provisional Artillery in the first line, the 14th New York Artillery in the second line, and the 179th New York and 3d Maryland, in the third line. . . . I shall never forget the terrible and magnificent sight. The earth around us trembled and heaved—so violently that I was lifted to my feet. Then the earth along the enemy's lines opened, and fire and smoke shot upward seventy-five or one hundred feet. The air was filled with earth, cannon, caissons, sand-bags and living men, and with everything else within the exploded fort. One large lump of clay as large as a hay-stack or small cottage was thrown out and left on top of the ground toward our own works. Our orders were to charge immediately after the explosion, but the effect produced by the falling of earth and the fragments sent heavenward that appeared to be coming right down upon us, caused the first line to waver and fall back, and the situation was one to demoralize most troops.

I gave the command "Forward," but at the outset a serious difficulty had to be surmounted. Our own works, which were very high at this point, had not been prepared for scaling. But scale them in some way we must, and ladders were improvised by the men placing their bayonets between the logs in the works and holding the other end at their hip or on shoulders, thus forming steps over which men climbed. I with others stood on top of the works pulling men up and forming line; but time was too precious to wait for this, and Colonel Marshall, who was standing below within our works, called to me to go forward. This was done very quickly and our colors were the first to be planted on the ruined fort. We captured several prisoners and two brass field-pieces, light twelve-pounders, which were in the left wing (their right) of the fort and had not been buried beneath the ruins.

Prisoners stated that about one thousand men were in the fort. If so, they were massed there over night, expecting an attack, as the fort could not accommodate so many men; but nearly all who were within it were killed or buried alive. We succeeded in taking out many—some whose feet would be waving above their burial place; others, having an arm, hand, or head only, uncovered; others, alive but terribly shaken. Being convinced that a magazine was near the two pieces of artillery, I detailed a sergeant and some men to search for it and to man the guns. The magazine, containing a supply of ammunition, was found. We then hauled back the pieces of artillery to get a range over the top of works on a Confederate gun on our left that was throwing canister and grape into us. We loaded and fired and silenced the gun, and at our first fire forty-five prisoners came in, whom I sent to our lines. We loaded and placed the other piece in position to use. . . . A charge was made upon us, and the fire from this piece did terrible execution on their advancing lines, and with the fire of our men they were repulsed. On the repulse of this charge we captured a stand of colors. . . . We charged and captured the works behind the crater, but our supports had not come. The delay in getting them over our own works gave the enemy a chance to recover their surprise and resume their stations at their guns, which they opened upon our men then crossing the field. When the colored troops advanced they could not be forced beyond the "crater" for some time, and when they were, were driven back to our lines, or into the pit. [*Battles and Leaders*, IV, pp. 561–562.]

Narrative of Major Powell, continued

The whole scene of the explosion struck every one dumb with astonishment as we arrived at the crest of the debris. . . . Before the brigade commanders could realize the situation, the two brigades became inextricably mixed in the desire to look into the hole.

However, Colonel Marshall yelled to the Second Brigade to move forward, and the men did so, jumping, sliding, and tumbling into the hole, over the debris of material, and dead and dying men, and huge blocks of solid clay. They were followed by General Bartlett's brigade. Up on the other side of the crater they climbed, and while a detachment stopped to place two of the dismounted guns of the battery in position on the enemy's side of the crest of the crater, a portion of the leading brigades passed over the crest and attempted to reform. In doing so members of these regiments were killed by musket-shots from the rear, fired by the Confederates who were still occupying the traverses and intrenchments to the right and left of the crater. . . . This coming so unexpectedly caused the forming line to fall back into the crater.

Had General Burnside's original plan, providing that two regiments should sweep down inside the enemy's line to the right and left of the crater, been sanctioned, the brigades of Colonel Marshall and General Bartlett could and would have reformed and moved on to Cemetery Hill before the enemy realized fully what was intended. . . . After falling back into the crater a partial formation was made by General Bartlett and Colonel Marshall with some of their troops, but owning to the precipitous walls the men could find no footing except by facing inward, digging their heels into the earth and throwing their backs against the side of the crater. . . . The enemy had not been idle. He had brought a battery from his left to bear upon the position, and . . . the crest of the crater was being swept with canister. . . . The firing on the crater now was incessant, and it was as heavy a fire of canister as was ever poured continuously upon a single objective point. It was as utterly impracticable to re-form a brigade in that crater as it would be to marshal bees into line after upsetting the hive; and equally as impracticable to reform outside of the crater, under the severe fire in front and rear. . . .

A brigade of the Second Division (Potter's) under the command of Brigadier-General S. G. Griffin advanced its skirmishers and followed them immediately, directing its course to the right of the crater. General Griffin's line, however, overlapped the crater on the left, where two of three of his regiments sought shelter in the crater. Those on the right passed over the trenches, but owing to the peculiar character of the enemy's works, which were not single, but complex and involuted and filled with pits, traverses, and bomb-proofs, forming a labyrinth as difficult of passage as the crater itself, the brigade was broken up, and, meeting the severe fire of canister, also fell back into the crater, which was then full to suffocation. Every organization melted away, as soon as it entered this hole in the ground, into a mass of human beings clinging by toes and heels to the almost perpendicular sides. [*Battles and Leaders*, IV, pp. 551–553.]

As Burnside's men futilely endeavored to regain the momentum of their assault, the remnants of *Elliott's* wrecked brigade (command of which passed to Col. *Fitz W. McMaster* after *Elliott* was shot leading a counterattack) put up a fierce fight, aided by the brigades to its left and right and Confederate artillery.

Report of Major General Johnson, continued

When the torrents of dust had subsided the enemy was found in the breach. Some four flags were counted, and a continuous column of white and black troops came pouring on from the enemy's lines to support those in the advance, while their artillery, mortars, and cannon, opened all along their lines, concentrating on our works and grounds adjacent to the crater one of the heaviest artillery fires known to our oldest officers in the field. Their heaviest fire was from batteries in the vicinity of the Baxter road. . . .

On the advancing column the Twenty-third and a part of the Twenty-second South Carolina Regiments, on the right, and the Seventeenth and part of the Eighteenth South Carolina Regiments, on the left, opened from our parapets a most destructive fire. The flanking arrangements of our works on both sides of the breach afforded peculiar advantages. Soon the fire along the line of the division, extending far out on each flank wherever the enemy's could be reached, swept the ground in front of the crater. To the men of *Wise's* brigade, occupying the eminence south of the Baxter road about 200 yards from the crater, the enemy's masses moving on the open ground up to the breach, presented a most inviting and accessible target, upon which their fire took unerring effect. [Brig. Gen. *Ambrose R.*] *Wright's* battery, of four guns, admirably located, and intrenched on the left of *Elliott's* brigade and in rear of our lines, poured its whole column of fire in the right flank of the enemy's masses. . . .

Major [*John C.*] *Haskell's* mortar batteries, in charge of Captain [*James*] *Lamkin*, consisting of four Coehorns on the Jerusalem plank road, one Coehorn and two 12-pounder mortars in the ravine some 200 yards to the left and in rear of the breach, and two mortars to the left of *Wright's* battery, were all opened promptly upon the enemy's columns. The practice of the four mortars on the plank road was admirable. Its shells were dropped with remarkable precision upon the enemy's masses clustering in disorder in front of and in the crater. Some three mortars on the right of the Baxter road, commanded by Lieutenant [*John*] *Langhorne*, also opened early in the engagement, and continued to fire at intervals with good effect until its close.

As soon as I was aware that the enemy had sprung the mine and broken my line near the center I immediately communicated with the brigades in both wings of the division and directed them to extend their intervals and re-enforce the wings of *Elliott's* brigade, so as to give as great strength as possible to the forces on which the weight of the enemy's columns must first fall. . . . As soon as the enemy occupied the breach they attempted to advance along our trenches upon the flanks of our broken line; but our men, sheltering themselves behind the angles and flanks of our works, in the boyaux running out perpendicular to the rear of our trenches, and behind the piles of earth above their bomb-proofs, opened a fatal fire on every point where the foe exposed themselves. Thus their advance was stayed, and they commenced the work of intrenching, while they still tried by more cautious means to press back our faithful and gallant men.

Brigadier General *S. Elliott*, the gallant commander of the brigade which occupied the salient, was making prompt disposition of his forces to assault the enemy and reoccupy the remaining portion of the trench cavalier when he was dangerously wounded. He had given the necessary orders for the Twenty-sixth and the left wing of the Seventeenth South Carolina Regiments to be withdrawn from the trenches, and had preceded them to the open ground to the left and in rear of the cavalier when he was struck by a rifle-ball. The command of this brigade now devolved upon Colonel *F. W. McMaster*, of the Seventeenth South Carolina Regiment. This officer (having received the re-enforcement of one regiment, sent to him by Colonel [*Lee*] *McAfee*, commanding [Maj. Gen. *Matthew*] *Ransom's* brigade) directed Colonel [*Alexander*] *Smith*, of the Twenty-sixth South Carolina Regiment, to form in a ravine on the left and rear of the breach a rear line consisting of the Twenty-fifth North Carolina, Twenty-sixth South Carolina, and three companies of the Seventeenth South Carolina Regiments, arranged from left to right in the order named.

Some fourteen Federal flags were now counted on our works, and it became evident that it would be better to endeavor to hold the enemy in check until larger re-enforcements arrived than risk the disaster that might follow from an unsuccessful assault by a very inferior force without any support.

The new line to the left and rear of the salient was scarcely formed when the enemy attempted, with a force thrown out to the rear of our works, with those in our trenches, and with a line in front of our trenches, to charge to our left along our breast-works and in rear and front. The Twenty-fourth and Forty-ninth North Carolina Regiments, *Ransom's* brigade, had promptly closed in on the part of the Seventeenth South Carolina Regiment remaining in the trenches when the intermediate regiments were drawn out to form the rear line, and now met and repulsed the charge in front, while the line under Colonel *Smith*, of the Twenty-sixth South Carolina Regiment, was equally successful in rear. Two companies of the Forty-ninth North Carolina Regiment, posted in the covered way near the main line, poured a heavy volley on the flank of the enemy in rear, and our men of the Seventeenth South Carolina and Forty-ninth North Carolina Regiments, under cover of angles, boyaux, &c., drove back the charge along the trenches. After this the enemy continued to fight along the parapet, keeping under cover; but, though our forces on the left failed in several attempts to throw up barricades in the trenches, the former made but slow progress in this movement.

In the meantime the Twenty-third South Carolina Regiment, under Captain [*E. R.*] *White*, and a few remaining men of the Twenty-second South Carolina Regiment, under Captain [*James*] *Shedd*, aided by the Twenty-sixth and part of the Forty-sixth

Virginia Regiments, gallantly defended the trenches on the right of the breach.

The South Carolina troops on that side succeeded in placing a barricade in the trenches on the side of the hill, and planting themselves behind it and in the boyaux running to the rear, maintained their position within thirty yards of the crater for about five hours, during which the enemy never drove them a foot to the right, though they made several assaults, and attempted several times to form a line in rear of our works, so as to move on the flank and rear of this gallant little band. In the events of the 30th of July there will perhaps be found nothing more heroic or worthy of higher admiration than this conduct of the Twenty-second and Twenty-third South Carolina Regiments.

Colonel [*John T.*] *Goode*, commanding *Wise's* brigade, caused the Fifty-ninth Virginia Regiment, under Captain [*Henry*] *Wood*, to be formed in a ditch running perpendicular to the rear of the main work, and when the enemy attempted some five times to form in rear of the breach for the purpose of charging to the right, and after they had planted four colors on the line, by which the movement designated was to be made, this regiment, under Captain *Wood*, and the Twenty-sixth Virginia Regiment, under Captain [*R. E.*] *Steele*, with the Twenty-second and Twenty-third South Carolina Regiments and two guns . . . near the junction of the Baxter and Jerusalem plank roads, opened with a fire that drove them precipitately back to the crater. [*O.R.*, XL, part 1, pp. 788–791.]

Narrative of Col. Fitz W. McMaster, CSA, commanding Elliot's Brigade, Johnson's Division, Anderson's Corps, Army of Northern Virginia

Pegram's salient, where four guns, under Captain *Pegram* of Richmond, forming part of Major [*J. C.*] *Coit's* battalion, was in the centre of *Elliott's* brigade. The brigade was arranged in the following order, from left to right—Twenty-sixth, Seventeenth, Eighteenth, Twenty-second and Twenty-third regiments. . . . The mine was exploded one-quarter of 5 a.m. 30th July 1864, with eight thousand pounds of powder. It overwhelmed the battery, the whole of the Eighteenth, three companies of the Twenty-third and part of company A, Seventeenth regiment.

For some minutes there was the utmost consternation among my men. Some scampered out of the lines; some, paralyzed with fear, vaguely scratched at the counter-scarp as if trying to escape. Smoke and dust filled the air. A few minutes afterward, General Ledlie's division began to charge. This aroused our officers; they began to cheer, and our men bounded on the banquette and commenced firing on the ranks of men who were rushing in without firing a gun. By this time some of the men of the gallant Eighteenth, who extricated themselves from the bank which covered them, came rushing down the trenches, and as many as could picked up guns and began firing. For a considerable time the firing was done entirely by the infantry.

In a few minutes after the explosion, Major *Coit*, who commanded the most effective artillery on our side, came up to me to see if any of his guns were uninjured.

As soon as he could reach *Wright's* battery of four guns, in the ravine to the rear of *Ransom's* brigade, which was at least half an hour after the explosion, he began to fire, and shot six hundred balls into the divisions of Potter, Willcox, and Ferrero, which succeeded Ledlie's division. These guns were the only ones on our lines which, besides enfilading the enemy at close range, could also *fire on the crater and part of our lines.* . . .

In fifteen or twenty minutes after the explosion General *Elliott* came up through the crowded ditch, followed by Colonel *Smith* of the Twenty-sixth regiment, with a few of his men, and ordered the Twenty-sixth and Seventeenth to form a line on the crest of the hill, and charge the crater. He and a few men gallantly jumped up on the crest of the hill, about fifty yards of the crater, he pointed out the line, and was in less than five minutes shot down and brought back. The command then devolved on your Colonel, who countermanded the order to form on the crest of the hill, which was utterly impracticable, and formed some of the men in the ditches, which went to the rear and commanded some yards in the rear of the crater. Courier after courier was sent to the division commander, and one courier to the regiments on the right of the crater. I ordered Colonel *Smith* to take his regiment, with three companies of the Seventeenth, under Captain [*E. A.*] *Crawford* (which then were larger than the Twenty-sixth regiment) to form in the ravine in the rear of the crater, and cover up the gap, there to lie down and to rise up and fire when necessary, so as to prevent the enemy from rushing down the hill and getting in the rear of our lines. This order was promptly executed, and gave the remainder of the Seventeenth in the main trench more room to use their guns. . . .

The negroes, numbering 4,300 muskets, under General Ferrero, rushed to the mine at 8 o'clock, and one distinct charge, as alleged soon after. Some of the officers allege their men got 200 yards towards the crest, which was 500 yards to the rear, but this is a clear mistake. None ever advanced 50 yards beyond, for I watched their efforts with great anxiety up to about 9 o'clock; as I believed the fate of Petersburg depended on it. The officers frequently attempted to urge their men forward, and some would rush across a few yards and then run back. . . . We saw at one time fourteen beautiful banners waving in the crater and gallant officers, trying to urge their men on in the direction of Cemetery Hill. But all efforts to reach this point, from the rear of the crater, failed by 9 o'clock. And they then attempted to effect their purpose by taking the lines north of the crater, which would secure them a chance to reach the point of their destination, by the ravine that passed through *Ransom's* lines. This, together with the conformation of the ground necessarily forced the burden of the battle on the Confederate line, north of the crater and in close proximity to it. And especially on *Elliott's* brigade; the right of *Ransom's* brigade and the artillery under the command of Major *Coit*.

The enemy, thus having changed their tactics, would occasionally rush on our right flank—we made barricades to oppose them; they then would run down the front of the line and jump over and were met with the bayonet and clubbed with the musket. Generally they were repelled, occasionally they succeeded and captured some men. Private [*W. A.*] *Hoke*, of Company A, was thus cut off, and refused to surrender, and struck down several of the enemy before he was bayoneted. Few battles would show more bayonet wounds than this. After a severe hand to hand fight, disputing every inch, and losing . . . many brave men, we were driven down the hill to *Ransom's* brigade, which at this time was pouring in an enfilading fire. . . .

At 10 o'clock I was ordered to the brigade headquarters to see General *Bushrod Johnson*, our division commander. . . . [Maj. Gen. *William*] *Mahone's* troops were formed in the line already there. (*SHSP*, X, pp. 119–123.)

From the overlook at the Crater, take the paved trail to the right to the large obelisk labeled "Mahone," and face toward the Crater.

STOP 4: THE MAHONE MONUMENT

THE CONFEDERATE COUNTERATTACK

News of the mine explosion reached *Robert E. Lee* shortly after six a.m. He immediately ordered two brigades from Maj. Gen. *William Mahone's* division of Lt. Gen. *Ambrose P. Hill's* corps to leave their position west of the Jerusalem Plank Road and rush to the scene. Meanwhile, around seven a.m., Burnside ordered fresh troops to join the assault. Included among these was Ferrero's division of African American troops—the one that had originally been designated to lead the assault. But these forces only made the situation worse by getting tangled up with Federals already in and about the Crater. (Making matters worse, instead of leading his men into the fight, Ferrero took shelter in the same bomb-proof to which Ledlie had personally retreated.)

In addition to the Crater itself, by nine a.m. the eight Federal brigades Burnside had thrown into the battle had managed to claim possession of about 500 yards of the Confederate line. Unfortunately, organizing a concerted effort to push forward to the Jerusalem Plank Road and the high ground on Cemetery Hill—the tactical objective identified by Army of the Potomac headquarters—proved hopeless. Consequently, by midmorning Grant and Meade were already seriously considering shutting down the battle.

Before they could do so, however, shortly before eight thirty a.m., *Mahone's* two brigades reached the scene. Within a half hour, *Mahone* had ordered his lead brigade, Col. *David Weisiger's*, to move across the Jerusalem Plank Road toward the Crater and launch a counterattack against the elements of Burnside's force that had managed to move beyond the Crater. Their fury exacerbated by information that they would find African American troops in their front, *Weisiger's* men first ran into Lt. Col. John A. Bross's regiment of African American soldiers, whose commander had managed to move them out of the Crater onto open ground and was trying to form them up in preparation for a push to the Jerusalem Plank Road. *Weisiger's* men drove Bross's command back into the Crater and then commenced clearing the trenches around the Crater of Federal troops in bitter hand-to-hand combat, in the process shoving even more of them into the already packed Crater.

Narrative of Captain McCabe, continued

Lee, informed of the disaster at 6:10 a.m., had bidden his aide, Colonel *Charles Venable*, to ride quickly to the right of the army

The Battle of the Crater (USAMHI)

and bring up two brigades of [Maj. Gen. *Richard H.*] *Anderson's*
old division, commanded by *Mahone*, for time was too precious
to observe military etiquette and send the orders through *Hill*.
Shortly after, the General-in-Chief reached the front in person,
and all men took heart when they descried the grave and gracious
face, and "Traveller" stepping proudly, as if conscious that he bore
upon his back the weight of the nation. [Gen. *Pierre G. T.*] *Beau-*
regard was already at the Gee House, a commanding position five
hundred yards in rear of the Crater. . . . *Venable* had sped upon his
mission and found *Mahone's* men already standing to their arms;
but the Federals, from their lofty "look-outs" were busily inter-
changing signals, and to uncover such a length of front without
exciting observation, demanded the nicest precaution. Yet was
this difficulty overcome by a simple device, for the men being ordered to drop back one by one, as if going for water, obeyed with
such intelligence, that Warren continued to report to Meade that
not a man had left his front.

   Then forming in the ravine to the rear, the men of the Virginia
and Georgia brigades came pressing down the valley with swift,
swinging stride. . . . Halting for a moment in rear of the "Ragland
House," *Mahone* bade his men strip off blankets and knapsacks
and prepare for battle. Then riding quickly to the front, while
the troops marched in single file along the covered way, he drew

rein at *Bushrod Johnson's* head-quarters, and reported in person to *Beauregard*. . . . He rode still further to the front, dismounted, and pushing along the covered-way from the Plank Road, came out into the ravine, in which he afterwards formed his men. Mounting the embankment at the head of the covered way, he descried within 160 yards a forest of glittering bayonets and beyond, floating proudly from the captured works, eleven Union flags. Estimating rapidly from the hostile colors the probable force in his front, he at once dispatched his courier to bring up the Alabama brigade from the right, assuming thereby a grave responsibility, yet was the wisdom of the decision vindicated by the event.

Scarcely had the order been given, when the head of the Virginia brigade began to debouch from the covered way. Directing Colonel *Weisiger*, its commanding officer, to file to the right and form line of battle, *Mahone* stood at the angle, speaking quietly and cheerily to the men. Silently and quickly they moved out, and formed with that precision dear to every soldier's eye—the Sharpshooters leading, followed by the Sixth, Sixteenth, Sixty-first, Forty-first, and Twelfth Virginia. . . . Now the leading regiment of the Georgia brigade began to move out, when suddenly a brave Federal officer, seizing the colors, called on his men to charge. Descrying this hostile movement on the instant, *Weisiger*, a veteran of stern countenance which did not belie the personal intrepidity of the man, uttered to the Virginians the single word— Forward.

Then the Sharpshooters and the men of the Sixth on the right, running swiftly forward, for theirs was the greater distance to traverse, the whole line sprang along the crest, and there burst from more than eight hundred warlike voices that fierce yell which no man ever yet heard unmoved on the field of battle. Storms of case-shot from the right mingled with the tempest of bullets which smote upon them from the front, yet was there no answering volley, for these were veterans, whose fiery enthusiasm had been wrought to finer temper by the stern code of discipline. . . . Still pressing forward with steady fury, while the enemy, appalled by the inexorable advance, gave ground, they reached the ditch of the inner works—then one volley crashed from the whole line, and the Sixth and Sixteenth, with the Sharpshooters, clutching their empty guns and redoubling their fierce cries, leaped over the retrenched-cavalier, and all down the line the dreadful work of the bayonet began. [*SHSP*, II, pp. 289–292.]

Narrative of Lt. Col. William H. Stewart, CSA, commanding Sixty-
first Virginia, Weisiger's Brigade, Mahone's Division, Third Corps,
Army of Northern Virginia

When nearly opposite the portion of the works then held by
the Federal troops, we met several soldiers who were in the works
at the time of the explosion. Our men began to ridicule them
for going to the rear, when one of them remarked: "Ah boys, you
have hot work ahead; they are negroes and show no quarter." This
was the first intimation that we had to fight negro troops, and it
seemed to infuse the little band with impetuous daring as they
pressed forward. . . .

I never felt more like fighting in my life. Our comrades had
been slaughtered in a most inhuman and brutal manner, and
slaves were trampling over their mangled and bleeding corpses.
Revenge must have fired every heart and strung every arm with
nerves of steel for the Herculean task of blood. We filed up a
ditch, which had been dug for a safe ingress and egress to and
from the earthworks, until we reached the vale between the elevation on which the breastworks were located and the one on
the banks of the little stream just mentioned—within two hundred yards of the enemy. . . . The Crater and a space of about
200 yards on the north were literally crammed with the enemy's
troops. . . .

Mahone's Old Brigade and part of the Georgia Brigade deployed, covered the enemy's front from about the centre of the
Crater to their right. The silken banners of the enemy proudly
floated on the breezes, supported by countless bayonets glistening in the sunlight. . . . As the soldiers filed into line, General *Ma-*
hone walked from right to left, commanding the men to reserve
their fire until they reached the brink of the ditch, and after delivering one volley to use the bayonet. Our line was hardly adjusted,
and the Georgians had not finished deploying, when the division
of negroes—the advance line of the enemy—made an attempt
to rise from the ditch and charge. Just at that instant, about 8:45
o'clock, a.m., a counter charge was ordered. The men rushed forward, officers in front, with uncovered heads and waving hats,
and grandly and beautifully swept onward over the intervening
space, with muskets at trail. The enemy sent a storm of bullets in
our ranks, and here and there a gallant fellow would fall, but the
files would close, still pressing onward, unwavering, into the jaws
of death. . . .

The orders of General *Mahone* were obeyed to the very letter. The brink of the ditch was gained before a musket was discharged. The cry "No quarter" greeted us, the one volley responded, and the bayonet was plied with such irresistible vigor that success was insured within a short space of time. Men fell dead in heaps, and human gore ran in streams that made the very earth mire beneath the tread of our victorious soldiers. The rear ditch being ours, the men mounted the rugged embankments and hurled their foes from the front line up to the very mouth of the Crater. [*SHSP*, XXV, pp. 78–82.]

Report of Col. Henry G. Thomas, USA, commanding Second Brigade, Fourth Division, Ninth Corps, Army of the Potomac

There was a white division in the pits into which we were ordered. The instant I reached the First Brigade I attempted to charge, but the Thirty-first was disheartened at its loss of officers and could not be gotten out promptly. . . . A partially successful attempt was then made to separate the Twenty-eighth and Twenty-ninth Regiments U.S. Colored Troops from the white troops of one of the brigades of the First Division, Ninth Corps, previous to attempting another charge. I then sent word that unless the enfilading fire on my right was stopped, by the moving of a force in that direction at the moment in which I moved, that no men could live to reach the crest. Immediately after this I was ordered by Brigadier-General Ferrero to advance in concert with Colonel [Joshua] Sigfried and take the crest. I ordered the Twenty-ninth this time to lead, which it did gallantly, closely followed by the Twenty-eighth and a few of the Twenty-third, when it was at once engaged by a heavy charging column of the enemy, and after a struggle driven back over our rifle-pits.

At this moment a panic commenced. The black and white troops came pouring back together. A few, more gallant than the rest, without organization, but guided by a soldier's instinct, remained on the side of the pits nearest our line and held the enemy at bay some ten or fifteen minutes, until they were nearly all shot away. . . . I desire, however, to pay a passing tribute to Lieutenant-Colonel Bross, Twenty-ninth U.S. Colored Troops, who led the charge of this brigade. He was the first man to leap over the works, and bearing his colors in his own hands he fell never to rise again. [*O.R.*, XL, part 1, pp. 598–599.]

Retrace your steps to return to the Crater.

Maj. Gen. William Mahone (USAMHI)

STOP 5: THE CRATER

THE BATTLE ENDS

The success of *Weisiger's* counterattack convinced Grant and Meade that it was time to break off the fight. Burnside was not ready to give up, though, and vehemently protested orders to pull his men back to their original lines. At about eleven a.m., while Burnside and his superiors debated the matter, *Mahone* threw Lt. Col. *Matthew Hall's* Georgia brigade into the battle. This attack was unable to accomplish much, but while they were engaged the Confederates managed to bring up more forces, including two mortars that began firing into the Crater from only a few yards away. After about two hours of this, a brigade of Alabamians commanded by Col. *John Sanders* advanced to the edge of the Crater, then rushed in with the bayonet. By then the Federals were already under orders to retreat, and many of the men had pulled back to their original lines, but the brigade commanders had determined that it would be too risky to order the full force to do so before night fell. However, the butchery *Sanders's* men and the other Confederates who joined in the fight inflicted—especially upon African American soldiers, many of whom were killed even though they were trying to surrender—put an end to Federal resistance in the Crater.

Report of Major General Johnson, continued

The first charge having failed in completely dislodging the enemy . . . between 11 and 12 a.m. a second unsuccessful charge having been made by *Wright's* brigade, of *Mahone's* division, I proceeded to concert a combined movement on both flanks of the crater, to which most of the enemy's troops were now drawn. By arrangement a third charge was made a little before 2 p.m., which gave us entire possession of the crater and the adjacent lines. This charge was made on the left and rear of the crater by *Sanders'* brigade, of *Mahone's* division, by the Sixty-first North Carolina, of *Hoke's* division, and Seventeenth South Carolina Regiments, of this division. The last two regiments, under Major [*John*] *Culp*, of the Seventeenth South Carolina Regiment, *Elliott's* brigade, advanced on the right of *Sanders'* brigade. These movements on the left were all placed under the direct supervision of General *Mahone*, while I proceeded to the right to collect what troops I could from the thin line on that flank to co-operate in the charge and divide the force of the enemy's resistance. The time allotted only permitted me to draw out the Twenty-third and the fragments of the Twenty-second South Carolina Regiment, under Captain *Shedd*. They moved gallantly forward as soon as the main line was seen advancing on the left, and entered the crater with the troops of that line, capturing 3 stand of colors and about 130 prisoners. Previous to this charge the incessant firing kept up by our troops on both flanks and in rear had caused many of the enemy to run the gauntlet of our cross-fires in front of the breach, but a large number still remained, unable to advance, and perhaps afraid to retreat. The final charge was therefore made with little difficulty, and resulted in the complete re-establishment of our lines and the capture of many additional prisoners. [*O.R.*, XL, pt 1, p. 792.]

Narrative of Capt. John C. Featherston, CSA, Ninth Alabama, Sanders's Brigade, Mahone's Division, Third Corps, Army of Northern Virginia

As we came out of the covered way we were met by General *Mahone*, himself on foot, who called the officers to him, explained the situation, and gave us orders for the fight. He informed us that the brigades of Virginians and Georgians had successfully charged and taken the works on the left of the fort, but that the fort was still in the possession of the enemy, as was also a part of the works on the right of it, and we of the Alabama brigade were expected to storm and capture the fort. . . . He further informed us that he had ordered our men, who then occupied the works on either side of the fort, to fire at the enemy when they should show themselves above the top of the fort or along their main line, so as to shield us as much as possible from their fire.

As we were leaving him he said: "General *Lee* is watching the result of your charge."

The officers then returned to their places in line and ordered the men to load and fix bayonets. Immediately the brigade moved up the ravine as ordered. . . . The Ninth Alabama, being on the right of the brigade, was in front as we ascended the ravine, or depression, to form line of battle. . . . This brigade of five regiments carried into the battle of the "Crater" 628 men. . . . After we had crawled up in front of the fort and about two hundred yards therefrom, we lay down flat on the ground, and our batteries, in the rear, opened fire on the enemy's artillery in order to draw their fire. This was done that we might charge without being subjected to their artillery fire. . . . Our guns soon ceased firing, and we at once arose and moved forward, as directed, in quick time at a trail arms, with bayonets fixed.

In a short distance we came in view of the enemy, both infantry and artillery, and then was presented one of the most awfully grand and cruel spectacles of that terrible war. One brigade of six hundred and twenty-eight men was charging a fort in an open field, filled with the enemy to the number of over five thousand, supported by a park of artillery said to number fifty pieces. . . . When we came within range we saw the flash of the sunlight on the enemy's guns as they were leveled above the walls of that wrecked fort. Then came a stream of fire and the awful roar of battle. This volley seemed to awaken the demons of hell, and appeared to be the signal for everybody within range of the fort to commence firing. We raised a yell and made a dash in order to get under the walls of the fort before their artillery could open upon us, but in this we were unsuccessful. . . . The Virginians, Georgians and South Carolinians commenced firing from the flanks at the fort and at the enemy's mainline, as did our artillery, and enemy's infantry and artillery from all sides opened upon us.

On we went, as it seemed to us, literally "into the mouth of hell." When we got to the walls of the fort we dropped down on the ground to get the men in order and let them get their breath. While waiting we could hear the Yankee officers in the fort trying to encourage their men, telling them, among other things, to "remember Fort Pillow." . . . There were quite a number of abandoned muskets with bayonets on them lying on the ground around the fort. Our men began pitching them over the embankment, bayonet foremost, trying to harpoon the men inside, and both sides threw over cannon balls and fragments of shot and earth, which by the impact of the explosion had been pressed as hard as brick. . . . Col. H[orace] H. King ordered the men near him to put their hats on their bayonets and quickly raise them above the fort, which was done, and, as he anticipated, they were riddled with bullets. Then he ordered us over the embankment, and over we went, and were soon engaged in a hand-to-hand struggle of life and death. The enemy shrank back, and the death grapple continued until most of the Yankees found in there were killed. This slaughter would not have been so great had not our men found negro soldiers in the fort with the whites. This was the first time we had met negro troops, and the men were enraged at them for being there and at the whites for having them there.

The explosion had divided the pit into two compartments. As soon as we had possession of the larger one the Yankees in the smaller one cried out that they would surrender. . . . This practically ended the fight inside the fort; but the two armies outside continued firing at this common center. . . . The slaughter was fearful. The dead were piled on each other. In one part of the fort I counted eight bodies deep. There were but few wounded compared with the killed. [*SHSP*, XXXVI, pp. 163–167.]

Report of Gen. Robert E. Lee, CSA, commanding Army of Northern Virginia

At 5 a.m. the enemy sprung a mine under one of the salients on General *B. R. Johnson's* front and opened his batteries upon our lines and the city of Petersburg. In the confusion caused by the explosion of the mine he got possession of the salient. We have retaken the salient and driven the enemy back to his lines with loss. . . . General *Mahone* in retaking the salient possessed by the enemy this morning recovered the four guns with which it was armed, captured 12 stand of colors, 74 officers, including Brigadier-General Bartlett and staff, and 855 enlisted men. Upward of 500 of the enemy's dead are lying unburied in the trenches. His loss slight. [*O.R.*, XL, part 1, pp. 752–753.]

Report of Lt. Gen. Ulysses S. Grant, USA, commanding Armies of the United States

The mine was sprung a few minutes before 5 o'clock this morning, throwing up four guns of the enemy and burying most of a South Carolina regiment. Our men immediately took possession of the crater made by the explosion, and a considerable distance of the parapet to the right of it, as well as a short work in front, and still hold them. The effort to carry the ridge beyond, and which would give us Petersburg and the south bank of the Appomattox, failed. As the line held by the enemy would be a very bad one for us, being on a side hill, the crest on the side of the enemy, and not being willing to take the chances of a slaughter sure to occur if another assault was made, I have directed the withdrawal of our troops to their old lines. . . .

It was the saddest affair I have witnessed in the war. Such opportunity for carrying fortifications I have never seen and do not expect again to have. . . . I am constrained to believe that had instructions been promptly obeyed that Petersburg would have

Interior of the Crater (USAMHI)

been carried with all the artillery and a large number of prisoners without a loss of 300 men. [*O.R.*, XL, part 1, pp. 17–18.]

To go to the Visitor Center, return to your vehicle by following the paved path to the parking area, then drive out of the parking area and along the park road to its terminus at Crater Road. Turn right, and proceed 0.8 mile to Wythe Street. Shortly before the intersection, make note of Blandford Church on your right. Turn right on Wythe Street, and drive 2.2 miles on VA 36 (which becomes Washington Street and then Oaklawn Boulevard) to the exit to Petersburg National Battlefield on the right. Take the exit, and at the top of the ramp turn left to return to the parking area. Due to the one-way park road, if you wish to now study the sites associated with First Petersburg or the Battle of Fort Stedman, you have to first return to the Visitor Center.

Optional excursion: After turning right onto Crater Road and proceeding 0.6 mile, you will see the parking area for Blandford Church on your right.

Originally built in 1735, Old Blandford Church and the hill on which it sits not only served as the objective of the Union attack at the Crater but had seen significant fighting during the American Revolution. Although it had been abandoned over seventy years earlier, in 1882 the City of Petersburg decided to repair and preserve the church. In 1901 the Ladies Memorial Association of Petersburg was authorized to develop it into a memorial chapel to honor the 30,000 Confederate soldiers buried in its cemetery. The Ladies Memorial Association managed to raise sufficient funds to commission Louis Comfort Tiffany's studio to design fifteen memorial stained-glass windows, each containing the image of a saint and symbols associated with that saint, to honor the Confederate soldiers from each of the fifteen states of the Confederacy. The first were unveiled in 1904. The magnificent church and cemetery are open to visitors, although there is a small fee for tours of the former. It is well worth a visit.

To travel to Stop 1 on the Westward Movements Excursion from the parking area for the Crater, follow the park road to its terminus at Crater Road. Turn left onto Crater Road, and drive 1.8 miles until you reach Flank Road. Turn right onto Flank Road; at 0.1 mile, make a sharp left-hand turn. Park at the pull-off, get out of your vehicle, and face north toward Fort Davis.

In 1864–1865, Crater Road was known as the Jerusalem Plank Road and was the point where the two siege lines were closest to each other. Fort Sedgwick, also known as "Fort Hell," was located to your left, just south of Morton Avenue, 1.3 miles from where you turn onto Crater Road. Today a Baptist church, converted from a department store, stands on the site.

PART II
EXCURSIONS

EXCURSION 1
FROM COLD HARBOR TO PETERSBURG

This excursion is designed to follow the Army of the Potomac from the battlefield at Cold Harbor to the outskirts of Petersburg, using some of the same roads traveled by Union forces in June 1864. This part of Virginia is rich in other aspects of American history as well, particularly from the colonial period.

SUMMARY OF PRINCIPAL EVENTS, 27 MAY–15 JUNE 1864

May

27—Federal cavalry crosses the Pamunkey River

28—Battle of Haw's Shop (Enon Church)

28–30—Battle of Totopotomoy Creek

30—Battle of Old Church (Matadequin Creek)

31—Initial confrontation at Cold Harbor

June

1–3—Battle of Cold Harbor

12—Army of the Potomac begins its movement to the James River

13—Skirmish at Riddell's Shop (Glendale) between Union Fifth Corps and cavalry and Confederate First and Third Corps

14—Union troops begin crossing the James River at Wilcox's Landing; construction begins on the pontoon bridge at Weyanoke Point

15—Union troops begin crossing the James via the pontoon bridge; initial attacks on the Petersburg defenses by Eighteenth Corps and Second Corps

Drive out of the parking area for the Petersburg National Battlefield Visitor Center and proceed down the park road to the exit for eastbound Route 36 (Oaklawn Boulevard). Take Oaklawn Boulevard 2.7 miles to Interstate 295, and take the northbound ramp toward Richmond. Drive 24.9 miles to exit 34A (Creighton Road eastbound). Follow Creighton Road 0.7 mile to the intersection with Cold Harbor Road (Route 156). Turn right onto Cold Harbor Road, and drive 1.8 miles to the Visitor Center for the Richmond National Battlefield Park (NBP), Cold Harbor Unit. Turn left onto Anderson-Wright Drive and pull into the parking area for the Visitor Center. Cold Harbor features the only Richmond NBP contact station that is open year-round, with exhibits, a short video on the Overland Campaign, books and maps, and restrooms.

STOP 1: COLD HARBOR

Report of Lieut. Gen. Ulysses S. Grant, USA, commanding Armies of the United States

From the proximity of the enemy to his defenses around Richmond it was impossible by any flank movement to interpose between him and the city. I was still in a condition to either move by his left flank and invest Richmond from the north side, or continue my move by his right flank to the south side of the James. While the former might have been better as a covering for Washington yet a full survey of all the ground satisfied me that it would be impracticable to hold a line north and east of Richmond that would protect the Fredericksburg railroad—a long, vulnerable line which would exhaust much of our strength to guard, and that would have to be protected to supply the army, and would leave open to the enemy all his lines of communication on the south side of the James. My idea, from the start, had been to beat *Lee's* army north of Richmond if possible; then, after destroying his lines of communication north of the James River, to transfer the army to the south side and besiege *Lee* in Richmond or follow him south if he should retreat. After the battle of the Wilderness it was evident that the enemy deemed it of the first importance to run no risks with the army he then had. He acted purely on the defensive behind breast-works, or feebly on the offensive immediately in front of them, and where, in case of repulse, he could easily retire behind them. Without a greater sacrifice of life than I was willing to make, all could not be accomplished that I had designed north of Richmond. I therefore determined to hold substantially the ground that we then occupied, taking advantage of any favorable circumstances that might present themselves, until the cavalry could be sent to Charlottesville and Gordonsville and to effectually break up the railroad connection between Richmond and the Shenandoah Valley and Lynchburg, and when the cavalry got well off to move the army to the south side of the James River, by the enemy's right flank, where I felt I could cut off all his sources of supply except by the [James River] canal. [U.S. War Department, The War of the Rebellion: A Compilation of the Official Records of the Union and Confederate Armies, 70 vols. in 128 parts and index (Washington, D.C.: Government Printing Office, 1880–1901), series 1, volume XLVI, part 1, pp. 20–21. Hereafter cited as *O.R.*; all references are to series 1 unless otherwise noted.]

Report of Brig. Gen. Rufus Ingalls, USA, Chief Quartermaster, Armies operating against Richmond

On the 12th [June] the army began another flank movement, to cross the Chickahominy at Long and Jones' Bridges, over pontoons laid by our engineers, and the James, at Fort Powhatan, another pontoon bridge, and to advance rapidly on Petersburg. The trains were conducted by Tunstall's Station on roads to White House and New Kent, thence by Slatersville, Barhamsville, and Diascond, to Cole's Ferry, where they crossed the Chickahominy over a pontoon bridge, constructed by the engineers, of more than 2,000 feet in length. They were then conducted to Charles City and down the neck to Douthat's, opposite Fort Powhatan, where they crossed the James over the pontoon bridge at that place, commencing at 2 p.m. on the 15th and closing at 7 a.m. on the 17th. The movement was very complicated, difficult, and arduous. It was one of the most important on record; but it was conducted with a skill and vigor by Captain [Luther H.] Pierce that crowned it with magnificent success. [*O.R.*, XL, part 1, pp. 37–38.]

Gen. Robert E. Lee, CSA, commanding Army of Northern Virginia, to Lieut. Gen. Ambrose P. Hill, CSA, commanding Third Corps, Army of Northern Virginia, June 1864

The time has arrived, in my opinion, when something more is necessary than adhering to lines and defensive positions. We shall be obliged to go out and prevent the enemy from selecting such positions as he chooses. If he is allowed to continue that course we shall at last be obliged to take refuge behind the works of Richmond and stand a siege, which would be but a work of time. You must be prepared to fight him in the field, to prevent him taking positions such as he desires, and I expect the co-operation of all the corps commanders in the course which necessity now will oblige us to pursue. It is for this purpose that I desire the corps to be kept together and as strong as possible, and that our absentees will be brought forward and every attention given to refreshing and preparing the men for battle. Their arms and ammunition should be looked to and cooked provisions provided ahead. [*O.R.*, XL, part 2, pp. 702–703.]

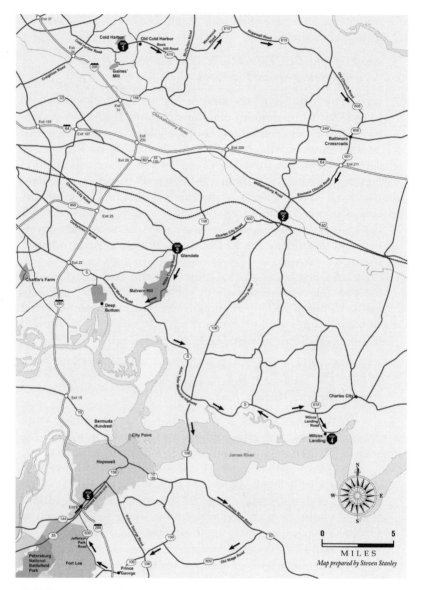

Cold Harbor to Petersburg overview

The Army of the Potomac began vacating its lines at Cold Harbor after nightfall on June 12. Grant conducted the movement to the south side of the James River in four separate elements. Maj. Gen. William F. Smith's Eighteenth Corps, Army of the James, moved to White House Landing on the Pamunkey River, where it boarded transports and sailed out to the Chesapeake Bay, then back up the James River to Bermuda Hundred. The remaining four army corps moved overland to the James, with two corps (Second and Fifth) crossing the Chickahominy River at Long Bridge and the other two (Sixth and Ninth) crossing at Jones Bridge farther east. The fourth element of the march, the army's trains, moved still farther east, guarded by a division of U.S. Colored Troops, and crossed the Chickahominy on a pontoon bridge.

Drive out of the parking lot at Cold Harbor, turning left onto Route 156, Cold Harbor Road. In 0.9 mile, continue straight at Old Cold Harbor Crossroads. At this point the road becomes Rock Hill Road (Route 619). After 2.6 miles, bear left at the intersection to continue on Rock Hill Road. In 0.3 mile Rock Hill Road ends at a T intersection. Turn left here, as Route 619 becomes McClellan Road. Travel 0.6 mile, and turn right onto Westwood Road, which is still Route 619. After 2.6 miles, turn right to continue on Route 619, now Hopewell Road. In 5.2 miles, turn right onto Route 606, Old Church Road. Old Church Road becomes Route 609 as you pass the turn to St. Peter's Episcopal Church. After 4.3 miles, Old Church Road reaches State Route 249 at Talleysville, or Baltimore Crossroads. Continue straight ahead at the traffic circle; the road becomes State Route 106, Emmaus Church Road.

A few miles to the northeast lies the site of White House Landing on the Pamunkey River. White House served as the primary supply and transportation hub for the Army of the Potomac during both the 1862 Peninsula Campaign and the latter stages of the Overland Campaign. The Richmond and York River Railroad, now part of the Norfolk Southern network, crosses the Pamunkey here. Baltimore Crossroads also figured in another Civil War event, Maj. Gen. *James E. B. Stuart's* 1862 ride around the Army of the Potomac. *Stuart* passed through this intersection on his way to Jones Bridge, near the modern community of Providence Forge.

All four of Meade's army corps making the movement to the James on foot passed through this intersection after following the route you just drove. Here Maj. Gen. Horatio Wright's Sixth Corps and Maj. Gen. Ambrose E. Burnside's Ninth Corps turned east and headed for Jones Bridge, while Maj. Gen. Winfield S. Hancock's Second Corps and Maj. Gen. Gouverneur K. Warren's Fifth Corps continued south to Long Bridge.

Continue driving on Route 106. You will arrive at two traffic circles, 0.5 mile and 1.2 miles from Baltimore Crossroads, respectively. Go straight through both of them and bear slightly left after the second, remaining on Route 106 at the Interstate 64 interchange. At 4.6 miles from Baltimore Crossroads, cross U.S. Route 60 to remain on Route 106. In another 0.4 mile you will see a turn-off on your left with a Virginia Civil War Trails marker; pull over to read this if you wish. When you are ready to continue, travel another 0.2 mile to the bridge over the Chickahominy River. Pull to the right side of the road just before the bridge and park. Watch for traffic as you walk to the bridge and face the river.

STOP 2: LONG BRIDGE

Hancock and Warren crossed the Chickahominy River on pontoons a short distance east of the modern road bridge, in front of you and to your left. The river seems unimposing now, but in 1864 the entire area was swampy and flooded, creating a major obstacle for Union engineers. After crossing the river early on the morning of June 13, Warren's corps headed southwest, toward Malvern Hill and the Glendale crossroads, with the mission of screening the Federal movement.

Report of Maj. Gen. Ambrose E. Burnside, USA, commanding Ninth Corps, Army of the Potomac

On the night of the 12th [June], in accordance with instructions, the corps was moved to Tunstall's Station, where we arrived about daylight on the 13th; finding there a considerable portion of the general trains of the different corps, this corps was halted until they were all under way, when we started for Jones' Crossing, on the Chickahominy, by way of Baltimore Crossroads and Olive Church, and halted about three-quarters of a mile from the crossing. The pontoon bridge being occupied with crossing the Sixth Corps we bivouacked here for the night and crossed at an early hour on the following morning, the 14th. [*O.R.*, XL, part 1, pp. 521–522.]

Daily memoranda taken at headquarters, Second Corps, Army of the Potomac

June 12, 1864.—Orders received this p.m. to be ready to march tonight, which is very agreeable to all of us, as there seems to be no hope of breaking the enemy's lines here, they are so strong and powerfully garrisoned. 11 p.m., the movement of Second Corps commenced, First Division taking the lead, moving in direction of Long Bridge, over the Chickahominy. Withdrawal from our lines effected very quietly and promptly. The pickets remain on our lines, under command of Colonel [John S.] Hammell, Sixty-Sixth New York Volunteers, officer of the day, until the line of battle is completely withdrawn, then to follow the corps. Major [Peter] Nelson, aide-de-camp, directed by the general to remain with Colonel Hammell. Marched all night—men and officers very weary.

June 13, 1864.—Head of column reached pontoon bridge over Chickahominy at Long Bridge at 9.30 a.m., and immediately commenced crossing, General [David B.] Birney in advance, having been directed to pass First and Second Divisions to permit them to cook breakfast. 11 a.m., wrote note, by direction of General Hancock, to General [John] Gibbon to protect pontoon bridge over Chickahominy until it was taken up. Marched rapidly all day. Head of column reached James River, near Wilcox's Landing, at 5.30 p.m. Corps formed line of battle for the night. Preparations making for transporting the troops over the James to-morrow. [*O.R.*, XL, part 1, p. 316.]

Gen. Robert E. Lee to Secretary of War James A. Seddon, CSA, 10 p.m., June 13, 1864

A dispatch just received from Maj Genl [*Wade*] *Hampton* states that he defeated the enemy's cavalry near Trevilian [Trevilian Station in Louisa County was the objective of a raid on the Virginia Central Railroad by Federal cavalry under Maj. Gen. Philip H. Sheridan] with heavy loss. . . . The enemy retreated in confusion, apparently by the route he came, leaving his dead and wounded on the field.

At daybreak this morning it was discovered that the army of Genl Grant had left our front. Our skirmishers were advanced between one and two miles, but failing to discover the enemy were withdrawn, and the army was moved to conform to the route taken by him. He advanced a body of cavalry and some infantry from Long Bridge to Riddell's Shop, which were driven back this evening nearly two miles, after some sharp skirmishing. [Clifford Dowdey and Louis Manarin, eds., *The Wartime Papers of Robert E. Lee* (1961; New York: Da Capo, 1987), pp. 776–777.]

General Robert E. Lee to President Jefferson Davis, CSA,
12:10 p.m., June 14, 1864

I think the enemy must be preparing to move south of James River. Our scouts and pickets yesterday stated that Genl Grant's whole army was in motion for the fords of the Chickahominy from Long Bridge down, from which I inferred that he was making his way to the James River as his new base. I cannot however learn positively that more than a small part of his army has crossed the Chickahominy. [Dowdey and Manarin, eds., *The Wartime Papers of Robert E. Lee*, pp. 776–777.]

Brig. Gen. James Dearing, CSA, commanding Dearing's Cavalry
Brigade, Department of North Carolina and Southern Virginia, to
Lt. Col. John M. Otey, CSA, Assistant Adjutant General, June 13,
1864

From scouts I learn that seven transports with troops passed up James River yesterday. I suppose they have either gone to Bermuda Hundred or were landed at City Point, to operate against Petersburg; most likely the latter. I am under the impression the late attack on Petersburg was nothing more than a reconnaissance in force, preparatory to a formidable attack. These re-enforcements arriving strengthen me in my opinion. [*O.R.*, XL, part 2, p. 649.]

Return to your vehicle and drive straight ahead, crossing the bridge. Cross the railroad tracks in 0.4 mile, and make an immediate right onto Route 600, Charles City Road. Proceed 4.2 miles along Charles City Road until you reach a stop sign. Continue straight ahead, remaining on Charles City Road. In another mile you will reach the Glendale crossroads, with Willis Church Road leading south to Malvern Hill. At this intersection, turn right and park immediately on the right beside the historical marker. Walk back to the intersection, facing west in your original direction of travel.

STOP 3: GLENDALE

This area, known as Riddell's Shop (or Riddle's, as reflected in the 1860 Census) during the war, was the scene of heavy fighting during the 1862 Peninsula Campaign. *Lee* struck Maj. Gen. George B. McClellan here as the Army of the Potomac moved toward the James River and again at Malvern Hill in the last of the Seven Days Battles. One of the "Freeman Markers," emplaced in the mid-1920s with captions written by Douglas Southall Freeman to commemorate battles around Richmond, lies at this important crossroads.

Warren's infantrymen, with a division of cavalry in support, constructed a 5-mile-long line of fieldworks here, stretching from Malvern Hill, on your left, to White Oak Swamp, to your right. Warren's mission at this point was to screen the Federal army's movement across the James, leaving *Lee* uncertain as to Grant's ultimate objective.

Journal of Maj. Gen. Gouverneur K. Warren, USA, commanding Fifth Corps, Army of the Potomac

Monday, June 13.—Our cavalry drove back the enemy's to New Market Cross-Roads. Crawford's division went to White Oak Swamp bridge to cover passage of trains and Second Corps. At 8 a.m. began to withdraw, bothered by [Col. John B.] McIntosh's cavalry brigade, and only got as far as Saint Mary's Church, though travelling nearly all night. Enemy did not follow. [*O.R.*, XL, part 1, p. 453.]

Report of Col. George H. Chapman, Third Indiana Cavalry, commanding Second Brigade, Third Division, Cavalry Corps, Army of the Potomac

Holding this position on White Oak Swamp until the arrival of a portion of General Crawford's division, of the Fifth Corps, by which I was relieved, I was directed to move my command out on the main road to Richmond. As near as I can now recollect this was about noon of the 13th [June]. Proceeding about a mile my advance came upon the enemy strongly posted in a belt of timber in front of Riddell's Shop. After some skirmishing, finding the enemy disposed to contest the position with obstinacy, I directed the Third Indiana and Eighth New York to prepare to fight on foot, and forming them in line of battle advanced into the woods at a double-quick. A brigade of rebel cavalry, dismounted and armed mainly with rifled muskets, held the position, but they soon gave way before the impetuosity of my men, leaving many of their dead and wounded on the field. By this advance I was enabled to cover the road to Malvern Hill (Quaker road), and was directed by the general commanding division not to advance farther. Patrols sent out on the roads to my front developed that the enemy had fallen back from my front some distance. . . . I formed line of battle . . . the right extending well across the road from Bottom's Bridge. . . . At about 6 p.m. the enemy were discovered advancing in strong line of battle and heavy column down the Bottom's Bridge road, the entire force, so far as it was developed, being infantry. Soon the entire line became heavily engaged. My ammunition being nearly exhausted, and the enemy showing vastly superior numbers, I deemed it prudent to retire to the position held by my second line, which was done in good order . . . At near dark the enemy advanced from the cover of the timber in strong line of infantry, and a regiment of our infantry, which had been posted on the right of my line, gave way rapidly and with scarcely a show of resistance, throwing the right of my line into considerable confusion. The left, however, retired in good order. . . . The command passed to the rear of the infantry and was massed in a field near by until about 10 p.m., when the brigade moved in rear of infantry in direction of Charles City Court-House. [*O.R.*, XL, part 1, pp. 643–644.]

Gen. Robert E. Lee to Secretary of War Seddon, 9 p.m., June 14, 1864

The force of the enemy mentioned in my last dispatch as being on the Long Bridge Road disappeared during the night. It was probably advanced to cover the movement of the main body, most of which, as far as I can learn, crossed the Chickahominy at Long Bridge and below, and has reached James River at Westover and Wilcox's Landing. A portion of General Grant's army, upon leaving our front at Cold Harbor, is reported to have proceeded to the White House and embarked at that place. Everything is said to have been removed, and the depot at the White House broken up. The cars, engine, railroad iron, and bridge timber that had been brought to that point have also been reshipped. [*O.R.*, XL, part 2, p. 651.]

Return to your car and make a U-turn when it is safe to do so. At the stop sign, continue straight ahead onto Willis Church Road, driving through the 1862 Glendale battlefield and the Malvern Hill battlefield. Willis Church Road ends at U.S. Route 5, the John Tyler Memorial Highway. Turn left, and proceed 13.2 miles until you see Wilcox Wharf Road (Route 618) on the right. Turn right onto Wilcox Wharf Road, and follow it for 1.2 miles to the parking area at the James River. Walk to the dock that extends into the river.

STOP 4: CROSSING THE JAMES

WILCOX'S LANDING AND THE PONTOON BRIDGE

In deciding where to cross the James, Grant had to take several considerations into account. He needed to cross his army far enough downstream to maintain his deception as to the objective of his march and to avoid Confederate cavalry probes. But he also needed to cross far enough upstream to complete his movement as quickly as possible, preferably before *Lee* had time to reinforce Petersburg from north of the James. On the morning of June 14, Grant decided to ferry the Second and Fifth Corps across the James at Wilcox's Landing, near where you stand now. From here, ferryboats crossed to Windmill Point on the south bank. Farther downstream, engineers began building a pontoon bridge at Weyanoke Point at noon on June 14; this bridge was to convey the remaining two army corps and the army's artillery and wagon trains.

The James River was 1,992 feet wide here in 1864, necessitating what is still known as the world's longest free-standing pontoon bridge. A mixed force of Regular Army and Fiftieth New York Engineers constructed the bridge and its approaches on both sides of the river, adding upstream and downstream anchors and three small boats upstream and downstream of the bridge to slow the river's current. The bridge itself consisted of 101 pontoons and was 10 feet wide; it was operational for crossing beginning on June 15. Both ends of the pontoon-bridge site are now on private property, but the next segment of this excursion will allow you to rejoin the Federal route of march on the other side of the river.

Lt. Gen. Ulysses S. Grant to Maj. Gen. Henry W. Halleck, Chief of Staff at Washington, 1:30 p.m., June 14, 1864

Our forces will commence crossing the James to-day. The enemy shows no signs yet of having brought troops to the south side of Richmond. I will have Petersburg secured, if possible, before they get there in much force. Our movement from Cold Harbor to the James River has been made with great celerity and so far without loss of accident. [*O.R.*, XL, part 1, p. 12.]

Report of Maj. Gen. Winfield S. Hancock, USA, commanding Second Corps, Army of the Potomac

The troops reached Wilcox's Landing, on the James River, at 5.30 p.m. on the 13th. Myself and the officers of my staff were busily engaged during that night and the following day and night in conducting the embarkation of the troops and material of my corps, which were all safely landed on the south bank of the James, at Wind-Mill Point, near upper landing, at an early hour on the morning of the 15th. My headquarters remained on the north bank of the river until the troops had crossed, communication being kept up by the signal telegraph.

I had been directed by General Meade on the evening of the 14th to hold my troops in readiness to move, and informed that it was probable I would be instructed to march toward Petersburg, and that rations for my command would be sent me from City Point. Later in the evening the following instructions reached me from General Meade:

> General Butler has been ordered to send to you at Wind-Mill Point 60,000 rations; so soon as they are received and issued you will move your command by the most direct route to Petersburg, taking up a position where the City Point railroad crosses Harrison's Creek, where we now have a work.
>
> On receipt of the above instructions I at once sent my chief commissary to the south bank of the James to receive and issue the expected rations. [*O.R.*, XL, part 1, p. 303.]

Daily memoranda taken at headquarters, Second Corps, continued

June 14, 1864.—11.10 a.m., Birney's troops commenced moving on board the transports and crossing James River, disembarking at Windmill Point and at upper landing. Crossing of troops (infantry and artillery) continued all day and night, Gibbon's division following, Birney's and [Gen. Francis C.] Barlow's following Gibbon's. Considering the facilities at hand the troops have been transported across the stream with remarkable promptitude and success. [*O.R.*, XL, part 1, p. 316.]

Journal of Major General Warren, continued

Tuesday, June 14.—Marched to Saint Charles [Charles City] Court-House. Took up position, built bridges, &c. Hancock ferrying across Chickahominy; too wide for wagon-train bridge. Lost a day by it.

Wednesday, June 15.—We lay all day in camp. Pontoon bridge built last night across the James River.

Thursday, June 16.—Commenced moving at 2 a.m. All the

corps ferried over at 1 p.m. Artillery and wagons all crossed on the pontoon bridge. Went on board *Atlanta*. Command marched toward Petersburg. Marched nearly all night and reached there before morning. [*O.R.*, XL, part 1, p. 453.]

Daily memoranda taken at headquarters, Second Corps, continued

June 15, 1864.—5 a.m., the last regiment of the corps has just been landed on the south side of the James. The whole corps now ready to move when ordered. We remained from 5 a.m. until 10.30 a.m. waiting for arrival of 60,000 rations of the corps which General Butler was to send from City Point. Orders received in the mean time to march toward Petersburg after we had received rations. As no rations arrived the head of the column (General Birney's division) moved out in direction of Petersburg at 10.30 a.m., or rather in the direction of Harrison's Creek, near Petersburg. [*O.R.*, XL, part 1, p. 316.]

Drive back out to Route 5, turning left. Drive 7 miles and turn left onto State Route 106, crossing the James River over the Benjamin Harrison Memorial Bridge. On the south side of the river, turn left onto U.S. Route 10, James River Drive. After 4.1 miles, turn right onto Route 609, Old Stage Road. As you make this turn, you are rejoining the Federal route of march from the bridge and ferry sites to Petersburg. At 5.6 miles, turn left onto Route 156 Bypass, Ruffin Road. At the turn you will notice an interpretive marker describing the September 1864 "Beefsteak Raid," in which Confederate cavalry under Maj. Gen. Wade Hampton captured hundreds of head of Union beef cattle. After 1.1 miles, continue straight ahead as Route 156 Bypass becomes Route 106, Courthouse Road. In another 1.5 miles you will pass through Prince George Court House. Note your mileage as you pass the courthouse, continuing on Route 106 as it passes under I-295. At 0.6 mile past the courthouse, you will reach a traffic circle. Make the first right onto Route 634, Allin Road, and then bear right after 0.5 mile as the road becomes Route 630, Jefferson Park Road. In 2.8 miles, turn right onto Oaklawn Boulevard and travel 0.7 mile, passing under I-295 once again. Turn left onto Colonial Corner Drive, and make an immediate right into the convenience-store parking lot in front of you. Leave your vehicle here, cross the street (minding traffic), and stand in the nearby trees with a view toward the I-295 overpass.

STOP 5: BAYLOR FARM

Facing west toward I-295, you are looking at the wartime site of the Baylor Farm. The modern highway interchange and other suburban sprawl has obliterated any trace of the farm, but you may discern a slight rise in the ground beyond the overpass, on top of which the Confederates placed their defenses. Here a small detachment of Confederate cavalry and artillery under Brig. Gen. *James Dearing* was charged with delaying the Union advance on Petersburg. The lead elements of Smith's Eighteenth Corps, composed primarily of the U.S. Colored Troops of Brig. Gen. Edward Hinks's division, reached this point early on June 15. Repeated attacks scattered the Confederate defenders, but *Dearing* gained valuable hours during which *Lee* began to reinforce the Petersburg defenses. At the same time, Maj. Gen. Winfield Scott Hancock's Second Corps was at the center of what would become a growing controversy: Grant's and Meade's failure to follow their successes on June 15 with the immediate capture of Petersburg.

Grant's efforts to screen his movement south of the James worked virtually to perfection and, when combined with other moves in central and western Virginia, placed *Lee* under extreme pressure. Sheridan's cavalry raid into Louisa County threatened the Virginia Central Railroad, forcing a response by a Confederate mounted force under Maj. Gen. *Wade Hampton*; the resulting loss of cavalry did not help *Lee's* efforts to figure out what his opponent was doing. Farther west, a Federal raiding force under Maj. Gen. David Hunter threatened the vital Confederate supply depot at Lynchburg. *Lee* was forced to dispatch Gen. *Jubal A. Early* with 8,000 men of his Second Corps to deal with the threat. Even while Gen. *Pierre G. T. Beauregard* opposed the initial Federal attacks on Petersburg with his local defense forces, *Lee* was unable to move the bulk of his army south of the James because he was unsure of Grant's ultimate objective.

Report of Major General Burnside, continued

The corps was concentrated near Jordan's house, where it halted till the road was cleared of the Sixth Corps trains, when it moved out by way of Vaiden's, Clopton's, and Tyler's Mill to its position on the right of the Sixth Corps, our right resting near the Jones house, on an arm of the James River, the line extending in a northwesterly direction until it joined the line of the Sixth Corps. This position was fortified.

At about 8 p.m. on the 15th we started under orders to reenforce Generals Hancock and Smith near Petersburg, crossing the James River on the pontoon bridge above Fort Powhatan. We marched up the road nearest the river until we reached the Old Court-House, when we turned to the left, our advance reaching a position occupied by our troops about 10 a.m. on the 16th. [*O.R.*, XL, part 1, p. 522.]

Report of Maj. Gen. William F. Smith, USA, commanding Eighteenth Corps, Army of the James

About 4 a.m. the head of my column left Broadway. Near Baylor's farm our cavalry came upon the enemy's artillery and infantry. General [August V.] Kautz being unable to dislodge them, General Hinks was ordered to make the attack. The rifle-pits were gallantly carried by General Hinks' command and one piece of artillery captured. My command was then ordered to move forward according to the original orders of the day, and got into position around the enemy's works at Jordan's house around 1.30 p.m. I found the enemy's artillery so arranged as to have a cross-fire on most of my entire front, and some batteries which I had ordered into position were immediately driven out by enemy's fire. As no engineer officer was ordered to report to me I was obliged to make the reconnaissance in person, and some time was unnecessarily wasted on that account, but not till about 7 p.m. were the final preparations completed for the assault. In about twenty minutes the works at Jordan's house and on its left were carried by the divisions of Generals [William T. H.] Brooks and Hinks, capturing guns, caissons, horses, ammunition, colors, camp and garrison equipage, and intrenching tools and prisoners. Some heavy profile works in rear of the line captured still keeping up a galling fire I ordered the colored troops to carry them by assault. This was gallantly done. About this time I learned that General Martindale, on my right, with Stannard's brigade in advance, had carried the enemy's works between Jordan's house and the Appomattox, capturing two pieces of artillery, with teams, caissons, &c., complete. By this time darkness had set in, and having learned some time before that re-enforcements were rapidly coming in from Richmond, and deeming that I held important points of the enemy's line of works, I thought it prudent to make no farther advance, and made my dispositions to hold what I already had. About midnight Gibbon's division, of the Second Corps, came up to relieve the part of my too extended lines. [*O.R.*, XL, part 1, p. 705.]

Report of Brig. Gen. Edward W. Hinks, USA, commanding Third Division, Eighteenth Corps

At about 1 a.m. of the 15th instant I had moved [Col. Samuel] Duncan's brigade consisting of the Fourth, Fifth and Sixth and Twenty-second Regiments U.S. Colored Infantry; [Col. John H.] Holman's (Provisional) brigade, consisting of the First U.S.

Colored Infantry and one wing of the Fifth Massachusetts Cavalry (dismounted); [Lt. Col. James R.] Angel's battery and [Capt. Francis C.] Choate's battery . . . to the immediate vicinity of Broadway, and at 2 a.m. reported in person to Maj. Gen. W. F. Smith at Broadway. In accordance with his orders I concentrated my command in the immediate vicinity of Cope's house, below Broadway, on the road from City Point to Petersburg, at about daylight, with directions to take my place in column immediately following Kautz's cavalry. . . .

About 5 o'clock, General Kautz's cavalry having passed, my division was ordered into column and proceeded as far as the railroad, when its march was obstructed by a halt of the cavalry, and sharp firing of musketry and artillery was heard toward the front. I immediately make a personal reconnaissance and found that the enemy had opened fire from a position in Baylor's field, which commanded the road, as it debouched from the wood and swamp near Perkinson's Saw Mill, and that the head of the cavalry column had been driven in. Having reported the state of affairs to General Smith, I was ordered to deploy in two lines of battle, with skirmishers in front, and force a passage of the swamp. Duncan's brigade was formed on the first line, Holman's in the second. Considerable delay was occasioned by the difficulty in getting the Fifth Massachusetts Cavalry into line by reason of its awkwardness in maneuver, it being composed of new recruits, and drilled only in Cooke's single rank cavalry formation, which entirely unfitted it to act as infantry in line. The lines, however, being formed, I ordered an advance. . . . The enemy was found to be in a hastily constructed work, occupying a very strong position in Baylor's field, with four pieces of artillery and some force of infantry in the field-works, and two pieces of artillery, with supports, upon the crest of the hill to the right. The distance from the edge of the woods to the works was about 400 yards over open, rising ground, which was speedily overcome, when the enemy fled toward Petersburg, leaving in our hands one 12-pounder gun. This line was carried at a little later than 8 a.m. About 9 a.m. I renewed my march (Colonel Holman's command in advance) by the road from the City Point road to the Jordan Point road. Having reached the Jordan Point road, I turned to the right and again met the enemy's pickets on Bailey's Creek. . . . This position was gained at about 11 a.m. . . . The enemy kept up an unremitting and very accurate and severe fire of artillery upon my position from the batteries now known as Batteries Nos. 6, 7, 8, 9, and 10. At about 5 o'clock I was informed by General Smith that he intended to charge the works with the skirmish line, and directed me to cause the proper disposition to be made to advance as soon as General Brooks' line commenced to advance. . . .

In the gallant and soldierly deportment of the troops engaged on the 15th instant under varying circumstances; the celerity with which they moved to the charge; the steadiness and coolness exhibited by them under heavy and long-continued fire; the impetuosity with which they sprang to the assault; the patient endurance of wounds, we have a sufficient proof that colored men, when properly officered, instructed, and drilled, will make most excellent infantry of the line, and may be used as such soldiers to great advantage. [*O.R.*, XL, part 1, pp. 721–723.]

Report of Major General Hancock, continued

About 4 a.m. on the 15th I wrote to General [Seth] Williams, assistant adjutant-general of the Army of the Potomac, that all of my troops, save one regiment of infantry and four batteries, were disembarked on the south side of the James, but the rations which I had been informed I would receive from City Point had not arrived, and that I feared that a good deal of time would be required to issue them when they came. About 6.30 a.m. I again reported to General Williams that no rations had arrived.

I delayed the order for my troops to march until 9 a.m., waiting to receive the rations from City Point, but as they did not arrive I gave the order by signal telegraph for the head of the column to move. . . . The column did not get in motion until 10.30 a.m. I notified the commanding general that the expected rations had not arrived, and that I had given orders for my troops to move at once; this order was approved, and I was instructed to push forward to the position designated for my command behind Harrison's Creek. Lieutenant-Colonel [Charles H.] Morgan, my chief of staff, was directed to remain with General Birney to conduct the march of the column. He was furnished with a map from headquarters of the army, on which our position behind Harrison's Creek was marked—by the map about four miles from Petersburg, and between that place and City Point. It is proper to say in this connection that it afterward appeared my orders were based on incorrect information, and the position I was ordered to take did not exist as it was described on my instructions; Harrison's

Creek proved to be inside the enemy's lines and not within miles
of where it was laid down on the map which I was furnished to
guide me. The map was found to be utterly worthless, the only
roads laid down on it being widely out of the way. . . . None of
the inhabitants could or would give any information concerning
the location of this [Harrison's] creek. . . . At 5.30 p.m., as the
column neared Old Court-House, Birney being about one mile
distant, a dispatch from General Grant, addressed to General Gibbon or any division commander of the Second Corps, reached me.
This dispatch directed all haste to be made in getting up to the
assistance of General Smith, who it stated had attacked Petersburg
and carried the outer works in front of that city. A few moments
later a note from General Smith was delivered to me by one of his
staff, which informed me that he (General Smith) was authorized
by Lieutenant-General Grant to call upon me for assistance and
requesting me to come up as rapidly as possible. Fortunately these
dispatches were received just when the head of Birney's division
was passing a country road leading directly toward Petersburg,
and the column (Birney's and Gibbon's troops) was turned in
that direction. No time had been lost on the march during the day
although it was excessively hot. The road was covered with clouds
of dust, and but little water was found on the route, causing severe
suffering among the men.

I desire to say here that the messages from Lieutenant-
General Grant and from General Smith, which I received between
5 and 6 p.m. on the 15th, were the first and only intimations I had
that Petersburg was to be attacked that day. . . .

My troops received no rations until the 16th, when they occupied the works in front of Petersburg, the rations having been
sent to City Point. I spent the best hours of the day on the 15th in
marching by an incorrect map in search of a designated position,
which, as described, was not in existence or could not be found.
[*O.R.*, XL, part 1, pp. 303–305.]

Narrative of Gen. Pierre G. T. Beauregard, CSA, commanding Department of North Carolina and Southern Virginia [and Defenses of Petersburg]

The Confederate forces opposed to Smith's corps on the 15th
of June consisted of the 26th, 34th, and 46th Virginia regiments,
the 64th Georgia, the 23d South Carolina, [Lt. Col. *Fletcher H.*]
Archer's militia, [*Cullen A.*] *Battle's* and [*William Henry*] *Wood's*

battalions, [Capt. *Nathaniel A.*] *Sturdivant's* battery, *Dearing's* small command of cavalry, and some other transient forces, having a real effective for duty of 2200 only. These troops occupied the Petersburg line on the left from Battery No. 1 to what was called Butterworth's Bridge, toward the right, and had to be so stationed as to allow but one man for every 4½ yards. From that bridge to the Appomattox—a distance of fully 4½ miles—the line was defenseless.

Early in the morning—at about 7 o'clock—General *Dearing*, on the Broadway and City Point roads, reported his regiment engaged with a large force of the enemy. The stand made by our handful of cavalry, near their breastworks, was most creditable to themselves and to their gallant commander, and the enemy's ranks, at that point, were much thinned by the accurate firing of the battery under [Capt. *Edward*] *Graham*. But the weight of numbers soon produced its almost inevitable result, and, in spite of the desperate efforts of our men, the cavalry breastworks were flanked and finally abandoned by us, with the loss of one howitzer. Still, *Dearing's* encounter with the enemy, at that moment and on that part of the field, was of incalculable advantage to the defenders of our line, inasmuch as it afforded time for additional preparation and the distribution of new orders by *Wise.* [Robert Underwood Johnson and Clarence Clough Buell, eds., *Battles and Leaders of the Civil War,* 4 vols. (New York: The Century Company, 1884–1887), volume IV, p. 540.]

Gen. Robert E. Lee to Gen. Pierre G. T. Beauregard, *10:30 a.m., June 16, 1864*

Your dispatch of 9.45 received. It is the first that has come to hand. I do not know the position of Grant's army, and cannot strip north bank of James River. Have you not force sufficient? [Dowdey and Manarin, eds., *Wartime Papers of Robert E. Lee,* p. 784.]

Gen. Robert E. Lee to General Beauregard, *6 a.m., June 17, 1864*

I am delighted at your repulse of the enemy. Endeavor to recover your lines. Can you ascertain anything of Grant's movements? I am cut off now from all information. [Dowdey and Manarin, eds., *Wartime Papers of Robert E. Lee,* p. 787.]

If you wish to continue your tour by examining the rest of the events of June 15, 1864, return to your vehicle and turn right onto Colonial Corner Drive, then

immediately left onto one-way westbound Woodlawn Street, which rejoins Oaklawn Boulevard (Route 36). Continue 2.7 miles on Oaklawn Boulevard until you
see the exit to Petersburg National Battlefield on your right. Take the exit, pass
through the kiosk, and proceed to the parking area. The Visitor Center serves as
the starting point for the excursions that cover the fighting within the present-
day boundaries of the Petersburg National Battlefield's Eastern Front Unit. Turn
to page 9 to continue your study of the events of June 15–18, 1864.

If you wish to visit City Point instead, turn left onto Colonial Corner Drive
and left onto one-way eastbound Oaklawn Boulevard for 2.9 miles; the street
becomes Winston Churchill Drive on the way. At the T intersection, turn left onto
Randolph Road, and proceed 0.6 mile to Broadway, crossing the City Point Railroad. Turn right, and take East Broadway for 0.6 mile. Turn left onto Cedar Lane,
and proceed 0.4 mile to the parking area for City Point Unit–Petersburg National
Battlefield on the left.

EXCURSION 2
CITY POINT

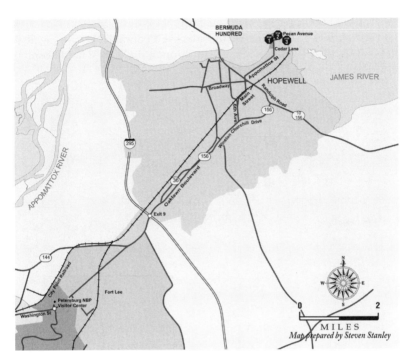

City Point overview

During the 1864–1865 Richmond-Petersburg Campaign, Lt. Gen. Ulysses S. Grant made his headquarters at City Point. Located near the confluence of the James and Appomattox Rivers, about 8 miles from the Union front lines, the property at the tip of the peninsula had been in the Eppes family for more than 225 years by the time of the Civil War. In 1860 the house in front of you was the center of a plantation of over 2,000 acres on which more than a hundred slaves lived and worked. The larger community of City Point (now Hopewell) at the beginning of the Civil War consisted of about twenty-five houses, five wharves, and the railroad that linked it with Petersburg.

In the months that followed Grant's arrival on June 15, 1864, a great supply depot grew up around City Point, and it became one of the busiest ports in the world. A massive bakery daily turned out about 100,000 rations of bread that were transported to the troops on the front lines by a special military railroad, while hundreds of ships brought supplies from the North. In addition to housing the headquarters of the commanding general of all of the Union armies and the depots that sustained the massive Federal operation against Petersburg, City Point was also the location of the largest field hospital in the country.

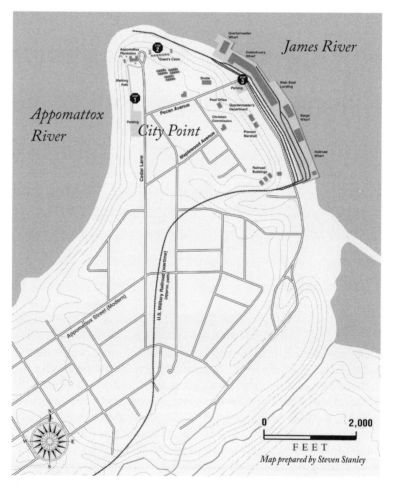

City Point, 1864–1865

To reach City Point from the Petersburg National Battlefield Visitor Center, drive out of the parking lot and cross the bridge over Route 36. When you come to a fork at 0.2 mile, take the left-hand road onto eastbound Route 36 (Oaklawn Boulevard). Proceed 5.1 miles on Route 36 (on the way it becomes Winston Churchill Drive [Route 156]) until you come to a light. Turn left at the light onto South 6th Avenue, drive 0.7 mile to Broadway, and turn right. Proceed 0.2 mile, turn left onto Main Street, and continue on Main until it becomes Appomattox Street. After 0.7 mile, turn left onto Cedar Lane, and proceed 0.3 mile to the parking area for the Grant's Headquarters at City Point Unit of Petersburg National Battlefield on the left. After parking, walk along the path that runs along the bluff of the Appomattox River to a point overlooking the bay.

STOP 1: APPOMATTOX OVERLOOK

Of the numerous facilities for treating sick and wounded Federal soldiers that were built during the war, the largest and perhaps the finest was the Depot Field Hospital at City Point. Located just across the bay from Appomattox Plantation on the modern site of John Randolph Medical Center, it covered nearly 200 acres and was capable of handling up to 10,000 patients, with the efforts of army surgeons supported by civilian organizations such as the U.S. Sanitary Commission and U.S. Christian Commission.

CITY POINT HOSPITAL

Report of Surg. Edward B. Dalton, USA, Chief Medical Officer of Depot Field Hospital

On the morning of the 14th [June] a large proportion of the medical officers, the commissary, and the quartermaster, together with the purveying department and most of the hospital property, started down the Pamunkey. . . . We reached Jamestown Island on the afternoon of the 15th. Here orders were received . . . to proceed to City Point and there establish the hospital depot.

On the 16th, upon reaching the pontoon bridge near Fort Powhatan, we were delayed, succeeded in getting above the bridge by means of a small boat and thence by tug to City Point on the 18th, just as a train of ambulances arrived, loaded with wounded from the assault upon Petersburg. These were at once attended to, and transportation to Washington procured for them, hospital transports being loaded for the purpose by Surgeon [Charles] McCormick, U.S. Army, medical director of the Department of Virginia and North Carolina. The hospital property was at once unloaded and conveyed to the site selected and there put in readiness as rapidly as possible for the reception of wounded, who still continued to come in large numbers. This site, which is the one still occupied, is located to the south of the James River, one mile from City Point toward Petersburg. It is situated upon a broad plain extending from the Petersburg pike to the high bluffs overlooking the basin of the Appomattox, just at the junction of the latter river with the James. The plan of the encampment, which still remains essentially unaltered, was mainly devised by Doctor [Alonzo J.] Phelps. Some irregularities occurred in its execution, in consequence of the embarrassment of laying out the camp and erecting tents at the same time that the presence of wounded called constantly for professional labor. By means of pontoons two temporary wharves were soon constructed at a convenient point a short distance up the Appomattox. These were for the exclusive use of the hospital, and were used respectively for the landing and issuing of supplies and for transferring wounded to the hospital transports. The services of the transports were immediately, and for a time, constantly in demand. Two of these, the *Connecticut* and *State of Maine*, were of sufficiently light draught to be able to come alongside the wharf. The *De Molay* could reach the mouth of the Appomattox and was there loaded by means of lighters. The *Atlantic, Baltic,* and *Western Metropolis* came no farther than Fort Monroe or Newport News and were there loaded by transfer from the *Connecticut* and *State of Maine.* All rendered most efficient service, especially the *Connecticut,* which has been throughout the campaign remarkable for the promptness and energy displayed in her management.

The purveying department met all necessary demands with promptness and liberality. Nothing really essential to the care of the wounded was wanting. Bedsacks and blankets were supplied without stint, although for a time bedsteads were dispensed with, excepting in the severer cases, a large proportion of the patients being placed upon sacks amply filled with straw and arranged upon the ground beneath the tents. None were without shelter. Drugs and dressings in abundance, hospital stores, ice, and even delicacies were constantly issued; cooking stoves, caldrons, and portable ovens were on hand in sufficient quantity for any emergency. Requisitions received prompt and full attention at all times. But a short time elapsed before the arrival of an abundant supply of bedsteads, when sheets and pillow-cases were at once made use

of in all cases where they could essentially add to the comfort of
the patient. The capacity of the hospital was rapidly increased until it became capable of accommodating 10,000 patients. At first
these were mainly wounded, but as the season advanced and the
prolonged duty in the trenches told upon the men, the proportion of sick became greater. Each successive engagement would
fill the beds with wounded, but these, especially the severely hurt,
were sent north as rapidly as possible, while the sick, as a general
rule, were removed only when the character of the case rendered
a change of climate essential to recovery.

The entire encampment now covers an area of some 200
acres and is composed of 1,200 hospital tents. The latter were
originally pitched in groups composed of two tents and an intervening fly, and placed end to end. These groups are arranged in
rows, side by side, divided by lateral interspace of fifteen feet in
width between the individual groups. The ends of the groups abut
upon streets sixty feet wide, running parallel with the river and
meeting at right angles a main avenue 180 feet in width, which
extends from the verge of the bluff directly through the center
of the camp to the Petersburg pike. Since the approach of cool
weather an entire tent has been substituted for the intervening
fly in each group.

Shortly after the establishment of the hospital at this point,
works were constructed by the quartermaster for supplying the
encampment with water. Two steam-engines of four horse-power
each were placed at the foot of the bluff at the edge of the river,
whence they force water into a tank capable of containing 6,000
gallons, which is raised thirty feet above the level of the bluff and
supported upon a strong wooden trestle-work. From this tank a
conducting pipe of two inches diameter descends to the ground
and is then conducted at a depth of eighteen inches below the
surface along the main avenue. At right angles to this main pipe
smaller ones diverge at intervals and enter the various divisions
of the hospital, where at the extremity of each pipe is a hydrant.
These works, which were completed on the 6th of July, have proved
entirely satisfactory. An abundance of river water was thus supplied
for laundry, bathing, and other coarser purposes. Wells were dug in
various parts of the hospital, and these, with numerous springs in
the vicinity, afforded a plentiful supply for drinking and cooking.

For several weeks subsequent to the arrival at City Point no
rain fell and the accumulation of dust became a source of the

greatest discomfort. Bodies of troops and wagons were constantly passing along the main road, and the dust thus disturbed was borne in dense clouds over and through the camp, filling the tents and penetrating even the bedclothes. This matter was represented at the Surgeon-General's Office and sprinkling carts applied for. Eight of these were promptly sent down from Washington and were immediately and constantly made use of. They afforded great relief not only in subduing the dust but also in moderating the intense heat of the atmosphere. As an additional means high, broad bowers were built continuously along the ends of the tents on each side of the streets. For purposes of drainage each group of tents was surrounded by a trench eight inches in depth. From these trenches the water is conducted into ditches which run parallel to and to each side of the streets, and terminate by means of still larger ones in various irregular ravines with which the ground is broken and which descend rapidly to the river. This system has proved entirely effectual.

It is impossible, by merely quoting the register, to convey an accurate idea of the number of sick and wounded who have received attention in this hospital. At Fredericksburg, at White House, and still later at City Point, hundreds passed through under circumstances which rendered it impracticable to register their names or even to accurately estimate their number. These instances occurred during or immediately subsequent to an engagement, when the accumulation of wounded and the constant calls for professional labor sometimes made it necessary to transfer at once from the ambulances to the hospital transports. In fact, as I have already stated, so unremitting were the professional duties of the medical officers during the first fortnight at Fredericksburg, that it was impossible even to prepare morning reports, and it was not until the 16th of May that even a numerical report was attempted. From that date to the present daily reports have been forwarded, and they show that from the 16th of May, 1864, to October 31, 1864, there have been received into this hospital and retained here under treatment for at least forty-eight hours, 68,540 sick and wounded officers and men. Of these 51,313 have been transferred to the various U.S. general hospitals at the North, and 11,706 have been returned direct from this hospital to duty with their commands. One thousand five hundred and sixteen have died. A large number of the wounded had when received here already suffered amputation or other capital operations at the immediate front, while in a great many other cases similar interference was still necessary. The experience here has given the most convincing evidence in favor of primary operations in gunshot wounds.

The majority of the sick received during the summer have suffered from dysentery, diarrhea, and malarial fevers. A small proportion of cases of typhoid fever have occurred and a very few, comparatively, of pneumonia and milder diseases of the chest. The manifestations of malarial influences have, as a general rule, been of a mild character, and evidently owing in great measure to the prolonged exposure and hard service to which the men have been subjected in the trenches. In fact, very many of these do not properly come under the head of either of the recognized classes of malarious fever, but were rather cases of a depressed condition not ineptly expressed by the term malarial malaise. A large proportion of these recovered rapidly and entirely under the influence of rest, cleanliness, and good nourishment, together with moderate administration of quinine and iron. A number of cases have arisen within the limits of the encampment, but not in sufficient number or of sufficient severity to impair the efficiency of the hospital or to throw any doubt upon the propriety of its establishment and continuance. On the contrary, the numbers who have recovered and been returned to duty within a few weeks after their admission, and without their removal to a distance from the seat of war, have proved this site a most eligible one. [U.S. War Department, *The War of the Rebellion: A Compilation of the Official Records of the Union and Confederate Armies*, 70 vols. in 128 parts and index (Washington, D.C.: Government Printing Office, 1880–1901), series 1, volume XL, part 1, pp. 269–272. Hereafter cited as *O.R.*; all references are to series 1 unless otherwise noted.]

Narrative of Adelaide W. Smith, Army Nurse

The hospital was situated half a mile from General Grant's headquarters at City Point, at the junction of the James and Appomattox Rivers, and about eight miles from Petersburg front. The hospital camp, then under the charge of Surgeon Edward Dalton and medical staff, was laid out with great precision. This field hospital was divided into the 9th, 2d, 6th, 5th corps, and corps d'Afric, and these again into divisions, avenues, and streets at right angles,—numbered and lettered. There were many

Post Hospital, City Point (USAMHI)

thousands of sick and wounded in these wards, nine thousand or
more at a time, I believe.

Convalescent soldiers did police, ward, nurse and kitchen
duty. There were hundreds of wards with stockade sides, covered
with canvas roofs upheld in the usual manner by ridge and tent
poles, each containing probably fifty or more bunks or cots. A
perfect system of order and policing by convalescent men was enforced, and not a particle of refuse or any scrap was allowed to
lie for a moment upon the immaculate streets or avenues of the
"Sacred Soil," which was generally beaten hard and dry, though
in wet weather this was a problem to try men's souls and women's
soles too. At such times we were obliged to wade through nearly a
foot of liquid mud, occasionally sticking fast till pulled out some-
how, perhaps with the loss of a high rubber boot.

The wards were wonders of cleanliness, considering the disad-
vantages of field life, and even at that time sanitation was of a high
order and, to a great degree, prevented local diseases. Men nurses,
soldiers unfit for active duty, took pleasure in fixing up their wards
with an attempt at ornamentation, when allowed. These men well
deserved their pay, as they worked cheerfully for the government
and for their sick comrades, doing their part faithfully during the
devastations of war. They were as much needed and as necessary
as their heroic comrades in the field. I never knew of one of these
faithful, hard-working amateur nurses being guilty of neglect or

unkindness, though chronic growlers and irritable sick men were often exasperating to the nurse's unfailing care and patience. They frequently conveyed some interdicted luxuries from the sutler, or extra rations, to make life more endurable and comfortable for the invalids. This was usually winked at by their officers. They were generally appreciated, and little dissatisfaction or complaint could have been expressed. Perfect discipline and sympathy seemed to prevail.

During my year in this Field Hospital I did not hear of any enforcement of severe punishment, but I remember, one day, while riding outside of hospital lines, past a post or camp in the woods, seeing in the distance a poor fellow hanging by his thumbs to the branch of a tree. It was said by the men of his regiment that "the fellow ought to have been hanged."

Just across the road on one side of the hospital was a row of State Agency tents. Larger tents of the Sanitary Commission,— that magnanimous gift of the people that so often, even in the far South, so nobly supplemented the regular hospital work and supplies, sometimes even with its own transports and its own official corps of workers,—headed this row. In the middle of the Agency row were the tents of the Christian Commission, supported chiefly by churches from all over the Northern States. They had built a large rough wooden structure where regular services were held on Sundays and on many evenings during the week, to the great relief and enjoyment of weary men seeking to find a word of hope and comfort, and a change from the monotony of ward life. Many ministers and other speakers came to look over the work, and many of them were very interesting and earnest.

Along this extensive row of tents were the Agencies, supported by the liberality of their several States, which also supplemented the government in giving special care to their own individual men. Capable men and refined women workers toiled uncomplainingly to make hospital life more endurable for the sick.

From Petersburg front sick and wounded were daily sent to the hospital, often on rough flat sand cars, over badly laid shaking tracks, being brought as hastily as possible that they might receive proper care and help. The sight of these cars, loaded with sufferers as they lay piled like logs, waiting their turn to be carried to the wards,—powder-stained, dust-begrimed, in ragged torn and blood-stained uniforms, with here and there a half-severed limb dangling from a mutilated body,—was a gruesome, sickening one, never to be forgotten, and one which I tried not to see when unable to render assistance.

Not only were the sick and wounded from nearby brought there, but large numbers came from more southerly points of the army of the Potomac. Many seriously or permanently injured were sent here to wait until able to be forwarded to Washington. Some came en route on sick furloughs, or to be discharged, or when fit returned to their regiments in the field. Every grade of suffering or weariness found temporary shelter and care here. All incurable cases were hurried forward as soon as possible to make room for the multitude still coming.

I found plenty of work to do, and attached myself to the Ninth Corps especially, though visiting all the wards and corps. I was invited by Mrs. Mayhew to work with her for some weeks in the Maine State Agency. While there I was asked later, in the absence of Miss [Helen L.] Gilson, of Lynn, Massachusetts, to take charge of the Corps d'Afric, but I soon found that the work was chiefly to look after refugee negroes, and to give them employment in laundry work, etc. Doctor Thomas Pooley was then in charge of that corps, and is now a distinguished oculist of Manhattan. I still see him, a very young man, resplendent in a new uniform with bright buttons, red sash, etc., as officer of the day.

Miss Gilson had come with Mr. [Frank B.] Fay, General Superintendent of the Sanitary Commission, in the field, and formerly Mayor of Chelsea, Massachusetts, and she chose to work for the Corps d'Afric. That was quite as well conducted as any other corps. Miss Gilson was a dainty young woman, and, while in camp, wore a short pretty dress of grey cloth and a white kerchief tastily arranged over her dark hair and one about her neck. She had a pure soprano voice, and frequently sang army songs and hymns to the men, making them quite happy, and with a sort of reverence, they seemed to find her an angel of peace. In her earnest devotion, Miss Gilson remained too long ministering to typhoid patients from whom she contracted the fever, and at last was compelled to leave her chosen work and go to her home, still hoping to recover and to return to the patients of her corps. Her strength was not equal to the waste of that burning fever, however, and she died in her early womanhood, a sacrifice to her benevolence and patriotism as truly and honorably as the men who died on the field of battle. [Adelaide W. Smith, *Reminiscences of an Army Nurse during the Civil War* (New York: Greaves Publishing, 1911), pp. 96–109.]

Continue walking toward the large house. This belonged to Dr. Richard Eppes, who at the beginning of the war volunteered his services to the Confederacy and by 1864 was working as a surgeon in one of the Confederate hospitals in Peters- burg. The house served as the headquarters for Quartermaster Rufus Ingalls and his staff during the operations against Richmond and Petersburg in 1864–1865, and ranger-guided tours are often available. There are also restrooms here. Upon reaching the opposite side of the house, facing the river, turn right and walk to the small wooden structure, Grant's Cabin, and upon reaching it turn left to face the river. Directly in front of you, you will see the James River as it flows to this point from Richmond and then continues to your right down to the Chesapeake Bay. Across the James to your left, you will see Bermuda Hundred at the tip of the peninsula formed by the confluence of the Appomattox and James.

STOP 2: GRANT'S CABIN

After establishing his headquarters at City Point in June 1864, Grant and his staff spent several months living out of tents set up on the grounds of Appomattox Manor. In November 1864 Grant's cabin, one of twenty-two that were built in this area to replace the tents, was constructed. Although simple and crude, the cabin was sturdy enough to see Grant through the winter of 1864–1865. In August 1865 it was relocated to Fairmount Park in Philadelphia and remained there for over a century. In 1983 the cabin returned to Appomattox Plantation,

Lt. Gen. Ulysses S. Grant and staff at City Point (USAMHI)

which the National Park Service had acquired few years earlier, and was reconstructed near its original site.

Narrative of Lt. Col. Horace Porter, USA, Aide-de-camp to Lt. Gen. Ulysses S. Grant, commanding Armies of the United States

The camp at City Point had now given place to winter quarters. . . . The tents, which were much worn, had become very uncomfortable as the cold weather set in; and they were removed, and log huts were erected in their stead. Each hut contained space enough for bunks for two officers, and had a small door in front, a window on each side, and an open fireplace at the rear end. General Grant's hut was as plain as the others, and was constructed with a sitting-room in front, and a small apartment used as a bedroom in rear, with a communicating door between them. An iron camp-bed, an iron wash-stand, a couple of pine tables, and a few common wooden chairs constituted the furniture. The floor was entirely bare. [Horace Porter, *Campaigning with Grant* (New York: Century, 1907), pp. 29–30.]

Narrative of Vice President Alexander Stephens, CSA

We were met on the evening of the same day, at that part of the lines at which we had, in the meantime, been notified to appear at 4 o'clock, by an escort under the conduct of Lieutenant-Colonel [Orville E.] Babcock of General Grant's staff, and were conveyed by railroad to City Point. Upon reaching that place we were immediately taken to the Head Quarters of the Commander-in-Chief. Here, for the first time, I met General Grant himself. . . . I was never so much disappointed in my life, in my previously formed opinions, of either the personal appearance or bearing of any one, about whom I had read and heard so much. The disappointment, moreover, was in every respect favorable and agreeable. I was instantly struck with the great simplicity and perfect naturalness of his manners, and the entire absence of everything like affectation, show, or even the usual military air or mien of men in his position. He was plainly attired, sitting in a log-cabin, busily writing on a small table, by a Kerosene lamp. It was night when we arrived. There was nothing in his appearance or surroundings which indicated his official rank. There were neither guards nor aids about him. Upon Colonel Babcock's rapping at his door, the response, "Come in," was given by himself, in a tone of voice, and with a cadence, which I can never forget.

His conversation was easy and fluent, without the least effort or restraint. In this, nothing was so closely noticed by me as the point and terseness with which he expressed whatever he said. He did not seem either to court or avoid conversation, but whenever he did speak, what he said was directly to the point, and covered the whole matter in a few words. I saw before being with him long, that he was exceedingly quick in perception, and direct in purpose, with a vast deal more of brains than tongue, as ready as that was at his command. . . . The more I became acquainted with him, the more I became thoroughly impressed with the very extraordinary combination of rare elements of character which he exhibited. During the time he met us frequently, and conversed freely upon various subjects. . . . He was, without doubt, exceedingly anxious for a termination of our war, and the return of peace and harmony throughout the country. It was through his instrumentality mainly, that Mr. Lincoln finally consented to meet us at Fortress Monroe. . . .

I will add: that upon the whole the result of this first acquaintance with General Grant . . . was, the conviction on my mind, that, taken all in all, he was one of the most remarkable men I had ever met with, and that his career in life, if his days should be prolonged, was hardly entered upon; that his character was not yet fully developed; that he himself was not aware of his own power, and that if he lived, he would, in the future, exert a controlling influence in shaping the destinies of this country, either for good or for evil. Which it would be, time and circumstances alone could disclose. That was the opinion of him then formed, and it is the same which has been uniformly expressed by me ever since. [Alexander H. Stephens, *A Constitutional View of the Late War between the States*, 2 vols. (Atlanta, Ga.: National Publishing, 1868–1870), volume II, pp. 596–599.]

During the nine months that Grant had his headquarters at City Point, President Abraham Lincoln visited him four times. Less than a week after the failure of the First Petersburg Offensive of June 15–18, Lincoln spent two days meeting with Grant and visiting troops. On July 31, 1864, Lincoln came down from Washington and spent the late morning and early afternoon talking with Grant about the command situation around Washington, D.C., in the aftermath of a Confederate offensive that reached the outskirts of the capital before being turned back at the Battle of Fort Stevens of July 11–12. On February 3, 1865,

Lincoln did not actually reach City Point but did use Grant's personal dispatch boat, the *River Queen*, for a meeting with representatives of the Confederate government. The longest of Lincoln's visits to City Point was his final one. He arrived at City Point late on March 24 and stayed in the area until April 8. During that time, he reviewed troops, met with his principal military commanders on board the *River Queen* to discuss how to handle the defeated Confederates, and visited both Richmond and Petersburg after they fell to Federal forces on April 3.

Narrative of Horace Porter, *continued*

On March 20 General Grant had telegraphed the President: "Can you not visit City Point for a day or two? I would like very much to see you, and I think the rest would do you good." This invitation was promptly accepted, and on the 24th word came that he was on his way up the James aboard the *River Queen*. About nine o'clock that evening the steamer approached the wharf, and General Grant, with those of us who were with him at the moment, including Robert Lincoln, went down to the landing and met the President, Mrs. [Mary Todd] Lincoln, their youngest son, "Tad," and several ladies who had come from Washington with the Presidential party. The meeting was very cordial. It lasted but a short time, however, as Mr. Lincoln and his family were evidently fatigued by the trip, and it was thought that they might want to retire at an early hour. His steamer was escorted by a naval vessel named the *Bat*, commanded by Captain John S. Barnes, an accomplished officer of the navy. . . .

About six o'clock the next morning, March 25, the camp was awakened and was soon all astir by reason of a message from the Petersburg front saying that the enemy had broken through our lines near Fort Stedman and was making a heavy attack. . . . The President, who was aboard his boat anchored out in the river, soon heard of the attack, and he was kept informed of the events which were taking place by his son Robert, who carried the news to him. . . . By half-past eight o'clock it was learned that our whole line had been recaptured, many prisoners taken, and that everything was again quiet. Mr. Lincoln now sent a telegram to the Secretary of War, winding up with the words: "Robert just now tells me there was a little rumpus up the line this morning, ending about where it began." . . .

General Grant proposed to the President that forenoon that he should accompany him on a trip to the Petersburg front. The invitation was promptly accepted, and several hours were spent in visiting the troops, who cheered the President enthusiastically. He was greatly interested in looking at the prisoners who had been captured that morning; and while at [Maj. Gen. George C.] Meade's headquarters, about two o'clock, sent a despatch to [Secretary of War Edwin M. Stanton] Stanton, saying: " . . . I have nothing to add to what General Meade reports, except that I have seen the prisoners myself, and they look like there might be the number he states—1600." The President carried a map with him, which he took out of his pocket and examined several times. He had the exact location of the troops marked on it, and he exhibited a singularly accurate knowledge of the various positions.

Upon the return to headquarters at City Point, he sat for a while by the camp-fire; and as the smoke curled about his head during certain shiftings of the wind, and he brushed it away from time to time by waving his right hand in front of his face, he entertained the general-in-chief and several members of the staff by talking in a most interesting manner about public affairs, and illustrating the subjects mentioned with his incomparable anecdotes.

At first his manner was grave and his language much more serious than usual. He spoke of the appalling difficulties encountered by the administration, the losses in the field, the perplexing financial problems, and the foreign complications; but said they had all been overcome by the unswerving patriotism of the people, the devotion of the loyal North, and the superb fighting qualities of the troops. . . . General Grant asked: "Mr. President, did you at any time doubt the final success of the cause ?" "Never for a moment," was the prompt and emphatic reply, as Mr. Lincoln leaned forward in his camp-chair and enforced his words by a vigorous gesture of his right hand. . . . The President now went aboard his boat to spend the night. The next morning he wandered into the tent of the headquarters telegraph operator, where several of us were sitting. . . .

Three tiny kittens were crawling about the tent at the time. The mother had died, and the little wanderers were expressing their grief by mewing piteously. Mr. Lincoln picked them up, took them on his lap, stroked their soft fur, and murmured: "Poor little creatures, don't cry; you'll be taken good care of," and turning to [Theodore S.] Bowers, said: "Colonel, I hope you will see that these poor little motherless waifs are given plenty of milk and treated kindly." Bowers replied: "I will see, Mr. President, that they are taken in charge by the cook of our mess, and are well cared for." Several times during his stay Mr. Lincoln was found fondling these kittens. He would wipe their eyes tenderly with his handkerchief, stroke their smooth coats, and listen to them purring their gratitude to him. It was a curious sight at an army headquarters, upon the eve of a great military crisis in the nation's history, to see the hand which had affixed the signature to the Emancipation Proclamation, and had signed the commissions of all the heroic men who served the cause of the Union, from the general-in-chief to the lowest lieutenant, tenderly caressing three stray kittens. It well illustrated the kindness of the man's disposition, and showed the childlike simplicity which was mingled with the grandeur of his nature. . . .

It was decided that upon this day [March 26] Mr. Lincoln would review a portion of the Army of the James on the north side of the James River, and Sheridan was invited to join the party from headquarters who were to accompany the President. The boat started from City Point at eleven o'clock. . . . The President was in a more gloomy mood than usual on the trip up the James. He spoke with much seriousness about the situation, and did not attempt to tell a single anecdote. As the boat passed the point where Sheridan's cavalry was crossing the river on the pontoon-bridge, he manifested considerable interest in watching the troopers, and addressed a number of questions to their commander. . . . Finally we reached our destination, but it was some minutes after the review had begun. Mrs. [Mary T.] Ord, and the wives of several of the officers who had come up from Fort Monroe for the purpose, appeared on horseback as a mounted escort to Mrs. [Mary Todd] Lincoln and Mrs. [Julia Boggs Dent] Grant. This added a special charm to the scene, and the review passed off with peculiar brilliancy. Mrs. Grant enjoyed the day with great zest, but Mrs. Lincoln had suffered so much from the fatigue and annoyances of her overland trip that she was not in a mood to derive much pleasure from the occasion. I made up my mind that ambulances, viewed as vehicles for driving distinguished ladies to military reviews, were not a stupendous success, and that thereafter they had better be confined to their legitimate uses of transporting the wounded and attending funerals.

Upon the return trip on the boat, the President seemed to recover his spirits. Perhaps the manifestation of strength on the part of the splendid Army of the James which he had witnessed at the review had served to cheer him up. . . . It was nearly dark when the party returned to City Point. After dinner the band was brought down to the steamboat, and a dance was improvised. Several ladies were aboard, and they and the officers danced till midnight. Neither the President nor General Grant joined, even in a square dance, but sat in the after part of the boat conversing. Sheridan stayed overnight at City Point, and started early in the morning for the cavalry headquarters on the Petersburg front. [Porter, *Campaigning with Grant*, pp. 402–416.]

During Lincoln's March–April 1865 visit, Maj. Gen. William T. Sherman, commander of Union forces then operating in the Carolinas, arrived on the scene to participate in a conference with Lincoln, Grant, and Rear Admiral David Porter.

Narrative of Horace Porter, continued

Sherman, in his correspondence, had intimated a desire to have a personal conference with his chief before the general movement of all the armies took place; and it was learned on March 27 that he had arrived at Fort Monroe, and was on his way up the James. . . . Late in the afternoon the *Russia*, a captured steamer, arrived with Sherman aboard, and General Grant and two or three of us who were with him at the time started down to the wharf to greet the Western commander.

Before we reached the foot of the steps, Sherman had jumped ashore and was hurrying forward with long strides to meet his chief. As they approached Grant cried out, "How d' you do, Sherman!" "How are you, Grant!" exclaimed Sherman; and in a moment they stood upon the steps, with their hands locked in a cordial grasp, uttering earnest words of familiar greeting. Their encounter was more like that of two school-boys coming together after a vacation than the meeting of the chief actors in a great war tragedy. Sherman walked up with the general-in-chief to headquarters, where Mrs. Grant extended to the illustrious visitor a cordial greeting. Sherman then seated himself with the others by the camp-fire, and gave a most graphic description of the stirring events of his march through Georgia. The story was the more charming from the fact that it was related without the manifestation of the slightest egotism. His field of operations had covered more than half of the entire theater of war; his orders always spoke with the true bluntness of the soldier; he had fought from valley depths to mountain heights, and marched from inland rivers to the sea. Never were listeners more enthusiastic; never was a speaker more eloquent. . . .

After the interview had continued nearly an hour, Grant said to Sherman: "I'm sorry to break up this entertaining conversation, but the President is aboard the *River Queen*, and I know he will be anxious to see you. Suppose we go and pay him a visit before dinner." "All right," cried Sherman; and the generals started down the steps, and were soon after seated in the cabin of the steamer with the President. In about an hour the two commanders came back and entered the general-in-chief's hut. . . . The next morning (March 28) Admiral Porter came to headquarters. . . . After spending a quarter of an hour together, General Grant said that the President was expecting them aboard his boat, and the two generals and the admiral started for the *River Queen*. No one accompanied them. . . . It was in no sense a council of war, but only an informal interchange of views between the four men who, more than any others, held the destiny of the nation in their hands. Upon the return of the generals and the admiral to headquarters, they entered the general-in-chief's hut. . . .

General Grant afterward told us the particulars of the interview. It began by his explaining to the President the military situation and prospects, saying that the crisis of the war was now at hand, as he expected to move at once around the enemy's left and cut him off from the Carolinas, and that his only apprehension was that [Gen. *Robert E.*] *Lee* might move out before him and evacuate Petersburg and Richmond, but that if he did there would be a hot pursuit. Sherman assured the President that in such a contingency his army, by acting on the defensive, could resist both [Gen. *Joseph E.*] *Johnston* and *Lee* till Grant could reach him, and that then the enemy would be caught in a vise and have his life promptly crushed out. Mr. Lincoln asked if it would not be possible to end the matter without a pitched battle, with the attendant losses and suffering; but was informed that that was a matter not within the control of our commanders, and must rest necessarily with the enemy. Lincoln spoke about the course which he thought had better be pursued after the war, and expressed an inclination to lean toward a generous policy. In speaking about the Confederate political leaders, he intimated, though he did not say so in express terms, that it would relieve the situation if they should escape to some foreign country. Sherman related many interesting incidents which occurred in his campaign. Grant talked less than any one present. The President twice expressed some apprehension about Sherman being away from his army; but Sherman assured him that he had left matters safe . . . and that he would start back himself that day.

That afternoon Sherman took leave of those at headquarters, and returned to his command. [Porter, *Campaigning with Grant*, pp. 417–424.]

To reach the next stop, turn right and walk over to the stairway and down to the shore of the James River. Then turn right, walk over to the dock at the end of Pecan Street, and face downriver.

STOP 3: THE WHARF

UNION LOGISTICS

Report of Brig. Gen. Rufus Ingalls, USA, Chief Quartermaster of Armies operating against Richmond

On reaching the James and coming in contact with the command of Major-General [Benjamin F.] Butler, I was announced on the 16th as chief quartermaster of "armies operating against Richmond," and immediately took post at City Point, which had been indicated the principal depot by Generals Grant and Meade.

After crossing the James over the pontoon bridge and by the ferries, the troops pressed forward into positions in front of Petersburg. The trains were placed in parks between the depot and those positions convenient to the railroad. Improvements were commenced at once to make the depot efficient and ample. Wharves and store-houses were constructed; the railroad to Petersburg was put in working order up to our lines; and supplies were brought to the depot in the required quantities, and issued. A uniform system of supply was put in force in both armies. [*O.R.*, XL, part 1, pp. 37–38.]

Report of Bvt. Maj. Gen. Rufus Ingalls, USA, Chief Quartermaster of Armies operating against Richmond

On the 1st of July, 1864, I was on duty at City Point, Va., at the headquarters of the lieutenant-general commanding the Armies of the United States, as chief quartermaster Armies operating against Richmond. These armies were composed of the Army of the Potomac and Army of the James, and our lines extended from the north side of the James River near Richmond to the southeast

City Point (USAMHI)

of Petersburg, a distance of over twenty-five miles, along the whole length of which was almost constant skirmishing night and day. . . . It became manifest that the defense of Richmond and Petersburg would be as protracted and stubborn as the resources and ability of the rebel commander could render it. I proceeded, therefore, under the written orders of the lieutenant-general, to create suitable depots for receiving and storing and issuing necessary supplies for the armies. The principal depot was established at City Point, on the James, at the mouth of the Appomattox, and was made one of the most . . . convenient, commodious, economical, and perfect ever provided for the supply of armies.

A secondary depot was kept up at Bermuda Hundred, and a still lesser one at Deep Bottom, more especially for the Army of the James. There was an average of some 40 steam-boats of all sorts including tugs, 75 sail vessels, and 100 barges daily in the James River, engaged in the transportation of supplies, and plying between that river and the Northern ports. With such facilities an army of 500,000 men could have been fully supplied within any reasonable distance of our base. I do not know the whole number of vessels employed in our supply. A daily line of boats was established between City Point and Washington for mail and passenger service. Besides this, our transport fleet was constantly engaged in bringing cavalry and artillery horses, mules, clothing, ammunition, subsistence, &c., and carrying back to Washington broken-down animals and other unserviceable property.

The depot was placed under the charge of Colonel P. P. Pitkin, who held the position of chief quartermaster of the depot until November 7, 1864, . . . and was succeeded by Colonel George W. Bradley. Both of the gentlemen were highly experienced, vigorous, and accomplished officers, and performed their very arduous and responsible duties with great credit to themselves and advantage to the service. The chief quartermaster at the principal depot always kept direct charge of the water transportation in James River. The other branches of the department, however, such as employes, forage, clothing, and railroad transportation, were in charge of subordinate quartermasters, selected for peculiar fitness, subject to the supervision of the chief depot quartermaster, who was required to report to me in writing every day, such as arrivals and clearances of shipping, receipts and issues of clothing, forage, &c. The chief quartermaster of each army was required to render, on or before the 25th of every month, a detailed, consolidated estimate, revised and approved by the army commander, of the supplies required for issue to the army the month following. Upon this data I prepared and submitted my estimate for the combined forces on or before the 1st of each month. This method had very many good results. It compelled all interested to ascertain the real wants of the troops, and to secure their regular and prompt supply. No quartermaster's stores were permitted to be sent to the armies, except over my signature. . . . My printed orders and circulars in the hands of my subordinates prescribed the manner in which they should perform their duties on all points where the regulations and general orders were silent. An extensive repair depot was established near City Point and placed in charge of Bvt. Lieutenant Colonel E. J. Strang, who received all serviceable animals and means of transportation from the Washington depot and made the issues to the armies, and who received from the armies unserviceable stock, wagons, ambulances, &c. and shipped back all that could not be repaired in his shops. He employed a force of about 1,800 carpenters, wheelwrights, blacksmiths, saddlers, corral hands, teamsters, laborers, and guards.

During the year ending June 30, 1865, he had repaired 3,653 army wagons and 2,414 ambulances. He had shod 19,618 horses and 31,628 mules. He received 27,116 serviceable horses and 10,893 mules, 436 wagons, and 36 ambulances. He received from the troops 16,344 unserviceable horses, 9,684 mules, 1,392 wagons, and 400 ambulances. He received also by the surrender of *Lee's* army 400 horses, 1,300 mules, 101 wagons, and 99 ambulances. He issued to the troops 31,386 horses, 18,891 mules, 1,536 wagons, and 370 ambulances. He sent back for recuperation and repair 13,575 horses, 4,313 mules, 743 wagons, and 36 ambulances, besides a great amount of harness and other property. I mention these items simply to convey an idea of the duties to be performed at depots. This was only one branch.

As soon as we occupied City Point, General [Daniel] McCallum, the able officer in charge of U.S. military railroads, had a strong construction corps on the spot prepared to rebuild the railroad up to our lines near Petersburg, and afterward as fast as the army gained ground to the southeast a temporary extension was laid close to our forces, until finally it extended to Hatcher's Run, a distance of about nineteen miles. Along this road were stations, as described in my last report on the Orange and Alexandria Railroad, where sidings and platforms were made for the prompt distribution of supplies to the different commands. This road saved much wear and tear of the wagon trains and enabled the lieutenant-general to concentrate troops rapidly at any desirable point. After the surrender of *Lee*, this road—the new portion— was dismantled and the material placed in depot to be disposed of in proper time. The great field hospital at City Point has been described in other reports. It was a very perfect one for the purpose. The medical officers in charge exercised great taste and judgment in its management. There was a somewhat similar field hospital for the Army of the James at Point of Rocks, on the Appomattox. The medical department of each army had its own wharves, storehouses, transports, and hospitals, under the control of its medical officers. The ordnance and subsistence departments had special wharves and store-houses, so also had General [Henry] Abbot, who had charge of siege guns and material for the entire line, all constructed by the quartermaster's department. . . .

On the 1st of July, 1864, there were on hand in the armies operating against Richmond means of land transportation as follows: 41,329 horses, 23,961 mules, 4,440 army wagons, 57 two-horse light wagons, and 915 ambulances.

At the beginning of the last campaign my returns show on hand as follows: 24,192 horses, 23,356 mules, 4,071 army wagons, 144 two-horse light wagons, and 907 ambulances.

After the close of the final campaign, say on May 1, 1865, the means of transportation were as follows: 33,948 horses, 25,093 mules, 4,207 army wagons, 140 two-horse light wagons, and 820 ambulances.

This property was used as prescribed in the orders of the lieutenant-general, a copy of which accompanied my last report, and most of it came to Washington with the last May and June, and was turned into the depot, as the troops were discharged, for final disposition. . . . This transportation was in most excellent condition and rendered services of vital importance on the last grand campaign from Petersburg and Richmond to Appomattox Court-House. There were many partial movements of the armies from July 1, 1864, to the opening of the last campaign, but they did not render many new dispositions necessary in our department as to the transportation. . . .

On the 9th of August near noon there occurred a fearful explosion in the midst of the City Point depot, killing and wounding some 250 employes and soldiers, throwing down over 600 feet in length of ware-houses, and tearing up some 180 linear feet of the wharf. It was found that a barge laden with ordnance stores had been blown up. Immense quantities of shot and shell were thrown into the air and much of it fell in the encampment of the lieutenant-general, wounding, however, only one, Colonel Babcock, of his staff. The lieutenant-general himself seems proof against the accidents of flood and field. It was assumed at the time that the explosion was the result of carelessness on the part of someone in or near the barge, but the developments made in the trial of the assassins of the late President would show that it was the dastardly work of that infernal rebel torpedo bureau in Richmond. The damages of the depot were soon repaired. . . . December 5 [7], the Fifth Corps, supported by the Ninth, made a march toward

Weldon. On such occasions the moving columns were generally directed in orders to be provided with a small stated allowance of subsistence, forage, and ammunition wagons and ambulances. The main trains remained parked in safe and convenient positions near the outer defenses of the City Point depot, but always loaded and fully prepared to move forward whenever and wherever needed. It was the rule, after having passed the James, in June, 1864, that each corps should generally be followed by its own trains.

On the evening of the 23rd of January, 1865, it was known that the rebels were apparently preparing to make a raid down the James with their fleet of iron-clads and wooden boats for the purpose of destroying our depots on the river, particularly that great one at City Point, where supplies had been accumulated and stores to meet the wants of the armies in case the James River and Northern ports should be closed by ice. The weather was already very inclement, and the Potomac and Delaware were then, or shortly afterwards, rendered entirely unnavigable by ice.

Early on the 24th the rebel fleet approached our obstructions, and one of the iron-clads passed them, but the one following got foul upon them. Our batteries made obstinate resistance, and blew up one of the smaller gun-boats. Our men even were led with great effort to the bank of the river, and poured volleys of musketry into the ram that had passed the obstructions. The navy at that point were not prepared at the moment for any effective resistance. Had the rebels persisted at that time they could, had they succeeded, have inflicted upon us incalculable losses, the result of which no one can pretend now to estimate; but most fortunately for us they abandoned the raid and retired to their former position. Two or three days later it was impossible for these boats to make a descent. The navy was thoroughly prepared, and I had sent, by order of the lieutenant-general, my aide-de-camp, Bvt. Captain J. W. French, Eighth Infantry, up the river with vessels laden with coal, who sunk two on the night of the 25th to fill up the gap made in the obstructions. He performed this service under the enemy's guns with great gallantry. . . .

I remained on duty at City Point, directing the reduction of employees, the discharge of transports, and the diminution of expenses generally in the quartermaster's department, until the 8th of May, when I received a telegraphic order from the lieutenant-general to report in person to him in Washington. [*O.R.*, LI, part 1, pp. 251–256.]

THE EXPLOSION AT CITY POINT, 9 AUGUST 1864

Perhaps the most spectacular episode in City Point's wartime experience came in August 1864, when a massive explosion, the work of Confederate saboteurs, occurred along the wharfs.

Lt. Gen. Ulysses S. Grant, commanding Armies of the United States, to Maj. Gen. Henry W. Halleck, Chief of Staff at Washington, August 9, 11, 1864

Five minutes ago an ordnance boat exploded, carrying lumber, grape, canister, and all kinds of shot over this point. Every part of the yard used as my headquarters is filled with splinters and fragments of shell. I do not know yet what the casualties are beyond my own headquarters. Colonel Babcock is slightly wounded in hand and 1 mounted orderly is killed and 2 or 3 wounded and several horses killed. The damage at the wharf must be considerable both in life and property. As soon as the smoke clears away I will ascertain and telegraph you. . . . The following is a list of casualties from the explosion of the ammunition barge on the 9th instant: Killed, 12 enlisted men, 2 citizen employed, 1 citizen not employed by Government, 28 colored laborers; wounded, 3 commissioned officers, 4 enlisted men, 15 citizen employed, 86 colored laborers. Besides these there were 18 others wounded, soldiers and citizens not belonging about the wharf. The damage to property was large, but I have not the means of reporting it. [*O.R.*, XLII, part 1, p. 17.]

Narrative of Horace Porter, continued

An event occurred in the forenoon of August 9 which looked for an instant as if the general-in-chief had returned to headquarters only to meet his death. He was sitting in front of his tent, surrounded by several staff-officers. General [George H.] Sharpe, the assistant provost-marshal-general, had been telling him that he had a conviction that there were spies in the camp at City Point, and had proposed a plan for detecting and capturing them. He had just left the general when, at twenty minutes to twelve, a terrific explosion shook the earth, accompanied by a sound which vividly recalled the Petersburg mine, still fresh in the memory of every one present. Then there rained down upon the party a terrific shower of shells, bullets, boards, and fragments of timber. The general was surrounded by splinters and various kinds of ammunition, but fortunately was not touched by any of the missiles. Babcock of the staff was slightly wounded in the right hand by a bullet, one mounted orderly and several horses were instantly killed, and three orderlies were wounded. In a moment all was consternation. On rushing to the edge of the bluff, we found that the cause of the explosion was the blowing up of a boat loaded with ordnance stores which lay at the wharf at the foot of the hill. Much damage was done to the wharf, the boat was entirely destroyed, all the laborers employed on it were killed, and a number of men and horses near the landing were fatally injured. The total casualties were forty-three killed and forty wounded. The general was the only one of the party who remained unmoved; he did not even leave his seat to run to the bluff with the others to see what had happened. Five minutes afterward he went to his writing-table and sent a telegram to Washington, notifying Halleck of the occurrence. No one could surmise the cause of the explosion, and the general appointed me president of a board of officers to investigate the matter. We spent several days in taking the testimony of all the people who were in sight of the occurrence, and used every possible means to probe the matter; but as all the men aboard the boat had been killed, we could obtain no satisfactory evidence. It was attributed by most of those present to the careless handling of the ammunition by the laborers who were engaged in unloading it; but there was a suspicion in the minds of many of us that it was the work of some emissaries of the enemy sent into the lines.

Seven years after the war, when I was serving with President Grant as secretary, a Virginian called to see me at the White House, to complain that the commissioner of patents was not treating him fairly in the matter of some patents he was endeavoring to procure. In the course of the conversation, in order to impress me with his skill as an inventor, he communicated the fact that he had once devised an infernal machine which had been used with some success during the war; and went on to say that it consisted of a small box filled with explosives, with a clockwork attachment which could be set so as to cause an explosion at any given time; that, to prove the effectiveness of it, he had passed into the Union lines in company with a companion, both dressed as laborers, and succeeded in reaching City Point, knowing this to be the base of supplies. By mingling with the laborers who were engaged in unloading the ordnance stores, he and his companion succeeded in getting aboard the boat, placing their infernal machine among the ammunition, and setting the clockwork so that the explosion would occur in half an hour. This enabled them to get to a sufficient distance from the place not to be suspected. I told him that his efforts, from his standpoint, had been eminently successful. At last, after many years, the mystery of the explosion was revealed.

This occurrence set the staff to thinking of the various forms of danger to which the general-in-chief was exposed, and how easily he might be assassinated; and we resolved that in addition to the ordinary guard mounted at the headquarters camp, we would quietly arrange a detail of "watchers" from the members of the staff, so that one officer would go on duty every night and keep a personal lookout in the vicinity of the general's tent. This was faithfully carried out. It had to be done secretly, for if he had known of it he would without doubt have broken it up and insisted upon the staff-officers going to bed after their hard day's work, instead of keeping these vigils throughout the long, dreary nights of the following winter. [Porter, *Campaigning with Grant*, pp. 273–274.]

Narrative in **Harper's Weekly**

The scene of the EXPLOSION AT CITY POINT, which occurred August 9 . . . was along the new pine wharf at the main steamboat landing. This wharf was one-third of a mile in length. Back from its edge ten or twelve feet was the large new Government warehouse, also of pine, nearly coextensive in length with the wharf, and answering as a depot for the railroad which conveys supplies to the army. Across the railroad, and at the foot of the hill on which the small town is situated, was a new row of buildings, accommodating the Post, office, Adams's Express office, and the Quarter-master's office. Upon the hill, besides about a dozen houses, were numerous tents for soldiers. On the morning of the explosion three barges, the *Major-General Meade*, the *J. E. Kendrick*, and the *J. C. Campbell* lay close to the wharf. The *J. E. Kendrick* was loaded with ammunition, and it was on this boat that the mischief developed from a too careless handling of the ammunition. The 11.30 a.m. train was just about to start out when a stunning shock was heard, and the air was piled thick with the ruinous fragments which in their fall rained down upon the tents and houses on the hill, and upon the heads of passengers on board the train, scattering the ground for a mile around with muskets, shells, bolt-heads, and the ribs of exploded barges. The *Kendrick* was blown to atoms with the loss of all on board—a dozen or more of souls. The captain was absent. The *General Meade* and the *Campbell* were destroyed and sunk with little if any loss of life. The wharf was torn up, the warehouse was destroyed, and the railroad cars shattered, though not irreparably, by the concussion. The row of buildings the other side of the railroad was crushed. The entire loss of property was about two millions. The loss of life was not so large as might have been expected. Upward of 50 were killed, 32 of whom were colored laborers. Besides these nearly a hundred were wounded, a great proportion slightly. It was altogether a melancholy and heart sickening accident. ["Before Petersburg," *Harper's Weekly,* August 27, 1864.]

Report of John Maxwell, Secret Service, CSA

I have the honor to report that in obedience to your order, and with the means and equipment furnished me by you, I left this city [Richmond] 26th of July last, for the line of the James River, to operate with the Horological torpedo against the enemy's vessels navigating that river. I had with me *Mr. R. K. Dillard,* who was well acquainted with the localities, and whose services I engaged for the expedition. On arriving in Isle of Wight County, on the 2nd of August, we learned of immense supplies of stores being landed at City Point, and for the purpose, by stratagem, of introducing our machine upon the vessels there discharging stores, started for that point. We reached there before daybreak on the 9th of August last, with a small amount of provisions, having traveled mostly by night and crawled upon our knees to pass the east picket-line. Requesting my companion to remain behind about half a mile I approached cautiously the wharf, with my machine and powder covered by a small box. Finding the captain had come ashore from a barge then at the wharf, I seized the occasion to hurry forward with my box. Being halted by one of the wharf sentinels I succeeded in passing him by representing that the captain had ordered me to convey the box on board. Hailing a man from the barge I put the machine in motion and gave it in his charge. He carried it aboard. The magazine contained about twelve pounds of powder. Rejoining my companion, we retired to a safe distance to witness the effect of our effort. In about an hour the explosion occurred. Its effect was communicated to

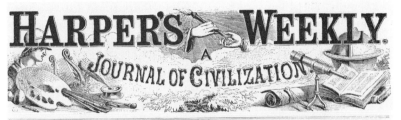

HARPER'S WEEKLY.
A JOURNAL OF CIVILIZATION

Vol. VIII.—No. 400.]   NEW YORK, SATURDAY, AUGUST 27, 1864.   [SINGLE COPIES TEN CENTS. $4.00 PER YEAR IN ADVANCE.

Entered according to Act of Congress, in the Year 1864, by Harper & Brothers, in the Clerk's Office of the District Court for the Southern District of New York.

Explosion at City Point (*Harper's Weekly*, August 27, 1864)

another barge beyond the one operated upon and also to a large wharf building containing their stores (enemy's), which was totally destroyed. The scene was terrific, and the effect deafened my companion to an extent from which he has not recovered. My own person was severely shocked, but I am thankful to Providence that we have both escaped without lasting injury. We obtained and refer you to . . . the enemy's newspapers, which afford their testimony of the terrible effects of this blow. The enemy estimates the loss of life at 58 killed and 126 wounded, but we have reason to believe it greatly exceeded that. The pecuniary damage we heard estimated at $4,000,000, but, of course, we can give you no account of the extent of it exactly.

I may be permitted, captain, here to remark that in the enemy's statement a party of ladies, it seems, were killed by this explosion. It is saddening to me to realize the fact that the terrible effects of war induce such consequence; but when I remember the ordeal to which our own women have been subjected, and the barbarities of the enemy's crusade against us and them, my feelings are relieved by the reflection that while this catastrophe was not intended by us, it amounts only, in the providence of God, to just retaliation. [*O.R.*, XLII, part 1, pp. 954–955.]

To return to the Petersburg National Battlefield Visitor Center, drive out of the parking area, turn right onto Cedar Lane, and drive 0.3 mile to Appomattox Street. Turn right onto Appomattox Street and proceed 0.7 mile onto Main Street, then turn right on Broadway. After driving 0.3 mile on Broadway, turn left onto 6th Street and proceed 0.7 mile to the light at Winston Churchill Drive (Route 156). Turn right onto Winston Churchill and drive 2.2 miles to the intersection of Routes 156 and 36. Continue straight onto Route 36 (Woodlawn Street, which then becomes Oaklawn Boulevard), and drive 7.1 miles to the exit on the right to Petersburg National Battlefield. Turn onto the ramp, and at the top turn right and proceed to the parking area for the Visitor Center.

To reach the first stop for the "Westward Movements" excursion, drive out of the parking area, turn right onto Cedar Lane, and drive 0.3 mile to Appomattox Street. Turn right onto Appomattox Street, proceed 0.7 mile onto Main Street, and then turn right onto Broadway. After driving 0.3 mile on Broadway, turn left onto 6th Street, and proceed 0.7 mile to the light at Winston Churchill Drive (Route 156). Turn left onto Winston Churchill, and drive 2.2 miles to the intersection of Routes 156 and 36. Continue straight onto Route 36 (Woodlawn Street, which then becomes Oaklawn Boulevard), and drive 6.6 miles to Crater Road (Route 301/460). Turn left onto Crater Road, and drive 1.8 miles to Flank Road. Turn right onto Flank Road, and after 0.1 mile turn left into the parking area for Fort Davis.

EXCURSION 3
DEEP BOTTOM

None of the battles that occurred north of the James River in July and August 1864 were decisive by themselves; however, one cannot understand Lt. Gen. Ulysses S. Grant's strategic and operational approach in the war's Eastern theater without viewing these actions in that context. Grant's objective, clearly stated in correspondence with Maj. Gen. George G. Meade, commander of the Army of the Potomac, was to destroy Gen. *Robert E. Lee's* Army of Northern Virginia. The capture of the Confederate capital, Richmond, and its primary logistical and transportation hub, Petersburg, became concomitant objectives because *Lee* had occupied and fortified those places with his forces. Throughout the summer and fall of 1864, Grant used a series of offensives north of the James to fix Confederate attention and divert Confederate reinforcements away from the Petersburg sector. Grant viewed any tactical success east and north of Richmond as an added benefit to be exploited appropriately.

For his part, *Lee* viewed the area north of the James River as an "economy of force" sector and garrisoned it with second-rate units from the Richmond defenses, mostly a mix of heavy artillery, dismounted cavalry, and local defense infantry units. During the 1862 Peninsula Campaign, Confederate engineers began the construction of a system of fortifications to protect Richmond. By 1864, this defensive system consisted of five distinct lines in various stages of construction and maintenance. Closest to the city, the twenty-four detached forts and batteries of the Interior Line completely encircled the capital. Next, the Intermediate Line was a system of earthen ramparts that protected the northern, eastern, and western approaches to the city, extending from the James River above Richmond to the river below, or downstream from, the city. This line covered the major roads that entered the capital from the east—the Osborne Turnpike and the New Market, Darbytown, and Williamsburg Roads. A short extension from the Intermediate Line ended in a large entrenched camp on Chaffin's Farm, just north of the James River. This camp and its major fortification, Fort Harrison, anchored the Southern defenses at the river. The Exterior Line, another earthen rampart, originated at Fort Harrison and covered the Charles City Road and the Mechanicsville Turnpike, ending at the Chickahominy River east of Richmond. Finally, two smaller lines, still under construction in the summer of 1864, left the Intermediate Line and strengthened Confederate defenses around New Market Heights. At the beginning of the campaign, a mixed Confederate force of infantry and cavalry occupied these entrenchments, which faced the Union bridgehead at Deep Bottom.

The operations north of the James River are of interest for two other reasons. First, these battles featured widespread participation by African American soldiers, led by white officers. The men of the U.S. Colored Troops (USCT) fought hard and well, suffering significant casualties. They also won acclaim from the army's senior leadership and decorations for valor, including the Medal of Honor. Their participation in combat against white Confederates during the Fifth Offensive, most notably at Fort Gilmer, provided compelling evidence of the war's racial component, as did the July 1864 fight at the Crater.

In addition, the Union Army of the James played a major role in the fighting north of its namesake river. Labeled an "Army of Amateurs," by one modern historian, Maj. Gen. Benjamin Butler's army performed creditably and acted as the primary headquarters for the Second Battle of Deep Bottom and the Union Fifth Offensive, which came nearer than any other to breaking through the Confederate defenses around Richmond. One cannot escape the feeling that this force was an underutilized asset that could have swung the balance of power in the Eastern Theater had it been employed more aggressively.

The battles and maneuvers around the city of Petersburg have traditionally captured the interest and attention of visitors to this area, mainly because the decisive events of the campaign happened there and because the holdings of the Petersburg National Battlefield are there. Only by visiting battle sites north of the James River, however, can one gain a full understanding of this great campaign and of Grant and *Lee's* operational thinking during it.

It is also north of the James that the modern visitor encounters many of the problems that can make this campaign difficult to understand and interpret. Only one of the major sites discussed in this excursion, Fort Harrison and its associated works, is maintained by the National Park Service, belonging to the Richmond National Battlefield Park. The rest of the sites are on private property and are not interpreted beyond a scattering of historical markers, making it a difficult task for the uninitiated to gain a full understanding of the campaign.

Richmond, Virginia (USAMHI)

Exit the parking area for the Petersburg National Battlefield Visitor Center, and proceed 0.2 mile down the park road to the exit for eastbound Route 36 (Oaklawn Boulevard), in the direction of Hopewell. Take Oaklawn Boulevard for 2.7 miles to Interstate 295, and take the northbound ramp to Richmond. Travel 12.2 miles to exit 22A, and take the ramp leading to eastbound Route 5 (New Market Road). Proceed 1.3 miles to Kingsland Road on the right. Turn and proceed 0.7 mile to Deep Bottom Road. Turn left onto Deep Bottom Road, and follow it for 1.3 miles to the parking area for Deep Bottom Park. Walk to the bank of the James River, noting the interpretive signs placed here by the Civil War Trust, which feature period photographs of the area. At the river, face to the right, upstream toward Richmond. At this spot you are approximately 11 miles southeast of the Confederate capital.

SUMMARY OF PRINCIPAL EVENTS, 18 JUNE–7 OCTOBER 1864

June
18—Skirmish at King and Queen Court-House; Maj. Gen. David B. Birney, U.S. Army, in temporary command of Second Army Corps; Brig. Gen. William T. H. Brooks, U.S. Army, assumes command of Tenth Army Corps
19–April 3, 1865—Siege of Petersburg and Richmond

20—Skirmish at White House; skirmish at King and Queen Court-House

21—Action at Howlett's Bluff; skirmishes at White House, or Saint Peter's Church, and Black Creek, or Tunstall's Station

22—Engagement near the Jerusalem Plank Road

22–July 2—Expedition against the South Side and Danville Railroads, with skirmishes at Reams Station (June 22) and Staunton River Bridge, or Roanoke Station (June 25), and engagements at Sappony Church, or Stony Creek (June 28–29), and at Reams Station (June 29)

23—Skirmish at Jones's Bridge

24—Engagement at Saint Mary's Church; action at Hare's Hill

27—Maj. Gen. Winfield S. Hancock, U.S. Army, resumes command of Second Army Corps

28—Action at Howlett's Bluff

30–July 1, 1864—Actions on Four-Mile Creek, at Deep Bottom

July

12—Skirmish at Warwick Swamp; skirmish at Turkey Creek

14—Action at Malvern Hill

16—Action at Four-Mile Creek; action at Malvern Hill

17—Skirmish at Herring Creek

18—Brig. Gen. Alfred H. Terry, U.S. Army, in temporary command of Tenth Army Corps

19—Brig. Gen. John H. Martindale, U.S. Army, in temporary command of Eighteenth Army Corps, vice Maj. Gen. William F. Smith relieved

22—Maj. Gen. Edward O. C. Ord, U.S. Army, assumes command of Eighteenth Army Corps

23—Maj. Gen. David B. Birney, U.S. Army, assumes command of Tenth Army Corps

27—Skirmish near Lee's Mill

27–29—Demonstrations on the north bank of the James River and engagement at Deep Bottom (or Darbytown, Strawberry Plains, and New Market Road)

28—Action at Four-Mile Creek

30—Explosion of the Mine and assault on the Crater; skirmish at Lee's Mill.

August

1—Skirmish at Deep Bottom

3—Action near Wilcox's Landing

4—Action near Harrison's Landing

5—Explosion of Confederate mine in front of Eighteenth Army
  Corps; skirmish at Cabin Point
7—Maj. Gen. Philip H. Sheridan, U.S. army, assigned to
  temporary command of Middle Military District
9—Explosion at City Point; affair near Sycamore Church
13—Actions at Four-Mile Creek and Dutch Gap
13–20—Demonstration on the north bank of the James River, at
  Deep Bottom (including combats at Fussell's Mill, Gravel Hill,
  Bailey's Creek, Deep Run [or Creek], White's Tavern, Charles
  City Road, New Market Road, and more)
14—Maj. Gen. John G. Parke, U.S. Army, in command of Ninth
  Army Corps
18–21—Battle of the Weldon Railroad (including combats at
  Globe Tavern, Yellow House, and Blick's Station)
22—Skirmish on the Vaughan Road
23—Action on the Dinwiddie Road, near Reams Station
24—Skirmish near Reams Station; action on the Vaughan Road,
  near Reams Station
25—Battle of Reams Station
27—Maj. Gen. Edward O. C. Ord, U.S. Army, in temporary
  command of the Army of the James
31—Skirmish near the Davis House
September
2—Reconnaissance beyond Yellow Tavern, on Weldon Railroad
3—Affair near Sycamore Church
4—Maj. Gen. John Gibbon, U.S. Army, in temporary command
  of Eighteenth Army Corps
5—Maj. Gen. David B. Birney, U.S. Army, in temporary
  command of the Army of the James
5–6—Reconnaissance to Sycamore Church
7—Maj. Gen. Benjamin F. Butler, U.S. Army, resumes command
  of the Army of the James
10—Assault on Confederate works at the Chimneys
13—Scout to Poplar Spring Church
15—Reconnaissance toward Dinwiddie Court-House and
  skirmish
16–17—Affair at Coggins's Point (September 16) and pursuit of
  the Confederates
19—Scout to Lee's Mill and Proctor's House
22—Maj. Gen. Edward O. C. Ord, U.S. Army, resumes command
  of Eighteenth Army Corps

29–30—Battle of Chaffin's Farm (including combats at Fort
    Harrison, Fort Gilmer, New Market Heights, and Laurel Hill)
29–October 2—Battle of Poplar Spring Church (including
    combats at Wyatt's, Peebles's, and Pegram's Farms, Chappell
    House, and Vaughan Road)
October
1—Bvt. Maj. Gen. Godfrey Weitzel, U.S. Army, in temporary
    command of Eighteenth Army Corps
7—Engagement on the Darbytown and New Market Roads
    (including combats at Johnson's Farm and Four-Mile Creek)

STOP 1: DEEP BOTTOM

FIRST DEEP BOTTOM, 26–29 JULY 1864

In front of you is the area of the James River known as Deep Bottom. In 1864 it was one of the major Union Army crossing points above
Richmond. Approximately where the modern boat landing now lies, a
pontoon bridge spanned the James. A second, "lower" bridge crossed
the river a short distance downstream, on the other side of Bailey's
Creek, out of sight behind you.

Through the summer of 1864, Lt. Gen. Ulysses S. Grant tried continually to stretch and break the Confederate defenses at Petersburg
with coordinated offensives against the northern and southern ends
of Gen. *Robert E. Lee's* defensive lines. Deep Bottom, which lies on the
north side of the James River opposite Jones's Neck, was an ideal location for a pontoon bridge, as it lay due north of the Federal lines in
Bermuda Hundred and formed a narrow, reasonably sheltered spot
in the river. On June 19, after the failure of the initial Federal assaults
to capture Petersburg, Grant decided to construct a pontoon bridge
here, giving Federal forces a direct avenue of approach to Richmond
via the roads that emanated, fanlike, from the Richmond defenses to
the northwest—the Charles City, Darbytown (or Central), and New
Market Roads.

Following the unsuccessful Bermuda Hundred campaign against
Richmond and Petersburg, Maj. Gen. Benjamin Butler's Army of the
James was positioned perfectly to operate north of the James. Engineers from Butler's Tenth Corps constructed the first pontoon bridge
at Deep Bottom on June 20, and Brig. Gen. Robert S. Foster's brigade
crossed to the north side on the next day. In response, *Lee* sent two
brigades of infantry to bolster the Richmond defenses, now under

the command of Lt. Gen. *Richard S. Ewell. Lee* clearly worried about
the threat this bridgehead posed to his defenses and was taking active
steps to contain it before Grant launched his Third Offensive.

**Gen. Robert E. Lee, CSA, commanding Army of Northern Virginia,
to Lt. Gen. Richard S. Ewell, CSA, commanding Department of
Richmond, July 6, 1864**

It is very important that we should gather the crops of wheat,
oats, and grass that are within our reach below Chaffin's Bluff,
and I think that all the assistance that we can give with men and
teams consistently with military operations should be applied to
that purpose. General [*Henry*] *Heth*, while stationed with two of
his brigades near Chaffin's Bluff, took steps to gather these crops,
which I hope will be continued by the two brigades now under
General [*James*] *Conner.* I think the other troops in your department should be employed as far as practicable in the same manner, and I need not tell you that that part of the country most
exposed to the ravages of the enemy should be first attended to.
I do not like the continuance of the enemy on the north side
of James River and the maintenance of the pontoon bridge at

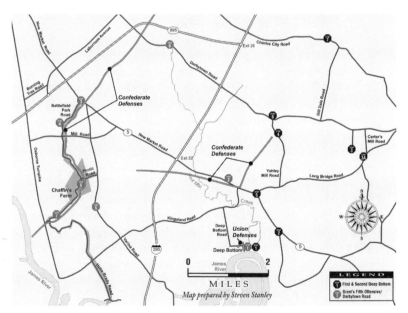

Confederate and Union Lines near Deep Bottom

Deep Bottom. I believe his force is not very large, and desire you to see if it cannot be driven away, and the bridge destroyed. I had hoped that Colonel [*Thomas*] *Carter* would have been able to have annoyed, if not injured, his transports on the river, and think that by the use of a four-gun battery, composed of pieces most suitable for the purpose, relieving the men and horses as occasion requires and operating in conjunction with [Gen. *Martin*] *Gary's* cavalry, he may do them great damage. The gunners might be mounted upon horses of other batteries, which by being relieved as proposed, would not be injured, if placed under a careful officer. Please see if anything can be done to drive the enemy from the north bank and interrupt his communications, &c. [U.S. War Department, *The War of the Rebellion: A Compilation of the Official Records of the Union and Confederate Armies*, 70 vols. in 128 parts and index (Washington, D.C.: Government Printing Office, 1880–1901), series 1, volume XL, part 3, p. 745. Hereafter cited as *O.R.*; all references are to series 1 unless otherwise noted.]

Gen. Robert E. Lee to Lieutenant General Ewell, July 24, 1864

Upon hearing that the enemy were re-enforcing their troops on the north side of the James River yesterday morning General [*Joseph*] *Kershaw's* division was ordered to Chaffin's Bluff. I directed him to assume command of the troops under General *Conner*, reconnoiter the enemy and ascertain his position, intentions, &c. He informs me that about two brigades intrenched themselves on Tilghman's farm last night and are still working; that it is reported that a second pontoon bridge has been constructed south of Bailey's Run, and that the enemy is apparently making a permanent lodgment on both banks of Bailey's Run with a view to future operations. He states that he has disposed of his troops so as to defend the Varina, New Market, and Darbytown roads. My object in sending troops there was to endeavor to dislodge the enemy, drive them across the river, and destroy the bridges, and if practicable I wish this done, and have sent a dispatch to General *Kershaw* to that effect. We cannot afford to sit down in front of the enemy and allow him to intrench himself wherever he pleases, and I wish you to see if you cannot break him up on the north side of the James River. [*O.R.*, XL, part 3, p. 797.]

Maj. Gen. Joseph B. Kershaw, CSA, commanding Division, First Corps, Army of Northern Virginia, to Lieutenant General Ewell, July 24, 1864

In accordance with General *Lee's* desires I shall attempt to dislodge the enemy from Bailey's Run. I shall attack them on the south of the run, and if successful will try Deep Bottom. As these operations may develop a counter attack it might be as well that you send to the works here any forces at your disposal. I expect to employ all my troops in these operations, and in the first part of the enterprise they will to some extent uncover the Varina road, though I hope to keep the enemy so well employed that he will hardly be in condition to avail himself of that circumstance, especially as I shall keep up my present line of pickets. [*O.R.*, XL, part 3, p. 797.]

FIRST DEEP BOTTOM: THE THIRD OFFENSIVE, 26–29 JULY 1864

As June turned to July and the fighting around Petersburg settled into trench warfare, Grant sought a way to break the developing stalemate. The Third Offensive would be the latest instance of a federal operational method that was used frequently in 1864: sequential offensive operations north and south of the James, designed to take advantage of the growing disparity of numbers between Grant's and *Lee's* forces. North of the James, Grant planned an offensive emanating from the Deep Bottom bridgehead. A force of infantry and cavalry would destroy railroads around Richmond and attempt to break into the city if the opportunity presented itself. At a minimum, this threat would force *Lee* to shift forces north of the river, increasing the chances of success opposite Petersburg, where a mine dug beneath Confederate lines by elements of Burnside's Ninth Corps would be exploded. Together, the movement north of the James and the mine attack would constitute Grant's third offensive against the Richmond-Petersburg lines.

For the attack out of Deep Bottom, Grant selected Maj. Gen. Winfield Scott Hancock's Second Corps of the Army of the Potomac, along with a cavalry force of three divisions under Maj. Gen. Philip H. Sheridan. This force would have to disengage from its positions facing Petersburg in order to move north and cross the James River.

Report of Lt. Gen. Ulysses S. Grant, USA, commanding Armies of the United States

With a view of cutting the enemy's railroad from near Richmond to the Anna rivers, and making him wary of the situation of his army in the Shenandoah, and, in the event of failure in this, to take advantage of his necessary withdrawal of troops from Petersburg to explode a mine that had been prepared in front of the Ninth Corps and assault the enemy's lines at that place, on the night of the 26th of July the Second Corps and two divisions of the Cavalry Corps and [Brig. Gen. August V.] Kautz's cavalry were crossed to the north bank of the James River and joined the force General Butler had there. [*O.R.*, XLVI, part 1, p. 25.]

Lieutenant General Grant to Maj. Gen. George G. Meade, USA, commanding Army of the Potomac

Before making an expedition down the Weldon road I propose to make a demonstration on the north side of the James River, having for its real object the destruction of the railroad on that side. To execute this, the Second Army Corps, two divisions of Sheridan's cavalry (Sheridan commanding in person), will be required. Kautz's cavalry will also be ordered to report to Sheridan for the occasion. This whole force should be got, if possible, to Deep Bottom without attracting the attention of the enemy and before our own people are allowed a clue as to what is really intended. There are now two pontoon bridges at Deep Bottom, and in the evening before the movement commences a second should be thrown across the Appomattox at Broadway. This would give two roadways the whole distance to be traveled. There are now two brigades at Deep Bottom and on the New Market and Malvern Hill road. These troops will continue to hold their present position, thus securing the crossing for our troops on their return. After crossing the James River, the cavalry will advance rapidly as possible on the Virginia Central Railroad (in fact the bridges over the Chickahominy on both roads should be destroyed) as near to the city as possible. From this point they will work north as far as the South Anna, unless driven off sooner. I will direct General [Rufus] Ingalls to send with the expedition 200 of his railroad men to aid in the work of destruction.

The Second Corps will also advance as rapidly as possible from Deep Bottom until they get opposite Chaffin's Bluff. Here they will take up a line to prevent the enemy throwing a force across the river to cut off the return of our cavalry. If, in the judgment of the commanding officer, his whole force is not necessary for this he will advance toward Richmond with his available force and hold such positions as he may think will insure the greatest security to the expedition. No wagons will be taken with the expedition except to carry necessary intrenching tools and tools for destroying roads. Wagons, however, to carry forty rounds of ammunition and five days' rations and three days' grain, may be sent in advance and parked near the pontoon bridge over the James, ready to be forwarded if required. The troops will carry four days' rations with them, commencing from the time they leave Deep Bottom. To give them these, the commissary at Deep Bottom will be instructed to have on hand 60,000 rations ready to issue.

When the work of destroying the railroad is accomplished the whole expedition will return and resume their present places. It is barely possible that by a bold move this expedition may surprise the little garrison of citizen soldiery now in Richmond and get in. This cannot be done, however, by any cautious movement, developing our force, and making reconnaissances before attacking. The only way it can be done, if done at all, is to ride up to the city boldly, dismount, and go in at the first point reached. If carried in this way, the prize could be secured by hurrying up the Second Corps and sending back word here, so that other dispositions could be made. This expedition has for its object, as first stated, to destroy the railroads north of Richmond. If anything more favorable grows out of it it will be due to the officers and men composing it, and will be duly appreciated. In the absence of the Second Corps and cavalry great watchfulness will be required on the part of the other troops and readiness to take advantage of any movement of the enemy. In preparing for this move let it be understood that it is for a grand raid toward Weldon. I do not mean to imply the necessity of saying anything untrue, but simply to make the necessary preparations for starting without giving out the idea of what is to be done and leave our troops to guess that it is to go south, as they will without contradiction. I should like this expedition to get off to-morrow night if possible; if not then, the night following. [*O.R.*, XL, part 3, p. 437.]

Major General Meade to Maj. Gen. Winfield S. Hancock, USA,
commanding Second Corps, Army of the Potomac, July 25, 1864

You will move your corps to-morrow afternoon at such time
and in such manner as to conceal the movement from the enemy,
and so as to reach the pontoon bridge at Point of Rocks soon
after dark. You will cross this bridge and proceed to the upper
bridge at Deep Bottom, crossing the James over this bridge and
moving from thence to Chaffin's farm, taking the position and
carrying out the orders indicated in the inclosed letter from the
lieutenant-general commanding. The object of this movement
and the details of its conduct are so clearly set forth in this letter
of the lieutenant-general commanding it is not deemed necessary to add any additional instructions from these headquarters.
Major-General Sheridan, in command of two divisions of cavalry,
will cross at the Broadway Landing bridge and the lower bridge at
Deep Bottom. He is directed to report his movements to you, and
in all matters of co-operation to take his orders from you. You will
keep me advised of your progress and all movements through the
nearest telegraph office. [*O.R.*, XL, part 3, p. 443.]

Return to your vehicle, and drive back out to Kingsland Road, returning to New
Market Road (Route 5). Turn right. As you drive southeast along New Market
Road, there is rising terrain on the left (north) side of the road; this is the eastern
end of New Market Heights, a wooded ridgeline that anchored the Confederate
defensive line running southeast from Richmond. After 1.7 miles, turn right into
the entrance road to Curles Neck Farm. As the farm is private property, you will
need to remain at this point, near the highway. Get out of your vehicle next to the
historical marker describing Curles Neck and Bremo, and face due south with
New Market Road to your back.

STOP 2: STRAWBERRY PLAINS

You are now in the northern portion of Strawberry Plains, the
assembly area for the Second Corps's attack out of the Deep Bottom
Bridgehead. The site of the "lower" (downstream) pontoon bridge is
out of sight in front of you (south).

After arriving at the bridgehead on the night of July 26, Hancock
changed his plan and decided to cross his entire command, with infantry followed by cavalry, by the lower pontoon bridge, leaving the
Tenth Corps troops garrisoning the bridgehead to demonstrate and
fix in place the Confederate defenders opposite the upper bridge.

The crossing went without incident, and Hancock's entire force was across the river before dawn on July 27.

Report of Maj. Gen. Winfield S. Hancock, USA, commanding
Second Corps, Army of the Potomac

On the afternoon of the 26th of July, about 4 o'clock, the head of my command, consisting of [Maj. Gen. John] Gibbon's, [Brig. Gen. Francis C.] Barlow's, and [Brig. Gen. Gershom] Mott's divisions, left its camp near the Deserted House for Point of Rocks, the column moving well to the rear to avoid being seen by the enemy. Just after dark we crossed the Appomattox by the pontoon bridge at Point of Rocks and proceeded to Deep Bottom, taking a rather difficult road to the left in order that the cavalry, which was crossing at Broadway Landing, might have an unobstructed road to Deep Bottom. Through the kindness of General Butler the road had been picketed, and small fires built to facilitate our march. I arrived at Deep Bottom a short time in advance of my command and met General Sheridan, commanding the cavalry, at the headquarters of Brigadier-General Foster, Tenth Corps, whose command held the bridge-heads on the north side of the James. My instructions were to move rapidly from Deep Bottom toward Chaffin's Bluff, and take up a position to prevent the enemy from crossing troops to the north side, and to hold the position while General Sheridan moved to the Virginia Central Railroad with two divisions of cavalry. Further than this my movements were to be contingent upon General Sheridan's success in operating toward Richmond. The success of this movement depended upon the contingency that the enemy's works would be thinly occupied, and the movement a surprise.

The information I derived from conversation with General Foster was briefly as follows: The upper and lower pontoon bridges were above and below Four-Mile Run, impassable near its mouth. The enemy held, apparently in considerable force, a strong position near the upper bridge, while their line appeared to terminate nearly opposite the lower bridge. The original plan was that the Second Corps should cross the upper bridge while the cavalry was crossing the lower. After consulting with General Sheridan, however, and referring the matter to the major-general commanding for his approval, I determined to cross the infantry at the lower bridge and turn the enemy's position, while General Foster with his force threatened the enemy in his front. The cavalry was directed to cross the river immediately after the Second Corps; the infantry commenced crossing about 2 a.m. on the 27th, and was massed behind a belt of oak timber near the bridge. [*O.R.*, XL, part 1, p. 308.]

Remain in place. Turn around and observe the tree line on the far side of New Market Road.

The wartime trace of the road was approximately 100 yards north of your position in what is currently a wooded area on private property; contemporary accounts located the "Sweeney Pottery" in this vicinity. It was here that the Confederate defenders of New Market Heights placed their advanced entrenchments, including a section of four 20-pounder Parrott rifled guns. At dawn on July 27, Hancock ordered his corps forward, with Brig. Gen. Francis C. Barlow's First Division leading the way. The assault was a complete success, carrying the Confederate line and capturing some artillery in the process. Hancock's infantry then pivoted to the west, moving up the New Market Road to your left and clearing the way for Sheridan's cavalry to begin a sweeping movement to the north and west, toward the Richmond defenses and the railroads beyond.

Report of Major General Hancock, continued

As soon as possible after daylight an advance was ordered, the First Division, Brigadier-General Barlow commanding, leading. At the same time a strong skirmish line from the Third Division was thrown out to our right to feel the woods bordering the New Market and Malvern Hill road, and one from General Gibbon's division in the timber along the bank of Four-Mile Run. The skirmish line of the Third Division from [Brig. Gen. Regis] De Trobriand's brigade, consisting of the Ninety-ninth and One hundred and tenth Pennsylvania Volunteers, became sharply engaged and was re-enforced by the Seventy-third New York Volunteers. Meanwhile the skirmish line of [Brig. Gen. Nelson A.] Miles' brigade, of Barlow's division (composed of the One hundred and eighty-third Pennsylvania, Twenty-eighth Massachusetts, and Twenty-sixth Michigan Volunteers), under command of Col. J. C. Lynch, One hundred and eighty-third Pennsylvania Volunteers, engaged the enemy farther to the left, driving him into the rifle-pits along the New Market and Malvern Hill road, and by a

Brig. Gen. Francis C. Barlow, Maj. Gen. David B. Birney, Brig. Gen. John Gibbon, and Maj. Gen. Winfield Scott Hancock (USAMHI)

well executed movement captured four 20-pounder Parrott guns, with their caissons, and drove the enemy from their works. [*O.R.*, XL, part 1, p. 309.]

Report of Maj. Gen. Francis C. Barlow, USA, commanding First Division, Second Corps, Army of the Potomac

At 4 p.m. on July 26 the division marched with the rest of the corps for Deep Bottom. During the night we crossed the pontoon bridge at that point, and massed in a concealed position on the north bank of the James River, near the earth-works held by Foster's brigade. The march was a severe one and the roads in some places bad, and considerable falling out occurred.

Early on the morning of July 27, in obedience to orders, the division, in conjunction with the remainder of the corps, pressed forward against the line of the enemy's rifle-pits, which covered the road running parallel to the river. The skirmish line of the division, consisting of regiments of Miles' brigade, advanced under a fire of musketry and artillery, and by a well executed movement drove the enemy from the rifle-pits in their front, capturing four pieces of artillery. The enemy held the line weakly. Subsequently we advanced through the woods about one mile to the New Market road, and went on the river road to the deserted hotel. The woods were deep and thick, and the advance through them occupied some time. [*O.R.*, XL, part 1, p. 330.]

Report of Brig. Gen. Nelson A. Miles, USA, commanding First Brigade, First Division, Second Corps, Army of the Potomac

At 4 p.m. of the 26th the command left camp near the Deserted House, marched to Point of Rocks, crossed the Appomattox at about 9 p.m., thence to the pontoon bridge across the James at Deep Bottom, and halted at about 3 a.m. of the 27th behind a grove at the edge of Strawberry Plains. At about 6 a.m. a line of skirmishers, consisting of the One hundred and eighty-third Pennsylvania, Twenty-eighth Massachusetts, and Twenty-sixth Michigan, under the command of Col. J. C. Lynch, One hundred and eighty-third Pennsylvania, was advanced across the Plains, supported by the remainder of the division. This line advanced without indication of the enemy until within a short distance of the Long Bridge road, when it was met by a fire from a force partially intrenched in this road. A fire was kept up by this force from four 20-pounder Parrott guns, stationed in the road at the line of General Mott, which connected with the right of this division, and at the same time sharp skirmishing was kept up with this skirmish line, which was covered by a crest from the fire of the artillery. Colonel Lynch moved his line by the right flank around the flank of this force in the road, and by a vigorous push drove it from its position and captured the pieces, with caissons and ammunition chests. [*O.R.*, XL, part 1, p. 332.]

Return to your vehicle. Turn left onto New Market Road, taking care to watch for traffic. Drive 1.3 miles to Long Bridge Road. Turn right onto Long Bridge Road, and travel for 2.7 miles. As you pass Gravel Hill Church on your left, prepare to turn left just past the church onto Carters Mill Road. Carters Mill Road ends in 0.6 mile at Darbytown Road; turn left. Travel 0.3 mile to the entrance for Mansfield Woods subdivision on your left. Turn into the subdivision, and take this road to its end, a distance of 0.5 mile. Park your vehicle here, and walk into the field next to you, proceeding in your original driving direction toward the tree line in front of you, a distance of approximately 200 yards. This tree line separates the field from another farm field; at the far end of the second field is a small white farmhouse. Stand in the shade of the trees with a view of the farmhouse.

Alternate site for Stop 3 with no view of the farm: After turning right onto Long Bridge Road, drive for 2.7 miles. As you pass the Gravel Hill Recreation Center on your right, prepare to turn left into the parking lot for Gravel Hill Church. Park in the shaded area nearest to the Recreation Center and get out of your vehicle, facing back along Long Bridge Road with a view of the open field before you.

STOP 3: THE DARBY/ENROUGHTY FARM

In Mansfield Woods subdivision: You are now standing north of the wartime Darby/Enroughty Farm, located in the woods approximately one-quarter mile before you. Note how the tree lines compartmentalize the fields.

At Gravel Hill Church: You are now standing east of the wartime Darby/Enroughty Farm, located in the woods approximately one-half mile before you. The area before you was a cleared farm field at the time of the battle.

After the Second Corps breakout from the Deep Bottom bridgehead, Hancock's three infantry divisions came into line against the main Confederate defenses along New Market Heights, about 3 miles to your right front (west). As they did so, the strength of the Confederate position became apparent, and Hancock was unable to turn it after a series of attacks on the 27th. *Lee* augmented his defenses with over 16,000 troops from the divisions of Maj. Gens. *Cadmus M. Wilcox* and *Joseph B. Kershaw*, placing his First Corps commander, Lt. Gen. *Richard H. Anderson*, in overall command to coordinate the effort. You may read the Federal accounts of this fighting here or save them for the Second Deep Bottom excursion, which visits the New Market Heights line.

The second component of Grant's initial foray north of the James was a cavalry raid by Sheridan's three divisions, commencing on the morning of July 28. As Hancock grappled with *Anderson's* infantry along New Market Heights, Sheridan's horsemen moved northeast on the Long Bridge Road, approaching the critical Glendale crossroads, scene of bitter fighting during the 1862 Seven Days Battles. Confederate infantry from *Wilcox's* division reached this position in the afternoon following a cross-country movement, encountering Federal cavalrymen moving northeast along the Long Bridge Road. Dismounted horsemen formed a battle line around the Darby Farm, and a see-saw fight developed between Confederate infantry and Federal horsemen equipped with repeating rifles.

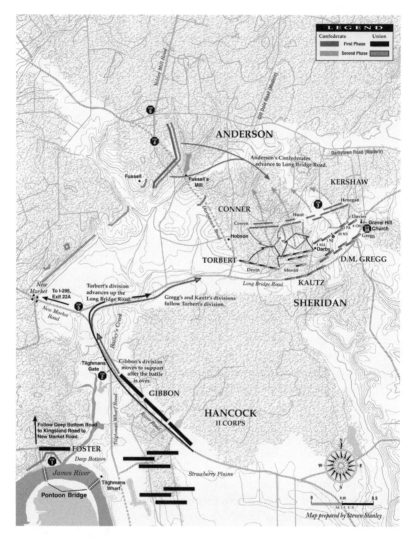

First Deep Bottom, July 28, 1864

NEW MARKET HEIGHTS

Gen. Robert E. Lee to Lt. Gen. Richard H. Anderson, CSA,
commanding First Corps, Army of Northern Virginia, July 27, 1864

A dispatch just received from Genl *Kershaw* has determined me to send Genl *Heth's* division to reinforce him. I wish you to proceed to Deep Bottom & take command of the troops belonging to this army there. Examine the enemy's position, endeavor to ascertain his strength, and if practicable drive him away and destroy his bridges. [Clifford Dowdey and Louis Manarin, eds., *The Wartime Papers of Robert E. Lee* (1961; New York: Da Capo, 1987), p. 826.]

Report of Major General Hancock, continued

As rapidly as the troops could be brought forward in the country, about which we then knew nothing, they were pushed up the New Market and Malvern Hill road in pursuit of the enemy, the Second Division in advance. The enemy brought a battery out opposite General Mott on our extreme right, but it was soon driven off by the fire of our artillery and General Mott's skirmish line, and retreated by a cross-road to the New Market and Long Bridge road. When we arrived at Bailey's Creek the enemy were found posted on the opposite bank in well-constructed works, in a position offering great advantages for defense. Bailey's Creek is so much of an obstacle that a line of battle could not well cross it under fire, and the distance from the creek to the works was about 1,000 yards, the intervening ground being perfectly open. The works appeared to be filled with men, and a number of pieces of artillery were in position. After a careful examination of the position it was decided that the chances of successful assault were unfavorable, and it was determined to maneuver to the right, with the view of turning the position.

Meanwhile the cavalry had moved to the right toward Malvern Hill and to the front on the New Market and Long Bridge road. Gibbon's division held the advance position on the New Market and Malvern Hill road while Barlow's and Mott's divisions were pushed forward to the New Market and Long Bridge road, connecting with the cavalry near the fork of the Central road. General Barlow, commanding First Division, made a close reconnaissance of the enemy's line, but was unable to find the flank. The cavalry, by one or two spirited charges on my right, gained possession of some high open ground, which it was hoped

might enable them to get in rear of the enemy's line, but, as subsequently ascertained, the enemy's line was refused on this flank,
turning sharply to their left near Fussell's Mill. About 3.30 p.m.
Lieutenant-General Grant visited the line, but I did not see him.
Having examined the position, he left me a note stating that he
did not see that much could be done, but that if it was possible
for me to roll up the enemy's left toward Chaffin's Bluff, and thus
release our cavalry, he desired it done. He stated that according
to his information the enemy had in my front seven brigades of
infantry and a small force of cavalry. Night coming on put a stop
to further operations. [*O.R.*, XL, part 1, p. 310.]

Report of Brigadier General Miles, *continued*

A skirmish line was then pushed through the woods in the
direction of the New Market road, which was reached after noon
with slight opposition. A line of battle was formed in the edge of
the woods along this road and one regiment (the Twenty-sixth
Michigan) sent on a reconnaissance up the Central road. The
enemy were observed building a line of works on a ridge nearly
parallel to the New Market road. This regiment came upon the
enemy in detached pits a short distance from the New Market
road and drove him into his main line, the position of which having been ascertained the regiment was withdrawn. [*O.R.*, XL, part
1, p. 333.]

Report of Major General Barlow, *continued*

Beyond the New Market road and crossing it and the river
road, the enemy occupied in considerable force a strong and
commanding line of rifle-pits. Pressing a skirmish line as close
as possible to this line, and made a reconnaissance with a view to
discover, if possible, the left flank of the enemy's works and a suitable place for an attack, I could not find the point where the line
ended on the enemy's left, and further operations were prevented
by night-fall. [*O.R.*, XL, part 1, p. 331.]

DARBY/ENROUGHTY FARM

Report of Major General Hancock, *continued*

During the night of the 27th I received intelligence that the
enemy were re-enforcing from the south side of the James. [Brig.

Gen. Henry W.] Birge's brigade, of the Tenth [Nineteenth] Corps
(a little over 2,500 strong), reported to me early on the morning
of the 28th and relieved Gibbon's division from its advanced position on the New Market and Malvern Hill road. General Sheridan
was also placed under my orders and it was decided that he should
advance up the Central or Charles City road, if either could be
opened. Brigadier-General Foster was directed by General Butler
to make a vigorous demonstration in his immediate front to at-
tract as many of the enemy as possible to that point. By a telegram
from General Grant to General Meade (a copy of which reached
me at 10 o'clock on the morning of the 27th), I was informed
that General Grant did not desire me to attack the enemy's works,
but to turn their position. The dispatch expressed the opinion of
General Grant that the cavalry by going well out might turn the
enemy's flank. Preparations were made to carry out the views of
General Grant, but it become evident at an early hour that the
enemy having been largely re-enforced would assume the offensive, and they were discovered moving to my right in strong force
about 8 a.m. The fire of the gun-boats in the river was directed on
the enemy by means of signals, and was effective in changing the
direction of their march.

About 10 a.m. the cavalry skirmish line was driven in on the
New Market and Long Bridge road and on the crossroad leading over the Charles City road by Ruffin's house, and a vigorous
attack was made by the enemy upon our cavalry at both points,
which compelled it to retire some distance. Gibbon's division
was hurried up to the support of the cavalry, but before it arrived the attacking force of the enemy had been disposed of by a
gallant advance of our cavalry (dismounted), driving the enemy
over a mile, capturing nearly 200 prisoners and several colors.
The prisoners belonged to *Kershaw's* division of infantry. [Brig.
Gen. David M.] Gregg's division of cavalry effected its withdrawal
from the Charles City road after a sharp fight with the enemy's
infantry, losing one gun. Anticipating a more determined attack,
I changed the disposition of my lines. Gibbon's division held the
approaches to the New Market and Long Bridge road, while the
cavalry was withdrawn to cover the New Market and Malvern Hill
road. The enemy having been reported as passing toward Malvern Hill, a garrison was placed in the bridge-head at the lower
bridge by General Foster, and artillery placed in position under
my direction to prevent the enemy from cutting me off from the

river. As soon as this was accomplished the infantry was withdrawn to a line following the general direction of the New Market and Malvern Hill road. Repeated dispatches showing that the enemy were concentrating against me were furnished me, and I made every preparation to receive them. They made no further demonstration during the day, however, other than to crowd the cavalry skirmishers a little. [*O.R.*, XL, part 1, pp. 310–311.]

Memoir of Lt. J. F. J. Caldwell, First South Carolina Volunteer Infantry

On the morning of the 28th of July, our brigades were formed, and marched rapidly up the lines, passing *Kershaw's* division, which lay in trenches from the Williamsburg Road to Fussel's mills. [Brig. Gen. *James H.*] *Lane's* brigade accompanied us. After passing the mills, two or three shell were thrown up the narrow country road by which we marched. . . . We had to advance through a close mass of wood for the distance of near two hundred yards. . . . There was now a wide gap between us and *Lane's* brigade. His men struggled and delayed a good while with the mud. Ours pressed on, in spite of their disordered line, across the bog, into the cornfield, and opened vigorously as they advanced. The confusion increased, as a matter of course. Finally, we cleared the corn and mounted an open hill. The enemy fled before us, taking refuge partly on the edge of the opposite farm [the Darby Farm], (some three hundred yards off,) partly in a strip of wood that ran up, from the north, to the crest of the open ridge we occupied.

. . . We were ordered to continue the advance. Let us look over this ground before we enter it. On our left a strip of sapling woods runs, meeting the left of the Fourteenth regiment. It widens as it runs back, but on each side of it is field. The Twelfth and Thirteenth captured their piece on the field on the left. On the right there is open ground for three hundred yards at least, then there is a house and farm-buildings, and, behind that, woods. The enemy are posted in and around that house. To the right of that house, and a hundred yards nearer us than it is, is a spring—a cool one, I judge, from the depth between the two hills, and the great oaks that shade it. From this spring, straight out eastward, runs a strip of heavy timber and a marsh. Between this wood strip and that on our left is an open, clear, smooth descent down the hill we are on, and an ascent up the hill where the farm-house is, of about three hundred yards.

. . . The enemy now fired upon us sharply, wounding and killing some, but generally overshooting. We fired as we advanced. *Lane's* brigade moved up, but did not connect with us, or even get quite on a line with us. . . . But the enemy observe the gap between us and *Lane*, and dispatch a small body of quick men to it. They strike at once, roll back Lane's men, swing around the right of the First regiment, and before they can think, have almost cut them off.

. . . There was a general break. On the extreme right, our men had almost run over the enemy's line. But, fortunately, it was a thin one—a strong skirmish, probably. Farther on the left, men could rally at intervals and delay the Federals, but so warm was the fire from these, and so strong the conviction of failure, that we gradually gave clear back, across the open field, and into the woods, where our advance commenced.

. . . The general carelessness of officers, and the excitement and stubbornness of the men, had lost us what should have been a brilliant success. We had surprised the enemy, terrified him, doubled him up in confusion, and yet we failed, because we were so foolish as not to keep a line. I am perfectly willing to take my share of the blame, and therefore I have a right to speak freely. This was the first time I had ever seen cause to be ashamed of the brigade, and, I am glad to say, it was the last. [J. F. J. Caldwell, *The History of a Brigade of South Carolinians, Known First as "Gregg's," and Subsequently as "McGowan's Brigade"* (Philadelphia: King and Baird, 1866), pp. 169–173.]

Report of Brig. Gen. David M. Gregg, USA, commanding Second Division, Cavalry Corps, Army of the Potomac

After crossing the James River the division was encamped near Light-House Point, picketing in rear and on left of the army until the 26th of July, on the evening of which day it marched with the First Division of the Cavalry Corps, the two divisions under command of Major-General Sheridan, from its camp across the Appomattox at Point of Rocks, and thence north of the James River, crossing at Deep Bottom. On the 27th the division occupied a position on Strawberry Plains. On the morning of the 28th an order from Major-General Sheridan directed me to move the division to Ridley's [Riddell's] Shop, near the intersection of the New Market and Charles City roads. The division moved from Strawberry Plains in the following order: The First Brigade, Brig.

Gen. H. E. Davies commanding, in advance, the Second Brigade, Col. J. I. Gregg commanding, following. Following a wood road leading from the Plains, the division struck the New Market road at the position occupied by the First Division, on the right of the Second Army Corps.

Having moved one mile and a half down the New Market road, and being within the picket-line of the First Division, the pickets on the left of the advance of my column were observed skirmishing with an enemy, and falling back slowly toward the road. The Second Division was at this time marching in a column of fours, and the country on either side of the road was densely wooded, save one small opening, from the farther side of which the enemy were advancing. I at once ordered a regiment of the First Brigade to turn out of the column and move to the support of the pickets of the First Division. In a very few minutes a line of battle of the enemy's infantry (*Kershaw's* division) emerged from the woods and advanced toward the road occupied by my command.

Without opportunity to form the command regiments were dismounted at once to oppose the enemy. Two guns of Light Battery A, Second U.S. Artillery, commanded by First Lieut. W. N. Dennison, were turned upon the enemy's line, and their fire, together with that of the carbines of the dismounted regiments, checked temporarily the advance of the enemy; the suddenness of the attack, and the impracticability of forming my Second Brigade so as to bring it into action at once, gave the enemy an advantage, which he used in forcing back the First Brigade to the road. At this time the Second Brigade, having formed in rear of the road, was brought forward, but the enemy had made a precipitate retreat across the field and through the woods. Mounted regiments were pushed forward rapidly in pursuit, but the enemy, under cover of the dense pines which mounted troops could not penetrate, effected their escape, leaving about 30 of their dead and a number of wounded on the field. In resisting the advance of the enemy the guns of Dennison's battery did most excellent service. Some of the horses attached to a rifled gun were killed and its support driven off by an overpowering force of the enemy, and the gun thus fell into the hands of the enemy. As soon as the narrow wood road upon which the gun was carried off by the enemy was discovered, a mounted regiment was sent to effect its recapture, but this was not accomplished. [*O.R.*, XL, part 1, p. 612.]

Major General Hancock to Lieutenant General Grant, July 28, 1864, 12:40 p.m.

The enemy's infantry after attacking our cavalry on the Long Bridge road was driven back by General [Alfred T. A.] Torbert's cavalry, which after a sharp fight, captured 2 colors and about 150 prisoners from *Lane's* brigade, *Wilcox's* command, which has been at Chaffin's Bluff for about three weeks and which marched from there last night. There has been considerable movements of infantry to-day, from the rear of the enemy's right toward the left. . . . Gibbon's division of infantry has reached the rear of the cavalry for the purpose of supporting it, but in front of Torbert the enemy appear to have retired to form a new line. In front of General Gregg, however, the enemy has continued to hold the position and fighting is still going on. . . .

The enemy seems to be extending his line a little farther to his left (our right). . . . I think it possible that I might be attacked next on the Central [Darbytown—ed.] road, but have a brigade watching it; Barlow's division near at hand. [*O.R.*, XL, part 3, p. 561.]।

Major General Hancock to Major General Meade, July 28, 1864, 2 p.m.

An intelligent prisoner has just been captured and brought in to me, a native of Ohio. He says that *Kershaw's* division, of [Lt. Gen. *James*] *Longstreet's* corps, and *Wilcox's* of [Lt. Gen. *Ambrose P.*] *Hill's*, moved to our right this morning from the positions they held yesterday, where they were relieved this morning by the rest of *Hill's* corps, which came over last night. He says that some of the officers told him (he does not know the truth of it) that [Maj. Gen. *George E.*] *Pickett's* and [Maj. Gen. *Charles W.*] *Field's* divisions, of *Longstreet's* corps, came over. [*O.R.*, XL, part 3, p. 562.]

Remain in place to consider the end of the first battle of Deep Bottom and its implications for the campaign.

STALEMATE NORTH OF THE JAMES

With the Second Corps's attack stalled at New Market Heights and continuing reports of additional Confederate defenders converging on the Glendale crossroads sector to contain Sheridan's cavalry sweep, Hancock became increasingly cautious, worrying primarily about a Confederate flanking movement cutting him off from the Deep Bottom bridgehead. Grant decided on June 28 to begin returning Hancock's force to Petersburg in anticipation of the impending mine explosion southeast of the city. The Federal position at Deep Bottom would remain a significant concern for *Lee*, as he had to use elements of his army to contain it, thus denuding his forces defending Petersburg and available to counter Grant's continual raids on the vital lines of supply and communication to the rest of the Confederacy. Though it was a tactical defeat for Grant, First Deep Bottom cost *Lee* an estimated 540 casualties against 210 Federals and did achieve one major operational objective—it forced *Lee* to transfer half of his army, more than five divisions, to the north side of the James to counter Hancock and Sheridan. It remained to be seen whether Grant and Meade could take advantage of this temporary mismatch in front of Petersburg.

Report of Lieutenant General Grant, continued

On the 28th our lines were extended from Deep Bottom to New Market Road, but in getting this position were attacked by the enemy in heavy force. The fighting lasted for several hours, resulting in considerable loss to both sides. The first objective of this move having failed, by reason of the very large force being thrown there by the enemy, I determined to take advantage of the diversion made, by assaulting Petersburg before he could get his force back there. One division of the Second Corps was withdrawn on the night of the 28th, and moved during the night to the rear of the Eighteenth Corps, to relieve that corps in the line, that it might be foot-loose in the assault to be made. The other two divisions of the Second Corps and Sheridan's cavalry were crossed over on the night of the 29th, and moved in front of Petersburg. On the morning of the 30th . . . the mine was sprung. [*O.R.*, XLVI, part 1, p. 25.]

Return to your vehicle, and turn right onto Darbytown Road. Travel 0.3 mile to Carters Mill Road; turn right. Carters Mill Road ends at Long Bridge Road; turn right, passing Gravel Hill Church. Drive 2.0 miles to Yahley Mill Road; turn right. Drive for 1.2 miles; as the road leaves the wooded low ground and goes uphill, pull off to the right where a large power line crosses the road. Park on the dirt service road near the power line, get out of your vehicle, and face down the power line with Yahley Mill Road at your back. Fussell's Mill pond is before you, out of sight behind the small ridgeline. The pond served as an impenetrable obstacle in front of the Confederate defensive line at this point. You are standing on New Market Heights.

SECOND DEEP BOTTOM: THE FOURTH OFFENSIVE, 13–20 AUGUST 1864

The modern Yahley Mill Road, on which you are stopped, was the wartime southern terminus of the Darbytown Road, one of the three roads leaving the Richmond fortifications to the southeast of the city. The low ridge upon which you are standing was defended by the Confederates of Maj. Gen. *Charles Field's* division of the First Corps.

During the First Deep Bottom fighting, the area where you are standing marked the northernmost extent of the Confederate defense; *Lee's* men were able to use the hilly and wooded terrain, combined with field fortifications, to prevent Hancock from turning their northern flank. Maj. Gen. *Cadmus M. Wilcox's* division passed through this area on July 28 to conduct the counterattack that halted Sheridan's cavalry movement.

STOP 4: FUSSELL'S MILL

Following the stunning and well-publicized Union failure at the Battle of the Crater on July 30, 1864, Grant continued to seek opportunities to break the Confederate position around Petersburg. From July through October Grant planned and executed a series of two-pronged offensives against Richmond and Petersburg, designed to pull the Confederates in opposite directions and complicate *Lee's* efforts to use his interior lines to move troops to each threatened point in turn. In mid-August, the Second Battle of Deep Bottom was a companion offensive to the Union effort to break the Weldon Railroad south of Petersburg. The two battles together made up the Union Fourth Offensive.

During the summer of 1864, *Lee* sent portions of his army to the Shenandoah Valley in an effort to relieve Federal pressure on the Richmond-Petersburg sector, taking the calculated risk that he could maintain a defensive posture against Butler's and Meade's forces and hold his lines of supply and communication while forcing Grant to detach forces for operations in the valley. In mid-June, Lt. Gen. *Jubal A. Early* took *Lee's* Second Corps west to the valley, where he had initial success against second-rate Union forces and even threatened Washington, D.C., in early July. Lt. Gen. *Richard H. Anderson*, *Lee's* First Corps commander, followed with his headquarters and additional reinforcements after the Third Offensive. *Early's* raid forced Grant to send seven veteran infantry divisions and the Sixth Army

Corps headquarters to defend the national capital and to deal with *Early*, creating more parity in front of Petersburg. As the summer and fall progressed and the Confederacy suffered the fall of Atlanta on its western front, *Lee* had fewer strategic options.

The second battle at Deep Bottom followed a similar script to that of the first, with Hancock's Second Corps and a division of cavalry (Sheridan and the rest of his force were operating against *Early* in the Shenandoah Valley) joining Butler's Tenth Corps north of the river once again. Maj. Gen. *Charles Field* remained the Confederate tactical commander along the New Market Heights, with a veteran force of Army of Northern Virginia infantry. Maj. Gen. *W. H. F. "Rooney" Lee's* Confederate cavalry picketed the roads into Richmond and secured *Field's* northern flank.

Report of Lieutenant General Grant, continued

Reports from various sources led me to believe that the enemy had detached three divisions from Petersburg to re-enforce *Early* in the Shenandoah Valley. I therefore sent the Second Corps and Gregg's division of cavalry, of the Army of the Potomac, and a force of General Butler's army, on the night of the 13th of August, to threaten Richmond from the north side of the James, to prevent him from sending troops away, and, if possible, to draw back those sent. In this move we captured six pieces of artillery and several hundred prisoners. . . . The enemy having withdrawn heavily from Petersburg to resist this movement, the Fifth Corps, General [Gouverneur K.] Warren commanding, was moved out on the 18th and took possession of the Weldon railroad. [*O.R.*, XLVI, part 1, p. 30.]

Report of Maj. Gen. Winfield S. Hancock, USA, commanding Second Corps, Army of the Potomac

At 12 m. August 12 I received instructions from the major-general commanding to move my corps to City Point, the artillery to cross the Appomattox at Point of Rocks, and to park in some concealed position within General Butler's lines. Great care was taken to conceal these movements from the enemy, and the idea was encouraged that the command was about embarking for Washington. On the morning of the 13th I received my instructions, which were nearly identical with those furnished me in July when operating from Deep Bottom. An estimate of General Butler's was furnished me, putting the enemy's strength north

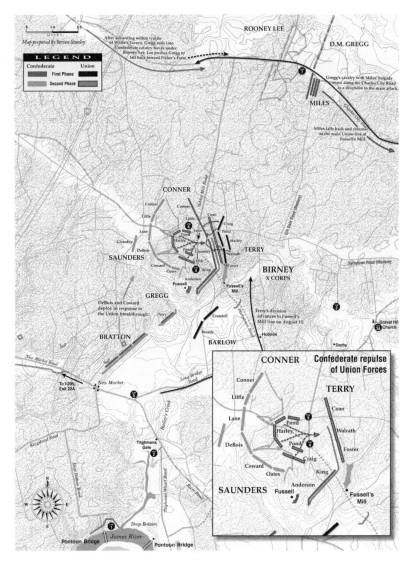

Second Deep Bottom, August 14–17, 1864

Pontoon bridge at Deep Bottom (USAMHI)

of the James at 8,500 men. General Gregg's division of cavalry was placed under my orders, and also the Tenth Corps, under Major-General [David B.] Birney. A portion of this corps was then holding the bridge-heads at Jones' Neck. It was supposed that my corps could be readily disembarked from boats by running along shore and throwing out gang-planks, while General Birney used the upper bridge and the cavalry the lower. Leaving Major [William G.] Mitchell, aide-de-camp, to superintend the embarkation of the infantry, I went up to Deep Bottom, accompanied by General Ingalls and a part of my staff, for the purpose of selecting places for landing the troops. I foresaw that the difficulties of disembarkation would be greater than were apprehended, and at my suggestions the transports left City Point at 10 p.m. instead of at midnight, as was originally contemplated. Colonel [Charles H.] Morgan, chief of staff, preceded them with a lighter and materials for constructing temporary wharves. As this expedition was one of considerable magnitude, and accomplished perhaps less than was hoped, I think proper to insert here extracts from the order issued to commanders on the afternoon of the 13th:

CONFIDENTIAL CIRCULAR. HEADQUARTERS SECOND
ARMY CORPS,
City Point, August 13, 1864

VI. At daybreak, or as soon [as] General Mott's division is
disembarked, he will proceed up the New Market and Malvern Hill
road, driving the enemy into his intrenched line behind Bailey's
Creek, or beyond it, if practicable. During this operation the cavalry
under General Gregg will cover the right flank of General Mott's
division. As soon as the Second and First Divisions, Second Corps, are
disembarked they will, under command of General Barlow, move to
General Mott's right, and assault the enemy's line near the Jennings
house. If the line is carried General Barlow will move to his left and
uncover General Mott's front, who will then advance along the New
Market road.

VII. The cavalry will cover the right flank of General Barlow's
command during this operation. As soon as the Central and Charles
City Court-House roads are uncovered by the advance of the infantry,
General Gregg will proceed to execute the orders already received by
him, identical with those of July 25.

VIII. General Birney, with his command, will be prepared to attack
the enemy in position behind Four-Mile Run at daybreak. The hour
for attack will, however, be specially designated to General Birney.
If successful, he will advance along the New Market and Kingsland
roads to the junction of the Varina road; then along the Varina road
to the Mill road, securing, if possible, the cross-roads at Osborne's old
turnpike.

By order of Major-General Hancock:
FRANCIS A. WALKER,
Assistant Adjutant-General

As I feared, the command was not able to disembark rapidly;
the boats could not run near enough to the shore, and the difficulty materially increased as the tide was running out. Many of
the boats were not adapted to the transportation of troops, and
considerable delay was caused in landing. I had taken the precaution to send all led and pack horses and all saddle-horses that
could possibly be spared around by Bermuda Hundred. Notwithstanding the exertions of the officers, it was 9 o'clock in the morning before the command was disembarked. One boat, containing
1,200 men of General Barlow's division, grounded in the river,
and the troops were not gotten ashore until some time later. I

had previously visited General Birney and postponed his assault. [*O.R.*, XLII, part 1, pp. 216–217.]

These delays in movement and debarkation would cost the Federal force any chance of quickly seizing the Confederate positions along New Market Heights.

Report of Brig. Gen. Francis C. Barlow, USA, commanding First Division, Second Corps, Army of the Potomac

On August 13 the division, together with the rest of the corps, proceeded by water to Deep Bottom, arriving there during the night of the 13th. The disembarkation of the troops occupied considerable time, for the reason that the greater part of the men were stowed upon the upper decks of steamers, from which they could descend only by ones or twos at a time. The whole division was not landed until broad daylight, and the greater part of one brigade (the Fourth) was delayed many hours by the grounding of the steamer in which it was transported. When landed, the division was pushed rapidly forward through the woods to the New Market road, together with the Second Division, which was temporarily placed under my command. [*O.R.*, XLII, part 1, p. 247.]

Narrative of Maj. Gen. Charles W. Field, CSA, commanding Division, First Corps, Army of Northern Virginia

The next day I returned to my original place in the trenches, and in about a week afterwards left for the north side of the James to resist a threatened attack there. I found upon the north side of the James, permanently stationed there, an artillery force and many guns at Chaffin's Bluff, the Richmond City battalion, and a Tennessee brigade (Maj. Gen. *Bushrod R. Johnson's*), all under the nominal command of Lieutenant-General *Ewell*. I say nominal, because, though General *Ewell* commanded the Department of Richmond, which embraced those troops, and everything which might be located there, in fact I commanded, and made disposition to suit myself, without consultations with him, and received no orders from him. When I first went over to the north side, Lieutenant-General *Anderson*, with *Kershaw's* and *Heth's* divisions, were there, but, the enemy withdrawing the most of his force to the south side during the night, on the following day Lieutenant-General *Anderson* and the two divisions last mentioned did the same, leaving my division, and the permanent force I have before mentioned, on the north side to watch the enemy.

At this time General *Anderson*, with *Kershaw's* division, marched
to join *Early* in the Valley. I believe it was proposed for me to follow in a few days, but at daylight on the 14th of August the enemy,
having thrown a heavy force to the north side during the previous night, attacked my lines. He made three assaults at different
times during the day, which were handsomely repulsed, with loss
to him; and, finding that he could not succeed by direct assault,
he determined to effect his purpose by turning my left flank. The
great superiority of his troops in numbers gave him bright prospects of doing this. Up to this time my lines extended from Chaffin's Bluff on the right to New Market Heights on the left, my
extreme left resting at this latter place. Covering so great a line,
it was of course, with the comparatively few troops at my disposal,
weak everywhere, the men being in extended single rank, and in
many places there being none at all. I omitted to include a small
brigade of cavalry, under Brigadier General *Gary*, as a part of the
permanent force on the north side, and which force rendered
me very important service on this occasion. [*Southern Historical
Society Papers*, 52 vols. (Millwood, N.Y.: Kraus reprint, 1876–1959),
volume XIV, p. 550. Hereafter cited as *SHSP*.]

Gen. Robert E. Lee to Major General Field, August 14, 1864

[Maj. Gen. *Wade*] *Hampton* will be with you this evening. Two
brigades go from here. Major [*Edward C.*] *Anderson*, with 500 cavalry, ordered from Richmond. This may be a feint to draw troops
from here. Watch closely and return the troops here at the earliest
moment. [Dowdey and Manarin, eds., *The Wartime Papers of Robert E.
Lee*, p. 836.]

Return to your vehicle, and turn left onto Yahley Mill Road. Drive 1.2 miles until
the road ends at Long Bridge Road. Turn right, and travel 0.4 mile to the intersection with U.S. Route 5, the New Market Road. Just before the stop sign, turn
right into the gravel turn-off beside the intersection. Park near the trees beside
Route 5, get out of your vehicle, and face south across Route 5 and the James
River.

STOP 5: THE CAPTURE OF THE ROCKBRIDGE ARTILLERY

The area where you are standing was the apex of the Confederate
New Market Heights defensive line. Here, the entrenched line bent
back to the north and followed the high ground behind you above
Bailey's Creek, roughly along the line of the modern Yahley Mill Road.

Grant's plan for August 13 again called for the Tenth Corps to hold the Confederate defenders in place along New Market Heights while the Second Corps searched to the north for an exposed or weakened Confederate flank. The infantry attack was again to clear the way for a cavalry foray north and west toward Richmond. Just as it had in late July, the Federal attack began promisingly.

Report of Major General Hancock, continued

On General Birney's front, on the other side of Bailey's Creek, we had gained some success. The enemy weakened their line at that point to such an extent to resist General Barlow's advance, which was always strongly threatening, that General Birney was enabled to seize a part of their line with trifling loss, capturing at the same time four guns (8-inch howitzers), three of which were brought off by General Birney, and one secured on the following day by the exertions of General Mott. [*O.R.*, XLII, part 1, p. 218.]

Report of Brig. Gen. Robert S. Foster, USA, commanding Third Brigade, First Division, Tenth Corps, Army of the James

At 3.25 a.m. August 14 I received an order from Brigadier-General [Alfred H.] Terry to advance with my brigade and engage the enemy on the right of my position at Deep Bottom. The regiments in camp were immediately formed, and those on picket ordered in, and at 5.10 a.m. I met the enemy, having the Eleventh Maine, One hundredth New York, Tenth Connecticut, and First Maryland [Cavalry (dismounted)] in line of battle, preceded by a heavy skirmish line, and the Twenty-fourth Massachusetts in column of division in support, driving them into their rifle-pits. At 7.15 a.m. I ordered a charge, which was gallantly made, at 7.35, by the Twenty-fourth Massachusetts, in column of division, supported by the other regiments of my command, and the Sixth Connecticut, Colonel [Alfred P.] Rockwell (who had been temporarily assigned to my command), in support, driving the enemy out of three lines of rifle-pits and into the main line of intrenchments, across a deep ravine, with considerable loss, capturing about 100 prisoners, their dead and wounded, and 200 small-arms. Skirmishing continued from this time until 3 p.m., when, by direction of Brigadier-General Terry, I ordered Col. G[eorge] B. Dandy, with the One hundredth New York, supported by the Sixth Connecticut, Colonel Rockwell, to move to the right, and, if possible, connect with the Second Corps on the lower bank of

Four-Mile Creek. The regiments moved across the field in line of battle under a very heavy fire of artillery, capturing four 8-inch siege howitzers, and forming the desired connection with the Second Corps. Colonel Dandy was subsequently re-enforced by Lieutenant-Colonel [William P.] Coan's brigade, of the Second Division, Tenth Army Corps, and remained in position until the morning of the 15th. (For details see report of Col. G. B. Dandy, One hundredth New York, accompanying.) At 10 p.m. the brigade moved to the right across Four-Mile Creek and formed *en masse* on Strawberry Plains, where they rested during the night. [*O.R.*, XLII, part 1, pp. 727–728.]

Report of Col. George B. Dandy, 100th New York Infantry, Third Brigade, First Division, Tenth Corps, Army of the James

On the morning of the 14th the regiment was relieved from picket and ordered to fall in with the brigade. The position assigned us was the right of the brigade and in the advance against the enemy's works. I was directed to keep my right flank as near as possible on Four-Mile Creek. This was not precisely possible on account of the nature of the ground and the presence of the enemy in rifle-pits on the opposite side of the creek. When the brigade moved forward the regiment advanced steadily, at no time halting until the outer works of the enemy were captured. In this assault the regiment took 35 prisoners and 40 muskets, most of the prisoners (21) being taken by Company G, Lieutenant [Benjamin F.] Hughson commanding. The regiment, after having occupied the enemy's pits, was subjected to a vigorous shelling, and his sharpshooters, from a belt of woods on our right on Four-Mile Creek, had a good fire on our flank and rear, and did us some damage. Between 2 and 3 p.m. I was directed by Brigadier-General Foster, commanding Third Brigade, to withdraw my regiment from the line for the purpose of executing a movement on our right, designed to clear the belt of woods on Four-Mile Creek of the enemy, and open communication with the corps of General Hancock on the opposite side. This wood was crowded with sharpshooters, and it was reported that the enemy had a battery there.

The Sixth Connecticut, Colonel Rockwell, was ordered to report to me as a re-enforcement. Having formed my own regiment and the Sixth Connecticut in two lines of battle, the One hundredth New York in front, I charged the woods at the double-quick, driving the enemy from it and the rifle-pits beyond it, capturing a battery of four 8-inch sea-coast howitzers in position at the edge of the wood, and established communication with the Second Corps. The line so taken was held and skirmishers established to defend it. In this assault I was supported by the brigade of Lieutenant-Colonel Coan, who reported to me after the assault and was placed on picket that night to hold the ground. The guns with limbers and a full supply of ammunition were brought off during the night. During the assault the enemy from his main work opened upon our flank very heavily with six or eight guns, but, fortunately, he had not time to inflict much damage. [*O.R.*, XLII, part 1, pp. 757–758.]

Return to your vehicle, and retrace your route to Stop 1 of this excursion, but continue past the parking area at Fussell's Mill. Pass under the power lines, and continue for 0.3 mile to the intersection with Darbytown Road. Continue straight ahead through the intersection, and make an immediate left into the driveway for Henrico County Fire Station 18. Park in the parking area and walk out to the Darbytown/Yahley Mill intersection. Face to the left (east) across Yahley Mill Road. You are now looking toward the site of Fussell's Mill, approximately one-half mile to your right before you.

A short distance in front of you, on the right-hand side of Darbytown Road, stands a Virginia state historical marker honoring the Thirty-ninth Illinois Veteran Volunteer Infantry Regiment, a unit that participated in the desperate fighting here on August 16, 1864. This marker was placed along the line of the Confederate defensive position and is thus a good reference point for understanding the fighting at Second Deep Bottom. From the sign's location, the Confederate defenses stretched southward, using Fussell's Mill and the dense terrain around it, to the New Market Road, where they turned westward to join the Confederate Intermediate Line.

STOP 6: NEW MARKET HEIGHTS AND FUSSELL'S MILL

After a successful assault out of the Deep Bottom bridgehead, the Second Corps encountered the main Confederate line on New Market Heights, along the modern Yahley Mill road over which you just drove. At this point in the offensive, Hancock's division commanders confused his intent. Brig. Gen. Francis C. Barlow employed his brigades piecemeal, giving *Ewell*, back in overall command following *Anderson's* departure to the Shenandoah Valley, time to shift additional forces from the western portion of the line. In three days of inconclusive fighting, the Second Corps could not fix and overwhelm the Confederate left flank. Late on August 15, Grant determined to shift the Tenth Corps, Army of the James, from its static role at Deep Bottom, moving it north behind the Second Corps and back into line to its right, opposite Fussell's Mill. Maj. Gen. David B. Birney's corps thus assumed the Federal main effort. The reports in this section of the guide discuss Hancock's attacks in the battle's first phase, followed by Union and Confederate perspectives on the action at Fussell's Mill.

NEW MARKET HEIGHTS

Report of Major General Hancock, continued

General Mott moved out on the New Market and Malvern Hill road, as directed, and proceeded with little opposition to Bailey's Creek, where the enemy were found, as on the previous occasion, in a very strong position. It was intended that General Barlow should keep the force under his command (nearly 10,000 men) well in hand, and not attempt to develop a line of battle from General Mott's right. The thick woods prevented my knowing accurately what disposition he was making. It appears, however, that he extended to the right, carrying one line held by the enemy's dismounted cavalry and finally assaulting near Fussell's Mill with one brigade of the Second Division, when I expected him to attack with the greater portion of two divisions. His report, herewith inclosed, reflects little credit on the troops, showing that he made several unsuccessful attempts on the enemy's line, but I must say that had they been kept more compact they ought to have broken through the line, then thinly held, by mere weight of numbers, and thus have opened a way for General Mott. General Barlow's example to the troops was all that could be expected or desired from his well-known gallantry and devotion to duty. I attribute the lack of cohesion in the troops, as set forth in General Barlow's report, to the large number of new men in the command and the small number of experienced officers. General Barlow's main assault was not made until about 4 p.m. and night put an end to further operations, my expectations having been considerably disappointed. [O.R., XLII, part 1, p. 217.]

Report of Brigadier General Barlow, continued

Upon reaching the New Market road without opposition I held it with one brigade as a protection to my left flank, and with

the greater part of my own and the Second Division as they successively came up I pushed up the Central road. The enemy's line of
rifle-pits crossing the Central road being held only by a very thin
line of skirmishers, I pushed forward the first troops that arrived
(the Second New York Heavy Artillery) as quickly as possible to occupy the line. This regiment failed entirely to execute my orders,
and instead of occupying the point indicated it proceeded to an
entirely different part of the line, where the skirmishers of the
First Brigade were pressing the enemy. The commanding officer
of this regiment, Major [George] Hogg, showed himself utterly
unfit for command, and the regiment did not behave with credit
to itself. Seeing this failure I ordered the Irish Brigade to take
the same point. I am compelled to say that these troops behaved
disgracefully and failed to execute my orders. They crowded off to
our right into the shelter of some woods, and there became shattered and broken to pieces. By this time the enemy had moved
troops into that part of the line which I was endeavoring to take,
and had brought artillery to bear upon us. I then moved two brigades (the Third and Fourth) farther to the enemy's left, to a hill
near Fussell's mill-pond. The enemy's works beyond the mill-pond
were very thinly occupied, and I prepared to advance upon them
with the Fourth Brigade of my division. The enemy opening upon
us with artillery from their extreme right the troops exhibited
such signs of timidity and demoralization that I was convinced
that it was out of the question to employ them in this work. Therefore I ordered the First Brigade of the Second Division to advance
upon the works. They were occupied only by a very thin line of
the enemy, and could have been easily carried had the troops advanced with reasonable vigor and courage. I am compelled to say
that they failed to do this. The mill-pond was an obstacle to the
advance of the line in one place, but such of the troops as had the
requisite courage easily succeeded in passing to our left of it; but
they were too few to drive out the enemy. The attack was repulsed,
and the enemy had time to move troops to occupy the threatened
points. [*O.R.*, XLII, part 1, p. 248.]

Narrative of Major General Field, *continued*

About a mile to the left of New Market Heights, where the
left of my infantry rested, the New Market and Darbytown roads
united at Fussell's mill. The line of works behind which I was,
continued to this point, but was, as I said before, not manned. The

enemy rightly judged that by getting possession of these abandoned, or rather unoccupied, works at this point, he could, with his large force, probably sweep us before him into the lines surrounding Richmond, as the line upon which we then were was perpendicular to this last line, and the enemy arriving on our left flank would roll us up before we could form line of battle facing him, because our right was at Chaffin's, several miles distant. Accordingly, under cover of a forest, the enemy dashed at this point, Fussell's mill, but *Gary* quickly dismounting two of his three regiments threw them behind the works and received the Yankees with a galling fire. Fortunately, I was at the moment at my extreme left, and learning the enemy's intention, had a few minutes before started with *Anderson's* Georgia brigade and two pieces of artillery at a double-quick to the assailed point.

Reaching near the point of attack a few minutes after it began, a part of *Anderson's* brigade and the two guns opened upon the enemy's left flank, whilst *Gary* poured in a galling fire in front; the enemy wavered a few minutes, and then gave way in confusion, and fell back out of range for the day. The conduct of *Gary* on this occasion was very judicious and gallant. Only a portion of the enemy had crossed from Petersburg during the previous night, but all this day (August the 14th), from the elevation at New Market Heights, a stream of reinforcements could be seen coming over. Telegraphing at once to General *Lee*, who was at Petersburg, the condition of things, he sent to me also large reinforcements which were reaching me at intervals during the 15th. During this day the enemy made no attack, but were hard at work fortifying in my front. By morning of the 16th all my reinforcements had arrived and were in position, my line extending considerably to the left of Fussell's mill in the direction of the Charles City road. [*SHSP*, XIV, p. 551.]

Report of Brig. Gen. John Bratton, commanding Bratton's Brigade, Field's Division, First Corps, Army of Northern Virginia

We remained in this position [New Market Heights, July 30] with our pickets well out in front, enjoying freedom from the presence of the enemy, until the morning of 13th [14] of August, when the enemy assaulted, and after three efforts succeeded in driving in my pickets, capturing and killing some of them. It was here that Captain [*Christopher L.*] *Beaty*, of the Palmetto Sharpshooters, one of the most efficient officers of this brigade, fell

mortally wounded. The enemy in his front were successfully repulsed, he was slain, and some of his men captured by the enemy,
who had driven in the pickets on our left and came up in rear of
his lines. I mention this as due to the gallant officers and men who
were captured there. Our picket-line was finally driven in, pretty
badly mutilated. The enemy opened a furious cannonade upon
our main line, which, however, did not last long. Our skirmishers
were advanced, and they threatened his left, resting near the Yarborough house, which perhaps induced him to withdraw. While
this was occurring here it seems that the enemy were moving heavy
columns up the Darbytown and Charles City roads, which necessitated a sliding of the whole division to the left. I was ordered
to follow and keep up connection with the brigade on my left.
This was done, and night found my brigade with its right resting
upon the Drill house, and extending along New Market Heights
beyond the Libby house. [The Drill House and field stood within
the southeastern corner of the New Market Heights position, on
the high ground due north of the Kingsland/New Market Road
intersection.] [*O.R.*, XLII, part 1, p. 878.]

BREAKTHROUGH AT FUSSELL'S MILL

It was here, on the afternoon of August 16, that Tenth Corps
troops, led by Brig. Gen. Alfred H. Terry's First Division, found the
weak point in the Confederate line. This area witnessed a temporary
rupture of the Richmond defenses and the death of a promising Confederate brigadier.

Gen. Robert E. Lee to Secretary of War James Seddon, CSA, August 16, 1864, 4:00 p.m.

The enemy has made a determined attack on our line between
the Darbytown and Charles City Roads. At one time he broke
through but was repulsed, and we now occupy our original positions. [Dowdey and Manarin, eds., *The Wartime Papers of Robert E.
Lee*, p. 838.]

Report of Major General Hancock, continued

About 10 a.m. General Terry's division, of Birney's corps, advanced against the enemy's works above Fussell's Mill, and after
a severe contest carried the line, capturing 3 colors and 200 or
300 prisoners, most of them from *Wright's* (Georgia) brigade and

Lane's brigade. [Col. Calvin A.] Craig's brigade, of Mott's division, and the colored troops under Brig. Gen. William Birney, attacked on the right of the line; both are said to have acquitted themselves gallantly. Colonel Craig, commanding the brigade of Mott's division, was unfortunately killed in this assault. He had but just returned from an absence on account of wounds received during the campaign. The enemy soon rallied and retook the line, but it was several hours before I could ascertain the exact state of affairs, the wooded nature of the country preventing any personal examination. We retained only an advanced line of skirmish pits from which the enemy had been driven. [Lt. Col. Oscar] Broady's brigade, of General Barlow's division, was sent to General Birney at his request, and was formed to cover his right flank. [*O.R.*, XLII, part 1, p. 219.]

Report of Brigadier General Foster, continued

On the morning of the 15th we moved to the right across the Long Bridge road to an open field, where we remained, formed *en masse*, until the morning of the 16th, when at daylight the command moved to the right and was ordered to support Colonel [Joseph R.] Hawley's brigade, but subsequently was ordered to engage the enemy on the right of Colonel Hawley's brigade in the woods. The Tenth Connecticut, Twenty-fourth Massachusetts, and the Eleventh Maine were placed in the front, preceded by a heavy skirmish line, with the One hundredth New York and First Maryland Cavalry as supports, and in this position advanced through the woods, crossing two almost impassable ravines, and driving the enemy from two lines of rifle-pits, capturing over 100 prisoners. In this advance my right was protected handsomely by Colonel Craig's brigade, of the Second Corps. After reforming, at 1.40 p.m. a charge was ordered on the enemy's line of works, situated on the opposite bank of a deep ravine, which was made by my brigade in line and Colonel Hawley's and Colonel [Francis B.] Pond's brigades *en masse* on my right. The enemy's line was gained and held for one hour and forty minutes, under a very heavy flank and front fire of musketry and artillery, when the re-enforcements which had been sent for not arriving, and my left flank being partially turned and the line on my right pierced, I fell back across the ravine and reformed in line about 200 yards from the enemy's works. Colonel Broady's brigade of the Second Corps soon after reported to me, and by my direction formed in line on my right.

About dark a line of intrenchments was commenced and thrown up in front of the line of the enemy's second line of rifle-pits, to which we retired about midnight. [*O.R.*, XLII, part 1, p. 728.]

Narrative of Major General Field, continued

There was now under my command about fifteen thousand troops, consisting of the permanent troops I have previously named, my own division, now immediately commanded by Brigadier-General [*John*] *Gregg*, and a brigade or two each, I think, from *Heth's*, *Wilcox's*, [Maj. Gen. *William*] *Mahone's*, and *Pickett's* divisions. I regret that I cannot recall just now precisely whose brigades they were, but one I know was [Brig. Gen. *Nathaniel H.*] *Harris's* Mississippi brigade, one was [Brig. Gen. *Victor J. B.*] *Girardey's* Georgia, one was Virginia, two were North Carolina, one commanded by General *Conner*, one [Brig. Gen. *Ambrose R.*] *Wright's*, and the other I do not recollect. I should add that *W. H. F. Lee's* division of cavalry had also reported to me, and covered my left on the Charles City road.

I think it was about 10 or 11 o'clock a.m. of the 16th that the enemy made an assault in heavy masses on a part of my line about six hundred yards to the left of Fussell's mill. He had hit upon the most unfavorable point in our line of defence, for the ground was irregular, and what was of much more consequence, there was a dense forest of oak and pines in this immediate front, which we had only had time to cut away for a few yards (about fifty) in front of our works, thus offering a secure shelter to, and screening the enemy from our men till he got within fifty yards of our works. But he was met with a heavy and well-directed fire as soon as he showed himself through the bushes, and quickly withdrew. It was about a half hour after this, that whilst sitting on the ground with my staff and couriers, about one hundred yards in rear of the centre of the assault, with our horses hitched to some bushes close by, that I heard a scattering fire and some cheering immediately in my front. I knew at once that the enemy was assaulting again, but as he had just been handsomely repulsed at that very point, I felt so sure that the result would be the same now that I did not even rise up from the ground.

Major *Willis F. Jones*, my Adjutant-General, who was standing up near me and could see all that was going on so near us, suddenly said, very excitedly, General, they are breaking: thinking he referred to the Yankees, I replied, Well, I knew they would;

but he immediately exclaimed, but, General, it's our men, and, jumping to my feet, I saw at a glance the most appalling, disheartening sight of my life. The brigade just before me—*Girardey's* Georgia—had, from some entirely inexplicable cause, given way without firing a shot hardly, and the brigade on its left, a North Carolina one, seeing this, immediately did the same, and, at the moment of my looking, both brigades were coming back in disordered squads, and the Yankees were jumping over the works they had just vacated in close pursuit, and cheering like all the world. Jumping on my horse in a moment, I dashed up the line to reach the left two brigades, which were now cut off, and which I wished to attack in flank, whilst with the rest of my disposable troops I met him in front. Though I rode parallel to, and not over fifty yards in front of the enemy for some distance, the motion of my horse, and the great excitement of the enemy, made him miss me, though numerous shots were fired at me. But I could not reach the brigade on my left—the enemy were between us—had broken the army in two, and were pouring through the gap left by the two brigades which had broken. These two brigades for a time at least seemed to dissolve, but they were afterwards rallied, and aided in restoring things, the North Carolina one particularly doing good service.

At this time not only the day but Richmond seemed to be gone. There were three roads (the New Market, Darbytown and Charles City) radiating from Fussell's mill and leading to Richmond. The enemy had possession of these roads, was fronting two of them in heavy masses, and with my left entirely cut off, I had not at hand a single regiment to oppose him. I felt that nothing but a miracle could save us. My own gallant division had never yet failed when called upon, and sending an order to General *Gregg* commanding it to bring me every available man he had, to leave only a skirmish line to hold his works, and to come quickly, in a few minutes this division had formed a line of battle (under cover of the forest) in the enemy's path; we advanced against the enemy, and after a hard and well contested battle drove him back a half mile to our works, which he had captured, over and beyond them, retook our works and continued to hold them forever afterwards. This glorious and scarcely to be hoped for result was accomplished by *Gregg*, commanding my division, attacking in front aided by such portions of the two broken brigades as could be rallied (a majority of the North Carolina fighting well, its Colonel commanding being badly wounded) and that portion of the army which had been cut off—Colonel *Conner*, afterwards General *Conner*, being the senior, and in command of it, attacking at the same time in flank. This ended the fighting for that day.

Our losses, as might be inferred from such open, hard fighting, were heavy—the enemy's, though, much more so. Among the casualties in my division which now, at this distance of time, recur to me were: Colonel [*F. H.*] *Little*, commanding Eleventh Georgia, wounded; Colonel *Jack Brown*, of Georgia, my aide-de-camp, Lieutenant *W. Roy Mason*, badly wounded, falling into the hands of the enemy, and General *Gregg's* aide de-camp killed. Brigadier-General *Girardey* was killed early in the action, at the time his brigade broke. He had only a few days before been raised from the rank of Major and assigned to that brigade, and fell in his first action with his new rank. He was said to be a gallant, meritorious officer. [*SHSP*, XIV, pp. 551–554.]

Memoir of Lieutenant Caldwell, continued

We took up the position assigned us, *Lane's* brigade being next to *Field's* division, and our brigade next to them—the extreme left of the Confederate line. Our sharpshooters were deployed in front as skirmishers, and the main line was ordered to erect defenses as rapidly as possible. We were in one rank, loosely dressed. Before long our skirmishers became slightly engaged, and the firing on our right waxed very hot. But, after some fierce volleys there, a comparative silence ensued; and then there came word along the line that the enemy had broken *Field's* line and captured his works. We were at once ordered out of the intrenchments, put into a rapid march toward the right, in rear of the works, and closed up in two ranks as we moved. . . . After a march of nearly half a mile through the woods, we were fronted and dressed. . . . The enemy now occupied a considerable line of works. . . . As we reached the pine thicket in which the works lay, the enemy, although we were still invisible to them, opened fire upon us. . . . We advanced slowly.

The Twelfth [South Carolina] regiment first struck the works. They plunged at them once and got in, driving off the enemy immediately before them. But the enemy on their right threw such an enfilade fire along them, that they were forced to withdraw. But they rallied and assailed the works again, but with the same result. Still they rallied on the rest of the brigade and pushed

forward with undiminished ardor. . . . Once the right of the brigade pushed up within twenty steps of the enemy. But the latter met them with unusual composure, firing a murderous volley
right in their faces. Stunned and confused with this sudden blow,
our line edged back for some paces, still, however, facing their
adversaries and returning their fire. The men of the brigade who
were shot down by the volley just described now lay between the
two fires, some of them calling loudly to their comrades to make
the charge. The whole line on the right had now come up close
to the works, firing all the while and keeping most of the enemy
hidden. The chief impetus came, at this juncture, from the right,
where some of *Field's* men (*Bratton's* South Carolina brigade, I
think) flung themselves into the works. The enthusiasm seized
the whole line. With a yell they dashed against the fortifications,
stormed out the dense line crowded there, and killed them by
scores as they fled away in irretrievable panic. A good many prisoners fell into our hands, and an amount of plunder unequalled
in any battle before or since. There were two lines of Federals in
the works, a white line and one of negroes. [Caldwell, *The History
of a Brigade of South Carolinians*, pp. 176–177.]

Return to your vehicle. Leave the parking lot, and turn left at the Yahley Mill/
Darbytown Road intersection. Drive east on Darbytown Road for 0.8 mile, turning left onto Gill Dale Road. Travel north for 1.6 miles until Gill Dale Road ends at
Charles City Road, and turn right. The open fields north of the intersection were
the wartime Fisher Farm. Drive 0.3 mile, and turn left into the parking lot for Poplar Springs Baptist Church and cemetery. Park in the large paved lower parking
lot. Note that the current church is out of sight beyond the cemetery; you have
turned into the parking lot before reaching it. Walk to the two markers to the left
of the parking lot before you reach the cemetery. Face back in the direction from
which you drove, noting the creek that crosses Charles City Road.

STOP 7: CAVALRY ENGAGEMENT ON THE CHARLES CITY ROAD

The church buildings near where you stand, Poplar Springs Baptist Church, replace several earlier incarnations of a church on this
spot. A group of Slovakian émigrés formed the First Slovak Baptist
Church here in 1913.

The original Poplar Springs Church served as a staging area for
Brig. Gen. David M. Gregg's Federal cavalry division. In accordance
with Hancock's plan, Gregg was to circumvent the Confederate defenses to their northeast, allowing Hancock's and Birney's corps to

clear a path to Richmond. Gregg would then turn northwest and exploit this opening and reach the Confederate capital if possible.

Looking west along Charles City Road, in the direction from which
you just came, you will see a slight rise along the far bank of Deep Run
Creek; it was here that Confederate cavalry occupied a picket line
covering the Charles City Road approach to Richmond. The Federal
attack scattered this picket line, and a running cavalry fight developed
along the road to the capital.

Report of Major General Hancock, continued

On the morning of the 16th General Birney was ordered to
attack. As a strong diversion, General Gregg was directed to move
up the Charles City road, and General Miles' brigade, of Barlow's
division, was placed under his orders with the understanding that
when Birney became engaged General Miles was to return by a
cross-road and form on Birney's right and take part in the main
attack. The advance of General Gregg was made at an early hour
and the enemy was driven rapidly before him beyond Deep Creek,
nearly to White's Tavern. General [*John R.*] *Chambliss*, of the Confederate cavalry, was killed during this advance, and his body fell
into our hands. [*O.R.*, XLII, part 1, p. 219.]

The historical marker near the site of *Chambliss's* death is titled "A
Sad Reunion." Union Brig. Gen. Gregg and Confederate Brig. Gen.
Chambliss had been classmates in the West Point class of 1853. When
Gregg reputedly spotted his friend's body lying near the road, he ar-
ranged for the body and personal effects to be sent through the lines
to *Chambliss's* family's home in Southside Virginia.

Gen. Robert E. Lee to President Jefferson Davis, CSA, August 16, 1864, 10:35 a.m.

Genl *Field*, on the Darbytown Road, reports that Genl [*W. H. F.*]
Lee's pickets at the swamp have been driven back, and that the
enemy in heavy force are advancing up the Charles City Road
and are nearly at White's Tavern. Enemy is in rear of *Field's* force,
and it will be thrown over on the left to attack enemy in flank. I
recommend the works at Richmond be manned. If *Hampton's* force is
accessible, please order it at once down Charles City Road. [Dowdey
and Manarin, eds., *The Wartime Papers of Robert E. Lee*, p. 838.]

Gen. Robert E. Lee to Secretary of War Seddon, August 16, 1864, 8:30 p.m.

The enemy did not renew the attack after his repulse mentioned in my first dispatch. His force on the Charles City Road, after advancing to within two (2) miles of White's Tavern, was driven back across White Oak Swamp. Our loss was small. [Dowdey and Manarin, eds., *The Wartime Papers of Robert E. Lee*, p. 839.]

Report of Major General Hancock, continued

About 1.30 p.m. the enemy's cavalry, strengthened by an infantry force, advanced on Gregg and Miles on the Charles City road. Our troops retired fighting to Deep Creek. Here General Miles withdrew his brigade, in accordance with my instructions, and moving in on General Birney's right, took command of his own and Broady's brigades. [Gen. Thomas A.] Smyth's brigade, of Gibbon's division, was formed on Birney's left, but was engaged only in brisk skirmishing. General Mott felt the enemy's line at intervals during the afternoon beyond Bailey's Creek, to prevent them from sending re-enforcements to our front. They showed on each occasion a strong line in Mott's front. General Birney proposed to attack again at 5 p.m., but reported at 6 p.m. that on advancing his skirmish line he found the enemy had massed in his front, and decided that he could not attack successfully. General Gregg was holding his position beyond Deep Creek in an old line of the enemy's rifle-pits. At 4.45 p.m. he was attacked by the enemy and forced back across the creek. Forming on the south bank he succeeded in holding the enemy in check, although they made a strong effort to cross. The remainder of the day passed without incident. [*O.R.*, XLII, part 1, p. 219.]

Remain in place at Poplar Springs Church.

WITHDRAWAL ACROSS THE JAMES

Report of Major General Hancock, continued

On the night of the 16th a fleet of steamers was sent from City Point to Deep Bottom, returning at 4 a.m. on the 17th, the object being to convey the impression to the enemy that we were withdrawing from Deep Bottom, and to induce them to come out of their works and attack us. There was no change in the disposition of my lines on the 17th, nor could any movements be detected on the part of the enemy. During the day General Birney sent me a note saying that our wounded and those of the enemy in the affair of the 16th were between the lines exposed to the fire of both parties, and requesting a flag of truce to cover their removal. Under the authority of General Grant a cessation of hostilities from 4 until 6 p.m. was arranged for the purpose indicated by General Birney. I was somewhat mortified to find that a mistake had been made in the matter, for not one wounded man was found, the enemy having removed all of ours and buried some of the dead. General *Chambliss'* body was delivered to the enemy during this truce.

At 5 p.m. I received a dispatch from Lieutenant-General Grant, saying that the position obtained by General Butler near Dutch Gap was of no practical importance. At 10.15 p.m. I received a dispatch from General Grant telling me that General Warren would move from our left to the Weldon railroad at 4 a.m. on the 18th, and desiring me to take advantage of any opportunity for success in my front. On the 18th General Barlow was compelled by sickness to give up the command of his division to General Miles. This day passed with skirmishing and reconnoitering the enemy's position until 5.30 p.m., when the enemy came out of their works above Fussell's Mill and attacked General Birney. The fight lasted about thirty minutes, when the enemy were repulsed with considerable loss. General Miles, with the First and Fourth Brigades of his command, took part in this affair, attacking the enemy on his left flank.

At the same time the enemy appeared in considerable force on the road from the Charles City road over White Oak Swamp, driving Gregg's cavalry away from the cross-roads and obtaining a position on the Charles City road some three miles in rear of General Gregg's position at Deep Creek. As usual, under such circumstances, the enemy were reported moving to my rear (toward Malvern Hill) with infantry and artillery, and the fire being brisk in that direction, I sent Miles' brigade out to support Gregg, but the brigade did not engage the enemy. General Gregg kept up his communication with Deep Creek by an interior wood road, and the enemy retired from the cross-roads on the following morning. At 8 p.m. General Mott was ordered to Petersburg to relieve the Ninth Corps from the intrenchments. This made a contraction of our lines necessary, and the following dispositions were made: Smyth's division held from Bailey's Creek, on the New

Market road, to the right along the wood road leading to the Long Bridge road, connecting with Miles' division, which held nearly to Ruffin's, on the Long Bridge road. The Tenth Corps occupied the high ground near Ruffin's, covering the approaches from the right. The picket-line remained unchanged, except that the right was withdrawn somewhat.

On the 19th, at 10.30 a.m., I received a dispatch from General Grant informing me that the enemy had sent a division to Petersburg, and advising me not to hesitate to attack with my whole force if I found a weak point. No such point had been discovered, but I spent two or three hours in a close examination of the line, and finally concluded to attack a little to the left of where General Barlow had failed on the 15th. The detailed order had been prepared for the assault, which was to be made by a portion of Miles' division and a brigade of colored troops from Birney, all under command of General Miles. I thought the chance of carrying the line a fair one, the main difficulty being in holding the position, or in gaining any decisive advantage from it. I described the position fully to General Grant, and at his suggestion the projected assault was abandoned. About 1 p.m. I was requested to send a brigade of cavalry to General Meade if I could spare it. General Gregg was at once ordered to send the brigade. Nothing of great interest occurred during the 20th. Immediately after dark I withdrew my command, in accordance with orders, the Tenth Corps covering the movement, and marched my two divisions by Point of Rocks to my old camp, near Petersburg. The cavalry moved by Broadway Landing, reporting to the major-general commanding when they had crossed the Appomattox. The Tenth Corps returned to its former camp. The night was extremely inclement, and the roads were in an exceedingly bad condition, but my command arrived at camp in very good order between 6 and 7 a.m. on the 21st. [*O.R.*, XLII, part 1, p. 219.]

A few days after the latest round of fighting died down north of the James, *Lee* summarized the recent actions for his commander in chief. The letter places the Federal defeat at Deep Bottom in a larger operational context, hinting that even though the Second Corps and Gregg's cavalrymen suffered a tactical defeat, Grant's campaign plan was having an effect on *Lee's* ability to hold the Richmond and Petersburg defenses.

General Robert E. Lee to President Davis, August 22, 1864

The enemy availed himself of the withdrawal of troops from Petersburg to the north side of James River, to take a position on the Weldon Railroad. He was twice attacked on his first approach to the road, and worsted both times, but the attacking force was too small to drive him off.

Before the troops could be brought back from north of James River, he had strengthened his position so much, that the effort made yesterday to dislodge him was unsuccessful, and it was apparent that it could not be accomplished even with additional troops, without a greater sacrifice of life than we could afford to make, or than the advantages of success would compensate for. . . . I think it is his purpose to endeavor to compel the evacuation of our present position by cutting off our supplies, and that he will not renew the attempt to drive us away by force.

His late demonstration on the north side of the James was designed I think in part, to cause the withdrawal of troops here to favor his movement against the road, but also to endeavor if possible to force his way to Richmond. Being foiled in the attempt, he has brought back all the troops engaged in it, except those at Dutch Gap, and it is possible that they too will be withdrawn to this side of the James. It behooves us to do everything in our power to thwart his new plan of reducing us by starvation, and all our energies should be directed to using to its utmost capacity our remaining line of communication with the south. . . .

I shall do all in my power to procure some supplies by the Weldon road, bringing them by rail to Stony Creek, and thence by wagons. One train has already been sent out, and others are prepared to go. I think by energy and intelligence on the part of those charged with the duty, we will be able to maintain ourselves until the corn crop in Virginia comes to our relief, which it will begin to do to some extent in about a month. . . .

Our supply of corn is exhausted today, the small reserve accumulated in Richmond having been used. I am informed that all the corn that was brought from the south was transported to this place and Richmond, but the supply was not sufficient to enable the Quartermaster Department to accumulate a larger reserve. . . .

I trust that Your Excellency will see that the most vigorous and intelligent efforts be made to keep up our supplies, and that all officers concerned in the work, be required to give their unremitting personal attention to their duty. [Dowdey and Manarin, eds., *The Wartime Papers of Robert E. Lee*, pp. 842–843.]

Narrative of Major General Field, continued

Though Richmond came at last so near being closely invested, and the result to us was so important, the people even in Richmond, a few miles off, were never aware how great their danger was, and never knew of nor appreciated the importance of the battle. Indeed, it was scarcely known that a battle had been fought and won. [*SHSP*, XIV, p. 553.]

Once again, *Lee* and his commanders were able to use interior lines and mission-type orders[7] to react quickly and stop a Federal offensive north of the James River. As he had in July at First Deep Bottom, Grant was able to continue his operational approach of simultaneous attacks at opposite ends of *Lee's* extended defensive lines, preventing the Confederates from concentrating reinforcements at one point. Grant had greater success to the south of Petersburg, capturing and holding a lodgment on the Weldon Railroad, cutting that major Confederate supply line and making the Fourth Offensive an overall success. The desperate fighting north of the James cost *Lee* hundreds of additional casualties and two generals, but the eastern approaches to Richmond remained secure.

Return to your vehicle. If you wish to continue with a look at Grant's Fifth Offensive north of the James, you may return directly to Deep Bottom Park, the first stop for that excursion, by taking the Charles City Road 0.5 mile back to Gill Dale Road. Turn left, and follow Gill Dale Road for 1.7 miles to its end at Darbytown Road. Turn right, and make an immediate left at 0.2 mile on Bradbury Road. After 1.4 miles, Bradbury Road ends at Long Bridge Road. Turn right, and follow your original route back to Deep Bottom Park via the New Market, Kingsland, and Deep Bottom Roads.

For an alternate route to Deep Bottom that shows you the site of *Chambliss's* death and the extent of the Federal cavalry penetration, turn right onto Charles City Road. At 1.3 miles you will pass the *Chambliss* marker on the right side of the road. Drive another 1.6 miles, passing under I-295, to reach White's Tavern, a white two-story frame building on the right side of the road, now a Henrico County facility. Make a U-turn when it is safe to do so, and drive back

---

[7] Mission-type orders give a subordinate the commander's intent for an operation, leaving the details of execution to the subordinate. These orders allow for changing situations in combat.

along the Charles City Road for 0.6 mile, turning right onto Turner Road. Drive 3.5 miles to the intersection with New Market Road, and turn left. Return to Deep Bottom via the Kingsland Road.

To return to the Petersburg National Battlefield Visitor Center, follow the directions above for a direct return to Deep Bottom, but continue straight ahead on New Market Road (U.S. Route 5) to the I-295 interchange. Take I-295 south for 12.2 miles to exit 9B, Westbound Route 36/Oaklawn Boulevard, proceeding on Oaklawn Boulevard to the Visitor Center.

EXCURSION 4
FORT HARRISON AND DARBYTOWN ROAD

After two months of successful operations south and west of Petersburg, which saw Maj. Gen. George G. Meade's Army of the Potomac cut the Weldon Railroad, one of the Confederate capital's principal lines of supply and communications with the Carolinas, Lt. Gen. Ulysses S. Grant continued to try to work his way around *Gen. Robert E. Lee's* right flank south of the Cockade City. As September ended, Grant's next objective was the Squirrel Level Road, one of the routes used by Confederate logisticians to move supplies by wagon into Petersburg. After the Fourth Offensive of August 1864 cut the Weldon Railroad, the northernmost point in Confederate hands was the depot at Stony Creek, in southern Virginia. Trains from the Carolinas stopped here, and their contents were transferred to wagons and brought into Richmond and Petersburg via the Squirrel Level Road and the Boydton Plank Road (modern U.S. Route 1).

Lee had to continually extend his defenses westward to cover these roads and the South Side Railroad, leaving him fewer reliable units to respond to a breakthrough anywhere along the line.

As *Lee* continued to fortify his position around Petersburg and transfer combat power to the Shenandoah Valley, Maj. Gen. Benjamin Butler, commander of Grant's Army of the James, saw an opportunity north of the James. Butler's well-developed intelligence network reported that *Lee* had diminished his force north of the James, leaving the defenses of Richmond in the hands of second-rate garrison artillery units and Virginia militia battalions. With Grant's support, Butler developed a plan to use his army to sweep into Richmond and end the war at a stroke.

SUMMARY OF PRINCIPAL EVENTS, 1 SEPTEMBER– 8 OCTOBER 1864

September
2—Reconnaissance beyond Yellow Tavern on Weldon Railroad
3—Affair near Sycamore Church
7—Maj. Gen. John Gibbon, U.S. Army, in temporary command
of Eighteenth Army Corps

Maj. Gen. Benjamin F. Butler (USAMHI)

5—Maj. Gen. David B. Birney, U.S. Army, in temporary
command of the Army of the James
5–6—Reconnaissance to Sycamore Church
7—Maj. Gen. Benjamin F. Butler, U.S. Army, resumes command
of the Army of the James
10—Assault on Confederate works at the Chimneys

13—Scout to Poplar Spring Church

15—Reconnaissance toward Dinwiddie Court-House and
skirmish

16–17—Affair at Coggins's Point (September 16) and pursuit of
the Confederates

19—Scout to Lee's Mill and Proctor's House

22—Maj. Gen. Edward O. C. Ord, U.S. Army, resumes command
of Eighteenth Army Corps

29–30—Battle of Chaffin's Farm (including combats at Fort
Harrison, Fort Gilmer, New Market Heights, and Laurel Hill)

29–October 2—Battle of Poplar Spring Church (including
combats at Wyatt's, Peebles's, and Pegram's Farms, Chappell
House, and Vaughan Road)

October

1—Bvt. Maj. Gen. Godfrey Weitzel, U.S. Army, in temporary
command of Eighteenth Army Corps

7—Engagement on the Darbytown and New Market Roads
(including combats at Johnson's Farm and Four-Mile Creek)

Drive out of the parking area for the Petersburg National Battlefield Visitor Center, and proceed 0.2 mile down the park road to the exit for eastbound Route 36 (Oaklawn Boulevard) in the direction of Hopewell. Take Oaklawn Boulevard for 2.7 miles to Interstate 295, and take the northbound ramp to Richmond. Travel 12.2 miles to exit 22A, and take the ramp leading to eastbound Route 5 (New Market Road). Proceed 1.3 miles to Kingsland Road on the right. Turn and proceed 0.7 mile to Deep Bottom Road. Turn left onto Deep Bottom Road, and follow it for 1.3 miles to the parking area for Deep Bottom Park. Walk to the bank of the James River, noting the interpretive signs placed here by the Civil War Trust, which feature period photographs of the area. At the river, face to the right, upstream toward Richmond. At this spot you are approximately 11 miles southeast of Richmond.

STOP 1: DEEP BOTTOM

Report of Lt. Gen. Ulysses S. Grant, USA, commanding Armies of the United States

By the 12th of September a branch railroad was completed from the City Point and Petersburg Railroad to the Weldon railroad, enabling us to supply without difficulty, in all weather, the army in front of Petersburg. The extension of our lines across the Weldon railroad compelled the enemy to so extend his that it seemed he could have but few troops north of the James for the

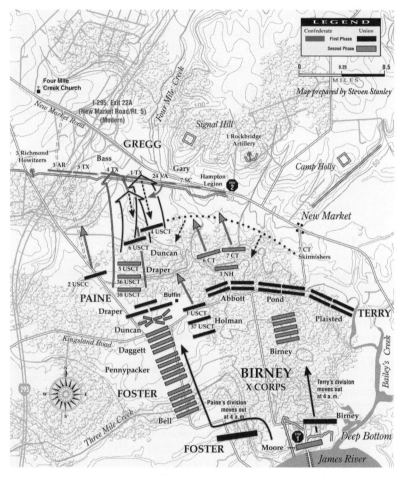

New Market Heights, September 29, 1864: First and second phases

defense of Richmond. On the night of the 28th the Tenth Corps, Major-General [David B.] Birney, and the Eighteenth Corps, Major-General [Edward O. C.] Ord commanding, of General Butler's army, were crossed to the north side of the James, and advanced on the morning of the 29th, carrying the very strong fortifications and intrenchments below Chaffin's Farm, known as Fort Harrison, capturing fifteen pieces of artillery and the New Market road and intrenchments. [U.S. War Department, *The War of the Rebellion: A Compilation of the Official Records of the Union and*

Confederate Armies, 70 vols. in 128 parts and index (Washington, D.C.: Government Printing Office, 1880–1901), series 1, volume XLVI, part 1, p. 30. Hereafter cited as *O.R.*; all references are to series 1 unless otherwise noted.]

Report of Maj. Gen. Edward O. C. Ord, USA, commanding Eighteenth Corps, Army of the James

On the 28th day of September, 1864, in obedience to orders, I selected from my corps—then on duty between the James and Appomattox Rivers—about 4,000 men, from Generals [George J.] Stannard's and [Charles A.] Heckman's divisions, for a movement on the north side of the James against Richmond, in co-operation with another column under Major-General Birney, composed of his corps and [Brig. Gen. Charles J.] Paine's division of mine; in all, that column was about 10,000 strong, and was designed to reach Richmond via Deep Bottom and the New Market road, while I was to engage the works nearer the river, and prevent the interruption of General Birney's column by re-enforcements which the enemy might send across from the south side of the James River, where they had a heavy force. The movement was to be a surprise, therefore I issued no written orders and my verbal orders were not communicated to the troops until after dark, when all communication should have ceased with our own picket-line. This precaution was deemed necessary to prevent the spies which abounded in our regiments from deserting and giving information of our movement to the enemy. [*O.R.*, XLII, part 1, p. 793.]

Return to your vehicle. Drive out to New Market Road (U.S. Route 5), and turn left. After 0.5 mile, turn right onto New Market Heights Lane and park immediately. Get out of your vehicle and remain at the side of the road, facing south across Route 5.

STOP 2: NEW MARKET HEIGHTS

In this area, the historic trace of the New Market Road matches the road bed of the current U.S. Route 5, putting the Confederate entrenchments on the south side of the highway. A 200-yard stretch of the entrenchments is visible in the tree line on the other side of the road; at the time of the battle, the area south of the road was cleared by the Confederate defenders of New Market Heights, with fallen trees left in the low ground as an abatis. The swampy course of

Maj. Gen. Edward O. C. Ord (USAMHI)

Four Mile Creek also runs across in front of you before turning north and crossing the road to your right, or west; in 1864 it was a significant obstacle to troop movement from Deep Bottom, over a mile to the south. The area where you are standing would have been completely cleared of trees, allowing signals to pass to and from the defenders of this part of the Southern defenses.

This section of the New Market Heights line was manned by the remnants of the famous Texas Brigade, augmented with some dismounted cavalry troopers. After the two battles of Deep Bottom over the summer of 1864, it was a quiet section of the Richmond-Petersburg defenses as fall came to Tidewater Virginia.

Opposite this line, a division of U.S. Colored Troops massed in the swampy ground around the Deep Bottom bridgehead. Brig. Gen. Charles J. Paine's Third Division, Eighteenth Corps of the Army of the James, was attached to Birney's right wing for the Fifth Offensive. Butler was known throughout the Army for his enlightened views on African American soldiers and employed them extensively throughout his army. Black troops had already seen combat during the Richmond-Petersburg campaign but had been controversially removed from the primary attack after the mine detonation on July 30.

A series of brave but disjointed Federal attacks by USCT regiments made no headway against the New Market Heights line until late morning, when Brig. Gen. *Martin Gary* withdrew after receiving word of the attack on Fort Harrison to the west. As the Texans withdrew, the black regiments swept into the works behind them, achieving well-deserved notoriety and praise as a result.

Report of Col. Alonzo G. Draper, USA, commanding Thirty-sixth U.S. Colored Troops, Third Division, Eighteenth Corps, Army of the James

On the morning of the 29th ultimo my brigade was massed in column in rear of the woods near Ruffin's house before daybreak. We were directed to lie down and wait for further orders. After the Third Brigade had preceded us for half a mile or more I received an order to form line of columns and advance. We advanced immediately across the open field, leaving Ruffin's house on our left. On this field we received a skirmish fire from the woods. When nearly down to the ravine I received an order from Brigadier-General Paine to move my brigade to the right, as "we were getting the worst of it there." We immediately moved by the right flank and again by the left (by the proper evolutions), and formed at the ravine, where the troops lay down in line. We were here subjected to the fire of the New Market batteries, which did little damage. After lying here about half an hour I was ordered to form my brigade into line of double columns and assault the enemy's works in front. The Twenty-second U.S. Colored Troops were to skirmish on our left. This they did for awhile, but did not continue to the works. After passing about 300 yards through young pines, always under fire, we emerged upon the open plain about 800 yards from the enemy's works.

Across this the brigade charged with shouts, losing heavily. Within twenty or thirty yards of the rebel line we found a swamp

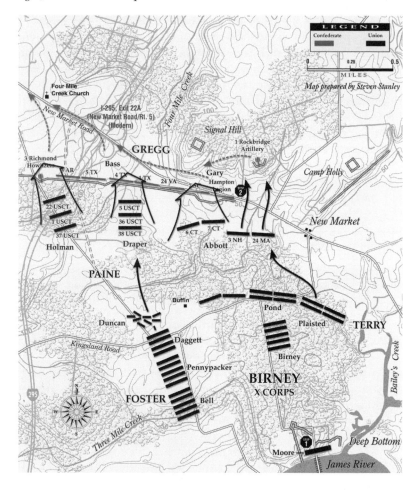

New Market Heights, September 29, 1864: Final phase

which broke the charge, as the men had to wade the run or stream and reform on the bank. At this juncture, too, the men generally commenced firing, which made so much confusion that it was impossible to make the orders understood. Our men were falling by scores. All the officers were striving constantly to get the men forward. I passed frequently from the right to the left, urging every regimental commander to rally his men around the colors and charge. After half an hour of terrible suspense, by starting the yell among a few, we succeeded in getting them in motion. The entire brigade took up the shout and went over the rebel works. When we reached the palisades the rebels fell back to the woods on the side of Signal Hill. We again assaulted and drove them out. I immediately formed for defense, and sent a courier to Brigadier-General Paine for re-enforcements, which arrived in about twenty minutes to a half hour. In this assault we had no supports. [*O.R.*, XLII, part 1, p. 819.]

Report of Brig. Gen. Robert S. Foster, USA, commanding Second Division, Tenth Corps, Army of the James

On the 28th of September, pursuant to orders from the major-general commanding the corps, broke camp near Petersburg at promptly 3 p.m. and took up the line of march, following in rear of First Division, Tenth Army Corps. Owing to delays in the wagon train of that division my progress was slow, and the head of my column only reached the pontoon bridge across the Appomattox at 8.35 p.m. and Deep Bottom at 1.30 a.m. on the 29th. On reaching Deep Bottom the Two hundred and third Pennsylvania Volunteers was detached from the Second Brigade and ordered to garrison the roads at that place. The balance of my command bivouacked outside the works until 5.50 a.m., when it was moved forward and formed in column of battalion in mass, the head of column resting on the Kingsland road about 300 yards on the right of the Grover house, in support of General William Birney's division, of the Tenth Army Corps. At 8.30 a.m. the division moved forward to Signal Hill and took the advance up the New Market and Richmond road, the First Brigade leading the column. [*O.R.*, XLII, part 1, p. 760.]

Diary of Sgt. Maj. Christian A. Fleetwood, Fourth U.S. Colored Troops

WEDNESDAY 28 on board a gunboat and debarked at Jones Landing. Marched up to works Bivouacked at Deep Bottom Dined and sup'd with 5. U.S.C.T. Trimonthly report made out slept with Kelly, Arnold, & Hawkins Letters came from Bradford & Est. & Cootus with carte

Stirred up Regt. and, Knap[s]acks C.G.E. packed away Coffe boiled and

THURSDAY, SEPTEMBER 29, 1864 line formed. Moved out & on Charged with the 6th at daylight and got used up. Saved colors. Remnants of the two gathered and Maneuvering under Col

[John W.] Ames of 6th U.S.C.T. Marching in line & flank all day saw Gen. Grant & Staff both Birneys [brother generals] and other "Stars" Retired at night. [http://nationalhumanitiescenter.org/pds/maai/identity/text7/fleetwooddiary.pdf]

General Orders, U.S. Army, April 6, 1865

The President of the United States of America, in the name of Congress, takes pleasure in presenting the Medal of Honor to Sergeant Major Christian A. Fleetwood, United States Army, for extraordinary heroism on 29 September 1864, while serving with 4th U.S. Colored Infantry, in action at Chaffin's Farm, Virginia. Sergeant Major Fleetwood seized the colors, after two Color Bearers had been shot down, and bore them nobly through the fight. [U.S. Government Printing Office, *Medal of Honor Recipients: 1863–1878* (Washington: U.S. Government Printing Office, 1979), p. 88.

If you wish to visit the remains of an earthen Confederate fort that served as a signal station in this area, return to your vehicle and drive 0.3 mile up New Market Heights Lane until you see a small gravel turnout on your left. Make a U-turn and park in this turnout, next to the woods. Walk approximately 200 yards west into the woods until you see a small earthen fortification. Go to the outside of the fort wall and face south, toward Route 5.

You are standing beside a Confederate signal station, part of the New Market Heights defenses. Period maps refer to this location as "Signal Hill," one of two such places in this area of the James River, and 1864 battle reports describe a signal tower as having stood here. These stations allowed the Confederate defenders to communicate along the length of the line via signal flags.

Return to your car. Drive back to New Market Road and turn right. Travel 3.4 miles on New Market Road. You will see a restaurant on the left side of the road. Turn into the parking lot, parking your vehicle at the southwestern end of the lot. Get out of your vehicle, and face in your original direction of travel along Route 5.

STOP 3: LAUREL HILL AND THE TENTH CORPS ATTACK

You are standing just east of the northern end of the Confederate Exterior Line. The remains of the earthen entrenchments are visible before you, where the modern Battlefield Park Road meets New Market Road. Battlefield Park Road conforms to the Exterior Line for most of its length down to Fort Harrison. Note the broken and rolling terrain around you, particularly to your left (south). There is also a slight rise before you, past Battlefield Park Road; this is Laurel Hill, a terrain feature the Confederate defenders used to their advantage after abandoning New Market Heights. This terrain made it difficult for the Federal Tenth Corps to mass combat power for its attacks here on September 29.

After capturing New Market Heights, elements of the Tenth Corps reorganized and pushed westward along New Market Road toward Fort Harrison. Brig. Gen. *Martin Gary's* mixed force of infantry and cavalry, the force that had occupied the New Market Heights trenches, conducted an effective delaying action, slowing the movement of Brig. Gen. Robert S. Foster's division. Union numbers began to tell, however, and by early afternoon blue regiments were astride the Exterior Line and ready to attack to the south.

Report of Brigadier General Foster, continued

At 9.25 the head of column met the enemy's picket along the line of works at the junction of the Mill and New Market and Richmond roads. A portion of the 142nd New York Volunteers, Lieut. Col. A. M. Barney, were deployed as skirmishers, and followed by the whole brigade charged the works at a run, the enemy falling back rapidly, leaving their works in our possession. After a short rest the column again moved forward through the woods, with but a few shots from the enemy's vedettes, to the open ground, when the head of the column was opened on with very severe artillery fire from the fort to the front and left and by their light 12-pounders in position at Laurel Hill Church. I attempted to form under cover of the wood in three lines of battle, but the formation of the ground threw them in echelon—the First Brigade in advance, the Second Brigade extending to the right, and Third to the right. This was done under a heavy fire of artillery, which did considerable execution. As soon as formed, I ordered an advance to dislodge the battery at Laurel Hill Church, which was promptly executed, the enemy retiring in such haste as to leave their killed on the field and the road strewn with artillery ammunition and implements. I formed my command along the New Market road, the right resting at Laurel Hill Church. [*O.R.*, XLII, part 1, p. 760.]

Return to your vehicle, and turn left onto New Market Road. Drive 0.1 mile to Battlefield Park Road; turn left. Follow the park road for 0.5 mile to Fort Gilmer, noting Cornelius Creek and the difficulties it would pose for an attacking force.

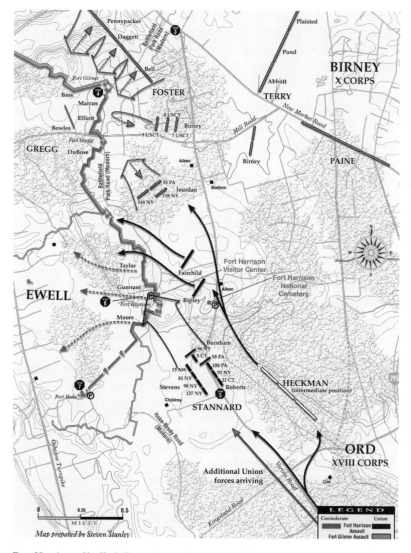

Fort Harrison–Chaffin's Farm, September 29–30, 1864

Park at Fort Gilmer, on the left side of the road, and stand on the sidewalk looking toward the earthen wall in front of you.

STOP 4: FORT GILMER

Fort Gilmer occupied a salient in the Exterior Line, where the
fortifications turned west and then north to follow the natural defensive terrain along Cornelius Creek. This fort, which had two heavy
guns (including a 64-pounder cannon) and Confederate troops from
the Richmond defenses, was reinforced by Georgians from Maj. Gen.
Charles Field's First Corps division. Foster's Tenth Corps division, after
capturing Laurel Hill Church, turned to attack Fort Gilmer from the
north, while U.S. Colored Troops from Brig. Gen. William B. Birney's
(the corps commander's brother) Third Division attacked from the
east. Birney's attack was unsupported from its left, as the remainder
of Brig. Gen. George Stannard's division became disoriented in the
woods east of the Varina Road and was unable to mount an effective
attack on either Fort Gregg or Fort Johnson, the next strong points on
the line between Fort Gilmer and Fort Harrison.

Report of Brigadier General Foster, continued

At 1.25 p.m. I received orders from Lieutenant-Colonel
[Richard H.] Jackson, assistant inspector-general Tenth Army
Corps, to charge and attempt the capture of the enemy's works,
supposed to be Fort Gilmer, and was informed that Brigadier-
General Birney was to advance simultaneously on my left, and
that I was to be supported by troops of Brigadier-General Paine's
command. I was to commence the movement in ten minutes from
the receipt of order. I at once formed my line, the Second Brigade, Col. G. Pennypacker, Ninety-seventh Pennsylvania Volunteers, on the right; the First, Col. R. Daggert, One hundred and
seventeenth New York Volunteers, on the center, and the Third,
Col. Louis Bell, Fourth New Hampshire Volunteers, on the left,
and at 1.35 p.m. moved forward, the distance from the road to
the fort being three-quarters of a mile. As we advanced I found
four ravines intervening and also that old trees and undergrowth
had been slashed, rendering our advance very slow, and requiring a halt at the second ravine, and again just after the crossing of
the Fourth to reform. During this time the command was subject
to a very severe enfilading fire of artillery from two forts on the
right and one gun from a fort on the left, and a front fire from

Fort Gilmer, which disabled many of my men. After reforming the last time the line moved forward to the assault and advanced rapidly under a heavy fire from infantry, an artillery fire of grape and canister from Fort Gilmer, and shell and case from the two forts to the right, but was obliged to fall back. With the assistance of the officers of my command the line was rallied and reformed, and one brigade of Brigadier-General Paine's command coming to my support another assault was made, which was again unsuccessful and the forces obliged to retire, which they did slowly and stubbornly to the New Market and Richmond road, when the line was again reformed. As my line advanced to the assault a body of troops of the enemy, apparently 500 or 600, moved from the fort on the right, and reached Fort Gilmer in season to assist the garrison in our repulse. In this assault the colors of the Third New York Volunteers were lost. I had the circumstances investigated and have the honor to forward here with the report of the commanding officer of the regiment, which with the indorsement of the brigade commander, would seem to show that it was not through any unworthy act on the part of the regiment. [*O.R.*, XLII, part 1, p. 760.]

Report of Col. James Shaw, commanding Seventh U.S. Colored Troops, First Brigade, Third Division, Tenth Corps, Army of the James

At about 2 p.m. we continued our march down the New Market road and was ordered to form to the left of the road in column by regiments in mass. I had passed down the regiment directing this formation and had reached the center on my return, when I found them moving to the right, and, hurrying to that flank, found we had filed to the left on the Varina road and that the enemy had opened heavily on our column with artillery. I was then directed by the general commanding to form in "right into line" on the right of the road and in a direction oblique to it, a slight descent in the ground partially covering the line, then to charge and take an earth-work some three-quarters of a mile in our front. Before the line was formed this order was countermanded, and I was directed to send out four companies as skirmishers for the same purpose. Companies C, D, G, and K were designated for this purpose, Capt. Julius A. Weiss, the senior captain, in command. Deploying these companies, Captain Weiss proceeded steadily to the front, under a heavy fire of artillery, and, as he approached the works, charged into the very trenches, but was unable to get farther. Not a man faltered, but all who did not fall reached the work, charged boldly, and did all in their power to take it. They are all missing. [*O.R.*, XLII, part 1, p. 772.]

Narrative of Maj. Gen. Charles W. Field, CSA, commanding Division, First Corps, Army of Northern Virginia

I think it was about the last of September that early one morning General *Lee* sent for me and directed me to proceed at once to Chaffin's Bluff, showing me at the same time a telegram from [Brig. Gen. *John*] *Gregg* stating that Fort Harrison had been captured.

On arriving on the north side that evening, and not having been met by any instructions from Lieutenant General *R[ichard] H. Anderson* (who had just returned from the Valley and was now in command), and believing the occasion too important to lose time in seeking them from him personally, I inquired of a staff-officer, who came galloping by me, where the enemy was most pressing, and receiving for reply that he thought near Fort Gilmer, I immediately, with [Brig. Gen. *William F.*] *Perry's* brigade (the only one then with me), marched in that direction. As I got in sight of the breastworks I saw beyond them two lines of the enemy (the leading line of negroes) moving up to assault Gilmer and the lines to the right and left of it. Ascertaining at once that [Brig. Gen. *Dudley M.*] *DuBose* held Gilmer and neighboring works, that *Gregg* with the Texas brigade was on his right, I threw at a double-quick *Perry* on the left of *DuBose*. Hardly had they got in the trenches when the enemy got within musket range. Fire was opened along the line, but the enemy, under cover of some little irregularities, continued to advance beautifully. But directly our fire got too hot, and he broke and fled in haste, leaving many dead and wounded before us.

It is worthy of remark that some of the negro troops got up to our breastworks and were killed there. In this affair the enemy's losses were heavy, ours scarcely anything. [*Southern Historical Society Papers*, 52 vols. (Millwood, N.Y.: Kraus reprint, 1876–1959), volume XIV, p. 555. Hereafter cited as *SHSP.*]

Walk to your right along the sidewalk until you leave the interior of Fort Gilmer. Stand where you can see the exterior of the fort wall and the ditch in front of it.

Narrative of Pvt. Charles Johnson, CSA, Salem Flying Artillery,
First Virginia Light Artillery Battalion, Artillery Brigade, First
Corps, Army of Northern Virginia

After the capture of "Fort Harrison," our troops were formed
upon the same line of works, but of course a new line had to be
formed in front of "Fort Harrison." "Fort Gilmer" was the next
fort in the line, which had some five or six heavy cannon, and was
manned by about forty men (of what command I never knew).
Between Forts "Harrison" and "Gilmer," a distance of nearly half
a mile, were stationed [Lt. Col. *Robert A.*] *Hardaway's* batteries,
[Capt. *Willis B.*] *Dance's* being the nearest to "Fort Harrison,"
[Capt. *Charles B.*] *Griffin's* next, and [Col. *Thomas H.*] *Carter* and
[Capt. *Archibald*] *Graham* to their left, supported by the Texans and
Tennesseeans, with the "City Battalion" deployed as skirmishers.
General [*Richard S.*] *Ewell* was with the skirmish line, constantly
encouraging them by his presence and coolness. I remember very
distinctly how he looked, mounted on an old gray horse, as mad as
he could be, shouting to the men, and seeming to be everywhere
at once. I do not remember at what time in the day the attack was
made, but it commenced by the Yankees making a furious charge
upon *Dance's* battery, and they came in such numbers and so rapidly that they got within forty yards of *Dance's* guns before our
fire told upon them. Here it was that the Tennesseeans did such
glorious work. They had trotted (or rather run) from another
part of the line when the attack first began, and by the time they
reached *Dance's* guns the Yankees were almost there, but the colonel in command of the brigade leaped across the works, followed
by his men, and after an almost hand to hand fight drove the
Yankees back. Too much praise cannot be given to this colonel (I
wish I could remember his name), for I was told by one of *Dance's*
men that he had never seen a man so entirely free from fear, and
that in front of his men he discharged every barrel of his pistol
right into the Yankees' faces. I do not now remember the loss in
this charge, but Captain *Dance* and a good many of his men were
wounded, and several of the men killed.

Almost immediately after the enemy retired from *Dance's*
front, an attack was made upon another part of the line to the left,
and the same Tennesseeans again double quicked to the point of
attack, and again the Yankees were forced to retire before their
fire and the canister of the artillery. . . . After this last repulse, the

Yankees did not renew the attack for some time (if I remember rightly not for several hours), and when they did come, it was away off to the left and in front of "Fort Gilmer." They advanced in three lines, one behind the other, the first line composed of negroes. Some said that the second line was also negroes, but I cannot speak positively of that, but the rear line was of white troops.

"Fort Gilmer" was on a hill, with quite an extensive flat in front, from which the trees had all been cut, and most of the trees were lying on the ground with their branches still attached. The "Louisiana Guard Artillery" on the left, and "Salem Artillery" on the right of the fort, occupied redoubts so constructed that each had an enfilade fire upon the Yankees as they advanced. The enemy came rather cautiously at first, but finally they came with a rush, our artillery firing shrapnel at first, but they soon begun to load with canister, and the way those negroes fell before it was very gratifying to the people on our side of the works. But the Yankees came on until they got to the ditch in front of "Fort Gilmer"—a dry ditch about ten (10) feet deep and twelve (12) feet wide. Into this ditch a great many of the negroes jumped, and endeavored to climb up on each other's shoulders, but were beaten back by our infantry, and almost all of them killed.

One negro, who was either drunk or crazy, crawled through a culvert which ran from the inside of the fort into the ditch, and was shot on the inside. No great number of negroes got into the ditch, and the rest of the attacking column having no shelter from the fire of both artillery and infantry, were forced to give way and retire. Thus ended the battle of "Fort Gilmer," and there was no more fighting done on this part of the line where we were that day, though I think the part of the line occupied by *Gary's* cavalry was attacked, but I never knew anything about that fight. [*SHSP*, I, p. 440.]

At this point the excursion will switch to the attack of Butler's left wing, Maj. Gen. Edward O. C. Ord's Eighteenth Corps, from Aiken's Landing to Fort Harrison. Return to your vehicle. Resume driving south on Battlefield Park Road for 1.5 miles. Turn left onto Picnic Road; bear left in 0.1 mile to remain on Picnic Road, which will end at Varina Road in 0.3 mile. Turn right. Drive 0.9 mile down Varina Road, turning right onto Old Level Farm Road, a dirt road that leads to a farm in the middle of the field. As this farm lane is private property, it is recommended that you remain in your vehicle to read the selections for this stop, or stand beside your vehicle facing north, back toward the direction from which you came.

STOP 5: VARINA ROAD

On the night of September 28–29, Ord's two divisions crossed the James River on a pontoon bridge at Aiken's Landing and advanced up Varina Road, driving in Confederate skirmishers as they went.

Report of Major General Ord, continued

My move began about 9 o'clock on the night of the 28th of September, when the men were drawn out of the trenches and marched to the river opposite Aiken's, where, between 9 and 12 p.m., a bridge was thrown over the James. By 12 p.m. my troops were at the bridge, and before daylight were across the river and formed. At the dawn of day I attacked the enemy's skirmish line with my skirmishers, and though the rebels were re-enforced we drove them right along toward Richmond, up the hills, and for three miles through the woods, until about 7.30 a.m., when we reached the open ground in front of Fort Harrison, the strongest rebel work on that front, which immediately opened upon us with several heavy guns. [*O.R.*, XLII, part 1, p. 793.]

Report of Bvt. Maj. Gen. George J. Stannard, USA, commanding division, Eighteenth Corps, Army of the James

In pursuance to verbal orders received from Major-General Ord, commanding corps, this division moved from its late camp, on the line between the Appomattox and James Rivers, at 9 p.m. on the night of 28th of September, and marched, without noise, in the direction of Aiken's Landing, on the James River. At 3 a.m. on the 29th, in obedience to written orders received at that hour, the division, with Brigadier-General [Hiram] Burnham's (Second) brigade leading, crossed the James River near Aiken's on a pontoon bridge, and taking the road to the left moved in the direction of the enemy's works at Chaffin's farm. Previous to breaking camp on the night of the 28th, two regiments of infantry, forming a part of Brigadier-General Burnham's brigade, had, under orders to that effect, exchanged the arms heretofore in use for the Spencer repeating rifle. These two regiments [Tenth New Hampshire and 118th New York] were at once, on reaching the north bank of the river, thrown out as skirmishers and flankers. . . . The remainder of the command, having been disposed in column by division, at once moved forward on the road running parallel to the course of the river, and at a few moments after daybreak encountered the enemy's pickets, which were driven in on the run. [*O.R.*, XLII, part 1, p. 798.]

Ord's divisions, under Brig. Gen. George J. Stannard and Brig. Gen. Charles A. Heckman, formed along the Varina Road in this field for the assault on the Exterior Line. Look to the north, and you will see that the road bends northeast a few yards before you. In 1864 the earthen ramparts of Fort Harrison, with the entrenchments of the Exterior Line on either side, would have been visible on the high ground to the left front, with an extensive belt of fallen trees left in place by the Confederate defenders to slow an attack.

At approximately 6:00 a.m., Stannard's division prepared for the attack behind a screen of skirmishers from Col. Michael T. Donohoe's brigade. Brig. Gen. Hiram Burnham's brigade would lead the attack, with Col. Aaron Stevens's and Col. Samuel H. Roberts's brigades to the left and right of the road, respectively. Ord planned for Heckman's division to continue northward along the road and swing in to attack the fort from the east. Complex terrain in the vicinity of the modern Picnic Road caused this element of the attack to fail, isolating the USCT units attacking Fort Gilmer.

Report of Major General Ord, continued

Here I reconnoitered and rapidly made dispositions to attack this work [Fort Harrison]. Stannard's division, Burnham's brigade leading, was directed to push forward in column by division over the open in front of the fort, on the left of the Varina road, covered with the same regiment which had so far and so well driven the enemy's skirmishers. Heckman was directed, as soon as it could be brought up, to move with his division through and along the edge of the timber, which skirted the Varina road on the right, keeping his men under cover, until he came opposite to the fort (Harrison), and then attack it on the front toward the wood (that is, the east front) as rapidly as possible. This would have enveloped the principal work on the south and east, and had General Heckman obeyed my orders many valuable lives would have been saved, and his division, reaching the work after Stannard's had taken it, would have been available to have attacked the only other work which intervened between us and Richmond in the rear; but he went too far into the woods, got his brigades scattered, and when found was not available in the right place. [*O.R.*, XLII, part 1, p. 793.]

Report of Brevet Major General Stannard, continued

The enemy now opened furiously from a powerful battery situated at the crest of the hill in my front and from other guns mounted in smaller redoubts situated at various points along the line of works which extended on the enemy's right to the river. The column here left the road, and, inclining to the left, moved directly across a heavy plowed field toward the principal work. The distance was about 1,400 yards, and while traversing this space my command, with the exception of my skirmishers, not having as yet discharged a musket, was exposed to a plunging fire of artillery and musketry, galling in the extreme, and caused them to become somewhat broken. The column, however, pushed gallantly forward until it reached the base of the hill upon which the battery was situated, when it came to a halt, from sheer exhaustion. The enemy were now moving up from their left considerable re-enforcements, and, fearing that the assault would fail by reason of the delay, I sent Captain [William L.] Kent, acting assistant adjutant-general of the division, to move the column at once to the assault. [*O.R.*, XLII, part 1, p. 798.]

Report of Maj. Normand Smith, commanding Thirteenth New Hampshire Infantry, First Division, Eighteenth Corps, Army of the James

The First Brigade, to which the regiment belongs, commanded by Colonel Stevens, broke camp at 9 p.m. of the 28th, and after several delays, during the night crossed the James at Aiken's Landing, about 3 a.m. . . . Just before daylight the column was advanced up the road on which our right rested. The skirmishers found the pickets of the enemy near the woods and drove them rapidly up the road some two miles to the open field in front of Fort Harrison, followed closely by the main column. The column was halted near the edge of the woods . . . and the First Brigade following. The Third Brigade was formed in a similar manner on the right of the road. The column was then advanced rapidly up the road, under a severe fire from the enemy's batteries until they obtained cover under the hill near the fort. Here the column was reformed by Colonel Roberts, of the Third, and Lieutenant-Colonel [J. B.] Raulston, of the First Brigade, Colonel Stevens having been severely wounded. We were again advanced under a heavy fire of musketry into the outer ditch of the fort without firing a shot. [*O.R.*, XLII, part 1, p. 805.]

Return to your vehicle, and execute a turn back to the north on Varina Road when it is safe to do so. Continue north on Varina Road for 0.9 mile, passing the Fort Harrison National Cemetery on your left. At 0.3 mile after the cemetery, turn left onto Picnic Road, reversing your trip from Fort Gilmer. Turn left at the intersection with Battlefield Park Road, drive 0.2 mile, and pull into the parking lot on your left opposite Fort Harrison. The small Visitor Contact Station and its restrooms are open seasonally. Follow the paved path into Fort Harrison, turning left at the small fork in the path. Follow this left fork until you see a cannon in a revetment on your left. Walk over and stand next to this cannon, looking over the barrel into the woods before you. Remember that the ground between the Varina Road (your last stop) and the fort was cleared of standing timber but that the fallen trees were left in place as an additional obstacle to the attackers.

STOP 6: FORT HARRISON

The lead brigade of Ord's Eighteenth Corps crossed the open ground from its jump-off point on the Varina Road (your last stop), sustaining heavy casualties as it did. The Thirteenth New Hampshire, Ninety-sixth New York, and Eighth Connecticut regiments made it into the ditch before you, clambered up the parapet here where you stand, and were inside Fort Harrison. The small defending force of reserve troops and heavy artillerists generally fought well but was overmatched.

The attack on Fort Harrison was locally successful, but it took a heavy toll in Federal casualties and leadership. Brig. Gen. Hiram Burnham was killed near this spot as he led his brigade over the wall; the entire work was renamed in his honor after the battle. Corps commander Ord was wounded as he arrived at the fort and assumed tactical control of the fighting, contributing to the loss of momentum that doomed the Federal effort on this day. Stannard's division attempted to attack south and clear the Intermediate Line to the James River but ran into determined Confederate resistance by small units.

September 29 was the best day of the war for Lt. Gen. *Richard S. Ewell,* the Department of Richmond commander and in charge of the defenses here. Once he was aware of the Federal breakthrough at Fort Harrison, he moved decisively to contain the damage, forming a scratch force across the interior of the Chaffin's Farm camp and effectively sealing off the breach. The new Confederate line connected the forts south of Fort Harrison with those north of it, restoring the integrity of the defenses north of the James.

The fort's interior contains a variety of markers describing both the action here on September 29 and the features that the Confederate

Fort Burnham, formerly Confederate Fort Harrison (USAMHI)

and Union defenders built into the fort over time. It is important to remember that the northern and western faces of the fort were constructed and improved by the Federal defenders following its capture.

Report of Major General Ord, continued

Stannard's division was ordered to advance across the open at quick time directly to the attack, and at double-quick when they had reached the hill. This they did beautifully, wavering a little just at the foot of the hill, which the fort crowned, when the fire of musketry and artillery was very severe. But I dispatched all my staff (just then around me) to urge the men forward, and followed them. The hill was ascended with heavy loss to us. Officers and men jumped into the ditch, followed it along round so as to cut off and capture the rebels in the extreme bastion, and helped each other up the parapet at that point. As soon as we entered this bastion or salient, I caused the guns to be turned upon the nearest adjacent parts of the enemy's works, and drove them out; and reconnoitering I saw through the smoke and fire what I supposed for some minutes was General Heckman's column entering the work next beyond Fort Harrison, Fort Gilmer; but it soon proved to be a large re-enforcement of the enemy.

The men who had got into the fort were scattered behind its parapets and in its ditches fighting the rebels, who had not left the adjacent parts. I tried to gather a party and form them with a view to swing round inside the rebel parapets behind them and drive the rebels out from the inside, but there were but few men to collect; all was confusion and excitement: The brigade which led in had lost mortally and badly wounded two commanders in succession. Nearly all the persons in the work were company officers, and with such as I could collect I pushed toward the river, inside the work still occupied by the rebels, with a view to reconnoiter and, if possible, get possession of the pontoon bridge by which any re-enforcements would have to cross to the fort. While doing so I was hit in the upper part of the leg, inside. Stanching the wound with an improvised tourniquet, I continued in command until a surgeon coming up remonstrated, and I sent for General Heckman, turned the command over to him, told him to gather all the division (Stannard's) and occupy the work with it. He reported his own division (which had not as yet engaged the enemy), to the right of and about half a mile up the road, just about to attack the work in front of it. I told him my orders were to occupy such works as we took, and with any spare forces we had to push on, attacking the works toward Richmond in succession. I learned that he afterward attempted to take the next work, Fort Gilmer, by an attack in front, but failed, with heavy loss. [*O.R.*, XLII, part 1, p. 794.]

Report of Major Smith, continued

Then came the struggle who should first plant their colors on the fort. The entire color guard of this regiment (six in number) were killed or wounded, four of them with the colors in their hands, and the regiment claims that their colors were first on the fort, which was carried a few minutes past 7 a.m. [Major Smith was wounded as he reached the ditch, and Capt. [Nathan D.] Stoodley, commander of Company G, continued the report.]

On entering the fort the regiment gathered around the colors, and some of them were sent to turn the guns in the fort, two of which were turned and fired several times on the retreating enemy. Soon after, we were formed on the left of the fort, placing the sentries on our left and toward the enemy. About 10 o'clock we joined the other regiments of the brigade and formed a line of battle in the rear, now front of the fort, posting pickets in advance of our present line, they remaining during the night. Late in the afternoon we commenced throwing up breast-works on the left of the fort. About an hour afterward we were moved out of the fort to the left, and worked all night on the Works, now running from the fort to the river. [*O.R.*, XLII, part 1, p. 805.]

When you are finished examining the interior of Fort Harrison, leave via the paved walking path and stand outside the northern wall, facing the parking lot where your vehicle is located.

Lee spent the night of September 29–30 arraying forces north of the James for a counterattack to recapture Fort Harrison. *Ewell* would lead this counterattack after his quick action had contained the Union breakthrough on the first day of the offensive, but the disjointed Confederate counterattack did not meet *Lee's* expectations.

Lee designed a complicated attack plan, predicated on using masking terrain to the north and west of the fort to bring two separate elements, divisions under *Field* and Maj. Gen. *Robert F. Hoke* (recently arrived from the Department of North Carolina and Southern Virginia), together in front of Fort Harrison in enough strength to overcome the defenders. *Field* set off first just before 2 p.m. from the north near Fort Johnson because he had farther to travel to come into line; *Hoke's* men sheltered in a ravine to the left in front of you. In the battle's enduring controversy, *Field's* men mistook their initial movement into position for an assault and proceeded past their juncture with *Hoke*, who failed to join in the attack. The piecemeal attacks were a disastrous failure, costing over 2,000 casualties compared to fewer than 300 for the Federals.

Narrative of Major General Field, continued

The enemy being driven completely out of sight and range at this point, I believed that that night was the time to attack and retake Fort Harrison. The gorge of the work was open on one side and there had not been sufficient time to close it up securely. General *Lee* just then arrived upon the ground from Petersburg and meeting him I told him what I proposed to do, but he thought it better to remain where I was for the present. Meanwhile the two other brigades ([Brig. Gen. *John C.*] *Bratton's* and [Brig. Gen. *George T.*] *Anderson's*) had come up. It was now sunset.

A little after dark Brigadier-General *Gregg* came to me, and said that he had just seen General *Lee*, who wished me to retake

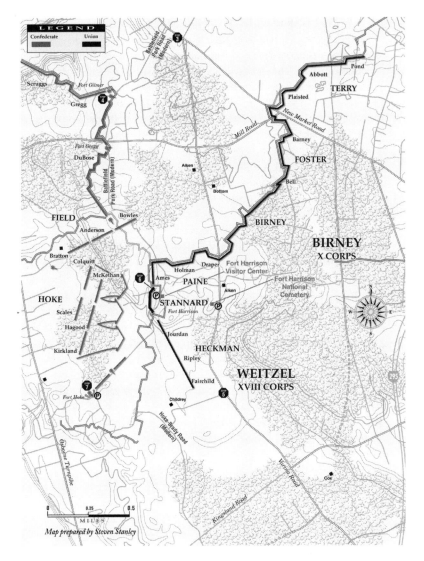

Fort Harrison–Chaffin's Farm, September 30, 1864

Fort Harrison that night, but that Lieutenant-General *Anderson* wished to see me for a moment before I made the assault. My men were worn out with a long day's march and excitement; were stretched upon the ground asleep. Rousing up the only three brigades which could be withdrawn for that purpose (*Bratton's*, *Anderson's*, and [Brig. Gen. *Edward*] *Perry's*), I started for Fort Harrison, two miles off, and, after reconnoitering, threw them up as close as possible, ready to assault. It was now one o'clock, and, all being ready, I went to report to Lieutenant-General *Anderson*, in pursuance of what I had been told was his desire. To my surprise, I found General *Anderson* asleep, and upon waking him and telling him what I came for, he said there was a mistake, that it was not intended I should attack that night. Directing the brigades to fall back a little, we went to sleep on our arms.

All night long we could distinctly hear the enemy in Fort Harrison hard at work strengthening it, and by next day it had become, in strength, a most formidable place. I have always thought it a great misfortune that it was not attacked that night. I believe that my division could have retaken it then. Next day, when we did attempt it, it cost us dearly. The plan of attack for the next day was as follows: portions of *Hoke's* division and my own were to be the assaulting column. *Hoke* was to attack one face, I the other. We were to get, unobserved, as near as possible to the work, and, after a severe artillery fire of twenty or thirty minutes' duration, I forget which, we were to rush upon the work simultaneously. There was a deep ravine, which ran within a hundred yards of the face which *Hoke* was to attack. Up this he could form and have his troops completely masked. On my side the ground was a level plain, and consequently I could not form nearer than five hundred yards of the work.

When the artillery fire was nearly over and the time for making the assault had nearly arrived, I directed General *Anderson*, commanding my leading brigade, to move up as close as possible to the work and let his men lay down, so as at the proper moment to spring up and reach the work simultaneously with *Hoke*, who had much less distance to charge than I. General *Anderson* failing to inform his men of his intention, they mistook the advance for an assault, and instead of halting and laying down rushed forward to attack. This brigade being in for it, necessitated my pushing *Bratton* and *Perry* to its assistance. *Hoke*, though aware that I was attacking prematurely, waited for the moment agreed upon, and thus the concentrated fire of the fort was poured upon my troops. The attack was, of course, unsuccessful, and my loss very heavy. Though *Hoke* made an effort after awhile, it was then too late. Had General *Anderson* sufficiently instructed his men to wait for the proper moment, or had *Hoke* attacked when I did, even though it did anticipate the time a few moments (and the chances for success were quite as good then as they could have been afterwards), the result might have been very different. General *Lee* now determined to attack upon the flank. [*SHSP*, XIV, p. 556.]

Report of Brig. Gen. John C. Bratton, CSA, commanding Brigade, Field's Division, First Corps, Army of Northern Virginia

On the morning of the 29th of September received orders to take cars for Rice's Station, which we did, and moved thence across the river at Drewry's to the Osborn turnpike. Reached there just before dark; started out from the works near New Market road on reconnaissance, but were ordered back, as night was coming on, and went into camp, but about 10 p.m. received orders to move down Osborn turnpike toward Battery Harrison, which had been taken by the enemy. We reconnoitered as well as we could at night, and were making dispositions to attack when orders came to move to the rear of Fort Gilmer and rest. We reached Fort Gilmer a little before daybreak; rested until about 8 a.m., and were ordered back to the vicinity of Battery Harrison.

The preliminaries were arranged for an assault, and the assault ordered at 2 p.m. In the meantime the enemy had thrown up a retrenchment, making Battery Harrison an inclosed work. I was to support *Anderson's* brigade. I occupied a rugged line on the right of *Anderson*. He was to move out to a ravine in his front and wait for me to file out of my rugged position and form in rear of him. (All the details are known to the major-general, but I mention this point for a purpose which will appear presently.) I gave full and explicit instructions to my brigade. Every officer and man knew exactly what he was to do. *Anderson* did not stop at the ravine, but passed on. To give my promised support and carry out my part in the arrangement it was necessary for my brigade to file out at the double-quick, and, without halting, or even moderating to quick time, to move by the right flank in line against the enemy. I deplored this and felt that my men were not having a fair chance, but it was too late to give new orders and instructions. All that was left me to do, I thought, under the circumstances, was to try to carry out the agreed-upon arrangement, and this [I] did. My brigade was ordered to follow about 100 yards in rear of *Anderson's*, and if they stopped to pass over them and charge the enemy's works.

My orders were obeyed, and my dead close under the enemy's works attest their honest efforts to achieve the object for which they were given. My right regiment (Colonel [*Reuben L.*] *Walker*) was streaming along at a run, unable to gain its position on the line of the brigade. This I halted for an instant, closed its ranks, and put it on the left against a little redan on the line a short distance in front of the enemy's retrenchments, and it was carried and much consternation produced among the enemy, who left one face of Fort Harrison—that looking toward B. Aiken's house—and did not occupy it again; but it was too late to help the main assault—that had failed; but it was a diversion, and more— sort of distraction to the enemy, which saved the lives of many of my retiring men. My shattered ranks were ordered to the rear to reform. I dispatched a staff officer to General *Hoke* to explain my situation and to say that l would make another effort in conjunction with him if he would assault. My four repulsed regiments, rallied by their gallant colonels, moved up, sadly reduced in numbers, but with firm and solid tread, as well in hand and obedient to orders as at the beginning. General *Hoke* assaulted, but so feebly, and was so quickly repulsed, that I did not put my regiments in again, but took up a position to support the troops in the redan in case they were assailed by the enemy. After dark, when all my dead and wounded except those immediately under the works of the enemy were brought off, the troops were withdrawn to the line of the morning. We failed to take the fort, and there is, therefore, no occasion for praise; but while I think it right that success should be, as it is, the measure of the soldier's merit, I would be ungrateful to the living and false to my glorious dead if I did not express my admiration of their heroic conduct in this action. They failed to take the fort, but it was because the difficulties from beginning to end of the attack were too much for human valor. Our loss here was severe, summing up in killed and wounded 377; some of the wounded are prisoners. I took into this action 1,165 muskets, 129 officers. [*O.R.*, XLII, part 1, pp. 879–880.]

Report of Col. James R. Hagood, CSA, First South Carolina Infantry, Bratton's Brigade, Field's Division, First Corps, Army of Northern Virginia

On the morning of the 30th, preparations were made to re-gain the fort, which lasted until midday, when the attack began. We were then 1,000 yards from the point to be carried. Immediately the regiment on my left began to double-quick, which soon increased to a run, thus exhausting the men and wasting their energies at a time when both should have been economized for the struggle on the parapet. I was opposed to this, but, believing it to be an order, acquiesced. The enemy shortly opened fire on us, which increased in effect every moment and soon began to tell fearfully in the ranks. At this critical moment the brigade which preceded us gave way, and rushing through our line caused immediate confusion. Added to this the village of soldiers' huts which lay in our track offered the temptation to skulk, which many failed to resist, and which was impossible in the confusion to prevent. With those of my men who still adhered to their colors I continued to advance until I attained a point within sixty yards of the fort. Here, owing to the little support which was accorded to me by the remainder of the brigade, I ordered a halt and began firing to divert my men. I waited here for ten or fifteen minutes for re-enforcements, but their failure to come up and the fearful destructiveness of the enemy's fire impressed me with the necessity of falling back, which I accordingly did. I rallied my men at the earliest practicable moment and reported to the brigadier-general commanding, who instructed me to return to my position of the morning. A short time afterward I was ordered to advance again on the enemy, bearing to the left so as to strike his works on the right of Colonel *Walker's* regiment, which was reported as having gained them. I executed this order, but discovered no enemy this side of the fort, the flank work having been manned by only a line of skirmishers, who were driven from it by [Brig. Gen. *Evander M.*] *Law's* brigade [commanded by Col. *Pinckney D. Bowles*] before the arrival of *Walker.* After dark we were withdrawn to our old position. [*O.R.,* XLII, part 1, p. 938.]

Report of Brevet Major General Stannard, continued

During the night previous the Third Division had made good progress in strengthening the position. A strong rifle-pit, with log traverses, had been thrown up on the left and along the center, but the right had no such protection. My command from the time that they entered the work in the morning had been busily engaged in strengthening and extending this line of defense, which, when completed, would make Battery Harrison an inclosed work. Before this portion of the line could be completed the enemy, at about 12.30 o'clock noon, threw himself in three lines upon my right, at the same time opening with two full batteries of field guns upon my center and left. I reserved my fire until they had emerged from the chaparral through which they advanced, when I opened a most effective fire of musketry. At the same time I replied to his artillery with the half battery mentioned in the report of operations for the 29th. . . . The enemy's furious onset had been in the meantime repulsed with musketry alone, driving him to cover, and leaving an immense number of dead and wounded in front of my right. He, however, quickly reformed, and with his accustomed yell tried the same position a second time. . . . My command was enabled to repulse the enemy's second and his successive assaults.

During the progress of this second attempt to carry our position, I received a musket ball in the right arm, which shattered the bone above the elbow and necessitated my removal from the field and amputation upon my arrival at the hospital. [*O.R.*, XLII, part 1, pp. 800–801.]

Return to your vehicle. Resume driving south along Battlefield Park Road. At 0.9 mile, bear right at the Y intersection to remain on Battlefield Park Road. In 0.2 mile, turn into the parking area for Fort Hoke on your right. Get out of your vehicle, and stand near the fort's exterior wall, facing back in the direction from which you drove.

STOP 7: FORT HOKE

Once Stannard's men captured Fort Harrison on September 29, elements of the division moved south along the entrenched line toward the James River, two small positions, Battery 10 and the White Battery. In the day's final action, the Fifth-eighth and 188th Pennsylvania Regiments of Col. Edgar M. Cullen's brigade attacked and captured Fort Hoke, driving off the Virginia heavy artillerists who manned it. This victory gained the Federals no lasting advantage, however, because the Confederates still occupied Fort Maury at the James River, reinforced by a gunboat, and held on to the positions north of Fort Harrison. With hard fighting and a timely response, *Ewell* was able to seal off the

Federal penetration. Stannard withdrew to Fort Harrison at nightfall, followed closely by a Confederate counterattack that retook Fort Hoke.

Report of Brevet Major General Stannard, continued

Moving with my Second Brigade, now commanded by Col. M[ichael] T. Donohoe, and my Third Brigade, commanded by Col. E[dgar] M. Cullen, Ninety-sixth New York Volunteers (Colonel Roberts having been relieved on account of severe illness), we drove the enemy successively from two lunettes which were thrown out from their main line of works at intervals of about 600 yards and compelled him to retire to his third and last remaining defense in this line of works. My First Brigade, meanwhile, now under the command of Lieut. Col. J. B. Raulston, Eighty-first New York Volunteers (Colonel Stevens having been severely wounded in the leg while leading his brigade in the assault—and I would here respectfully recommend that this officer be promoted for bravery and efficiency on the battle-field), remained in the captured work, throwing out a strong line of skirmishers toward the enemy's inner line of works, and to which his main body had retreated. The work which the enemy now held in his first line was situated directly on the river-bank, and was covered by the fire of one of his gun-boats, as well as by a field battery so stationed as to be able to take the work in reverse should it be captured. The work itself mounted three heavy guns, and in view of the serious loss which must follow an attempt to dislodge the party holding it, I withdrew my troops. The enemy, seeing the movement, which occurred just before sunset, followed up his supposed advantage, until I opened upon him from the battery on the hill with a half battery of light 12s belonging to the Third Regiment of New York Light Artillery. A few rounds of canister sent the pursuing party quickly to cover, and my troops were quietly withdrawn to Battery Harrison for better defense during the night. [*O.R.*, XLII, part 1, p. 799.]

Remain in position at Fort Hoke.

CONFEDERATE HEADQUARTERS NORTH OF THE JAMES

The Fifth Offensive north of the James was a clear tactical victory for the Federal army, but the fighting of September 29–30 did not appreciably change the operational calculus of the campaign. *Lee simply built and fortified a new line to the west of Fort Harrison and* continued to look for opportunities to expel the Army of the James from the northside. The most significant of these opportunities occurred a week later.

After Fort Harrison, *Lee* moved his field headquarters to Chaffin's Farm, to the west of you on the other side of Osborne Turnpike, in a sign of his concern for developments in this sector.

Reminiscences of Col. Edward Porter Alexander, CSA, Chief of Artillery, First Corps, Army of Northern Virginia

The next active hostilities occurred upon the north side of the James, where Gen. *Lee* was not content to permit the enemy to continue to occupy Fort Harrison, as it was now called, without another effort to dislodge them. On the afternoon of Thurs., Oct. 6th, I was ordered to send two battalions of artillery across the Darbytown Road, with *Field's* & *Hoke's* divisions, which were to go across and bivouac on that road that night, in order to make an advance at daylight upon the enemy's flank. Late in the afternoon I called at Gen. *Lee's* headquarters, & had an interview with him as to the proposed operation. To get across to the Darbytown Road it was necessary to take a cross road from the Osborne Pike opposite the Gunn house, near which I was encamped, about 100 yards from the pike, in a pine thicket. [Edward Porter Alexander, *Fighting for the Confederacy: The Personal Recollections of General Edward Porter Alexander*, ed. Gary W. Gallagher (Chapel Hill: University of North Carolina Press, 1989), p. 481.]

Return to your vehicle and drive straight ahead to Osborne Turnpike; turn right. Drive 3.0 miles to Burning Tree Road, and turn right. After 0.5 mile, this road ends at Laburnum Avenue. Turn left, and drive 2.1 miles to Darbytown Road. Turn right, and follow Darbytown Road 1.6 miles to Pioneer Baptist Church on your left. Turn into the parking lot, park, and walk to the Virginia state historical marker near the road.

STOP 8: DARBYTOWN ROAD, 7 OCTOBER 1864

As you drove along Darbytown Road from Laburnum Avenue, you followed the axis of the Confederate attack. At 1.3 miles from Laburnum you passed the entrance to Dorey Park recreational complex and may have noticed several Virginia Civil War Trails markers. The Dorey Park access road runs along the trace of the Exterior Line entrenchments; after the Fifth Offensive, Federal forces used these lines to consolidate their gains north of the James. On October 7, *Lee* attacked the Federal cavalry positions here both from along Darbytown Road and from the wooded ground to the south, in the direction of New Market Road. This attack had some initial success, but Grant's cavalry, fighting dismounted and armed with repeating weapons, quickly turned the tide. *Lee* lost yet another one of his generals, Texan *John Gregg.* After the October 7 fight, both sides settled back into largely static warfare north of the James while operations continued south of Petersburg.

Report of Lieutenant General Grant, continued

On the 7th of October the enemy attacked [Brig. Gen. August V.] Kautz's cavalry north of the James and drove it back with heavy losses in killed, wounded, and prisoners, and the loss of all the artillery—eight or nine pieces. This he followed up with an attack on our intrenched infantry line, but was repulsed with severe slaughter. [*O.R.*, XLVI, part 1, pp. 30–31.]

Report of Col. Robert M. West, commanding First Brigade, Kautz's Cavalry Division, Army of the James

We had been apprised of the attack the night previous by the general commanding division, and were up early, expecting it. All was quiet during the early morning and until about 6.30 o'clock, when couriers from the outposts gave notice of the approach of the enemy, both by the Central road and from the Charles City road through a small road which debouches near Mr. Gerhardt's house onto the open field whereon was our position. The picket reserves harassed the advance of the enemy, fighting on foot in the woods, and, as I believe, deceived them as to the kind of troops they would encounter. The enemy consumed about one hour driving in our outposts, and determining where to strike us. Our picket reserve on the Central road divided and came in by the left and right; Captain [George F.] Dern, Third New York Cavalry, commanding on the right; Captain [Colin] Richardson, same regiment, commanding on the left. Captain Dern came in by the Gerhardt house and made a stand at the works near there, fighting every step as he came. Now, the enemy having felt us all along our front moved rapidly to our right with nearly his whole force, coming out of the woods near the house I have named in masses, driving Captain Dern with his small party from the works and occupying them. Our men opened and kept up a well directed fire from their position near the road. The enemy halted

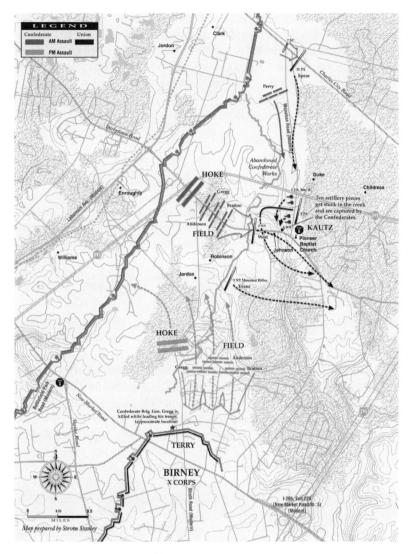

Darbytown Road, October 7, 1864

Brig. Gen. August V. Kautz and Brig. Gen. Godfrey Weitzel (USAMHI)

and reformed at the works, which were a continuation of the line we were holding, and from which they had driven Captain Dern. They edged down toward us so long as they could find cover in the sinuosities of the line; then swinging around their left they formed in three lines and advanced directly upon our flanks. Observing this, I ordered a change of front, which was effected in remarkably good order, considering the circumstances, the new line being the embankment of the ditch along the road. The Third New York now came up from where they had been supporting the artillery and got into position on the right of the Fifth Pennsylvania. The Fifth up to this time had done nearly all the fighting. The two regiments held their ground gallantly for a time, but their line was too long. The enemy pierced it exactly in the center. The Third New York rallied on its right at the unfinished redoubt of the Fourth Wisconsin Battery and did some further execution there. The Fifth Pennsylvania, being out of ammunition by this time, retired from the field under a withering fire from the enemy. [*O.R.*, XLII, part 1, pp. 826–827.]

Narrative of Major General Field, continued

Accordingly, *Hoke's* and my division having been relieved in the trenches by the Richmond militia during the night of the 6th of October, daylight next morning found us massed on the Darbytown road. The enemy's right, consisting of Kautz's division of cavalry, rested on this road. My division having the advance, upon approaching our old exterior line of works, found Kautz with his division dismounted and with twelve or sixteen pieces of artillery behind them. Having previously detached *Perry*, who, with *Gary's* cavalry, was to turn the enemy's right and come in behind him with the rest of the division (*Bratton* leading), I assaulted in front. After a sharp fight of twenty minutes Kautz was routed, ten guns and caissons complete, and more than one hundred artillery and cavalry horses, being among the spoils. The enemy, being now perfectly aware of our force and intentions, massed about two miles to the rear of the point from which Kautz had been routed a large force of infantry and artillery behind breastworks, protected in front by a line of abattis. *Hoke* now came up and formed in line of battle on my right, and, I understood, was to assault simultaneously with me. My gallant fellows, led by the brigade commanders on foot, rushed forward and penetrated to the abattis, facing a most terrific fire, delivered, as I afterwards learned from a Yankee officer of rank, who was present, from those new repeating Spencer rifles. *Hoke*, from some unexplained cause, did not move forward. The consequence was that the whole fire was concentrated on my fellows. We were repulsed with heavy loss. Among the killed and wounded was Brigadier-General *Gregg*, commanding Texas brigade, shot through the neck dead, and Brigadier-General *Bratton*, commanding South Carolina brigade, wounded in the shoulder. These gentlemen were both brave and able officers, and the fall of General *Gregg* was felt as a great calamity by the whole army, and was a misfortune from which his brigade never recovered. Had he lived a few days he would doubtless have been promoted, as I had recommended him for a Major-Generalcy for previous distinguished services. [*SHSP*, XIV, p. 557.]

Report of Colonel Hagood, continued

At sunrise on the morning of the 7th of October we attacked the enemy on the Darbytown Pass and drove him from the line of works. My regiment and Colonel [*Robert E.*] *Bowen's* were

advanced to storm the redoubt on the enemy's extreme right, occupied by his dismounted cavalry, which was carried in fine style.
General *Field* then directed me to change front to the right and
attack in flank with the two regiments (Second [Rifles] and First)
a redoubt farther to the right, which was defying the efforts of
Anderson's entire brigade. I executed this order, the men charging
with great spirit and driving from the work a body of the enemy.
Anderson's brigade then came up, and we awaited further orders.
I was now ordered by the brigadier-general commanding to move
on the enemy's artillery, posted on the farther edge of the field,
and which was still resisting. We reached it after double-quicking
for three fourths of a mile; shot down the horses and secured the
cannon. After long delay, which has never been explained to me,
we followed the enemy nearly to the New Market road, where he
had retired after his reverse of the morning and fortified. His
re-enforcements had arrived, and his position, surrounded by a
dense undergrowth impassable to a line of battle, was thus rendered almost impregnable. We attacked it, and, after a hard fight,
were repulsed. A short time afterward we were withdrawn, abandoning all the ground we had gained in the morning. [*O.R.*, XLII,
part 1, p. 938.]

Gen. Robert E. Lee, CSA, commanding Army of Northern Virginia, to Secretary of War James Seddon, October 7, 1864

Genl *Anderson* today drove the enemy from his position near
exterior line of defenses at Charles City Road to vicinity of New
Market Road, where he was found strongly entrenched, and was
not dislodged. Ten (10) pieces of artillery, with their caissons,
some horses, & prisoners were captured. Our loss said to be small;
enemy's not known. The brave Genl *Gregg*, of the Texas Brigade,
fell dead at the head of his men. [*O.R.*, XLII, part 1, p. 852.]

To return to the Petersburg National Battlefield Visitor Center, resume driving
east on Darbytown Road. In 0.4 mile, turn right onto Doran Road, which ends at
New Market Road (U.S. Route 5) in 2.1 miles. Turn left, and in 0.4 mile take the
ramp for southbound I-295. In 12.2 miles, take exit 9B for Westbound Route 36
(Oaklawn Boulevard). In 2.6 miles, bear right onto the ramp for the Visitor Center.

EXCURSION 5
WESTWARD MOVEMENTS

With the failure of the First Petersburg Offensive of June 15–18, 1864, the focus of Union operations south of the James River for much of the next nine months would be on securing control of the roads and rail lines south and west of Petersburg. If these were in Federal hands, the Confederates could not sustain the army defending Petersburg. While Richmond might still have operating rail lines west of the city as well as defensive works south of the city from which to continue the struggle, with the rail lines that ran through Petersburg gone, the Confederate capital's days would probably be numbered as well.

The series of offensives that occurred during this time followed a general pattern in which Lt. Gen. Ulysses S. Grant would initiate operations by taking advantage of his superior numbers and ability to quickly mass Union forces north of the James River to threaten Richmond. Gen. *Robert E. Lee* would have no choice but to respond to Grant's move by shifting Confederate forces north of the James to protect his capital, which would enable the Federals around Petersburg to advance from their fortified positions to seize footholds on the roads and railroads. *Lee* would then shift forces south to try to drive the Federals from their advanced positions before they had been securely fortified.

These Confederate counterattacks often achieved enough tactical success to inspire sufficient caution in the Union corps and division commanders responsible for fighting them off to limit Federal gains. Nonetheless, these operations almost invariably ended with the Federals having extended their lines westward to render secure fortified footholds on, in sequence, the Jerusalem Plank Road, Weldon Railroad, and Squirrel Level Road, and with the Union and Confederate lines having been extended to Hatcher's Run south and west of Petersburg. By February 1865, the Federals would be in striking distance of the last two major lines of communication, the Boydton Plank Road and South Side Railroad, that sustained Petersburg and *Lee's* army.

This excursion will take you along the route laid out by the National Park Service that follows the Union line south of Petersburg as it was extended between June and October 1864 from the vicinity of the Jerusalem Plank Road out to the forts the Federals built to consolidate their hold on territory near Peebles's Farm, with a side trip down to

Reams Station. It will then depart from the Park Service road to take you to sites associated with operations in October 1864 and February 1865 that extended the Federal lines to Hatcher's Run. In sequence, you will study the Second Petersburg Offensive of June 1864 (also known as the Battle of Jerusalem Plank Road), Fourth Petersburg Offensive of August 1864 (Battles of the Weldon Railroad/Globe Tavern and Reams Station), Fifth Petersburg Offensive of September–October 1864 (Battles of Fort Archer/Peebles's Farm), Sixth Petersburg Offensive of October 1864 (Battle of Boydton Plank Road/Hatcher's Run), and Seventh Petersburg Offensive of February 1865 (Battle of Dabney's Mill/Hatcher's Run).

SUMMARY OF PRINCIPAL EVENTS, 18 JUNE 1864–7 FEBRUARY 1865

June 1864
18—Skirmish at King and Queen Court-House; Maj. Gen. David B. Birney, U.S. Army, in temporary command of Second Army Corps; Brig. Gen. William T. H. Brooks, U.S. Army, assumes command of Tenth Army Corps
19–April 3, 1865—Siege of Petersburg and Richmond
20—Skirmish at White House; skirmish at King and Queen Court-House
21—Action at Howlett's Bluff; skirmishes at White House or Saint Peter's Church and Black Creek, or Tunstall's Station
22—Engagement near the Jerusalem Plank Road
22–July 2—Expedition against the South Side and Danville Railroads, with skirmishes at Reams Station (June 22) and Staunton River Bridge, or Roanoke Station (June 25), and engagements at Sappony Church, or Stony Creek (June 28–29) and at Reams Station (June 29)
23—Skirmish at Jones's Bridge
24—Engagement at Saint Mary's Church; action at Hare's Hill.
27—Maj. Gen. Winfield S. Hancock, U.S. Army, resumes command of Second Army Corps
28—Action at Howlett's Bluff
30–July 1, 1864—Actions on Four-Mile Creek, at Deep Bottom
July
12—Skirmish at Warwick Swamp; skirmish at Turkey Creek
14—Action at Malvern Hill
16—Action at Four-Mile Creek; action at Malvern Hill

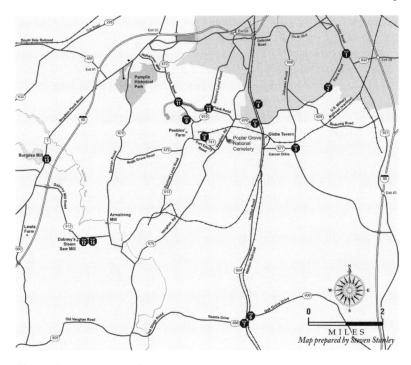

Westward movements overview

17—Skirmish at Herring Creek

18—Brig. Gen. Alfred H. Terry, U.S. Army, in temporary command of Tenth Army Corps

19—Brig. Gen. John H. Martindale, U.S. Army in temporary command of Eighteenth Army Corps, vice Maj. Gen. William F. Smith, relieved

22—Maj. Gen. Edward O. C. Ord, U.S. Army, assumes command of Eighteenth Army Corps

23—Maj. Gen. David B. Birney, U.S. Army, assumes command of Tenth Army Corps

27—Skirmish near Lee's Mill

27–29—Demonstrations on the north bank of the James River and engagement at Deep Bottom (or Darbytown, Strawberry Plains, and New Market Road)

28—Action at Four-Mile Creek

30—Explosion of the Mine and assault on the Crater; skirmish at Lee's Mill

August

1—Skirmish at Deep Bottom
3—Action near Wilcox's Landing
4—Action near Harrison's Landing
5—Explosion of Confederate mine in front of Eighteenth Army Corps; skirmish at Cabin Point
7—Maj. Gen. Philip H. Sheridan, U.S. Army, assigned to temporary command of Middle Military District
9—Explosion at City Point; affair near Sycamore Church
13—Actions at Four-Mile Creek and Dutch Gap
13–20—Demonstration on the north bank of the James River, at Deep Bottom (including combats at Fussell's Mill, Gravel Hill, Bailey's Creek, Deep Run [or Creek], White's Tavern, Charles City Road, New Market Road, and more)
14—Maj. Gen. John G. Parke, U.S. Army, in command of Ninth Army Corps
18–21—Battle of the Weldon Railroad (including combats at Globe Tavern, Yellow House, and Blick's Station)
22—Skirmish on the Vaughan Road
23—Action on the Dinwiddie Road, near Reams Station
24—Skirmish near Reams Station; action on the Vaughan Road, near Reams Station
25—Battle of Reams Station
27—Maj. Gen. Edward O. C. Ord, U.S. Army, in temporary command of the Army of the James
31—Skirmish near the Davis House

September

2—Reconnaissance beyond Yellow Tavern, on Weldon Railroad
3—Affair near Sycamore Church
7—Maj. Gen. John Gibbon, U.S. Army, in temporary command of Eighteenth Army Corps
5—Maj. Gen. David B. Birney, U.S. Army, in temporary command of the Army of the James
5–6—Reconnaissance to Sycamore Church
7—Maj. Gen. Benjamin F. Butler, U.S. Army, resumes command of the Army of the James
10—Assault on Confederate works at the Chimneys
13—Scout to Poplar Spring Church
15—Reconnaissance toward Dinwiddie Court-House and skirmish
16–17—Affair at Coggins's Point (September 16) and pursuit of the Confederates

19—Scout to Lee's Mill and Proctor's House

22—Maj. Gen. Edward O. C. Ord, U.S. Army, resumes command of Eighteenth Army Corps

29–30—Battle of Chaffin's Farm (including combats at Fort Harrison, Fort Gilmer, New Market Heights, and Laurel Hill)

29–October 2—Battle of Poplar Spring Church (including combats at Wyatt's, Peebles's, and Pegram's Farms, Chappell House, and Vaughan Road)

October

1—Bvt. Maj. Gen. Godfrey Weitzel, U.S. Army, in temporary command of Eighteenth Army Corps

7—Engagement on the Darbytown and New Market Roads (including combats at Johnson's Farm and Four-Mile Creek)

8—Reconnaissance on the Vaughan and Squirrel Level Roads

11—Bvt. Maj. Gen. Alfred H. Terry, U.S. Army, in temporary command of Tenth Army Corps

11–12—Scout toward Stony Creek Station

13—Engagement on the Darbytown Road

17—Lieut. Gen. *James Longstreet*, C.S. Army, ordered to resume command of his army corps

27—Skirmish in front of Fort Morton and Fort Sedgwick

27–28—Engagement at Fair Oaks and Darbytown Road; engagement at Boydton Plank Road and Hatcher's Run

29—Skirmish at Johnson's Farm

November

1–5—Scout from Bermuda Hundred into Charles City County

5—Skirmishes in front of Forts Haskell and Morton

7—Reconnaissance toward Stony Creek

16—Skirmish near Lee's Mill

24—Skirmish near Prince George Court House

25—Maj. Gen. Andrew A. Humphreys, U.S. Army, assigned to temporary command of Second Army Corps

28—Scout toward Stony Creek Station; Maj. Gen. Winfield S. Hancock, U.S. Army, assigned to command of a new veteran volunteer army corps (to be organized)

December

1—Expedition to Stony Creek Station, and skirmish

3—Tenth and Eighteenth Army Corps discontinued and Twenty-fourth and Twenty-fifth Army Corps organized, to be commanded, respectively, by Maj. Gens. Edward O. C. Ord and Godfrey Weitzel, U.S. Army

4—Skirmish near Davenport Church

7–12—Expedition to Hicksford, and skirmishes

8—Skirmish at Hatcher's Run

9–10—Reconnaissance to Hatcher's Run, and skirmishes

10—Skirmish in front of Fort Holly

14—Maj. Gen. Edward O. C. Ord, U.S. Army, in temporary command of the Army of the James

24—Maj. Gen. Benjamin F. Butler, U.S. Army, resumes command of the Army of the James

30—Maj. Gen. John G. Parke, U.S. Army, in temporary command of the Army of the Potomac and Bvt. Maj. Gen. Orlando B. Willcox, U.S. Army, of Ninth Army Corps

January 1865

2—Bvt. Maj. Gen. Samuel W. Crawford, U.S. Army, in temporary command of Fifth Army Corps; Brig. Gen. Charles Devens, U.S. Army, in temporary command of Twenty-fourth Army Corps

8—Maj. Gen. Edward O. C. Ord, U.S. Army, assumes command of the Department of Virginia and North Carolina and the Army of the James, vice Major General Benjamin F. Butler, relieved

9—Skirmish near Disputant Station

11—Maj. Gen. George G. Meade, U.S. Army, resumes command of the Army of the Potomac

12—Maj. Gen. John G. Parke, U.S. Army, resumes command of Ninth Army Corps

15—Maj. Gen. John Gibbon, U.S. Army, assumes command of Twenty-fourth Army Corps

17—Bvt. Maj. Gen. George W. Getty, U.S. Army, in temporary command of Sixth Army Corps

23–24—Action at Fort Brady, James River

24—Bvt. Maj. Gen. Orlando B. Willcox, U.S. Army, in temporary command of Ninth Army Corps

25—Skirmish near Powhatan

27—Maj. Gen. Gouverneur K. Warren, U.S. Army, resumes command of Fifth Army Corps

30—Scout to Long Bridge and Bottom's Bridge

February

2—Maj. Gen. John G. Parke, U.S. Army, resumes command of Ninth Army Corps

5–7—Battle of Hatcher's Run (otherwise known as Dabney's Mill, Armstrong's Mill, Rowanty Creek, and Vaughan Road)

6—Maj. Gen. Edward O. C. Ord, U.S. Army, assigned to command of the Department of Virginia

From the Petersburg National Battlefield Visitor Center, leave the parking area and take the exit onto Washington Street (Route 36). Drive 2.2 miles to the intersection with Crater Road (Route 301/460). Turn left onto Crater Road, and drive 2.8 miles south to Flank Road. (At 1.3 miles after turning onto Crater Road, you will pass the location of Fort Sedgwick, all remnants of which were obliterated in the 1960s to build a shopping center. Because of its location on the critical Jerusalem Plank Road [modern Crater Road] and proximity to Confederate Fort Mahone, Fort Sedgwick attracted so much fire from the Confederates that Union soldiers posted in it during the campaign of 1864–1865 referred to it as "Fort Hell.") Turn right onto Flank Road, then at 0.2 mile turn left. Park at the pull-off next to the historical marker that immediately appears on the left side of the road. Get out of your vehicle and face toward Fort Davis.

STOP 1: FORT DAVIS

After the Federals secured a foothold on the Jerusalem Plank Road during the First Petersburg Offensive of June 15–18, 1864, they commenced construction of a 3-acre fort on this site that was designed to accommodate over 500 men and 8 guns, the remnants of which are before you. Initially named in honor of Maj. Gen. Gouverneur Warren, commander of the Union Fifth Corps, it was shortly thereafter renamed Fort Davis in honor of Col. P. Stearns Davis of the Thirty-ninth Massachusetts, who was mortally wounded nearby on July 11, 1864.

SECOND PETERSBURG OFFENSIVE: BATTLE OF JERUSALEM PLANK ROAD, 22 JUNE 1864

On June 22, the Federals initiated the Second Petersburg Offensive. The Second Corps, commanded by Maj. Gen. David Birney while Maj. Gen. Winfield Scott battled complications from a wound he had suffered at the July 1863 Battle of Gettysburg, was ordered to cross the Jerusalem Plank Road south of the end of the Federal line, held by the Fifth Corps, then pivot to the right and move north to establish contact with the Fifth Corps and extend the Union line westward. Meanwhile, Maj. Gen. Horatio Wright's Sixth Corps was directed to cross the Jerusalem Plank Road farther south, then push west cross-country— to a position that it was hoped would enable him to extend the Federal lines all the way to the Appomattox River west of Petersburg.

Fort Sedgwick (USAMHI)

Report of Brig. Gen. David B. Birney, USA, commanding Second Corps, Army of the Potomac

On the 22nd instant I began a movement involving a change in the First and Third Divisions of the corps as then established. Its object was to advance the left and center of the corps to envelop the enemy's position.... General [Gershom] Mott advanced to the position assigned him, keeping connection with General [John] Gibbon's (Second) division, which remained in its entrenchments. General [Francis C.] Barlow, following the movements of General Mott's left, threw his whole line forward, effecting nearly a right half wheel through the dense woods in his front and completely severing connection with the Sixth Corps, as his orders required him to do. [U.S. War Department, *The War of the Rebellion: A Compilation of the Official Records of the Union and Confederate Armies*, 70 vols. in 128 parts and index (Washington, D.C.: Government Printing Office, 1880–1901), series 1, volume XL, part 1, pp. 325–326. Hereafter cited as *O.R.*; all references are to series 1 unless otherwise noted.]

Fortifications at Fort Davis (USAMHI)

Reminiscence of Maj. Gen. William Mahone, CSA, commanding division, Third Corps, Army of Northern Virginia

On the morning of the 21st June Gen. [Cadmus M.] *Wilcox* was sent out with his division of four brigades, passing on the west side of the Johnson House into the woodland beyond to feel for the left flank of the enemy's line. . . . I was directed to move out of the trenches and co-operate with *Wilcox* in any attack he should make upon the enemy, as he should in it, uncover my front. Genl. *Wilcox* went out and returned that night failing to find the enemy's line. On the morning of the 22nd June, Genl *Wilcox* was sent again out to find the left flank of the enemy's army and to strike it a blow and my instructions were, for that day, as for the day before.

My division occupied the intrenched line from the Rives Salient to the ravine of Lieutenant Run. . . . I saw the Federal troops moving orderly across the plank-road in the direction of the Johnson House, the leading regiment halting, stacking arms, and the men going deliberately to intrenching and the next regiment passing on and after clearing the leading regiment, halting, stacking arms, and then proceeding to intrench. . . . At this juncture, that is while the enemy was deliberately projecting their line, Genl. [*Robert E.*] *Lee* came upon the ground and expressed a desire that something should be done to arrest the progress of the Federal prolongation. . . . In response to Genl *Lee's* expressed desire, I caused the two right brigades of my division to drop quietly to the rear, so as to avoid discovery and then moved up the ravine of Lieutenant Run, all the way out of view till reaching the open field in front of the Johnson House and there they were formed in line of battle, skirmish line put out and the march commenced, so as to strike the head of the Federal projecting column, meanwhile sending an intelligent staff officer to find Genl. *Wilcox* and explain to him what I was about and to request that he bear down on my firing; that he was in the right position to take the Federals in the rear. [Mahone Family Papers, Library of Virginia, Richmond, Virginia.]

Drive out of the Fort Davis area and proceed straight to Crater Road. Turn left onto Crater Road. Proceed 0.1 mile to the traffic light, then turn left onto Flank Road. Proceed 1.0 mile on Flank Road to a parking area on the right side of the road. Walk over to the park service sign: "Fort Hays: A Silent Witness."

STOP 2: FORT ALEXANDER HAYS

Fort Alexander Hays was built in August and September 1864 as part of the effort to extend the fortified Federal line to the foothold the Army of the Potomac had secured on the Weldon Railroad in late August. It was named after Brig. Gen. Alexander Hays, who was killed leading a division during the May 1864 Battle of the Wilderness, and had five sides with a bomb-proof shelter in the interior. Although it was designed to accommodate ten pieces of artillery, only four were actually installed to support the 300-man garrison.

SECOND PETERSBURG OFFENSIVE: BATTLE OF JERUSALEM PLANK ROAD, 22 JUNE 1864

Birney's three divisions encountered little difficulty as they crossed the Jerusalem Plank Road on June 22 and then made their pivot north to reach a position where it connected with the left flank of the Fifth Corps. However, in the process, the division on Birney's left, Maj. Gen. Francis Barlow's, lost contact with Wright's corps. The

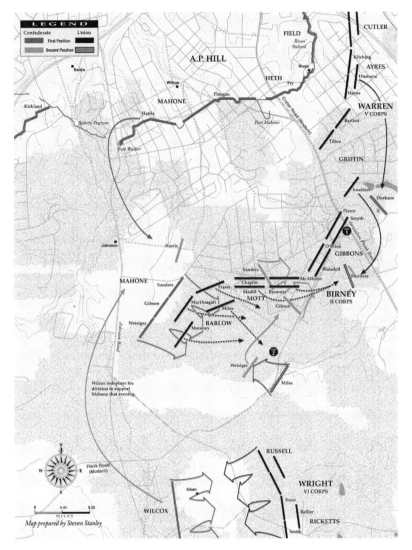

Jerusalem Plank Road, June 22, 1864

Confederates did not hesitate in taking advantage. Under *Lee's* personal supervision, two divisions from Lt. Gen. *Ambrose P. Hill's* corps were dispatched to the scene.

Then, taking advantage of a ravine located about a mile and a half west of the Jerusalem Plank Road that allowed it to penetrate into the gap between Barlow and the Sixth Corps undetected, Brig. Gen. *William Mahone's* division reached a position around three p.m. from which it was able to smash into Barlow's flank and rear. Barlow's command quickly fell apart, as did all of the division next in line, Brig. Gen. Gershom Mott's, and part of Maj. Gen. John Gibbon's. The routed Federals fled back to a line of fortifications near the Jerusalem Plank Road. There Birney's men managed to rally, but the Confederates were able to claim 1,700 prisoners and 4 pieces of artillery.

These events did not dampen Maj. Gen. George G. Meade's determination to salvage something from the operation, though, and on June 23 he had Wright continue fighting through the rugged terrain west of the Jerusalem Plank Road toward the Weldon Railroad. A detachment from Brig. Gen. Lewis Grant's brigade was able to establish a foothold on the road and begin tearing up track. However, during the afternoon a Confederate infantry force attacked Grant's force and managed to capture nearly 400 Federal soldiers. Despite being egged on by Meade to continue the operation, Wright, understandably anxious about the isolation of his command, prudently decided to pull back to the Jerusalem Plank Road.

Report of Brigadier General Birney, continued

In order to protect [Barlow's] left, thus exposed, two small brigades were held behind that part of the line, following the movement by the flank. . . . The line of the corps had nearly conformed to the enemy's position, when a body of their troops, from *Hill's* corps (whose number cannot be definitely ascertained, so dense were the woods) advanced upon the left flank of General Barlow and into the interval between his line and the Sixth Corps, which had become so great as to prevent any timely or intelligent co-operation. The advance of the enemy, in whatever force made, was proceeded by a strong skirmish line, which opened a sharp fire on the left and rear of our troops, advancing in line and directly upon the troops moving to the front by the flank. The unexpectedness of the fire and the trying character of the country might have excused a momentary confusion, but the troops on this part of the line seem to have been seized with panic, and to have only attempted to regain the breastworks, in which they rallied enough and showed a disposition to defend them. The breaking of the First Division communicated the panic in a less degree to the Third Division, which fell back rapidly and in some confusion, the enemy still pressing sharply along the advanced line taken by the corps, and striking everything on it by the flank.

There was no proper effort made by the immediate commanders to effect a change of front and meet the fire of the enemy. . . . As the rapid advance of the enemy reached the right of General Mott and the left of General Gibbon it seems to have been combined with a movement of other troops directly in front, whether preconcerted or excited by it is impossible to say. So far the prisoners taken had been chiefly individuals who preferred to give themselves up rather than run the risk of getting back under who were broken off from their commands in the thick woods and brush. The left of the Second Division consisted of the Second Brigade, Major [Timothy] O'Brien, One hundred and fifty-second New York Volunteers, commanding. This brigade is very small, very deficient in officers, and the conduct of Major O'Brien seems to have been wanting in force and promptness. The brigade met a fire from the front, but was curled up rapidly before the advance of the enemy, who had now got behind the first line of battle and were rolling it up. The breaking of this brigade let the enemy in on the flank of Captain [George] McKnight's (Twelfth New York Independent) battery, which was captured without any fault of officers or men. The panic along the line had become such that three or four small regiments (hardly averaging 100 muskets) surrendered in a body when summoned to do so.

The next regiment in line was the Twentieth Massachusetts Volunteers, whose commander, Captain H. L. Patten, taking advantage of a slight turn in the breast-works, and making a partial change of front, checked the enemy's advance and stopped all further retreat and loss. There seems to have been no time during this most unfortunate and disgraceful affair when the same promptness and spirit might not have ended the disasters of the day. Efforts were at once made by the division commanders and myself to restore the line within the breast-works. The enemy attacked smartly on two or three points, but were easily repulsed. At 4 p.m. I reported to the major-general commanding that my lines were re-established and the troops again in condition. My first information of the attack of the enemy was through a staff officer

of General Mott reporting that General Barlow's line had been
broken and his own left had been turned. I immediately rode
to the line, where I learned that General Gibbon's battery had
been taken. . . . There was no reason, either in the force engaged
or in the character of the ground—equally unfavorable to them
as to us—why the enemy's attack should not have been promptly
repelled. I attribute failure to the extraordinary losses among the
commanding, staff, and other officers in this command, to the
large proportion of new troops assigned to this corps to replace
veterans, to the fact that the Sixth Corps did not advance simultaneously, and that in consequence my line was taken in flank,
and at points even in reverse, creating a panic, and completing
a withdrawal to my line of that morning, with considerable loss.
[*O.R.*, XL, part 1, pp. 326–327.]

Report of Brig. Gen. Francis C. Barlow, USA, commanding First Division, Second Corps, Army of the Potomac

On June 22, instant, I moved to the right and front to connect
with and prolong the line of General Mott's division in obedience to orders. This necessarily severed my connection with the
Sixth Corps. My left flank being thus unprotected I placed one
brigade on the left of General Mott's line and threw back two
small brigades at nearly a right angle to General Mott's line as a
protection to my flank. I had scarcely got into position before the
enemy's skirmishers began pressing into the gap between me and
the Sixth Corps. They were driven back from that part of my flank
which was covered by the two brigades which were thrown back,
but soon extended farther to my right and rear. I immediately
brought my second line (General Miles' brigade) back into the
rifle-pits to reestablish, as far as possible, the connection with the
Sixth Corps. Before I could execute any change of position with
my advanced line the great part of that line (Second, Third, and
Fourth Brigades) came back in confusion to the rifle-pits. The
enemy pressed in vigorously, capturing a considerable number
of the troops that broke, and such parts of the troops as stood
fast; the troops on my right came in also. I had hardly arranged
my division in the rifle-pits before the enemy made a smart attack
upon one part of them, but were repulsed; a few of their dead
and wounded were left in our front. Prisoners say the attack was
in line of battle preceded by a skirmish line. Our advance separa-
tion from the Sixth Corps exposed us to be attacked under very

unfavorable circumstances. At the same time it must be admitted that the troops did not meet the attack with vigor courage and determination. The brigades of my front line (Second and Third) are too unsteady, from loss of commanding and other officers and other causes, to be much depended on in circumstances requiring much nerve and determination. [*O.R.*, XL, part 1, pp. 328–329.]

Report of Brig. Gen. George Getty, USA, commanding Second Division, Sixth Corps, Army of the Potomac

On the night of the [21st] . . . the corps was relieved by the Eighteenth Corps and moved to the left of the army. This division was on the extreme left, and formed in two lines, thrown back at right angles to the general line, to protect the flank. [Col. Oliver] Edwards' brigade (Fourth) was thrown out half a mile on the Jerusalem plank road to guard against an attack from that quarter, and held this position until the 29th. After some maneuvering toward night the lines were advanced a mile, the division moving up by the right flank, and keeping its connection with the main line.

On the 23rd Captain [Alexander M.] Beattie, Third Vermont, commanding the division sharpshooters, pushed forward on a scout, reached the Weldon railroad, driving before him a small force of the enemy's cavalry, cut the telegraph line, and tore up a small portion of the track. About noon he was attacked by the enemy in force, and slowly retired, skirmishing. A heavy skirmish line was immediately thrown out in front of the division, and intrenchments hastily thrown up. The enemy advanced in strong force and, driving back simultaneously the left of our skirmish line and the skirmishers of the Third Division on our right, succeeded in cutting off and capturing the Fourth Vermont and Major [C. K.] Fleming's battalion of the Eleventh Vermont, in all, 400 men. After feeling our lines strongly the enemy then withdrew. At 10 p.m. the lines were thrown back to the position first taken up on the 22nd covering the Jerusalem plank road; intrenchments were thrown up the following day, and the division remained in this position until the 29th. [*O.R.*, XL, part 1, p. 495.]

Lt. Gen. Ulysses S. Grant, USA, commanding Armies of the United States, to Maj. Gen. Henry W. Halleck, Chief of Staff at Washington, June 23, 1864

Yesterday and this morning have been consumed in extending our lines to the left to envelop Petersburg. The Second and

Sixth Corps are now west of the Jerusalem Plank Road. Yesterday, in moving to this position, the two corps became separated. The enemy pushed out between them and caused some confusion in the left of the Second Corps, and captured 4 pieces of artillery. Order was soon restored and the enemy pushed back. This morning no enemy is found on the left. This will be pushed forward until the enemy is found. [*O.R.*, XL, part 1, pp. 13–14.]

I find the affair of the 22nd was much worse than I had heretofore learned. Our losses (nearly all captures) were not far from 2,000, and 4 pieces of artillery. The affair was a stampede and surprise to both parties and ought to have been turned in our favor. [*O.R.*, XL, part 1, pp. 14.]

Report of Gen. Robert E. Lee, CSA, commanding Army of Northern Virginia

Yesterday a movement of infantry, cavalry and artillery was made toward the right of our forces at Petersburg in the direction of the Weldon railroad. The enemy was driven back, and his infantry is reported to have halted. . . . The enemy's infantry was attacked this afternoon on the west side of the Jerusalem plank road and driven from his first line of works to his second on that road by General *Mahone* with a part of his division. About 1,600 prisoners, 4 pieces of artillery, and a large number of small arms were captured. [*O.R.*, XL, part 1, pp. 749–750.]

Continue driving west on Flank Road for 1.3 miles until you reach its intersection with Johnson Road. Turn left onto Johnson Road (Route 608). After traveling 1.1 miles on Johnson Road, turn right into the driveway for Ernst Hall on the campus of Richard Bland College (it will appear just before you exit the campus). Proceed to the parking area, park, and walk over to the railroad section and sign: "The Petersburg Railroad."

STOP 3: RICHARD BLAND COLLEGE

FOURTH PETERSBURG OFFENSIVE: MOVEMENT TO THE WELDON RAILROAD, 18 AUGUST 1864

After the failure of the Third Richmond-Petersburg Offensive on July 28–30 (highlighted by the battles of First Deep Bottom and the Crater), Grant resumed looking for ways to get at the roads south of the Appomattox that connected Petersburg with the rest of the

Confederacy. He sent the Second Corps, once again commanded by Hancock, north of the James at Deep Bottom on August 14. While Hancock spent six days fruitlessly endeavoring to gain a decisive advantage north of the James in what became known as the Battle of Second Deep Bottom, on August 18 Maj. Gen. Gouverneur Warren's Fifth Corps pushed west with orders to reach the Weldon Railroad and tear up as much of the track as it could.

After passing the Gurley farm, on the current grounds of Richard Bland College, Warren's lead division, commanded by Maj. Gen. Charles Griffin, reached the Weldon Railroad near a small structure known as the Globe Tavern around nine a.m. Griffin then pushed a skirmish line about 500 yards to the east and a battle line a few hundred yards north of the tavern to cover the rest of his division as it went to work tearing up track. When Brig. Gen. Romeyn Ayres's and Brig. Gen. Samuel Crawford's divisions reached the Globe Tavern (which was also known as Yellow House), Warren ordered them to move north toward Petersburg.

Report of Maj. Gen. George G. Meade, USA, commanding Army of the Potomac

On the 14th of August Major-General Hancock, commanding Second Corps, [Brig. Gen. David M.] Gregg's division of cavalry, and a detachment of troops of the Department of Virginia and North Carolina, under Major-General Birney, crossed the James River at Deep Bottom, attacking the enemy in position. Birney carried the lines in front of him, capturing 6 pieces of artillery, 4 colors, and many prisoners. Barlow's attack with part of the Second Corps was not so successful. On the 15th Hancock maneuvered to the right, to develop the enemy's position and select a point of attack. On the 16th an attack was again made with partial success. . . . The 17th and 18th, and 19th were spent by Hancock in continual skirmishing, constantly threatening the enemy, but finding him too strongly posted to justify an attack. On the 20th Hancock was withdrawn, having previously sent Mott's division to Petersburg.

During these operations of Hancock on the north side of the James, advantage was taken of the weakening of the enemy's line south of the Appomattox to effect a lodgment on the Weldon railroad. For this purpose the Fifth Corps, having been previously withdrawn from the lines, its place being supplied by an extension of the Ninth, Warren moved on the 18th, and by a detour to the rear, struck the Weldon railroad near the Globe Tavern without much opposition, except from a small force of the enemy's cavalry. [*O.R.*, XLII, part 1, pp. 30–31.]

Report of Maj. Gen. Gouverneur K. Warren, USA, commanding
Fifth Army Corps, Army of the Potomac

Pursuant to orders, we set out at 4 a.m. on the 18th instant. We reached the enemy's cavalry pickets, at Doctor Gurley's house . . . at 7 a.m. General Griffin's division, in advance, was immediately formed in line of battle by brigade, with skirmishers deployed. We then, at 8 a.m., advanced rapidly. By the aid of the support of the cavalry picket belonging to the Third New York Cavalry we captured several of [Brig. Gen. *James*] *Dearing's* brigade of the enemy's cavalry, and reached the railroad without opposition. Griffin's division was immediately disposed to cover the position toward the south and west, and General [Romeyn] Ayres advanced to the north along the railroad. In about one mile this division found the enemy in line of battle, with artillery, which showed a firm disposition to contest our farther advance. General [Samuel] Crawford's division was then ordered up on the right of General Ayres to outflank the enemy. [*O.R.*, XLII, part 1, pp. 428–429.]

Return to your vehicle, and turn left back onto Johnson Road (Route 608). At the first intersection, turn left onto Carson Drive (Route 677), and proceed 0.8 mile to Halifax Road (Route 604). Turn right, and drive 1.0 mile on Halifax Road to the parking area for Free Temple Full Gospel Ministries, Inc., on the right. En route, if you look to the right at 0.3 mile from where you turn onto Halifax Road, you will see the wartime location of the Globe Tavern. Note that the railroad and road have switched positions since 1864. At the time of the war, the modern Halifax Road was the actual railroad bed, whereas the modern railroad follows the line of the old Halifax Road and has been straightened out.

STOP 4: GLOBE TAVERN

FOURTH PETERSBURG OFFENSIVE: BATTLE OF THE WELDON RAILROAD, 18 AUGUST 1864

As it had in June during the Second Offensive, the Confederate high command responded quickly and decisively when news arrived that the Federals were on the Weldon Railroad. By noon two Confederate brigades under the overall command of Maj. Gen. *Henry Heth* were pushing south along the railroad toward Warren's position. At that point, Ayres's and Crawford's divisions had moved into a belt of woods about a half mile north of the Globe Tavern. Federal skirmishers had reached the W. P. Davis House north of the woods when *Heth's* men launched their attack. Ayres's division was attacked by Brig. Gen. *Joseph Davis's* brigade, which quickly drove it back through the woods. Meanwhile, part of Col. *Robert M. Mayo's* brigade managed to penetrate the Federal line east of the railroad and force Crawford's division to retreat. Warren, however, managed to quickly rally his command and maintain his foothold on the railroad.

Report of Maj. Gen. Henry Heth, CSA, commanding Heth's Division, Third Corps, Army of Northern Virginia

On August 18, I was ordered to take two brigades—[Brig. Gen. *Joseph R.*] *Davis'* and [Brig. Gen. *Henry H.*] *Walker's*—and attack the enemy, who had made a lodgment on the Petersburg and Weldon Railroad at or near the Yellow Tavern, distance about four miles from Petersburg. I formed line of battle near the Davis House on the Weldon Railroad, *Davis'* Brigade (Brigadier-General *Davis* commanding) on the right of the railroad, its left resting on the railroad, *Walker's* Brigade (Colonel [*Robert Murphy*] *Mayo* commanding) on *Davis'* left, the right of *Walker's* Brigade resting on the railroad. Skirmishers were thrown out and soon encountered those of the enemy. I directed an advance, which was made in good order. The enemy was driven about three-fourths of a mile, and several lines of breastworks were carried by storm. Some 200 prisoners were captured. The enemy was found to be in much stronger force than was at first supposed, and the two brigades had done all that could be expected of them. [Janet B. Hewett et al., eds., *Supplement to the Official Records of the Union and Confederate Armies*, 51 vols. (Wilmington, N.C.: Broadfoot Publishing, 1994–1997). *Part I—Reports*, volume VII, p. 473.]

Report of Bvt. Maj. Gen. Romeyn B. Ayres, USA, commanding Second Division, Fifth Army Corps, Army of the Potomac

[On August 18] the division took the advance along the road after reaching it, the First and Second Brigades forming the line of battle. . . . The division advanced about 100 yards into a dense woods. Soon after reaching the front edge of the woods the enemy's line of battle struck mine, outflanking it. I have been informed that the brigade commanders (one has since been killed and the other captured) at this time gave the order to fall back.

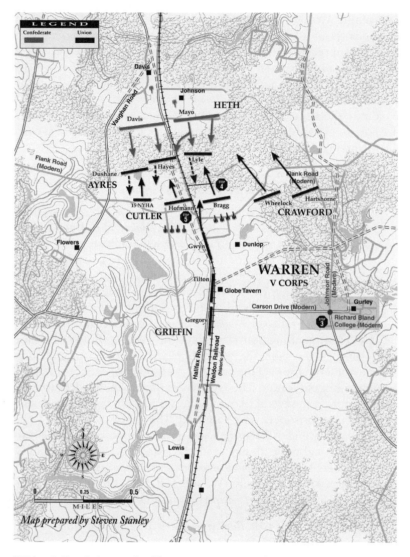

Confederate   Union

Davis

Johnson

Vaughan Road

Mayo   HETH

Davis

Flank Road (Modern)

Dushane   Hayes   Lyle

AYRES   STEP 4

Flank Road (Modern)

Hartshorne

15·NYHA   Hofmann   Bragg   Wheelock   CRAWFORD

CUTLER   STEP 5

Flowers

Gwyn   Dunlop

WARREN

Tilton   V CORPS

Globe Tavern

Johnson Road (Modern)

Gregory   Carson Drive (Modern)   Gurley

GRIFFIN   STEP 3   Richard Bland College (Modern)

Halifax Road

Weldon Railroad (historic path)

Lewis

Map prepared by Steven Stanley

Weldon Railroad, August 18, 1864

This was done for about 100 yards. I threw forward the Fifteenth New York into line and the two brigades were formed on it. The second was in some confusion on arriving upon this new line, but were rallied and soon engaged the enemy. The enemy after persistent efforts was repulsed, leaving his dead in our hands. During the engagement I deemed it advisable to re-enforce my left. This was furnished promptly, Colonel [J. William] Hofmann's brigade, of General [Lysander] Cutler's division, being sent to me for that purpose. A short time after this the engagement was over. After the first flush the division behaved handsomely. The Fifteenth New York Heavy Artillery was steady and cool. Colonel Hofmann's brigade moved as on drill. During the night rifle-pits were constructed along my front, which was disposed as follows, viz: The First Brigade on the right of the railroad; on the left the Fifteenth New York Artillery; then Hofmann's brigade; the Maryland Brigade being on the left, curving to the rear. [*O.R.*, XLII, part 1, p. 471.]

Report of Brig. Gen. Samuel W. Crawford, USA, commanding Third Division, Fifth Corps, Army of the Potomac

Having reached the Globe Tavern (or Yellow House) about noon on the 18th ultimo, I received instructions to mass my command in the immediate vicinity, and to hold them in readiness to move at a moment's notice. My division consisted of the First Brigade, Colonel P[eter] Lyle commanding; the Second Brigade, Colonel [Richard] Coulter commanding, and the Third, a provisional brigade, consisting of two regiments (the One hundred and ninetieth and One hundred and ninety-first Veteran Pennsylvania Reserve Volunteers, Colonel [William R.] Hartshorne commanding), numbering in the aggregate about 3,000 effective men. In about an hour I received orders to advance. The Second Division under General Ayres was advancing on the left of the railroad. My orders were to advance on the right in line of battle and form connection with the Second Division on my left. The ground in my immediate front was low, and in front ended in a dense and almost impenetrable thicket which ran along the whole line from right to left. The thicket was cut up with swampy grounds, and was almost impassable.

The First Brigade, under Colonel Lyle, was on the left, the Second, under Colonel Coulter, was in the center, and the Third Brigade, under Colonel Hartshorne, advanced in support on the right. I at once directed that a strong skirmish line should be deployed and thrown into the woods. The One hundred and seventh Pennsylvania Volunteers was deployed and advanced, the line of battle following. Meantime the enemy's batteries stationed near the Davis House had opened and obtained range of the command. Finding that the regiment deployed as skirmishers did not properly cover my front, I ordered it to be relieved by the One hundred and ninetieth Pennsylvania, or First Pennsylvania Reserve Veteran Volunteers, under Colonel Hartshorne, and directed the One hundred and seventh Pennsylvania to rejoin its brigade.

While superintending this movement and the general advance of my line, I sent a staff officer to find the right of the Second Division and to insure a firm connection with it on my left. This was thoroughly effected by the Sixteenth Maine Regiment, of Lyle's brigade (see report of Colonels Lyle, [Thomas] McCoy, and [Charles] Tilden). It was raining heavily as we advanced. On the right of the Sixteenth Maine was the Thirty-ninth Massachusetts. . . . Hardly had the connection been made and the brigade advanced into position on the right when the enemy threw himself on the right of the Second Division and forced it back. The woods and undergrowth on the right of the railroad were so thick on the left of my line as to be almost impenetrable. The enemy, however, after having driven back the right of the Second Division, seeing his advantage in regard to the troops on the right of the road, advanced directly on my left flank. The line fell back, continuing to fight until it entirely confronted the enemy, when a stand was made and the enemy retired, and the line again advanced to its original position. At this time I received an order from the major-general commanding the corps . . . to throw forward my right, and, as far as possible, advance toward the railroad and strike the enemy on his left flank. This was at once ordered, and the line moved forward on the right. The skirmish line, strongly supported, advanced. We met the enemy on the right and center and drove him back from two chains of hastily-constructed rifle-pits to his entrenchments beyond a large corn-field in front of the thicket of woods. To advance my line was a matter of the greatest difficulty. So dense and tangled was the undergrowth, and so interspersed with swamps, that it was almost impossible to keep up the congestion or to see beyond twenty or thirty feet. The line was established, however. I reported to the general commanding the corps the result of my advance. . . . The line was entrenched during the night in front of the First Brigade. [*O.R.*, XLII, part 1, pp. 491–492.]

Report of Major General Warren, continued

The enemy, at 2 p.m., advanced against General Ayres and forced his line to fall back to prevent being flanked. General Ayres contested the ground firmly, and finally drove the enemy back. Colonel Hofmann's brigade, Fourth Division, was sent to support General Ayres. Colonel Lyle's brigade, of General Crawford's division, also received a part of this attack. General Crawford continued to move forward his right until dark, but his advance was all the way through dense woods. . . . The enemy's loss must have exceeded our own, as he left his dead and some wounded on the ground. [*O.R.*, XLII, part 1, pp. 428–429.]

Return to your vehicle, and turn left onto Halifax Road. Drive 0.3 mile to Fort Wadsworth on the right, and pull into the parking area.

STOP 5: FORT WADSWORTH

The fortification in front of you was constructed in the aftermath of the Battle of the Weldon Railroad to strengthen the Federal hold on the railroad and anchor the left of the Union line south of Petersburg. Built on the site of the wartime Blick House, the rectangular fort had four bastions as well as a bomb-proof shelter and magazine in the interior. It was named after Brig. Gen. James S. Wadsworth, a division commander in the Army of the Potomac who had been mortally wounded on May 6, 1864, during the Battle of the Wilderness.

FOURTH PETERSBURG OFFENSIVE: BATTLE OF THE WELDON RAILROAD, 19 AUGUST 1864

Encouraged by their tactical achievements the day before, the Confederates decided to make an even stronger effort against Warren's command on August 19. As rain soaked the ground south of Petersburg, *Heth* once again advanced on the Federals from the north while three brigades under the command of *Mahone* maneuvered against their right. Fortunately for the Confederates, units from the Ninth Corps that were supposed to secure Crawford's right flank had not reached the field yet. Thus, *Mahone* was able once again, aided by the cover provided by the same ravine he had used in June, to deliver a devastating attack. Crawford's right flank was shattered, and the brigade on *Mahone's* left was able to reach the railroad in the rear of the Federals, who were fighting off *Heth's* attack. By the time they did so, however, Brig. Gen. Orlando Willcox's division from the Ninth Corps was on the field and quickly moved forward to bring *Mahone's* attack to a halt. Then, aided by Brig. Gen. Julius White's division, the Federals forced *Mahone* to fall back. The Federals had lost 2,700 prisoners, but their grip on the railroad remained firm.

Report of Major General Heth, continued

On August 19 General *Mahone* was directed to move around and attack the enemy on his right flank. At the same time, I was to make a diversion by an attack in front, passing over the same ground that we had fought over the day previous. As soon as *Mahone* attacked, I directed *Davis'* Brigade (Colonel [*William Steptoe*] *Christian* commanding, Colonel *Mayo* being sick) to advance. This was done and the enemy driven from his works on both sides of the railroad. The enemy in retreating before Colonel *Christian's* attack, struck *Mahone's* advancing column and enabled his troops to swell the number of prisoners they had already captured. The enemy, however, still held the railroad. [*O.R. Supplement*, VII, p. 473.]

Report of Major General Warren, continued

August 19, at 4 a.m. I sent General [Edward S.] Bragg's brigade to the right to support General Crawford and establish a connection on the shortest line, with skirmishers, between my right and the pickets near the Jerusalem plank road. The order General Bragg did not execute as directed, but took up another line a mile or more to the rear. I at once directed General Bragg to correct his line and sent the best officers of my staff to assist.

At 4.15, before this was accomplished and reported to me, the enemy broke through this picket-line with heavy force in column of fours, left in front, and facing to the right swept rapidly down to our left in rear of General Crawford's line. At the same time General Ayres and signal officers reported a heavy force on my front, along the railroad. My line was so extended that two regiments of the Pennsylvania Reserve Veterans of General Crawford's division were all on as a skirmish line, and the enemy passed quite in their rear. Colonel [Charles] Wheelock's brigade fought

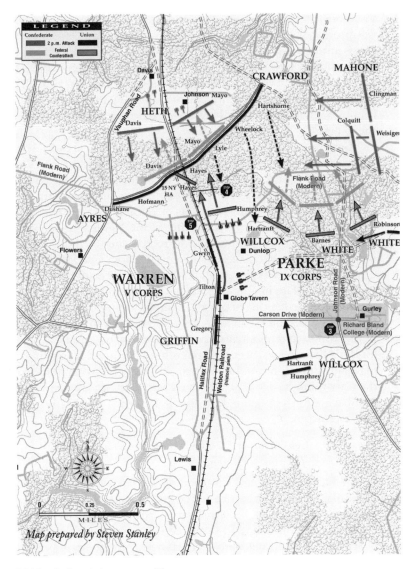

Weldon Railroad, August 19, 1864

well and lost comparatively little. So much confusion, however, was produced by the men falling back, and masking the fire of those in line, that all General Crawford's line was compelled to fall back, and also the right of General Ayres' division. Colonel Lyle's brigade lost very heavily in prisoners, and General [Joseph] Hayes, commanding First Brigade of General Ayres' division, was captured. General Crawford was at one time quite surrounded by the enemy.

General Willcox's division, of the Ninth Corps, about 1,200 strong, was immediately ordered up to attack the enemy, and the lines of Generals Ayres and Crawford, being reformed, moved forward at the same time, driving back the enemy, regaining the ground lost, and capturing prisoners. . . . About the same time the troops under General [Julius] White, of the Ninth Corps, about 1,000 strong, on our right, were formed facing to the right to oppose any further flanking, and engaged [Brig. Gen. Alfred H.] *Colquitt's* brigade of the enemy, and drove it back, capturing about 40 prisoners. The enemy in great confusion rapidly fell back to his intrenchments, carrying with them the disorganized parts of the command, which had become so by the attack from the rear in the woods, and also a large portion of those on picket. . . . Before this flank attack began, signal officers reported troops moving against my front on the railroad, and General Ayres reported their arrival in his front. These made repeated attempts to force him back after he regained his line but failed. [*O.R.*, XLII, part 1, pp. 429–430.]

Report of Lt. Gen. Ambrose P. Hill, CSA, commanding Third Corps, Army of Northern Virginia

I attacked the enemy this evening at 4 o'clock with the brigades of *Davis* and *Walker*, under Major-General *Heth*, the brigades of *Colquitt*, [Brig. Gen. *Thomas L.*] *Clingman*, and *Mahone*, under Major-General *Mahone*, and three batteries, under Colonel [*William J.*] *Pegram*, and defeated him, capturing about 2,700 prisoners, including one brigadier-general. . . . *Colquitt's* and *Clingman's* brigades in their advance through the thick undergrowth became so much scattered as to lose their organization. I was consequently compelled to order them to their original camps as a rallying point. *Mahone's* brigade was also ordered inside the lines. *Heth's* two brigades I have left occupying the ground they were to-day.

I have also directed General *W. H. F. Lee* to move at 3 o'clock in
the morning down to the Davis house. We will then be in position to push them again in the morning if we can get more
troops. . . . The blow struck them has been a very severe one.
[*O.R.*, XLII, part 1, p. 940.]

Maj. Gen. Gouverneur K. Warren (USAMHI)

FOURTH PETERSBURG OFFENSIVE: BATTLE OF THE WELDON RAILROAD, 21 AUGUST 1864

The Confederates made another effort on August 21 to break Warren's grip on the Weldon Railroad. The plan was that *Heth* would again attack from the north, this time with three brigades, while *Mahone* would try to dislodge the Federals by attacking from the west. As the Confederates prepared their offensive, Warren's men spent August 20 working through torrential rains to shorten their lines, dig strong fieldworks, and bring up artillery. Thus, *Heth's* attack on August 21 was unable to even reach the Federal works before Union artillery fire brought it to a bloody halt. *Mahone*, however, managed to get six brigades into a position beyond the Federal left undetected. He was surprised when, after ordering his men forward, he learned that the Federal line was not as far west as he had expected. Nonetheless, he continued his attack, ordering Brig. Gen. *Johnson Hagood's* brigade off to the right in the hope that it would find and hit Warren's flank while the other five brigades attacked the Federal position directly. Like *Heth's* attack, *Mahone's* did not come close to achieving its objectives, as the well-positioned Federal infantry and artillery tore great holes in his command and brought its advance to a bloody halt. *Hagood's* command suffered especially. Instead of finding the Federal flank, it found itself taking fire on three sides and was decimated. Thus ended the Battle of the Weldon Railroad.

Report of Major General Warren, continued

August 20, having become satisfied that our position here was one the enemy was determined to force us from, I posted my lines in position favorable for artillery defense, which gave me a considerable infantry reserve, and then awaited an attack. The day passed off without any. August 21, the enemy at 9 a.m. drove in my pickets on the north and west and opened with about thirty pieces of artillery, crossing his fire at right angles over my position. The timber, however, prevented his artillerymen from having any good view of our lines. At 10 a.m. he made an assault all along the north and west of my position, but was everywhere repulsed. His intention to outflank us on the left was completely frustrated. Our artillery did excellent execution and broke the enemy's line in place before coming in good musketry range. Our skirmish line was immediately advanced, and 339 men and 39 officers taken on prisoners, besides 139 rebel wounded were

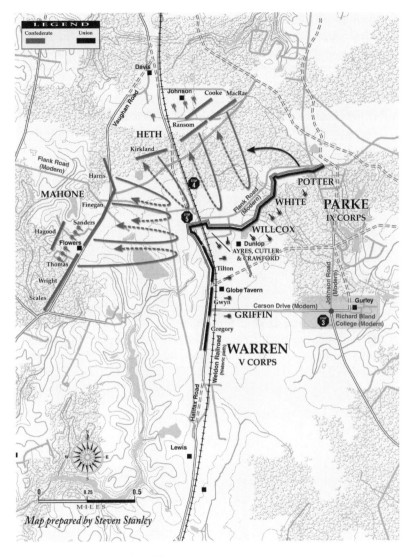

Weldon Railroad, August 21, 1864

brought in, among whom were Colonel *E. C. Council*, Sixteenth Mississippi, and Lieutenant Colonel *S. B. Thomas*, Twelfth Mississippi. General *Hagood's* brigade struck a part of our line where the troops were in echelon and they found themselves almost surrounded, and every one thinking they had surrendered, ceased firing. Troops immediately advanced to bring them in when their officers commenced firing, and Captain [Dennis] Dailey, provost-marshal of the Fourth Division, was shot by General *Hagood*. In the mixed condition of our men and the enemy, our line could not fire, and many of the enemy escaped. . . . We buried 211 of the enemy's dead. The rebel Generals [*Thomas B.*] *Lamar* and [*John C. C.*] *Sanders* were said by the prisoners to be killed. . . .

During these four days' operations men and officers performed their duties as well as any ever did under the circumstances. The heat of the first day was excessive, and on the march many fell out that are here reported among the missing, but who will soon rejoin us; about fifty were completely prostrated by sunstroke. The men were kept working night and day, and were every day and night wet through with the rains. The side roads and fields were almost impassable for artillery. . . . The position we have gained, besides fighting for three days and maintaining, we have by our work rendered unassailable, and a portion of the corps is available for other service. [*O.R.*, XLII, part 1, pp. 430–432.]

Narrative of Brig. Gen. Johnson Hagood, CSA, commanding Brigade, Mahone's Division, Hill's Corps, Army of Northern Virginia

At 2 a.m. (of the 21st of August) the brigade was aroused, and, moving out at half-past three, followed the column destined for the day's engagement. It still rained; and after a toilsome march through mud and water, first down the Squirrel Level road and then across toward the Poplar Spring Church, more or less skirmishing going on all the time by the flankers on our left, the brigade was directed to halt by the roadside and remain in reserve, while the column passed on. It had now ceased raining, and shortly afterwards, about a mile in front of us, the fire of skirmishers was heard, and a heavy fire of artillery opened. The men laid down and rested from the unwonted fatigue of the march. . . . in about half an hour a courier from General *Hill* arrived and directed us to hasten to the front and report to Major-General *Mahone*.

Proceeding by a short cut into the Vaughan road, under the guidance of the courier, and up that toward Petersburg until within six hundred yards of the Flowers' house, we turned across the field to the right and proceeded towards the railroad, in the vicinity of the Globe Tavern. A number of pieces were in position in this field, shelling the railroad, and the enemy's batteries in that direction, though not visible from woods intervening, were replying vigorously. General *Hagood* moving in columns of fours, passed at double quick across this field . . . and as he reached its further border, a major-general rode up to him announcing himself as General *Mahone.* Then leading the column, he himself placed it in position in line of battle along the edge of the wood and facing the railroad. "Now," said he to *Hagood,* "you are upon the flank and rear of the enemy. I have five brigades fighting them in front and they are driving them. I want you to go in and press them all you can." Some fifty yards within the woods the swamp of a rivulet (or "branch") was to be seen; beyond nothing was visible, and firing both of artillery and infantry was then going on. General *Mahone* added, "when you have crossed the branch swamp you will come upon a clearing in which some 300 yards further is the enemy's line, and they are not entrenched." He also urged promptness in the attack.

General *Hagood* immediately gave the order to advance, and the men moving in line made their way across the swamp. Upon arriving on the other side, we found ourselves in the clearing, but the enemy still not visible. We were under a hill and they were upon the open plateau sufficiently far beyond to prevent the view. The advance of the brigade had, however, evidently attracted attention from the fire drawn in our direction. The line had been much broken in crossing the swamp, and *Hagood* immediately pushed skirmishers up the hill for protection and ordered one of his staff to accompany them and reconnoiter. . . .

In a few minutes the brigade was formed, and the report coming at the same time from the skirmishers that the enemy was but a short distance ahead of them, and only in rifle pits, thus confirming General *Mahone's* statement. *Hagood,* cautioning his men to move only at a quick step till he himself gave the order to charge, moved his brigade forward. He had dismounted, and, placing himself in front of the center to steady the men and repress excitement, moved backward in front of the line for a short distance as if on a drill. Himself halting before reaching the crest of the hill, the line passed and he followed with his staff behind the right of the Twenty-first regiment. The Twenty-fifth was on the left of the Twenty-first, and the other three regiments on its right. As soon as the brigade became visible, ascending the hill, a rapid fire was opened upon it, to which in reply not a shot was fired, but moving forward steadily at quick time with arms at "right shoulder shift," as we approached the line of enemy's pits, they broke from them and fled. With one accord a battle yell rang out along our line, and the men, as if by command, broke into "double quick" in pursuit. At the same moment, General *Hagood* discovered that the line in front of us had only been an entrenched skirmish line, though so heavy as to have deceived his skirmishers into the notion that it was a line of battle; and that 250 yards beyond was a strongly entrenched line, crowded with men and artillery, extending right and left as far as he could see; and the five Confederate attacking brigades nowhere visible. It also appeared to him that he was moving upon a re-entering angle of the enemy's line. In this, however, he was partially mistaken. An examination of the field after the war . . . showed that the enemy's line crossing the railroad from the east, at this time bent immediately southward, and followed its course in a comparatively straight line at some forty yards on its western side. . . .

Immediately to the right of where we struck their line, a small bastioned work for field artillery was thrust forward, and our line of advance was oblique to the enemy's general line and toward its junction with the flank of this work. Thus, in fact, we were going into a reentering made more by the vicious direction of our advance than by the actual construction of the enemy's works. The flank fire from the bastioned work we could not have avoided, but from our oblique attack we had also more or less a flank fire from the straight line, which was an infantry parapet of fully five feet command with an exterior ditch eight or ten feet wide and artillery at intervals. Perceiving at a glance the hopelessness of assault under such circumstances, General *Hagood* stopping himself, shouted again and again the command to halt; but the crash and rattle of twelve or fifteen pieces of artillery, and probably 2,500 rifles, which had now opened upon us at close range, drowned his voice and the fury of the battle was upon his men. Moving forward with the steady tramp of the double quick, and dressing upon their colors, these devoted men, intent only on carrying the position before them, neither broke their alignment until it was broken by the irregular impact upon the enemy's works, nor stopped to fire their guns until their rush to obtain the parapet was repelled.

When General *Hagood* saw his men thus rushing upon certain destruction and his efforts to stop them unavailing, he felt that if they were to perish he should share their fate. . . . *Hagood* and [Orderly *J. D.*] *Stoney* alone reached the works—the latter shot in the shoulder but not disabled. The Twenty-fifth and Twenty-first regiments being on the left from the oblique direction of the advance, first struck the works; and while they struggled to get in, the other three regiments swept on. When they reached the ditch, there was from 75 to 100 yards interval between the two divisions into which the brigade had broken.

General *Hagood* was with Major [*S. H.*] *Wilds*, commanding the Twenty-first, who was cheering on his men to renewed assault (success being now their only hope of safety), when looking to the right he saw a mounted Federal officer among the men on the left portion of the brigade to the right, with a regimental color in his hands, and a confusion and parleying immediately around him that betokened approaching surrender. The fight was still raging to *Hagood's* right and left; there was no cessation on our part except in the squad just around this officer, and none whatever that was perceptible on the part of the enemy. They had pushed out from the right and left a line behind us to cut off our retreat, and this officer (Captain [William] Daly of General Cutler's staff) had galloped out of a sally port, seized a color from the hands of its bearer, and demanded a surrender. Some officers and men surrendered, but were not carried in; others refused, but just around him ceased fighting. General *Hagood* called to the men to shoot him and fall back in retreat. They either did not hear him or bewildered by the surrender of part of their number, failed to obey. It was a critical moment and demanded instant and decided action. In a few minutes the disposition to surrender would have spread and the whole brigade have been lost. Making his way across the intervening space as speedily as he could, exposed to a regular fire by file from the enemy's line, scarce thirty yards off, and calling to his men to fall back—which they did not do—General *Hagood* approached the officer and demanded the colors, and that he should go back within his own lines, telling him he was free to do so. He commenced arguing the hopelessness of further struggle, and pointed out the lines in our rear. *Hagood* cut him short, and demanded a categorical reply—yes, or no. Daly was a man of fine presence and sat with loosened rein upon a noble-looking bay that stood with head and tail erect and flashing eye and distended nostrils, quivering in every limb with excitement, but not moving in his tracks. In reply to his abrupt demand, the rider raised his head proudly and decisively answered, "No!" Upon the word General *Hagood* shot him through the body, and, as he reeled from the saddle upon one side, sprang into it from the other, Orderly *Stoney* seizing the flag from Daly's falling hands.

There was no thought of surrender now. The yell from the brigade following the act and ringing out above the noise of battle told their commander that they were once more in hand and would go now wherever ordered—whether to the front or rear.

Shouting to them to face about, *Hagood* led them at a run against the line in his rear, *Stoney* holding aloft in the front the recaptured flag which he had torn from its staff. This line melted before our charge; but the fire was terrific after breaking through it, until the shelter of the valley of the branch was reached. Upon its margin a fragment from a shrapnel shell tore open the loin of the horse upon which *Hagood* rode; and struggling, as he fell, he kicked Lieutenant *William Taylor* of the Seventh battalion upon the head, rendering him for the time so confused that he had to be led from the field by one of his men. . . . This ended the fighting for the possession of the Weldon Road. The Confederate losses had been very insignificant, until today, and now it was confined principally to our brigade. Grant had lost 5,000 men, but he had the road. [Johnson Hagood, *Memoirs of the War of Secession: From the Original Manuscripts of Johnson Hagood* (Columbia, S.C.: The State Company, 1910), pp. 290–295.]

Report of Gen. Robert E. Lee, CSA, commanding Army of Northern Virginia

The enemy abandoned . . . his position north of James River and returned to the south side. This morning General *Hill* attacked his position on Weldon Railroad. Drove him from his advanced lines to his main intrenchments, from which he was not dislodged. Over 300 prisoners, exclusive of wounded, were captured. Our loss was principally in Hagood's brigade. [*O.R.*, XLII, part 1, p. 851.]

Return to your vehicle, and turn right onto Halifax Road (Route 604). Proceed 4.9 miles until you reach Oak Grove Road, and turn left. Turn right onto Acorn Drive, and park at Oak Grove United Methodist Church. Walk to the signs adjacent to the church cemetery. These markers describe the June 1864 Wilson-Kautz Raid and provide strategic and operational background information for the August 1864 Battle of Reams Station.

STOP 6: OAK GROVE CHURCH

WILSON-KAUTZ RAID, 21 JUNE–1 JULY 1864

Launched in conjunction with the Second Petersburg Offensive of June 22–23 (which produced the Battle of Jerusalem Plank Road described earlier in this chapter), the Wilson-Kautz Raid was an ambitious cavalry operation that Federal commanders hoped would hasten the fall of Petersburg by wrecking the railroads south and west of the town. In the course of the raid, Brig. Gen. James H. Wilson's and

Front lines of Petersburg (USAMHI)

Brig. Gen. August V. Kautz's forces fought engagements near Blacks and Whites (modern Blackstone) and Nottoway Court House on June 23, the Staunton River Bridge on June 25, Sappony Church on June 28, and here in what became known as the First Battle of Reams Station. In the last of these engagements, fought on June 29, Wilson's and Kautz's men took a terrible beating at the hands of Confederate infantry commanded by Maj. Gen. *William Mahone* and Confederate cavalry commanded by Maj. Gen. *Fitzhugh Lee.* Wilson's and Kautz's forces were split and forced to abandon their artillery and burn their supply wagons in order to evade the forces surrounding them. While the raid did inflict some damage on Confederate logistics, tearing up about sixty miles of railroad track, the results did not offset the losses in men and material.

WILSON-KAUTZ RAID, 21–27 JUNE 1864

Report of Brig. Gen. James H. Wilson, USA, commanding Third Division, Cavalry Corps, Army of the Potomac

On the 20th I received instructions from General Meade to prepare my command for an expedition against the South Side and Danville railroads. On the 21st Brigadier-General Kautz reported to me with his division of four regiments. I was ordered to strike the railroad as close as practicable to Petersburg and destroy it in the direction of Burkeville and the Roanoke River. The High Bridge on the South Side road and Roanoke bridge on the Danville road were especially to be aimed at. . . . General [Andrew A.] Humphreys, chief of staff, informed me it was intended that the Army of the Potomac should cover the Weldon road the next day, the South Side road the day after. . . .

At 3 a.m. of the 22nd the expedition, consisting of about 5,500 cavalry and twelve guns, began the march by the way of Reams' Station and Dinwiddie Court-House. The troops were supplied with five days' light rations, and about 100 rounds of ammunition in wagons. At 2 p.m. the advance . . . of Kautz's division, struck the South Side road at the Sixteen-Mile Turnout. At Reams Station [Col. George H.] Chapman's brigade, covering the rear of the column, was attacked by the enemy's cavalry pursuing; sharp skirmishing was kept up till the rear arrived at the South Side road. But the advance, encountering no opposition, pushed on rapidly to Ford's Station, where it captured two trains of cars

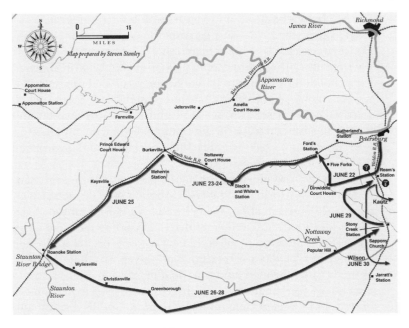

Wilson-Kautz Raid, June 22–30, 1864

with locomotives, burned the depot, water-tanks, and wood piles. The First Brigade of my division was kept employed from the time it reached the road till late at night in tearing up and burning railroad track. . . .

At 2 a.m. the next day I ordered Kautz's division to push on with the utmost rapidity for Burkeville Junction, and followed with the balance of the command as rapidly as it could march and destroy the road. At Blacks and Whites, following the trail of Kautz's division, we were misled and marched several miles on the direct road to Burkeville. I soon discovered the error and returned to the main road, but the rebel cavalry in pursuit, having kept straight forward, were met at the crossing of the railroad track near Nottoway Court-House. Chapman's brigade, in advance, attacked them with spirit and drove them back some distance. The rebels were re-enforced and in return compelled Chapman to fall back to the railroad. They attacked with great vigor, but were repulsed. Chapman was then re-enforced by the Fifth New York, but it being by that time quite dark, and the troops fatigued by their labor and marching, I determined not to renew the engagement. . . .

Just before daylight of the 24th, having heard of Kautz's success at Burkeville . . . I withdrew from the position near Nottoway Court-House, and by a rapid march through Hungarytown struck the Danville railroad near Meherrin Station. Kautz having burned the depot and stores at the Junction, and destroyed the tracks for several miles in all directions, had just passed Prices' Station when I arrived there. I sent an order to him to halt his division and tear up the railroad track till the command could be united. After working with great perseverance the whole command bivouacked that night in the vicinity of Keysville.

Early the next morning the march was resumed, heavy details engaged in destroying the railroad. About 2 p.m. the advance arrived at Roanoke Station, near the Roanoke or Staunton River. The bridge was found well defended—500 or 600 men and a battery of six guns strongly posted in earth-works on the south side of the river. The day was very hot, and the approach to the head of the brigade through a bottom field of growing grain. I posted the batteries on the hills, nearly three-quarters of a mile from the bridge, and directed General Kautz to dismount his division and endeavor to push close enough to the end of the bridge to set fire to it. After a most gallant and exhausting effort he was compelled to give up the task. Many of the men fainted from exhaustion, thirst, and heat . . . and were in no condition to overcome the natural defenses of the bridge, under a heavy fire of artillery and musketry.

But while General Kautz's men were doing their utmost to reach the bridge, the rebel cavalry unsuccessfully attacked Chapman's brigade, near the crossing of Little Roanoke. He had been directed to look out for the rear, in anticipation that they would endeavor to strike us while operating against the bridge. Having . . . convinced myself by personal inspection of the great difficulty and loss we should necessarily experience in again endeavoring to carry the bridge, I determined to withdraw to the eastward and march back to the James River. The objects of the expedition had in the main been accomplished. Every railroad station, depot, water-tank, wood pile, bridge, trestle-work, tool-house, and saw-mill, from fifteen miles of Petersburg to the Roanoke River, had been burned. Most of the track of the South Side road north of Burkeville and all of the Danville road from the Junction to the Roanoke bridge were destroyed. The temporary interposition of *Lee's* division of cavalry between different parts of our column prevented General Kautz from moving against the High Bridge near Farmville, on the upper Appomattox. The Danville road from Burkeville to the Roanoke having been constructed by laying flat iron rails upon tramway of pitch pine, was completely destroyed, with great ease, by piling fence-rails along both sides of the track and setting them on fire.

. . . Under cover of the night I withdrew my command to Wylliesburg and halted about daylight, fed, and rested. The enemy no longer pressing upon us, the column returned to the northeast by easy marches; passing through Christianville and Greensborough, crossed the Meherrin at Saffold's Bridge, and thence through Smoky Ordinary and Poplar Hill, to the Nottoway at the Double Bridges on the direct road to Prince George Court-House. The whole command arrived at this place by the middle of the afternoon of June 28. From all the information I could gather I was led to believe that [Maj. Gen. *Wade*] *Hampton's* cavalry had not yet made its appearance in that vicinity, and that the only force barring the march of my command was a battalion of infantry and a remnant of *W. H.* [*F.*] *Lee's* division of cavalry, stationed at Stony Creek Depot, in all not to exceed 1,000 men. The road to Prince George Court-House passed two miles and a half to the west of the depot, and a picket of fifty men was reported to be stationed at Sappony Church. . . . I determined, therefore, to lose no time, but push on with rapidity to that place, drive the pickets back to the Stony Creek Depot, and under cover of darkness march the whole command as rapidly as possible toward Prince George Court-House. The advance guard, under the direction of Captain [Edward] Whitaker, of my staff, found the picket posted as I expected at the church, and by a spirited dash drove it toward the depot.

This success had scarcely been reported before the enemy received re-enforcements and in turn drove back the advance guard to the head of the column. Colonel [John] McIntosh hastily dismounted his brigade and attacked the rebels with great spirit, driving them rapidly back to Sappony Church, where they had constructed a rail breast-works. A few prisoners were captured, from whom I learned that *Hampton's* and *Fitzhugh Lee's* divisions of cavalry had just arrived. Knowing from the character of the enemy's resistance this information to be correct, I determined to hold the position with my own division till the balance of the command with the train could move by the left flank through the country to the road leading to Reams' Station. I hoped to march entirely around the cavalry at Stony Creek, and reach the left of our infantry before *Hampton* could discover my intention. I therefore directed Chapman to support McIntosh, while Kautz should conduct the column in its new march. In the mean time the enemy, finding that my troops had ceased to advance, made his dispositions and attacked them with great fury, but were repulsed with heavy loss. . . .

Sharp skirmishing continued throughout the night; the enemy attacked three times with spirit, but were met with determination equal to their own and each time repulsed with loss. By dawn everything had been withdrawn, except a part of Chapman's brigade. The enemy, discovering the state of affairs, pushed in on Chapman's left flank and broke through. Colonel Chapman gathered his command and marching rapidly on a large circuit rejoined the column near Reams' Station. [*O.R.*, XL, part 1, pp. 620–623.]

Report of Maj. Gen. Wade Hampton, CSA, commanding Cavalry Corps, Army of Northern Virginia

On the morning of 27th of June the general commanding ordered me to move my command from Drewry's Tavern to Stony Creek in order to intercept Wilson, who was returning from Staunton River bridge to rejoin Grant's army. In obedience to these orders I moved rapidly in the direction indicated with my division, [Brig. Gen. *John R.*] *Chambliss'* brigade having been sent forward the evening previous.

At 12 m. the next day I reached Stony Creek Depot, where I found *Chambliss.* From this point scouts were sent out to find the position of the enemy and to ascertain what route he was pursuing, and at 12.30 I wrote the general commanding, suggesting that a force of infantry and artillery be placed at Reams' Station, as the enemy would have to cross the railroad then at Jarratt's or at Belfield. The scouts having reported what road the enemy were marching on, I notified the general commanding of their position, and informed him that I should attack them at Sappony Church, asking him at the same time to place the infantry at Reams' Station and to order Major General *Fitz Lee* to take position near there. These dispositions were made by the general commanding, and in the meantime my command was put in motion.

Chambliss, who was in front, was ordered to push on to the church and to charge the enemy as soon as he met him. Soon after crossing Sappony Creek the enemy was encountered, and he was gallantly charged by the Ninth Virginia and driven back behind the church. Here he occupied a strong position, with dismounted men, and he succeeded in checking the charge. General *Chambliss* dismounted his men and took up a line near the church, when in a few moments he was heavily attacked. I brought up a portion of the Seventh Virginia to re-enforce him, and the attack was repulsed along the whole line. [Brig. Gen. *Pierce M. B.*] *Young's* brigade, under Colonel [*Gilbert J.*] *Wright*, was then dismounted and put into position, the enemy in the meantime using his artillery and small-arms rapidly. Soon after my line was established, Lieutenant-Colonel [*William J.*] *Crawley*, commanding the Holcombe Legion (infantry), brought 200 men of his command to join me, and he was placed in the center of the line. With these troops the line, which was not a strong one, was held steadily all night, the enemy constantly making demonstrations and attacks upon it, but without the least impression. The fire of their artillery becoming very hot I directed Major [*R. Preston*] *Chew* to place two guns (all I had) under Captain [*Edward*] *Graham*, where they could respond. These guns were well served and rendered me great assistance. The position of the enemy, who had two line of works, was so strong that I could not attack it in front, so at daylight I threw portions of [Brig. Gen. *Matthew*] *Butler's* and [Brig. Gen. *Thomas L.*] *Rosser's* brigades, under the immediate direction of Brigadier-General *Butler*, on the left flank of the enemy. At the same moment *Chambliss* advanced the whole of the front line, and in a few moments we were in possession of both lines of works, the enemy retreating in confusion and leaving their dead and wounded on the ground. They were followed closely for two miles, when, finding that they had taken the road to Reams' Station, I moved by Stony Creek Depot, in order to get on the Halifax road to intercept them, should they attempt to cross below Reams'. [*O.R.*, XL, part 1, pp. 807–808.]

WILSON-KAUTZ RAID, 29 JUNE–1 JULY 1864/FIRST BATTLE OF REAMS STATION, 29 JUNE 1864

Report of Brigadier General Wilson, continued

At 7 a.m. June 29 General Kautz's advance arrived in the neighborhood of [Reams Station], but instead of finding it in the possession of the infantry of the Army of the Potomac found [Maj. Gen. *Robert*] *Hoke's* division of rebel infantry strongly posted. He attacked them at once but after capturing about 60 prisoners was compelled to withdraw his troops. By 9 a.m. the entire command was united. . . . I determined to mass the entire command on the road leading to Petersburg—artillery behind the cavalry, ambulance next to the artillery, ammunition wagons last—and make a bold push to break through the enemy; having done this, to cross the railroad three miles north of Reams' Station and join the left of the army. But before the necessary dispositions could be made the enemy covered this road also with a strong force of infantry. The scouts soon after reported a heavy body of cavalry moving around our left flank. In company with Colonel McIntosh I carefully reconnoitered the enemy's line, but after examining it closely could see not reasonable hope of breaking through it or turning it. I therefore directed the troops to take all the ammunition required, and after leaving the ambulances and setting fire to the train, withdraw from their position by the Boydton road to the Double Bridges on the Nottoway—unless in the meantime something should be done by General Meade to relieve us. . . . The situation was critical. *Hampton* with two divisions of cavalry at Stony Creek Depot, *Hoke's* division of infantry at Reams' Station, on our right flank, connecting with another large force formed in two lines of battle in our front, and *W. H. F. Lee's* division of cavalry marching around our left flank, were clear enough indications of the rebel intentions.

It was plain nothing but great celerity of motion could extricate the command. I therefore clearly indicated the route to be pursued, and directed General Kautz and Colonels McIntosh and Chapman to withdraw their commands as soon as possible. All dispositions had been made and the movement fairly begun when the rebels, by passing to the left under cover of the woods, attacked the left and rear of the two regiments yet in line to cover the movement. Lieutenant [Charles] Fitzhugh turned his battery upon them and compelled them to retire, but their presence in that locality caused him as well as the two regiments to withdraw to the rear by the right flank and march parallel to the road. Kautz did not attempt to reach the road again, but pushed through the woods with the larger part of his command, till finally, by bearing to the left, crossed the railroad, between Reams' Station and Rowanty Creek, that night and bivouacked behind the army.

I received no information, however, of his movements, except through stragglers from the regiments of his division, 300 or 400. They knew nothing of his movements, but represented the balance of the command captured. My own division was finally assembled in column with as little confusion as could be expected, and after passing Sappony Creek suffered but little annoyance from the enemy. The guns of Fitzhugh's and [Capt. William M.] Maynadier's batteries as well as those attached to Kautz's division fell into the hands of the enemy, but were not captured in the fight. Having been compelled by the movement on our flank to withdraw through the woods, the officers and men could not get them through the swamp of Hatcher's Run and Rowanty Creek, and only abandoned them after every effort to extricate them had failed. Lieutenant [Thomas] Ward, of Maynadier's battery, succeeded in getting two of his guns away, but his horses having become exhausted by the rapid and long continued march he was compelled to throw the guns in the Nottoway River.

After withdrawing from the vicinity of Reams' Station, the march was continued without intermission, by the Double Bridges to Jarratt's Station, on the Weldon railroad, where the command arrived about daylight of the 30th. A small picket of the enemy was dispersed and the march continued eastward directly toward Peters' Bridge, on the Nottoway, and forded the river at that place. Thence bearing to the northward it marched as rapidly as possible toward Blunt's Bridge, on the Blackwater, arriving there at midnight. The bridge had been previously destroyed, but after an hour's hard labor was rebuilt. The entire command crossed by daylight, and after burning the bridge marched to the vicinity of Cabin Point, on the James River. The entire command arrived at 2 p.m. of the 31st [July 1] and encamped till the next day.

During this expedition the command marched 335 miles, 135 between 3 a.m. of the 28th and 2 p.m. of the 31st of June [July 1]. During this interval of eighty-one hours the command rested from marching and fighting not to exceed six hours. [*O.R.*, XL, part 1, pp. 623–624.]

FOURTH PETERSBURG OFFENSIVE/BATTLE OF REAMS' STATION, 23–25 AUGUST 1864

Encouraged by Warren's success in the operations of August 18–21, Grant and Meade ordered Hancock, now back in command of the

Second Corps, to move south and make a lodgment on the Weldon Railroad at Reams Station about 5 miles south of the Globe Tavern. From there, Hancock's men were to tear up track between Reams Station and Rowanty Creek 8 miles to the south. By the time the sun set on August 24, Hancock had two divisions of infantry and a force of about 2,000 cavalry at Reams Station. The following day, he sent a division south to tear up track. Confederate cavalry commander Maj. Gen. *Wade Hampton* quickly found out about Hancock's move, reported it to *Lee*, and persuaded him to authorize a counterattack. Eight infantry brigades from Lt. Gen. *Ambrose P. Hill's* corps were quickly dispatched south to deal with the Federals at Reams Station.

Report of Maj. Gen. Winfield Scott Hancock, USA, commanding Second Corps, Army of the Potomac

It is proper to premise that the Second Corps, with part of the Tenth Corps and General Gregg's cavalry, had been operating on the north side of the James River from the morning of the 14th instant, engaged daily in skirmishing with the enemy and on several occasions in considerable affairs, which at an earlier period of the war would have been dignified by the name of battles. General Mott's division (the Third) recrossed the James on the 18th and relieved a portion of the troops holding the intrenched line in front of Petersburg. The remaining divisions withdrew from Deep Bottom immediately after dark on the 20th, marching directly to their old camp near the Deserted House, where they arrived about 6.30 a.m. on the 21st. This march was one of the most fatiguing and difficult performed by the troops during the campaign, owing to the wretched condition of the roads, and the men arrived in camp greatly fatigued. They were permitted to rest barely long enough to cook breakfast, when the two divisions were ordered to a position near the Strong house, from which they were again speedily removed to the vicinity of the Gurley house, in rear of General Warren's position, arriving there about 3 o'clock in the afternoon. The following morning, August 22, both divisions were placed on fatigue duty repairing the roads. About noon, the First Division, General Miles commanding, General Barlow being absent sick, was ordered to move on to the Weldon railroad to aid in covering the working party and to assist in the destruction of the road. Nearly two miles was destroyed during the afternoon.

The work was prosecuted on the following day without material incident as far as Reams' Station. The cavalry under Colonel

[Samuel] Spear, consisting of two regiments, and the division of General Gregg, were engaged with the enemy's cavalry on the roads leading toward Dinwiddie Court-House, in which affairs the enemy were repulsed. General Barlow, who had assumed command of his division during the day, occupied the entrenchments at Reams' Station at night. The Second Division, Major-General Gibbon commanding, moved from the vicinity of the Aiken house shortly before dark on the 23rd, bivouacking for the night on the plank road and arriving at Reams' Station at an early hour on the morning of the 24th, relieving the First Division from the entrenchments. General Barlow was again obliged to relinquish command of his division to General Miles on account of sickness. On being relieved from the entrenchments, the First Division proceeded with the work of destroying the railroad toward Rowanty Creek, my instructions being to destroy the railroad as far as that point, if practicable.

During the 24th the road was destroyed beyond the crossroad known as Malone's Crossing, and to a point, say, three miles beyond Reams'. The advance of the working party was covered by two regiments of cavalry under Colonel Spear, while General Gregg, with his cavalry, held the approaches from the direction of Dinwiddie and Petersburg, picketing to General Warren's left and to my left as far as the plank road. Colonel Spear had some skirmishing with the enemy's cavalry on the road to Stony Creek and Malone's road, but with the assistance of 200 infantry from General Miles' division, drove them from the immediate vicinity of the road. At dark the working party and the division were withdrawn to the entrenchments at Reams', Colonel Spear holding the cross-roads. Orders were issued for the further destruction of the road on the following day by the Second Division. [*O.R.*, XLII, part 1, pp. 221–222.]

Report of Maj. Gen. Wade Hampton, CSA, commanding Cavalry Corps, Army of Northern Virginia

In pursuance of orders from the general commanding, I moved with the First and Third Divisions of Cavalry, under the command of Brigadier-Generals *Butler* and [*Rufus*] *Barringer*, to co-operate with Lieutenant-General *Hill* in an attack on the enemy at Reams' Station, at 5 a.m. August 25. After consultation with General *Hill* I was directed to strike the Petersburg and Weldon Railroad, with my main force on the left flank of the enemy, whilst another portion of my command was to cover the approach of General *Hill* on Reams' Station. I ordered General *Barringer* to take his own brigade up the Halifax road toward Malone's Crossing, and to send *Chambliss'* brigade, under command of Colonel *J. Lucius Davis*, up Malone's road, across Malone's Bridge, to the same point. This latter brigade was supported by *Rosser's* and *Young's* brigades, under command of Major-General *Butler*, General *Rosser* commanding his own, and Colonel *Wright Young's* brigade.

[Brig. Gen. *John*] *Dunovant's* brigade was left in reserve to protect the rear and flank of General *Hill*. These dispositions having been made, I crossed with the column at Malone's Bridge, and met the advance pickets of the enemy a short distance beyond at 9 a.m. These were driven in, when the enemy, in a strong position and some force, was encountered. Colonel *Davis* dismounted a portion of his brigade, and immediately engaged them. After a sharp fight the enemy gave way, falling back toward Malone's Crossing. We pursued him vigorously and rapidly, forcing all the cavalry we met to retreat toward Reams' Station, leaving their dead and wounded on the ground. [Capt. *William*] *McGregor* brought a section of his battery up at this moment, and by a rapid and well-directed fire contributed greatly to the confusion of the enemy. Their guns were admirably served during the whole engagement, and I beg to express my entire satisfaction at the conduct of Captain *McGregor* and his men. The enemy brought their infantry to take the place of their cavalry, deploying a heavy force in my front, whilst they attempted to turn both my flanks. In this they were foiled, and I held my ground steadily. [*O.R.*, XLII, part 1, pp. 942–943.]

Retrace your route to the Halifax Road, and turn left. Drive 0.2 mile, and turn right onto Reams Road (Route 606). Pull into the parking area on the right by the Civil War Trust. Exit your vehicle, and either do the stop here or follow the trail to the right until you reach the "Battle of Reams Station: Exposed Position of the Federal Artillery" marker (indicated as location 7a on the map).

STOP 7: REAMS STATION BATTLEFIELD

FOURTH PETERSBURG OFFENSIVE/BATTLE OF REAMS STATION, 24–25 AUGUST 1864

Hancock intended to spend August 25 tearing up railroad track, but when word arrived of the approach of the Confederates, he pulled his men back into a U-shaped defensive position at Reams Station.

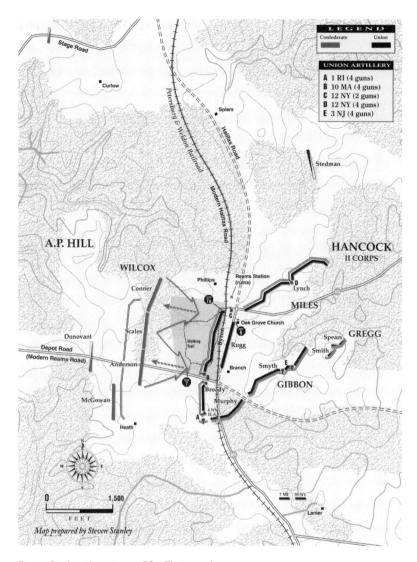

Reams Station, August 25, 1864: First assault

Maj. Gen. *Cadmus Wilcox* attacked the northern end of the Federal position with three brigades during the afternoon but was repulsed by Brig. Gen. Nelson Miles's division, while to his left Maj. Gen. John Gibbon's division fought off *Hampton's* cavalry. By 5:30, *Heth's* and *Mahone's* divisions had reached the field and, after a short bombardment by Col. *William Pegram's* artillery, launched an attack against the Federal position. After a bitter fight, the Confederates finally broke into and overwhelmed Miles's defenses, while to the south *Hampton's* command managed to drive Gibbon's men from their position. Hancock was able to rally his routed command sufficiently to make an orderly withdrawal to Petersburg that night, but there was no question that the Second Corps had suffered a humiliating defeat. The Fourth Petersburg Offensive was over.

Report of Major General Hancock, continued

At daylight of the 25th General Miles relieved the pickets of the Second Division, but the order for the work on the railroad was postponed until the result of the reconnaissances General Gregg had been directed to make could be ascertained. . . . On the receipt of the reports from the squadrons sent out by General Gregg, it was determined to send General Gibbon's division out to work, so as to lose no time that could be avoided. The division accordingly started, but had hardly gotten out of the entrenchments when a report was received from Colonel Spear that the enemy were advancing on him in force. He was very soon driven away from the cross-roads. General Gibbon deployed a heavy skirmish line on the right of the road to Stony Creek and advanced against the enemy, developing the fact that his cavalry was supported by infantry. While the skirmishing was going on here a part of the enemy's cavalry passed to my left and rear, breaking through General Gregg's picket-line, then running from Reams' to Gary's Church, on the plank road. They were speedily driven back by a regiment of cavalry and a small force from General Miles' division. At this juncture it was deemed prudent to recall General Gibbon's division, and he took post in the entrenchments on the left of the First Division, extending the breast-work to better protect the left and rear. It is proper to say here that the defensive position at Reams' was selected on another occasion by another corps, and was, in my judgment, very poorly located, the bad location contributing very materially to the subsequent loss of the position, and particularly to the loss of the artillery. . . .

At 12 o'clock the enemy drove in the pickets of the First Division on the Dinwiddie road, and at about 2 p.m. made a spirited advance against Miles' front, but were speedily repulsed. A second and more vigorous attack followed at a short interval and was likewise repulsed, some of the enemy falling within a few yards of the breast-work.

Dispatches were . . . sent at 3.30 p.m. to General Meade. The first stated that the prisoners thus far belonged to *Wilcox's* division, and that *A. P. Hill* was himself present. The second dispatch gave an account of the second attack on General Miles' position, and stated that [Brig. Gen. *George T.*] *Anderson's* brigade, of [Maj. Gen. *Charles W.*] *Field's* division, was present. . . . Meanwhile the enemy were preparing their forces for a final attack, which was inaugurated about 5 p.m. by a heavy artillery fire, which, while it did little actual damage, had its effect in demoralizing a portion of the command exposed to a reverse fire, owing to the faulty location of the rifle-pits, as before explained. The shelling continued for about fifteen minutes, when it was followed by an assault on General Miles' front, opposite the position held by the Consolidated Brigade and the Fourth Brigade.

Just at the time when a few minutes' resistance would have secured the repulse of the enemy, who were thrown into considerable disorder by the severity of the fire they were subjected to and the obstacles to their advance, a part of the line (composed of the Seventh, Fifty-second, and Thirty-ninth New York) gave way in confusion. At the same time a break occurred on the right of the One hundred and twenty-fifth and One hundred and twenty-sixth New York. A small brigade of the Second Division, under command of Lieutenant-Colonel [Horace] Rugg, which had previously been sent as a reserve to General Miles, was ordered forward at once to fill up the gap, but the brigade could neither be made to go forward nor fire. McKnight's battery, under Lieutenant [George K.] Dauchy, Twelfth New York Artillery [Battery], was then turned on the opening, doing great execution, but the enemy advanced along the rifle-pits, taking possession of the battery and turning one gun upon our own troops. On the left of the break in the line was [Col. Matthew] Murphy's brigade, of the Second Division, which was driven back, and two batteries (B, First Rhode Island Artillery, Lieutenant [Walter] Perrin, and the Tenth Massachusetts Battery, Captain [J. Henry] Sleeper) fell into the hands of the enemy after having been served with marked gallantry and losing a very large proportion of officers, men, and horses.

I immediately ordered General Gibbon's division forward to retake the position and guns, but the order was responded to very feebly by his troops, the men falling back to their breast-works on receiving a slight fire from the enemy. By the loss of this position the remainder of General Gibbon's division was exposed to an attack in reverse and on the flank and were obliged to occupy the reverse side of the breast-work they had constructed. Affairs at this juncture were in a critical condition, and but for the bravery and obstinacy of a part of the First Division and the fine conduct of their commander (General Miles) would have ended still more disastrously. General Miles succeeded in rallying a small force of the Sixty-first New York Volunteers, and forming a line at right angles with the breast-works swept off the enemy, recapturing McKnight's guns, and retook a considerable portion of his line. General Miles threw about 200 men across the railroad and toward the enemy's rear, but the force was too small to accomplish anything. . . .

An attempt was made to get some of the troops of Gibbon's division to assist in this operation, but the commanders reported that their men could not be brought up to the advance. The enemy's dismounted cavalry now made an attack on the left, driving General Gibbon's division from its breast-works. This division offered very little resistance, though the attack was feeble compared with that of the enemy's infantry, and the enemy, elated at their easy success at this point, were pressing on with loud cheers when they were met by a heavy flank fire from the dismounted cavalry, occupying the extreme left, and their advance summarily checked. General Gregg, with his own command and one regiment and a squadron from Colonel Spear's command, rendered invaluable services at this point, and the steadiness of his men contrasted more than favorably with the conduct of some of the infantry commands. The enemy turned their attention now to General Gregg's command, which was not able to hold its position after General Gibbon's division had fallen back, and accordingly the cavalry was withdrawn by him and formed on the left of the new line which General Gibbon had succeeded in forming a short distance in the rear of the rifle-pits. [Capt. Christian] Woerner's battery, First New Jersey Artillery, rendered efficient service during and after this attack. With the aid of this battery and the troops under General Miles the road running to the plank road was held until dark, the enemy being checked in every attempt to advance beyond that part of the line they had captured. . . . A part of the captured guns were held by the enemy's skirmishers, and General Miles succeeded in recapturing one, drawing it from the field to the wood within our lines.

Owing to some failure to make it known that the piece had been recovered it was unfortunately abandoned when the troops withdrew, making a total of nine guns lost during the action. At this time General Miles and General Gregg offered to retake their breast-works entire, but General Gibbon stated that his division could not retake any of his line. It being necessary to reoccupy the lost works to protect the only communication then open to the rear, and no reenforcements having arrived, the troops were ordered to withdraw at dark, General Miles covering the rear. General Willcox's division was formed about one mile and a half in rear of the field, and after the troops had passed became a rear guard. This command, with the one under Colonel [Robert] McAllister, on the plank road, withdrew during the night, returning to their respective camps. The troops of my own corps went into camp about midnight near the Williams house. The cavalry under General Gregg held the plank road and the country between the plank road and General Warren's left. The enemy made no attempt to follow up their advantage, except to throw out a small force of cavalry on the morning of the 26th to pick up stragglers.

Had my troops behaved as well as heretofore, I would have been able to defeat the enemy on this occasion. . . . I attribute the bad conduct of some of my troops to their great fatigue, owing to the heavy labor exacted of them and to their enormous losses during the campaign, especially in officers. The lack of the corps in this respect is painfully great and one hardly to be remedied during active operations. The Seventh, Fifty-second, and Thirty-ninth New York are largely made up of recruits and substitutes. The first-named regiment in particular is entirely new, companies being formed in New York and sent down here, some officers being unable to speak English. The material compares very unfavorably with the veterans absent. [*O.R.*, XLII, part 1, pp. 223–228.]

Report of Major General Heth, continued

On the night of August 24 we bivouacked at Armstrong's Mill on the Rowanty. On August 25 the march was resumed at daybreak, reaching a point about one mile from Reams' Station, on

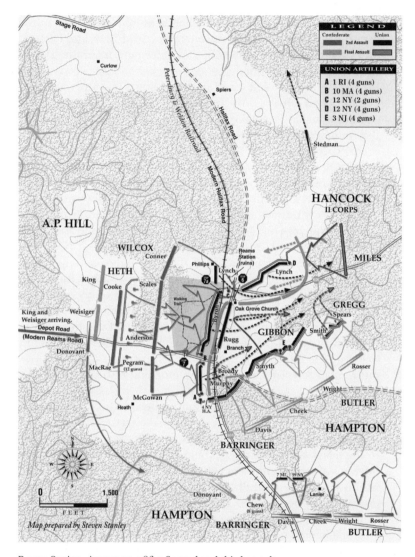

Reams Station, August 25, 1864: Second and third assaults

the Petersburg and Weldon Railroad, about 3 o'clock p.m. When within one mile of Reams' Station, we heard brisk skirmishing going on between our troops, under General [*Cadmus M.*] *Wilcox*, and the enemy. About half an hour before sunset I received an order from General [*Ambrose P.*] *Hill* to attack the enemy, who were strongly entrenched at Reams' Station, his works running parallel to the railroad for about one-half mile and then suddenly bending back at a considerable angle. Behind these works the enemy had in position numerous batteries. A portion of the enemy's breastworks were protected by obstructions formed by felling timber for 150 yards in front, rendering the works seemingly unapproachable from the front.

General *Wilcox* kindly pointed out to me the enemy's position, and the difficulties to be encountered were very formidable. [Brig. Gen. *William*] *MacRae's* Brigade was ordered to take position about 300 yards in front of the enemy's works, partially concealed by pine woods. [Gen. *John R.*] *Cooke* was ordered to take position on *MacRae's* left, a portion of his front as he advanced coming in direct contact with the obstructions above mentioned. Lieutenant-Colonel [*William J.*] *Pegram*, with his artillery, took position in a field to the right of *MacRae* and somewhat in rear of *MacRae's* line of battle. My attacking column was assisted by [Brig. Gen. *James H.*] *Lane's* North Carolina Brigade, which was formed on *Cooke's* left. The plan of attack was that *Pegram* should open for a certain length of time, after which the assault was to be made. After *Pegram* had opened for about twenty minutes, the attack was made and the works carried, our men not firing a shot until the enemy broke from his works.

This charge and its results had proved to me that nothing is impossible to men determined to win. The coolness and determination as evinced by all and expressed by many officers and men as I passed down the line, a few minutes before the attack was made, carried with it a conviction of success. *MacRae's* Brigade reached the works first, there being no abatis in his front; his loss was small. *Cooke* had to advance over an almost impenetrable entanglement. His gallant men, under severe fire, in squads, picked their way through this abatis. Some idea can be formed of the character of the obstacles to be overcome when it is correctly stated that five to ten minutes elapsed from the time the first man of men reached the line occupied by the enemy until a sufficient number had formed to enable the brigade to scale the works successfully, this under a sheet of fire from both infantry and artillery. *Cooke's* loss was, consequently heavy. The result of this battle was over 2,000 prisoners, nine pieces of artillery, and flags captured.

Cooke's and *MacRae's* Brigades won for themselves on this day fresh laurels, sufficient indeed to have given them a most enviable reputation among the most gallant brigades of the Army of Northern Virginia. . . . After the works were carried by *Cooke* and *MacRae* and the enemy was withdrawing—or so shaken as to render his position untenable—the dismounted cavalry charged and carried a portion of the works on my right, capturing many prisoners. [*O.R. Supplement*, VII, pp. 474–476.]

Report of Major General Hampton, continued

General *Hill* was notified of the condition of affairs and the position of the enemy, with a suggestion that he should attack promptly. He replied that he would do so, and he desired me to endeavor to draw the enemy down the railroad, so that he could take them in the rear. I withdrew my lines about 400 yards, but the enemy followed with great caution. General *Barringer*, whom I had sent with his brigade to the east of the railroad, reported that he had met a strong force of infantry, with cavalry, on the road by which he was advancing. I ordered him to picket the road strongly and to join me with his command at Malone's Crossing. This he did just as my line was retired, and I dismounted the Second North Carolina Regiment, under Colonel [*William*] *Roberts*, ordering him to take position on the right of the line and to attempt to turn the flank of the enemy if an opportunity offered.

At 5 p.m. the artillery of General *Hill* opened fire, and I at once ordered an advance of my whole line, which was then formed across the railroad at Malone's Crossing. This order was promptly obeyed, and the enemy gave way. They were driven to their works near Reams' Station, giving up several positions which they had fortified. Colonel *Roberts*, with his regiment, charged here one line of rifle-pits, carrying it handsomely, and capturing from 60 to 75 prisoners. In the meantime, seeing that General *Hill* was forcing the enemy back from the west side of the railroad into their works around the station, I withdrew all my force from that side of the road and formed a line, with *Chambliss'* brigade on the left, the North Carolina brigade in the center, and *Young's* brigade on the right. *Rosser* formed a second line to support the first, all being dismounted. Some regiments were kept mounted in case cavalry should be needed. The line being formed, the commanding officers were directed to keep the left flank on the railroad, advancing slowly, while the right swung round to strike the rear of the enemy, who were in position behind the railroad bank, and in a work which ran east perpendicularly to the railroad for some distance; then turning north kept parallel with the railroad, enveloping Oak Grove Church.

The ground over which my troops advanced was very difficult, and it had been rendered more so by the enemy, who had cut down the timber. In spite of this, and under a heavy fire of artillery and musketry, the line advanced steadily, driving the enemy into his works. Here he made a stubborn stand, and for a few moments checked our advance, but the spirit of the men was so fine that they charged the breast-works with the utmost gallantry, carried them, and captured the force holding them. This ended the fighting of the day, my men having been engaged for twelve hours. After the fight General *Hill* directed me to put my command in the trenches to cover the withdrawal of the infantry. This was done, and I remained with seven regiments at the station until 6.30 the next morning, when, finding that the enemy had withdrawn, I left General *Butler* to remove our wounded and to collect arms. [*O.R.*, XLII, part 1, pp. 943–944.]

Report of General Robert E. Lee, continued

General *A. P. Hill* attacked the enemy in his entrenchments at Reams' Station yesterday evening, and at the second assault carried his entire line. *Cooke's* and *MacRae's* North Carolina brigades, under General *Heth*, and *Lane's* North Carolina brigade of *Wilcox's* division, under General [*James*] *Conner*, with *Pegram's* artillery, composed the assaulting column. One line of breast-works was carried by the cavalry under General *Hampton* with great gallantry, who contributed largely to the success of the day. Seven stand of colors, 2,000 prisoners, and 9 pieces of artillery are in our possession. [*O.R.*, XLII, part 1, p. 851.]

Report of Major General Meade, continued

On the 22nd of August, Hancock having moved up to the vicinity of the Weldon railroad, Miles' division, Second corps, and Gregg's division of cavalry were sent to Reams' Station with instructions to destroy the road. On the 23rd General Hancock, with Gibbon's division, was sent to re-enforce Miles. The work of destruction was continued on the 24th; but on the 25th, the enemy appearing, Hancock concentrated his force at Reams'

Station, where, late in the afternoon, he was heavily attacked by a superior force of cavalry and infantry and pressed with so much vigor that a part of his line was broken, and five pieces of artillery fell into the hands of the enemy. Upon learning the condition of affairs Willcox's division, Ninth corps, was sent to support Hancock, but did not reach the ground till the action was over. At night Hancock withdrew, the enemy leaving the ground at the same time. This terminated the efforts of the enemy to dislodge us from the Weldon railroad. A line was at once formed connecting the Jerusalem plank road with our new position and the necessary defensive works laid out and constructed. [*O.R.*, XLII, part 1, p. 31.]

Return to your vehicle. Drive out of the parking area, and turn left to return to the Halifax Road. Turn left onto Halifax Road, and proceed 5.3 miles to Flank Road. Turn left onto Flank Road (it is just past the parking area for Fort Wadsworth), and drive 0.6 mile to the intersection with Vaughan Road (Route 675). Turn left onto Vaughan Road, and proceed 0.9 mile until you see Fort Emory Road on your right. Turn right onto Fort Emory Road (Route 741), and proceed 0.4 mile to Sharon Baptist Church on the right-hand side of the road. Pull into the parking area.

STOP 8: SHARON CHURCH

FIFTH PETERSBURG OFFENSIVE/BATTLE OF PEEBLES'S FARM, 30 SEPTEMBER–2 OCTOBER 1864

Grant began planning the operations north and south of the James River that would produce what is known as the Fifth Petersburg Offensive in early September. The offensive opened with Maj. Gen. Benjamin F. Butler's Army of the James launching a two-pronged offensive against New Market Heights and Fort Harrison north of the James, capturing both, on September 29. The Confederates were able to scrape together sufficient forces to contain the damage, but to do so *Lee* had to shift several brigades from Petersburg. This left only a small force in the defenses covering the vital Boydton Plank Road when the Fifth and Ninth Corps of the Army of the Potomac began moving west on September 30 with the objective of seizing that road—and perhaps even the South Side Railroad just beyond it. Leading the advance was Griffin's division of Warren's Fifth Corps, which marched passed Poplar Spring Church (modern Sharon Church) early on September 30, then deployed into line when they reached the Confederate defensive line along the Squirrel Level Road.

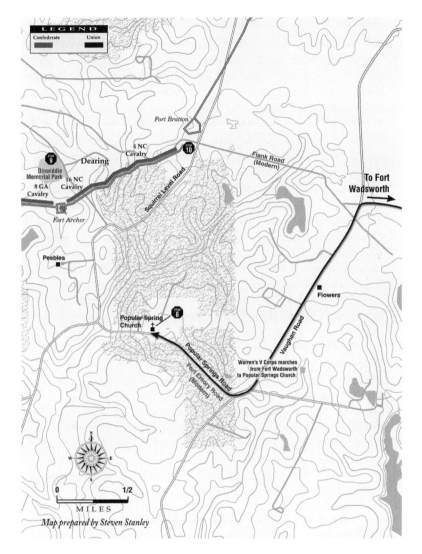

Peebles Farm: Union advance

Report of Major General Meade, continued

No further movement of consequence, beyond reconnaissances, was made until September 30, when orders were received
from the lieutenant-general commanding to make a demonstration on the left, with a view of preventing detachments to the
north side of the James, where operations were being carried on.
For this purpose Major-General Warren, with two divisions of the
Ninth, moved from the left toward Poplar Spring church and Peebles's farm. Gregg's division of cavalry at the same time moved
farther to the left and rear.

Griffin found the enemy entrenched on Peebles' farm, and
attacking carried a redoubt and line of rifle-pits, taking 1 gun and
about 100 prisoners. At the same time Ayres carried a small work
on the Squirrel Level road. In the afternoon [Maj. Gen. John G.]
Parke, moving on Warren's left toward the Boydton road, was
fiercely attacked by the enemy and for a time compelled to fall
back, but Griffin coming to his support the enemy was checked
and repulsed. Early in the day, October 1, Gregg met the enemy's
cavalry and forced them back, reporting his disappearance in the
afternoon.

On October 1 Mott's division, Second Corps, was withdrawn
from the lines and sent to re-enforce Parke, but could not reach
the ground in time for operations. On this day Gregg was heavily attacked on the Duncan road, where he was guarding the left
and rear; but repulsed the enemy, inflicting heavy losses on him
and killing Brigadier-General *Dunovant.* On the 2nd of October
the whole force advanced, but found the enemy had withdrawn
to his main entrenched line. A position was then taken up and
the necessary works laid out to extend our entrenched line to the
position gained. [*O.R.*, XLII, part 1, pp. 31–32.]

*Narrative of Maj. William H. Powell, USA, Fifth Corps, Army of
the Potomac*

The Army of the Potomac was got under arms at 4 o'clock on
the morning of the 29th, Generals Warren and Parke, each with
two divisions of his corps, ready to move. All the corps commanders made dispositions to withdraw from the intrenchments, leaving
garrisons in the redoubts and enclosed batteries. General Gregg
was sent to the crossing of Hatcher's Run by the Vaughan road and
the Squirrel Level road to the vicinity of the Peebles and Pegram
farms. At the former point the Confederates had a redoubt at the

Maj. Gen. Horatio G. Wright, Maj. Gen. Charles Griffin, Maj. Gen. George G. Meade, Maj. Gen. John G. Parke, and Maj. Gen. Andrew A. Humphreys (USAMHI)

termination of the intrenchments they had constructed and were still going on with. This intrenchment was nearly parallel with the Weldon Railroad and joined the Petersburg intrenchments. Peebles' farm was two miles west of the Union intrenchments on the railroad. It was not deemed advisable by General Grant that Meade should move on the 29th, nor until 8 o'clock a.m. of the 30th, and the object in view was to secure the junction of the Squirrel Level and Poplar Spring Church roads, coming from the southwest. The redoubt at the junction of these roads was known as Fort McRae, and was flanked by intrenchments and protected by abatis.

General Warren, with Griffin's and Ayres' divisions, and Hofmann's brigade of Crawford's division, accompanied by Batteries B, D, and H, 1st New York Light Artillery, was directed against Fort McRae, while General Parke was to follow with Willcox's and [Brig. Gen. Robert] Potter's divisions. At 7 o'clock a.m. of the 30th, therefore, Griffin and Ayres moved out of their intrenchments at Globe tavern, with [Brig. Gen. Joseph J.] Bartlett's brigade, temporarily under the command of Colonel [James] Gwyn, in the lead. Through a thick growth of woods and scrubby pine the command cautiously pursued its way for about two and one half miles, when skirmishers were thrown out under the personal direction of General Griffin. They had not proceeded far, when the Confederate pickets were encountered behind light works thrown up along the road in front of Poplar Grove Church. [William H. Powell, *The Fifth Army Corps (Army of the Potomac): A Record of Operations during the Civil War in the United States of America, 1861–1865* (New York, 1896; London: G. P. Putnam's Sons, 1986), pp. 729–730.]

Narrative of Bvt. Brig. Gen. Charles S. Wainwright, USA, commanding Artillery Brigade, Fifth Corps, Army of the Potomac

This morning [September 30], however, we did get off. General Griffin leading, followed by [Capt. Robert] Rogers's battery; Ayres with Hoffman's brigade next; then the remaining five batteries. The two divisions of the Ninth Corps followed close behind. We did not take a single wagon of any sort with us, not even an ambulance, leaving all parked in rear of the tavern. . . . The whole force of the two corps comprised about 12,000 muskets. . . . General Warren had got all the pioneers of the Fifth Corps in a body under his own command directly in rear of his advance, and as soon as we entered the wood he set them to work widening the road, and cutting a second one alongside of it, so that there should be no blocking in case of wheeled vehicles of any kind having to go back and forth. This was done without stopping the advance of the column at all, and even the men seemed to realize that their work was better laid out for them than usual, which incited them to greater activity.

About two hundred yards beyond Poplar Spring Church the road crossed by descending into a deep ravine; here Griffin's advance first struck the rebel pickets. A few shots drove in these outlying posts, and another hundred yards or so brought them to a large open space on the north of the road, known as the Peeble farm. [Charles S. Wainwright, *A Diary of Battle: The Personal Journals of Colonel Charles S. Wainwright, 1861–1865*, ed. Allan Nevins (New York, 1962), pp. 466–467.]

Return to your vehicle, and turn right onto Fort Emory Road until at 0.2 mile it ends at Squirrel Level Road (Route 613). Turn right onto Squirrel Level Road, and proceed 0.4 mile to Church Road. Turn left, proceed 0.2 mile on Church Road to the Dinwiddie Memorial Park, and pull into the parking area on the left.

STOP 9: FORT ARCHER

After the Federals seized their foothold on the Weldon Railroad in August, the Confederates constructed two lines of fortifications running south and west from the original Dimmock Line. The first covered the Boydton Plank Road and South Side Railroad. Forward of that line was one that roughly followed the Squirrel Level Road. A small square redoubt, Fort Archer, was one of the keys to this position, for it was located next to the Church Road that ran perpendicular to and connected the two Confederate lines.

Fort Archer was incomplete when the Federals launched the Fifth Petersburg Offensive on September 30 and fell relatively easily to an assault by Griffin's division. The Federals then renamed it Fort Wheaton, after an officer in the First Michigan who was killed during the Fifth Petersburg Offensive, and reconfigured it into a six-sided redoubt with six field guns. The fort covers about an acre and is National Park Service property. It is accessible from modern-day Church Road by following a narrow strip of land that belongs to the Park Service, which runs through the thick woods along the outer edge of the ditch that connects the fort with the road.

FIFTH PETERSBURG OFFENSIVE/BATTLE OF FORT ARCHER AND JONES FARM, 30 SEPTEMBER 1864

Lee's shifting of troops from the Petersburg defenses to the Richmond front in response to Butler's offensive against New Market Heights and Fort Harrison meant that the defenses along the Squirrel Level Road were manned by only a small force of dismounted cavalry and horse artillery. Nonetheless, Warren waited until the afternoon on September 30 before ordering Griffin to attack Fort Archer. The fort quickly fell to a determined assault by Col. James Gwyn's brigade, as did a large section of the Squirrel Level Road works on either side of Fort Archer to the rest of Griffin's command.

Narrative of Brevet Brigadier General Wainwright, continued

About two hundred yards beyond Poplar Spring Church the road crossed by descending into a deep ravine; here Griffin's advance first struck the rebel pickets. A few shots drove in these outlying posts, and another hundred yards or so brought them to a large open space on the north of the road, known as the Peeble farm. Skirmishing up the hill across this field they drew, as soon as reaching the top of a little crest, an artillery fire from a redoubt about six hundred yards north of where they left the road. There was no place into which I could get a battery to reply at that time, and even Griffin did not ask for one; or, if he did, General Warren did not order any out. There was skirmishing here for the better part of an hour, our men working up the ravine which brought them near to the redoubt without exposing them to its fire. . . .

The rebs made a fair fight; it was [Brig. Gen. *James J.*] *Archer's* brigade with one battery, but at last our men worked around to the right so as not to have more than fifty steps to go after leaving cover, when they carried the redoubt with a rush. I had never seen a work with a ditch carried before, and it certainly was different from the ideas we got from books and pictures. There was no line of men marching up to the work, nor any contest on the crest of the parapet; half a dozen men straggling to the top seemed to carry the work, so far as I could see—not but what there were plenty more close behind them. The work proved to be a square redoubt of some one hundred feet to the side, with a high parapet nearly finished. . . . Our loss had been a mere nothing. One hundred or so killed and wounded. We had got forty or fifty prisoners, one three-inch gun, one limber, three horses and three sets of harness. [Wainwright, *A Diary of Battle*, pp. 466–467.]

Narrative of Major Powell, continued

The Confederate pickets were encountered behind light works thrown up along the road. . . . The pickets were driven in and under a sharp fire from the works the line advanced. Under the crest of a small hill it halted to prepare for the assault. In a few moments the troops left the cover and were greeted with a heavy fire of grape and canister from a four-gun battery, and a furious discharge of musketry. After passing over about 500 yards of open ground, the 16th Michigan and 118th Pennsylvania, being in the lead, encountered some abatis. A passage was speedily cut wide enough for eight men, and through this the 16th went by fours by the left flank, and the 118th by the right flank.

The two commanders, Colonel [Norval] Welch and Captain [James B.] Wilson, led their regiments. Both climbed the parapet together and Welch fell dead from a carbine bullet. [Brig. Gen. *James*] *Dearing's* dismounted cavalry brigade, with infantry, was holding this point. As the troops crossed the works the Confederates fled. The 20th Maine had, as usual, pressed forward gallantly and lent its aid in the capture. Colonel Gwyn's horse fell on him as he mounted the works, and for a time he was severely disabled. This work had been well done, but more was to come. Griffin went into position some 200 yards beyond the captured works. General Ayres had in the meantime pressed forward with his division and gallantly carried the redoubt on the right of Griffin. [Powell, *Fifth Army Corps*, pp. 729–731.]

Narrative of Michigan Correspondent

"A more magnificent charge was never made by any corps in any war," said General Warren, speaking of the charge made to-day by General Griffin's division upon a redoubt and line of formidable breastworks fronting upon our headquarters. The place is called Peeble's Farm, from this being the name of the owner and late occupant of a large deserted house nearby, five miles from Petersburg and about the same distance from the Danville railroad. . . . Everyone who saw the charge, or who has expressed an opinion on it,—and there are none who have not passed an opinion,—speak in the highest terms of the dash, courage, and impetuosity of the men engaged. There were two charges made, and subsequently some fighting. I will recite the events in the order of their occurrence. The story is not lengthy, for in each case the rout was short and decisive.

At 9 a.m. the 1st and 2nd divisions of the corps, Colonel Hofman's brigade of the 3d division, and several batteries took up their line of march. The other troops of General Crawford's division and most of the corps batteries, together with a division of the 9th corps, remained to hold the works and forts at our old position, the latter troops, as well as the batteries, being under General Crawford's command. Arriving at the edge of a piece of woods, fronting which was an open space, beyond Peeble's house was seen a redoubt and a line of the enemy's entrenchments. The enemy's pickets, meantime, had fallen back before our advancing column to the redoubt. The enemy opened with six pieces of artillery. To this redoubt and the earthworks in the distance was not over 600 yards, and a line of battle was formed.

It was determined to charge this redoubt and the works. The charge was made solely by General Griffin's division. General Ayres's division was on the right of General Griffin's, and Colonel Hoffman's brigade on the right of the former division; but the latter troops did not charge. The 18th Massachusetts battalion,

Captain [Luther S. Bent] commanding, was first sent forward as skirmishers, but found too weak, and was subsequently strengthened by the 155th Pennsylvania, Colonel [Alfred Pearson], and the 1st Michigan, Major [George C.] Hopper commanding. The order being given to charge, the skirmish battle lines soon advanced across the open ground. The charging column pressed steadily, earnestly, persistently forward. Rebel shell and bullets had no dismaying effect.

"A commission to him who first mounts the parapet of that redoubt," shouted Colonel Welch, of the 16th Michigan, to his men. "Follow me!" . . . He was the first to mount the parapet, when he waved his sword. In an instant a rebel bullet penetrated his brain, and he lay dead. The men followed simultaneously and mounted the works at different points, the colors of some half dozen regiments floating triumphantly where a few moments before rebel colors had flaunted their traitorous folds to the breeze. It is no wonder that there should be different claimants for the honor of being the first to plant the Stars and Stripes on the works! All behaved magnificently, and all are deserving of life and honor. Nearly one hundred prisoners were captured, and one cannon. The enemy got off his remaining guns, but not all his horses.

"'We have taken the enemy's first line of works; can you take the second?" shouted General Griffin. "Yes, yes," was the responsive shout from a thousand throats, and they did take the second line, as bravely as they took the first. In the second line was a second redoubt. Brave heroes had fallen, but a splendid victory, a double victory, had been won. It was all the work of a few minutes, a work requiring less time than I have taken to write it. The second line was on the farther edge of the open field, and beyond were woods. Through the latter woods the beaten enemy fled in haste. Two brigades of *Heth's* division were in the force opposing us. No artillery was used on our side. Both lines of earthworks were very strong, and the redoubts were substantially put up. The 9th corps troops were shortly after placed in front of the 5th corps.

Desultory firing was kept up between the opposing pickets until about 5 p.m., when the enemy charged on the 9th corps, causing them to fall back in confusion. Quickly the 5th corps rushed to the rescue of the 9th, and sent the enemy back beyond the ground he had recovered. Night and darkness and rain ended the day's conflict. But it has been a day of splendid successes, and our troops—as well they may be—are jubilant over their victory. [John Robertson, compiler, *Michigan in the War* (Lansing, Mich.: W. S. George & Company, 1882), pp. 369–370.]

Wary of pushing too far and rendering his force vulnerable to a counterattack, Warren decided to spend some time consolidating his position after capturing Fort Archer. This gave Lt. Gen. *Ambrose P. Hill*, who, with *Lee* north of the James, commanded the defense of Petersburg, time to assemble a four-brigade strike force from *Heth's* and *Wilcox's* divisions. *Heth's* and *Wilcox's* men reached the scene as Brig. Gen. Robert Potter's division from Maj. Gen. John G. Parke's Ninth Corps was pushing forward from Peebles's Farm toward the Confederate defenses guarding the Boydton Plank Road. Late in the afternoon, Potter's men reached the Jones Farm about a mile from the Boydton Plank Road. There his hopes of carrying the Confederate defenses along the road were frustrated by the arrival of *Heth's* and *Wilcox's* commands, which launched a counterattack that drove the Federals back to the Squirrel Level Road defenses. There, assisted by Warren's men, they managed to rally as night fell.

Report of Major General Heth, continued

On September 30 I was directed to take two brigades of my division, *Archer's* (Brigadier-General *Archer* commanding) and *MacRae's* Brigade (Brigadier-General *MacRae* commanding) and drive back the enemy, who was approaching the Boydton Plank Railroad by the Church Road. Major-General *Wilcox* reported to me for duty, with two brigades of his division. On reaching a point about half a mile from where the Church Road intersects the Boydton Plank Road, the enemy was discovered to be in force in the pine woods south of the Jones House.

Some pieces of artillery from [Capt. *Edward*] *Graham's* Battery were placed in position, but before my troops could form line of battle, the enemy advanced, but was driven back and scattered by a few well-directed shots from *Graham's* guns.

Line of battle was now formed. *Wilcox's* Brigades (*Lane's* and [Brig. Gen. *Samuel*] *McGowan's*) forming the front line, *Archer's* and *MacRae's* a second and supporting column. As the line advanced *Archer* gained ground to the left until he formed on *McGowan's* left. *MacRae* gained ground to the right, forming on *Lane's* right.

The enemy was found in line of battle a short distance south of the Jones House.

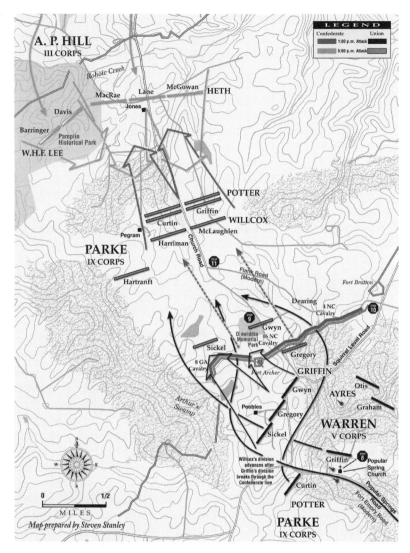

LEGEND

Confederate	Union
1:00 p.m. Attack	1:00 p.m. Attack
5:00 p.m. Attack	5:00 p.m. Attack

A. P. HILL
III CORPS

Rohoic Creek

MacRae   Lane   McGowan   **HETH**
Jones

Davis

Barringer
Pamplin
Historical Park
W.H.F. LEE

POTTER
Griffin
Curtin   **WILLCOX**
McLaughlen
Pegram
Harriman

Church Road

PARKE
IX CORPS

Hartranft

STOP 11

Flank Road
(Modern)

Fort Bratton

Dearing   4 NC
Cavalry

STOP 9

STOP 10

Gwyn
Dinwiddie   16 NC
Memorial   Cavalry
Park

Sickel
8 GA
Cavalry
Fort Archer

Gregory

Squirrel Level Road

GRIFFIN

Gwyn

Otis

Arthur's
Swamp

Peebles

Gregory

Sickel

AYRES

Graham

Griffin

WARREN
V CORPS

Willcox's division
advances after
Griffin's division
breaks through the
Confederate line.

Griffin

STOP 8

Popular
Spring
Church

Curtin

Popular Springs Road
Fort Emory Road
(Modern)

POTTER

N
W   E
S

0   1/2
MILES

PARKE
IX CORPS

Map prepared by Steven Stanley

Peebles Farm, September 30–October 2, 1864

He scarcely waited to receive our charge before he broke and fled. General *Hampton* came up and charged the routed enemy, capturing many prisoners who would otherwise have escaped. The number of prisoners taken on this occasion [numbered] some 1,600 or 1,700. Night put an end to further operations. [*O.R. Supplement*, VII, pp. 476–477.]

Report of Maj. Gen. John G. Parke, USA, commanding Ninth Corps, Army of the Potomac

On the morning of 30th of September I moved with the First and Second Divisions, following the Fifth Corps out from the Weldon railroad, on the road leading by the Poplar Spring Meeting-House, in pursuance of the following instructions from the major-general commanding: "General Warren is ordered to move out the Poplar Spring Church road and endeavor to secure the intersection of the Squirrel Level road. . . . Move out after and co-operate with him in endeavoring to secure a position on the right of the enemy's position." . . .

Closing up on the rear of Griffin's division, of the Fifth Corps, at the meeting-house, he being at that time engaged skirmishing with the enemy, I made an examination and started a force to open a road to the left of our present road, in order that I might pass Warren and take up a position on his left. Before this was completed General Griffin succeeded in driving the enemy from his intrenched position at the Peebles house. I then moved rapidly my advance division to his support, and as soon as the other division came up preparations were at once made to follow up the enemy and reach the Boydton plank road if possible.

Leaving the enemy's works on the Peebles farm, we moved northwest through a narrow belt of timber and came to a large opening in which stood the Pegram house, near the eastern edge. The Second Division advanced beyond the Pegram house, facing to the north and entered the timber. The First Division was deployed in support of the Second, having one brigade in support to move to the left, that being, in my opinion, the most exposed and vulnerable part of our line. Orders were then sent to General Potter, commanding the Second Division, to advance and attack, which was promptly done, but the movement was met by an advance of the enemy.

The enemy attacked vigorously, and having been re-enforced he overlapped Potter's division and forced it to retire, Griffin's division not having effected the connection with Potter's right. Some considerable confusion ensued, but a new line was at once established, facing north and forming directly in front of the Pegram house. Here the First Division was posted and the Second Division rallied. The enemy's advance was checked by this line, aided by Griffin's division, which had taken position on the right. Night closing in all firing ceased. Orders were received to take up a position along the line of works captured from the enemy, connecting with the Fifth Corps on the right and the left refused, covering the Squirrel Level road at the Clements house. This line was taken up during the night and intrenched. [*O.R.*, XLII, part 1, pp. 545–546.]

Report of Gen. Robert E. Lee, continued

Yesterday evening General *Heth* attacked the enemy's infantry, who had broken through a portion of the line held by our artillery on the Squirrel Level road, and drove them back. General *Hill* reports that they were severely punished and 400 prisoners captured. General *Hampton*, operating on *Heth's* right, also drove the enemy, capturing 2 stand of colors and about 500 prisoners, including 4 colonels and 13 other officers. [*O.R.*, XLII, part 1, p. 852.]

Turn right onto Church Road, and drive 0.2 mile back to the intersection with Squirrel Level Road (Route 613). Turn left onto Squirrel Level Road and proceed north 0.6 mile to Flank Road. Turn left onto Flank Road, and then pull immediately into the parking area on the left side of the road for Fort Urmston, which is on your right.

STOP 10: FORT URMSTON

Fort Urmston was constructed in October 1864 in the aftermath of the Fifth Petersburg Offensive. Named for a soldier in the Twelfth U.S. Infantry who was killed in fighting at Peebles's Farm, it was a six-sided redoubt that had positions for six guns and was designed to cover the approaches to Squirrel Level Road from the north. Its remnants are National Park Service property.

FIFTH PETERSBURG OFFENSIVE/BATTLES OF CHAPPELL'S FARM AND VAUGHAN ROAD, 1 OCTOBER 1864

On October 1, the Confederates made two efforts to try to reclaim possession of the Squirrel Level Road line. The first was made by Maj. Gen. *Henry Heth's* division against Brig. Gen. Romeyn Ayres's division, which had moved north up Squirrel Level Road to the right of Brig. Gen. Charles Griffin's division after the latter's capture of Fort Archer on September 30. Just north of where Fort Urmston was constructed, at the Chappell Farm, the Confederates made contact with Ayres's men and forced the Federals to fall back. However, *Heth* was unable to make any further progress when he found the enemy in fortified positions, and he broke off his offensive.

Report of Major General Heth, continued

On the morning of October 1, I moved my division down the Squirrel Level Road with the design of attacking the enemy at the Chappell House. General *Mahone* had reconnoitered the position the day before and found the enemy weak at that point, and it was supposed that here a successful blow might be struck. Line of battle was formed across the Squirrel Level Road, near the Davis house. Lieutenant-Colonel *Pegram* reported to me with a portion of his battalion of artillery.

Near the Chappell House an enclosed fort had been erected, being one of several similar works in a fortified line thrown up by our troops which the enemy now occupied. The design was to drive the enemy from the works at this point, and then sweep down the works in the direction of the Church Road, where *Wilcox* was in position. On advancing, the enemy was driven back to the works above mentioned, but after a close and careful reconnaissance he was found to be in heavy force, having strengthened this point as well as the entire line during the night. I concluded not to make a determined assault which, if successful, would have been with such heavy loss that no further attack could have been made successfully on these series of enclosed forts. The division was withdrawn during the night. [*O.R. Supplement*, VII, p. 477.]

Report of Maj. Robert Fauntleroy, CSA, Fifty-fifth Virginia Infantry, Walker's Brigade, Heth's Division, Third Corps, Army of Northern Virginia

On the morning of the 1st of October we were ordered to move at 3 a.m., when we took up line of march for the left and halted at Battery No. 45, where we remained until daybreak, when we again moved, taking the Squirrel Level road until its intersection with our lines of earth-works, where we crossed, advancing into the open field, where we formed line of battle, and moved forward on the enemy's position through a wood in front

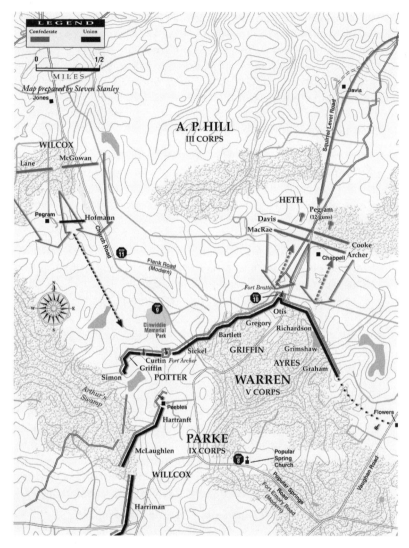

First Battle of Squirrel Level Road, October 1, 1864

obstructed with abatis. In this wood we encountered a considerable force of the enemy, who were soon repulsed and retired to our line of fortifications—or, rather, theirs, since they (the enemy) now have them—when they opened a heavy fire, causing our troops to recoil, and producing great confusion in my regiment, the men of different commands mixing with it and straggling to the rear, causing the same effect in mine, in spite of the best efforts of myself and officers to rally and arrange it. [*O.R.*, XLII, part 1, p. 942.]

While *Heth's* effort to drive in the Union right was coming to naught, *Hampton's* Confederate cavalry tried to achieve something against the Union left flank. While operating on the Vaughan Road, they encountered Brig. Gen. Henry E. Davies's Federal cavalry brigade during the afternoon. This meeting touched off a terrific cavalry fight that, although costly for the Federals in terms of casualties, foiled *Hampton's* attempt to significantly disrupt the operations of Union forces at and around Peebles's Farm.

Report of Major General Hampton, continued

Upon consultation with General *Heth*, it was determined to attack the enemy, he to strike them in front and I to move on their left flank. I moved [Maj. Gen. *W. H. F.*] *Lee's* division down the Harman . . . road and occupied some works which were found there. In the meantime the infantry had become engaged, and as the enemy moved up to re-enforce he exposed his flank to me. I at once ordered General *Lee* to attack, which he did with the Ninth and Tenth Virginia Regiments in the handsomest style, leading his men in person. These regiments went in line of battle, dismounted, and reserved their fire until very near the enemy. Delivering it regularly, they charged, routing the enemy completely, capturing about 900 prisoners and 10 standards. [Capt. *William*] *McGregor* kept his guns on the line of battle, charging with the troops, and keeping up a steady and accurate fire. The whole affair was one of the handsomest I have seen, and it reflects the highest credit on the troops engaged in it. To show the effect of this flank attack I may mention that *The Army and Navy Gazette*, a paper of the enemy, in reviewing the operations of their army, attributed the failure of their whole movement on this side of the James River to the fact that a flanking column was thrown between two of their divisions and swept off many men. We captured here and in the attack the night previous nearly 1,000 prisoners, including a very large number of commissioned officers.

Expecting that we would make an attempt the next morning to recapture the lines we had lost, I placed my command, or rather *Lee's* division and *Dearing's* brigade, near Fort MacRae, in the works. Whilst resting here *Butler* was attacked on the Vaughan road. Taking two of General *Lee's* regiments (the Ninth and Thirteenth Virginia) I crossed the country, struck the Squirrel Level road, and charged the enemy in rear. They fell back on the Vaughan road and took a very strong position near McDowell's house. I determined to attack them here and sent to General *Lee* to bring up two more regiments. Before these were put in the enemy was driven from our lines of works and my men had got within a few yards of their main line. Here it was that General *Dunovant* was killed, at the head of his brigade, whilst gallantly leading them, and Doctor [*John B.*] *Fontaine*, my medical director, who went to his assistance, was mortally wounded. Each of these officers, in his own sphere, was an admirable one; both were zealous in the performance of their duties and both were a loss to the service and to the country. Just as we were about to charge the breast-works it was reported that the enemy had gained my rear. This involved new dispositions to meet the expected attack and before it was ascertained that the report was groundless it was too late in the day to carry out my original plan of attack. The command was withdrawn at dusk. [*O.R.*, XLII, part 1, pp. 947–948.]

From the parking area, turn left onto Flank Road. Along Flank Road you will pass the remains of Fort Conahey, with an interesting interpretive marker, should you wish to stop and view it. Travel west on Flank Road for 0.7 mile to the parking area for Fort Fisher on the right side of the road.

STOP 11: FORT FISHER

Initial construction of Fort Fisher, the largest of the preserved earthworks in Petersburg National Battlefield, began during the first week of October 1864 as the Fifth Petersburg Offensive was coming to an end. Named for Otis Fisher, a lieutenant in the Eighth U.S. Infantry who had been killed during the fighting for Peebles's Farm, it was completed in mid-October and constructed to cover the Church Road. Initially a modest square redoubt designed to hold seven guns, in early 1865 it was expanded into a multibastioned earthwork that covered more than 4 acres and had positions for nineteen pieces of artillery. Behind Fort Fisher, Union engineers began construction on an observation and signal tower on the Peebles Farm in late December 1864. When completed in early 1865, the tower offered Federal officers an unmatched vantage point for monitoring events and gathering intelligence.

If you wish to further explore this area, the trail across Church Road from Fort Fisher will take you to the well-preserved remnants of Fort Welch and Fort Gregg, which were also constructed in the aftermath of the Fifth Petersburg Offensive. The former, named for Col. Norval Welch of the Sixteenth Michigan, who was killed at Peebles's Farm, is a pentagonal earthwork that had positions for nine field guns and covers a little less than an acre. It also marks the point where the Union fortified lines around Petersburg made a sharp bend to the south. Fort Gregg, named for James P. Gregg, a lieutenant in the Forty-fifth Pennsylvania who was killed in the fighting at Pegram's Farm, is a six-sided redoubt that covers about a half acre and had positions for six field guns. The trail linking Church Road and Fort Welch crosses what in 1864 was Pegram's Farm, which was located about midway between Fort Fisher and Fort Welch.

FIFTH PETERSBURG OFFENSIVE/BATTLE OF PEGRAM'S FARM, 2 OCTOBER 1864

After thwarting Confederate efforts to drive his forces from their new position of October 1, Warren put his men to work constructing works, evidently content to hold on to what he had gained to that point. That evening, however, Meade ordered Gen. Gershom Mott's division from the Second Corps to Warren and directed Warren to resume offensive operations on October 2. Warren complied by pushing his and Parke's commands forward from the Peebles's Farm line toward the Boydton Plank Road and directing Mott to advance along the Harmon Road (modern Duncan Road), hoping he might fall on the right flank of any Confederate forces in the area. After leaving their works, Warren's and Parke's men easily drove the Confederates in front of them, but, understandably wary of pushing forward too far too fast and giving the Confederates an opportunity to deliver a successful counterattack, were only able to reach a point just north of Pegram's Farm before finding enough Confederates posted in a line of strong entrenchments at the Jones Farm to make pushing to the Boydton Plank Road unfeasible. During the afternoon, Parke ordered

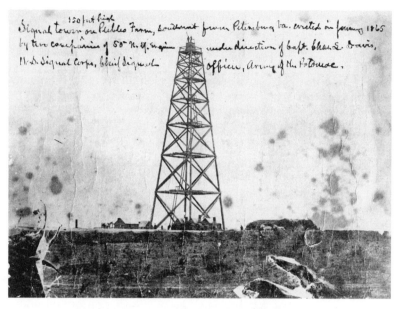

150-foot-high signal tower near Petersburg, Virginia (USAMHI)

Mott to conduct a reconnaissance in force, which provoked a sharp fight near the Hart House. Concluding that the Confederates were in too strong a position for much more to be accomplished, the Federal high command ended the Fifth Petersburg Offensive.

Report of Major General Parke, continued

During the 1st of October no further advance was made. A heavy rain continued throughout the day. The Third Division, Second Corps, Brevet Major-General Mott commanding, arrived in the afternoon, and was massed in the rear of our main line.

On the morning of the 2nd an advance was made for the purpose of developing the force of the enemy and position of his works. The Second Division was directed to take a position on Pegram house line, the First Division to connect with the left of the Second Division and advance the left of the division, pivoting on the Second Division so as to form a line facing northward, and the Third Division, Second Corps, was instructed to move out on the Squirrel Level road, and after taking position on the left of the

First Division to advance in connection with it. The movement was made in a satisfactory manner, and the enemy was found in force occupying a line extending northeast and southwest, covering the Boydton plank road, with artillery in position and infantry behind entrenchments. The losses fell mainly upon the Third Division, Second Corps. . . .

Having developed this force of the enemy, by direction of the major-general commanding, General Mott's and Willcox's divisions were retired, and the line was retained through the Pegram house, connecting with the Fifth Corps on the right, and the left covering the Squirrel Level road at the Clements house. October 3, work was at once commenced on redoubts, rifle-pits, and slashing, and continued daily.

October 5, General Mott's division was relieved by the Third Division (General [Edward] Ferrero), and General Mott was instructed to report to his own corps commander. The work on the entrenchments was pushed vigorously. Heavy details were finished by the three divisions. Two redoubts were constructed on the front line, three on the flank, and two on the rear line, with strong infantry parapet connections and heavy slashing in front. [*O.R.*, XLII, part 1, pp. 546–547.]

Report of Bvt. Maj. Gen. Gershom Mott, USA, commanding Third Division, Second Corps, Army of the Potomac

About 12 m. on the 1st instant I received orders from the major-general commanding the Second Corps, that I, with my division, would take the cars to the Yellow House of General Warren's headquarters, there procuring a guide, would march to the vicinity of the Ninth Corps, reporting to Major-General Parke. . . . The head of the column reported to General Parke at 2.30 p.m.; the rear was up at 5 p.m. I with my staff reported at 4 p.m., having remained to superintend the embarkation. The march from the railroad terminus to the headquarters Ninth Corps was severe owing to its raining very hard and the muddy condition of the roads. My division was massed in the rear of the Peebles house and remained until next morning.

On Sunday, the 2nd, having received orders from the major-general commanding the Ninth Corps to be in readiness to move at 5:30 a.m., and to report in person at 6 a.m. to his headquarters, my command was ready at said time, and I reported accordingly.

The orders I received were to form on the left of General Will-cox's division, of the Ninth Corps, and to advance with said division, keeping up the connection on my right, and to keep a good lookout for my left flank.

At 8 a.m. I deployed the Second Brigade (General [Byron] Pierce) on the left of General Willcox's division, with skirmishers well thrown out, followed closely by the Third Brigade (Colonel McAllister), with instructions to deploy as soon as the movement commenced and the nature of the ground would admit, the First Brigade (General [Regis] De Trobriand) in reserve, with instructions to throw out flankers and to leave a regiment at the point where the roads forked near the Clements house. Advancing a mile, I came upon a line of the enemy's works, which was carried at once, the enemy making but little resistance. After taking this line of works I advanced about a mile, driving the enemy's skirmishers, when I came upon a second and stronger line of works. These works were manned by infantry and artillery.

After skirmishing with the enemy for some little time, I received orders from General Parke to develop the force and ascertain how much of the enemy were in the position. I immediately ordered General Pierce to carry out the order, which he did by advancing the First Massachusetts Heavy Artillery, One hundred and fifth Pennsylvania Volunteers, One hundred and forty-first Pennsylvania Volunteers, and the Eighty-fourth Pennsylvania Volunteers, with the First U.S. Sharpshooters on the right flank. I also instructed Colonel McAllister to move a regiment of his brigade to the left of the position occupied by the battery, and when the attack was made by General Pierce to open a severe fire upon the battery, in order to draw part of the fire and relieve the attacking column as much as possible. At 3 p.m. the line was ordered forward, when it charged most gallantly to within a few rods of the work under a concentrated fire from musketry and artillery. At 3.10 p.m. I received a communication from Major-General Parke saying that he had just seen Major-General Meade, who did not wish me to run any great risk, but to take up a line and intrench. The attacking column was immediately recalled. [*O.R.*, XLII, part 1, pp. 344–345.]

Report of Major General Heth, continued

The division was withdrawn during the night [of October 1–2] and assumed the position it [had taken] the previous

WESTWARD MOVEMENTS [363

evening. Fearing that the enemy would attempt to gain the Boydton Road by a road to the right of and parallel to the Church
Road known as the [Harman] Road, I directed General *MacRae*
to move to a point on the road where he had some weeks previous
thrown up temporary works. General *MacRae* had not reached
the point indicated before the enemy attacked in force our cavalry on the Harman Road, rapidly driving it before him. General *MacRae* reached his works just in time to repel the advancing
enemy.

Davis and *Cooke* were now ordered in position on *MacRae's*
left. The enemy was evidently well informed of the extent of the
works *MacRae* occupied and made their dispositions to turn his
left but, in their attempt, struck *Davis'* Brigade and were easily
repulsed. From this time until October 27 my division was occupied in constructing breastworks extending in the direction of
Hatcher's Run. [*O.R. Supplement*, VII, pp. 477–478.]

Drive out of the parking area for Fort Fisher, and return to Church Road. Turn
left onto Church Road, and proceed 0.7 mile to Squirrel Level Road (Route 613).
Turn right onto Squirrel Level road, and drive 4.6 miles. Turn right onto Duncan
Road. Proceed 0.5 mile on Duncan Road to Dabney Mill Road, and turn left.
Proceed 0.5 mile to the parking area for the Civil War Trust site marked with signs
for "Hatcher's Run Battlefield" on the left. Pull in here and park.

STOP 12: DABNEY'S MILL

In October, Grant made yet another attempt to reach the Boydton
Plank Road and South Side Railroad. He directed Butler to make a
demonstration north of the James to distract the Confederates, while
south of the James, he ordered three corps from Meade's army forward on October 27. Parke's corps was directed to advance west from
the Peebles's Farm line to probe the Boydton Plank line, with Warren's command supporting his left. The main effort, however, was to
be made by Hancock's command. Supported by a division of cavalry,
it was to swing south and then west to reach the Boydton Plank Road.
Upon doing so, Hancock was to push north and east toward Petersburg to connect with Warren's left and, hopefully, extend the Union
line to the South Side Railroad. Evidence of the Federal move reached
the Confederate high command soon after it commenced, which led
to the dispatch of four brigades under *Heth* to the scene with orders to
arrest the Federal movement and, if an opening were found, deliver
a strong blow.

SIXTH PETERSBURG OFFENSIVE/BATTLE OF BOYDTON PLANK ROAD, 27–28 OCTOBER 1864

Report of Major General Meade, continued

On October 27 part of the Ninth, Fifth, and Second Corps, together with Gregg's division of cavalry, moved from the left in reconnaissance. The enemy was found in a line strongly entrenched, extending in front of the Boydton Plank Road down nearly to Armstrong's Mill. Wherever he was confronted by the Ninth and Fifth Corps his position was deemed too strong to attack. The Second Corps and Gregg's division, under Major-General Hancock, succeeded in crossing Hatcher's Run on the Vaughan road, and reaching the Boydton plank near Burgess' Tavern, encountering only slight opposition from the enemy's cavalry. About 4 p.m., however, the enemy attacked Hancock and Gregg with great force, but was in every instance repulsed. Crawford's division, Fifth Corps, had been crossed at Armstrong's Mill and had moved up Hatcher's Run, with a view of connecting with Hancock, but the serpentine nature of this stream, and the dense thicket through which Crawford had to move, prevented the junction being made. No object being attainable by remaining in the positions gained, the troops were on the 28th, withdrawn to the lines of entrenchments. [*O.R.*, XLII, part 1, p. 32.]

Report of Major General Hancock, continued

The order of movement prescribed that I should move down the Vaughan road with my two divisions, cross Hatcher's Run; thence by Dabney's Mill to the Boydton plank road; thence by the White Oak road, recrossing Hatcher's Run, and, finally, that I should strike the South Side Railroad. Gregg's division of cavalry was placed under my orders, and was to move on my left flank by way of Rowanty Post-Office and the Quaker road. The operations of the Ninth and Fifth Corps were intended, I presume, to occupy the enemy to an extent that would forbid their concentration against me.

The cavalry bivouacked near me on the night of the 26th. At 3.30 a.m. it moved out by the Halifax road, while the infantry ([Brig. Gen. Thomas W.] Egan's division in advance) moved over to the Vaughan road, where the enemy's vedettes were first encountered. The march was somewhat delayed by obstructions in the road, but the head of Egan's column reached Hatcher's Run very soon after daylight; and Egan at once made his arrangements to force the crossing. The enemy were posted in a rifle-pit on the opposite bank. They were in small force, but the approaches were difficult, trees having been felled in the stream, which was waist deep, above and below the ford. [Gen. Thomas] Smyth's brigade was deployed in the first line, and went forward in gallant style, carrying the works, with a loss of about 50 men. . . . As soon as the command was in hand on the opposite bank, Egan moved by the nearest road to Dabney's Mill, while Mott's division followed the Vaughan road for a mile, and then struck over to the mill by a cross-road. About the time we arrived at the mill I received a dispatch from General Gregg, telling me he had crossed the run, and the sound of his guns could be heard on our left.

At the ford I sent a dispatch to the major-general commanding stating that I had effected a crossing, and expressing some uneasiness at not hearing the firing of the Ninth Corps. As soon as Mott reached Dabney's Mill Egan moved on toward the Boydton road. The sound of Gregg's guns became more distinct, and it was hoped that we might strike the plank road in time to inflict some damage to the enemy, but we arrived in season only to hurry up their rear guard. [*O.R.*, XLII, part 1, pp. 230–231.]

Report of Major General Heth, continued

From October 2 until October 27, 1864, my division was kept at work, assisted by Major-General *Hampton's* Cavalry Corps, constructing breastworks from the Harman Road to Hatcher's Run. This long line of earth works was barely completed on October 27 when the enemy in heavy force moved from his entrenchments towards our right flank. When the cavalry pickets were driven in on the morning of October 27; of course the strength and designs of the enemy were unknown. Soon it became apparent that he was moving with a very heavy force and that his design was to cut the South Side Railroad. To effect this, general Grant crossed Hatcher's Run with six divisions of infantry, a division of cavalry, and a large amount of artillery.

His crossing was effected at Armstrong's Mill and where the Vaughan Road crosses Hatcher's Run, driving from these points the dismounted cavalry, who held these crossings. At the same time, and in order to cover the above movement, he deployed in front of a parallel to my line of works in heavy force, which continued to move by the left flank until it reached Hatcher's Run on the Creek Road, which road leaves the Boydton Plank Road at Burgess' Mill running along Hatcher's Run to Armstrong's Mill. From the accounts of the enemy subsequently published, it was evident that he did not suppose our breastworks extended as far west as Hatcher's Run.

His plans were, on reaching the right of our works, to turn them with the column deployed immediately in our front and move up the east side of Hatcher's Run, using the Creek Road for his artillery, this column uniting at Burgess' Mill with the column which had crossed the Creek at Armstrong's Mill and on the Vaughan Road. In the event of the enemy not being able to turn our right and get possession of the Creek Road with his covering columns, he supposed at least that this force would be able to hold in check all our disposable infantry, enabling him to move with his six divisions on the west side of Hatcher's Run, directly on the South Side Railroad via Burgess' Mill and the White Oak Road.

To oppose this combined movement of from 15,000 to 18,000 infantry, I had, early in the morning of October 27 under my orders, my own division and two brigades of *Wilcox's* Division (*Lane's* and *McGowan's*), *Dearing's* Brigade of Cavalry, and about 600 or 800 dismounted cavalry, the cavalry occupying the extreme right of the line. As soon as it became apparent that the enemy was moving down and feeling for the right of my line, I directed Brigadier-General *Davis* to move down our breastworks and reinforce the cavalry. General *Davis* reached the Creek Road and Hatcher's Run in opportune time, checking the enemy's advance.

About this time Brigadier-General *Dearing* informed me that he had received orders from General *Hampton* to draw off the mounted portion of his brigade and report to him. I informed General *Dearing* that it would be impossible for him to carry out his order until I replaced his brigade by an infantry force. General *Cooke* was ordered to move by the right flank down the works and relieve Dearing, after which *Dearing* withdrew. Colonel *Mayo*, commanding *Archer's* and [*Henry Harrison*] *Walker's* Brigade, was ordered to close in on *Cooke* and *MacRae* to close in on *Mayo*. *Lane* and *McGowan* were directed to fill up any interval on the left which might be created by the movement by the brigades of *Heth's* Division.

General *Dearing*, on reaching the plateau on the west side of Hatcher's Run, [which] overlooks Burgess' Mill and the bridge across the stream at this point, discovered that the enemy had reached the Boydton Plank Road. He was thus cut off from General *Hampton*. General *Dearing* reported this to me which was the first information that I had received that the enemy had crossed Hatcher's Run. General *Hampton* had sent repeated messages to me to this effect, but no messenger had reached me; some of them falling into the enemy's hands.

Communication was subsequently opened with General Hampton, by means of couriers, and a plan of attack agreed upon.

About a quarter of a mile from the point where the right of our works rested on Hatcher's Run and in the direction of Burgess' Mill, Major-General *Hampton* had constructed a dam across the stream. Leading from the dam a blind path, or abandoned road, ran diagonally through dense woods, intersecting the Boydton Plank Road . . . west of Burgess' Mill. I had passed along this path on several occasions in reconnoitering the west of the Rowanty and Hatcher's Run, and it was this knowledge thus obtained that enabled me with General *Hampton's* cooperation to defeat the plans of the enemy. [*O.R. Supplement*, VII, pp. 479–481.]

Drive out of the parking area, and turn left onto Dabney Mill Road. Proceed 2.3 miles to the intersection with Boydton Plank Road (U.S. 1). Turn right, and drive 0.7 mile to a small pull-off on the left side of the road just before the bridge over Hatcher's Run. This pull-off is not marked, and this road carries fast-moving traffic, so be careful. In light of the relatively small size of the pull-off and the noise from the road, it is probably best to read the selections for this stop in your vehicle.

STOP 13: BURGESS'S MILL

Hancock's command reached the Boydton Plank Road and secured its intersection with the White Oak Road by noon on October 27. Shortly thereafter orders arrived from army headquarters to pause and await further directions before moving north. In the meantime, Parke's men reached the Boydton Plank Road line but failed to find any weak spots that could be exploited, while, due to the nature of the terrain, Warren's command was unable to make decent progress as it tried to fill the space between Hancock and Parke. Grant and Meade directed Hancock to hold his position a few hundred yards south of where the road crossed Hatcher's Run at Burgess's Mill.

During the late afternoon, *Heth's* men took advantage of the gap between Hancock and the rest of the Federal army to reach a position

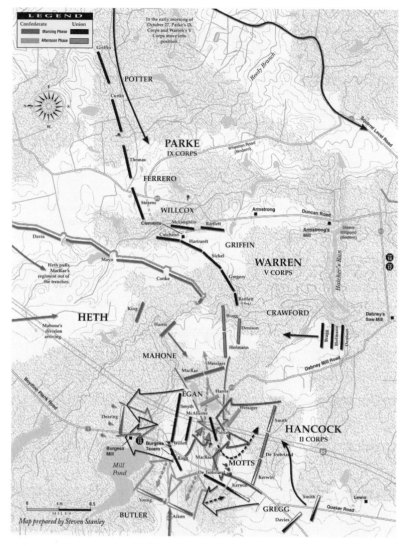

Boydton Plank Road, October 27, 1864

from which they were able to deliver a powerful blow to Hancock's right flank. Hancock's men were able to fight the Confederates off, but the battle exacerbated Grant and Meade's anxiety over the Second Corps's isolation. Thus, they approved Hancock's decision to give up his hold on the Boydton Plank Road and withdraw his command. The Confederates did nothing to interfere.

SIXTH PETERSBURG OFFENSIVE/BATTLE OF BOYDTON PLANK ROAD, 27–28 OCTOBER 1864

Report of Major General Hancock, continued

As soon as we emerged into the clearing at the plank road the enemy opened fire on us from near Burgess' Tavern and from our left. . . . Soon after my arrival at the Boydton road General Gregg came in by the Quaker road, and preparations were at once made for continuing the march by the White Oak road. General Egan's division moved down the Boydton road toward the bridge, for the purpose of driving the enemy across the run. Mott's division was put in motion for the White Oak road, and a brigade of cavalry sent down to relieve Egan, in order that he might follow Mott.

At this juncture, about 1 p.m., I received instructions from the major-general commanding to halt at the plank road. General Mott formed one brigade in line, looking toward the upper bridge, while General Egan continued to press the enemy's dismounted cavalry, who held their ground with tenacity, but were finally driven over the run by a charge from a part of Smyth's brigade. Very soon after the order to halt was received, General Meade came on the field, accompanied by Lieutenant-General Grant. General Meade informed me that Crawford's division, of the Fifth Corps, was feeling its way up along the south bank of the run, and desired me to assist in making the connection by extending to the right. The same information substantially, and a caution concerning the vacant space between the Fifth Corps and my right, had been received from General Humphreys, chief of staff, but a few minutes before General Meade's arrival.

Under instructions from me, General Egan deployed two of his brigades to the right of the plank road, and subsequently deployed two regiments as far as they would reach to the right. . . . Major [Henry] Bingham, of my staff, was sent to communicate with General Crawford, and states that he found him . . . a short three-fourths of a mile from my right. The enemy meanwhile were not idle. They placed nine guns in position in front of Egan on the north bank of the run, and five more about 800 yards from Egan's left, on the White Oak road, from which they opened a very annoying artillery fire. [Lt. Butler] Beck, with four guns of his battery, replied gallantly. General Gregg was directed to send one of his brigades to drive away or capture the battery on our left, but on making a reconnaissance of the position thought he discovered infantry protected by hastily constructed works, and did not advance against the battery. . . . As soon as Major Bingham returned from General Crawford and reported his (General Crawford's) whereabouts, Lieutenant-General Grant and General Meade left the field, giving me verbal orders to hold my position until the following morning, when I was to fall back by the same road I had come. . . .

I had determined to assault the bridge and gain possession of the high ground beyond. General Egan, whose division occupied the crest of the ridge near Burgess' Tavern, had been intrusted with the necessary preparations, and McAllister's brigade, of Mott's division, had gone forward to support him. De Trobriand's brigade, of Mott's division, was still in line of battle, facing the approaches from the upper bridge. The remaining brigade of Mott's division (General Pierce's) had been moved up to support a section of Beck's artillery, under Lieutenant [Richard] Metcalf, which was in position on a secondary ridge about midway between Mott and Egan. Constant firing had been heard on my right, which was attributed to Crawford's advance. Becoming uneasy, I ordered two regiments of Pierce's brigade to advance well into the wood and ascertain what was there. Lieutenant [May] Stacey, of my staff, was sent to General Crawford to inform him that I was about to assault the bridge, for which preparations were complete. A section of [Lt. Henry] Granger's battery had been advanced to cover the bridge; the artillery had already opened, and a small party of the One hundred and sixty-fourth New York, the advance of the storming party, had pushed across the bridge, capturing a 10-pounder Parrott gun.

Just at this time, about 4 p.m., a volley of musketry immediately on my right, which was followed by a continuous fire, left no doubt that the enemy were advancing. The small force of Pierce's brigade in the woods were overrun by weight of numbers, and the enemy broke out of the woods just where Metcalf's section was placed. Metcalf changed front, and fired a few rounds, and the part of Pierce's brigade in support endeavored to change front, but were unable to do so successfully, and most of the brigade was driven back in confusion, rallying at the plank road, the section falling into the hands of the enemy. . . . I sent Major [William] Mitchell, my senior aide, to General Egan, with orders for General Egan to desist from his assault on the bridge and to face his command to the rear and attack the enemy with his whole command. When Major Mitchell reached General Egan he found that the general, with the instinct of the true soldier, was already in motion to attack the force in his rear.

I do not think the enemy comprehended the situation precisely. They pushed rapidly across the ridge, resting their right across the Boydton road, and facing south, commenced firing. De Trobriand's brigade was quietly formed just in front of the Dabney's Mill road, with [Col. Michael] Kerwin's brigade of dismounted cavalry on its left. [Bvt. Capt. John] Roder's and Beck's batteries were opened on the enemy. Major Mitchell in returning from General Egan found the enemy in possession of the road, and taking the First Minnesota, of Rugg's brigade, Second Division, opened fire on them. This was perhaps the earliest intimation they had of the presence of any considerable force in their rear; and they immediately directed a part of their fire in that direction. General Egan swept down upon the flank of the enemy with Smyth's and [Col. James M.] Willett's brigades, of his own division, and McAllister's brigade of Mott's division, while the line formed along the Dabney Mill road advanced at the same time, as did the dismounted cavalry on the left. Some of the new troops, of which McAllister's brigade was largely composed, faltered but were speedily reformed. The general advance of Egan was, however, irresistible, and the enemy were swept from the field, with a loss of two colors and several hundred prisoners. The Thirty-sixth Wisconsin Volunteers are particularly mentioned for good conduct, capturing more prisoners than the regiment had men. The captured guns were recaptured by us. . . .

[Lt. Col. Horace] Rugg's brigade, of Egan's division, did not advance with the division as was expected and desired. . . . Had the brigade advanced the rout of the enemy would have been greater, and a larger number of prisoners would have fallen into our hands. The enemy were driven into the woods in complete confusion, and another brigade advancing against them would have secured many trophies. . . . Almost instantaneously with this attack the enemy commenced pressing my left and rear heavily. Mott's skirmishers in the direction of the upper bridge were sharply engaged, and several valuable officers were lost on this line. The enemy in front had hardly been repulsed when the firing in rear became so brisk that I was obliged to send to General Gregg all of his force I had used to meet the attack in front as well as another of his brigades, which I was about putting in on my right to cover the Dabney's Mill road, constantly threatened by the enemy.

The attack on Gregg was made by five brigades of *Hampton's* cavalry, and was persevered in until some time after dark. I desired to send infantry to Gregg's assistance . . . but I feared a renewal of the attack in my front, and I therefore trusted to General Gregg to hold his own, and I was not disappointed. About 5 p.m. I sent Major Bingham, of my staff, to communicate with General Warren or Crawford, to state what had occurred, and to say that unless the Fifth Corps moved up and connected with me, I could not answer for the result, as I was pressed by the enemy in heavy force. Unfortunately, Major Bingham was captured by the enemy . . . and though he subsequently escaped saw neither General Warren nor Crawford. At 5:20 p.m. I received a dispatch from Major-General Humphreys, chief of staff, telling me that our signal officers had discovered the enemy moving down the Boydton plank road, undoubtedly concentrating against me. . . .

Having moved in the morning, by order, without any reserve ammunition, I found myself seriously crippled for lack of it. . . . Quite a heavy rain was falling, and the wood road to Dabney's Mill, my only communication with the rest of the army, was seriously threatened by the enemy, and was becoming very bad. . . . Re-enforcements were offered to me, [but] the question of their getting to me in time, and of getting ammunition up in time to have my own command effective in the morning was left for me to decide, and I understood that if the principal part of the fighting in the morning would be thrown upon these re-enforcements it was not desired that they should be ordered up. They would at least have been called upon to do the fighting until my own command could have replenished their ammunition, which I was quite certain would not be in time. . . . Reluctant as I was to leave the field, and by so doing lose some of the fruits of my victory, I felt compelled to order a withdrawal rather than risk disaster by awaiting an attack in the morning only partly prepared. The hour for the movement to commence was fixed at 10 p.m.

At 10 o'clock General Mott moved out, followed by General Egan. Egan's division halted at Dabney's Mill until after daylight to cover the withdrawal of Crawford's division, Fifth Corps. The cavalry commenced withdrawing by the Quaker road at 10.30. The pickets did not commence withdrawing until 1 a.m. on the 28th, when they were brought off under the direction of Brigadier-General De Trobriand. [*O.R.*, XLII, part 1, pp. 231–236.]

Report of Major General Heth, continued

About 2 o'clock p.m. I received a message from Lieutenant-General *Hill*, through a staff officer, that Major-General *Mahone* had been ordered to report to me with three brigades of his division. General *Mahone* in compliance with this order reported to me about 3 o'clock with two brigades, informing me that his third brigade ([Brig. Gen. *Nathaniel H.*] *Harris's*) would not be up for some time owing to the difficulties incident to its withdrawal from the lines in front of Petersburg. It was evident to me that our only chance of driving the enemy from the Boydton Plank Road (the possession of which at the point now held, would have enabled him to have cut the South Side Railroad at his leisure) [was] to attack him at once with all my available forces.

Reinforcing *Mahone's* two brigades by *MacRae's* Brigade of my own division, I directed Major-General *Mahone*, with these three brigades to attack the enemy, approaching him by [a] blind path. . . . I piloted General *Mahone* for some distance on this path, giving him all the information in my possession and informing him that by a preconceived arrangement, between General *Hampton* and myself, that General *Hampton* would attack from the opposite direction as soon as he (General *Mahone*) opened, at the same time *Dearing* was to attack with any of his disposable force, *Harris'* and [Brig. Gen. *Alfred M.*] *Scales'*, if they were up, crossing Hatcher's Run at, Burgess' Mill.

About this time I received a note from General *Dearing* stating that the enemy had driven him from the bridge at Burgess' Mill, that he had fallen back, and that all the roads leading to the rear of my lines were open to his advance. This information was of such critical importance that I immediately proceeded to the threatened point. On entering Creek Road, to its intersection with the Boydton Plank Road, I found that the enemy had not, as

yet, possession of the bridge and apparently was making no effort
to cross Hatcher's Run in force. I immediately sought General
Dearing and found him, with his command, in line of battle perpendicular to the plank road, some third or half a mile from the
creek. *Harris'* Brigade was with him.

I ordered *Dearing* and *Harris* to advance with all possible
speed and prevent the enemy from crossing Hatcher's Run, and
hold the bridge at all hazards, also to attack vigorously by crossing
the creek, as soon as *Mahone* opened. About this time it was reported to me, by scouts, that the enemy had crossed an additional
force to the west of Hatcher's Run, and that this force was moving
up the creek, either for the purpose of turning the right flank of
my lines resting on Hatcher's Run or probably seeking to establish
communication with his force, which, from the firing he knew
had reached the Boydton Plank Road.

It was necessary to check this movement as it would enable
him to take the force under *Mahone* in reverse. I found that General *Davis* had anticipated the orders necessary to be given and had
thrown a force across the Creek checking the enemy and causing
him to commence fortifying. *Mahone* now opened, *Hampton* attacking from the opposite direction at the same time. *Mahone's* attack
was successful. He broke the enemy's line.... *MacRae's* Brigade
and a portion of [Brig. Gen. *David A.*] *Weisiger's* reached the Plank
Road, penetrating his center. *MacRae* reformed his brigade in the
woods on the north side of the Plank Road, but finding that it was
isolated and that the enemy was enveloping him, he judiciously
withdrew, cutting his way back to the point from which he started.

General *Mahone* was unable to follow up the advantage he
had gained for want of adequate force. *MacRae* and *Weisiger* in
regaining their positions lost heavily in prisoners, which, from the
overwhelming force of the enemy, and the scattered condition
of the men, was unavoidable. At the time that *Mahone* attacked,
Dearing and *Harris* attacked. This attack was feeble and without result. General *Dearing* behaved with conspicuous gallantry, leading
a portion of his command to the west side of Hatcher's Run, but
the rest of the force failed to assist him. It is doubtful in my mind
if *Dearing* and *Harris* had succeeded in gaining the works on the
west side of Hatcher's Run whether or not, with their forces, they
could have held them. *Harris* [afterward] deploying the necessary
number of skirmishers, numbering only 150 men, and *Dearing's*
men being much scattered.

After *MacRae* had regained his position, General *Mahone* projected a second attack upon that portion of the enemy occupying the plateau overlooking Burgess' Mill, but it was found impossible to carry out his plans, a creek impassible for troops in line of battle intervening between the attacking force and the enemy. Night then set in. I deemed it hazardous for General *Mahone* to continue longer in his isolated position and ordered him to withdraw his force to the east side of Hatcher's Run. During the night I visited General *Hampton's* camp, and a combined plan of attack was agreed upon for the succeeding day, all the necessary arrangements being made during the night. On the morning of October 28, it was discovered that the enemy had retreated during the night. [*O.R. Supplement*, VII, pp. 481–485.]

Report of Gen. Robert E. Lee, continued

The attack of General *Heth* upon the enemy on the Boydton plank road . . . was made by three brigades under General *Mahone* in front, and General *Hampton* in the rear. *Mahone* captured 400 prisoners, 3 stand of colors, and 6 pieces of artillery. The latter could not be brought off, the enemy having possession of the bridge. In the attack subsequently made by the enemy General *Mahone* broke three miles of battle, and during the night the enemy retired from the Boydton road, leaving his wounded and more than 250 dead on the field. [*O.R.*, XLII, part 1, p. 853.]

Turn around, and drive south on Boydton Plank Road. After 0.6 mile, turn left onto Dabney Mill Road (Route 613). Proceed 2.3 miles until you are back at the parking area for the Civil War Trust's Hatcher's Run Battlefield Site on the right.

STOP 14: HATCHER'S RUN

In February 1865, Grant and Meade launched another effort to get at the roads that supported Petersburg and its defenders. Early on the morning of February 5, Gregg's cavalry division moved out with orders to ride to Dinwiddie Court-House and interdict Confederate wagons using the Boydton Plank Road. Warren's corps received the task of supporting Gregg's effort, while the Second Corps, now commanded by Maj. Gen. Andrew Humphreys, was to move to the crossing of Hatcher's Run at Armstrong's Mill to cover Warren. Once again, the Confederates responded by rushing a force commanded by *Heth* to the scene. By the time they arrived, however, Humphreys

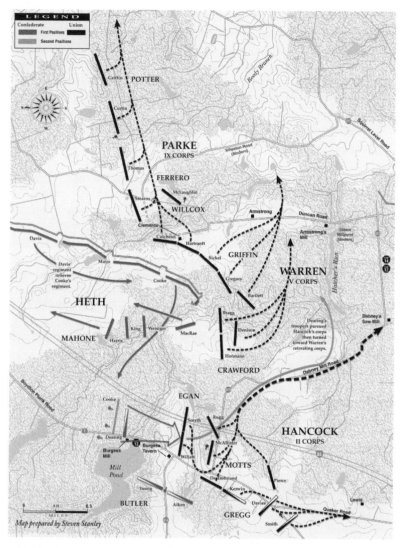

Boydton Plank Road, October 28, 1864

had his men posted in a fortified position. During the afternoon, the Confederates launched three separate attacks through sleet against Humphreys's position but never once reached the Federal lines. Although Gregg had reached Dinwiddie Court-House and captured some wagons, Grant decided to abandon that part of the plan and ordered Warren to pull back and take up a position south of Humphreys that covered the Dabney Mill Road and the Vaughan Road crossing of Hatcher's Run.

SEVENTH PETERSBURG OFFENSIVE/BATTLE OF HATCHER'S RUN, 5 FEBRUARY 1865

Report of Maj. Gen. George G. Meade, USA, commanding Army of the Potomac

I moved out this morning on the Vaughan road the Second Corps to the crossing of Hatcher's Run; on the road from Reams' Station to Dinwiddie Court-House, the Fifth Corps; and on a road crossing Hatcher's Run still lower down, the cavalry division under General Gregg. General Gregg was ordered to move to Dinwiddie Court-House, and to move up and down the Boydton road to intercept and capture the enemy's trains, and was further ordered to determine whether or not he could in any way inflict damage upon the enemy. General Warren to support General Gregg; General Humphreys, to support General Warren. All other available troops of this army were to be held ready to move at short notice.

The different commands reached their post in due season, but it was found difficult to open communication between Generals Humphreys and Warren along the Vaughan road. General Gregg proceeded to Dinwiddie Court-House, and moved up and down the Vaughan road and captured some 18 wagons and 50 prisoners, including 1 colonel. Finding that the Boydton road was but little used since the destruction of the bridges on that road and on the Weldon railroad, he returned to Malone's Bridge, on Hatcher's Run. At 4.15 p.m. the enemy, with what was reported to be *Hill's* corps and [Maj. Gen. *John B.*] *Gordon's* and [Brig. Gen. *John*] *Pegram's* divisions, attacked Humphreys. They were handsomely repulsed, with a loss to Humphreys of 300. Since this force had attacked Humphreys' right, consisting of but one division entire and one brigade, it became necessary to send for men enough to hold our communications with our rear line. One division of

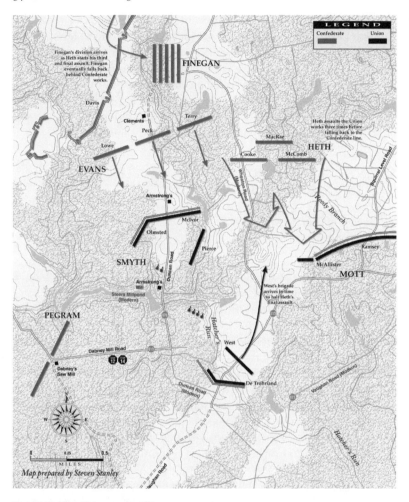

Hatcher's Run, February 5, 1865

the Ninth and one division of the Sixth Corps were therefore ordered to re-enforce Humphreys. Warren, with the cavalry, has been ordered to connect with his left and to report to him. [*O.R.*, XLVI, part 1, pp. 150–151.]

Report of Maj. Gen. Andrew A. Humphreys, USA, commanding Second Army Corps, Army of the Potomac

I was instructed on the 4th instant to move at 7 a.m. of the 5th, with the two divisions of my corps not in the entrenchments and two batteries of artillery, to the crossing of Hatcher's Run at the Vaughan road and at Armstrong's Mill, to hold those crossing, keep open the communication with the Fifth Corps, under General Warren, when it reached the intersection of the Vaughan and stage roads, some three or four miles distant, and support him, if required. In accordance with those instructions, I moved at 7 a.m. of the 5th, with General Mott's (Third) division, 5,961 officers and enlisted men, and General Smyth's (Second) division, 4,607 officers and enlisted men, and Battery K, Fourth U.S. Artillery, Brevet Captain Roder, and the Tenth Massachusetts Battery. . . . Major [Frank] Hess, Third Pennsylvania Cavalry, with 220 officers and men, joined me at 6 a.m. He was placed in advance, to drive in the enemy's cavalry pickets, and secure the crossing of Hatcher's Run, so as to conceal temporarily the fact from the enemy that the movement was made by an infantry force.

Major Hess found the enemy's infantry in small force holding the Vaughan road crossing, the run being dammed and obstructed by fallen trees. Being unable to use his cavalry with any effect, General De Trobriand's skirmishers, under his personal supervision, quickly drove the enemy from their rifle-pits, and secured the position at 9.30 a.m. This brigade was then rapidly crossed on the dam and put in position, covering the road, and his pickets extended to meet those of General Smyth, ordered to the crossing at Armstrong's Mill. With considerable difficulty a bridge about 100 feet in length was thrown across the stream. [Brig. Gen. George W.] West's brigade, of Mott's division, followed De Trobriand's, and was subsequently crossed to the south side of Hatcher's Run, completing the security of the position. Captain Roder's battery of 12-pounders was put in position here.

Smyth's division had been directed by me to diverge to the right from the Vaughan road near the Cummings house, secure the crossing at Armstrong's Mill, cover it and extend to the right past the Armstrong house, and rest his right upon the small swamp in that vicinity. Lieutenant [J. Webb] Adams' battery of rifled guns was sent with him. These instructions General Smyth executed at once, finding directly in front of his right, about 1,000 yards distant, the enemy's entrenchments, a redoubt, with the connecting curtains, being in full view. . . . Mott, by my direction, sent his rear brigade, McAllister's, to the vicinity of the Tucker house, with instructions to take position covering the Vaughan road a small parallel road connecting the Squirrel Level road with Armstrong's Mill, the right to rest near the swamp west of and rear to the Squirrel Level road, and the left to extend toward the swamp, on which Smyth's right was to rest. Smyth's division was relied upon to fill up the interval, should there be one. These orders were promptly executed. All the troops were directed to intrench immediately upon taking up position. Major Hess, Third Pennsylvania Cavalry, was ordered to open communication, on the south side of Hatcher's Run, between Mott's right and Smyth's left, and to move out to Dabney's Mill, and establish a post of observation there, and upon effecting this to move out the Vaughan road and communicate with Major-General Warren. . . .

I proceeded to examine Smyth's and McAllister's positions. It was here that I expected the attack of the enemy. Finding that McAllister was unable to cover the ground assigned to him, with the concurrence of the commanding general of the army, I telegraphed to Major-General Miles, whose division had remained in the entrenchments, to send out a strong brigade quickly to the Tucker house, to relieve McAllister's right and enable that officer to extend to his left and connect with Smyth. Major Hess was unable to carry out the first part of his instructions, but the pickets of the two divisions connected along the south branch of Hatcher's Run. The enemy's infantry pickets were driven from the Vaughan road, and communication established with Major-General Warren.

At about 4 p.m. the enemy opened with artillery from one of his redoubts that enfiladed the road leading to Armstrong's Mill from the Vaughan road, but doing no damage, and receiving no reply, the fire ceased. At 4.30 p.m. [Col. John] Ramsey's brigade (Fourth Brigade, First Division) 1,100 strong, reached the Tucker house, and enabled McAllister to extend toward Smyth's right. He had not yet quite completed this change of position when, at 5.15 p.m., the enemy, having concentrated a strong force in the vicinity of the Thompson house (since ascertained to be the chief parts of *Hill's* and *Gordon's* corps), made a sudden attack upon the right of Smyth and the left of McAllister. This attack was promptly and skillfully met by General Smyth and General McAllister, and the enemy's leading troops quickly repulsed, but the action was continued by those more distant until after 7 o'clock. The enemy's artillery opened from the redoubt already mentioned and from a battery near the Thompson house, both of which were effectually replied to. Early in the action I ordered up West's brigade, of Mott's division, to strengthen McAllister's left, which it did before the termination of the engagement; I also used two of Smyth's regiments as supports. The enemy withdrew to his entrenchments shortly after the engagement ceased.

Our loss (125 killed and wounded) was small, while that of the enemy was comparatively severe and must have been six or seven times greater than ours. . . . During the evening Hartranft's division, of the Ninth Corps, 3,200 strong, and [Brig. Gen. Frank] Wheaton's division of the Sixth Corps, 4,500 strong, reported to me and were posted along the Squirrel Level road, connecting with the entrenchments of the army. [*O.R.*, XLVI, part 1, pp. 191–193.]

SEVENTH PETERSBURG OFFENSIVE/BATTLE OF HATCHER'S RUN, 6 FEBRUARY 1865

By dawn on February 6, Warren had his command in the position designated by Grant and Meade the day before and soon thereafter ordered Crawford's division to push west along the Dabney Mill Road. Crawford quickly ran into a significant Confederate force, Brig. Gen. *John Pegram's* division of Maj. Gen. *John B. Gordon's* Second Corps, but was able to drive it from a line of defensive works just east of the Dabney Saw Mill. A counterattack by Brig. Gen. *Clement Evans's* division enabled the Confederates to reclaim their works temporarily, but then Ayres's division came up to help Crawford recapture the mill. They were unable to hold on, however, when *Mahone's* division, commanded on this day by Brig. Gen. *Joseph Finegan,* joined the fight and forced Crawford and Ayres to fall back until they encountered a division from the Sixth Corps that had been sent to their support.

Report of Major General Meade, continued

Warren advanced about 2 p.m. on the Dabney's Mill and Vaughan roads. Both columns had a spirited contest with the enemy, and steadily drove him before them till about 6 p.m., when the column on the mill road, having forced the enemy beyond Dabney's Mill and until he opened on them with artillery, indicating he was in his line of works, when, being re-enforced, Warren's troops were, in turn, compelled to retire in considerable confusion. The enemy was, however, checked before reaching the position occupied this morning, and Warren's troops rallied in this position. The column on the Vaughan road was recalled when the others were forced back. The troops are now formed in the lines occupied this morning. [*O.R.*, XLVI, part 1, p. 152.]

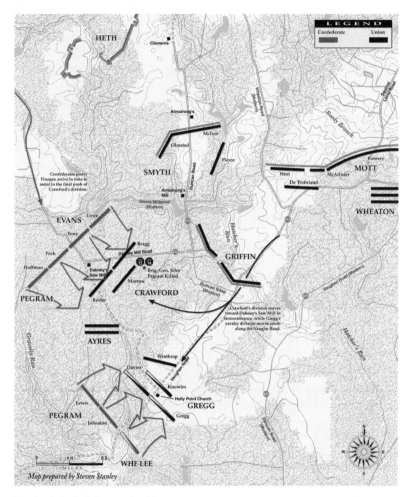

Hatcher's Run, February 6, 1865

Report of Major General Gouverneur K. Warren, USA, commanding Fifth Army Corps, Army of the Potomac

I, at 9 p.m. [on February 5], received orders to move up and join General Humphreys at the Vaughan road crossing of Hatcher's Run, to be prepared for any concentration of the enemy in the morning. This gave me specific instructions about the posting of my divisions and of General Gregg's cavalry, which was ordered up to join me for that purpose. I, as soon as practicable, ordered General [Charles] Griffin's division in motion, but the relieving of pickets, &c., made it nearly midnight before he was fairly on the road. My train all followed him, then General Ayres' division and the artillery, and then General Crawford's division.

General Gregg reached me on the Vaughan road at 4 a.m. on the 6th instant, and his troops filling up the road which my instructions required his forage train to return by, I directed it to follow General Crawford. The cavalry then brought up the rear, skirmishing with the enemy and punishing him severely when he came close enough. The night was very cold and the roads were frozen hard before morning. The troops had little rest and no sleep. The enemy's cavalry followed General Gregg up the Vaughan road, but were easily repulsed in their attempt to crowd us. . . . At 8 a.m. I received notification to feel the enemy along my front, and fight him if outside his lines. This I took to refer to the enemy in front of General Humphreys' troops, where the fighting had been the evening previous. . . . Before I could make any definite arrangements I received notice from General Humphreys that he was about to attack the enemy if outside his works; and then I thought it best to await the result of his operations and hold all the Fifth Corps and cavalry in hand to co-operate with him if needed. . . . At 11 a.m. General Humphreys informed me that the enemy on his front had retired to his entrenched lines, and I then waited further instructions from the general commanding after his receiving this information.

At 12.15 I received orders to make a reconnaissance south and west of Hatcher's Run, to ascertain the whereabouts of the enemy's lines in that direction. . . . At 1.15 p.m., I issued instructions to General Crawford to move out on the Vaughan road to where it turns off to Dabney's Mill, and then follow up that road toward the mill, drive back the enemy, and ascertain the position of his entrenched lines said to be there; also, to General Ayres to follow General Crawford with his division, taking with him General [Frederick] Winthrop's brigade, then with the cavalry down the Vaughan road. General Gregg was directed to send a force of cavalry and drive the enemy down the Vaughan road across Gravelly Run, and also to watch the left flank of the infantry column (composed of General Crawford and General Ayres) as it advanced.

This I thought the cavalry could easily do, as no considerable force of the enemy had been reported to me to be in that direction. General Griffin's division was left in reserve to support either the column toward Dabney's Mill or the cavalry on the Vaughan road, and posted where the road diverged. General Humphreys informed me also that [Brig. Gen. Frank] Wheaton's division, 4,500 strong, at the Cummings house, was available as support, as well as General De Trobriand's brigade, 2,500 strong. My orders were obeyed very promptly.

General Crawford had not proceeded far before the enemy's entrenched picket-line was encountered. This was soon carried by General [Edward] Bragg's brigade of his division. Having intrusted the direction of affairs on the Vaughan road to General Gregg with his cavalry, I went with the infantry column toward Dabney's Mill. We had proceeded but a short distance when heavy firing began on the Vaughan road, and reports came that General Winthrop's brigade had been attacked by the enemy in force and could not rejoin General Ayres, as both he and General Gregg had all they could do to maintain themselves. . . . I then directed General Griffin to re-enforce General Winthrop by a brigade and to take command of operations on the Vaughan road, reserving to myself General Griffin's Third Brigade (his largest and best), which was on his right, to send to General Ayres, in place of General Winthrop's, if it was needed there. Being again called upon by General Gregg for re-enforcements, as the enemy was turning his left, I sent over to order across the run the supports from General Humphreys. Having made these arrangements, I went along with the movement toward Dabney's Mill, to which place General Crawford soon drove the enemy. Rallying there, the enemy forced back General Crawford's left somewhat, when General Ayres was sent in to his support on that flank with his two brigades. The enemy was again driven and to some distance beyond Dabney's Mill. The firing continuing now to be constant and severe I brought up the Third Brigade of General Griffin's division in close support, and was obliged to put it all with General Ayres to hold our left. I sent then also, at once, for at least a brigade of General Wheaton's division, intending to order the whole division up if affairs on the Vaughan road would permit. Unfortunately, however, the enemy got up re-enforcements faster than I could, and when a brigade of General Wheaton's division was nearing the scene of action a charge was made by the enemy in a force (according to the *Petersburg Express* consisting of three divisions) against which I had but six brigades opposed.

Our line, despite all the exertions of the prominent officers and much good conduct among those in the ranks, gave way and fell back rapidly, but with little loss after the movement began; portions of the line continued to fire as it retired, and General Wheaton got his brigade in line, and with it a portion of the others reformed, so that the enemy was checked before our old lines were reached by us. . . . On the whole, it was not a bad fight and in no way discouraged me. [*O.R.*, XLVI, part 1, pp. 253–256.]

SEVENTH PETERSBURG OFFENSIVE/BATTLE OF HATCHER'S RUN, 7 FEBRUARY 1865

After a bitterly cold night Warren once again ordered Crawford to advance his division west on February 7 along the Dabney Mill Road. Crawford quickly found that the Confederates not only were still in place but had strengthened their positions. Nonetheless, during the afternoon, Warren directed Crawford to push forward a reconnaissance in force. Conducted in a driving hailstorm, the results of the reconnaissance confirmed Grant's and Meade's growing sense that they had accomplished all they could and it was time to end the Seventh Petersburg Offensive. Federal losses in the operation were around 1,500, while Confederate losses are estimated at around 1,000. The most prominent casualty was General *Pegram*, who was killed on February 6.

Report of Major General Warren, continued

About 10 a.m., having got my troops in hand and arranged, I directed General Crawford to attack the enemy from the right of our entrenchments, and by 12 m. he had again carried the enemy's advanced rifle-pits near the mill, which were considerably strengthened since the preceding day and were now defended by a portion of *Mahone's*.

At 12.30 p.m. I received dispatch that, "in view of the weather and the instructions of the lieutenant-general commanding, it was not advisable to make any attack to-day, unless I was satisfied great advantages could be gained." We had now drawn the enemy's fire, and his artillery fire from his main works. I then directed General Crawford to hold his main line on top of the hill and push a strong line of skirmishers as close to Dabney's Mill as possible. I then sent two brigades of General Wheaton to his support, and at 3.15 p.m. instructed him to drive the enemy as far as he could just before

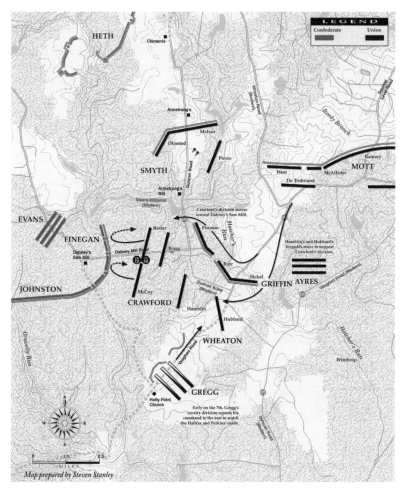

Hatcher's Run, February 7, 1865

dark. This brought on a spirited fight about 6 p.m., driving the enemy back nearly as far as we had done on the preceding day, nearly to Dabney's Mill. Some of our dead were thus recovered and buried. The enemy had artillery near Dabney's Mill, and I did not think it advisable to assault the position.

At midnight I withdrew General Crawford behind our line of breast-works without molestation from the enemy. General Crawford lost about sixty killed and wounded. General Wheaton's division was not engaged. Colonel [Michael] Kerwin's cavalry brigade also drove the enemy drown the Vaughan road across to the south side of Gravelly Run. The troops behaved most commendably during the trying weather, with no opportunity for rest or sleep. [*O.R.*, XLVI, part 2, p. 487.]

To return to the Visitor Center, turn left upon leaving the parking area for Hatcher's Run, and proceed 2.3 miles to Boydton Plank Road (Route 1). Turn right, and drive 3.4 miles on Boydton Plank Road to the intersection with U.S. Route 460 (Airport Street). Turn left, and immediately join Interstate 85 north toward Petersburg. Drive 6.4 miles to where I-85 joins I-95, and continue northbound. At exit 69, take the ramp to Wythe Street, and follow it to Washington Street. Bear right onto Washington Street (which becomes Oaklawn Boulevard), and drive 2.2 miles to the exit for Petersburg National Battlefield.

To reach the first stop for the Fall of Petersburg excursion, turn right onto Dabney Mill Road upon leaving the parking area for Hatcher's Run. Drive 0.5 mile until you reach Duncan Road (Route 670). Turn right onto Duncan Road, and proceed 0.4 mile to a T intersection. Turn right to continue on Duncan Road, and drive 0.5 mile to Vaughan Road (Route 675). Turn right onto Vaughan Road, and drive 1.7 miles until you see Old Vaughan Road (Route 605) on the right. Turn onto Old Vaughan Road, and proceed to the parking area for Dinwiddie Church of the Nazarene on the right-hand side of the road.

EXCURSION 6
THE FALL OF PETERSBURG

The unsuccessful attempt on March 25, 1865, to break the Federal line at Fort Stedman marked Gen. *Robert E. Lee's* final offensive effort in the Richmond/Petersburg area. Lt. Gen. Ulysses S. Grant worried, though, in late March that one morning he would find the Confederate lines at Richmond and Petersburg deserted and his foe on the move once again. Thus, Grant endeavored to impress upon his subordinates a sense of urgency as they planned what proved to be the final westward movement south of Petersburg, which began on March 27. He also planned to march Maj. Gen. William T. Sherman's army group north from North Carolina and combine it with the Armies of the Potomac and the James against *Lee's* Army of Northern Virginia. Infantry and cavalry divisions arrayed along Hatcher's Run southwest of Petersburg in anticipation of what would become the final battles of the war in the east. Grant's objective was to seize and hold *Lee's* remaining supply lines, the Boydton Plank Road and the South Side Railroad, forcing *Lee* either to evacuate Richmond and Petersburg or to remain in place and be destroyed. *Lee* responded to the Federal move with aggressive counterattacks by infantry and cavalry under the overall command of Lt. Gen. *Richard H. Anderson*, including cavalry under Gen. *W. H. F. Lee* and the small infantry division of Maj. Gen. *George Pickett*. Despite their efforts, by late on the evening of March 31, Dinwiddie Court-House was in Union hands. *Pickett's* small force still occupied the crucial Five Forks intersection, though, with an admonition from *Lee* to hold the intersection "at all hazards." April 1, 1865, became known as the "Waterloo of the Confederacy" when Maj. Gen. Philip H. Sheridan struck the entrenched Confederate position at Five Forks and destroyed it, leaving the Federals a clear path to the South Side Railroad. Grant realized that the time had come to end the siege. Before dawn on April 2, he launched an overwhelming assault on the Confederate lines south of Petersburg, splintering the Army of Northern Virginia into pieces. *Lee* began evacuating Richmond and Petersburg that night, setting the stage for the final campaign of the war in the Eastern Theater.

Several key roads and pieces of terrain form the background for the fighting of March 29–April 2. The Boydton Plank Road (modern-day

U.S. Route 1), the White Oak Road, and the South Side Railroad are the major wartime north-south and east-west thoroughfares in the area of operations; the Five Forks intersection, northwest of Dinwiddie Court-House, is the key piece of terrain in the area. Sutherland Station, northeast of Five Forks on the railroad, was an important point of concentration as *Lee* gathered forces to defend his exposed right flank. Nowadays, the modern-day Interstates 85 and 95 and U.S. Route 460 make moving around the battlefield relatively easy for the traveler. Gravelly Run and Hatcher's Run appear today to be minor waterways, but at the time of the campaign, they compartmentalized the terrain and had a profound effect on the fighting in early 1865.

The visitor to sites associated with the fall of Petersburg will benefit from a number of National Park Service properties, including most of the Five Forks battlefield and Fort Gregg in the city's main defenses. The Commonwealth of Virginia, Civil War Trust, and other private organizations have also contributed to the preservation effort west of the city, creating a patchwork of small interpreted sites that gives the modern-day visitor a fairly clear understanding of the final operations around Petersburg. This excursion takes the battles leading to the fall of Petersburg in chronological order, beginning with the clash at Lewis's Farm, moving on to the White Oak Road battlefield, and returning to Sheridan's staging base at Dinwiddie Court-House before moving on to Five Forks. After a short stop at Sutherland Station, the excursion ends at Forts Gregg and Whitworth, scenes of desperate fighting after the Union breakthrough on April 2, 1865.

SUMMARY OF PRINCIPAL EVENTS, 6 FEBRUARY–3 APRIL 1865

February

6—Maj. Gen. Edward O. C. Ord, U.S. Army, assigned to command of the Department of Virginia

9—Gen. *Robert E. Lee* assumes command of the Confederate Armies

26—Maj. Gen. Winfield S. Hancock, U.S. Army, assigned to the command of the Department of West Virginia and temporarily of all troops of the Middle Military Division not under the immediate command of Maj. Gen. Philip H. Sheridan

27–March 28, 1865—Expedition from Winchester to the front of Petersburg, Va.

March

25—Assault on Fort Stedman

26—Sheridan's command crosses the James River

29—Engagement at Lewis's Farm, near Gravelly Run; skirmish at the junction of the Quaker and Boydton Roads; skirmish on the Vaughan Road

30—Skirmishes on the line of Hatcher's Run and Gravelly Run

31—Engagement at the White Oak Road; engagement at Dinwiddie Court-House

April

1—Battle of Five Forks; Brig. Gen. Charles Griffin relieves Maj. Gen. Gouverneur K. Warren in the command of Fifth Corps

2—Assault upon and capture of fortified lines in front of Petersburg; engagements at Forts Gregg and Whitworth and at Sutherland's Station

3—Occupation of Richmond and Petersburg by Union forces; President Abraham Lincoln visits Petersburg, Va.

Readers may want to study the operations leading to the Fall of Petersburg covered in this section of the guide together with the engagement at Fort Stedman that immediately preceded them. Directions to Fort Stedman from the Petersburg National Battlefield Visitor Center and from Fort Stedman to the first stop for this excursion are provided in the Fort Stedman section of the guide.

To reach the first stop for the Fall of Petersburg excursion from the Petersburg National Battlefield Visitor Center, drive out of the parking area, and turn right onto the ramp just after the kiosk to take Route 36 (Oaklawn Boulevard) toward Petersburg. Proceed 2.2 miles on Route 36 (which turns into Washington Street) to the exit to southbound I-95. Take the exit, and proceed 0.3 mile to the exit for I-85; you are now at the northern terminus of I-85, where it joins with I-95. After taking the exit onto I-85 southbound, drive 2.3 miles, and take exit 65 for Squirrel Level Road, Route 115. At the top of the ramp, turn left, crossing the interstate, proceed 0.2 mile to the intersection with Squirrel Level Road, and turn right. At 2.3 miles from the last turn, bear left to remain on Squirrel Level Road. At 6.3 miles, remain straight ahead as Squirrel Level Road becomes Duncan Road. At 6.9 miles, turn right at the T intersection, remaining on Duncan Road. At 8.6 miles, turn right onto Old Vaughan Road (Route 605). Drive 0.1 mile to Dinwiddie Church of the Nazarene on the right side of the road, and pull into the parking area.

This excursion does not include a visit to Pamplin Historical Park, which has won enthusiastic—and well-deserved—acclaim as one of the truly outstanding Civil War sites in the country and whose 363 acres include the ground where the Union Sixth Corps broke through the Confederate lines on April 2, 1865. There is an entrance fee for Pamplin Park and the National Museum of the Civil

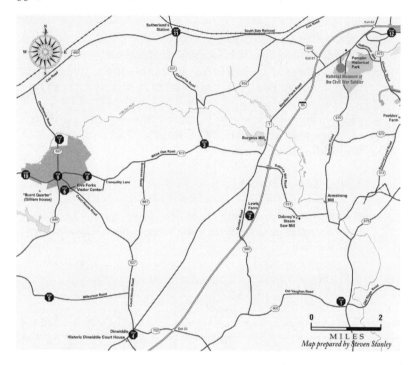

Fall of Petersburg overview

War Soldier located on its grounds, which is a real bargain if one has the time. Because of the additional fee and, more importantly, the fact that it requires an entire day to take full advantage of all that there is to see and do at Pamplin Park, we have reluctantly decided not to include it on this itinerary. Still, we would be remiss if we did not call attention to Pamplin Park and strongly urge anyone interested in the Civil War and the history of the area to make a point of setting aside plenty of time to see it during a visit to Petersburg.

Pamplin Historical Park is located on U.S. Route 1, the Boydton Plank Road. To reach the park from the Petersburg National Battlefield Visitor Center, follow the directions to Stop 1 of this itinerary, but leave I-85 at exit 63A for U.S. 1 southbound. Proceed south on U.S. 1 for 1.5 miles, and the park entrance will be on your left. If you wish to visit the sites at Pamplin Historical Park in chronological sequence, directions are provided both from Stop 11, Sutherland Station, and Stop 12, Fort Gregg.

STOP 1: DINWIDDIE CHURCH OF THE NAZARENE

The wartime church on this site was named Gravel Hill Church and served as Grant's forward headquarters in early 1865.

THE FIFTH CORPS ADVANCES, 29–31 MARCH 1865

The Federal plan for what proved to be the climactic final offensive of the Richmond-Petersburg Campaign built upon the fighting around Hatcher's Run in early February, during which Maj. Gen. George G. Meade's Army of the Potomac had gained a lodgment that threatened the Boydton Plank Road, one of the primary Confederate lines of supply and communication. Beginning on March 29, Grant planned to have Maj. Gen. Gouverneur Warren's Fifth Corps move north up the Quaker Road with the objective of seizing a position on the White Oak Road. Maj. Gen. Philip Sheridan's cavalry was to attack northwest toward Five Forks and the South Side railroad a few miles beyond.

Lee recognized the threat posed by this movement and reacted quickly to deal with it. He augmented Lieut. Gen. *Richard H. Anderson's* provisional corps, consisting of one infantry division (Brig. Gen. *Bushrod Johnson's*), with some artillery and cavalry. He also moved *Pickett's* division from the Howlett Line on Bermuda Hundred to Sutherland Station and recalled Maj. Gen. *W. H. F. Lee's* cavalry division from northwest of Richmond and Maj. Gen. *Fitzhugh Lee's* cavalry from Stony Creek, under the overall command of *Fitzhugh Lee. Anderson* and *Pickett* were to hold Five Forks and the White Oak Road line and to protect Boydton Plank Road, if possible.

Report of Lt. Gen. Ulysses S. Grant, USA, commanding Armies of the United States

General Sherman having got his troops all quietly in camp about Goldsborough and his preparations for furnishing supplies to them perfected, visited me at City Point on the 27th of March, and stated that he would be ready to move, as he had previously written me, by the 10th of April, fully equipped and rationed for twenty days, if it should become necessary to bring his command to bear against *Lee's* army, in co-operation with our forces in front of Richmond and Petersburg. . . . I explained to him the movement I had ordered to commence on the 29th of March; that if it should not prove as entirely successful as I hoped, I would cut the cavalry loose to destroy the Danville and South Side Railroads, and thus deprive the enemy of further supplies, and also prevent the rapid concentration of *Lee's* and [*Joseph E.*] *Johnston's* armies.

I had spent days of anxiety lest each morning should bring the report that the enemy had retreated the night before. I was firmly convinced that Sherman's crossing the Roanoke would be

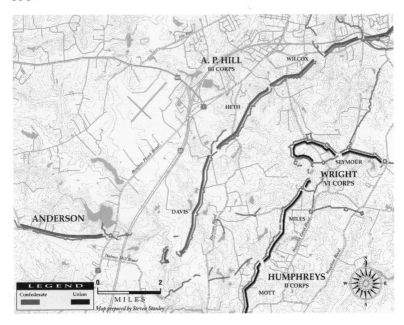

Positions of the armies, March 25, 1865

the signal for *Lee* to leave. With [Gen. *Joseph E.*] *Johnston* and him combined, a long, tedious, and expensive campaign, consuming most of the summer, might become necessary. By moving out I would put the army in better condition for pursuit, and would at least, by the destruction of the Danville road, retard the concentration of the two armies of *Lee* and *Johnston*, and cause the enemy to abandon much material that he might otherwise save. I therefore determined not to delay the movement ordered. On the night of the 27th, Major-General [Edward O. C. Ord], with two divisions of the Twenty-fourth Corps, Major-General [John] Gibbon commanding, and one division of the Twenty-fifth Corps, Major-General [William B.] Birney commanding, and [Brig. Gen. Ranald S.] Mackenzie's cavalry, took up his line of march in pursuance of the foregoing instructions, and reached the position assigned him near Hatcher's Run on the morning of the 29th.

On the morning of the 29th, the movement commenced. At night the cavalry was at Dinwiddie Court-House, and the left of our infantry line extended to the Quaker road, near its intersection with the Boydton plank road. The position of the troops, from left to right, was as follows: [Maj. Gen. Philip H.] Sheridan, [Maj. Gen. Gouverneur K.] Warren, [Maj. Gen. Andrew A.] Humphreys, Ord, [Maj. Gen. Horatio Wright], [Maj. Gen. John C. Parke]. Everything looked favorable to the defeat of the enemy and the capture of Petersburg and Richmond, if the proper effort was made.

From the night of the 29th to the morning of the 31st, the rain fell in such torrents as to make it impossible to move a wheeled vehicle, except as corduroy roads were laid in front of them. During the 30th, Sheridan advanced from Dinwiddie Court-House toward Five Forks, where he found the enemy in force. General Warren advanced and extended his line across the Boydton plank road to near the White Oak road, with a view of getting across the latter; but finding the enemy strong in his front and extending beyond his left, was directed to hold on where he was and fortify. General Humphreys drove the enemy from his front into his main line on the Hatcher, near Burgess' Mills. Generals Ord, Wright, and Parke made examinations in their fronts to determine the feasibility of an assault on the enemy's lines. The two latter reported favorably. The enemy confronting us, as he did, at every point from Richmond to our extreme left, I conceived his lines must be weakly held, and could be penetrated if my estimate of his forces was correct. I determined, therefore, to extend our line no farther, but to re-enforce General Sheridan with a corps of infantry, and thus enable him to cut loose and turn the enemy's right flank, and with the other corps assault the enemy's lines. [U.S. War Department, *The War of the Rebellion: A Compilation of the Official Records of the Union and Confederate Armies*, 70 vols. in 128 parts and index (Washington, D.C.: Government Printing Office, 1880–1901), series 1, volume XLVI, part 1, pp. 23–60. Hereafter cited as *O.R.*; all references are to series 1 unless otherwise noted.]

Report of Maj. Gen. George G. Meade, USA, commanding Army of the Potomac

On the 29th ultimo, in pursuance of orders received from the lieutenant-general commanding, the Second and Fifth Corps were moved across Hatcher's Run, the former by the Vaughan road, the latter by the old stage-road crossing at Perkins'. The Second Corps, holding the extreme left of the line before Petersburg prior to moving, was relieved by Major-General Gibbon, commanding two divisions of the Twenty-fourth Corps.

Major-General Humphreys, commanding Second Corps, was directed, after crossing Hatcher's Run, to take position, with his right resting on Hatcher's Run, and his left extending to the Quaker road. Major-General Warren, commanding Fifth Corps, was directed at first to take position at the intersection of the Vaughan and Quaker roads, and subsequently, about noon of the 29th, he was ordered to move up the Quaker road beyond Gravelly Run.

These orders were duly executed, and by evening Major-General Humphreys was in position, his right resting near Dabney's Mill and his left near Gravelly Meeting-House, on the Quaker road. [*O.R.*, XLVI, part 1, pp. 601–602.]

Report of Maj. Gen. Gouverneur K. Warren, USA, commanding Fifth Corps, Army of the Potomac

The map which we possessed of the country into which the Fifth Corps was about to operate, was what was known as the Dinwiddie County map, prepared many years ago, and republished for our use on a scale of one inch to the mile. It gave no topography except the main streams and main roads. The names of the occupants of the houses did not now all correspond to those on the map; some of them, too, had disappeared, and others had been erected in places not noted. The map contained no distinction of the forest and clearings or swamps, all which have ever played a most important part in the Virginia campaigns. . . .

The country in which we were to operate was of the forest kind common to Virginia, being well watered by swampy streams. The surface is level and the soil clayey or sandy, and, where these mix together, like quicksand. The soil, after the frosts of winter leave it, is very light and soft, and hoofs and wheels find but little support. [*O.R.*, XLVI, part 1, p. 797.]

Drive out of the parking area for Dinwiddie Church of the Nazarene, and turn right onto Old Vaughan Road. Proceed 2.9 miles until you see Quaker Road (Route 660) on your right. Turn right onto Quaker Road, and drive 2.6 miles to the Lewis Farm on the right side of the road; 1.4 miles after turning onto Quaker Road, you will cross Gravelly Run, mentioned in Meade's orders to Warren for the movement of March 29. Please be mindful of traffic at this stop, as the road shoulder is very narrow. Use the shoulder and driveway on the right side of the road just after the marker labeled "Quaker Road Engagement 29 March 1865." Get out of your vehicle, and face north in your original direction of travel.

STOP 2: LEWIS FARM

Warren made contact with the Confederates on March 29 with his lead brigade, commanded by Brig. Gen. Joshua L. Chamberlain of Gettysburg fame. Chamberlain added significantly to his reputation during the 1864–1865 campaign, leading an attack and sustaining a grievous wound on June 18 during the First Battle of Petersburg. The wound was so serious, in fact, that Chamberlain's division surgeon predicted that he would perish, and newspapers in Maine reported his death in battle. Grant issued Chamberlain a battlefield promotion to brigadier general, thinking that he would soon die, but Chamberlain recovered and resumed field service in November 1864. He took command of his brigade in early 1865.

The see-saw fighting at the Lewis Farm involved three of four brigades of Maj. Gen. *Bushrod Johnson's* Confederate division. Brig. Gen. Charles Griffin reinforced Chamberlain with four regiments from his other two brigades, plus the guns of Battery B, Fourth U.S. Artillery, which unlimbered on either side of the Lewis House, now in ruins in the grove of trees in the center of the open field. Chamberlain used these additional regiments to push forward from his initial defensive position on the farm, reaching the Boydton Plank Road intersection by nightfall at a cost of some 380 casualties, compared with an estimated 371 Confederate casualties. Warren entrenched on the Boydton Plank Road with the divisions of Griffin and Brig. Gen. Samuel W. Crawford. The division of Brig. Gen. Romeyn B. Ayres remained at the Quaker Road crossing of Gravelly Run. Chamberlain received another serious wound on March 29 but remained in the fight.

Report of Brig. Gen. Joshua L. Chamberlain, USA, commanding First Brigade, First Division, Fifth Army Corps, Army of the Potomac

The brigade broke camp on the morning of the 29th ultimo and marched at 6 a.m. by way of Arthur's Swamp and the old stage road and Vaughan road, toward Dinwiddie Court-House; turning to our right, we went into position near the Chappell house. Soon after this we returned to the Vaughan road and moved up the Quaker road in a northerly direction. On reaching Gravelly Run Major-General Griffin directed me to form my brigade in order of battle and advance against some works which were in sight on the opposite bank. . . . Major [Edwin A.] Glenn pushed forward vigorously and drove the enemy's skirmishers out of their works

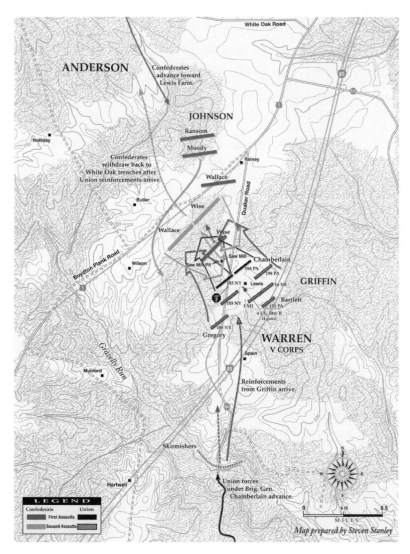

Lewis Farm, March 29, 1865

without any difficulty, and succeeded in pressing them through the woods and as far as the Lewis house. The enemy making considerable show of force in the edge of the woods beyond, I halted Major Glenn and brought my line of battle up to supporting distance. Here I was directed to halt. In a short time I was ordered by General Griffin to resume the advance. There being at that time no firing of any consequence on the skirmish line I brought my line of battle up to that point, reformed it on the buildings, re-enforced the skirmishers . . . and commenced a rapid advance with my whole command. The skirmishers reached the edge of [the] woods before the firing became at all severe. I was exceedingly anxious that the troops should gain the cover of the woods before receiving the shock of the fire, but the obstacles to be overcome were so great that this could not be fully accomplished, and my men were obliged to gain the woods against a heavy fire. They advanced, however, with great steadiness and drove the enemy from their position and far into the woods.

It was not long, however, before another attack was made upon us, evidently by a greatly superior force, and we became completely enveloped in a withering fire. We replied with spirit and persistency, holding our ground, taking rather the defensive at this stage of the action. In the course of half an hour my left became so heavily pressed that it gradually gave way, and at last was fairly turned, and driven entirely out of the woods to a position parallel with the road by which we advanced. This position could not be held ten minutes, and nothing but the most active exertions of field and staff officers kept the men where they were. . . . I was assured by Major-General Griffin, who was on the line, that if we would hold on five minutes he could bring up the artillery. Upon this I succeeded in rallying the men, and they once more gained the woods. Battery B of the Fourth U.S. Artillery now came into position and opened a most effective fire. By this assistance we held our line until the enemy fell heavily upon our right and center, and my men being by this time out of ammunition, many of them absolutely without a cartridge, began to yield ground. Seeing that this was inevitable I dispatched an aide to General [Edgar M.] Gregory [commander, Second Brigade] asking him for a regiment, and at the same time Major-General Griffin ordered up three regiments of the Third Brigade. These regiments came promptly to our assistance. . . .

This action lasted nearly two hours before any support reached us. I need not speak of the severity of the engagement . . . but I may be permitted to mention the fact that more than 400 of my men and 18 officers killed and wounded marked our line with too painful destructiveness. [*O.R.*, XLVI, part 1, pp. 847–848.]

Report of Maj. Gen. Bushrod Johnson, CSA, commanding Division, Anderson's Corps, Army of Northern Virginia

On Wednesday, the 29th of March, 1865, the cavalry having reported the enemy advancing in force with cavalry, artillery, and infantry on the Quaker (or military) road, west of Hatcher's Run, I was ordered by Lieut. Gen. *R. H. Anderson* to move my command down the road, attack them, and drive them back to the Vaughan road. . . . I advanced [Brig. Gen. *Henry A.*] *Wise's* brigade in line of battle, stretching across the Quaker road, and moved [Brig. Gen. *William H.*] *Wallace's*, [Brig. Gen. *Young M.*] *Moody's*, and [Brig. Gen. *Matthew W.*] *Ransom's* brigades, in the order named, by the flank in rear of *Wise's* brigade. Upon entering the skirts of the woods, south of the forks of the Boydton plank road and the Quaker road, *Wise's* brigade came under the fire of the enemy's skirmishers and charged forward until they encountered a line of battle posted with artillery. The engagement was commenced at 3.20 p.m. In a few moments a portion of *Wise's* brigade, on the Quaker road, was driven back from the woods to the open ground, and, by direction of Lieutenant-General *Anderson*, who had arrived on the ground about the time of the charge of *Wise's* brigade, I sent forward *Wallace's* brigade to the support of the part of *Wise's* brigade still contesting the ground with the enemy. Finding that the left of *Wise's* brigade had encountered a battery, which they had well-nigh captured, and were very hardly pressed, I directed Brigadier-General *Moody* to move his brigade up on the left of *Wise's* and *Wallace's*, but before this movement could be carried out, *Wallace's* brigade, with *Wise's*, was repulsed by a heavy fire from the left. Lieutenant-General *Anderson* now directed my division to be withdrawn, at about 5 p.m., and to take position across the Boydton plank road in the margin of the woods north and east of the Bevill house. In this position we remained until dusk, when . . . pickets were left in front and division retired into the breastworks adjacent to Burgess' Mill and west of Hatcher's Run. Our losses were about 250 men, mainly from *Wise's* and *Wallace's* brigades. [*O.R.*, XLVI, part 1, pp. 1286–1287.]

Brig. Gen. Joshua L. Chamberlain (USAMHI)

Return to your vehicle, and continue north along Quaker Road for 0.8 mile. When the road ends at U.S. Route 1, the Boydton Plank Road, turn right. Prepare to make a left turn in 0.8 mile onto State Route 613, the White Oak Road. Travel 1.6 miles to the intersection with State Route 631, Claiborne Road, and turn right, then immediately right into the gravel parking lot for the White Oak Road Battlefield. Leave your vehicle and walk over to White Oak Road, facing south across the road.

STOP 3: WHITE OAK ROAD

You are standing at the western end of the 30-mile Confederate defensive ring around Petersburg. To your left, on the north side of the road, are remnants of the Southern entrenchments. At this road intersection, the line angled northward along Claiborne Road to Hatcher's Run. The Civil War Trust has created a short hiking trail across a portion of the White Oak Road battlefield. To take this tour, follow the interpreted walking trail that leads eastward out of the parking area and crosses White Oak Road. Even though the terrain is now heavily forested, the walk south of White Oak Road affords some sense of the commanding position of the Confederate entrenchments in this area and provides excellent views of the strength of this defensive position. There is a pronounced downhill slope toward Gravelly Run; the troops of the Fifth Corps attacked uphill toward *Richard H. Anderson's* lines, which in this area conformed to the road trace. It is recommended that you read the selections for this stand from your position at the road, taking the hiking trail if time and interest permit.

Possession of White Oak Road was critical for the Confederates. It served as a major east-west line of communication along the defensive front, connecting the Confederate extreme right flank near Five Forks and the South Side Railroad with the defensive positions along Hatcher's Run. Once Sheridan's cavalry secured possession of Dinwiddie Court-House on March 29 and prepared to move northwest, the next step was for Warren's Fifth Corps to attack north and seize a position on the White Oak Road. *Anderson* stood in the way with his provisional corps.

Recognizing the critical nature of the situation on March 31, *Robert E. Lee* arrived at the entrenchments here early in the morning. Seeing that the Fifth Corps's left flank was exposed in the low ground south of White Oak Road, he planned a counterattack involving the four brigades of [Brig. Gen.] *Henry A. Wise*, [Brig. Gen.] *Young M. Moody*, [Brig. Gen.] *Eppa Hunton*, and [Brig. Gen.] *Samuel McGowan*. Maj. Gen. *Bushrod Johnson* was in command of the attack, under the supervision of *Anderson*, his corps commander.

At 10:30 a.m., soldiers of Ayres's Fifth Corps division set off for the Federal advance, reaching a position 50 yards south of White Oak Road and away to the west (your right) beyond the Claiborne Road intersection. The Federals began digging hasty entrenchments as they came into the open ground. Ayres had his brigades arranged *en echelon* to the right as he advanced, creating an opportunity for

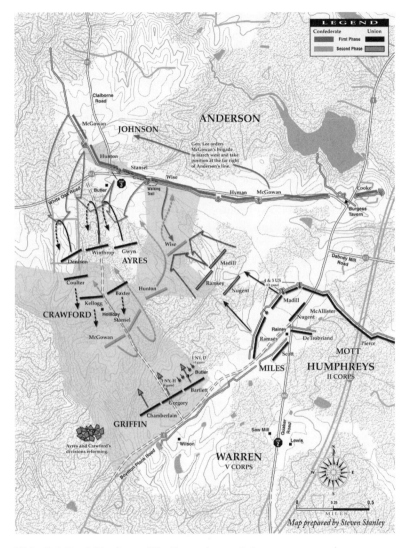

White Oak Road, March 31, 1865: First and second phases

the Confederate counterattack, which began at virtually the same time. The Confederate line burst from the woods and overlapped the left flank of the Federals, breaking three successive lines and driving the divisions of Ayres and Crawford back upon their supports at Gravelly Run. *Johnson's* troops began reversing the temporary Federal entrenchments so that they faced south. Griffin, reinforced by the Second Corps divisions commanded by Brig. Gens. Nelson Miles and Gershom Mott, picked up the remnants of Crawford's and Ayres's divisions and counterattacked from the Boydton Plank Road, with Chamberlain's brigade once again in the lead, reaching the White Oak Road west of Claiborne Road late in the afternoon. *Anderson* remained in the defensive lines where you are standing now, but the White Oak Road was effectively cut, preventing his direct link-up with *Pickett,* who was fortifying the Five Forks position a few miles to the west. This sharp fight, which cost the Federals almost 2,000 casualties and the Confederates more than 800, split *Lee's* front southwest of Petersburg and set the conditions for the disastrous defeat at Five Forks the next day.

Warren's conduct of this battle added to Grant's and Meade's growing dissatisfaction with the Fifth Corps commander. By the spring of 1865, Grant had developed an intense frustration with Warren and what he perceived to be his argumentative, cautious approach to battle command. The seeds of this frustration had been planted as far back as the fall of 1863, when, as the temporary commander of the Second Corps following Maj. Gen. Winfield S. Hancock's wounding at Gettysburg, Warren refused to attack prepared Confederate positions at Mine Run. Even though Warren was undoubtedly correct in this situation, he developed a characteristic that Grant described later in his memoirs. Warren, he declared, "could see every danger at a glance before he had encountered it. He would not only make preparations to meet the danger which might occur, but he would inform his commanding officer what others should do while he was executing his move" (Grant, *Personal Memoirs*).

Brig. Gen. Alexander Webb, USA, Chief of Staff, Army of the Potomac, to Maj. Gen. Gouverneur K. Warren, 10:30 a.m., March 31, 1865

Your dispatch giving Ayres' position is received. General Meade directs that should you determine by your reconnaissance that you can get possession of and hold the White Oak road you are to do so, notwithstanding the order to suspend operations today. [*O.R.*, XLVI, part 1, p. 813.]

Report of Major General Warren, continued

General [Frederic] Winthrop, with his brigade, of General Ayres' division, advanced about 10.30 a.m. and was repulsed, and simultaneously an attack which had been preparing against General Ayres was made by the enemy in heavy force, both from the north and west, and he was forced back. General Ayres and General Crawford did all that was in their power to stay the enemy. I hastened toward the point of attack, but on arriving near General Crawford's division it was also being forced back, and all our efforts to hold the men in the woods were unavailing. I am unable to give a more detailed account of this affair, not having reports of it from General Ayres and General Crawford. I then directed the formation of General Griffin's division along the bank of Gravelly Run, with [Capt. Charles E.] Mink's battery on his right. General Crawford's and General Ayres' divisions formed behind and in this line, and many of them took part in the engagement there. There Colonel [William] Sergeant, of the Two hundred and tenth Pennsylvania Volunteers, of Ayres' division, was mortally wounded.

Severe fighting at the creek now ensued and the advance of the enemy [was] completely checked.

I had early in these occurrences sent word of them to General Humphreys, on my right. He at once ordered up General Miles' division on my right, and a brigade of this advanced gallantly against the enemy, but was at first driven back.

The temporary result of this attack by the enemy was such as different portions of our army had experienced on many former occasions in taking up new and extended lines, but our loss was not great, and was probably quite equaled by the enemy.

The prospect of fighting the enemy outside of his breastworks, instead of having to assail him behind his defenses and through his obstructions, was one sufficiently animating to our hopes to more than compensate for the partial reverse we had sustained, and preparations were at once instituted for an advance with the whole corps. [*O.R.*, XLVI, part 1, pp. 814–815.]

Report of Bvt. Maj. Gen. Romeyn B. Ayres, USA, commanding Second Division, Fifth Army Corps, Army of the Potomac

I took up a position in a field lying east of Dabney's and extending to the White Oak road, posting the Second Brigade on the left and facing the Dabney place. Soon after I received from the corps commander an order . . . to take the White Oak road and intrench a brigade upon it. . . . I ordered forward the First Brigade, supported on the right by the Third. As the troops arrived within about fifty yards of the White Oak road the enemy's lines of battle rose up in the woods and moved forward across the road in the open. I saw at once that they had four or five to my one. The First Brigade was at once faced about (I presume by General Winthrop's order) and marched back across the field in good order. I expected to form my lines along the southern line of the field and fight it out, but the supports could not be held. This was partly due to the fact that the enemy sent a division past Dabney's and attacked my left at the same time that the front attack was made. I then endeavored to form the troops along a ravine which ran north and south along the eastern edge of the field, but in this I also failed. The result was that the troops fell back to the position occupied the day before, behind the swamp, and where the First Division, with artillery, was in line of battle. My three brigade commanders deserve credit for extricating their little brigades from their difficult positions, threatened by overwhelming numbers.

. . . Later in the day the entire corps moved forward over the field on the White Oak road finding no obstacle but some of the enemy's skirmishers, his main body having moved off. [*O.R.*, XLVI, part 1, pp. 868–869.]

Report of Bvt. Maj. Gen. Charles Griffin, USA, commanding First Division, Fifth Corps, Army of the Potomac

March 31, the division was relieved by the Second Corps, and directed to move to the left and mass upon the ground the Second Division had previously occupied. About 11 a.m., heavy musketry being heard in our front toward the White Oak road, the division was immediately put in motion in the direction of the firing, and had scarcely reached the bank of Gravelly Run when it was met by the Third Division running to the rear in a most demoralized and disorganized condition, soon after followed by the Second Division. The First Division was formed in line of battle along the bank of the run with the utmost difficulty, and two batteries placed in position, when the enemy pursuing our troops were checked and driven back. The command was then pushed across the run, supported by the Second and Third Divisions, and the First Brigade, leading, regained the position first taken by the troops in the morning. The enemy demonstrating in his rifle-pits,

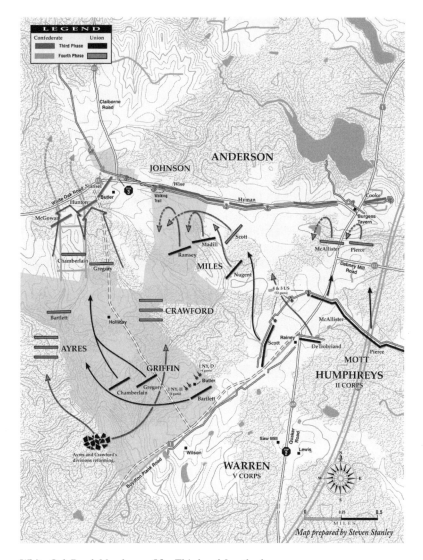

White Oak Road, March 31, 1865: Third and fourth phases

still in our front, General Chamberlain pushed boldly forward, carrying them in a handsome manner, taking one flag and about 135 prisoners, and gaining possession of the White Oak road. [*O.R.*, XLVI, part 1, p. 846.]

Report of Maj. Gen. Bushrod Johnson, CSA, commanding Division, Anderson's Corps, Army of Northern Virginia

At about 11 a.m. on the 31st of March, finding the enemy in two lines in the field west of Halter Butler's house, I at once ordered out *Hunton's* brigade, and notified Lieutenant-General *Anderson* and Major-General [*Henry*] *Heth* that I would make an attack as soon as I could form my line of battle. While forming this line, Brigadier-General *McGowan*, of [Maj. Gen. *Cadmus*] *Wilcox's* division, reported to me with his brigade. My line was formed with *McGowan's* brigade on the right, *Moody's* brigade, commanded by Colonel [*Martin L.*] *Stansel*, of the Forty-first Alabama Regiment, in the center, and *Hunton's* brigade on the left.

Having ascertained that an admirable movement might be made on the enemy's left flank, I had ordered *McGowan's* brigade to move behind a woods for that purpose; but this movement had only commenced when I discovered that the enemy were advancing. I immediately ordered my command to advance and meet the enemy's attack. The movement was handsomely and gallantly made, and Brigadier-General *McGowan*, in advancing, moved on the enemy's flank, as proposed, for a preparatory movement. The enemy's line immediately gave way, and my command followed up their advantage in a most spirited manner. By 2 p.m. the enemy were driven about one mile and a half to a position west of a branch of Gravelly Run, which skirts the Boydton road in vicinity of the bridge on that road over the latter stream. In this position the enemy's line, in strong force, was formed on vantage ground. During this advance *Wise's* brigade was moved out on the left of *Hunton's* brigade, by order of General *Lee*, and gallantly participated in the fight; but encountering a superior force, and having its left flank exposed, its left was driven back. . . . The next brigade on the right, that of General *Hunton*, repulsed (with the aid of the right of *Wise's* brigade) three charges by the enemy. . . . Our troops persistently continued to fight, but were unable to advance, and orders were first sent to hold the position they had gained. It, however, became evident that our troops were being exhausted, and needed re-enforcements, of which there was none available. Lieutenant-General *Anderson* now ordered my command to be withdrawn to the enemy's line of rifle-pits, thrown up by his skirmishers south of the White Oak road during the previous night. . . . The enemy's attack fell with force upon this angle, and carried it, and all our forces were then, at about 5 p.m., drawn into the main breast-works, where they lay during the night, with pickets well out on the White Oak road and to the right and left of it. The losses of the enemy were heavy, including about 470 prisoners. Our losses were about 800, including killed, wounded, and prisoners. [*O.R.*, XLVI, part 1, pp. 1287–1288.]

Memoir of Lt. J. F. J. Caldwell, CSA, First South Carolina Volunteer Infantry

But we drove through the woods, moved upon the Federal skirmishers, broke and routed them, and, swinging round the right of the brigade, so as to enfilade the Federal line, poured such volleys of musketry along their ranks as speedily set them flying. . . . We cheered continuously, and followed up the retreating enemy, firing the most accurate volleys, and preserving the most perfect order I ever witnessed in a charge. . . . They might oppose some effectual barrier to the unaided advance of the left of the Confederate force, but soon the right of our brigade would swing upon the flank and roll them back with slaughter. . . . I have no idea that the brigade ever killed more men, even in the most sanguinary engagements, than it did this day. Our loss was slight, the furious volleys of the enemy generally passing overhead. [J. F. J. Caldwell, *The History of a Brigade of South Carolinians Known First as "Gregg's," and Subsequently as "McGowan's Brigade"* (Philadelphia: King and Baird, 1866), pp. 272–273.]

When you have finished exploring the White Oak Road battlefield, return to your vehicle. Drive out of the parking area, and turn left on Claiborne Road, then left again on White Oak Road. Proceed 1.6 miles to Boydton Plank Road, and turn right to proceed for 6.2 miles to Dinwiddie Court-House. At 2.3 miles from the turn onto U.S. 1, you will cross Gravelly Run, which in March 1865 was a much more significant obstacle than it is today. Upon entering Dinwiddie, turn left onto Sycamore Drive, and park in the parking area on your immediate right. Walk across Sycamore Drive to the monument in front of the historic Dinwiddie Court-House Building.

STOP 4: DINWIDDIE COURT-HOUSE

SHERIDAN'S CAVALRY, 29–31 MARCH 1865

As Warren's Fifth Corps moved northwest along the Vaughan Road/Quaker Road axis, seizing the Boydton Plank Road and the White Oak Road, Sheridan's cavalry operated to Warren's west and south. Sheridan's objective was the Five Forks intersection, a few miles south of the South Side Railroad, but in the course of March 31 he ran into *Pickett's* force of infantry and cavalry. A spirited fight took place in the marshy creek beds west of the Boydton Plank Road, and Sheridan was hard-pressed to maintain possession of Dinwiddie Court-House, but as darkness fell on March 31, he and his men held. Torrential rains during the night raised Gravelly Run to the point that a pontoon bridge was required to span it. Meade ordered Warren to march to Sheridan's, initiating a controversy that led to Warren's removal from command on April 1.

Lieutenant General Grant to Maj. Gen. Sheridan, USA, commanding Cavalry Corps, Army of the Potomac, March 30

If your situation in the morning is such as to justify the belief that you can turn the enemy's right with the assistance of a corps of infantry, entirely detached from the balance of the army, I will so detach the Fifth Corps, and place the whole under your command for the operation. Let me know as early in the morning as you can your judgment in the matter, and I will make the necessary orders. Orders have been given Ord, Wright, and Parke to be ready to assault at daylight to-morrow morning. They will not make the assault, however, without further direction. The giving of this order will depend upon receiving confirmation of the withdrawal of a part of the enemy's forces on their front. If this attempt is made it will not be advisable to be detaching troops at such a distance from the field of operations. If the assault is not ordered in the morning, then it can be directed at such time as to come in co-operation with you on the left. *Pickett's* entire division cannot be in front of your cavalry. Deserters from [Brig. Gen. *George H.*] *Steuart's* brigade, of that division, came into Humphreys' front this afternoon. [*O.R.*, XLVI, part 3, p. 325.]

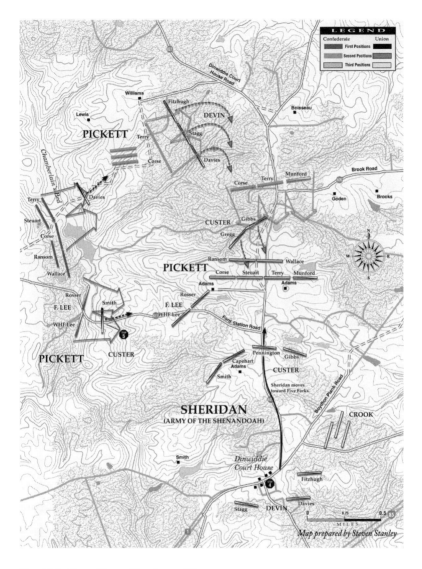

Dinwiddie Court-House, March 31, 1865

Maj. Gen. Philip H. Sheridan, Lt. Col. James W. Forsyth, Maj. Gen. Wesley Merritt,
Brig. Gen. Thomas C. Devin, Maj. Gen. George A. Custer (USAMHI)

Report of Maj. Gen. Philip H. Sheridan, USA, commanding Cavalry Corps, Army of the Potomac

Next morning, March 31, General [Wesley] Merritt advanced
toward the Five Forks with the First Division, and, meeting with
considerable opposition, General [Henry E.] Davies' brigade, of
[Maj. Gen. George] Crook's division, was ordered to join him,
while General Crook, advancing on the left with the two other brigades of his division, encountered the enemy's cavalry at Chamberlain's Creek, at a point a little north and west of Dinwiddie,
making demonstrations to cross. [Brig. Gen. Charles H.] Smith's
brigade was ordered to hold them in check, and [Col. J. Irvin]
Gregg's brigade to a position on his right. The advance of the First
Division got possession of the Five Forks, but in the meantime
the Fifth Army Corps, which had advanced toward the White Oak
road from the Vaughan road, was attacked and driven back, and
withdrawing from that point, this force of the enemy marched
rapidly from the front of the Fifth Corps to the Five Forks, driving

in our cavalry advance, and moving down on roads west of Chamberlain's Creek, attacked General Smith's brigade, but were unable to force his position. Abandoning the attempt to cross in his front, this force of the enemy's infantry succeeded in effecting a crossing higher up the creek, striking General Davies' brigade, of the Second Division, which after a gallant fight, was forced back upon the left flank of the First Division, thus partially isolating all this force from my main line covering Dinwiddie Court-House. Orders were at once given to General Merritt to cross this detached force over to the Boydton plank road and march down to Dinwiddie Court-House and come into the line of battle.

The enemy, deceived by this movement, followed it up rapidly, making a left wheel and presenting his rear to my line of battle. When his line was nearly parallel to mine, General [Alfred] Gibbs' brigade, of the First Division, and General Irvin Gregg's brigade, of the Second Division, were ordered to attack at once, and General [George A.] Custer was directed to bring up two of his brigades rapidly, leaving one brigade of his division with the trains, that had not yet reached Dinwiddie Court-House. In the gallant attack made by Gibbs and Gregg the enemy's wounded fell into our hands, and he was forced to face by the rear rank and give up his movement, which, if continued, would have taken in flank and rear the infantry line of the Army of the Potomac. When the enemy had faced to meet this attack, a very obstinate and handsomely contested battle ensued, in which, with all his cavalry and two divisions of infantry, the enemy was unable to drive five brigades of our cavalry, dismounted, from an open plain in front of Dinwiddie Court-House. As the enemy's infantry advanced to the attack, our cavalry threw up slight breast-works of rails at some points along our lines, and when the enemy attempted to force this position, they were handsomely repulsed and gave up the attempt to gain possession of the Court-House. It was after dark when the firing ceased, and the enemy lay on their arms that night not more than 100 yards in front of our lines. . . .

During the night of the 31st of March my headquarters were at Dinwiddie Court-House, and the lieutenant-general notified me that Fifth Corps would report to me and should reach me by midnight. This corps had been offered to me on the 30th instant, but very much desiring the Sixth Corps, which had been with me in the Shenandoah Valley, I asked for it, but on account of the delay which would occur in moving that corps from its position in the lines in front of Petersburg it could not be sent me. . . . I understood that the Fifth Corps, when ordered to report to me, was in position near S. Dabney's house, in the angle between the Boydton road and the Five Forks road. Had General Warren moved according to the expectations of the lieutenant-general, there would appear to have been but little chance for the escape of the enemy's infantry in front of Dinwiddie Court-House. Ayres' division moved down the Boydton plank road during the night, and in the morning moved west by R. Boisseau's house, striking the Five Forks road about two miles and a half north of Dinwiddie Court-House. General Warren, with Griffin and Crawford's divisions, moved down the road by Crump's house, coming into the Five Forks road near J. Boisseau's house between 7 and 8 o'clock on the morning of the first of April. Meantime I moved my cavalry force at daylight against the enemy's lines in my front, which gave way rapidly, moving off by the right flank, and crossing Chamberlain's Creek. . . .

The following were the instructions sent to General Warren:

CAVALRY HEADQUARTERS
Dinwiddie Court-House, April 1, 1865—3 a.m.
Major-General Warren, Commanding Fifth Army Corps:

I am holding in front of Dinwiddie Court-House, on the road leading to Five Forks, for three-quarters of a mile, with General Custer's division. The enemy are in his immediate front, lying so as to cover the road just this side of A. Adams' house, which leads out across Chamberlain's bed or run. I understand you have a division at J. Boisseau's; if so, you are in rear of the enemy's line and almost on his flanks. I will hold on here. Possibly they may attack Custer at daylight; if so, attack instantly and in full force. Attack at daylight tomorrow, and I will make an effort to get the road this side of Adams' house, and if I do you can capture the whole of them. Any force moving down the road I am holding, or on the White Oak road, will be in the enemy's rear, and in all probability get any force that may escape you by a flank attack. Do not fear my leaving here. If the enemy remains I shall fight at daylight.

P. H. SHERIDAN
Major-General.

. . . I then determined that I would drive the enemy with the cavalry to the Five Forks, press them inside of their works, and make a feint to turn their right flank, and meanwhile quietly move up the Fifth Corps with a view to attacking their left flank, crush the whole force, if possible, and drive westward those who might escape, thus isolating them from their army at Petersburg. [*O.R.*, XLVI, part 1, pp. 1102–1104.]

Report of Maj. Gen. George E. Pickett, CSA, commanding Division, First Corps, Army of Northern Virginia

On March 29, a telegram from Headquarters, Army of Northern Virginia, was received at my Headquarters, then at Swift Creek, ordering me to proceed with the two brigades ([Brig. Gen. *Montgomery D.*] *Corse's* and [Brig. Gen. *William Richard*] *Terry's*) at that point to cross the Appomattox and take the cars on the South Side Railroad for Sutherland's Station. *Steuart's* Brigade, then in position in front of Petersburg, [was] to join me in [the movement]. [Brig. Gen. *Eppa*] *Hunton's* Brigade was at this time on the North Side of the James.

Accordingly the column was put in motion, the three brigades reaching Sutherland's about 9 p.m. Shortly afterward came an order from Lieutenant-General *Anderson* to come on to the White Oak Road and take position on the right of Major-General *Bushrod Johnson's* Division. This was done by daybreak through a drenching rain, the three brigades extending some distance up the road. The Commander-in-Chief, about 12 m. in the day, ordered me to move on with my three brigades and two brigades under command of Brigadier-General [*Matthew W.*] *Ransom* (his own and *Wallace's*) and a battery of artillery, under Colonel [*William J.*] *Pegram*, to the Five Forks, where Major-General [*Fitzhugh*] *Lee* was with his division of cavalry, and at which point Major General [*W. H. F.*] *Lee* and [Brig. Gen. *Thomas L.*] *Rosser* were to join him with their divisions.

The march was necessarily slow on account of the continued skirmishing with the enemy's cavalry, both in front and flank. The enemy at one time charged in on the wagon train but were driven off by *Ransom*. In front we had to drive the enemy out of the way nearly the whole distance until we joined *Fitz Lee* at the Five Forks about sunset.

I learned then that parts of the ordnance train had been turned back, it was said, by orders of the Commander-in-Chief. General *Ransom* had his ordnance wagons and on these we had to depend for supplying the whole command in the engagements that followed. I was about to push on toward Dinwiddie

Court-House when upon consultation with General *Fitz Lee* (the other cavalry not having joined him and as it was so nearly dark, the men much in need of rest—having been marching nearly continuously for eighteen hours) I determined merely to throw out a couple of brigades on the Court-House Road so as to keep the enemy at a respectable distance during the night. This was done, *Corse* and *Terry* advancing some three-quarters of a mile, driving the enemy's cavalry who, however, being dismounted and armed with repeating rifles, made quite a stout little fight. [*O.R. Supplement*, VII, pp. 779–781.]

Report of Maj. Gen. Fitzhugh Lee, CSA, commanding Cavalry Corps, Army of Northern Virginia

On the 28th of March my division moved from its position on the extreme left of our lines in front of Richmond, on the north side of the James River, marched to Petersburg and up the South Side Railroad, reaching Sutherland's Station, nineteen miles from Petersburg, on the 29th. In compliance with verbal instructions received . . . I marched the next day (30th) toward Dinwiddie Court-House, via Five Forks, to watch and counteract the operations threatened by the massing of the Federal cavalry at Dinwiddie Court-House under Sheridan. After passing Five Forks a portion of the enemy's cavalry were encountered with success, and driven back upon their large reserves near the Court-House. Night put an end to further operations, and my division was encamped in the vicinity of Five Forks. My loss, though slight, included Brig. Gen. *W. H. Payne*, among the wounded; and the loss of the services of this bold, capable officer was severely felt in all subsequent movements. I was joined during the evening by the divisions of Maj. Gens. *W. H. F. Lee* and *Rosser*, and by order of the commanding general, took command of the Cavalry Corps.

On the 31st of March, *Pickett* coming up with five small brigades of infantry, we attacked the very large force of the enemy's cavalry in our front at Five Forks, killed and wounded many, captured over 100 prisoners, and drove them to within half a mile of Dinwiddie Court-House. [Maj. Gen. *Thomas T.*] *Munford*, in command of my old division, held our lines in front of the enemy's position, whilst the remaining two divisions of cavalry, preceding the infantry, moved by a concealed wooded road to turn and attack their flank. A short stream [Chamberlain's Bed], strongly defended at its crossing, presented an unexpected obstacle to the sudden attack contemplated. It was finally carried, however, with loss in *W. H. F. Lee's* and *Rosser's* divisions. *Munford*, attacking about the same time, also successfully carried the temporary works thrown up in his front, and by a gallant advance again united his command with the other divisions. Darkness put an end to our further advance. [*O.R.*, XLVI, part 1, pp. 1298–1299.]

During your drive to Dinwiddie from the White Oak Road battlefield, at a point 2.3 miles from turning onto Boydton Plank Road, you crossed Gravelly Run. On your left before the bridge was "Evergreen," the home of a Mrs. Butler, as sketched by Warren in his report of the campaign. Evergreen served as Warren's headquarters starting the night of March 29, after the fight at the Lewis Farm. Gravelly Run appears now to be an inconsequential stream, but in March 1865 two days of heavy rain had turned it into a 40-foot-wide, deep, and fast-moving obstacle to troop movement. The bridge at this site was out. This road represented the most direct route from the Fifth Corps position after the fighting at White Oak Road to Sheridan's position at Dinwiddie Court-House. Warren was relieved of command of Fifth Corps on April 1, largely because of a perceived lack of energy in supporting Sheridan. A postwar court of inquiry largely exonerated Warren for his conduct at Five Forks, though its findings were not published until after the general's death in 1882.

Report of Major General Warren, continued

At 5.15 p.m. I received the following from General Webb . . . which directed what before had only been suggested:

> The major-general commanding directs that you push a brigade down the White Oak road, to open it for General Sheridan, and support the same, if necessary.

About 6.30 p.m. I received the following from General Webb:

> A staff officer of General Merritt has made a report that the enemy has penetrated between Sheridan's main command and your position. This is a portion of *Pickett's* division. Let the force ordered to move out the White Oak road move down the Boydton plank road as promptly as possible.

It was then nearly dark. . . . I then gave directions to secure the position we had gained, by intrenching, and proceeded with my staff back about two miles to the Boydton plank road, at which place I could communicate by telegraph with General Meade during the night. General Meade's headquarters were distant four miles and a half . . . General Sheridan's at Dinwiddie Court House, distant five miles and a half, and separated from me by a stream not fordable for infantry, where it crossed the Boydton plank road, and the bridge broken down . . .

At 9.17 p.m. I received the following by telegraph dispatch, written by General Webb at 9 p.m.:

> You will, by the direction of the major-general commanding, draw back at once to your position within the Boydton plank road. Send a division down to Dinwiddie Court-House to report to General Sheridan. This division will go down the Boydton plank road. Send Griffin's division. General Humphreys will hold to Mrs. Butler's.

At 9.50 p.m. I received by telegraph the following from General Webb, written 9.20 p.m.:

> The division to be sent to Sheridan will start at once. You are to be held free to act within the Boydton plank road. General Humphreys will hold the road and the return [at White Oak Road].

To this I immediately replied:

> Your dispatch of 9.20 is just received. . . . The bridge is broken on the plank road, and will take I hardly know how long to make practicable for infantry. I sent an officer to examine it as soon as your first order was received. He now reports it not fordable for infantry. It requires a span of forty feet to complete the bridge, and the stream is too deep to ford. Nevertheless, I will use everything I can get to make it passable by the time General Griffin's division reaches it.

> General Griffin's division, in addition to the delay of assembling General [Joseph J.] Bartlett's brigade, had to withdraw his picket-line in front of the enemy, and if he moved first, the others, pending it, had to relieve his picket line.

Over the next two hours, Warren made the decision to replace Griffin's division with Ayres's.

> . . . I had no pontoons with me now. The supply with which I had started on the 29th had been used. . . . I directed a house to be torn to pieces to supply materials. . . . It must be remembered that our troops, so near the enemy, could not be roused by drums and bugles and loud commands, but each order had to be

communicated from each commander to his subordinate—from the general till it reached the non-commissioned officers, which latter could only arouse each man by shaking him. The obstacles to overcome in carrying out so many orders and changes of orders in the darkness of a stormy, starless night, when the moon had set, requires a statement of them in detail. . . .

At 11:45 p.m., Meade inquired whether Warren could move his force to Dinwiddie via the Quaker Road; Warren judged this route too long to be practicable (10 miles instead of 5) and disregarded the inquiry.

At 2.05 a.m. I learned the following, which I sent General Webb:

> The bridge over Gravelly Run Captain [William] Benyaurd reports now practicable for infantry, and General Ayres advancing across it toward Dinwiddie Court-House. I have given General Ayres orders to report to General Sheridan.

At 4.30 a.m. I received information that General Ayres had communicated with General Sheridan. . . . It will be remembered that General Ayres began to move back from the White Oak road by an order from me, sent at 9.35 p.m., and which was the first intimation of sending troops to General Sheridan. No orders stopped him, nor did anything delay him but physical obstacles, such as the darkness, bad roads, and broken bridge. . . .

This actual trial disposes of the question of the ability of my troops to reach General Sheridan by midnight. It took General Ayres till daybreak. It may be said in support of the "expectations" that the state of this bridge and stream were not known when the expectations were formed, but they should have been, as the route was used for communications between General Grant and General Sheridan the two preceding days. . . . To join General Sheridan by midnight on this route I then had to capture or destroy whatever of this force [*Pickett's* division and the Confederate cavalry] was between me and General Sheridan. Any expectation more unreasonable could not have been formed, nor would I attribute them to any one not wholly ignorant of the true state of the case.

While awaiting with General Griffin for instructions from General Sheridan, who had advanced with the cavalry toward Five Forks, I received, about 9.30 a.m., the following order, written by General Webb, at 6 a.m.:

General Meade directs that in the movements following your junction with General Sheridan you will be under his orders and report to him. Please send in a report of progress. [*O.R.*, XLVI, part 1, pp. 817–826.]

Return to your vehicle. Make a left onto Sycamore Drive and an immediate right back onto U.S. 1. In 0.2 mile, turn left onto Courthouse Road, State Route 627. After 0.9 mile, turn left onto Wilkinson Road, and drive 1.1 miles until you reach the bridge over Chamberlain Run. The best parking place is a small shoulder on the far side of the bridge and on the right side of the road. Be mindful of traffic if you choose to get out of your vehicle at this stop.

Many wartime residents referred to this terrain feature as "Chamberlain's Bed," using a local term for creek. The Union commander in this engagement referred to the creek as "Little Stony Creek."

STOP 5: CHAMBERLAIN'S BED

Pickett attacked at 2 p.m. on March 31 with two wings. Here at Fitzgerald's Ford, the southernmost force was composed of Confederate cavalry under the command of *Robert E. Lee's* nephew, Maj. Gen. *Fitzhugh Lee.* To the north, a force of infantry from the divisions of *Johnson* and *Pickett* forced a crossing at Danse's Ford. The Federal cavalry brigades of Brig. Gen. Henry E. Davies and Col. Charles H. Smith, the former reinforced during the course of the afternoon, put up stout resistance for several hours but eventually retired to Dinwiddie Court-House as an additional Confederate cavalry brigade under Brig. Gen. *Thomas T. Munford* moved south from Five Forks and struck the right flank of Davies's position as he fell back. *Pickett's* entire force then advanced to within a mile of Dinwiddie Court-House before darkness fell. However, at the conclusion of the fighting on March 31, the Federals certainly held the upper hand, possessing Boydton Plank Road and White Oak Road and occupying a dangerous position on the flank and rear of *Pickett's* force. Ayres's division of Fifth Corps arrived at Dinwiddie Court-House at dawn on April 1, consolidating the position.

Report of Bvt. Brig. Gen. Charles H. Smith, USA, commanding Third Brigade, Second Cavalry Division, Army of the Potomac

At 10.30 a.m. the 31st, the Second New York Mounted Rifles, on picket, were attacked and the brigade was moved out for support. The Second New York Mounted Rifles and Sixth Ohio

Cavalry were ordered to dismount and take position on the left bank of Little Stony Creek at which the enemy seemed to retire. One battalion of the First Maine was ordered to cross the creek and reconnoiter for the enemy. It effected a crossing without opposition, but as soon as it deployed and began to advance it was met by strong lines of the enemy, both mounted and dismounted, and driven back in confusion, the men seeking refuge among the led horses and fording the stream up to their necks. The enemy pursued in hot haste, plunged into the stream in heavy force, both mounted and dismounted, with such recklessness that some were drowned, drove back the two regiments posted on the bank and effected a lodgment on our side. At this juncture the two remaining battalions of the First Maine and the Thirteenth Ohio were ordered to dismount and deploy, the First Maine on the left of the road in the open field, the Thirteenth Ohio on the right of the road in the woods. As the line advanced the two regiments that had been driven back rallied, and the whole brigade charged, broke the enemy and drove him in confusion and with considerable loss across the stream. . . .

The entire brigade was then put in position along the bank of the creek dismounted, where it constructed a slight breast-work with rails and such other material as was at its command. At 5.30 p.m. the enemy opened briskly with four pieces of artillery, and the brigade suddenly discovered that it was confronted by *Pickett's* division of infantry. The brigade maintained its ground under the hottest fire of which the enemy was capable, losing heavily all the while, till nearly dark, when it ran entirely out of ammunition, in consequence of the train being delayed by the bad roads, and was forced to fall back to the main road leading from Dinwiddie Court-House to Five Forks, where it reformed and intimidated the advance of the enemy by presenting a good front, without a cartridge. Had a less determined resistance been made on the bank of the creek, and the strong force of the enemy been allowed to gain possession of the main road above referred to, the result must have proved quite disastrous to our cause that day. [*O.R.*, XLVI, part 1, pp. 1156–1157.]

Report of Maj. Gen. George Pickett, CSA, commanding Division, First Corps, Army of Northern Virginia

It rained throughout the night and up to about 12 the next day. General *Fitz Lee's* scouts and guides could not find out exactly the enemy's strength, but from the prisoners taken up to this time I knew we had no infantry in our front. He discovered at daylight that the enemy were pretty strongly posted in the Court-House Road, having quite a good position.

The rest of the cavalry having gotten up about 10 a.m., I determined to push on a road still further to the right, cross the stream higher up with Generals *W. H. F. Lee's* and *Rosser's* Cavalry and with the infantry, leaving *Fitz Lee's* Division to come up the direct road towards the Court-House as we advanced on the right. The rain had swollen the streams very much, which was the chief reason for the delay in the cavalry coming up.

General *W. H. F. Lee*, with his division, very gallantly charged over the creek, but the enemy were in too great number, and the infantry not being able to cross at that point (the stream not being fordable) they were compelled to back down. I pushed the infantry across lower down, *Terry's* Brigade leading, Colonel [*Joseph*] *Mayo* [*Jr.*], with the Third Virginia in advance. This regiment suffered a great deal, but the men gallantly dashed over the creek and swamp, killing and capturing, after a sharp engagement, about a hundred of the enemy.

Our whole force then moved on. The enemy in [the] meanwhile, strongly reinforced, made a determined resistance, and it was dark when we arrived within a half mile of the Court-House. *W. H. F. Lee's* cavalry had again crossed at the same point and *Fitz Lee's* Division had come up on the left. This engagement was quite a spirited one, the men and officers behaving most admirably. Our loss was principally confined to *W. H. F. Lee's* Cavalry and *Terry's* and *Corse's* Brigades, among them many valuable officers. The enemy were severely punished—half an hour more of daylight and we would have gotten to the Court-House; as it was, some prisoners were taken belonging to the Fifth Corps (Warren's). [*O.R. Supplement*, VII, pp. 779–781.]

Make a U-turn back onto Wilkinson Road (Route 611), and proceed 1.1 miles to Courthouse Road (Route 627). Turn left onto Courthouse Road, and drive 3.7 miles to the Five Forks Visitor Contact Station on your left. The Contact Station, a satellite of the Petersburg National Battlefield, contains exhibits about the Battle of Five Forks, books and reference materials, Park Service staff, and restrooms. You may also obtain a map of an 8-mile network of walking trails that covers the entire battlefield. The Devin Trail leads from the Contact Station to the Five Forks intersection and involves a 0.9-mile round-trip walk.

STOP 6: THE FEDERAL PLAN, 1 APRIL 1865

FIVE FORKS

On the morning of April 1, Grant sent a short situation update to President Lincoln, who was at the Federal supply depot at City Point. The hard-fought engagements at White Oak Road and Dinwiddie Court-House on March 31 had left *Robert E. Lee's* forces somewhat overextended and given the Federals a distinct opportunity.

Lieutenant General Grant to President Abraham Lincoln, April 1, 1865, 9:15 a.m.

Yesterday, as reported, the left of the Fifth Corps attempted to push north so as to cross the White Oak road about W. Dabney's house, but were driven back. Sheridan at the same time was pushing up the right branch of the two roads from J. Boisseau's north to the same road. He was at the same time holding Dinwiddie Court-House and the line of Chamberlains Creek. He was met by all the enemy's cavalry and four or five brigades of infantry, and gradually forced back until at 8 p.m. last evening he was holding a line from Chamberlains Creek to the Boydton road, probably not more than one mile from the Court-House. After the falling back of two divisions of the Fifth Corps they again pushed forward and gained the position on the White Oak road first sought. Finding, however, the situation Sheridan was in, orders were sent Warren after dark to leave the position he held, and to push two divisions down by J. Boisseau's and one down the Boydton to his relief. I had much hopes of destroying the force detached by the enemy so far to our rear. I have not yet heard the result, but I knew that Sheridan took the offensive this a.m. Ord yesterday pushed the enemy's pickets from the left of his (Ord's) line next to Hatcher's Run, capturing 189 men and two officers, with but very little loss to us. This put Ord so close to the enemy that he cannot put out pickets in front. This morning before day the enemy attempted to drive him from his position, but was repulsed without loss on our side, and leaving over sixty prisoners in our hands. [*O.R.*, XLVI, part 3, p. 393.]

Report of Maj. Gen. George G. Meade, USA, commanding Army of the Potomac

During the night [March 31–April 1], having been directed to send support to Major-General Sheridan at Dinwiddie Court-

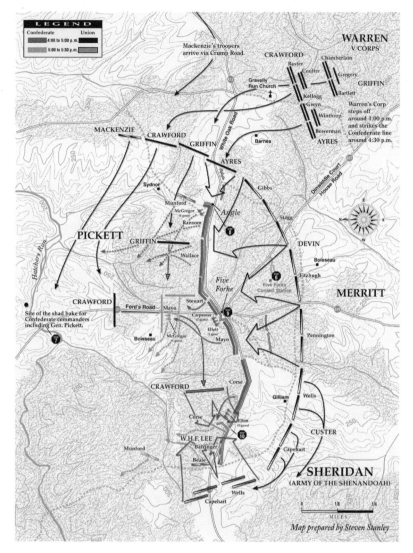

Five Forks, April 1, 1865

House, Major-General Warren was ordered to move with his whole corps, two divisions by the White Oak road and one by the Boydton plank road. Major-General Humphreys was ordered to extend his left as far as practicable consistent with its security.

During the foregoing operations the Sixth and Ninth Corps remained in the lines in front of Petersburg, with orders to watch the enemy closely, and, in the event of the lines in their front being weakened, to attack. [*O.R.*, XLVI, part 1, pp. 602–603.]

Sheridan's plan at Five Forks was to use his cavalry, six brigades under Brig. Gen. George Armstrong Custer and Brig. Gen. Thomas Devin, to demonstrate against the Confederate center and right while Warren's Fifth Corps attacked the Confederate left. The cavalry moved up the Scotts and Courthouse Roads, and the Fifth Corps used the Gravelly Run Church Road to move into position opposite the angle in the Confederate entrenchments. A short skirmish along the White Oak Road east of the entrenchments cleared away the Confederate cavalry screen linking *Pickett* and *Anderson*, making any direct reinforcement of the former impossible. At about 4:30, the attack got under way.

Report of Maj. Gen. Sheridan, continued

I then determined that I would drive the enemy with the cavalry to the Five Forks, press them inside of their works, and make a feint to turn their right flank, and meanwhile quietly move up the Fifth Corps with a view to attacking their left flank, crush the whole force, if possible, and drive westward those who might escape, thus isolating them from their army at Petersburg. Happily, this conception was successfully executed. About this time General Mackenzie's division of cavalry, from the Army of the James, reported to me, and consisted of about 1,000 effective men. I directed General Warren to hold fast at J. Boisseau's house, refresh his men, and be ready to move to the front when required; and General Mackenzie was ordered to rest in front of Dinwiddie Court-House until further orders. Meantime General Merritt's command continued to press the enemy, and by impetuous charges drove them from two lines of temporary works, General Custer guiding his advance on the Widow Gilliam's house and General Devin on the main Five Forks road. The courage displayed by the cavalry officers and men was superb, and about 2 o'clock the enemy was behind his works on the White Oak road, and his skirmish line drawn in.

I then ordered up the Fifth Corps on the main road, and sent Brevet Major [George L.] Gillespie, of the Engineers, to turn the head of the column off on the Gravelly Church road, and put the corps in position on this road obliquely to and at a point but a short distance from the White Oak road and about one mile from the Five Forks. Two divisions of the corps were to form the front line, and one division was to be held in reserve, in column of regiments, opposite the center. I then directed General Merritt to demonstrate as though he was attempting to turn the enemy's right flank, and notified him that the Fifth Corps would strike the enemy's left flank, and ordered that the cavalry should assault the enemy's works as soon as the Fifth Corps became engaged, and that would be determined by the volleys of musketry. I then rode over to where the Fifth Corps was going into position, and found them coming up very slowly. I was exceedingly anxious to attack at once, for the sun was getting low, and we had to fight or go back. It was no place to intrench, and it would have been shameful to have gone back with no results to compensate for the loss of the brave men who had fallen during the day.

In this connection I will say that General Warren did not exert himself to get up his corps as rapidly as he might have done, and his manner gave me the impression that he wished the sun to go down before dispositions for the attack could be completed. As soon as the corps was in position I ordered an advance in the following formation: Ayres' division on the left, in double lines; Crawford's division on the right, in double lines; and Griffin's division in reserve, behind Crawford; and the White Oak road was reached without opposition. [*O.R.*, XLVI, part 1, pp. 1104–1105.]

Report of Major General Warren, continued

The order of General Meade in the morning of April 1, to serve under General Sheridan, gave me much satisfaction at the time of its receipt. I was then completely ignorant of his having a preference for another corps, or the slightest objection to myself. I had never served with him before. When I met him at about 11 a.m. his manner was friendly and cordial. After talking with me a short time at the place where I found him (during which time he was occasionally receiving reports from his cavalry commanders) he mounted and rode off to the front. At 1 p.m. an officer brought me an order to bring up the infantry. I at once dispatched

Col. (now brevet brigadier-general) H. C. Bankhead to give the orders to the division commanders to bring up their commands, specifying the relative order in which I thought they could move the most rapidly. I then went up the Five Forks road, in advance of the infantry, to see General Sheridan, and to inform myself of the use to be made of my troops, so that no time would be lost on their arrival. General Sheridan explained to me the state of affairs and what his plan was for me to do. This I entered upon most cordially. He had placed a staff officer back on the road to mark the point where my command was to turn off. I then rode back to the point indicated, turned up the road (which led by Gravelly Run Church), and examined the ground. . . . General Sheridan's order was to form the whole corps before advancing, so that all of it should move simultaneously. He specially stated that the formation was to be oblique to the road, with the right advanced, with two divisions in front, and the third in reserve behind the right division. . . . Upon examination I determined on an equivalent of three lines of battle, for each of the front divisions, arranged as follows: Each division was to place two brigades in front, each brigade in two lines of battle, and the third brigade in two lines of battle behind the center of the two front lines; the Third Division was to be posted in column of battalions in mass behind the right. To General Ayres I assigned my left; General Crawford, my right; and General Griffin, my reserve, behind the right. In moving they were instructed to keep closed to the left and to preserve their direction in the woods, by keeping the sun, then shining brightly, in the same position over their left shoulders. . . . While the troops were forming I prepared the accompanying sketch, with explanations, for each division commander, and directed them, as far as time would admit, to explain it to the brigade commanders:

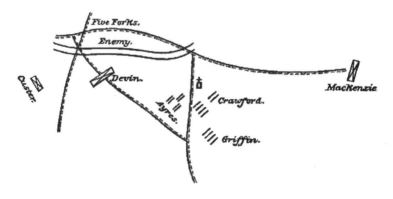

. . . During the formation of my troops I used all the exertions possible to hasten their arrival, and everything was so prepared for them that they marched at once to their assigned position without a halt. . . . His impatience was not greater apparently than I felt myself, and which I strove to repress and prevent any exhibition of, as it would tend to impair confidence in the proposed operations. . . .

Against General Sheridan's most ungenerous statement that I gave the impression that I wanted the sun to go down, I simply place my denial, and trust that my whole conduct in life, and especially in this war, sustains me in it. The sun did not set until two hours and a half after the formation was completed. [*O.R.*, XLVI, part 1, pp. 829–831.]

Return to your vehicle and leave the Contact Station parking lot, turning left onto Courthouse Road. You will arrive at the Five Forks intersection in 0.3 mile. Continue straight ahead on Courthouse (Fords) Road. After 1.0 mile, you will approach a bridge over Hatcher's Run; pull off and park on the right just before the bridge. Get out of your vehicle, taking care to watch for traffic, and walk to the bluff overlooking Hatcher's Run.

STOP 7: THE SHAD BAKE AND THE CONFEDERATE PLAN

One enduring curiosity from the engagement at Five Forks concerns the location and actions of *Pickett* and his subordinate commanders when the battle began. As their men prepared defenses along the White Oak Road to cover Five Forks on April 1, Confederate officers, including *Pickett* and *Fitz Lee*, gathered in the vicinity of Hatcher's Run for a shad bake. The exact site of this gathering has been lost to history but was probably very near where you are now standing.

Pickett's management of affairs on April 1 was driven both by *Robert E. Lee's* orders and the enemy disposition as he understood it. As the fighting at Dinwiddie Court-House ended on the evening of March 31, *Pickett* saw that he was in a dangerous position, with a strong Federal force to his front at the courthouse and an additional enemy force on his left flank and rear between Rowanty Creek and Boydton Plank Road. Accordingly, he began withdrawing to the north at around 4 a.m. Shortly after personally arriving at Five Forks, *Pickett* received a dispatch from *Lee*.

General Robert E. Lee, CSA, commanding Army of Northern Virginia, to Major General Pickett, April 1, 1865

Hold Five Forks at all hazards. Protect road to Ford's Depot and prevent Union forces from striking the South-side Railroad. Regret exceedingly your forced withdrawal, and your inability to hold the advantage you had gained. [LaSalle Corbell Pickett, *Pickett and His Men* (Philadelphia: J.B. Lippincott Company, 1913 [1899]), p. 266.]

Once he reached Five Forks after the withdrawal from Dinwiddie Court-House, *Pickett* responded to *Lee's* message by directing his men to begin constructing a line of earth-and-log breastworks along White Oak Road, extending about 1 mile to the east and west of the intersection. *Pickett* had a force of 9,000 to 10,000 men at his disposal. His three infantry brigades, under Brig. Gens. *Montgomery Corse, William Terry,* and *George Steuart,* augmented by two of *Bushrod Johnson's* brigades under Brig. Gens. *William Wallace* and *Matthew Ransom,* manned the defensive line from west to east. Two of Maj. Gen. *W. H. F. "Rooney" Lee's* three cavalry brigades protected the Confederate right flank at the end of the line opposite "Burnt Quarter," the Gilliam plantation, while the third occupied the 4-mile gap between Five Forks and the White Oak Road entrenchments. Maj. Gen. *Thomas T. Munford's* cavalry division provided security on the Confederate left flank. Col. *William J. Pegram* positioned three guns at the intersection and three more at the Confederate right flank; Capt. *William McGregor's* battery supported *Ransom* on the left. The Confederate supply wagons remained north of Hatcher's Run along Fords Road, guarded by Maj. Gen. *Thomas L. Rosser's* cavalry division.

As the afternoon of April 1 wore on, the Confederates apparently believed that no action would occur that day and accordingly began baking some fish that *Rosser's* staff had caught. *Pickett* and *Fitz Lee,* the overall cavalry commander on the field, left the line and went to *Rosser's* camp on Hatcher's Run. Some commentators have pointed to an anomaly that prevented the group from hearing the sounds of battle from the Five Forks crossroads; defenders of *Pickett* believe that the division commander moved to the sound of the guns as quickly as was practicable. As a consequence of the events of April 1, 1865, the "Shad Bake" at Five Forks has enjoyed an enduring notoriety in Civil War lore.

Report of Major General Pickett, continued

The fact being thus developed that the enemy were reinforcing with infantry and knowing the whole of Sheridan's and [Brig. Gen. August V.] Kautz's Cavalry were in our front, induced me to fall back at daylight in the morning to Five Forks, where I was directed by telegram from the Commander-in-Chief to hold so as to protect the road to Ford's Depot. The movement was made in perfect order, bringing off all of our wounded and burying all of our dead. The enemy were, however, pressing upon our rear in force.

I had all trains parked in rear of Hatcher's Run and would have preferred that position, but that from the telegram referred to, I supposed the commanding General intended sending up reinforcements. I had in the meantime reported by telegraph and informed the General commanding of the state of affairs, that the enemy were trying to get in between the main Army and my command and asking that a diversion be made or I would be isolated. This evidently was intended, as *Hunton's* Brigade did come up to Sutherland's, but not till after dark.

The best arrangements were made which the nature of the ground [permitted], *W. H. F. Lee's* Cavalry on the right, then *Corse, Terry, Steuart, Ransom* and *Wallace.* General *Fitz Lee* was ordered to cover the ground between *Wallace's* left and the creek with his cavalry dismounted. The enemy pushed up steadily from the Court-House and commenced extending to our left. General *Ransom* moved still further to the left, and I extended *Steuart's* Brigade so as to cover his ground. He (General *Ransom*) sent word to me that the cavalry were not in position. [*O.R. Supplement*, VII, p. 781.]

Report of Maj. Gen. Fitzhugh Lee, continued

Our position in the vicinity of Dinwiddie Court-House brought us in rear of the left of the infantry confronting the right of our line of battle at Burgess' Mills, and ascertaining during the night that that force, consisting of the Fifth Corps, had about-faced and was marching to the support of Sheridan and his discomfited cavalry, which would have brought them directly upon our left flank, at daylight on the 1st we commenced moving back to our former position at Five Forks, where *Pickett* placed his infantry in line of battle. *W. H. F. Lee* was on his right, one regiment of *Munford's* command on his left, united with the pickets of General [*William P.*] *Roberts'* command, who filled the gap between our position and

Maj. Gen. George E. Pickett (USAMHI)

the right of our main army, then at Burgess' Mills. *Rosser* was placed just in rear of the center as a reserve, Hatcher's Run intervening between him and our line. Everything continued quiet until about 3 p.m., when reports reached me of a large body of infantry marching around and menacing our left flank. I ordered *Munford* to go in person, ascertain the exact condition of affairs, hold his command in readiness, and if necessary order it up at once. He soon sent for it, and it reached its position just in time to receive the attack. A division of two small brigades of cavalry was not able long to withstand the attack of a Federal corps of infantry, and that force soon crushed in *Pickett's* left flank, swept it away, and before *Rosser* could cross Hatcher's Run the position at the Forks was seized and held and an advance toward the railroad made. It was repulsed by *Rosser. Pickett* was driven rapidly toward the prolongation of the right of his line of battle by the combined attack of this infantry corps and Sheridan's cavalry, making a total of over 26,000 men, to which he was opposed with 7,000 men of all arms. Our forces were driven back some miles, the retreat degenerating into a rout, being followed up principally by the cavalry, whilst the infantry corps held the position our troops were first driven from, threatening an advance upon the railroad, and paralyzing the force of reserve cavalry by necessitating its being stationary in an interposing position to check or retard such an advance. [*O.R.*, XLVI, part 1, pp. 1299–1300.]

Return to your vehicle, and make a U-turn onto Courthouse Road when it is safe to do so. Proceed 1.0 mile back to the Five Forks intersection, and turn left onto Route 613, White Oak Road. Proceed 0.7 mile to a parking area on the left side of the road. Pull into the parking area. Walk over to the interpretive signs in the parking lot, and face into the woods.

STOP 8: THE ANGLE

In the underbrush a short distance from this parking lot lie the remains of the angle where the Confederate defensive line stopped and turned north for a short distance. If you choose to explore the area, please remember not to walk on these remains. The Fifth Corps's assault crossed the White Oak road from southeast to northwest, hitting this angle with a force of three divisions and overlapping it to the north. A thin line of Confederate infantry from *Pickett's* division, augmented by *Munford's* cavalry, faced them.

At the point of the angle, the divisions of Ayres and Griffin overwhelmed *Ransom's* men, who were spread out along the breastworks at a rate of one man every 8 to 10 feet. Brig. Gen. Frederic Winthrop, one of Ayres's brigade commanders, was among the first Federals over the wall and was mortally wounded almost immediately. The Southern defenders here were simply swept away, forcing the units to their left to progressively face left to fight for their lives and then retreat to the west.

On the outside of the Federal wheeling movement, Crawford's division had a greater distance to travel and became focused on scattered Confederate defenders to the north. As a result, that formation gradually detached itself from the main Fifth Corps line and began moving north. Seeing this, Warren moved toward Griffin's division in an attempt to bring it back into line. Sheridan interpreted this movement as a further dereliction of duty by Warren, who he believed was tacitly stalling the attack so as to see no further action that day. Later, as the battle was concluding, the cavalry commander sent a dispatch to Warren via courier relieving him of command. First Division commander Griffin assumed corps command.

Report of Major General Sheridan, continued

The Fifth Corps on reaching the White Oak road made a left wheel and burst on the enemy's left flank and rear like a tornado, and pushed rapidly on, orders having been given that if the enemy was routed there should be no halt to reform broken lines. . . . The enemy were driven from their strong line of works and completely routed, the Fifth Corps doubling up their left flank in confusion. . . .

During this attack I again became dissatisfied with General Warren. During the engagement portions of his line gave way when not exposed to a heavy fire, and simply from want of confidence on the part of the troops, which General Warren did not exert himself to inspire. I therefore relieved him from the command of the Fifth Corps, authority for this action having been sent to me before the battle, unsolicited. [*O.R.*, XLVI, part 1, p. 1105.]

Report of Major General Warren, continued

After the forward movement began a few minutes brought us to the White Oak road, distant about 1,000 yards. There we found the advance of General Mackenzie's cavalry, which, coming up the White Oak road, had arrived there just before us. This showed us for the first time that we were too far to our right of the enemy's left flank. General Ayres' right crossed the road in the open field, and his division commenced changing front at once, so as to bring his line on the right flank of the enemy's position. Fortunately for us the enemy's left flank so rested in the woods that he could not fire at us as we crossed this open field, and the part of it that faced us formed a very short line. This General Ayres attacked at once, the firing being very heavy, but less than usually destructive, on account of the thick woods. The rapid change of front by General Ayres caused his right flank at first to get in advance of General Crawford's owing to the greater distance the latter had to move, and exposed the former to being taken in flank by the enemy. Orders were sent by me to General Crawford to oblique his division to the left and close up this interval. As soon as I had found the enemy's left flank orders were sent to General Griffin by several staff officers to move also obliquely to the left and come in to the support of General Ayres. But as Griffin's division was moving out of sight in the woods the order only reached him in the neighborhood of the place marked "Chimneys" on the map.

While giving orders thus I did not think it proper to leave my place on the open field, because it was one where my staff officers, sent to different parts of the command, could immediately find me on their return, and thus I could get information from all points at once, and utilize the many eyes of my staff, and those of my commanders, instead of going to some special point myself and neglect all others. The time had not arrived, in my judgment, for me to do that. It may be that at this time it was that General Sheridan thought I did not exert myself to inspire confidence in the troops that broke under a not very severe fire. There was no necessity for my personal presence for such purpose reported from any part of the field. [*O.R.*, XLVI, part 1, pp. 832–833.]

Report of Brevet Major General Ayres, *continued*

The division was ordered to move down the Boydton pike during the night of March 31, and report to General Sheridan at Dinwiddie Court-House. Before arriving there it was met by a staff officer of General Sheridan with instructions to turn off on a road leading west into a road leading from Dinwiddie Court-House to the White Oak road, and thus come upon the left and rear of the enemy, who was facing General Sheridan's command, near

Dinwiddie. As we approached, just after daylight, the enemy hastily decamped. The cavalry pursued, and this corps, having united, followed northward about 2 p.m. Arriving near the White Oak road the enemy were found in line of battle, with breast-works along that road facing south. Our troops were formed in line of battle for the attack. . . . Advancing through woods into an open the skirmishers engaged those of the enemy, pushing them back. Soon after crossing the White Oak road, finding the enemy's fire to come from the left, I changed front to the left by facing the Second Brigade to the left and filing it to the left. . . . After this change of front the troops were pushed forward, and soon came upon the left flank of the enemy, which was thrown back at right angles with his main line and covered by a strong breast-work, screened behind a dense undergrowth of pines and about 100 yards in length. This breast-work my troops charged and carried at the bayonet's point, capturing in carrying it over 1,000 prisoners and several battle-flags. Halting there a short time by General Sheridan's order, till it was apparent the enemy were giving way generally, I pushed forward rapidly . . . till orders were received to halt. The division was then retired to camp near the Five Forks. It took in this battle some 2,000 prisoners and 8 battle-flags.

That distinguished soldier, Bvt. Brig. Gen. Fred[eric] Winthrop, U.S. Volunteers, fell mortally wounded just as his brigade was gallantly charging the enemy's breast-works, and in the moment of triumph freely laid down his life for his country. His dying thoughts were for his comrades, and his last anxious inquiries were concerning the fate of the day. [*O.R.*, XLVI, part 1, pp. 869–870.]

Report of Bvt. Maj. Gen. Samuel W. Crawford, USA, commanding Third Division, Fifth Corps, Army of the Potomac

Early in the morning, while still in camp near the White Oak road, it was announced to me by the major-general commanding the corps that he was about to move with his entire command toward Dinwiddie Court-House, to operate in connection with the cavalry, then in the neighborhood of a place called Five Forks. . . . Upon arriving at Boisseau's Cross-Roads the command was massed for a short time, when by an order received from Major-General Warren the division took the lead on a road leading directly to Five Forks. . . . Upon arriving at Gravelly Run Church the division was formed with two brigades, namely: Second Brigade (General [Henry] Baxter's) on the right, the First Brigade

(Colonel [John A.] Kellogg's) on the left, each in two lines, supported by Colonel [Richard] Coulter's (Third) brigade, in the rear of the center. . . . We were in a short distance, less than half a mile, of the White Oak road. When the troops were in hand . . . the command moved at once. We crossed Gravelly Run, crossed the White Oak road and changed direction to the left and advanced directly to the west. We encountered the enemy's skirmishers shortly after moving driving them steadily back. Our way led through bogs, tangled woods, and thickets of pine, interspersed with open spaces here and there. [*O.R.*, XLVI, part 1, pp. 879–881.]

Report of Brevet Major General Griffin, continued

Immediately after the order to advance against the enemy was given (who was supposed to be intrenched at Five Forks), with instructions to the division that after it had crossed the [White Oak] road it was to change direction to the left, so as to strike the enemy in flank or rear. After advancing about a mile and finding nothing in front save a few cavalry vedettes, and there being heavy volleys of infantry to the left and rear, the division was halted, and upon a personal examination it was found that the enemy was moving up the White Oak road. Immediately the division was faced by the left flank, and marched some 400 or 500 yards, when its direction as to the line of battle was changed perpendicularly to the left and moved down on a double-quick upon the enemy. . . . The enemy's rifle-pits were taken, together with about 1,500 prisoners and several battle-flags. Here a little confusion resulted from the troops exchanging shots with the cavalry who were coming up in front of the enemy's works. This change brought the First Division on the left of the Third. The command was then pushed forward along the rifle-pits, capturing prisoners and driving the enemy before it, until it advanced to the Five Forks, where the cavalry and the infantry met, capturing five guns, several caissons, and the Third Brigade, First Division, taking on the Ford road a train of wagons and ambulances belonging to *Pickett's* division. At about this point Major-General Sheridan in person directed me to take command of the Fifth Corps and push the enemy down the White Oak road. I immediately directed General Ayres and the other commanders to push forward with all possible dispatch, and the pursuit was kept up until after dark, when the command was halted, the cavalry having pushed to the front out of sight and hearing of the infantry. [*O.R.*, XLVI, part 1, pp. 838–839.]

Make a U-turn back onto White Oak Road, and proceed 0.6 mile to the Five Forks intersection. Cross straight through the intersection to remain on White Oak Road, and immediately pull into the small parking area to your left across from the cannon. Walk across the road to the cannon, and face in the direction the gun is pointing.

STOP 9: THE WATERLOO OF THE CONFEDERACY

You will notice several Confederate memorials in the vicinity, most notably to Colonel *William J. Pegram.* Most of the Confederate guns at Five Forks belonged to his battalion, with a section of three of them at this spot, the center of *Pickett's* defensive line.

Crawford's northward movement took him clear of organized Confederate resistance along White Oak Road. His division reached Ford's Road at the Ben Boisseau clearing after scattering some cavalry pickets and capturing wagons along the road. Warren caught up with Crawford at this time and ordered him to turn his division to the south to attack down the road toward the forks. At the southern end of the Boisseau clearing, he encountered *McGregor's* four-gun battery, now firing north after having escaped from the angle. *Pickett* was back on the scene, having seen the fighting and taken a roundabout path from the Shad Bake to Five Forks. He formed a hasty defensive line oriented north, using the remnants of *Corse's* brigade. Col. Richard Coulter's brigade overran *McGregor's* battery and captured the guns, scattering the defenders and capturing many of them.

Here at the Five Forks intersection, *Pegram's* small battery of 3-inch rifles fought on virtually alone against Col. Charles Fitzhugh's cavalry brigade in his front. The twenty-three-year-old colonel sat his horse, directing fire, until wounded and carried from the field on a stretcher. *Pegram* died the next day at Ford's Station on the South Side Railroad. He had survived his brother John, a Confederate brigadier who was killed on February 6 at Hatcher's Run, by less than two months. The *Pegrams* were Petersburg natives.

Report of Brevet Major General Crawford, continued

The connection between the Second Division and my line could not be maintained. I received orders from both General Sheridan and General Warren to press rapidly forward. . . . I pressed immediately on and found myself in the enemy's rear on the Ford road, which I crossed. Here I captured seven ambulances and several wagons of *Wallace's* brigade, which I sent to the rear, and many prisoners. No exact number can be reported, as they were sent to the rear as fast as taken. Just at this point the enemy opened upon my center and left flank a very heavy fire. Major-General Warren, arriving on the field at that moment, directed me to advance immediately down the Ford road, and General Coulter's brigade was selected for that purpose. Two regiments, commanded by Major [West] Funk, were placed on what was then the left of the road, and the rest of the brigade were on the right, supported by the other two brigades in echelon. I advanced at once and captured a battery of four guns, the commanding officer of which was killed at that point, and also the battle-flag of the Thirty-second Virginia Infantry, which was captured by Sergt. Hiram A. Delavie, Company I, Eleventh Pennsylvania Volunteers. They then changed direction, and advanced again in a southwest direction, the enemy flying before us, though keeping up a desultory firing. [*O.R.*, XLVI, part 1, p. 881.]

Report of Major General Sheridan, continued

As stated before, the firing of the Fifth Corps was the signal to General Merritt to assault, which was promptly responded to, and the works of the enemy were soon carried at several points by our brave cavalrymen . . . and the cavalrymen of General Merritt dashing on to the White Oak road, capturing their artillery, and turning it upon them and riding into their broken ranks so demoralized them that they made no serious stand after their line was carried, but took to flight in disorder. Between 5,000 and 6,000 prisoners fell into our hands, and the fugitives were driven westward, and were pursued until long after dark by Merritt's and Mackenzie's cavalry for a distance of six miles. [*O.R.*, XLVI, part 1, p. 1105.]

Report of Bvt. Maj. Gen. Wesley Merritt, USA, commanding Cavalry Corps, Army of the Shenandoah

April 1, early in the morning an advance of the Third Division showed that the enemy had withdrawn a short distance from our front during the night. The Third Division was ordered to dismount, the country being impracticable for mounted operations, and move with its left resting on Chamberlain's Bed, toward the Five Forks. The First Division was ordered to move, mounted, to its old position near Boisseau's house and form connection with the Third Division, press the enemy in the same direction (toward the Five Forks). The infantry (Fifth Corps), which had formed a junction and was under the orders of the major-general commanding, was to move up on our right flank toward the White Oak road. The cavalry pressed the enemy back to his intrench-ments at the Five Forks, which intrenchments run parallel to the White Oak road. It was a great source of satisfaction to our gal-lant men to drive the enemy, outnumbering us as he did, over the same ground from which he had forced us the day before. Every man fought with a will, and not until the enemy's breast-heighths, glistening with bayonets, were within fifty yards of our front, did the brave cavalrymen, baptized with the blood of fifty battles, cease the advance, and then only for a moment. The time was occupied in supplying the commands with ammunition and resting the men, who had marched and fought on foot for miles. Word was received from the major-general commanding that the infantry would attack the enemy's works on our right in a very short time, and that the cavalry must co-operate. . . .

It could not have been earlier than 3 o'clock when the infantry fire opened. The cavalry, without a moment's hesitation, rushed into close quarters with the enemy, who, having fought the cavalry all day, evidently had concentrated their strength on the works im-mediately opposed to us. The enemy's artillery in the works com-menced firing rapidly, but owing to the woods obscuring the view where the cavalry line was operating, this fire was necessarily inac-curate and not very destructive. A hotter musketry fire than on this day has seldom been experienced during the war. Fortunately for us the enemy, firing from breast-works, aimed high, else the casualties in the command must have been very much greater. Gen-eral Custer was directed to keep one brigade mounted, in order to make the most of a pursuit when the enemy was dislodged from his works. Every thing worked well. The right of [Col. Alexander C. M.] Pennington's brigade, which was thrown into some confusion on account of a deficiency in ammunition, was soon restored, and, the desired ammunition supplied, the attack was prosecuted and soon crowned with success, Fitzhugh's brigade, of the First Divi-sion, mounting the works in the face of the enemy, tearing down their colors and planting the brigade standard over two pieces of artillery, which, together with nearly 1,000 prisoners, remained substantial indication of the prowess of this gallant brigade and its accomplished commander. [*O.R.*, XLVI, part 1, pp. 1117–1118.]

Report of Brevet Major General Crawford, continued

The men advanced through the woods with the utmost enthusiasm until we came in rear of the works on the enemy's right flank, where a few shots were received. The command pressed steadily onward until after dark, when it was halted at a point on the White Oak road and subsequently marched back along that road to the neighborhood of the Gravelly Run road, from which we had started, where we passed the night. [*O.R.*, XLVI, part 1, p. 881.]

Report of Major General Pickett, continued

General *Fitz Lee* was again ordered to cover the ground at once, and I supposed it had been done, when suddenly the enemy in heavy infantry column appeared on our left front, and the attacks, which had up to that time been confined principally to our front toward the Court-House, now became general. Charge after charge of the enemy was repulsed, but they still kept pushing up, division after division, and pressing round our left. General *Ransom*, perceiving this, took his brigade from behind his temporary breastworks and boldly charged the heavy column of the enemy, committing great havoc and temporarily checking their movement. In this he had his horse killed, he falling under him, and his Assistant Adjutant-General, the brave but unfortunate Captain [*Stirling H.*] *Gee* killed.

The few cavalry, however, which had gotten in position gave way, and the enemy came pouring in on *Wallace's* left, causing his men to give back. *Pegram* had been mortally wounded, the captain of the battery killed, and many of the men killed or wounded. I succeeded nevertheless in getting a sergeant with men enough for one piece, put it in position on the left, and fired some eight rounds into the head of the enemy's column, when the axle broke disabling the piece. I had also immediately withdrawn *Terry's* Brigade from its position and threw them on the left flank, charging over *Wallace's* men and forcing them back to their positions. Even then, with all the odds against us, we might have held till night, which was fast approaching, but the ammunition was fast giving out. Colonel [*Charles C. Flowerree's*] Regiment fought hand-to-hand with the enemy after their cartridges were expended, but it was of no avail, and although the enemy's dead lay in heaps, we were obliged to give way, our left being completely turned.

Wallace's Brigade again broke, though some of the officers in it behaved most gallantly and used their utmost exertions to re-form them, but in vain! And everything assumed the appearance of a panic when, by dint of great personal exertion on the part of my staffs, together with the general officers and their staff officers, we compelled a rally and stand on *Corse's* Brigade, which was still in perfect order and had repelled, as had *W. H. F. Lee's* Cavalry, every attempt of the enemy against them. [*O.R. Supplement*, VII, p. 782.]

Cross the road back to your vehicle. Continue on White Oak Road in your original direction of travel for 0.9 mile to the parking area on your left. Walk to a point overlooking the open field.

STOP 10: MUNFORD'S STAND

Beyond the tree line to your left before you lies "Burnt Quarter," the Gilliam home. As the Confederate left and center collapsed farther to the east along White Oak Road, Major General *Munford's* cavalry division (called *Fitzhugh Lee's* division because he originally commanded it), with some of *Corse's* infantry and a section of *Pegram's* guns in support, conducted a desperate delaying action against Custer's Federal horsemen. The brigades of Cols. William Wells and Henry Capehart used the wooded ravine to the right before you to make a concealed movement to the Confederate right flank; two Southern brigades, led by Brig. Gen. *Rufus Barringer*, stopped this attack along the road to your right. One Federal regiment, the Fifteenth New York, emerged from the ravine before you, arranged its lines, and charged the guns at this location to facilitate the flanking attack of Wells and Capehart.

Report of Bvt. Maj. Gen. George A. Custer, USA, commanding Third Division, Army of the Shenandoah Cavalry

About one hour and a half before dark a staff officer informed me that the major-general commanding had placed the Fifth Corps in position to assault the enemy's left. The First Cavalry Division had been dismounted and were to attack in the center, while my command was to engage the enemy on his right, keeping up the connection with the First Cavalry Division. An examination of the ground in front and on the enemy's right seemed to favor a movement by a mounted force against the enemy's right and rear. With this object in view I deployed the First Brigade dismounted,

Colonel Pennington commanding, along the entire line held by my division. The Second and Third Brigades, commanded, respectively, by Colonels Wells and Capehart, were mounted and moved opposite the extreme right of the enemy, and waited the opening of the general assault before advancing to turn the enemy's right flank. As soon as the firing on the line held by the Fifth Corps indicated the inauguration of the attack the Second and Third Brigades were moved at a gallop against the right of the enemy's line of battle. To cover the movement and to draw the fire of the enemy's batteries in front Lieutenant-Colonel [James] Bliss, of the Eighth New York Cavalry, was directed to charge with his regiment upon the enemy's batteries.

Without a hope of successfully carrying the enemy's position Lieutenant-Colonel Bliss gallantly led his regiment up to the very muzzles of the enemy's guns, at the same moment exposed to a terrible cross-fire from the enemy's infantry posted in rifle-pits and behind barricades within easy range. Although suffering a heavy loss in men and horses and compelled to retire the object of the charge was accomplished. Before the enemy could shift the position of his batteries my columns had pushed past the extreme right of his line and were moving rapidly to place themselves directly in rear of his position. Although this movement was almost entirely under the view of the enemy it was so rapid he was unable to prevent it. *W. H. F. Lee's* division of cavalry was discovered to be moving upon us. Portions of each command moved simultaneously to the attack. For some time success was varied and uncertain. My line was then facing in the same direction toward which that of the enemy had faced two hours before, the enemy being between my command and the line of battle of the Fifth Corps and First Cavalry Division. The gradual nearing of the firing indicated that the enemy's left was being forced back. This fact had its influence on the position of the enemy with whom we were engaged and aided us in effecting a total rout of the entire force of the enemy. . . . The pursuit was maintained over a distance of six miles and only ended on account of the darkness. [*O.R.*, XLVI, part 1, pp. 1130–1131.]

Report of Major General Pickett, continued

One of the most brilliant cavalry engagements of the war took place on this part of the field near Mrs. Gilliam's residence. The enemy made a most determined attack, in heavy force (cavalry) but were in turn charged by General *W. H. F. Lee*, completely driving them off the field. This, with the firm stand made by General *Corse's* men and those that could be rallied at this point, enabled many to escape capture.

Thus the shades of the evening closed on the bloody fields. Had the cavalry on the left done as well as those on our right the day would probably have been ours; as it was, it was most stubbornly contested against great odds. . . . Our loss in killed and wounded was very severe and a good many were captured. [*O.R. Supplement*, VII, pp. 781–783.]

The Confederate stand here allowed the remnants of *Pickett's* force to withdraw north along Ford's Road and across Hatcher's Run. *Pickett* escaped the battlefield with approximately 2,500 men and later joined with *Bushrod Johnson's* division to move west to Amelia Court-House, where they would join the rest of the Army of Northern Virginia on the retreat from Richmond and Petersburg that ended at Appomattox Court-House. As night fell on April 1, the Federals were in possession of Five Forks and the White Oak Road as far east as Claiborne Road. *Anderson* learned of the outcome at Five Forks and began his own withdrawal during the night, occupying a new defensive line at Sutherland Station on the South Side Railroad.

Five Forks was an unmitigated disaster for the Confederate cause. In addition to approximately 550 Confederates killed and wounded, Sheridan captured over 2,000 Southerners and, at a cost of 634 casualties of his own, had a clear path to the South Side Railroad.

Return to your vehicle. Turn right onto White Oak Road, and drive 0.9 mile back to the Five Forks intersection. Turn left onto Courthouse Road, and travel 2.4 miles to U.S. Route 460 (Cox Road). Turn right, and drive 4.4 miles to Namozine Road (Route 708); turn left, and pull into the parking area for Sutherland Tavern. Get out of your vehicle and face south across Cox Road toward the intersection with Claiborne Road.

STOP 11: SUTHERLAND STATION

THE BREAKTHROUGH AND FALL OF PETERSBURG, 2 APRIL 1865

You are standing just south of wartime Sutherland Station on the South Side Railroad. As discussed earlier in this excursion, Sutherland was the concentration point for the infantry and cavalry forces assembled by *Lee* to counter Meade's attack northward from Dabney's Mill, and in the aftermath of Five Forks, part of *Anderson's* provisional corps established a position here to protect the last remaining Confederate line of communication with Gen. *Joseph E. Johnston's* army in North Carolina.

As night fell on April 1, 1865, Grant was poised to end the campaign for Petersburg. The Army of the Potomac's Fifth Corps and Sheridan's cavalry occupied Five Forks. The Union Second Corps supported them north and west of Dinwiddie Court-House, threatening *Anderson* as he withdrew from the White Oak Road entrenchments. Closer to the city, the Sixth and Ninth Corps of the Army of the Potomac and the Twenty-fourth Corps, Army of the James, had orders to initiate an all-out assault before daybreak. A preparatory bombardment began at about 3:00. At 4:40, Maj. Gen. Horatio Wright's Sixth Corps attacked and broke the Confederate line, reaching the Boydton Plank Road after daybreak. (The site of the Sixth Corps breakthrough is preserved and interpreted on the grounds of Pamplin Historical Park; directions to the park and its museum are provided at the end of this excursion. The site is not a National Park Service property, and a separate entrance fee is required.) Wright's men pivoted left and moved southwest down the Boydton Plank Road toward Hatcher's Run, where they encountered the leading elements of the Twenty-fourth Corps. The entire force then doubled back and moved on Petersburg. Maj. Gen. John C. Parke's Ninth Corps attacked in the Jerusalem Plank Road sector and captured Fort Mahone.

The Federal divisions south and west of Petersburg were then delayed in their advance on the town by swampy, flooded terrain around Rohoic Creek and by a series of Confederate delaying actions. These actions allowed the rest of *Lee's* army and the Confederate government to evacuate Richmond and Petersburg during the night of April 2–3, 1865, setting the stage for the war's final campaign in the East.

One of these delaying actions occurred here at Sutherland Station. On April 2, after helping to overrun the Confederate defenses around Hatcher's Run, the Federal Second Corps moved north across the White Oak Road, with its objective being the South Side Railroad.

Report of Major General Meade, continued

On April 1, after consultation with the lieutenant-general commanding, believing from the operations on his right that the enemy's lines on his left must be thinly held, orders were sent to Major-Generals Wright and Parke to attack the next morning at 4.

About 7 p.m., intelligence having been received of the brilliant success of the cavalry and Fifth Corps at Five Forks, orders were sent to Generals Parke and Wright to open their batteries and press the enemy's picket-line. At the same time [Brig. Gen. Nelson A.] Miles' division, Second Corps, was detached to the support of Major-General Sheridan, and Major-General Humphreys advised of the intended attacks of the Twenty-fourth, Sixth, and Fifth Corps, and directed to hold his two remaining divisions ready to co-operate in the same, should they prove successful.

On the 2d of April Major-General Wright attacked at 4 a.m., carrying everything before him, taking possession of the enemy's strong line of works, and capturing many guns and prisoners. After carrying the enemy's line in his front, and reaching the Boydton plank road, Major-General Wright turned to his left and swept down the enemy's line of intrenchments till near Hatcher's Run, where, meeting the head of the Twenty-fourth Corps, General Wright retraced his steps and advanced on the Boydton plank road toward Petersburg, encountering the enemy in an inner line of works immediately around the city. Major-General Wright deployed his corps confronting their works, in conjunction with the Twenty-fourth and part of the Second Corps.

Major-General Parke's attack at 4 a.m. was also successful, carrying the enemy's lines, capturing guns and prisoners, but the position of the Ninth Corps confronting that portion of the enemy's line the longest held and most strongly fortified, it was found he held a second and inner line, which Major-General Parke was unable to carry. Receiving a dispatch during the morning from Major-General Parke, reporting his being pressed by the enemy, the troops left in the City Point defenses, under Brigadier General [Henry W.] Benham and Brevet Brigadier-General [Charles H. T.] Collis, were ordered up to General Parke's support, their prompt arrival enabling them to render material assistance to General Parke in holding his lines.

So soon as Major-General Wright's success was reported Major-General Humphreys was ordered to advance with the remaining divisions of his corps—[Brig. Gen. William] Hays on the right, advanced and captured a redoubt in front of the Crow house, taking a gun and over 100 prisoners; Mott, on the left, on advancing on the Boydton plank road, found the enemy's line evacuated. Hays and Mott pushed forward and joined the Sixth Corps, confronting the enemy. Early in the morning Miles, reporting his

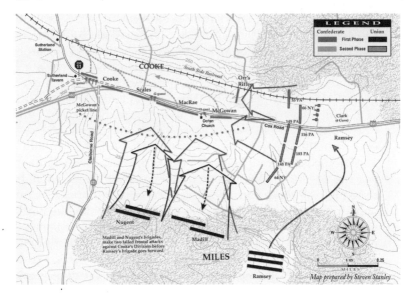

Sutherland Station, April 2, 1865

return to his position on the White Oak road, was ordered to advance on the Claiborne road simultaneously with Mott and Hays. Miles, perceiving the enemy were moving to his right, pursued and overtook him at Sutherland's station, where a sharp engagement took place, Miles handling his single division with great skill and gallantry, capturing several guns and many prisoners. On receiving intelligence of Miles being engaged, Hays was sent to his support, but did not reach the field till the action was over.

At 3 a.m. of the 2d [3rd] of April Major-Generals Parke and Wright reported no enemy in their front, when, on advancing, it was ascertained Petersburg was evacuated. [Brig. Gen. Orlando B.] Willcox's division, Ninth Corps, was ordered to occupy the town, and the Second, Sixth, and Ninth Corps immediately moved up the river, reaching that night the vicinity of Sutherland's station. [*O.R.*, XLVI, part 1, pp. 603–604.]

Report of Bvt. Maj. Gen. Nelson A. Miles, USA, commanding First Division, Second Corps, Army of the Potomac

April 2, at 7.30 a.m. moved upon the White Oak road to the point left the previous night. The picket-line left here by me the night previous had in the meantime, by orders, fallen back. At 9 a.m. the enemy abandoned his works, and they were immediately occupied by my men. The pursuit of the enemy was at once commenced, and he was followed closely to a point near Sutherland's Station, where he was found in position behind breast-works with artillery. The Second and Third Brigades were immediately ordered to charge the position, and they advanced promptly to the attack, but owing to the natural strength of the position and the difficult nature of the ground intervening the assault was unsuccessful. It was in this attack that Brevet Brigadier-General [Henry J.] Madill, commanding Third Brigade, was wounded severely, while gallantly urging his men forward to the enemy's works. At 12.30 p.m. a second assault was made by the Third Brigade, Brevet Brigadier-General [Clinton D.] MacDougall having been placed in command. The artillery of the division had at this time come up, and being placed in position assisted in the attack by a vigorous shelling of the enemy's line. This attack was also repulsed, the enemy being able to concentrate his force opposite any threatened point. The brigade was withdrawn to its former position—a crest about 800 yards from that occupied by the enemy.

I now determined to carry the position by an attack on the enemy's flank. A strong skirmish line was pushed forward upon the extreme right flank of the enemy, overlapping it and threatening the railroad. Indeed, a portion of this skirmish line was on the railroad at 1.10 o'clock. The attention of the enemy being thus diverted from his left flank, the Fourth Brigade (Brevet Brigadier-General [John] Ramsey) was moved rapidly around it through a ravine and wood, and massed in the woods without being discovered by the enemy. At 2.45 p.m. the brigade advanced at double quick, with a hearty cheer and in magnificent order, striking the enemy in flank, and sweeping rapidly down inside the breast-works, capturing large numbers of prisoners and putting to precipitous flight the remainder. That portion of the enemy who escaped were driven to the woods near the river, where they were picked up the next morning. . . . The division captured 600 prisoners, 1 battle-flag, and 2 pieces of artillery. As I was directed by General Sheridan to drive the enemy toward Petersburg, I advanced in that direction by the River and the South Side roads about two miles, when I was met by the Second Division, who were moving on the latter road in the opposite direction. I therefore returned to the vicinity of Sutherland's Station toward evening,

Maj. Gen. Horatio G. Wright (USAMHI)

disposed my troops so as to hold the railroad, and bivouacked for the night. [*O.R.*, XLVI, part 1, pp. 711–712.]

Memoir of Lieutenant Caldwell, continued

After a march of about three miles we came in sight of the railroad. The enemy, following us with energy, now opened with artillery upon the rear of the Confederate column, and a few pieces of the latter replied to them. It was evident that we must give them battle. The trains of wagons and artillery were hurried up past us, and Gen. *Heth* selected a line of defence. This line ran, for nearly half its length, just on the edge of a highway, and for its whole length, was almost parallel with the South Side Railroad. The right of the Confederate line rested by a large house on the west of the road by which we came; our left against a country church, whose name I have forgotten. The railroad was a hundred yards in rear of the left of the line, and passed through a deep cut here. We were on the summit of a perfectly smooth, open ridge, which commanded the slope towards our enemy for six or eight hundred yards. At about that distance ran a small stream and a ravine. Beyond the ravine rose a ridge, similar to the one we occupied, but covered partly with large oaks, partly with pines.

I am not informed of the presence of more than four brigades on our line—[Brig. Gen. *John R.*] *Cooke's*, [Brig. Gen. *Alfred M.*] *Scales'*, [Brig. Gen. *William*] *M[a]cRae's*, [Brig. Gen. *Samuel*] *Mc-Gowan's*. We were allowed a few pieces of artillery, principally on the flanks and near the center of the line. Gen. *Heth* received an order to return to Petersburg, and take command of *Hill's* corps or some portion of it [Lt. Gen. *Ambrose P. Hill* had been killed earlier on April 2 while reconnoitering his lines.] . . . Upon its appearing that Gen. *Cooke* was here, the command devolved on him as the senior brigadier general. We formed a straight line, and fortified with rails from the neighboring fences. . . . We certainly had not more than four thousand troops, and probably not so many. Our brigade could number about a thousand. We were on the extreme left of the line, our left resting on the church I have already mentioned.

. . . We were not long left in suspense. All the length of the crest of the ridge before us began, in a few minutes, to glitter with arms, and then to grow blue with the long lines of the enemy swarming to attack. . . . Their line was oblique to ours; so that they first struck the extreme right. They were expected calmly and silently, and they themselves ceased cheering after a time; but when within three or four hundred yards of the Confederates, they raised the shout with greater vigor than ever, and stormed towards the works. At once a unanimous yell of defiance burst from the Confederate line, and all our troops within rifle range opened on them. They replied volley to volley and shout to shout, and pushed a desperate charge. But *Lee's* veterans were not to be frightened by sounds or appearances. They rolled a perfect sheet of lead across the open interval, striking down scores of the enemy. . . .

The enemy then moved a line against the left wing of the Confederates. . . . The impetuosity of the Federals was absolutely irresistible. The skirmish line fired with remarkable precision, and held their position with a tenacity worthy of their reputation; but they were forced back upon the main body. Then the enemy dashed violently against us, cheering as if already seeing victory. The scene of the right wing was repeated. . . . The enemy struggled and groped awhile, but, at last, ran clear off the field.

The enemy paused for perhaps an hour before renewing the attack, but they were visible massing troops opposite the left of our line. . . . On came the Federal lines, like the converging currents of a storm, cheering, firing, sweeping over the whole field.

Now was the most disorderly movement I ever saw among Confederate troops. We had to pass over two or three hundred yards of clear field, under the fire of infantry on our flank and in rear, and under the shelling of their artillery. The whole air shrieked with missiles, the whole earth trembled with the tumult of sounds. It is useless to protract the description. Suffice it to say, we fled to the cover of woods and distance, and sought the unfriendly banks of the Appomattox. [Caldwell, *The History of a Brigade of South Carolinians*, pp. 218–224.]

Gen. Robert E. Lee to John C. Breckenridge, Secretary of War, CSA, April 2, 1865, 10:40 a.m.

I see no prospect of doing more than holding our position here till night. I am not certain that I can do that. If I can I shall withdraw to-night north of the Appomattox, and, if possible, it will be better to withdraw the whole line to-night from James River. The brigades on Hatcher's Run are cut off from us; enemy have broken through our lines and intercepted between us and them, and there is no bridge over which they can cross the Appomattox this side of Goode's or Beaver's which are not very far from the

Danville Railroad. Our only chance, then, of concentrating our forces, is to do so near Danville railroad, which I shall endeavor to do at once. I advise that all preparation be made for leaving Richmond to-night. I will advise you later, according to circumstances. [*O.R.*, XLVI, part 1, p. 1264.]

Drive out of the parking area, and turn left onto Cox Road (Route 460). Proceed 3.0 miles until you reach the fork where it meets with Airport Street (Route 460). Follow the fork to the right onto Airport Street and drive 1.4 miles until you reach Boydton Plank Road (Route 1). Turn left onto Boydton Plank Road, and proceed 1.4 miles to Simpson Road (Route 603). At 0.4 mile after turning onto Boydton Plank Road, the entrance to Pamplin Historical Park, site of the Sixth Corps breakthrough on April 2, is on the right. At 0.5 mile after turning onto Boydton Plank Road, you will see signs to the left indicating the site of *A. P. Hill's* death on April 2. At 1.2 miles, just before reaching the I-85 interchange, turn right onto Simpson Road (Route 142), and then bear left, continuing on Route 142. Proceed 0.6 mile to Seventh Avenue (Route 319), and turn left, then immediately pull into the parking area on the right. Walk 200 yards to Fort Gregg, and stand outside the ramparts with a view toward the southwest, approximately toward where you are parked.

STOP 12: FORT GREGG

Forts Gregg and Whitworth stood on the western approaches to Petersburg, just west of the original Dimmock Line and north of the line of trenches covering the Boydton Plank Road.

On the afternoon of April 2, a "forlorn hope" of 300 Confederates from Lt. Gen. *James Longstreet's* First Corps, primarily belonging to Georgia and Mississippi regiments in Maj. Gen. *Cadmus M. Wilcox's* division, held the forts for several hours against an overwhelming Federal force streaming through the breach in the Petersburg defenses. This short but heroic defense bought critical time for the evacuation of Richmond and Petersburg.

The Boisseau House, scene of some critical moments in this engagement, is located on the grounds of Pamplin Park, which is south of your current position. The Harmon House was located on the side of Boydton Plank Road opposite the entrance to Pamplin Park.

Report of Maj. Gen. John Gibbon, USA, commanding Twenty-fourth Corps, Army of the James

On reaching the vicinity of Fort Welch, where the Sixth Corps had broken through, I found [Brig. Gen. Robert S.] Foster already in line of battle perpendicular to the enemy's old line and confronting two strong works, Forts Gregg and Baldwin [Whit-worth], which the enemy had erected to protect his right of the town. [Brig. Gen. Thomas M.] Harris' brigade was formed on Foster's left, and as soon as they arrived [Brig. Gen. John W.] Turner's other two brigades were formed in rear of Foster. As the Sixth Corps came up it went into position, two divisions on my left and one on my right, and as soon as they reached within sup-porting distance Foster's line was ordered to charge the works in its front. The troops moved steadily and rapidly forward, under a very heavy fire of both artillery and musketry, and gained Fort Gregg, to find it surrounded by a deep, wide ditch partially filled with water and flanked by a fire from both right and left. Turner's two brigades were pushed rapidly up in support from the second line, whilst Harris at the same time rushed against Fort Baldwin. The enemy made a most desperate resistance, and it was not until Fort Gregg was almost entirely surrounded and our brave men had succeeded in climbing upon the parapet under a most mur-derous fire, that the place was finally taken by the last of several determined dashes with the bayonet, Harris and a portion of the First Division at the same time carrying Fort Baldwin. This assault, certainly one of the most desperate of the war, succeeded by the obstinate courage of our troops, but at a fearful cost. Fifty-five of the enemy's dead were found inside Fort Gregg, whilst my own loss during the operations of the day, most of which occurred around these two forts, was 10 officers and 112 men killed and 27 officers and 565 men wounded. We captured 2 pieces of artillery, several colors, and about 300 prisoners. [*O.R.*, XLVI, part 1, p. 1174.]

Report of Col. James C. Briscoe, USA, commanding 199th Pennsylvania Infantry, Osborn's Brigade, Foster's Division, Twenty-fourth Corps, Army of the James

Our line now rested at a point about 800 yards distant from Fort Gregg, a very difficult swamp between us and the fort, and the whole intervening space swept by the enemy's musketry and artillery fire. About noon we received orders to attack and carry the fort, and the whole line advanced in good style. The ground in front of the southeast salient of the work forms a perfect natural glacis for about 300 yards; passing over this space my regiment suffered its severest loss—canister, shot, and minie bullets tore through the ranks, yet not a man faltered. I was struck down by a glancing ball about seventy-five yards from the work, and although

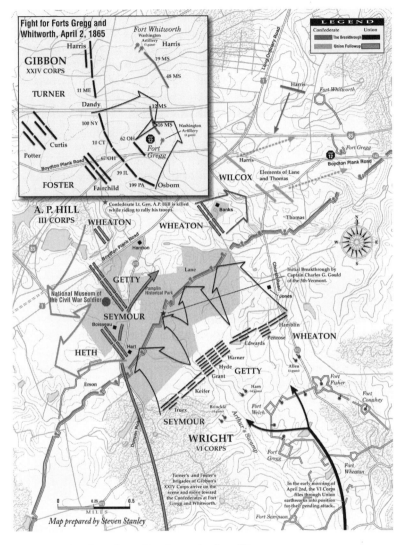

Breakthrough at Petersburg–Fort Gregg, April 2, 1865

I lost but a moment in recovering myself, the men were already in the moat and clambering up the exterior slope; were fighting hand to hand across the parapet, the enemy refusing to surrender, though surrounded on all sides. This sort of thing lasted nearly twenty minutes, when we finally burst over the parapet and the fort was ours. [*O.R.*, XLVI, part 1, p. 1190.]

Reminiscences of Maj. Gen. Cadmus M. Wilcox, CSA, commanding Division, First Corps, Army of Northern Virginia

Inasmuch as I was present at the time, and gave the order to occupy both batteries, Gregg and Whitworth, and made such other disposition of the small number of men at my disposal as would best answer the purpose in view, and finally, when this was accomplished, directed the withdrawal to the main line in rear, and as my official report has never been published, I will now give some of the facts connected with the defence of these two batteries. . . . Early in October, 1864, *Heth's* division and two brigades, [Brig. Gen. *James E.*] *Lane's* and *McGowan's*, of my division, were placed in position with orders to entrench, the line being east of the Boydton Plank Road, which ran to Dinwiddie Courthouse. . . . The right rested on Hatcher's run, a mile below Burgess' mill, this being at the crossing of the run by the Dinwiddie Courthouse road. This new line guarded the road—Boydton plank road—over which we received supplies from Hicksford, on the Weldon railroad, in rear or south of the point where the Federal line crossed this road.

All during the night of April 1st the enemy's batteries around Petersburg kept up an almost incessant cannonade. . . . The infantry pickets were also wide awake and kept up more than their usual firing. About day-light it was increased, and of such volume as to make the impression that it was not a mere skirmish-line engagement. I started for the front, and on reaching the vicinity of Battery Gregg met a number of my men coming to the rear. They reported that our lines had been broken. Portions of [Brig. Gen. *Edward L.*] *Thomas'* and [Brig. Gen. *James H.*] *Lane's* brigades were in and near Batteries Gregg and Whitworth. I learned that the lines had been pierced on *Lane's* front near Boisseau's house and at a point to his right. Most of the enemy then turned to their left, sweeping up every thing as far as Hatcher's run; part had filed to their right and had driven our line back; not, however, without suffering seriously. Gen. [Horatio G.] Wright, commanding the Sixth corps, informed me subsequently that he lost 1,200 men in getting over the line. The enemy had reached the plank road in small numbers. One of *Lane's* regiments was forced back to the Southside road. The enemy were seen along our captured lines and on the plank road. *Lane's* and *Thomas'* men were reformed—in all about 300—moved forward in good spirits, and recaptured the lines in the vicinity of Boisseau's house, together with the artillery of the different batteries along it. This was reported to Gen. *Lee.*

Col. [*Charles*] *Venable,* aide-de-camp to Gen. *Lee,* soon joined me with the message that *Harris'* brigade would report in a few minutes; he numbers little over 500 muskets. Heavy masses of the enemy were soon seen moving forward from their entrenched lines. . . . It was useless to attempt engaging them with the force I had; *Harris* was, therefore, ordered forward a little beyond the Widow Clark's house, advanced skirmishers, but with orders not to become engaged with his line of battle. It was the purpose to delay the forward movement of the enemy as much as possible, in order that troops from the north side of the James River might arrive and fill in the gaps between the right of our own Petersburg lines and the Appomattox. . . . The lines of battle of the enemy, imposing from their numbers and strength, advanced. Slowly but steadily our artillery—that in rear of *Harris'* brigade, was withdrawn, and the brigade, after a slight skirmish, retired.

It was now that a little detachment was ordered to occupy Battery Gregg. It was made up of two pieces of artillery, and in all about 200 men, the infantry being composed of detachments from *Thomas', Lane's* and *Harris'* brigades; the number from *Thomas'* brigade, as now remembered, being less than that from either of the other two. The most of *Harris'* brigade was ordered to Battery Whitworth. At the time the detachments were placed in Gregg I did not know who was the ranking officer; did not regard it of much consequence, as I had determined to remain either in it or near it. I was in Gregg about 10 minutes. Saw that it has as many men as could fire, conveniently. Extra ammunition was supplied, and the little detachments ordered to hold these two batteries to the last. Battery Gregg was a detached lunette, with a ditch about eight or ten feet deep, and about the same width, and the parapet of corresponding height and thickness. . . . It was the intention to have connected these two batteries with a rifle trench, and earth had been excavated for a distance of thirty yards, commencing at the right end of the palisading of Gregg. The connection was never made; but it was by means of the parapet of this short, unfinished trench, that the enemy reached the crest of Battery Gregg. As the enemy's attacking force advanced, a few guns on the main lines at Battery 45, the two guns in Gregg, and the three in Whitworth delivered a rapid fire. The enemy's battery in the open field beyond Old Town creek was in the meantime directing a brisk and well-directed fire upon Gregg and Whitworth. The enemy's front line coming within good range, the musketry from the two little garrisons began, and with decided effect, to be easily seen. This inspired with increased courage our men, greatly diminished in numbers. The enemy drew nearer, but close in front of Whitworth were the cabins of a brigade that had passed the winter there. Our men set these on fire, and enemy attacking this part of the line, halted near by. Against Gregg, however, they continued to advance, nearer and nearer, till they were within less than sixty yards. The two guns in it ceased firing; those on the main line also. The three in Whitworth were withdrawn without any authority from myself, and the enemy's battery beyond Old Town Creek was forced to desist, their own troops being between it and Gregg. The latter was now nearly surrounded. The heroism displayed by the defenders of Battery Gregg has not been exaggerated by those attempting to describe it. A mere handful of men, they beat back repeatedly the overwhelming numbers assailing them on all sides. [*Southern Historical Society Papers*, 52 vols. (Millwood, N.Y.: Kraus reprint, 1876–1959), volume IV, pp. 27–28.]

Account of Lt. Gen. Ambrose P. Hill's death by Sgt. George Tucker, CSA, Chief of Couriers, Third Corps, Army of Northern Virginia

About midnight the cannonading in front of Petersburg, which had begun at nightfall, became very heavy, increasing as the hours went by. Colonel [*William H.*] Palmer, Chief of Staff, woke Major [*Norborne*] Starke, Acting Adjutant General, and requested him to find out the cause and effect of the prolonged firing. This was between 2 and 3 o'clock on the morning of April 2. Major *Starke* returned before daylight and reported "that the enemy had part of our line near the Rives' salient, and that matters looked critical on the lines in front of the city." This he communicated to General *Hill* at Venable's.

Before sunrise General *Hill* came over and asked Colonel *Palmer* if he had any report from Generals *Wilcox* and *Heth*, whose divisions on the right extended from the front of Fort Gregg to and beyond Burgess's Mill, on Hatcher's Run. The Colonel told him that he had heard nothing from them, and had nothing further to report beyond Major *Starke's* statement.

The General then passed on to his tent, and a few minutes later the Colonel, noticing his colored servant, Charles, leading the General's saddled horse to his tent, ran to him just as he was mounting and asked permission to accompany him. He told the Colonel no, and desired him to wake up the staff, get everything in readiness and have the headquarters' wagons hitched up. He added that he was going to General *Lee's*, and would take Sergeant *Tucker* and two couriers, and that as soon as he could have an interview with General *Lee*, he would return.

General *Hill* then rode to the couriers' quarters and found me in the act of grooming my horse. (I did not then have the slightest intimation of what had taken place since our return from the lines the night before.) He directed me to follow him with two couriers immediately to General *Lee's* headquarters. He then rode off rapidly. It was our custom, in critical times, to have, during the night, two of the couriers' horses always saddled. I called to *Kirkpatrick*[8] and [Pvt. *William H.*] *Jenkins*, the couriers next in turn, to follow the General as quickly as possible. I saddled up at once and followed them. *Kirkpatrick* and *Jenkins* arrived at General *Lee's* together, only a few minutes after General *Hill*, who at once directed *Kirkpatrick* to ride rapidly back to our quarters (I met him on the road, going at full speed) and tell Colonel *Palmer* to follow him to the right, and the others of the staff, and couriers, must rally the men on the right. This was the first information received at corps headquarters that our right had given way. General *Hill* then rode, attended only by *Jenkins* to the front gate of General *Lee's* headquarters (Turnbull House, on the Cox road, nearly one and a half miles westerly from General *Hill's*), where I met them. We went directly across the road into the opposite field, and riding due south a short distance the General drew rein, and for a few moments used his field glass, which, in my still profound ignorance of what had happened, struck me as exceedingly queer. We

---

[8] Even the foremost student of the final battles around Petersburg, A. Wilson Greene of Pamplin Historical Park, has, despite diligent and thorough research, "been unable to further identify Kirkpatrick." A. Wilson Greene, *Breaking the Backbone of the Rebellion: The Final Battles of the Petersburg Campaign* (Knoxville: University of Tennessee Press, 2008), p. 478, n. 14.

then rode on in the same direction down a declivity toward a small branch running eastward to Old Town Creek, and a quarter of a mile from General *Lee's*. We had gone little more than half this distance, when we suddenly came upon two of the enemy's armed infantrymen. *Jenkins* and myself, who, up to this time, rode immediately behind the General, were instantly upon them, when, at the demand, "surrender," they laid down their guns. Turning to the General, I asked what should be done with the prisoners? He said: "*Jenkins*, take them to General *Lee*." *Jenkins* started back with his men, and we rode on.

Though not invited, I was at the General's side, and my attention having now been aroused and looking carefully ahead and around I saw a lot of people in and about the old log hut winter quarters of [Maj. Gen. *William*] *Mahone's* division, situated to the right of Whitworth House and on top of the hill beyond the branch we were approaching. Now as I knew that those quarters had been vacant since about March 15th by the transfer of *Mahone* to north of the Appomattox, and feeling that it was the enemy's troops in possession, with nothing looking like a Confederate anywhere, I remarked, pointing to the old camp: "General, what troops are those?" He quickly replied: "The enemy's." Proceeding still further and General *Hill* making no further remark, I became so impressed with the great risk he was running that I made bold to say: "Please excuse me, General, but where are you going?" He answered: "Sergeant, I must go to the right as quickly as possible." Then, pointing southwest he said: "We will go up this side of the branch to the woods, which will cover us until reaching the field in rear of General *Heth's* quarters, I hope to find the road clear at General *Heth's*."

From that time on I kept slightly ahead of the General. I had kept a Colt's army pistol drawn since the affair of the Federal stragglers. We then made the branch, becoming obscured from the enemy, and crossing the Bowdtoin (not "Boydtown," as some writers have called it) plank road, soon made the woods, which were kept for about a mile, in which distance we did not see a single person, and emerged into the field opposite General *Heth's*, at a point two miles due southwest from General *Lee's* headquarters, at the Turnbull House, and at right angles with the Bowdtoin plank road, at the "Harman" House, which was distant half a mile. When going through the woods, the only words between General *Hill* and myself, except a few relating to the route, were by himself.

He called my attention and said: "Sergeant, should anything happen to me you must go back to General *Lee* and report it."

We came into the field near its corner, at the foot of a small declivity, rising which I could plainly see that the road was full of troops of some kind. The General, raising his field glass, said: "They are there." I understood perfectly that he meant the enemy, and asked: "Which way now, General?" He pointed to that side of the woods parallel to the Bowdtoin plank road, about one hundred yards down hill from where our horses stood, saying: "We must keep on to the right." I spurred ahead, and we had made two thirds of the distance, and coming to a walk, looked intently into the woods, at the immediate edge of which were several large trees. I saw what appeared to be six or eight Federals, two of whom, being some distance in advance of the rest, who halted some forty or fifty yards from the field, ran quickly forward to the cover of one of the large trees, and, one above the other on the same side, leveled their guns.

I looked around to General *Hill.* He said: "We must take them," at the same time drawing, for the first time that day, his Colt's navy pistol. I said: "Stay there, I'll take them." By this time we were within twenty yards of the two behind the tree and getting closer every moment. I shouted: "If you fire, you'll be swept to hell! Our men are here—surrender!" When General *Hill* was at my side calling "surrender," now within ten yards of the men covering us with their muskets (the upper one the General, the lower one myself), the lower soldier let the stock of his gun down from his shoulder, but recovered quickly as his comrade spoke to him (I only saw his lips move) and both fired. Throwing out my right hand (he was on that side) toward the General, I caught the bridle of his horse, and, wheeling to the left, turned in the saddle and saw my General on the ground, with his limbs extended, motionless.

Instantly retracing the ground, leading his horse, which gave me no trouble, I entered the woods again where we had left them, and, realizing the importance, and of all things most desirous of obeying my General's last order "to report to General *Lee*," I changed to his horse a very superior one and quite fresh, and letting mine free kept on as fast as the nature of the ground would permit. But after sighting and avoiding several parties of Federal stragglers and skirmishers, I felt that it would be best to take to the open country and run it. After some distance of this I made for the *Mahone* division log hut winter quarters, which were still full of the enemy, upon the principle of greater safety in running through its narrow streets than taking their leisurely fire in the open. Emerging thence down hill to the branch, along the north side of which General *Hill* had so shortly ridden in his most earnest endeavor to reach our separated and shattered right, and in a straight line for General *Lee's* headquarters, I came in sight of a mounted party of our own people, who, when the branch was crossed and the hill risen, proved to be Lieutenant General [*James*] *Longstreet* and staff, just arrived from north of the Appomattox. Meanwhile, meeting Colonels *Palmer* and [*R. J.*] *Wingate* and others of General *Hill's* staff and couriers, and halting a moment to answer the kindly expressed inquiries of General *Longstreet,* we rode on and found General *Lee* mounted at the Cox road in front of army headquarters. I reported to him General *Hill's* last order to me. General *Lee* then asked for details, received which and expressing his sorrow he directed me to accompany Colonel *Palmer* to Mrs. *Hill.* General *Lee* said: "Colonel, break the news to her as gently as possible."

The Fifth Alabama battalion, provost guard to General *Hill's* corps, skirmishing, found the General's body, which was still slightly warm, with nothing about it disturbed. The Federal party were doubtless alarmed at what had been done and must have instantly fled. The writer did not again see General *Hill's* body, which was brought to Venable's by a route still further to our rear, having, with the staff and courier of the Third corps, been ordered to General *Longstreet,* who soon became very actively engaged. I learned that the ball struck the General's pistol hand and then penetrated his body just over the heart. Captain *Frank Hill,* aide de camp (and nephew) to the General, in charge, and Courier *Jenkins* were of the party detailed to escort the body, with Mrs. *Hill* and her children, to "a Mr. Hill's," near the banks of James river, in Chesterfield county, where the General's body was temporarily buried and afterwards removed to Hollywood Cemetery, Richmond, Virginia. ["Accounts of the Death of A. P. Hill," And Then A. P. Hill Came Up: The Life and Career of General Ambrose Powell Hill, http://www.aphillcsa.goellnitz.org/death2.html.]

Memoir of Lieutenant Caldwell, continued

During this day (Sunday) the enemy had stormed the line in front of Petersburg and north of the Appomattox. *Mahone's* division had driven them back, with heavy loss, at the latter point; but along the southern line they had been fearfully successful. It is true, that just in front of Petersburg they were repulsed; but, farther down the line, they carried the infantry works, carried (with a slaughter unparalleled during the war) Forts Mahone and Gregg, swept around the remaining line, and compelled the abandonment of the city of Petersburg. With Petersburg fell the line between the Appomattox and the James, and with it, Richmond. Both Petersburg and Richmond were evacuated on this (Sunday) night, and, of course, the whole forty miles of the Confederate line. The great arc which we had so ably defended for nine months was lost, and the army was in retreat for a new position. Yet even retreat was not permitted by the enemy to go on undisturbed. Sheridan's immense force of cavalry drove upon the left wing of the army, and *Pickett* and *Bushrod Johnson* barely prevented them from entirely cutting off our retirement up the Appomattox. Such was the state of our affairs, while we attempted to sleep on the night of April 2. [Caldwell, *The History of a Brigade of South Carolinians,* p. 225.]

Gen. Robert E. Lee to Breckenridge, April 2, 1865, 7:00 p.m.

It is absolutely necessary that we should abandon our position to-night, or run the risk of being cut off in the morning. I have given all the orders to officers on both sides of the river, and have taken every precaution that I can to make the movement successful. It will be a difficult operation, but I hope not impracticable. Please give all orders that you find necessary in and about Richmond. The troops will all be directed to Amelia Court-House. [*O.R.*, XLVI, part 1, p. 1265.]

If you wish to see the other fort in this area that figured in the fighting of April 2, return to your vehicle and turn right onto Seventh Avenue, entering the grounds of Central State Hospital. At 0.2 mile, on your right is a picnic area situated within the remains of Fort Whitworth. Park in the area, and walk into the fort.

If you wish to visit either the Pamplin Historical Park and its National Museum of the Civil War Soldier or the location of *A. P. Hill's* death, retrace your route past Fort Gregg and back to Boydton Plank Road. Turn left onto Boydton Plank Road. To visit *A. P. Hill's* death site, drive 0.7 mile, and turn right onto A. P. Hill Drive, which turns into Sentry Hill Court. Turn either left or right (Sentry Hill Court is a loop), and park on the far side of the loop after 0.2 mile. The marker is located in the woods a few hundred feet from where you are parked. The entrance to Pamplin Park is another 0.2 mile along Boydton Plank Road past the A. P. Hill Drive intersection. As previously mentioned, there is a fee for Pamplin Park, but its wonderful exhibits, remarkably well-preserved entrenchments, and informative living history programs make for an interesting and enjoyable half- or full-day separate excursion.

Capture of Confederate works at Petersburg (USAMHI)

To return to the main visitor center for Petersburg National Battlefield, re-trace your route back to Fort Gregg, and turn right onto Simpson Road. Return to Boydton Plank Road, and turn right, exiting immediately onto northbound I-85. Take I-85 to its junction with northbound I-95. At exit 69, take the ramp to Wythe Street, and follow it to Washington Street. Turn right onto Washington Street, and drive 2.2 miles (Washington Street becomes Oaklawn Boulevard) to the exit for Petersburg National Battlefield Park.

APPENDIX I
ORDER OF BATTLE, 15 JUNE 1864

UNITED STATES ARMY

Lt. Gen. Ulysses S. Grant, Commanding

ARMY OF THE POTOMAC

Maj. Gen. George G. Meade, Commanding

GENERAL HEADQUARTERS

Provost Guard (Brig. Gen. Marsena Patrick)
Volunteer Engineer Brigade (Brig. Gen. Henry W. Benham)
Signal Corps
    Artillery (Brig. Gen. Henry J. Hunt)
    Artillery Park (Lt. Col. Freeman McGilvery)
Independent Company Oneida Cavalry

SECOND ARMY CORPS (MAJ. GEN. WINFIELD SCOTT HANCOCK)

FIRST DIVISION (BRIG. GEN. FRANCIS C. BARLOW)

First Brigade (Brig. Gen. Nelson A. Miles)
MacDougall's Brigade (Col. Clinton D. MacDougall)
Fourth Brigade (Lt. Col. John Hastings)

SECOND DIVISION (MAJ. GEN. JOHN GIBBON)

First Brigade (Lt. Col. Francis E. Pierce)
Second Brigade (Col. James P. McIvor)
Third Brigade (Col. Thomas A. Smyth)

THIRD DIVISION (MAJ. GEN. DAVID B. BIRNEY)

First Brigade (Col. Henry J. Madill)
Second Brigade (Brig. Gen. Byron R. Pierce)
Third Brigade (Brig. Gen. Gershom Mott)
Fourth Brigade (Col. William R. Brewster)
Artillery Brigade (Maj. John G. Hazard)

FIFTH ARMY CORPS (MAJ. GEN. GOUVERNEUR K. WARREN)

FIRST DIVISION (BRIG. GEN. CHARLES GRIFFIN)

First Brigade (Col. William S. Tilton)
Second Brigade (Col. Jacob B. Sweitzer)
Third Brigade (Brig. Gen. Joseph J. Bartlett)

SECOND DIVISION (BRIG. GEN. ROMEYN B. AYRES)

First Brigade (Brig. Gen. Joseph Hayes)
Second Brigade (Col. Nathan T. Dushene)
Third Brigade (Col. J. Howard Kitching)

THIRD DIVISION (BRIG. GEN. SAMUEL W. CRAWFORD)

First Brigade (Col. Peter Lyle)
Second Brigade (Brig. Gen. Henry Baxter)
Third Brigade (Col. James Carle)

FOURTH DIVISION (BRIG. GEN. LYSANDER CUTLER)

First Brigade (Col. Edward S. Bragg)
Second Brigade (Col. J. William Hofmann)
Artillery Brigade (Col. Charles S. Wainwright)

SIXTH ARMY CORPS (MAJ. GEN. HORATIO G. WRIGHT)

FIRST DIVISION (BRIG. GEN. DAVID A. RUSSELL)

First Brigade (Col. William H. Penrose)
Second Brigade (Brig. Gen. Emory Upton)
Third Brigade (Lt. Col. Gideon Clark)
Fourth Brigade (Col. Joseph E. Hamblin)

SECOND DIVISION (BRIG. GEN. GEORGE W. GETTY)

First Brigade (Brig. Gen. Frank Wheaton)
Second Brigade (Brig. Gen. Lewis Grant)
Third Brigade (Col. Daniel D. Bidwell)
Fourth Brigade (Col. Oliver Edwards)

THIRD DIVISION (BRIG. GEN. JAMES B. RICKETTS)

First Brigade (Col. William S. Truex)
Second Brigade (Col. Benjamin F. Smith)
Artillery Brigade (Col. Charles H. Tompkins)

NINTH ARMY CORPS (MAJ. GEN. AMBROSE E. BURNSIDE)

FIRST DIVISION (BRIG. GEN. JAMES LEDLIE)

First Brigade (Col. Jacob P. Gould)
Second Brigade (Col. Ebenezer W. Pierce)

SECOND DIVISION (BRIG. GEN. ROBERT B. POTTER)

First Brigade (Lt. Col. Henry Pleasants)
Second Brigade (Brig. Gen. Simon G. Griffin)

THIRD DIVISION (BRIG. GEN. ORLANDO B. WILLCOX)

First Brigade (Col. John F. Hartranft)
Second Brigade (Col. William Humphrey)

FOURTH DIVISION (BRIG. GEN. EDWARD FERRERO)

First Brigade (Col. Joshua K. Sigfried)
Second Brigade (Col. Henry G. Thomas)
Artillery Brigade (Lt. Col. John A. Monroe)

CAVALRY CORPS (MAJ. GEN. PHILIP H. SHERIDAN)

FIRST DIVISION (BRIG. GEN. ALFRED T. A. TORBERT)

First Brigade (Brig. Gen. George A. Custer)
Second Brigade (Col. Thomas C. Devin)
Reserve Brigade (Brig. Gen. Wesley Merritt)

SECOND DIVISION (BRIG. GEN. DAVID McM. GREGG)

First Brigade (Brig. Gen. Henry E. Davies Jr.)
Second Brigade (Col. J. Irvin Gregg)

THIRD DIVISION (BRIG. GEN. JAMES H. WILSON)

First Brigade (Col. John B. McIntosh)
Second Brigade (Col. George H. Chapman)
Horse Artillery Brigade (Capt. James M. Robertson)

DEPARTMENT OF VIRGINIA AND NORTH CAROLINA (MAJ. GEN. BENJAMIN F. BUTLER)

Naval Brigade (Brig. Gen. Charles K. Graham)
Engineers (Maj. Joseph Walker)
Siege Artillery (Col. Henry L. Abbott)
Signal Corps (Capt. Lemuel B. Norton)

TENTH ARMY CORPS (BRIG. GEN. WILLIAM T. H. BROOKS)

FIRST DIVISION (BRIG. GEN. ALFRED H. TERRY)

First Brigade (Col. Joshua B. Howell)
Second Brigade (Col. Joseph R. Hawley)
Third Brigade (Col. Harris M. Plaisted)
Artillery (Capt. Loomis L. Langdon)

SECOND DIVISION (BRIG. GEN. JOHN W. TURNER)

First Brigade (Col. N. Martin Curtis)
Second Brigade (Col. William B. Barton)
Third Brigade (Col. Louis Bell)
Artillery (Capt. George T. Woodbury)

THIRD DIVISION (BRIG. GEN. ORRIS S. FERRY)

First Brigade (Brig. Gen. Gilman Marston)
Second Brigade (Col. James B. Armstrong)

EIGHTEENTH ARMY CORPS (MAJ. GEN. WILLIAM F. SMITH)

FIRST DIVISION (BRIG. GEN. GEORGE J. STANNARD)

First Brigade (Col. Edgar M. Cullen)
Second Brigade (Brig. Gen. Hiram Burnham)
Third Brigade (Col. Guy V. Henry)

SECOND DIVISION (BRIG. GEN. JOHN H. MARTINDALE)

First Brigade (Col. Alexander Piper)
Second Brigade (Col. Griffin A. Stedman Jr.)

Third Brigade (Brig. Gen. Adelbert Ames)
THIRD DIVISION (BRIG. GEN. EDWARD W. HINKS)
First Brigade (Col. John H. Holman)
Second Brigade (Col. Samuel Duncan)
Artillery Brigade (Col. Henry S. Burton)

CAVALRY DIVISION (BRIG. GEN. AUGUST V. KAUTZ)
First Brigade (Col. Robert M. West)
Second Brigade (Col. Samuel M. Spear)

CONFEDERATE STATES ARMY

Gen. Robert E. Lee, Commanding

ARMY OF NORTHERN VIRGINIA

Gen. Robert E. Lee, Commanding
Provost Guard (Maj. D. B. Bridgford)
Engineers (Col. T. M. R. Talcott)

FIRST ARMY CORPS (LT. GEN. RICHARD H. ANDERSON)

PICKETT'S DIVISION (MAJ. GEN. GEORGE E. PICKETT)
Steuart's Brigade (Brig. Gen. George H. Steuart)
Corse's Brigade (Brig. Gen. Montgomery D. Corse)
Hunton's Brigade (Brig. Gen. Eppa Hunton)
Terry's Brigade (Col. William R. Terry)

FIELD'S DIVISION (MAJ. GEN. CHARLES W. FIELD)
Bratton's Brigade (Brig. Gen. John C. Bratton)
Anderson's Brigade (Brig. Gen. George T. Anderson)
Law's Brigade (Col. William F. Perry)
Gregg's Brigade (Brig. Gen. John Gregg)
Benning's Brigade (Col. Dudley M. DuBose)

KERSHAW'S DIVISION (BRIG. GEN. JOSEPH B. KERSHAW)
Kershaw's Brigade (Col. John W. Henagan)
Humphreys's Brigade (Brig. Gen. Benjamin G. Humphreys)
Wofford's Brigade (Brig. Gen. William T. Wofford)
Bryan's Brigade (Col. James P. Simms)
Artillery (Brig. Gen. E. Porter Alexander)
    Huger's Battalion (Lt. Col. Frank Huger)
    Haskell's Battalion (Maj. John C. Haskell)
    Cabell's Battalion (Col. Henry C. Cabell)
    Gibbes's Battalion (Maj. Wade H. Gibbes)

THIRD ARMY CORPS (LT. GEN. AMBROSE P. HILL)

ANDERSON'S DIVISION (BRIG. GEN. WILLIAM MAHONE)

Sanders's Brigade (Col. John C. C. Sanders)
Mahone's Brigade (Col. David A. Weisiger)
Harris's Brigade (Brig. Gen. Nathaniel H. Harris)
Wright's Brigade (Brig. Gen. Ambrose R. Wright)
Perry's Brigade (Brig. Gen. Joseph Finegan)

HETH'S DIVISION (MAJ. GEN. HENRY HETH)

Davis's Brigade (Brig. Gen. Joseph R. Davis)
Cooke's Brigade (Brig. Gen. John R. Cooke)
Kirkland's Brigade (Col. William MacRae)
Fry's Brigade (Col. Robert M. Mayo)

WILCOX'S DIVISION (MAJ. GEN. CADMUS M. WILCOX)

Thomas's Brigade (Brig. Gen. Edward L. Thomas)
Lane's Brigade (Brig. Gen. James H. Lane)
McGowan's Brigade (Brig. Gen. Samuel McGowan)
Scales's Brigade (Brig. Gen. Alfred M. Scales)
Artillery (Col. R. Lindsay Walker)
    Cutts's Battalion (Lt. Col. Allen S. Cutts)
    Richardson's Battalion (Lt. Col. Charles Richardson)
    McIntosh's Battalion (Lt. Col. David G. McIntosh)
    Pegram's Battalion (Lt. Col. William J. Pegram)
    Poague's Battalion (Lt. Col. William T. Poague)
    Washington Artillery (Lt. Col. Benjamin Eshelman)

CAVALRY CORPS (MAJ. GEN. WADE HAMPTON)

HAMPTON'S DIVISION (MAJ. GEN. WADE HAMPTON)

Dunovant's Brigade (Brig. Gen. John Dunovant)
Young's Brigade (Brig. Gen. Pierce M. B. Young)
Rosser's Brigade (Brig. Gen. Thomas L. Rosser)

FITZHUGH LEE'S DIVISION (MAJ. GEN. FITZHUGH LEE)

Wickham's Brigade (Brig. Gen. Williams C. Wickham)
Lomax's Brigade (Brig. Gen. Lunsford L. Lomax)

W.H.F. LEE'S DIVISION (MAJ. GEN. W. H. F. LEE)

Barringer's Brigade (Brig. Gen. Rufus Barringer)
Chambliss's Brigade (Brig. Gen. John R. Chambliss Jr.)
Horse Artillery (Maj. R. Preston Chew)
    Breathed's Battalion (Maj. James Breathed)

ARTILLERY (BRIG. GEN. WILLIAM N. PENDLETON)

Second Corps Artillery (Brig. Gen. Armistead L. Long)
    Carter's Battalion (Lt. Col. Thomas H. Carter)
    Cutshaw's Battalion (Maj. Wilfred E. Cutshaw)
    Brown's Battalion (Lt. Col. Robert A. Hardaway)

DEPARTMENT OF NORTH CAROLINA AND SOUTHERN VIRGINIA (GEN. PIERRE G. T. BEAUREGARD)

JOHNSON'S DIVISION (MAJ. GEN. BUSHROD R. JOHNSON)

Elliott's Brigade (Brig. Gen. Stephen D. Elliott)
Gracie's Brigade (Brig. Gen. Archibald Gracie)
Johnson's Brigade (Col. John S. Fulton)
    Moseley's Artillery Battalion (Maj. Edgar F. Moseley)
    Coit's Artillery Battalion (Maj. James C. Coit)

HOKE'S DIVISION (MAJ. GEN. ROBERT F. HOKE)

Clingman's Brigade (Brig. Gen. Thomas L. Clingman)
Colquitt's Brigade (Brig. Gen. Alfred H. Colquitt)
Hagood's Brigade (Brig. Gen. Johnson Hagood)
Martin's Brigade (Brig. Gen. James G. Martin)
    Read's Artillery Battalion (Maj. John P. W. Read)

FIRST MILITARY DISTRICT (BRIG. GEN. HENRY A. WISE)

Wise's Brigade (Col. Powhatan R. Page)
Dearing's Cavalry Brigade (Brig. Gen. James Dearing)
    Bogg's Artillery Battalion (Maj. Francis J. Boggs)

DEPARTMENT OF RICHMOND (LT. GEN. RICHARD S. EWELL)

Ransom's Brigade (Brig. Gen. Matthew W. Ransom)
Cavalry Brigade (Brig. Gen. Martin W. Gary)
Local Defense Troops and Reserves (Brig. Gen. George W. C. Lee)

RICHMOND FORCES (MAJ. GEN. JAMES L. KEMPER)

BARTON'S DIVISION (BRIG. GEN. SETH M. BARTON)

ARTILLERY DEFENSES (LT. COL. JOHN C. PEMBERTON)

FIRST DIVISION (LT. COL. JOHN W. ATKINSON)

SECOND DIVISION (LT. COL. JAMES HOWARD)

Light Artillery (Lt. Col. Charles E. Lightfoot)
Chaffin's Farm (Maj. Alexander W. Stark)
Chaffin's Bluff (Lt. Col. J. M. Maury)
Drewry's Bluff (Maj. F. W. Smith)
James River Naval Squadron (Comdr. John K. Mitchell)

APPENDIX II
ORDER OF BATTLE, 29 SEPTEMBER 1864

UNITED STATES ARMY

Lt. Gen. Ulysses S. Grant, Commanding

ARMY OF THE POTOMAC

Maj. Gen. George G. Meade, Commanding

SECOND CAVALRY DIVISION (BRIG. GEN. DAVID McM. GREGG)

First Brigade (Brig. Gen. Henry E. Davies Jr.)
Second Brigade (Col. Charles H. Smith)
Remount Camp (Capt. Andrew H. Bibber)
Artillery Reserve (Brig. Gen. Henry Hunt)
Artillery Park (Capt. Calvin Shaffer)
Detachment, Sixth Corps (Capt. William Harn)
Engineers (Brig. Gen. Henry W. Benham)
Provost Guard (Brig. Gen. Marsena R. Patrick)
Signal Corps Detachment (Maj. Benjamin F. Fisher)

SECOND ARMY CORPS (MAJ. GEN. WINFIELD SCOTT HANCOCK)

FIRST DIVISION (BRIG. GEN. NELSON A. MILES)

First Brigade (Col. James C. Lynch)
Consolidated Brigade (Lt. Col. James McGee)
Fourth Brigade (Lt. Col. William Glenny)

SECOND DIVISION (MAJ. GEN. JOHN GIBBON)

First Brigade (Brig. Gen. Thomas W. Egan)
Second Brigade (Col. Matthew Murphy)
Third Brigade (Col. Thomas A. Smyth)

THIRD DIVISION (BRIG. GEN. GERSHOM MOTT)

First Brigade (Brig. Gen. Regis De Trobriand)
Second Brigade (Brig. Gen. Byron R. Pierce)
Third Brigade (Col. Robert McAllister)
Artillery Brigade (Maj. John G. Hazard)

FIFTH ARMY CORPS (MAJ. GEN. GOUVERNEUR K. WARREN)

FIRST DIVISION (BRIG. GEN. CHARLES GRIFFIN)

First Brigade (Col. Horatio G. Sickel)
Second Brigade (Col. Edgar Gregory)

Third Brigade (Col. James Gwyn)

SECOND DIVISION (BRIG. GEN. ROMEYN B. AYRES)

First Brigade (Lt. Col. Elwell S. Otis)
Second Brigade (Col. Samuel Graham)
Third Brigade (Col. Arthur Grimshaw)

THIRD DIVISION (BRIG. GEN. SAMUEL W. CRAWFORD)

First Brigade (Brig. Gen. Edward S. Bragg)
Second Brigade (Brig. Gen. Henry Baxter)
Third Brigade (Col. J. William Hofmann)
Artillery Brigade (Col. Charles S. Wainwright)

NINTH ARMY CORPS (MAJ. GEN. JOHN G. PARKE)

FIRST DIVISION (BRIG. GEN. ORLANDO B. WILLCOX)

First Brigade (Col. Samuel Harriman)
Second Brigade (Brig. Gen. John F. Hartranft)
Third Brigade (Col. Napoleon B. McLaughlen)

SECOND DIVISION (BRIG. GEN. ROBERT B. POTTER)

First Brigade (Col. John I. Curtin)
Second Brigade (Brig. Gen. Simon G. Griffin)

THIRD DIVISION (BRIG. GEN. EDWARD FERRERO)

First Brigade (Col. Ozora P. Stearns)
Second Brigade (Col. Charles S. Russell)
Artillery Brigade (Lt. Col. John Albert Monroe)

ARMY OF THE JAMES

Maj. Gen. Benjamin F. Butler, Commanding

CAVALRY DIVISION (BRIG. AUGUST V. KAUTZ)

First Brigade (Col. Robert M. West)
Second Brigade (Col. Samuel P. Spear)
Independent Brigade (Brig. Gen. Gilman Marston)
Naval Brigade (Brig. Gen. Charles K. Graham)
Siege Train (Col. Henry L. Abbot)
Engineers (Col. Edward W. Serell)
Pontoneers (Capt. John Pickering)
Signal Corps Detachment (Capt. Henry R. Clum)

TENTH ARMY CORPS (MAJ. GEN. DAVID B. BIRNEY)

FIRST DIVISION (BRIG. GEN. ALFRED H. TERRY)

First Brigade (Col. Francis B. Pond)
Second Brigade (Col. Joseph C. Abbott)
Third Brigade (Col. Harris M. Plaisted)

SECOND DIVISION (BRIG. GEN. ROBERT S. FOSTER)

First Brigade (Col. Rufus Daggett)
Second Brigade (Col. Galusha Pennypacker)
Third Brigade (Col. Louis Bell)

THIRD DIVISION

First Brigade (Brig. Gen. William B. Birney)
Artillery Brigade (Lt. Col. Richard H. Jackson)

EIGHTEENTH ARMY CORPS (MAJ. GEN. EDWARD O. C. ORD)

FIRST DIVISION (BRIG. GEN. GEORGE J. STANNARD)

First Brigade (Col. Aaron F. Stevens)
Second Brigade (Brig. Gen. Hiram Burnham)
Third Brigade (Col. Samuel H. Roberts)

SECOND DIVISION (BRIG. GEN. CHARLES A. HECKMAN)

First Brigade (Col. James Jourdan)
Second Brigade (Col. Edward H. Ripley)
Third Brigade (Col. Harrison Fairchild)

THIRD DIVISION (BRIG. GEN. CHARLES J. PAINE)

First Brigade (Col. John H. Holman)
Second Brigade (Col. Alonzo G. Draper)
Third Brigade (Col. Samuel A. Duncan)
Temporary Brigade (Maj. David B. White)
Artillery Brigade (Maj. George B. Cook)
Provisional Brigade (Col. Joseph Potter)

CONFEDERATE STATES ARMY

Gen. Robert E. Lee, Commanding

ARMY OF NORTHERN VIRGINIA

Gen. Robert E. Lee, Commanding
Provost Guard (Maj. D. B. Bridgford)
Engineers (Col. T. M. R. Talcott)

FIRST ARMY CORPS (MAJ. GEN. RICHARD H. ANDERSON)

FIELD'S DIVISION (MAJ. GEN. CHARLES W. FIELD)

Gregg's Brigade (Brig. Gen. John Gregg)
Benning's Brigade (Col. Dudley M. DuBose)
Anderson's Brigade (Brig. Gen. George T. Anderson)
Law's Brigade (Col. Pinckney D. Bowles)
Bratton's Brigade (Brig. Gen. John C. Bratton)

PICKETT'S DIVISION (MAJ. GEN. GEORGE E. PICKETT)

Terry's Brigade (Brig. Gen. William R. Terry)
Hunton's Brigade (Brig. Gen. Eppa Hunton)
Steuart's Brigade (Brig. Gen. George H. Steuart)
Corse's Brigade (Brig. Gen. Montgomery D. Corse)
Provisional Brigade (Col. Edgar B. Montague)
Artillery Brigade (Brig. Gen. Edward Porter Alexander)
 Cabell's Battalion (Col. Henry C. Cabell)
 Huger's Battalion (Maj. Frank Huger)
 Haskell's Battalion (Maj. John C. Haskell)
 Thirteenth Virginia Light Artillery Battalion (Maj. William M. Owen)
 First Virginia Light Artillery Battalion (Lt. Col. Robert A. Hardaway)
 Johnson's Battalion (Maj. Marmaduke Johnson)

THIRD ARMY CORPS (LT. GEN. AMBROSE P. HILL)

HETH'S DIVISION (MAJ. GEN. HENRY HETH)

MacRae's Brigade (Brig. Gen. William MacRae)
Cooke's Brigade (Brig. Gen. John R. Cooke)
Davis's Brigade (Brig. Gen. Joseph R. Davis)
Archer's Brigade (Brig. Gen. James J. Archer)

LIGHT DIVISION (MAJ. GEN. CADMUS M. WILCOX)

Lane's Brigade (Brig. Gen. James H. Lane)
McGowan's Brigade (Brig. Gen. Samuel McGowan)
Scales's Brigade (Brig. Gen. Alfred M. Scales)
Thomas's Brigade (Brig. Gen. Edward L. Thomas)

MAHONE'S DIVISION (MAJ. GEN. WILLIAM MAHONE)

Mahone's Brigade (Col. David A. Weisiger)
Harris's Brigade (Brig. Gen. Nathaniel H. Harris)
Finegan's Brigade (Brig. Gen. Joseph Finegan)
Sanders's Brigade (Col. J. Horace King)
Girardey's Brigade (Col. William Gibson)
Artillery Brigade (Col. Reuben L. Walker)
 Pegram's Battalion (Lt. Col. William J. Pegram)
 McIntosh's Battalion (Lt. Col. David G. McIntosh)
 Richardson's Battalion (Lt. Col. Charles Richardson)
 Eleventh Georgia Light Artillery Battalion (Maj. John Lane)
 Poague's Battalion (Lt. Col. William Poague)
 Washington Artillery Battalion (Lt. Col. Benjamin Eshelman)

CAVALRY CORPS (MAJ. GEN. WADE HAMPTON)

FIRST DIVISION (BRIG. GEN. MATTHEW C. BUTLER)

Dunovant's Brigade (Brig. Gen. John Dunovant)
Young's Brigade (Brig. Gen. Pierce M. B. Young)

THIRD DIVISION (MAJ. GEN. W. H. F. LEE)

Chambliss's Brigade (Col. J. Lucius Davis)
Barringer's Brigade (Brig. Gen. Rufus Barringer)

Dearing's Brigade (Col. Joel R. Griffin)
 Horse Artillery Battalion (Maj. R. Preston Chew)

DEPARTMENT OF NORTH CAROLINA AND SOUTHERN VIRGINIA

HOKE'S DIVISION (MAJ. GEN. ROBERT F. HOKE)

Clingman's Brigade (Col. Hector M. McKethan)
Colquitt's Brigade (Brig. Gen. Alfred H. Colquitt)
Hagood's Brigade (Brig. Gen. Johnson Hagood)
Kirkland's Brigade (Brig. Gen. William W. Kirkland)

JOHNSON'S DIVISION (MAJ. GEN. BUSHROD R. JOHNSON)

Wise's Brigade (Col. John T. Goode)
Ransom's Brigade (Col. Lee McAfee)
Gracie's Brigade (Brig. Gen. Archibald Gracie)
Wallace's Brigade (Brig. Gen. William H. Wallace)

FIRST MILITARY DISTRICT (BRIG. GEN. HENRY A. WISE)

Walker's Brigade (Brig. Gen. James A. Walker)
Garnett's Brigade (Lt. Col. John J. Garnett)
Post of Petersburg (Maj. William Ker)
Fort Clifton (Lt. Col. Henry Guion)
Artillery Brigade (Col. Hilary P. Jones)
 Twelfth Virginia Light Artillery Battalion (Maj. Francis J. Boggs)
 Thirty-eighth Virginia Light Artillery Battalion (Lt. Col. John Read)
 Coit's Battalion (Maj. James C. Coit)
 Moseley's Battalion (Lt. Col. Edgar Moseley)
 Drewry's Bluff (Lt. Col. George Terrett)
 Smith's Artillery Battalion (Maj. Francis Smith)

DEPARTMENT OF RICHMOND (LT. GEN. RICHARD S. EWELL)

Johnson's Brigade (Col. John M. Hughs)
 First Virginia Reserve Battalion (Maj. James Strange)
 Second Virginia Reserve Battalion (Lt. Col. John H. Guy)
 Twenty-fifth Virginia Battalion (Maj. Wyatt Elliot)
Gary's Cavalry Brigade (Brig. Gen. Martin W. Gary)
Richmond Forces (Maj. Gen. James L. Kemper)

BARTON'S DIVISION (BRIG. GEN. SETH M. BARTON)

Local Defense Brigade (Brig. Gen. Patrick T. Moore)
Barton's City Brigade (Col. Meriwether Lewis Clark)
Independent Richmond Infantry
Independent Richmond Cavalry
Artillery Defenses (Lt. Col. John C. Pemberton)

FIRST DIVISION (LT. COL. JOHN W. ATKINSON)

SECOND DIVISION (LT. COL. JAMES M. HOWARD)

 Lightfoot's Battalion (Lt. Col. Charles E. Lightfoot)
 Stark's Battalion (Maj. Alexander W. Stark)
 Chaffin's Bluff Battalion (Lt. Col. John Minor Maury)
James River Naval Squadron (Comdr. John K. Mitchell)

APPENDIX III
ORDER OF BATTLE, 1–2 APRIL 1865

UNITED STATES ARMY

Lt. Gen. Ulysses S. Grant, Commanding

ARMY OF THE POTOMAC

Maj. Gen. George G. Meade, Commanding
Provost Guard (Brig. Gen. George N. Macy)
Engineer Brigade (Brig. Gen. Henry W. Benham)
Independent Brigade (Brig. Gen. Charles H. T. Collis)
Artillery (Brig. Gen. Henry J. Hunt)
Siege Train (Brig. Gen. Henry L. Abbott)

SECOND ARMY CORPS (MAJ. GEN. ANDREW A. HUMPHREYS)

FIRST DIVISION (BRIG. GEN. NELSON A. MILES)

First Brigade (Col. George W. Scott)
Second Brigade (Col. Robert Nugent)
Third Brigade (Col. Henry J. Madill)
Fourth Brigade (Col. John Ramsey)

SECOND DIVISION (BRIG. GEN. WILLIAM HAYS)

First Brigade (Col. William Olmsted)
Second Brigade (Col. James P. McIvor)
Third Brigade (Brig. Gen. Thomas A. Smyth)

THIRD DIVISION (BRIG. GEN. GERSHOM MOTT)

First Brigade (Brig. Gen. Regis de Trobriand)
Second Brigade (Brig. Gen. Byron R. Pierce)
Third Brigade (Col. Robert McAllister)
Artillery Brigade (Lt. Col. John G. Hazard)

FIFTH ARMY CORPS (MAJ. GEN. GOUVERNEUR K. WARREN)

FIRST DIVISION (BRIG. GEN. CHARLES GRIFFIN)

First Brigade (Brig. Gen. Joshua L. Chamberlain)
Second Brigade (Col. Edgar M. Gregory)
Third Brigade (Maj. Gen. Joseph J. Bartlett)

SECOND DIVISION (BRIG. GEN. ROMEYN B. AYRES)

First Brigade (Brig. Gen. Frederick Winthrop)
Second Brigade (Brig. Gen. Andrew W. Denison)

Third Brigade (Brig. Gen. James Gwyn)

THIRD DIVISION (BRIG. GEN. SAMUEL W. CRAWFORD)
First Brigade (Col. John A. Kellogg)
Second Brigade (Brig. Gen. Henry Baxter)
Third Brigade (Col. Richard Coulter)
Artillery Brigade (Brig. Gen. Charles S. Wainwright)

SIXTH ARMY CORPS (MAJ. GEN. HORATIO G. WRIGHT)

FIRST DIVISION (BRIG. GEN. FRANK WHEATON)
First Brigade (Col. William H. Penrose)
Second Brigade (Col. Joseph E. Hamblin)
Third Brigade (Col. Oliver Edwards)

SECOND DIVISION (BRIG. GEN. GEORGE W. GETTY)
First Brigade (Col. James M. Warner)
Second Brigade (Brig. Gen. Lewis A. Grant)
Third Brigade (Col. Thomas W. Hyde)

THIRD DIVISION (BRIG. GEN. TRUMAN SEYMOUR)
First Brigade (Col. William S. Truex)
Second Brigade (Col. J. Warren Keifer)
Artillery Brigade (Maj. Andrew Cowen)

NINTH ARMY CORPS (MAJ. GEN. JOHN G. PARKE)

FIRST DIVISION (BRIG. GEN. ORLANDO B. WILLCOX)
First Brigade (Col. Samuel Harriman)
Second Brigade (Lt. Col. Ralph Ely)
Third Brigade (Lt. Col. Gilbert P. Robinson)

SECOND DIVISION (BRIG. GEN. ROBERT B. POTTER)
First Brigade (Col. John I. Curtin)
Second Brigade (Brig. Gen. Simon G. Griffin)

THIRD DIVISION (BRIG. JOHN F. HARTRANFT)
First Brigade (Lt. Col. William H. H. McCall)
Second Brigade (Col. Joseph A. Mathews)
Independent Brigade (Col. Charles H. T. Collis)
Artillery Brigade (Col. John C. Tidball)

CAVALRY CORPS

SECOND DIVISION (MAJ. GEN. GEORGE CROOK)
First Brigade (Brig. Gen. Henry E. Davies Jr.)
Second Brigade (Col. J. Irvin Gregg)
Third Brigade (Col. Charles H. Smith)

ARMY OF THE SHENANDOAH

Maj. Gen. Philip H. Sheridan, Commanding

CAVALRY CORPS (BRIG. GEN. WESLEY MERRITT)

FIRST DIVISION (BRIG. GEN. THOMAS C. DEVIN)

First Brigade (Col. Peter Stagg)
Second Brigade (Col. Charles L. Fitzhugh)
Third (Reserve) Brigade (Brig. Gen. Alfred Gibbs)

THIRD DIVISION (BRIG. GEN. GEORGE A. CUSTER)

First Brigade (Col. Alexander C. M. Pennington)
Second Brigade (Col. William Wells)
Third Brigade (Col. Henry Capehart)

ARMY OF THE JAMES

Maj. Gen. Edward O. C. Ord, Commanding

BERMUDA HUNDRED DEFENSES (MAJ. GEN. GEORGE L. HARTSUFF)

INFANTRY DIVISION (MAJ. GEN. EDWARD FERRERO)

First Brigade (Col. Gilbert H. McKibbin)
Second Brigade (Col. George C. Kibbe)
Independent Brigade (Brig. Gen. Joseph B. Carr)
Artillery (Col. Henry L. Abbott)
Fort Pocahontas (Lt. Col. Ashbel W. Angel)
Harrison's Landing (Col. Wardwell G. Robinson)
Fort Powhatan (Col. William J. Sewell)

TWENTY-FOURTH ARMY CORPS (MAJ. GEN. JOHN GIBBON)

FIRST DIVISION (BRIG. GEN. ROBERT S. FOSTER)

First Brigade (Col. Thomas O. Osborn)
Third Brigade (Col. George B. Dandy)
Fourth Brigade (Col. Harrison S. Fairchild)

THIRD DIVISION (BRIG. GEN. CHARLES DEVENS)

First Brigade (Col. Edward H. Ripley)
Second Brigade (Col. Michael T. Donohoe)
Third Brigade (Col. Samuel H. Roberts)

INDEPENDENT DIVISION (BRIG. GEN. JOHN W. TURNER)

First Brigade (Lt. Col. Andrew Potter)
Second Brigade (Col. William B. Curtis)
Third Brigade (Brig. Gen. Thomas M. Harris)
Artillery (Maj. Charles C. Abell)

TWENTY-FIFTH ARMY CORPS (MAJ. GEN. GODFREY WEITZEL)

FIRST DIVISION (BRIG. GEN. AUGUST V. KAUTZ)

First Brigade (Col. Alonzo G. Draper)
Second Brigade (Brig. Gen. Edward A. Wild)
Third Brigade (Brig. Gen. Henry G. Thomas)
Attached Brigade (Col. Charles S. Russell)

SECOND DIVISION (BRIG. GEN. WILLIAM B. BIRNEY)

First Brigade (Col. James Shaw Jr.)
Second Brigade (Col. Ulysses Doubleday)
Third Brigade (Col. William W. Woodward)
Artillery Brigade (Capt. Loomis L. Langdon)

CAVALRY DIVISION (BRIG. GEN. RANALD S. MACKENZIE)

First Brigade (Col. Robert M. West)
Second Brigade (Col. Andrew W. Evans)

CONFEDERATE STATES ARMY

Gen. Robert E. Lee, Commanding

ARMY OF NORTHERN VIRGINIA

Gen. Robert E. Lee, Commanding
Provost Guard (Maj. D. B. Bridgeford)
Engineers (Col. T. M. R. Talcott)

FIRST ARMY CORPS (LT. GEN. JAMES LONGSTREET)

PICKETT'S DIVISION (MAJ. GEN. GEORGE E. PICKETT)

Steuart's Brigade (Brig. Gen. George H. Steuart)
Corse's Brigade (Brig. Gen. Montgomery D. Corse)
Hunton's Brigade (Brig. Gen. Eppa Hunton)
Terry's Brigade (Maj. William W. Bentley)

FIELD'S DIVISION (MAJ. GEN. CHARLES W. FIELD)

Perry's Brigade (Brig. Gen. William F. Perry)
Anderson's Brigade (Brig. Gen. George T. Anderson)
Benning's Brigade (Brig. Gen. Henry L. Benning)
Gregg's Brigade (Col. Robert M. Powell)
Bratton's Brigade (Brig. Gen. John C. Bratton)

KERSHAW'S DIVISION (MAJ. GEN. JOSEPH B. KERSHAW)

DuBose's Brigade (Brig. Gen. Dudley M. DuBose)
Humphreys's Brigade (Col. William H. FitzGerald)
Simms's Brigade (Brig. Gen. James P. Simms)
Artillery (Brig. Gen. Edward Porter Alexander)
    Haskell's Battalion (Lt. Col. John C. Haskell)
    Huger's Battalion (Maj. Tyler C. Jordan)

SECOND ARMY CORPS (MAJ. GEN. JOHN B. GORDON)

GRIMES'S DIVISION (MAJ. GEN. BRYAN GRIMES)

Battle's Brigade (Col. Edwin L. Hobson)
Grimes's Brigade (Col. David G. Cowand)
Cox's Brigade (Brig. Gen. William R. Cox)
Cook's Brigade (Col. Edwin A. Nash)
     Archer's Battalion (Lt. Col. Fletcher H. Archer)

EARLY'S DIVISION (BRIG. GEN. JAMES A. WALKER)

Johnston's Brigade (Col. John W. Lea)
Lewis's Brigade (Capt. John Beard)
Walker's Brigade (Maj. Henry Kyd Douglas)

GORDON'S DIVISION (BRIG. GEN. CLEMENT A. EVANS)

Evans's Brigade (Col. John H. Lowe)
Terry's Brigade (Col. Titus V. Williams)
York's Brigade (Col. Eugene Wagaman)
Artillery (Brig. Gen. Armistead L. Long)

THIRD ARMY CORPS (LT. GEN. AMBROSE P. HILL)

HETH'S DIVISION (MAJ. GEN. HENRY HETH)

Davis's Brigade (Col. Andrew M. Nelson)
Cooke's Brigade (Brig. Gen. John R. Cooke)
MacRae's Brigade (Brig. Gen. William MacRae)
McComb's Brigade (Brig. Gen. William McComb)

LIGHT DIVISION (MAJ. GEN. CADMUS M. WILCOX)

Thomas's Brigade (Brig. Gen. Edward L. Thomas)
Lane's Brigade (Brig. Gen. James H. Lane)
McGowan's Brigade (Brig. Gen. Samuel McGowan)
Scales's Brigade (Brig. Gen. Alfred M. Scales)

MAHONE'S DIVISION (MAJ. GEN. WILLIAM MAHONE)

Forney's Brigade (Brig. Gen. William H. Forney)
Weisiger's Brigade (Brig. Gen. David A. Weisiger)
Harris's Brigade (Brig. Gen. Nathaniel H. Harris)
Sorrel's Brigade (Col. George E. Taylor)
Finegan's Brigade (Col. David Lang)
Artillery Brigade (Brig. Gen. Reuben L. Walker)

ANDERSON'S CORPS (LT. GEN. RICHARD H. ANDERSON)

JOHNSON'S DIVISION (MAJ. GEN. BUSHROD R. JOHNSON)

Wise's Brigade (Brig. Gen. Henry A. Wise)
Wallace's Brigade (Brig. Gen. William H. Wallace)
Moody's Brigade (Brig. Gen. Young M. Moody)
Ransom's Brigade (Brig. Gen. Matthew W. Ransom)
Artillery (Col. Hilary P. Jones)

CAVALRY CORPS (MAJ. GEN. FITZHUGH LEE)

FITZHUGH LEE'S DIVISION (BRIG. GEN. THOMAS T. MUNFORD)

Payne's Brigade (Col. Reuben B. Boston)
Munford's Brigade (Brig. Gen. Thomas T. Munford)
Gary's Brigade (Brig. Gen. Martin W. Gary)

W. H. F. LEE'S DIVISION (MAJ. GEN. WILLIAM H. FITZHUGH LEE)

Barringer's Brigade (Brig. Gen. Rufus Barringer)
Beale's Brigade (Capt. Samuel H. Burt)
Roberts's Brigade (Brig. Gen. William P. Roberts)

ROSSER'S DIVISION (MAJ. GEN. THOMAS L. ROSSER)

Dearing's Brigade (Brig. Gen. James Dearing)
McCausland's Brigade
Artillery (Lt. Col. R. Preston Chew)

DEPARTMENT OF RICHMOND (LT. GEN. RICHARD S. EWELL)

G. W. C. LEE'S DIVISION (MAJ. GEN. GEORGE W. C. LEE)

Barton's Brigade (Brig. Gen. Seth M. Barton)
Moore's Brigade (Brig. Gen. Patrick T. Moore)
Artillery Brigade (Col. Stapleton Crutchfield)
Light Artillery (Lt. Col. Charles E. Lightfoot)
Chaffin's Bluff (Lt. Col. J. M. Maury)
Drewry's Bluff (Maj. F. W. Smith)
James River Naval Squadron (Rear Adm. Raphael Semmes)

BIBLIOGRAPHY

Alexander, Edward Porter. *Fighting for the Confederacy: The Personal Recollections of General Edward Porter Alexander.* Edited by Gary W. Gallagher. Chapel Hill: University of North Carolina Press, 1989.

Basler, Roy P., ed. *The Collected Works of Abraham Lincoln,* 9 vols. New Brunswick, N.J.: Rutgers University Press, 1953–1955.

Bearss, Edwin C., and Chris Calkins. *The Battle of Five Forks.* Lynchburg, Va.: H. E. Howard, 1985.

Bearss, Edwin C., with Bryce A. Suderow. *The Petersburg Campaign, Volume 1: The Eastern Front Battles, June–August 1864.* El Dorado Hills, Calif.: Savas-Beatie, 2012.

Bernard, George S., ed. *War Talks of Confederate Veterans.* Petersburg, Va.: Fenn and Owen, 1892.

Bowery, Charles R. *Lee and Grant: Profiles in Leadership from the Battlefields of Virginia.* New York: AMACON, 2005.

Caldwell, J. F. J. *The History of a Brigade of South Carolinians Known as "Gregg's," and Subsequently as "McGowen's Brigade."* Philadelphia, Pa.: King and Baird, 1866.

Calkins, Chris. *History and Tour Guide of Five Forks, Hatcher's Run and Namozine Church.* Columbus, Ohio: Blue and Gray Magazine, 2003.

Catton, Bruce. *Grant Takes Command.* Boston: Little, Brown, 1968.

Cavanaugh, Michael A., and William Marvel. *The Battle of the Crater: "The Horrid Pit," June 25–August 6, 1864.* Lynchburg, Va..: H. E. Howard, 1989.

Dowdey, Clifford, and Louis H. Manarin, eds. *The Wartime Papers of Robert E. Lee.* New York: Da Capo, 1987.

Fox, John J., III. *The Confederate Alamo: Bloodbath at Petersburg's Fort Gregg on April 2, 1865.* Winchester, Va..: Angle Valley Press, 2010.

Freeman, Douglas Southall. *R. E. Lee,* 4 vols. New York: Charles Scribner's Sons, 1934–1935.

Gallagher, Gary W., ed. *Lee the Soldier.* Lincoln: University of Nebraska Press, 1996.

Gordon, John B. *Reminiscences of the Civil War.* New York: Charles Scribner's Sons, 1903.

Grant, Ulysses S. *Personal Memoirs of Ulysses S. Grant.* Edited by Brooks D. Simpson. Lincoln: University of Nebraska Press, 1996 [1885].

Greene, A. Wilson. *Breaking the Backbone of the Rebellion: The Final Battles of the Petersburg Campaign,* 2nd ed. Knoxville: University of Tennessee Press, 2008.

———. *Civil War Petersburg: Confederate City in the Crucible of War.* Charlottesville: University of Virginia Press, 2006.

Grimsley, Mark, and Brooks D. Simpson, eds. *The Collapse of the Confederacy.* Lincoln: University of Nebraska Press, 2002.

Hagood, Johnson. *Memoirs of the War of Secession: From the Original Manuscripts of Johnson Hagood.* Columbia, S.C.: The State Company, 1910.

Hattaway, Herman, and Archer Jones. *How the North Won: A Military History of the Civil War.* Urbana: University of Illinois Press, 1983.

Hess, Earl J. *In the Trenches at Petersburg: Field Fortifications and Confederate Defeat.* Chapel Hill: University of North Carolina Press, 2009.

————. *Into the Crater: The Mine Attack at Petersburg.* Columbia: University of South Carolina Press, 2010.

Hewett, Janet B., et al., eds. *Supplement to the Official Records of the Union and Confederate Armies,* 51 vols. Wilmington, N.C.: Broadfoot Publishing, 1994–1997.

Horn, John. *The Destruction of the Weldon Railroad: Deep Bottom, Globe Tavern, and Reams Station, August 14–25, 1864.* Lynchburg, Va.: H. E. Howard, 1991.

————. *The Petersburg Campaign, June 1864–April 1865.* New York: Da Capo Press, 1993.

Howe, Thomas J. *The Petersburg Campaign: Wasted Valor: June 15–18, 1864.* Lynchburg, Va.: H. E. Howard, 1988.

Humphreys, Andrew A. *The Virginia Campaign of '64 and '65.* New York: Charles Scribner's Sons, 1883.

Johnson, Robert U., and Clarence C. Buel, eds. *Battles and Leaders of the Civil War,* 4 vols. New York: Century, 1887–1888.

Levin, Kevin M. *Remembering the Battle of the Crater: War as Murder.* Lexington: University Press of Kentucky, 2012.

Longacre, Edward G. *Army of Amateurs: General Benjamin F. Butler and the Army of the James, 1863–1865.* Mechanicsburg, Pa.: Stackpole Books, 1997.

Nevins, Allan, ed. *A Diary of Battle: The Personal Journals of Colonel Charles S. Wainwright, 1861–1865.* New York: Da Capo, 1962.

Newsome, Hampton. *Richmond Must Fall: The Richmond-Petersburg Campaign, October 1864.* Kent, Ohio: Kent State University Press, 2013.

Newsome, Hampton, John Horn, and John G. Selby, eds. *Civil War Talks: Further Reminiscences of George S. Bernard and His Fellow Veterans.* Charlottesville: University of Virginia Press, 2012.

Pickett, LaSalle Corbell. *Pickett and His Men.* Philadelphia: J. B. Lippincott Company, 1913 [1899].

Porter, Horace. *Campaigning with Grant.* New York: Century, 1897.

Powell, William H. *The Fifth Army Corps (Army of the Potomac): A Record of Operations during the Civil War in the United States of America, 1861–1865.* London: G. P. Putnam's Sons, 1986.

Power, J. Tracy. *Lee's Miserables: Life in the Army of Northern Virginia from the Wilderness to Appomattox.* Chapel Hill: University of North Carolina Press, 1998.

Rafuse, Ethan S. *Robert E. Lee and the Fall of the Confederacy, 1863–1865.* Lanham, Md.: Rowman and Littlefield, 2008.

Robertson, James I., ed. *The Civil War Letters of General Robert McAllister.* New Brunswick, N.J.: Rutgers University Press, 1965.

Robertson, John, compiler. *Michigan in the War.* Lansing, Mich.: W. S. George & Company, 1882.

Simpson, Brooks D. *Ulysses S. Grant: Triumph over Adversity, 1822–1865.* New York: Houghton Mifflin, 2000.

Slotkin, Richard. *No Quarter: The Battle of the Crater, 1864.* New York: Random House, 2009.

Smith, Adelaide W. *Reminiscences of an Army Nurse during the Civil War.* New York: Greaves Publishing, 1911.

Sommers, Richard J. *Richmond Redeemed: The Siege at Petersburg.* Garden City, N.Y.: Doubleday, 1981.

Southern Historical Society Papers, 52 vols. Millwood, NY: Kraus Reprint, 1977 (1876–1959).

Stephens, Alexander H. *A Constitutional View of the Late War between the States,* 2 vols. Atlanta, Ga.: National Publishing, 1868–1870.

Thomas, Emory M. *Robert E. Lee: A Biography.* New York: W. W. Norton, 1995.

Trudeau, Noah Andre. *The Last Citadel: Petersburg, Virginia, June 1864–April 1865.* Boston: Little, Brown, 1991.

U.S. War Department. *War of the Rebellion: A Compilation of the Official Records of the Union and Confederate Armies,* 70 vols. in 128 parts. Washington, D.C.: Government Printing Office, 1880–1901.

INDEX

Abbot, Henry, 189
Acorn Drive, 321
Adams, A., house of, 414
Adams, J. Webb, 379
Adams, Samuel, 80–81
Adams Express, 193
Aiken house, 276, 331
Aiken's Landing, Va., 265, 266, 268
Airport Street, 387, 451
Alabama troops
    Fifth Alabama, 460
    Ninth Alabama, 139
    Forty-first Alabama, 408
Alexander, Edward Porter, 74, 280
Allin Road, 159
Amelia Court-House, Va., 443, 461
American Revolution, 142
Ames, John W., 258
Anderson, Edward C., 229, 235
Anderson, George T., 272, 274, 275,
    276, 284–285, 335
Anderson, Richard H., 31, 69, 118,
    129, 133
    and Deep Bottom operations, 213,
        215, 223, 228, 229, 232
    and Final Petersburg Offensive, 389,
        393, 400, 415, 425, 443, 444
    and Fort Harrison/New Market
        Heights, Battle of, 263, 272, 274,
        275
    and White Oak Road, Battle of, 402,
        404, 408, 409
Anderson-Wright Drive, 147
Angel, James R., 16, 162
Anna Rivers, 206
A. P. Hill Drive, 461
Appomattox Court-House, Va., 189, 443

Appomattox Manor, 177
Appomattox Plantation, 169, 177
Appomattox River, xx, xxiii, 11, 14, 18,
    22, 29, 30, 31, 35, 39, 49, 56, 74,
    79, 90, 100, 141, 161, 165, 167,
    169, 170, 173, 177, 186, 188,
    206, 209, 212, 219, 224, 253,
    266, 293, 302, 303, 325, 450,
    455, 458, 460, 461
Appomattox Street, 196
Archer, Fletcher H., 18, 20, 164
Archer, James J., 348, 351, 366
Armstrong house, 379
Armstrong's Mill, 292, 337, 364, 365,
    366, 375, 379, 380
Army and Navy Gazette, 357
Army of Northern Virginia, 3, 9, 23, 71,
    81, 118, 120, 129, 135, 139, 149,
    197, 205, 215, 224, 228, 235,
    263, 275, 277, 280, 285, 295,
    302, 305, 312, 316, 320, 326,
    331, 355, 389, 393, 400, 408,
    415, 416, 421, 429, 443, 454
Army of the James, 4, 9, 12, 15, 106,
    151, 161, 182, 185, 186–187,
    188, 198, 201, 202, 230, 231,
    232, 249, 250, 253, 255, 257,
    262, 266, 268, 280, 281, 290,
    292, 342, 389, 425, 444, 451, 452
Army of the Potomac, 3, 4, 10, 12, 14,
    26, 30, 35, 36, 41, 42, 43, 44, 46,
    51, 53–54, 55, 60, 62, 65, 66, 67,
    74, 78, 82, 84, 87, 90, 95, 107,
    109, 121, 123, 136, 147, 151,
    152, 154, 155, 157, 163, 176,
    185, 197, 206, 208, 209, 211,
    212, 219, 224, 228, 249, 292,

Army of the Potomac, *continued*
294, 296, 301, 303, 304, 305, 307,
309, 322, 328, 330, 342, 344, 346,
353, 361, 378, 382, 389, 393, 395,
396, 397, 404, 405, 406, 410, 412,
413, 420, 435, 444, 446
Army of the Shenandoah, 438, 441
Arthur's Swamp, 397
Atlantic, 170
Avery house, 31, 33, 43, 58, 68, 90, 93
Avery, M. P., 46
Ayres, Romeyn B., 66, 397
and Five Forks, Battle of, 426, 427,
433, 434–435, 436
and Hatcher's Run/Dabney's Mill,
Battle of, 381, 383, 384
and Peebles Farm/Poplar Spring
Church, Battle of, 344, 345, 346,
349, 355
and Weldon Railroad, Battle of the,
303, 304, 305–307, 309, 310, 312
and White Oak Road, Battle of, 402,
404, 405–406, 418, 419

Babcock, Orville E., 178, 189, 191, 192
Bailey's Creek, 30, 162, 201, 202, 204,
205, 215, 227, 229, 230, 233,
243, 244, 290
Baltic, 170
Baltimore Crossroads, 151, 152
Bankhead, H. C., 427
Barhamsville, Va., 149
Barlow, Francis C.
and Deep Bottom operations, 209,
210, 211 (photo), 211–212, 215,
216, 221, 227, 228, 230, 232,
233–234, 237, 244, 245
and First Petersburg Offensive, 31,
33, 36, 39, 41, 42, 46, 62
and Jerusalem Plank Road, Battle of,
294, 296, 298, 300–301, 303

and movement from Cold Harbor to
Petersburg, 58
and Reams Station, Second Battle of,
330, 331
Barnard, John G., 41
Barnes, Joseph H., 44
Barney, A. G., 259
Barney, B. G., 45
Barringer, Rufus, 331, 332, 340, 441
Bartlett, Joseph J., 67, 345, 418
Bartlett, William F., 121, 122, 125, 141
Battery No. 1 (C.S.), 18, 27, 32, 33, 165
Battery No. 2 (C.S.), 27, 28, 31, 32, 33
Battery No. 3 (C.S.), 24, 27, 32
Battery No. 4 (C.S.), 11, 23
Battery No. 5 (C.S.), 10, 11, 20, 23, 24,
27, 28
Battery No. 5 (U.S.), 86
Battery No. 6 (C.S.), 10, 11, 20, 23, 24,
25, 27, 163
Battery No. 7 (C.S.), 11, 23, 24, 25, 26,
27, 32, 33, 163
Battery No. 8 (C.S.), 24–28, 163
Battery No. 9 (C.S.), 24, 25, 27, 28–38, 163
Battery No. 9 (U.S.), 80, 86, 87, 88, 93,
94, 96
Battery No. 10 (C.S.), 24, 25, 163, 278
Battery No. 10 (U.S.), 79, 82, 84, 87, 89
Battery No. 11 (C.S.), 24, 25, 27
Battery No. 11 (U.S.), 82, 83, 86, 87, 88,
90, 94
Battery No. 12 (C.S.), 31
Battery No. 12 (U.S.), 82, 83, 86, 87, 88,
89, 94
Battery No. 14 (C.S.), 27, 44
Battery No. 15 (C.S.), 32, 44
Battery No. 16 (C.S.), 44
Battery No. 23 (C.S.), 20
Battery No. 25 (C.S.), 49
Battery No. 45 (C.S.), 355, 456
Battle, Cullen A., 18, 20, 164

Battlefield Park Road, 258, 259, 265, 269, 278

Baxter, Henry, 435

Baxter Road, 63, 64, 119, 126, 127, 129

Baylor Farm, 15, 17, 20, 159–166, 162

Beattie, Alexander M., 301

Beaty, Christopher L., 23, 53

Beauregard, Pierre G. T., 3, 133, 134
  and First Petersburg Offensive, 9, 18, 19 (photo), 22, 23, 29–30, 31, 32, 37, 49–52, 55, 68–69, 160, 164–165

Beaver's Bridge, 450

Beck, Butler, 370, 371

Beefsteak Raid, 159

Bell, Louis, 23, 261

Bellfield, Va., 326

Benham, Henry W., 445

Benjamin Harrison Memorial Bridge, 159

Bent, Luther S., 350

Bentonville, N.C., 73

Benyaurd, William, 419

Bermuda Hundred, 4, 9, 10, 12, 14, 31, 37, 39, 48, 151, 154, 177, 186, 202, 227, 291, 393

Bermuda Hundred Campaign, 9

Bertolette, John D., 93, 94

Bevill house, 400

Bingham, Henry, 369, 370, 372

Birge, Henry W., 217

Birney, David B., 103, 104, 199, 200, 201, 250, 288, 289, 290
  and Deep Bottom operations, 211 (photo), 226, 227, 228, 230, 233, 236, 241, 243, 244, 245
  and First Petersburg Offensive, 10, 26, 29, 30, 31, 33, 35, 36, 38, 39, 41, 52
  and Fort Harrison assault, 252, 253, 255, 258

and Jerusalem Plank Road, Battle of, 293, 294, 296, 298–300, 303
  and movement from Cold Harbor to Petersburg, 153, 158, 159, 163, 164

Birney William B., 237, 257, 258, 261, 394

Black Creek, 200, 288

Blacks and Whites, Va., 322, 323

Blackwater River/Swamp, 65, 66, 329

Blandford Church, xxiii, 101, 142

Blick house, 309

Blick's Station, 201, 290

Bliss, James, 442

Blunt's Bridge, 329

Boisseau, Ben, 437

Boisseau, J., house of, 414, 423, 425

Boisseau, R., house of, 414

Boisseau house, 438, 451, 454, 455

Boisseau's Crossroads, 435

Book, David P., 89

Bottom's Bridge, 156, 292

Boughton, John C., 95–96

Bowen, Robert E., 284

Bowers, Theodore S., 181

Bowles, Pinckney D., 277

Boydton Plank Road, 249, 287, 288, 328, 342, 344, 347, 351, 353, 359, 361, 363, 364, 365, 366, 367, 369, 371, 372, 373, 374, 375, 377, 387, 389, 391, 392, 393, 395, 397, 400, 401, 404, 408, 409, 410, 413, 414, 417, 418, 420, 423, 425, 428, 434, 444, 445, 451, 454, 458, 459, 461, 462

Boydton Plank Road, Battle of, 288, 291, 364, 369–375

Brackett, Levi C., 92

Bradbury Road, 247

Bradley, George W., 187

Bragg, Braxton, 37

Bragg, Edward S., 66, 310, 384

Bratton, John, 235–236, 241, 272, 274, 275, 277, 284

Breckenridge, John C., 450, 461

Bremo, 208

Briscoe, James C., 452–454

Broadway Landing, Va., 15, 161, 162, 206, 208, 209, 245

Broadway Road, 18, 20, 165, 166, 169, 196

Broady, Oscar, 237, 243

Brooks, William T. H., 10, 14, 23, 24, 25, 26, 28, 29, 39, 104, 161, 163, 199, 288

Bross, John A., 132, 136

Brown, Jack, 240

Bryant house, 30

Burch, John F., 81

Burgess Mill, 366, 367–375, 395, 400, 430, 432, 454, 457

Burgess Tavern, 364, 369, 370

Burkeville, Va., 322, 323, 324, 325

Burnham, Hiram, 23, 266, 267, 269

Burning Tree Road, 280

Burnside, Ambrose E., 117 (photo)
    and Crater, Battle of the, 103, 105, 106, 107, 109, 112–114, 115, 121–122, 125, 126, 132, 138, 205
    and First Petersburg Offensive, 31, 33, 35, 37, 38, 39, 43, 52, 57, 60–61, 65, 160
    and movement from Cold Harbor to Petersburg, 151, 152

Burt, Mason W., 67

Butler, Benjamin F., 4, 9, 10, 106, 185, 198, 201, 202, 249, 250, 290, 292, 363
    and Cold Harbor to Petersburg movement, 158, 159
    and Deep Bottom operations, 206, 209, 217, 223, 224, 244

and First Petersburg Offensive, 12, 14, 18, 37, 41–42, 48, 158, 159
    and New Market Heights/Fort Harrison assaults, 252, 265, 342

Butler, Halter, 408

Butler house, 408

Butler, M., house of, 417, 418

Butler, Matthew, 327, 331, 332, 341

Butterworth's Bridge, 18, 20, 165

Cabin Point, Va., 201, 290, 329

Caldwell, J. F. J., 218–219, 240–241, 409, 449–450, 460–461

Capehart, Henry, 441, 442

Carle, James, 46–47

Carolinas, xxiii, 10, 183, 249

Carson Drive, 304

Carter, Joseph F., 89

Carter, Thomas, 204, 264

Carters Mill Road, 212, 222

Cavalry Corps, C.S., 326, 331, 365, 416

Cavalry Corps, U.S., 155, 219, 322, 410, 412, 438

Cedar Lane, 166, 169, 196

Cemetery Hill, 60, 61, 113, 115, 125, 131, 132, 142

Central Road, 215, 217, 221, 227, 234, 281

Central State Hospital, 461

Chaffin's Bluff, 203, 204, 206, 209, 216, 221, 228, 229, 263

Chaffin's Farm, 197, 201, 208, 235, 251, 252, 258, 266, 269, 280, 291

Chamberlain, Joshua L., 67, 397–400, 401 (photo), 404, 408

Chamberlain's Creek/Bed, 412, 413, 414, 416, 420–422, 423, 438

Chambliss, John R., 242, 244, 326, 327, 332, 340

Chapman, George H., 155–156, 322, 323, 324, 326, 328

Chappell Farm, 354, 355

Chappell house, 202, 251, 291, 355, 397

Charles City County, Va., 291

Charles City Court-House, Va., 14, 149, 156, 158

Charles City Road, 154, 197, 201, 202, 217, 219, 227, 235, 236, 239, 241–243, 244, 247, 248, 281, 285, 290

Charlottesville, Va., 148

Chelsea, Mass., 176

Chesapeake Bay, 151, 177

Chesterfield, Va., 58, 460

Chew, R. Preston, 327

Chickahominy River, 12, 14, 74, 149, 151, 152, 153, 154, 156, 158, 197, 206

Chimneys, 434

Chimneys, the, 201, 250, 290

Choate, Francis C., 162

Christ, Benjamin, 42, 44

Christian, William Steptoe, 310

Christianville, Va., 325

Church Road, 346, 347, 351, 354, 355, 358, 359, 363

City Point, Va., xx, xxiii, 9, 12, 14, 15, 24, 35, 74, 154, 158, 159, 162, 163, 164, 166, 167–196, 186 (photo), 201, 224, 226, 227, 243, 290, 393, 423, 445

City Point Railroad, 11, 14, 23, 158, 166, 251

City Point Road, 14, 17, 18, 20, 27, 32, 56, 57, 162, 165

City Reservoir (Petersburg), 68

Civil War Trust, 199, 251, 332, 363, 375, 390, 402

Claiborne Road, 401, 402, 404, 409, 443, 446

Clements house, 354, 361, 362

Clingman, Thomas L., 24, 31, 32, 47–48, 312

Clopton's, 160

Coan, William P., 231, 232

Coggin's Point, 201, 251, 290

Coit, J. C., 129, 130, 131

Cold Harbor, Battle of, 4, 10, 147

Cold Harbor, Va., xx, 10, 12, 14, 147, 148, 151, 156, 157

Cold Harbor Road, 147, 151

Cole's Ferry, 149

Collis, Charles H. T., 445

Colonial Corner Drive, 159, 165, 166

Colquitt, Alfred H., 24, 31, 33, 53, 56, 57, 118, 119, 312

Colquitt's Salient, 57, 72, 76, 77, 81

Columbia, S.C., 73

Committee on the Conduct of the War, 114

Connecticut (transport ship), 170

Connecticut troops

    Sixth Connecticut, 230, 231

    Eighth Connecticut, 269

    Tenth Connecticut, 230, 237

Conner, James, 203, 238, 240, 341

Cook, John B., 26

Cooke, Giles B., 51

Cooke, John R., 339, 340, 341, 363, 366, 449

Cooke, Philip St. George, 16, 162

Cooper, Frederick, 55

Cope house, 162

Cornelius Creek, 259, 261

Corps d'Afric, 173, 176

Corse, Montgomery, 415, 416, 422, 429, 430, 437, 441, 443

Coulter, Richard, 307, 436, 437, 438

Council, E. C., 316

Courthouse Road, 159

Court-House Road, 416, 420, 422, 425, 428, 432, 443

Cox Road, 443, 451, 457, 460

Craig, Calvin, 237

Crater, Battle of the, xx, xxiii, 4, 5, 9, 57, 58, 65, 101, 103–143, 198, 200, 223, 289, 302

Crater Road, xxiii, 70, 101, 142, 143, 196, 293, 296

Crawford, E. A., 130

Crawford, Samuel, 292
    and Boydton Plank Road, Battle of, 364, 369, 370, 372, 373
    and Dabney's Mill/Hatcher's Run, Battle of, 381, 383, 384, 385, 386
    and Final Offensive, 397, 404, 405, 426, 427, 433, 434, 435–436, 437, 437–438, 440
    and First Petersburg Offensive, 42, 44, 46–47, 58, 61, 62, 65
    and movement from Cold Harbor to Petersburg, 155
    and Peebles Farm/Poplar Spring Church, Battle of, 345, 349
    and Weldon Railroad, Battle of the, 303, 304, 305, 307–309, 310, 312

Crawley, William J., 327

Creek Road, 366, 373

Creighton Road, 147

Crook, George, 412

Cullen, Edgar M., 278, 279

Culp, John, 138

Cummings house, 379, 384

Curles Neck Farm, 208

Curtin, John, 43, 62, 63

Custer, George A., 412 (photo), 413, 414, 425, 439, 441–442

Cutler, Lysander, 65–66, 307, 319

Dabney, S., house of, 414

Dabney, W., house of, 423

Dabney Mill Road, 363, 367, 371, 372, 375, 377, 381, 385, 387

Dabney's Mill, 363–367, 372, 373, 380, 381, 383, 384, 385, 386, 396, 405, 406, 444

Dabney's Mill, Battle of. See Hatcher's Run/Dabney's Mill, Battle of

Daggert, R., 261

Dailey, Dennis, 316

Dalien, Prosper, 90

Dalton, Edward B., 169–173

Daly, William, 319, 320

Dance, Willis B., 264

Dandy, George B., 231–232

Danse's Ford, 420

Danville Railroad, 104, 200, 288, 322, 324, 325, 349, 393, 394, 451

Darby/Enroughty Farm, 213, 218

Darbytown Pass, 284

Darbytown Road, xx, 104, 197, 200, 202, 204, 212, 221, 222, 223, 232, 234, 236, 239, 241, 242, 247, 249, 281, 283, 289

Darbytown Road, Battle of, 280–285, 291

Dauchy, George K., 335

Davenport Church, 292

Davies, Henry E., 220, 357, 412, 413, 420

Davis, J. Lucius, 332

Davis, Jefferson, 154, 242, 246

Davis, Joseph R., 305, 310, 312, 363, 366, 374

Davis, P. Stearns, 293

Davis, W. P., house of, 305, 308, 313

Davis house, 201, 290, 355

Dawson, Matthew M., 45

Dearing, James A., 15, 18, 20, 22, 154, 160, 165, 304, 348, 357, 366, 367, 373, 374

Deep Bottom, xx, 104, 105, 106, 112, 186, 197–248, 226 (photo), 251–253, 254, 257, 288, 289, 290, 303, 330

Deep Bottom, First, 105, 106, 112, 202–222, 223, 247, 302

Deep Bottom, Second, 198, 213, 223–247, 303

Deep Bottom Park, 199, 247, 251

Deep Bottom Road, 199, 247, 251

Deep Run, 201, 242, 243, 244, 290

Delaware River, 190

De Molay, 170

Dennison, W. N., 220

Department of North Carolina and South Carolina, 18, 20, 32, 55, 58, 63, 154, 164

Department of North Carolina and Southern Virginia, 154, 272

Department of Richmond, 10, 202, 228, 269

Department of Virginia, 72, 293, 390

Department of Virginia and North Carolina, 169, 292, 303

Department of Western Virginia, 10

Department of West Virginia, 72, 390

Depot Field Hospital at City Point, 169–176, 174 (photo), 188

Dern, George F., 283

Deserted House, 209, 212, 330

De Trobriand, Regis, 35, 210, 362, 370, 371, 373, 379, 384

Devane, William Stewart, 47, 48

Devens, Charles, 292

Devin, Thomas C., 412 (photo), 422, 425

Diascond, Va., 149

Dictator, the, 24, 25

Dillard, R. K., 194

Dimmock, Charles, 11

Dimmock Line, 11, 20, 31, 32, 38, 49, 347, 451

Dinwiddie Church of the Nazarene, 101, 387, 391, 392–396

Dinwiddie County, Va., 396

Dinwiddie Court-House, Battle of, 410–422

Dinwiddie Court-House, Va., 201, 250, 290, 322, 331, 375, 377, 389, 390, 391, 394, 395, 397, 402, 409, 410–420, 421, 423–425, 428, 429, 430, 434–435, 440, 444, 454

Dinwiddie Memorial Park, 346–354

Dinwiddie Road, 201, 290, 335

Disputant Station, 292

Donohoe, Michael T., 267, 279

Doran Road, 285

Dorey Park, 280

Double Bridges, 328, 329

Douglas, Hugh, 109

Douthat's, 149

Draper, Alonzo G., 255

Drewry's Bluff, 22, 275

Drewry's Tavern, 326

Drill house, 236

DuBose, Dudley M., 263

Duncan, Samuel, 15, 25, 161, 162

Duncan Road, 101, 344, 359, 363, 387, 391

Dunn house, 30, 32, 79, 87, 88, 90, 92

Dunovant, John, 332, 344, 358

Dutch Gap, 201, 244, 246, 290

Early, Jubal, 51, 81, 105, 160, 223, 224, 229

Edwards, Oliver, 301

Egan, Thomas W., 31, 33, 35, 364, 365, 369, 370, 371, 373

Eighteenth Army Corps, U.S., 104, 115, 200, 201, 202, 222, 289, 290, 291, 301

and First Petersburg Offensive, 12, 15, 17, 30, 36, 39, 48, 52–53, 57, 147, 151, 160, 161

and New Market Heights/Fort Harrison assaults, 249, 251, 252, 253, 255, 265, 266, 268, 269

Elliott, Stephen D., 32, 58, 64, 106, 119,
    120, 121, 126, 127, 129, 130,
    131, 138
Elliott's Salient, 106, 109, 120
Ely, Ralph, 86, 87, 88
Emancipation Proclamation, 182
Emmaus Church Road, 151
Enon Church, 147
Eppes, Richard, 177
Eppes family, 167
Ernst Hall, 302
Evans, Clement, 381
Ewell, Richard S., 10, 203, 204, 205, 228,
    232, 264, 269, 272, 278

Fairmount Park, 177
Fair Oaks, 291
Farmville, Va., 325
Fauntleroy, Robert, 355–357
Fay, Frank B., 176
Fayetteville, N.C., 73
Featherston, John C., 139–141
Felder, R. F., 57
Ferrero, Edward, 112, 114, 130, 131,
    132, 136, 361
Field, Charles W., 51, 52, 119, 335
    and Darbytown Road, Battle of, 284,
        285
    and Deep Bottom operations, 221,
        223, 224, 228–229, 234–235,
        238–240, 241, 242, 247
    and Fort Harrison/New Market
        Heights, Battle of, 261, 263, 272–
        275, 277, 280
Fifth Army Corps, U.S., 147, 173, 189,
    224, 292, 293, 296, 391
    and Boydton Plank Road, Battle of,
        364, 369, 372, 373
    and Crater, Battle of the, 115
    and Final Offensive, 393, 395, 396,
        397, 444, 445

and First Petersburg Offensive, 11,
    14, 38, 39, 42, 44, 46, 52, 53, 58,
    61–62, 65, 67
and Five Forks, Battle of, 410, 412,
    413, 414, 415, 417, 420, 422,
    423, 425, 426, 430, 432, 433,
    435, 436, 438, 439, 441, 442
and Hatcher's Run/Dabney's Mill,
    Battle of, 377, 379, 382, 383
and movement from Cold Harbor to
    Petersburg, 151, 152, 155, 157
and Peebles Farm/Poplar Spring
    Church, Battle of, 342, 344, 346,
    350, 353, 354, 361, 363
and Weldon Railroad, Battle of the,
    303, 305, 307
and White Oak Road, Battle of, 402,
    404, 405, 406
Finegan, Joseph, 381
First Army Corps, C.S., 147, 205, 215,
    223, 228, 235, 261, 263, 275,
    276, 280, 415, 421, 451, 454
First Maine Heavy Artillery Monument,
    49–57
First Slovak Baptist Church, 241
Fisher, Otis, 358
Fisher Road, 241
Fitzgerald's Ford, 420
Fitzhugh, Charles, 328, 329, 437, 439
Five Forks, xxiii, 389, 390, 391, 393, 395,
    402, 404, 410, 412, 414, 415,
    416, 419, 420, 421, 422, 425,
    426, 428, 429, 430, 432, 435,
    436, 437, 439, 443, 444
Five Forks, Battle of, 389, 390, 391,
    423–443, 444, 445
Five Forks Road, 414, 425, 427
Flank Road, 143, 196, 293, 295, 302,
    342, 354, 358
Fleetwood, Christian A., 257–258
Fleming, C. K., 301

Flowerree, Charles C., 440

Flowers house, 317

Fontaine, John B., 358

Force, Jacob B., 26

Fords Road, 428, 429, 436, 437, 438, 443

Ford's Station, 322, 429, 430, 437

Forsyth, James W., 412 (photo)

Fort Archer, 288, 347–351, 355

Fort Brady, 292

Fort Clifton, 10

Fort Conahey, 358

Fort Davis, 143, 196, 293–296, 295 (photo), 296

Fort Emory Road, 342, 346

Fort Fisher, 358–363

Fort Gilmer, 198, 202, 251, 259, 260–265, 267, 269, 270, 271, 275, 291

Fort Gregg, Battle of, 451–456

Fort Gregg (Confederate), xxiii, 261, 390, 391, 392, 451–461, 462

Fort Gregg (Union), 359

Fort Harrison, xx, xxiii, 197, 198, 202, 249, 251, 252, 255, 258, 259, 261, 263, 264, 265, 266, 267, 268, 269–278, 270 (photo), 280, 291, 342, 347

Fort Harrison National Cemetery, 269

Fort Harrison/New Market Heights, Battle of, 249, 251, 252, 255, 258, 259, 261, 263, 264, 265, 266, 267, 268, 269–278, 270 (photo), 275, 276, 277, 278, 279, 280

Fort Haskell, 80, 82, 84, 86–87, 88, 89, 93, 96, 97, 291

Fort Hays, 79, 90, 296–302

Fort Hoke, 278–279

Fort Holly, 292

Fort Howard, 79, 90

Fort Johnson, 261, 272

Fort Mahone, 293, 444, 461

Fort Maury, 278

Fort McGilvery, 86, 94, 96

Fort McRae, 345, 357

Fort Meikel, 79

Fort Monroe, 83, 170, 179, 182, 183

Fort Morton, 291

Fort Pillow, 140

Fort Powhatan, 41, 148, 149, 160, 169

Fort Prescott, 90

Fort Sedgwick, 143, 291, 293, 294 (photo)

Fort Stedman, xxiii, 9, 39, 49, 57, 71, 72, 74, 76, 77, 78, 79, 80, 81, 82, 83, 84, 86, 87, 88, 89, 91, 92, 93, 94, 95, 96, 97, 98, 100, 101, 180, 389, 391

Fort Stedman, Battle of, xx, xxiii, 9, 71–101, 142, 389, 391

Fort Stevens, 105

Fort Stevens, Battle of, 179

Fort Urmston, 354–358

Fort Wadsworth, 309–313, 342

Fort Welch, 359, 451

Fort Wheaton, 347

Fort Whitworth, 390, 391, 451, 452, 454, 455, 456, 461

Foster, Robert S., 451, 452

  and Deep Bottom operations, 202, 209, 211, 217, 230, 231, 237–238

  and Fort Harrison/New Market Heights, Battle of, 257, 259, 261–262

Four Mile Creek, 104, 200, 202, 209, 210, 227, 230, 251, 254, 288, 289, 290, 291

Frank, Paul, 53

Fraser, John, 53

Fredericksburg, Va., 172

Freeman, Douglas Southall, 155

Free Temple Full Gospel Ministries, Inc., 304

French, J. W., 190
Friend house, 30, 87, 88, 91, 92
Friend's Field, 32
Funk, West, 438
Fussell's Mill, 201, 216, 218, 222, 223–
    229, 232–241, 290

Gary, Martin, 204, 229, 235, 255, 259, 284
Gary's Church, 334
Gee, Stirling H., 440
Gee house, 133
Georgia troops
    Eleventh Georgia, 240
    Sixty-fourth Georgia, 18, 20, 164
Gerhardt house, 281
Getty, George W., 292, 301
Gettysburg, Battle of, 3, 36n6, 293,
    397, 404
Gibbon, John, 201, 249, 290, 292
    and Deep Bottom operations, 209,
        211 (photo), 215, 217, 221, 243
    and Final Petersburg Offensive, 394,
        395, 451–452
    and First Petersburg Offensive, 29,
        30, 33, 36, 39, 52, 53
    and Jerusalem Plank Road, Battle of,
        294, 298, 299, 300
    and movement from Cold Harbor to
        Petersburg, 153, 158, 161, 164
    and Peebles Farm/Poplar Spring
        Church, Battle of, 201, 290
    and Reams Station, Second Battle of,
        331, 334, 336, 337, 341
Gibbs, Alfred, 413
Gill Dale Road, 241, 247
Gillespie, George L., 426
Gilliam Farm, 249, 441, 442
Gillmore, Quincy A., 10
Gilmer, J. F., 11
Gilson, Helen L., 176
Girardey, Victor J. B., 238, 239, 240

Glendale, 151, 152, 154–156, 221
Glenn, Edwin A., 397, 399
Globe Tavern, 201, 288, 290, 303, 304,
    305, 307, 317, 330, 345
Goldsborough, N.C., 73, 393
Goode, John T., 22, 129
Goode's Bridge, 450
Gordon, John B.
    and Fort Stedman, Battle of, 74–78,
        79–80, 81, 83, 84, 97, 98, 100–101
    and Hatcher's Run/Dabney's Mill,
        Battle of, 377, 380, 381
Gordon, Rebecca H., 77
Gordonsville, Va., 148
Gould, J. P., 44
Gracie, Archibald, 119
Graham, Archibald, 264
Graham, Edward, 18, 20, 165, 327, 351
Granger, Henry, 370
Grant, Julia Boggs Dent, 182, 183
Grant, Lewis, 298
Grant, Ulysses S., 1, 2, 3, 287
    and Boydton Plank Road, Battle of,
        363, 365, 367, 369, 370
    and City Point, 167, 168, 177, 177
        (photo), 178, 179, 180, 181, 183,
        184, 185, 191, 192, 193
    and Crater, Battle of the, 105, 106–
        107, 112, 113, 114, 115, 132,
        138, 141
    and Darbytown Road, Battle of, 320,
        326, 329, 342, 345, 363, 365,
        367, 369, 370, 375, 377
    and Deep Bottom operations, 197,
        198, 202, 203, 205, 206, 213,
        215, 217, 221, 222, 223, 224,
        230, 233, 244, 245, 247
    and Final Petersburg Offensive, 389,
        392, 393–395, 397, 404, 410,
        419, 423, 444
    and First Petersburg Offensive, 9, 10,

11, 12, 13 (photo), 33, 36, 37, 39, 48–49, 51, 56
and Fort Harrison/New Market Heights, Battle of, 249, 251, 258, 280, 281
and Fort Stedman, Battle of, 71, 72–74, 76, 77, 98, 100–101
and Hatcher's Run/Dabney's Mill, Battle of, 375, 377, 381, 385
and Jerusalem Plank Road, Battle of, 301–302
and movement from Cold Harbor to Petersburg, 148–149, 153, 154, 155, 156, 157, 160, 164, 165
and Peebles Farm/Poplar Spring Church, Battle of, 326, 342, 345
and Weldon Railroad, Battle of the, 320, 329
Grant's Headquarters/Cabin, 169, 173, 177–185, 177 (photo)
Gravel Hill, 201, 290
Gravel Hill Church, 212, 213, 222, 392
Gravel Hill Recreation Center, 213
Gravelly Meeting-House, 396
Gravelly Run, 383, 387, 390, 391, 396, 397, 402, 404, 406, 408, 409, 410, 417, 436
Gravelly Run Church, 435
Gravelly Run Church Road, 425, 426, 427, 440
Greene, A. Wilson, 457n
Greensborough, Va., 325
Gregg, David M., 217, 219–220, 221, 224, 226, 227, 241, 242, 243, 244, 245, 303, 330, 331, 334, 336, 337, 341, 344, 364, 365, 369, 370, 372, 375, 377, 382, 383, 384
Gregg, J. Irvin, 220, 412, 413
Gregg, James P., 359
Gregg, John I., 238, 239, 240, 263, 272, 281, 284, 285

Gregory, Edgar M., 399
Griffin, Charles, 345 (photo)
and Dabney's Mill/Hatcher's Run, Battle of, 383, 384, 391, 397, 399
and First Petersburg Offensive, 41, 43, 58, 65, 66
and Five Forks, Battle of, 418, 419, 426, 427, 433, 434, 436
and Peebles Farm/Poplar Spring Church, Battle of, 342, 344, 345, 346, 347, 348, 349, 350, 353, 354, 355
and Weldon Railroad, Battle of the, 303, 304
and White Oak Road, Battle of, 404, 405, 406–408
Griffin, Charles B., 264
Griffin, Simon, 121, 126
Gurley Farm, 303, 304, 330
Gwyn, James, 345, 347, 348

Hagood, James R., 277, 284–285
Hagood, Johnson, 24, 27, 31, 32–33, 55–57, 314, 316–320
Hagood Line, 31, 38, 39, 49
Halifax Road, 304, 309, 321, 327, 332, 342, 364
Hall, Matthew, 138
Halleck, Henry W., 12, 48, 157, 191, 192, 301
Hammell, John S., 153
Hampton, Wade
and Boydton Plank Road, Battle of, 365, 366, 367, 372, 373, 374, 375
and Deep Bottom operations, 229, 242
and movement from Cold Harbor to Petersburg, 153, 159, 160
and Peebles Farm/Poplar Spring Church, Battle of, 353, 354, 357–358

Hampton, Wade, *continued*
  and Reams Station, Battle of, 330,
    331–332, 334, 340–341
  and Wilson-Kautz Raid, 325, 326–
    327, 328
Hancock, Winfield Scott, 72, 104, 114,
    200, 291, 293, 390, 404
  and Boydton Plank Road, Battle of,
    363, 364–365, 367, 369–373
  and Cold Harbor to Petersburg
    movement, 151, 152, 153, 157–
    158, 160, 163
  and Deep Bottom operations, 105,
    106, 112, 205, 208, 209–210,
    210–211, 211 (photo), 213,
    215–216, 216–218, 221, 222, 223,
    224–228, 230, 231, 232, 236–237,
    241, 243, 288, 303
  and First Petersburg Offensive, 12,
    28–29, 30–31, 33, 35, 36, 37, 38,
    39–41, 52, 61, 160, 163
  and Reams Station, Second Battle
    of, 329, 330–331, 332, 334–337,
    341, 342
Hardaway, Robert A., 264
Hardy, John, 95
Hare house/Hill, 36, 39, 49, 52, 55,
    56, 57, 60, 61, 65, 98, 100, 104,
    200, 288
Harman Road, 359, 363, 365
Harmon house, 451, 458
Harney, George, 68
Harper's Weekly, 193–194, 195 (photo)
Harriman, Samuel, 86, 89, 90
Harris, David B., 32, 49, 58
Harris, Nathaniel H., 238, 373, 374
Harris, Thomas M., 452, 455
Harris Line, 52, 58
Harrison's Creek, 31, 38–49, 158, 159,
    163–164
Harrison's Landing, Va., 10, 37, 200, 290

Hart house, 360
Hartranft, John F., 91 (photo), 121, 381
  and First Petersburg Offensive, 41,
    42, 43, 44, 61, 62–63
  and Fort Stedman, Battle of, 79, 86,
    87, 88, 89, 90–95
Hartshorne, William R., 307
Harvey, William A., 57
Haskell, John C., 127
Hatcher's Run, 73, 188, 287, 288,
    292, 329, 344, 363, 364, 365,
    366, 367, 373, 374, 375–387,
    389, 390, 391, 393, 394, 395,
    400, 402, 423, 428, 429, 430,
    432, 443, 444, 445, 450, 454,
    455, 457
Hatcher's Run/Dabney's Mill, Battle
    of, 72, 288, 291, 292, 363, 375,
    377–387, 437
Hawley, Joseph R., 237
Haw's Shop, Battle of, 147
Hayes, Joseph, 312
Hays, Alexander, 296
Hays, William, 445, 445
Heckman, Charles A., 253, 267, 270, 271
Henrico County, Va., 247
Henrico County Fire Station 18, 232
Herring Creek, 104, 200, 289
Hess, Frank, 379, 380
Heth, Henry
  and Boydton Plank Road, Battle of,
    365–367, 373–375
  and Deep Bottom operations, 203,
    215, 228, 238
  and Final Petersburg Offensive, 408,
    449, 454, 456, 458
  and Peebles Farm/Poplar Spring
    Church, Battle of, 350, 351–353,
    354, 355, 357, 362–363
  and Reams Station, Second Battle of,
    334, 337–340, 341

and Weldon Railroad, Battle of the, 304, 305, 309, 310, 312, 314

Hicksford, Va., 73, 292, 454

High Bridge, 322, 325

Hill, Ambrose P., 69, 77, 132, 133, 149, 221, 298, 351, 354, 373, 377, 380

death of, 456–460

and Final Petersburg Offensive, 449, 451, 456, 457, 458, 459, 460, 461

and Reams Station, Second Battle of, 330, 331, 332, 335, 339, 340, 341

and Weldon Railroad, Battle of the, 312–313, 316, 320

Hill, Frank, 460

Hill, Kitty, 460

Hinks, Edward W., 14, 15, 17, 23, 24–26, 28, 29, 30, 36, 160, 161, 161–163

Hodgkins, Joseph A., 94

Hofmann, J. William, 66, 67–68, 307, 309, 345, 346, 349

Hogg, George, 234

Hoke, Robert, 18, 22, 23, 24, 27, 28, 30, 31, 32, 33, 47, 55, 119, 138, 272, 274, 275, 276, 280, 284, 328

Hoke, W. A., 131

Holcombe Legion, 327

Hollywood Cemetery, 460

Holman, John H., 15–16, 25, 161, 162

Holston, William F. H., 96

Hopewell, Va., 24, 167, 199, 251

Hopewell Road, 151

Hopewell Visitor Center, 17

Hopper, George C., 350

Houghton, Charles H., 123–125

Howlett house, 58

Howlett Line, 31, 39, 393

Howlett's Bluff, 104, 200, 288

Hughson, Benjamin F., 231

Humphrey, William, 46

Humphreys, Andrew A., 291, 322, 345 (photo), 369, 372

and Dabney's Mill/Hatcher's Run, Battle of, 375, 377, 378–381, 382, 383, 384

and Final Petersburg Offensive, 395, 396, 405, 410, 418, 425, 445

Hungarytown, Va., 324

Hunter, David, 160

Hunton, Eppa, 402, 408, 415, 430

Illinois troops
    Thirty-ninth Illinois, 232

Indiana troops
    Third Indiana Cavalry, 155
    Twentieth Indiana, 35

Ingalls, Rufus, 149, 177, 185–190, 206, 226

Interstate 64, 152

Interstate 85, 387, 390, 391, 392, 462

Interstate 95, xix, 101, 387, 390, 391, 462

Interstate 295, xix, 147, 159, 199, 247, 248, 251, 285

Irish Brigade, 234

Isle of Wight County, Va., 194

Jackson, Richard H., 261

James River, xx, xxiii, 1, 2, 3, 4, 10, 12, 13, 14, 18, 38, 41, 48, 51, 74, 98, 103, 104, 105, 106, 107, 112, 147, 148, 149, 151, 153, 154, 155, 156, 157, 158, 159, 160, 163, 166, 167, 170, 173, 177, 180, 182, 185, 186, 187, 190, 194, 197, 198, 199, 200, 201, 202, 203, 204, 205, 206, 207, 208, 209, 211, 212, 213, 216, 219, 224, 226, 228, 229, 246, 247, 251, 252, 253, 258, 265, 266, 268, 269, 272, 278, 280, 281, 287, 289, 290, 292, 303, 320, 324, 329, 330, 342, 344, 351, 357, 363, 391, 415, 416, 450, 455, 460, 461

James River and Kanawha Canal, 14, 148
James River Drive, 159
Jamestown Island, 169
Jarratt's Station, 326, 329
J. C. Campbell, 193, 194
Jefferson Park Road, 159
J. E. Kendrick, 193, 194
Jenkins, William H., 457, 458, 460
Jennings house, 227
Jerusalem Plank Road, xxiii, 49, 51, 65,
    104, 127, 129, 132, 133, 143,
    200, 287, 293, 296, 298, 301,
    302, 310, 337, 342, 444
Jerusalem Plank Road, Battle of, 288,
    293–302, 321
John Randolph Medical Center, 169
Johnson, Bushrod R., 84, 228, 393, 397,
    400, 429, 443, 461
    and Crater, Battle of the, 118, 126–
        129, 131, 134, 138–139, 141
    and First Petersburg Offensive, 22,
        31, 32, 37, 63–64, 65
    and White Oak Road, Battle of, 402,
        404, 408–409, 415, 420
Johnson, Charles, 263–265
Johnson, John L., 89
Johnson house, 295, 296
Johnson Road, 302, 304
Johnson's Farm, 202, 251, 291
Johnston, Joseph E., 71, 72, 73, 74, 76,
    98, 184, 393, 394, 444
John Tyler Memorial Highway, 156
Jones, Hilary P., 49
Jones, Willis F., 238
Jones Farm, 347, 351, 359
Jones' Landing, Va., 74, 257
Jones's Bridge, 104, 149, 151, 152,
    200, 288
Jones's Neck, 202, 226
Jordan house, 23, 29, 161
Jordan Point Road, 162

Kautz, August V., 14, 15, 106, 161,
    162, 206, 281, 283 (photo), 284,
    322, 323, 324, 325, 326, 327,
    328, 329, 430
Kellogg, John A., 436
Kent, William L., 268
Kershaw, Joseph, 51, 204, 205, 213, 215,
    217, 218, 220, 221, 228, 229
Kerwin, Michael, 371, 387
Keysville, Va., 324
Kiddoo, Joseph B., 17, 26
King, Horace H., 140
King and Queen Court-House, Va., 10,
    103, 104, 199, 200, 288
Kingsland Road, 199, 208, 227, 236,
    247, 248, 251
Kirkpatrick, 457

Laburnum Avenue, 280
Ladies Memorial Association of
    Petersburg, 142–143
Lamar, Thomas B., 316
Lamkin, James, 127
Lane, James H., 218, 219, 221, 237, 240,
    339, 341, 351, 366, 454, 455
Lang, William, 96
Langhorne, John, 127
Laurel Hill, 202, 251, 258–259
Laurel Hill Church, 259, 291
Law, Evander M., 277
Ledlie, James H., 39, 41, 44–46, 47, 115,
    121, 122, 130, 132
Lee, Fitzhugh, 322, 324, 325, 326, 393
    and Dinwiddie Court-House, Battle
        of, 415, 416, 416–417, 420, 421
    and Five Forks, Battle of, 422, 428,
        429, 430–432, 440, 441
Lee, Robert E., 2, 4, 99 (photo),
    184, 188
    and Crater, Battle of the, 106, 112,
        132, 133, 139, 141

and Dabney's Mill, Battle of, 375
and Darbytown Road, Battle of, 280,
    285, 287
and Deep Bottom operations, 197,
    198, 202, 203, 204, 213, 215,
    222, 223, 224, 229, 235, 236,
    242, 243, 245, 246–247, 247
and Final Offensive, 389, 390, 393,
    394, 402, 404, 408, 415, 420,
    423, 428, 429, 430, 444, 450,
    455, 457, 458, 459, 460, 461
and First Petersburg Offensive, 9, 10,
    18, 31, 37–38, 39, 49, 51, 52, 65,
    68, 69
and Fort Harrison/New Market
    Heights, Battle of, 249, 263, 272,
    275, 280
and Fort Stedman, Battle of, 71, 72,
    74, 76, 77, 81, 98–100, 101
and Hatcher's Run, Battle of, 363,
    365, 367, 369, 370
and Jerusalem Plank Road, Battle of,
    296, 298, 302
and movement from Cold Harbor to
    Petersburg, 148, 149, 153, 154,
    155, 156, 157, 160, 165
and Peebles Farm/Poplar Spring
    Church, Battle of, 342, 347,
    351, 354
and Weldon Railroad, Battle of the,
    320, 330, 341
Lee, W. H. F., 224, 238, 242, 313, 325,
    328, 357, 358, 389, 393
and Dinwiddie Court-House, Battle
    of, 415, 416, 417
and Five Forks, Battle of, 422, 429,
    430, 441, 442, 443
Lee's Mill, 104, 200, 201, 251, 289, 291
Lewis Farm, 390, 391, 396, 397–400, 417
Lewis Farm, Battle of, 397–400
Lewis house, 397, 399

Libby house, 236
Libby Prison, 83
Lieutenant Run, 295, 296
Light-House Point, 219
Lincoln, Abraham, 105, 391
    at City Point, 179–180, 181, 182,
        183, 185, 189, 423
Lincoln, Mary, 182
Lincoln, Robert, 180
Lippitt, James W., 48
Little, F. H., 240
Little Roanoke River, 324
Little Stony Creek, 421
Long Bridge, 14, 149, 151, 152, 153,
    154, 156
Long Bridge Road, 156, 212, 213,
    215, 217, 221, 222, 229, 236,
    245, 247, 292
Longstreet, James, 77, 221, 291, 451,
    460
Loring, Charles G., 93
Louisa County, Va., 153, 160
Louisiana troops
    Louisiana Guard Artillery, 265
Lyle, Peter, 47, 307, 308, 309, 312
Lynch, J. C., 210, 212
Lynchburg, Va., 51, 148, 160
Lynn, Mass., 176

MacDougall, Clinton D., 447
Mackenzie, Ranald, 394, 425, 433, 438
MacRae, William, 339, 340, 341, 351,
    363, 366, 373, 374, 375, 449
Madill, Henry J., 35, 447
Mahone, William, 101, 137 (photo),
    238, 458, 459
    and Boydton Plank Road, Battle of,
        373, 374, 375
    and Crater, Battle of the, 131,
        132, 133, 134, 135, 136, 138,
        139, 141

Mahone, William, *continued*
   and Dabney's Mill Battle of, 381, 385
   and Jerusalem Plank Road, Battle of,
      295–296, 298, 302
   and Peebles Farm/Poplar Spring
      Church, Battle of, 355
   and Reams Station, Second Battle
      of, 334
   and Weldon Railroad, Battle of the,
      309, 310, 312, 314, 316, 317
   and Wilson-Kautz Raid, 322
Maine, 397
Maine State Agency, 176
Maine troops
   First Maine Cavalry, 421
   First Maine Heavy Artillery, 49, 53, 55
   Eleventh Maine, 230, 237
   Sixteenth Maine, 308
   Twentieth Maine, 348–349
   Thirty-first Maine, 43
   Thirty-second Maine, 43
Main Street, 169, 196
Major-General Meade, 193, 194
Malone Road, 332
Malone's Bridge, 332, 377
Malone's Crossing, 331, 332, 340
Malvern Hill, 10, 104, 152, 154, 155,
      156, 200, 206, 210, 215, 217,
      218, 227, 233, 244, 288
Mansfield Woods, 212, 213
Marshall, Elisa G., 121, 122, 123, 124, 125
Martin, James G., 31
Martindale, John H., 14, 23, 24, 28, 29,
      39, 52, 104, 161, 200, 289
Maryland, 105
Maryland troops, (U.S.)
   First Maryland Cavalry, 230, 237
   Second Maryland, 43
   Third Maryland, 81, 88, 89, 122, 123
Mason, W. Roy, 240
Massachusetts troops
   First Massachusetts Heavy Artillery, 362

Fifth Massachusetts Cavalry, 16, 162
Tenth Massachusetts Artillery, 335, 379
Sixteenth Massachusetts, 55, 67
Eighteenth Massachusetts, 349
Twentieth Massachusetts, 299
Twenty-first Massachusetts, 45, 122
Twenty-fourth Massachusetts, 230, 237
Twenty-eighth Massachusetts, 210, 212
Twenty-ninth Massachusetts, 83, 86,
    88, 121
Thirty-fifth Massachusetts, 122
Thirty-sixth Massachusetts, 43
Thirty-ninth Massachusetts, 293, 308
Fifty-sixth Massachusetts, 122
Fifty-seventh Massachusetts, 82, 86,
    87, 90, 92, 122
Fifty-eighth Massachusetts, 43
Fifty-ninth Massachusetts, 83, 122
Matadequin Creek, 147
Mathews, Joseph A., 88, 94
Maxwell, John, 194–196
Maxwell, Norman, 89
Mayhew, Mrs., 176
Maynadier, William M., 329
Mayo, Joseph, Jr., 422
Mayo, Robert M., 305, 310, 366
McAfee, Lee, 128
McAllister, Robert, 53, 54–55, 337, 362,
    371, 379, 380
McCabe, W. Gordon, 120, 132–134
McCallum, Daniel, 188
McClellan, George B., 154
McClellan Road, 151
McCormick, Charles, 169
McCoy, Thomas, 308
McDowell house, 358
McGowan, Samuel, 351, 366, 402, 408,
    437, 449, 454
McGregor, William, 332, 357, 429
McIntosh, John, 155, 325, 326, 328
McLaughlen, Napoleon B., 77, 79, 82–
    84, 86, 87, 88, 90, 91, 93

McKethan, Hector, 48

McKnight, George, 299, 335, 336

McMaster, Fitz W., 126, 128, 129–131

Meade, George G., 3, 4, 9, 181, 185, 197,
    249, 345 (photo)
  and Boytdton Plank Road, Battle of,
    363, 364, 367, 369, 370
  and Cold Harbor to Petersburg
    movement, 151, 158, 160
  and Crater, Battle of the, 105, 106,
    112, 114, 115, 132, 133, 138
  and Dabney's Mill/Hatcher's Run,
    Battle of, 375, 377–378, 381, 385
  and Deep Bottom operations, 206,
    208, 217, 221, 222, 223, 245
  and Final Petersburg Offensive, 393,
    395–396, 404, 410, 418, 419,
    420, 423–425, 426, 444–446
  and First Petersburg Offensive, 10,
    11–12, 31, 33, 35, 36, 38, 39, 52,
    58, 69
  and Fort Stedman, Battle of, 100
  and Jerusalem Plank Road, Battle of,
    292, 298
  and Peebles Farm/Poplar Spring
    Church, Battle of, 344, 345,
    359, 362
  and Reams Station, Second Battle of,
    329, 335, 341
  and Weldon Railroad, Battle of the,
    303–304
  and Wilson-Kautz Raid, 322, 328

Meade's Station, 86, 87, 90, 91, 93

Mechanicsville Turnpike, 197

Medal of Honor, 198

Meherrin River, 325

Meherrin Station, 324

Merritt, Wesley, 412 (photo), 412, 413,
    417, 425, 426, 438–439

Metcalf, Richard, 370, 371

Michigan troops
  First Michigan, 347, 350

First Michigan Sharpshooters, 46, 87

Second Michigan, 46, 86, 87, 88, 95

Sixteenth Michigan, 348, 350

Twentieth Michigan, 88, 93

Twenty-sixth Michigan, 210, 212, 215

Middle Military Division, 72, 201, 290, 390

Miles, Nelson A., 242, 243, 244, 245,
    300, 330, 380, 404, 405
  and Deep Bottom operations, 210,
    211, 212, 216
  and Reams Station, Second Battle of,
    331, 334, 335, 336, 337, 341
  and Sutherland Station, Battle of,
    445, 446–449

Miller, John O., 63

Milliken, William D., 26

Mill Road, 259

Mine Run Campaign, 404

Mink, Charles E., 405

Minnesota troops
  First Minnesota, 371

Mississippi troops
  Twelfth Mississippi, 316
  Sixteenth Mississippi, 316

Mitchell, William G., 226, 371

Moody, Young M., 400, 402, 408

Morgan, Charles H., 163, 226

Morton, J. St. Clair, 43, 44

Morton Avenue, 143

Mott, Gershom, 303, 330, 344, 359, 360,
    361–362, 404, 445, 446
  and Boydton Plank Road, Battle of,
    365, 369, 370, 371, 372, 373
  and Dabney's Mill/Hatcher's Run,
    Battle of, 379, 380
  and Deep Bottom operations, 209,
    212, 215, 227, 230, 233, 237,
    243, 244
  and First Petersburg Offensive, 52,
    53, 54
  and Jerusalem Plank Road, Battle of,
    294, 298, 299, 300

Munford, Thomas T., 416, 417, 420, 429, 430, 432, 441
Murphy, Matthew, 335

Namozine Road, 443
National Museum of the Civil War Soldier, 391–392, 461
National Park Service, xxi, xxiii, xxiv, 178, 198, 287, 288, 347, 354, 390, 444
Neill, Thomas, 39
Nelson, Peter, 153
New Hampshire troops
    Fourth New Hampshire, 261
    Sixth New Hampshire, 43
    Ninth New Hampshire, 43
    Eleventh New Hampshire, 43
    Tenth New Hampshire, 266
    Thirteenth New Hampshire, 268, 269
New Jersey troops
    First New Jersey Artillery, 336
    Second New Jersey, 55
    Third New Jersey Light Artillery, 96
    Eleventh New Jersey, 54
New Kent Court-House, 149
New Market Crossroads, 155
New Market Heights, 198, 202, 208, 210, 213, 215–216, 221, 222, 224, 228, 229, 230, 232–236, 251, 253–259, 291, 342, 347
New Market Heights, Battle of. See Fort Harrison/New Market Heights, Battle of
New Market Heights Lane, 253, 258
New Market Race Course, 56
New Market Road, 104, 197, 199, 200, 201, 202, 204, 206, 208, 210, 212, 215, 216, 217, 218, 219, 220, 222, 227, 228, 229, 233, 234, 239, 244–245, 247, 248, 251, 252, 253, 257, 258, 259, 262, 275, 281, 285, 289, 290, 291

Newport News, Va., 170
New York troops
    First New York Light Artillery, 345
    Second New York Heavy Artillery, 234
    Second New York Mounted Rifles, 43, 420
    Third New York, 262
    Third New York Cavalry, 281, 283, 304
    Fifth New York Cavalry, 323
    New York Light Artillery, 279
    Seventh New York, 335, 337
    Eighth New York Cavalry, 155, 442
    Twelfth New York Artillery, 299, 335
    Fourteenth New York Heavy Artillery, 81, 82, 84, 122, 123
    Fifteenth New York, 307, 441
    Fifteenth New York Heavy Artillery, 307
    Twenty-fourth New York Cavalry, 62
    Thirty-ninth New York, 335, 337
    Forty-fourth New York, 67
    Fiftieth New York Engineers, 157
    Fifty-second New York, 335, 337
    Sixty-first New York, 336
    Sixty-sixth New York, 153
    Seventy-third New York, 210
    Eighty-first New York, 279
    Ninety-sixth New York, 269, 279
    100th New York, 230, 233, 237
    109th New York, 89
    117th New York, 261
    118th New York, 266
    125th New York, 335
    126th New York, 335
    142nd New York, 259
    147th New York, 65
    152nd New York, 299
    155th New York, 36–37
    164th New York, 370
    179th New York, 122, 123
Nineteenth Corps, U.S., 217

Ninth Army Corps, U.S., 151, 152,
   173, 176, 189, 201, 205, 206,
   244, 290, 292, 303, 309, 377–
   378, 380
   and Boydton Plank Road, Battle of,
      363, 364, 365
   and Crater, Battle of the, 103, 105,
      109, 121, 123, 136
   and Final Petersburg Offensive, 425,
      444, 445, 446
   and First Petersburg Offensive, 11,
      31, 36, 38, 39, 41, 42, 43, 44, 46,
      48, 52, 53, 58, 62, 66
   and Fort Stedman, Battle of, 78, 82,
      84, 87, 90, 92, 95, 100
   and Peebles Farm/Poplar Springs
      Church, Battle of, 342, 344, 346,
      350, 353, 361, 362
Norfolk and Petersburg Railroad, 22, 33,
   58, 61, 62–63, 64–65, 66, 67, 68,
   105, 106
Norfolk Turnpike, 67
North Anna, Battle of the, 9
North Carolina, 71, 76, 389, 444
North Carolina troops
   Second North Carolina Cavalry, 340
   Twenty-fourth North Carolina, 128
   Twenty-fifth North Carolina, 128
   Thirty-fifth North Carolina, 46
   Thirty-ninth North Carolina, 46–47
   Forty-ninth North Carolina, 128
   Fifty-first North Carolina, 48
   Sixty-first North Carolina, 47, 138
Nottoway Court-House, Va., 322,
   323, 324
Nottoway River, 325, 328, 329

Oak Grove Methodist Church,
   321–332, 341
Oak Grove Road, 321
Oaklawn Boulevard, xix, 142, 147, 159,

166, 169, 196, 199, 248, 251,
   285, 387, 391, 462
O'Brien, Timothy, 299
Offensives
   First, xx, xxiii, 9, 11–69, 71, 101,
      105, 142, 147–165, 179, 287,
      293, 397
   Second, 288, 293–302, 304, 321
   Third, xx, 9, 103, 105, 103–143,
      203–222, 223, 302
   Fourth, 223–247, 249, 288, 302–320,
      329–342
   Fifth, 198, 247, 251–280, 288,
      342–363
   Sixth, 288, 364–375
   Seventh, 288, 377–387
   Final, xviii, 389–462
Ohio troops
   Sixth Ohio Cavalry, 420–421
   Thirteenth Ohio, 421
   Sixtieth Ohio, 46
Old Church, Battle of, 147
Old Church Road, 151
Old Cold Harbor Crossroads, 151
Old Court-House, 164
Old Level Road, 265
Old Stage Road, 159, 397
Old Town Creek, 456, 458
Old Vaughan Road, 101, 387, 391, 396
Olive Church, 152
Oliver, Charles, 89
Orange and Alexandria Railroad, 188
Ord, Edward O. C., 72, 74, 104, 112,
   200, 201, 251, 254 (photo), 289,
   290, 291, 292, 293, 390, 394,
   395, 410, 423
   and Fort Harrison, Battle of,
      252, 253, 265, 266, 267, 269,
      270–271
Ord, Mary T., 182
Osborn, Thomas O., 452

Osborne Turnpike, 197, 227, 275, 280

Otey, John M., 154

Overland Campaign, 2, 4, 9, 147, 151

Page, P. R., 22

Paine, Charles J., 253, 255, 257, 261, 262

Palmer, William H., 456, 457, 460

Pamplin Historical Park, 391–392, 444, 451, 457, 461

Pamunkey River, 12, 147, 151, 169

Parke, John G., 43, 61, 201, 290, 292, 345 (photo), 345, 395, 410
  and Boydton Plank Road, Battle of, 363, 367
  and Crater, Battle of the, 78–79, 84–87, 91, 93, 94
  and Final Petersburg Offensive, 444, 445, 446
  and Peebles Farm/Poplar Spring Church, Battle of, 344, 351, 353–354, 359, 360–361, 362

Patten, H. L., 299

Paul, Samuel B., 18

Payne, W. H., 416

Pearson, Alfred, 350

Pecan Street, 185

Peebles house, 349, 353, 361

Peebles's Farm, 202, 251, 287, 344, 345, 346, 347, 349, 351, 353, 354, 357, 359, 360 (photo), 363

Peebles's Farm, Battle of, 288, 291, 342–354

Pegram, John, 377, 381, 385, 437

Pegram, Richard G., 58–60, 63, 64–65, 106, 119, 120, 129

Pegram, William J., 312, 334, 339, 355, 415, 429, 437, 440, 441

Pegram house, 353, 354, 360, 361

Pegram's Farm, 202, 251, 291, 344, 359–363

Pegram's Salient, 106, 119, 129

Peninsula Campaign, 151, 154, 197

Pennington, Alexander C. M., 439, 442

Pennsylvania, 3

Pennsylvania troops
  Second Pennsylvania Heavy Artillery, 122, 123
  Third Pennsylvania Cavalry, 379, 380
  Fifth Pennsylvania Cavalry, 283
  Eleventh Pennsylvania, 438
  Forty-fifth Pennsylvania, 43, 359
  Forty-eighth Pennsylvania, 43, 107, 109
  Fifty-eighth Pennsylvania, 278
  Sixty-second Pennsylvania, 67
  Eighty-third Pennsylvania, 67
  Eighty-fourth Pennsylvania, 362
  Ninety-seventh Pennsylvania, 261
  Ninety-ninth Pennsylvania, 210
  100th Pennsylvania, 45, 81, 86, 88, 89, 93, 122
  105th Pennsylvania, 362
  107th Pennsylvania, 308
  110th Pennsylvania, 210
  118th Pennsylvania, 348
  140th Pennsylvania, 53
  141st Pennsylvania, 35, 362
  155th Pennsylvania, 350
  183rd Pennsylvania, 210, 212
  187th Pennsylvania, 67
  188th Pennsylvania, 278
  190th Pennsylvania, 307, 308
  191st Pennsylvania, 307
  199th Pennsylvania, 452
  200th Pennsylvania, 86, 87, 90, 91–92, 93, 94
  204rd Pennsylvania, 257
  205th Pennsylvania, 90, 93
  207th Pennsylvania, 90, 93–94
  208th Pennsylvania, 90, 91, 93, 94
  209th Pennsylvania, 87, 90, 91, 92, 93, 94
  210th Pennsylvania, 405
  211th Pennsylvania, 90, 94

Pennypacker, Galusha, 261

Pentecost, Joseph H., 88

Perkins, 395

Perkinson's Saw Mill, 15, 162

Perrin, Walter, 335

Perrine, Isaac, 96

Perry, William F., 263, 274, 284

Peters Bridge, 329

Petersburg, Va., xviii (photo), xix, xx, xxii, xxiii, 2, 3, 4, 5, 9, 10, 11, 12, 14, 15, 17, 23, 29, 30, 33, 35, 36, 37, 38, 39, 41, 48, 49, 51, 52, 58, 65, 66, 69, 71, 72, 73, 74, 76, 83, 101, 105, 106, 112, 141, 142, 147, 149, 154, 155, 157, 158, 159, 160, 162, 163, 164, 167, 168, 169, 170, 173, 175, 177, 180, 184, 185, 186, 188, 189, 191, 197, 202, 205, 206, 222, 223, 224, 235, 245, 247, 249, 251, 254, 255, 272, 281, 287, 288, 293, 301, 302, 303, 305, 309, 317, 321 (photo), 322, 324, 328, 330, 331, 345, 347, 349, 351, 360, 373, 375, 387, 389, 390, 391, 392, 393, 395, 402, 404, 414, 415, 416, 425, 437, 443, 444, 445, 447, 451, 454, 455, 456, 460, 461, 462

Petersburg Express, 384

Petersburg National Battlefield, xx, xxi, xxii, xxiii, 57, 71, 101, 141, 166, 169, 196, 198, 358, 387, 392, 462

Petersburg Pike, 170, 171

Phelps, Alonzo J., 170

Philadelphia, Pa., 177

Pickett, George E., 221, 238, 389, 393, 417, 419, 431 (photo), 461
    and Dinwiddie Court-House, Battle of, 404, 410, 415–416, 420, 421–422
    and Five Forks, Battle of, 425, 428, 429, 430, 432, 436, 437, 440–441, 442–443

Picnic Road, 265, 267, 268

Pier, C. K., 46

Pierce, Byron R., 53, 54, 362, 370, 371

Pierce, Luther H., 149

Pioneer Baptist Church, 280

Pitkin, P. P., 187

Pleasants, Henry, 106, 107, 109–111, 112, 116–118

Point of Rocks, Va., 14, 188, 208, 209, 212, 219, 224, 245

Pond, Francis B., 237

Pooley, Thomas, 176

Poor Creek, 57, 58, 105, 107, 109

Poplar Grove Church, 346, 348

Poplar Hill, 325

Poplar Spring Church, 201, 202, 241, 251, 290, 291, 316, 342, 344, 346, 347, 353

Poplar Spring Church Road, 345

Porter, David, 183, 184

Porter, Horace, 178, 180–183, 183–185, 191–193

Potomac River, 105, 190

Potter, Robert, 79
    and Crater, Battle of the, 107, 109, 114, 121, 126, 130
    and First Petersburg Offensive, 38, 41–43, 44, 58, 60, 61, 62, 63
    and Peebles Farm/Poplar Spring Church, Battle of, 345, 351, 353, 354

Powell, William H., 114–115, 118, 125–126, 344–346, 348–349

Powhatan, Va., 292

Preston, Samuel D., 48

Prices' Station, 324

Prince George Court-House, Va., 159, 291, 325

Prince George Court-House Road, 30, 31, 32, 35, 53, 57, 79

Proctor's house, 201, 251, 291

Providence Forge, Va., 151

Quaker Road, 155, 364, 369, 373, 391, 393, 394, 396, 397, 400, 401, 410, 419

Ramsey, John, 36–37, 53, 380, 447
Randall, George M., 84
Randolph Road, 166
Ransom, Matthew W., 88, 119, 128, 130, 131, 400, 415, 429, 430, 440
Ransom, Robert, Jr., 10
Rapidan River, 3
Raulston, J. B., 268, 279
Raulston, William C., 62
Reams Road, 332
Reams Station, 104, 200, 201, 288, 290, 321, 322, 325, 326, 327, 328, 329, 330, 331, 332, 334, 337, 339, 340, 341–342, 377
Reams Station, First Battle of, 322, 327–329
Reams Station, Second Battle of, 288, 290, 329–342
Reese, Henry, 109
Rhines, L. C., 46
Rhode Island troops
   First Rhode Island Artillery, 335
   Seventh Rhode Island, 43
Richard Bland College, 302–304
Richardson, Charles T., 83
Richardson, Colin, 281
Richmond, Fredericksburg, and Potomac Railroad, 148
Richmond, Va., xix, xxiv, 2, 3, 4, 5, 9, 12, 13, 29, 37, 48, 51, 52, 71, 72, 74, 83, 101, 105, 112, 147, 148, 149, 155, 161, 167, 177, 180, 184, 185, 186, 189, 194, 197, 198, 199 (photo), 202, 205, 206, 207, 208, 209, 210, 222, 223, 224, 228, 229, 230, 235, 236, 239, 242, 245, 246, 247, 249, 251, 252, 253, 254, 255, 257, 259, 261, 262, 266, 267, 271, 287, 288, 347, 389, 391, 393, 395, 416, 443, 444, 451, 455, 460, 461
Richmond and Petersburg Railroad, 32
Richmond and York River Railroad, 151
Richmond National Battlefield, xxiii, 147, 198
Riddell's Shop, 10, 147, 153, 154, 155, 219
Rion, James H., 57
River Queen (boat), 180, 184
River Road, 447
Rives Salient, 295, 456
Roanoke Bridge, 322, 324
Roanoke River, 322, 324, 325, 393
Roanoke Station, 104, 200, 288, 324
Roberts, Samuel H., 267, 268, 279
Roberts, William, 340, 430
Robinson, Gilbert P., 88
Rockbridge Artillery, 229–232
Rock Hill Road, 151
Rockwell, Alfred P., 230, 231
Roder, John, 371, 379
Roemer, Jacob, 61, 88
Rogers, Charles H., 96
Rogers, Robert, 346
Rohoic Creek, 444
Rosser, Thomas L., 327, 332, 340, 415, 416, 417, 422, 429, 432
Rowanty Creek, 292, 328, 329, 330, 331, 337, 367, 428
Rowanty Post Office, 364
Ruffin house, 217, 245, 255
Ruffin Road, 159
Rugg, Horace, 335, 371
Russia (steamer), 183

Saffold's Bridge, 325
Saint Mary's Church, 104, 155, 200, 288
Saint Peter's Church, 104, 151, 200, 288
Salem Flying Artillery, 264, 265
Sanders, John, 138, 139, 316

Sappony Church, 104, 200, 288, 322, 325, 326

Sappony Creek, 327, 329

Scales, Alfred M., 373, 449

Schuylkill County, 107

Scott's Road, 425

Second Army Corps, C.S., 81, 223

Second Army Corps, U.S., 94, 100, 103–104, 147, 173, 199, 200, 288, 291, 330, 344, 359, 395, 404, 406
  and Boydton Plank Road, Battle of, 363, 364, 369
  and Cold Harbor to Petersburg movement, 151, 152–153, 155, 157, 158, 159, 161, 164
  and Deep Bottom operations, 105, 106, 205, 206, 207, 208, 209, 210, 211, 212, 213, 220, 222, 224, 227, 228, 230, 232–233, 237, 238, 245, 303
  and First Petersburg Offensive, 10, 11, 12, 14, 26, 27, 28–29, 30, 33, 35, 36, 38, 41, 44, 48, 52–53, 54, 55, 57, 58, 61, 62, 65, 66
  and Hatcher's Run/Dabney's Mill, Battle of, 375, 377, 378
  and Jerusalem Plank Road, Battle of, 293, 294, 300, 301, 302
  and Peebles Farm/Poplar Springs Church, Battle of, 360, 361
  and Reams Station, Second Battle of, 341
  and Sutherland Station, Battle of, 444, 445, 446

Seddon, James A., 153, 156, 236, 243, 285

Sentry Hill Court, 461

Sergeant, William, 405

Seven Days' Battles, 154, 213

Seventh Avenue, 451, 461

Seventh South Carolina Battalion, 57

Seventh U.S. Colored Troops, 262

Seventeenth Maine, 35

Seventeenth Michigan, 88, 89

Seventeenth Michigan Engineers, 87

Shand house, 31, 38, 41, 42, 43, 44, 60

Sharon Baptist Church, 342–346

Sharpe, George H., 191

Shaw, James, 262

Shedd, James, 128, 139

Shenandoah Valley, 51, 71, 105, 148, 206, 223, 224, 229, 232, 249, 263, 413

Shepherd, Russell B., 53

Sheridan, Philip H., 72, 73, 74, 106, 112, 182, 183, 201, 290, 389, 390, 391, 393, 395, 444, 445, 447, 461
  and Deep Bottom operations, 205, 206, 208, 209, 210, 213, 217, 219, 221, 222, 223, 224
  and Dinwiddie Court-House, Battle of, 410, 412 (photo), 412–415, 416, 417, 418, 420
  and Five Forks, Battle of, 423, 425–426, 427, 428, 430, 432, 433, 434, 435, 436, 437, 438, 443

Sherman, William T., 71, 73, 98, 183, 184, 185, 389

Shorkley, George, 92

Short, William H., 27

Sigfried, Joshua, 136

Signal Hill, 257, 258

Simpson Road, 451, 462

Sixteen-Mile Turnout, 322

Sixth Army Corps, U.S., 11, 39, 52–53, 57, 100, 151, 152, 160, 173, 223–224, 292, 293, 294, 298, 300, 301, 302, 378, 381, 391
  and Final Petersburg Offensive, 413, 425, 444, 445, 446, 451, 455

Slatersville, Va., 149

Sleeper, J. Henry, 335

Smith, Adelaide W., 173–176

Smith, Alexander, 128, 130

Smith, Charles H., 412, 413, 420, 420–421

Smith, Normand, 268, 271–272

Smith, William F. "Baldy," 104, 151, 160, 161, 162, 163, 164, 200, 289
    and First Petersburg Offensive, 11, 12, 14, 15, 16 (photo), 18, 20, 23, 24, 25, 28, 29, 30, 31, 35, 37, 39, 41, 57

Smithfield, N.C., 73

Smith's Store, 10

Smoky Ordinary, 325

Smyth, Thomas A., 53, 243, 244, 365, 369, 371, 379, 380, 381

South Anna River, 206

South Carolina troops
    First South Carolina, 218, 219, 284, 409
    Second South Carolina Rifles, 284
    Eleventh South Carolina, 56
    Twelfth South Carolina, 218, 240
    Thirteenth South Carolina, 218
    Fourteenth South Carolina, 218
    Seventeenth South Carolina, 119, 126, 128, 129, 130, 131, 138
    Eighteenth South Carolina, 119, 120, 121, 126, 129, 130
    Twenty-first South Carolina, 56, 318, 319
    Twenty-second South Carolina, 119, 120, 121, 126, 128, 129, 139
    Twenty-third South Carolina, 18, 20, 119, 126, 128, 129, 139, 164
    Twenty-fifth South Carolina, 57, 318, 319
    Twenty-sixth South Carolina, 119, 127, 128, 129, 130
    Twenty-seventh South Carolina, 33, 56
    Palmetto Sharpshooters, 235

South Side Railroad, 104, 200, 249, 287, 288, 322, 324, 342, 347, 363, 364, 365, 366, 373, 389, 390, 393, 402, 410, 415, 416, 429, 437, 443, 444, 449, 454

South Side Road, 447

South Sixth Avenue, 169

Spear, Samuel, 330–331, 334, 336

Spotsylvania, Battle of, 9

Spring Hill, 17, 96

Squirrel Level Road, 101, 249, 287, 291, 316, 342, 344, 345, 346, 347, 351, 353, 354, 355, 358, 360, 361, 363, 379, 380, 381, 391

Stacey, May, 370

Stannard, George J., 29, 161, 253, 261, 266, 267–268, 269, 270, 271, 277–278, 278–279

Stansel, Martin L., 408

Stanton, Edwin M., 181

Starke, Norborne, 456, 457

State of Maine (transport ship), 170

Staunton River, 324

Staunton River Bridge, 104, 200, 288, 322, 326

Steele, R. E., 129

Stephens, Alexander, 178

Steuart, George H., 410, 415, 429, 430

Stevens, Aaron, 267, 268, 279

Stevens, Walter, 11

Stewart, William H., 135–136

Stoodley, Nathan D., 271

Stoney, J. D., 319, 320

Stony Creek, 104, 200, 246, 249, 288, 291, 326, 331, 334, 393

Stony Creek Station, 291, 325, 326, 327, 328

Strang, E. J., 187

Strawberry Plains, 104, 200, 208–212, 219, 231, 289

Strong house, 330

Stuart, James E. B., 151

Sturdivant, Nathaniel A., 18, 165

Sturgis, Thomas, 83
Surgeon General's Office, 172
Susquehanna River, 3
Sutherland Station, 390, 392, 393, 415,
     416, 430, 443–451
Sutherland Station, Battle of, 391,
     446–451
Sutherland Tavern, 443
Sweeney Pottery, 210
Sweitzer, Jacob B., 67
Swift Creek, 415
Swords, Henry L., 83
Sycamore Church, 201, 249, 250, 290
Sycamore Drive, 409, 419

Tabb, William B., 33
Talleysville, 151
Taylor, William, 320
Taylor Farm, 57–70, 101, 105–107
Taylor house, xxiii, 57, 60, 61, 63, 64
Taylor's Creek, 63, 64, 69
Tenth Army Corps, U.S., 10, 103, 121,
     199, 200, 202, 208, 209, 219,
     224, 226, 230, 231, 233, 236,
     245, 252, 257, 258–259, 261,
     262, 288, 289, 291, 330
Terrett, George H., 37
Terry, Alfred H., 10, 104, 200, 230, 236,
     289, 291
Terry, William Richard, 415, 416, 422,
     429, 430, 440
Texas Brigade, 254
Third Army Corps, C.S., 120, 135, 139,
     147, 149, 295, 305, 312, 316, 355
Thomas, Edward L., 454, 455
Thomas, Henry G., 136
Thomas, S. B., 316
Thompson house, 380
Tidball, John C., 86
Tiffany, Louis Comfort, 143
Tilden, Charles, 308

Tilghman's Farm, 204
Tilton, William S., 66–67
Torbert, Alfred T. A., 221
Totopotomoy Creek, Battle of, 147
Traveller, 133
Trevilian Station, 153
Tucker, George, 456–460
Tucker house, 379, 380
Tunstall's Station, 104, 149, 152, 200, 288
Turnbull house, 457, 458
Turner, John W., 452
Turner Road, 248
Turkey Creek, 104, 200, 288
Twenty-fourth Army Corps, U.S., 291,
     292, 394, 395, 444, 445, 451, 452
Twenty-fifth Army Corps, U.S., 291, 394
Tyler's Mill, 160

U.S. Army troops
     First U.S. Sharpshooters, 362
     Second U.S. Artillery, 220
     Fourth U.S. Artillery, 379, 397, 399
     Eighth U.S. Infantry, 358
     Twelfth U.S. Infantry, 354
U.S. Christian Commission, 169, 175
U.S. Colored Troops, 5
     First U.S. Colored Troops, 26,
          161–162
     Fourth U.S. Colored Troops, 17, 24,
          26, 161, 257
     Fifth U.S. Colored Troops, 17, 161, 257
     Sixth U.S. Colored Troops, 161
     Twenty-second U.S. Colored Troops,
          17, 161, 255
     Twenty-third U.S. Colored Troops,
          136
     Twenty-eighth U.S. Colored Troops,
          136
     Twenty-ninth U.S. Colored Troops,
          136
     Thirty-sixth U.S. Colored Troops, 255

U.S. Route 1, 249, 367, 375, 387, 390, 392, 401, 451
U.S. Route 5, 156, 159, 199, 208, 229, 251, 253, 258
U.S. Route 10, 159
U.S. Route 60, 152
U.S. Route 460, 387, 390, 443, 451
U.S. Sanitary Commission, 169, 175, 176

Vaidan's, 160
Van Buren, James L., 91, 93
Varina Road, 204, 205, 227, 261, 262, 266–269
Vaughan Road, 201, 202, 251, 290, 291, 292, 317, 342, 344, 354, 357, 358, 364, 365, 366, 377, 379, 380, 381, 382, 383, 384, 387, 391, 395, 396, 397, 400, 410, 412
Venable, Charles, 133, 455
Vermont troops
    Third Vermont, 301
    Fourth Vermont, 301
    Eleventh Vermont, 301
    Seventeenth Vermont, 43
Vicksburg Campaign, 103
Virginia, 2, 10, 147, 246, 249, 390, 396
Virginia Central Railroad, 106, 153, 160, 206, 209
Virginia Route 36, xix, 17, 70, 105, 142, 147, 169, 196, 199, 247, 251, 285, 293, 391
Virginia Route 106, 159
Virginia troops
    First Virginia Light Artillery, 264
    Third Battalion, Virginia Reserves, 20
    Third Virginia, 422
    Sixth Virginia, 134
    Seventh Virginia Cavalry, 327
    Ninth Virginia Cavalry, 327, 357, 358
    Tenth Virginia Cavalry, 357

Twelfth Virginia, 134
Thirteenth Virginia Cavalry, 358
Sixteenth Virginia, 134
Twenty-sixth Virginia, 18, 20, 22, 129, 164
Thirty-second Virginia, 438
Thirty-fourth Virginia, 18, 20, 22, 164
Forty-first Virginia, 134
Forty-fourth Battalion Virginia Infantry, 20
Forty-sixth Virginia, 18, 129, 164
Fifty-fifth Virginia, 355
Fifty-ninth Virginia, 27, 129
Sixty-first Virginia, 134
Petersburg Battery, 58, 63, 120
Visitor Center, Petersburg National Battlefield, xxi, xxiii, 10, 24, 70, 72, 84, 101, 105, 142, 147, 166, 169, 196, 199, 248, 251, 285, 293, 387, 391, 462
Visitor Center, Richmond National Battlefield Park, Cold Harbor, 147, 151
Visitor Center, Richmond National Battlefield Park, Fort Harrison, 269
Visitor Contact Station, Petersburg National Battlefield, Five Forks, 422, 428

Wadsworth, James S., 309
Wainwright, Charles S., 346, 347–348
Walker, Francis A., 227
Walker, Henry H., 305, 312, 366
Walker, James A., 81, 97–98
Walker, Reuben L., 276, 277
Wallace, William H., 400, 415, 429, 430, 437, 440, 441
Ward, Thomas, 329
Warren, Gouverneur K., 292, 293, 329, 330, 331, 337

and Boydton Plank Road, Battle of, 363, 367, 372, 375

and Cold Harbor to Petersburg movement, 151, 154, 155, 158–159

and Crater, Battle of the, 112, 133

and Deep Bottom operations, 224, 244

and Final Offensive, 391, 393, 395, 396, 397, 402, 404, 405, 410, 414, 417–420, 422, 423, 425, 426–428, 433–434, 435, 437, 438

and First Petersburg Offensive, 38, 39, 52, 58, 61, 65

and Five Forks, Battle of, 391, 414, 417–420, 422, 423, 425, 426–428, 433–434, 435, 437, 438

and Hatcher's Run/Dabney's Mill Battle of, 377, 378, 379, 380, 381, 382–385, 385–387

and Peebles Farm/Poplar Spring Church, Battle of, 342, 344, 345, 346, 347, 348, 349, 351, 359, 361

and Weldon Railroad, Battle of the, 224, 244, 303, 304, 305, 309, 310–312, 313 (photo), 314–316

and White Oak Road, Battle of, 393, 402, 404, 405

Warwick Swamp, 104, 200, 288

Washington, D.C., 12, 105, 148, 157, 169, 172, 176, 179, 187, 188, 189, 190, 191, 192, 223, 224, 301

Washington, George, 101

Washington Street, xix, 70, 142, 293, 387, 391, 462

Watts, Richard A., 94

Webb, Alexander, 404, 417, 418, 419

Webb house, 32

Weisiger, David, 132, 134, 135, 138, 374

Weiss, Julius A., 262

Weitzel, Godfrey, 202, 251, 283 (photo), 291

Welch, Norval, 348, 350, 359

Weldon, 190, 207

Weldon Railroad, 73, 201, 206, 223, 224, 244, 246, 247, 249, 251, 287, 290, 296, 298, 301, 302, 303, 304, 305, 314, 320, 322, 329, 330, 331, 339, 341, 342, 345, 347, 353, 377, 454

Weldon Railroad, Battle of the, 201, 246, 288, 290, 304–320

Wells, William, 441, 442

West, George W., 379, 380

West, Robert M., 281

Western Metropolis, 170

Westover, 156

Westwood Road, 151

Weyanoke Peninsula, 12, 147, 157

Wheaton, Frank, 381, 384, 385, 386

Wheelock, Charles, 310

Whitaker, Edward, 325

White, E. R., 128

White, Julius, 310, 312

White Battery, 278

White House, Va., 12, 14, 48, 73, 74, 104, 149, 151, 156, 172, 200, 288

White Oak Road, 364, 366, 367, 369, 370, 390, 391, 393, 395, 401, 402, 404, 405, 406, 408, 409, 410, 412, 414, 415, 417, 418, 419, 420, 423, 425, 426, 428, 429, 432, 433, 434, 435, 436, 437, 438, 439, 440, 441, 443, 444, 446

White Oak Road, Battle of, 402–409, 423

White Oak Swamp, 10, 14, 155, 243

White's Tavern, 201, 242, 243, 247, 290

Whitworth house, 458

Widow Clark house, 455

Widow Gilliam house, 425

Wilcox, Cadmus M., 120, 213, 221, 223, 238, 366
 and Final Petersburg Offensive, 408, 451, 454–456, 457
 and Jerusalem Plank Road, Battle of, 295, 296
 and Peebles Farm/Poplar Spring Church, Battle of, 351, 355
 and Reams Station, Battle of Second, 334, 335, 339, 341
Wilcox's Landing, 2, 12, 14, 147, 153, 156, 57–159, 200, 289
Wilcox Wharf Road, 156
Wilds, S. H., 319
Wilkinson Road, 420, 422
Willcox, Orlando B., 292, 337
 and Crater, Battle of the, 114–115, 121, 130
 and Final Offensive, 446
 and First Petersburg Offensive, 38–39, 41, 42, 43–44, 58, 60, 61–62
 and Fort Stedman, Battle of, 79, 81, 82, 86, 87–90, 91, 92, 93
 and Peebles Farm/Poplar Spring Church, Battle of, 342, 345, 361, 362
 and Weldon Railroad, Battle of the, 310, 312
Willett, James M., 371
Williams, Seth, 163
Williamsburg Road, 197, 218
Williams house, 337
Willis Church Road, 154, 156
Wilderness, Battle of, 9, 12, 148, 296, 309
Wilson, James B., 348
Wilson, James H., 14, 321, 322–326, 327–329
Wilson-Kautz Raid, 321–329

Winchester, Va., 72, 73, 390
Windmill Point, 157, 158
Wingate, R. J., 460
Winston Churchill Drive, 166, 169, 196
Winthrop, Frederick, 383, 384, 405, 406, 433, 435
Wisconsin troops
 Fourth Wisconsin Battery, 283
 Thirty-second Wisconsin, 371
 Thirty-seventh Wisconsin, 89
 Thirty-eighth Wisconsin, 46
Wise, Henry A., 119, 126, 129, 165, 400, 402, 408
 and First Petersburg Offensive, 19, 20, 22, 23, 27–28, 32, 33, 47, 63
Woerner, Christian, 96–97, 336
Wood, Henry, 129
Wood, William H., 18, 22, 164
Woodlawn Street, 166, 196
World War I, 5
Wright, Ambrose R., 127, 130, 236, 238
Wright, Elias, 26, 27, 138
Wright, Gilbert J., 327
Wright, Horatio G., 35, 57, 151, 155, 293, 296, 298, 345 (photo), 395, 448 (photo)
 and Final Petersburg Offensive, 410, 444, 445, 446
Wyatt's Farm, 202, 251, 291
Wylliesburg, Va., 325
Wythe Street, xix, 70, 101, 142, 387, 462

Yahley Mill Road, 222, 223, 229, 232, 241
Yarborough house, 236
Yellow House, 201, 290, 303, 307, 361
Yellow Tavern, 201, 249, 290, 305
Young, Pierce M. B., 327, 332, 340
Young, Wright, 332